THE CONSTITUTION
AND WHAT IT MEANS TODAY

Edward S. Corwin's
THE
CONSTITUTION
AND WHAT IT MEANS
TODAY

Revised by Harold W. Chase
and Craig R. Ducat

FOURTEENTH EDITION

PRINCETON UNIVERSITY PRESS

To: Alpheus T. Mason

*The third in a line of extraordinary
teacher-scholars who have served as
McCormick Professors of Jurisprudence,
Princeton University:*

Woodrow Wilson 1898-1910

Edward S. Corwin 1918-1946

Alpheus T. Mason 1947-1968

PREFACE TO EDITION XIV

We who have had the responsibility for revising this classic work of Edward S. Corwin wish to acknowledge what a great and rare privilege it has been. Working with a classic is not easy; for it carries with it the heavy responsibility of attempting to maintain the quality of the work. Even so, for us who have long admired the work of Professor Corwin and, particularly for the one for whom Professor Corwin was a remarkable, lovable, and inspiring teacher, it was truly a labor of love.

As we worked on the manuscript, two initial impressions were reinforced day by day. The first was the enormous change in the meaning of the Constitution over the last twenty years. One does not fully appreciate the full impact of that change until he goes over the Constitution provision by provision. The second impression was how very good the work of Corwin had been in earlier editions both as to substance and style. He had a very special skill for being pithy. Words were used sparingly, and every word carried meaning. His summaries of historical development, his evaluations and judgments were remarkably good as measured by hindsight. Consequently, even in the face of great change, we endeavored to preserve as much of the original Corwin as was possible. Where we added to his work we tried to emulate his style and the quality of his work. Nothing would make us more proud than acceptance of this edition as a worthy successor to the first thirteen.

Corwin's words in a Preface to an earlier edition serve as the best explication of his approach: "Although *The Constitution and What It Means Today* utilizes now and then other materials, decisions of the Supreme Court contribute its principal substance. . . . I have endeavored, especially in connection with such important subjects as judicial review, the commerce clause, executive power, freedom of speech, press and religion, etc., to accompany explanation of currently prevailing doctrine and practice with a brief summation of the historical development thereof. The serviceability of history to make the present more understandable has been remarked upon by writers from Aristotle to the late Samuel Butler, famed author of *Erewhon and The Way of All Flesh*; and the idea is particularly pertinent to legal ideas and institutions." While being faithful to his approach, we felt it was important to constitutional interpretation to add citations of significant lower court decisions.

We owe some special thanks to those who helped in their own ways to make this edition a reality: Herbert Bailey of the Princeton University Press; Bernice M. Chase, whose varied editorial skills were put to good use; Vera M. Fadden; and to O. James Werner and his staff at the most accommodating library we have ever worked in, the San Diego County Law Library. We owe particular thanks to William B. Rohan of that library, who served as well as a

first and on-going critic as well as devil's advocate, and to Gail
Filion, an editor of extraordinary skill and understanding. Others
to whom we owe thanks are: Victor E. and Carol Flango, Eric L.
Chase, Sylvia Lindgren and Fay Manger.

H.W.C.
C.R.D.

CONTENTS

Some Judicial Diversities

"In *the Constitution of the United States—the most wonderful instrument ever drawn by the hand of man—there is a comprehension and precision that is unparalleled; and I can truly say that after spending my life in studying it, I still daily find in it some new excellence.*"—JUSTICE JOHNSON. In Elkinson v. Deliesseline, 8 Federal Cases 593 (1823)

"The *subject is the execution of those great powers on which the welfare of a nation essentially depends. . . . This provision is made in a Constitution intended to endure for ages to come and, consequently, to be adapted to the various crises of human affairs.*"—CHIEF JUSTICE MARSHALL. In McCulloch v. Maryland, 4 Wheaton 316 (1819)

"It *[the Constitution] speaks not only in the same words, but with the same meaning and intent with which it spoke when it came from the hands of its framers, and was voted on and adopted by the people of the United States. Any other rule of construction would abrogate the judicial character of this Court and make it the mere reflex of the popular opinion or passion of the day.*"—CHIEF JUSTICE TANEY. In the Dred Scott Case, 19 Howard 393 (1857)

"We *read its [the Constitution's] words, not as we read legislative codes which are subject to continuous revision with the changing course of events, but as the revelation of the great purposes which were intended to be achieved by the Constitution as a continuing instrument of government.*"—CHIEF JUSTICE STONE. In United States v. Classic, 313 U.S. 299 (1941)

"Judicial *power, as contradistinguished from the power of the laws, has no existence. Courts are the mere instruments of the law, and can will nothing.*"—CHIEF JUSTICE MARSHALL. In Osborn v. U.S. Bank, 9 Wheaton 738 (1824)

"We *are under a Constitution, but the Constitution is what the judges say it is. . . .*"—FORMER CHIEF JUSTICE HUGHES when Governor of New York

---

"When *an act of Congress is appropriately challenged in the courts as not conforming to the constitutional mandate the judicial branch of the Government has only one duty,—to lay the article of the Constitution which is invoked beside the statute which is challenged and to decide whether the latter squares with the former.*"—JUSTICE ROBERTS. In United States v. Butler, 297 U.S. 1 (1936)

"While *unconstitutional exercise of power by the executive and legislative branches of the Government is subject to judicial restraint, the only check on our own exercise of power is our own sense of self-restraint.*"—JUSTICE STONE (dissenting), *ibid.*

"The *glory and ornament of our system which distinguishes it from every other government on the face of the earth is that there is a great and mighty power hovering over the Constitution of the land to which has been delegated the awful responsibility of restraining all the coordinate departments of government within the walls of the governmental fabric which our fathers built for our protection and immunity."* —CHIEF JUSTICE EDWARD DOUGLASS WHITE when Senator from Louisiana. In 23 *Cong. Rec.* 6516 (1892)

"JUDICIAL *review, itself a limitation on popular government, is a fundamental part of our constitutional scheme. But to the legislature no less than to courts is committed the guardianship of deeply cherished constitutional rights.*"—JUSTICE FRANK-FURTER. In Minersville School Dist. *v.* Gobitis, 310 U.S. 586 (1940)

"CASE-BY-CASE *adjudication gives to the judicial process the impact of actuality and thereby saves it from the hazards of generalizations insufficiently nourished by experience. There is, however, an attendant weakness to a system that purports to pass merely on what are deemed to be the particular circumstances of a case. Consciously or unconsciously the pronouncements in an opinion too often exceed the justification of the circumstances on which they are based, or, contrariwise, judicial preoccupation with the claims of the immediate leads to a succession of* ad hoc *determinations making for eventual confusion and conflict. There comes a time when the general considerations underlying each specific situation must be exposed in order to bring the too unruly instances into more fruitful harmony. The case before us presents one of those problems for the rational solution of which it becomes necessary, as a matter of judicial self-respect, to take soundings in order to know where we are and wither we are going.*"—JUSTICE FRANKFURTER (dissenting). In Larson *v.* Domestic & Foreign Corp., 337 U.S. 682, 705 (1949)

"ORDINARILY *it is sound policy to adhere to prior decisions but this practice has quite properly never been a blind, inflexible rule. Courts are not omniscient. Like every other human agency, they too can profit from trial and error, from experience and reflection. As others have demonstrated, the principle commonly referred to as* stare decisis *has never been thought to extend so far as to prevent the courts from correcting their own errors. Accordingly, this Court has time and time again from the very beginning reconsidered the merits of its earlier decisions even though they claimed great longevity and repeated reaffirmation. . . . Indeed, the Court has a special responsibility where questions of constitutional law are involved to review its decisions from time to time and where compelling reasons present themselves to refuse to follow erroneous precedents; otherwise its mistakes in interpreting the Constitution are extremely difficult to alleviate and needlessly so.*"—JUSTICE BLACK (dissenting). In Green *v.* US., 356 U.S. 165, 195 (1958)

"TO *give blind adherence to a rule or policy that no decision of this Court is to be overruled would be itself to overrule many decisions of the Court which do not accept that view. But the rule of* stare decisis *embodies a wise policy because it is often more important that a rule of law be settled than that it be settled right.*"—CHIEF JUSTICE STONE (dissenting). In U.S. *v.* Underwriters Assn., 322 U.S. 533, 579 (1944)

"A MILITARY *order, however unconstitutional, is not apt to last longer than the military emergency. Even during that period a succeeding commander may revoke it all. But once a judicial opinion rationalizes such an order to show that it conforms to the Constitution, or rather rationalizes the Constitution to show that the Constitution sanctions such an order, the Court for all time has validated the principle of racial discrimination in criminal procedure and of transplanting American citizens. The principle then lies about like a loaded weapon ready for the hand of any authority that can bring forward a plausible claim of an urgent need. Every repetition imbeds that principle more deeply in our law and thinking and expands it to new purposes. All who observe the work of courts are familiar with what Judge Cardozo described as 'the tendency of a principle to expand itself to the limit of its logic.' A military commander may overstep the bounds of constitutionality, and it is an incident. But if we review and approve, that passing incident becomes the doctrine of the Constitution. There it has a generative power of its own, and all that it creates will be in its own image."*—JUSTICE JACKSON (dissenting). In Korematsu v. U.S., 323 U.S. 214, 246 (1944)

"ONE who belongs to the most vilified and persecuted minority in history is not likely to be insensible to the freedoms guaranteed by our Constitution. Were my purely personal attitude relevant I should wholeheartedly associate myself with the general libertarian views in the Court's opinion, representing as they do the thought and action of a lifetime. But as judges we are neither Jew nor Gentile, neither Catholic nor agnostic. We owe equal attachment to the Constitution and are equally bound by our judicial obligations whether we derive our citizenship from the earliest or the latest immigrants to these shores. As a member of this Court I am not justified in writing my private notions of policy into the Constitution, no matter how deeply I may cherish them or how mischievous I may deem their disregard. The duty of a judge who must decide which of two claims before the Court shall prevail, that of a State to enact and enforce laws within its general competence or that of an individual to refuse obedience because of the demands of his conscience, is not that of the ordinary person. It can never be emphasized too much that one's own opinion about the wisdom or evil of a law should be excluded altogether when one is doing one's duty on the bench." —JUSTICE FRANKFURTER (dissenting). In Board of Education v. Barnette, 319 U.S. 624, 646-647 (1943)

"THE case confronts us again with the duty our system places on this Court to say where the individual's freedom ends and the State's power begins. Choice on that border, now as always delicate, is perhaps more so where the usual presumption supporting legislation is balanced by the preferred place given in our scheme to the great, the indispensable democratic freedoms secured by the First Amendment. . . . That priority gives these liberties a sanctity and a sanction not permitting dubious intrusions. And it is the character of the right, not of the limitation, which determines what standard governs the choice."—JUSTICE RUTLEDGE. In Thomas v. Collins, 323 U.S. 516, 529-530 (1945)

THE PREAMBLE

WE, THE PEOPLE OF THE UNITED STATES, IN ORDER TO FORM A MORE PERFECT UNION, ESTABLISH JUSTICE, INSURE DOMESTIC TRANQUILLITY, PROVIDE FOR THE COMMON DEFENSE, PROMOTE THE GENERAL WELFARE, AND SECURE THE BLESSINGS OF LIBERTY TO OURSELVES AND OUR POSTERITY, DO ORDAIN AND ESTABLISH THIS CONSTITUTION FOR THE UNITED STATES OF AMERICA

THE Preamble, strictly speaking, is not a part of the Constitution, but "walks before" it. By itself alone it can afford no basis for a claim either of governmental power or of private right.[1] It serves, nevertheless, two very important ends: first, it indicates the source from which the Constitution comes, from which it derives its claim to obedience, namely, the people of the United States; second, it states the great objects which the Constitution and the Government established by it are expected to promote: national unity, justice, peace at home and abroad, liberty, and the general welfare.[2]

"We, the people of the United States," in other words, We, the citizens of the United States, whether voters or nonvoters.[3] In theory the former represent and speak for the latter; actually from the very beginning of our national history, the constant tendency has been to extend the voting privilege more and more widely: Woman's suffrage was established by the addition of the Nineteenth Amendment. More recently the right to vote in national elections has been extended to residents of the District of Columbia by the Twenty-Third Amendment, and in 1971 the Twenty-Sixth Amendment was passed insuring that citizens eighteen years of age or older shall not be denied the right to vote "by the United States or by any state on account of age." More vigorous implementation of the Fifteenth Amendment and passage of the Twenty-Fourth Amendment have enabled an ever-increasing percentage of Black citizens to vote. Consequently, the terms "voter" and "citizen" are becoming practically interchangeable as applied to the adult American.

"We, the People"

"Do ordain and establish," not *did* ordain and establish. As a *document* the Constitution came from the generation of 1787; as a *law*

---

[1] Jacobson v. Mass., 197 U.S. 11 (1905).

[2] "Its true office," says Story, "is to expound the nature and extent and application of the powers actually conferred by the Constitution, and not substantively to create them." Joseph Story, *Commentaries on the Constitution* (Cambridge, Mass., 1833), 462.

[3] "The words 'people of the United States' and 'citizens' are synonymous terms. . . . They both describe the political body who, according to our republican institutions, form the sovereignty, and who hold the power and conduct the government through their representative. They are what we familiarly call the 'sovereign people,' and every citizen is one of this people, and a constituent member of this sovereignty." Chief Justice Taney, in Dred Scott v. Sandford, 19 How. 393, 404 (1857). On the relationship between citizenship and voting, *see* Chief Justice Chase in Minor v. Happerset, 21 Wall. 162 (1874).

it derives its force and effect from the present generation of American citizens, and hence should be interpreted in the light of present conditions and with a view to meeting present problems.[4]

The term "United States" is used in the Constitution in various senses (*see e.g.* Article III, Section III). In the Preamble it signifies, as was just implied, the States which compose the Union, and whose voting citizens directly or indirectly choose the government at Washington and participate in amending the Constitution.[5]

The Frame-work of Government   Articles I, II, and III set up the framework of the National Government in accordance with the doctrine of the Separation of Powers of "the celebrated Montesquieu," which teaches that there are three, and only three, functions of government, the "legislative," the "executive," and the "judicial," and that these three functions should be exercised by distinct bodies of men in order to prevent an undue concentration of power. The importance of this doctrine as a working principle of government under the Constitution has been much diminished by Presidential actions in foreign affairs particularly with respect to employing United States forces abroad, by the growth of Presidential leadership in legislation, by the increasing resort by Congress to the practice of delegating what amounts to legislative power to the President and other administrative agencies, and by the mergence in the latter of all three powers of government according to earlier definitions. But responding to what it regarded as the excesses of the Nixon presidency, Congress has sought in recent years to recover some of its powers vis-à-vis the President. Following a decisive electoral victory in 1972, President Nixon impounded in wholesale fashion funds appropriated by Congress, made extraordinary claims for executive privilege, unilaterally reorganized the executive branch, and dealt cavalierly with Congressional reaction to his foreign and military policies. At the height of his assertions of executive power, the revelations constituting the "Watergate Affair" blossomed into full flower; Nixon's resignation, forced in part by the threat of impeachment, provided the ultimate testimony to the fact that Presidential power, no matter how it had grown, could not overwhelm Congress. As to the specific Nixon claims to power, discussion is provided in the exposition of the pertinent constitutional provisions (*see* pp. 108, 134, 157, 179, and 184).

So broad a principle as the doctrine of the Separation of Powers has naturally received at times conflicting interpretation by the Supreme Court, occasionally from the same judges.[6] The most recent

---

[4] *See* the words of Chief Justice Marshall in 4 Wheat. 316, 421 (1819).

[5] The most comprehensive discussion of this subject is that by counsel and the Court in Downes *v.* Bidwell, the chief of the famous Insular Cases of 1901. *See* 182 U.S. 244 (1901).

[6] *Cf.* in this connection Chief Justice Taft's opinion for the Court in *ex parte* Grossman, 267 U.S. 87, 119-120 (1925) with the same Justice's opinion in Myers *v.* U.S., 272 U.S. 52, 116 (1926); also Justice Black, for the Court, in Youngstown Sheet and Tube Co., 343 U.S. 579, 585-589, with Chief Justice Vinson, for the minority, *ibid.*, 683-700 (1952).

pronouncement of the Supreme Court on the subject recalled its decision in United States *v.* Nixon, 418 U.S. 683 (1974), saying: "Although acknowledging that each branch of the government has the duty initially to interpret the Constitution for itself, and that its interpretation of its powers is due great respect from the other branches, the Court squarely rejected the argument that the Constitution contemplates a complete division of authority between the three branches." The Court went on: "Like the District Court, we therefore find that appellant's argument rests upon an 'archaic view of the separation of powers as requiring three airtight departments of government.' Rather, in determining whether the Act disrupts the proper balance between the coordinate branches, the proper inquiry focuses on the extent to which it prevents the Executive Branch from accomplishing its constitutionally assigned functions. Only where the potential for disruption is present must we then determine whether that impact is justified by an overriding need to promote objectives within the constitutional authority of Congress."[7]

The Nixon years and their aftermath raises a perplexing question as to the future of the doctrine of separation of powers. Are the vigorous efforts of Congress to reassert itself a harbinger of the future or an anomaly to fend off the assertions of power of the only American President to resign while in office?[8] The response to the Carter presidency, free of the Nixon taint, should go far to answer that question.

[7] Nixon *v.* Administrator of General Services, 433 U.S. 425 (1977).
[8] *See* pp. 108-109. Also, it is noteworthy that some Congressmen were deeply disturbed by President Nixon's directive giving the Subversive Activities Control Board new functions without apparent legislative authority. For the President's Order see 36 *Fed. Reg.* 1283 (1971); for report of Congressional concern, *see* 1971 *Cong. Quart. Weekly Report*, 1549-1552. For report of Senate's retribution (voting to cut off funds for SACB), *see* 1972 *Cong. Quart. Weekly Report*, 1553. *See* 118 *Cong. Rec.* No. 175, S17968ff. (1972).

ARTICLE I

Article I defines the legislative powers of the United States, which it vests in Congress.

SECTION I

¶All legislative powers herein granted shall be vested in a Congress of the United States, which shall consist of a Senate and House of Representatives.

This seems to mean that no other branch of the Government except Congress may make laws; but as a matter of fact, by Article VI, ¶2, treaties which are made "under the authority of the United States" have for some purposes the force of laws, and the same has on a few occasions been held to be true of "executive agreements" entered into by the President by virtue of his diplomatic powers.[1] Also, of course, judicial decisions make law since later decisions may be, by the principle of *stare decisis*, based upon them. Indeed, the Supreme Court, by its decisions interpreting the Constitution, constantly alters the practical effect and application thereof. As Woodrow Wilson aptly put it, the Supreme Court is "a kind of Constitutional Convention in continuous session." Likewise, regulations laid down by the President, heads of departments, or administrative bodies, such as the Interstate Commerce Commission, the Securities and Exchange Commission, and so on, are laws and will be treated by the courts as such when they are made in the exercise of authority validly "delegated" by Congress. — "Law" in the Constitution

From this section, in particular, is derived the doctrine that the National Government is one of "enumerated powers," a doctrine which was given classic expression by Chief Justice Marshall in 1819 in the following words: "This government is acknowledged by all, to be one of enumerated powers. The principle, that it can exercise only the powers granted to it, would seem too apparent, to have required to be enforced by all those arguments, which its enlightened friends, while it was depending before the people, found it necessary to urge; that principle is now universally admitted."[2] The doctrine is today subject to many exceptions. In particular, "the executive power" and "the judicial power" have not been confined to "enumerated powers" (*see* p. 148 and p. 204). Indeed, in 1828 Marshall himself held that "the Constitution confers absolutely on the government of the Union, the powers of making war, and of making treaties; consequently, that government possesses — "A Government of Enumerated Powers"

---

[1] B. Altman & Co. *v.* U.S., 224 U.S. 583 (1912); United States *v.* Belmont, 301 U.S. 324 (1937); United States *v.* Pink, 315 U.S. 203 (1942). *Cf.* Tucker *v.* Alexandroff, 183 U.S. 424, both opinions (1902).
[2] McCulloch *v.* Md., 4 Wheat. 316, 405 (1819).

the power of acquiring territory, either by conquest or by treaty."[3] And from the power to acquire territory, he continued, arose as "the inevitable consequence" the right to govern it.[4] Subsequently powers have been repeatedly ascribed to the National Government by the Court on grounds which ill accord with the doctrine of enumerated powers: the power to legislate in effectuation of the "rights expressly given, and duties expressly enjoined" by the Constitution;[5] the power to impart to the paper currency of the Government the quality of legal tender in the payment of debts;[6] the power to acquire territory by discovery;[7] the power to legislate for the protection of the Indian tribes wherever situated in the United States;[8] the power to exclude and deport aliens;[9] and to require that those who are admitted be registered and fingerprinted;[10] and finally the complete powers of sovereignty, both those of war and peace, in the conduct of foreign relations.[11]

For the most part, the great expansion of the power of the National Government has not come about by breaching the *doctrine* of enumerated powers as it pertains to Congress, but rather by broad interpretation of those specific powers, notably the commerce clause, and by a liberal interpretation of the "necessary and proper" clause. Nonetheless, the Supreme Court has, in the main, limited Congress to its enumerated powers.

Relevant to this discussion is the recognition that several of the Constitutional amendments confer specific powers on the Congress. For example, the Thirteenth, Fourteenth, and Fifteenth Amendments each state that "Congress shall have power to enforce this article by appropriate legislation."

Also ascribable to Section I is the doctrine that "the legislature" (*i.e.* Congress) "may not delegate its powers," which was once expounded by Chief Justice Taft as follows: "The well-known maxim '*Delegata potestas non potest delegari,*' applicable to the law of agency in the general and common law, is well understood and has had

---

[3] 1 Pet. 511, 542 (1828).   [4] *Ibid.*, 543.

[5] Prigg *v*. Pa., 16 Pet. 539, 616, 618-619 (1842).

[6] Julliard *v*. Greenman, 110 U.S. 421, 449-450 (1884). *See also* Justice Bradley's concurring opinion in Knox *v*. Lee, 12 Wall. 457, 565 (1871).

[7] United States *v*. Jones, 109 U.S. 513 (1883).

[8] United States *v*. Kagama, 118 U.S. 375 (1886); Mescalero Apache Tribe *v*. Jones, 489 P. 2d. 666, 668 (1971). More recently the Supreme Court has attributed the source of Federal authority over Indian matters to the Federal responsibility for regulating commerce with Indian tribes and for treaty making. McClanahan *v*. Arizona Tax Com'n, 411 U.S. 164 (1973). *But see* Robinson *v*. Wolff, 349 F.Supp. 514, 521 (1972). (See p. 83.)

[9] Fong Yue Ting *v*. U.S., 149 U.S. 698 (1893).

[10] Hines *v*. Davidowitz *et al.*, 312 U.S. 52 (1941).

[11] United States *v*. Curtiss-Wright Export Corp., 299 U.S. 304, 315, 316-318 *passim* (1936). For anticipations of this conception of the powers of the National Government in the field of foreign relations, *see* Pennhallow *v*. Doane, 3 Dall. 54, 80, 81 (1795); *also ibid.*, 74 and 76 (argument of counsel); *also* Chief Justice Taney's opinion in Holmes *v*. Jennison, 14 Pet. 540, 575-576 (1840).

wider application in the construction of our Federal and State Constitutions than it has in private law. The Federal Constitution and State Constitutions of this country divide the governmental power into three branches . . . in carrying out that constitutional division . . . it is a breach of the National fundamental law if Congress gives up its legislative power and transfers it to the President, or to the Judicial branch, or if by law it attempts to invest itself or its members with either executive power or judicial power. This is not to say that the three branches are not co-ordinate parts of one government and that each in the field of its duties may not invoke the action of the two other branches in so far as the action invoked shall not be an assumption of the constitutional field of action of another branch. In determining what it may do in seeking assistance from another branch, the extent and character of that assistance must be fixed according to common sense and the inherent necessities of the governmental coordination."[12]

As indicated above, this doctrine, too, considered as a judicially enforcible constitutional limitation, has suffered enfeeblement, especially within recent years. This results, in the first place, from the vast expansion of the national legislative power over private enterprise and industrial relations, through the independent regulatory agencies, such as the I.C.C., the F.T.C., the S.E.C., the N.L.R.B., etc. From the nature of the case a good deal of latitude must be accorded such bodies in the discharge of their duties. In the second place, war has eroded the doctrine. Legislation conferring upon the President and his subordinates powers to deal with a fluid war situation must necessarily be couched in fluid terms. The subject is illustrated in later pages.[13]

Although the Supreme Court has insisted that Congress must set an "intelligible standard"[14] in delegating power, it has not been loathe to accept such general terms as "public interest" and "public convenience," "interest" or "necessity" as meeting constitutional requirements.[15]

The extent to which the doctrine of non-delegation has been enfeebled was demonstrated in recent decisions of the Supreme Court. The Trade Expansion Act of 1962 as amended by the Trade

[12] Hampton Jr. & Co. *v.* U.S., 276 U.S. 394, 405, 406 (1928). *See also* the excellent article by P. W. Duff and Horace E. Whiteside, "Delegata Potestas non Potest Delegari," in Douglas B. Maggs (ed.), *Selected Essays on Constitutional Law*, IV (Chicago, 1938), 291-316.

[13] *See infra* pp. 107-110 and 157-163.

[14] Sunshine Coal Co. *v.* Adkins, 310 U.S. 381, 398 (1940); U.S. *v.* Rock Royal Co-op, 307 U.S. 533, 577 (1939).

[15] N.Y. Central Securities Co. *v.* U.S., 287 U.S. 12, 24 (1932); Radio Com'n *v.* Nelson Bros. Co., 289 U.S. 266, 285 (1933); Nat. Broadcasting Co. *v.* U.S., 319 U.S. 190, 225 (1943); Federal Com'n *v.* Broadcasting Co., 309 U.S. 134, 138 (1940); U.S. *ex. rel.* Knauff *v.* Shaughnessy, 338 U.S. 537 (1950). *But see* Panama Refining Co. *v.* Ryan, 293 U.S. 388 (1935); Schechter Corp. *v.* U.S., 295 U.S. 495 (1935); Kent *v.* Dulles, 357 U.S. 116 (1958); Justice Brennan's separate opinion in Robel *v.* U.S., 389 U.S. 258, 274 (1967) and dissenters' rejoinder at 288, note 2.

Act of 1974 provides that, if the Secretary of the Treasury finds that an "article is being imported into the United States in such quantities or under such circumstances as to threaten to impair the national security," the President is authorized to take such action to "adjust the imports . . . so that . . . [they] will not impair the national security." In a challenge to a Presidential action that, among other things, raised the license fees on imported oil, the Supreme Court decided that "Taken as a whole then, the legislative history . . . belies any suggestion that Congress, despite its use of broad language in the statute itself, intended to limit the President's authority to the imposition of quotas and to bar the President from imposing a license fee system like the one challenged here. To the contrary [the history] lead[s] to the conclusion that . . . [the act] does in fact authorize the actions of the President challenged here. Accordingly, the judgment of the Court of Appeals to the contrary cannot stand."[16] But the Court did warn in conclusion that the "holding today is a limited one" that the act "in no way compels the further conclusion that *any* action the President might take, as long as it has even a remote impact on imports, is also so authorized."

Further, against the contention that it was an unconstitutional delegation of power, the Court in 1975 upheld a Congressional statute that allowed Indian tribes, with the approval of the Secretary of the Interior to regulate the introduction of liquor into "Indian country," so long as state law was not violated. Justice Rehnquist speaking for the Court explained that limitations on Congress's power to delegate are "less stringent in cases where the entity exercising the delegated authority itself possesses independent authority over the subject matter" and "that when Congress delegated its authority to control the introduction of alcoholic beverages into Indian country, it did so to entities which possess a certain degree of independent authority over matters that affect the internal and social relations of tribal life."[17]

In view of the extraordinary extent of the power delegated to the President in the Stabilization Act of 1970, a decision of the Temporary Emergency Court of Appeals holding that the act was not an unconstitutional delegation of legislative power to the President is noteworthy.[18]

Lastly, the term "legislative powers" connotes certain powers of the individual houses of Congress which are essential to their satisfactory performance of their legislative role. Some of these are conferred upon them in specific terms in the following sections, some are "inherent," or more strictly speaking are *inherited*. The subject is treated below.

[16] Federal Energy Administration *v*. Algonquin SNG, Inc., 426 U.S. 548 (1976).
[17] United States *v*. Mazurie, 419 U.S. 544, 556-557 (1975).
[18] DeRieux *v*. Five Smiths, Inc., 499 F. 2d. 1321 (1974).

SECTION II

¶1. The House of Representatives shall be composed of members chosen every second year by the people of the several States, and the electors in each State shall have the qualifications requisite for electors of the most numerous branch of the State legislature.

The House of Representatives

"Electors" are voters. The right here conferred is extended by Amendment XVII to the choice of Senators. While the enjoyment of this right is confined by these provisions to persons who are able to meet the requirements prescribed by the States for voting, provided these do not transgress the Constitution (*e.g.* Amendments XV, XIX, and XXIV), yet the right itself comes, not from the States, but from the Constitution, and so is a "privilege and immunity" of national citizenship, about the exercise of which Congress may throw the protection of its legislation and which, under Section I of the Fourteenth Amendment, no State may "abridge."[1]

In 1964, in the landmark case Wesberry v. Sanders, the Supreme Court further enhanced the meaning of this provision by its decision that "we hold that, construed in its historical context, the command of Art. I§2, that representatives be chosen 'by the people of the several states' means that as nearly as practicable one man's vote in a congressional election is to be worth as much as another's."[2]

In 1973, Justice Rehnquist, speaking for the Court, indicated that the cases following in the wake of Wesberry v. Sanders interpreted the "command" that one man's vote be worth as much as another's to mean that it "permits only the limited population variances which are unavoidable despite a good faith effort to achieve absolute equality, or for which justification is shown."[3] Significantly, the opinion explicitly distinguished between the requirements of Article I, Section II, and the Fourteenth Amendment in regard to apportionment stating that "in the implementation of the basic constitutional principle—equality of population among the districts—more flexibility was constitutionally permissible with respect to state legislative reapportionment than in congressional redistricting." (*See* p. 522.)

¶2. No person shall be a Representative who shall not have attained the age of twenty-five years, and been seven years a citizen of the United States, and who shall not, when elected, be an inhabitant of that State in which he shall be chosen.

---

[1] *Ex parte* Yarbrough, 110 U.S. 651 (1884); United States v. Classic, 313 U.S. 299 (1941); United States v. Saylor, 322 U.S. 385 (1944).
[2] 376 U.S. 1 (1964).
[3] Mahan v. Howell, 410 U.S. 315, 320 (1973).

It was early established in the case of Henry Clay, who was elected to the Senate before he was thirty years of age, that it is sufficient if a Senator possesses the qualifications of that office when he takes his seat; and the corresponding rule has always been applied to Representatives as well.[4]

An "inhabitant" is a resident. Custom alone has established the rule that a Representative must be a resident of the *district* from which he is chosen.[5]

In 1974 the Supreme Court held as constitutional the provision of the California Code forbidding a ballot position to an independent candidate for elective public office if he had registered affiliation with a qualified party within one year prior to the immediately preceding primary election. Clearly, the Court did not believe that the provision as applied to candidates for Congress added qualifications for office contrary to Article I, Section II, ¶2. Justice White speaking for the Court reasoned: "A state need not take the course California has, but California apparently believes with the founding fathers that splintered parties and unrestrained factionalism may do significant damage to the fabric of government. . . . It appears obvious to us that the one-year disaffiliation provision furthers the State's interest in the stability of its political system. We also consider that interest not only permissible, but compelling and as outweighing the interest the candidate and his supporters may have in making a later rather than an early decision to seek independent ballot status. . . ."[6]

Justice Brennan was joined by Justices Douglas and Marshall in a vigorous dissent, suggesting that with respect to both issues vital State objectives could "be served equally well in significantly less burdensome ways."

Also, in 1974, a California court held that a State constitutional provision that a judge had to take a leave of absence without pay prior to filing for elective office "does not add a fourth eligibility requirement to run for Congress and may reasonably be construed in a manner consistent with Article I, Section 2, Clause 2 of the federal Constitution. . . ."[7]

¶3. Representatives and direct taxes shall be apportioned among the several States which may be included within this Union, according to their respective numbers, which shall be determined by adding to the whole number of free persons, including those bound to serve for a term of years, and excluding Indians not taxed, three-fifths of all other persons. The actual

---

[4] U.S., 74th Congress, 1st Sess., Senate Report 904 (1935); 79 *Cong. Rec.* 9651-9653 (1935).

[5] Asher C. Hinds, *Precedents of the House of Representatives*, I (Washington, 1907-1908), §414.

[6] Storer *v.* Brown, 415 U.S. 724, 736 (1974).

[7] Alex *v.* County of Los Angeles, 111 Cal.Rptr. 285, 293 (1974).

enumeration shall be made within three years after the first meeting of the Congress of the United States, and within every subsequent term of ten years, in such manner as they shall by law direct. The number of Representatives shall not exceed one for every thirty thousand, but each State shall have at least one Representative; and until such enumeration shall be made, the State of *New Hampshire* shall be entitled to choose three, *Massachusetts* eight, *Rhode Island and Providence Plantations* one, *Connecticut* five, *New York* six, *New Jersey* four, *Pennsylvania* eight, *Delaware* one, *Maryland* six, *Virginia* ten, *North Carolina* five, *South Carolina* five, and *Georgia* three.

This paragraph embodies one of the famous compromises of the Constitution. The term "three-fifths of all other persons" meant three-fifths of all slaves. Amendment XIII has rendered this clause obsolete and Amendment XIV, Section II, has superseded it.

The basis of representation following the census of 1910 was one Representative for substantially 212,000 inhabitants. Following the census of 1920 Congress ignored its constitutional duty to make a reapportionment, but reapportionment on the basis of the census of 1930 was provided for beforehand, by the Act of June 18, 1929. Under this act, the size of the House was restricted to 435 members, who were allotted among the States by the same method as was employed in the apportionment of 1911, the so-called "method of major fractions." The problem—obviously one for the statistical expert—was to find a number, or "electoral quotient," to divide into the population of each State which would give the predetermined total of Representatives—435—when, for each remainder in a State which was in excess of one-half of such number or "electoral quotient," an additional representative was allotted. By an act passed in 1941, however, this cumbersome method is replaced by the original "method of equal proportions," which is made possible by permitting Congress to depart from the number 435 within moderate limits.[8]

The Basis of Apportionment

In a noteworthy decision in 1976, a U.S. district court held that "Thus both the historical background and the plain meaning of the Constitution support the power of Congress to fix the number of representatives at a figure less than the maximum of one for every 30,000 inhabitants."[9]

The duty of Congress created by this paragraph to provide for an "enumeration" of population every ten years has grown into a vast, indefinite power to gratify official curiosity respecting the belongings and activities of the people. Thus in the decennial survey of 1940 a near revolt was provoked in upstate New York by the

The Census

[8] For a detailed description and analysis of the various modes of apportionment, *see* the document prepared for the Senate in 1940 by a Harvard mathematician, Edward V. Huntington, 76th Congress, 3rd Sess., Senate Document 304 (1940).

[9] Whelan *v*. Cuomo, 415 F.Supp. 251, 258 (1976).

rumor that 232 questions would be put by the enumerators. But popular irritation was allayed when it turned out that only (!) sixty-four questions would have to be answered and after the President had issued a proclamation warning people of the legal penalties they would incur if they failed to cooperate.[10]

A different kind of complaint emerged from the census of 1970. In hearings before the House Census and Statistics Subcommittee of the Post Office and Civil Service Committee, it was charged that there was an "undercount" of 15% in the ghettos.[11]

¶4. When vacancies happen in the representation from any State, the executive authority thereof shall issue writs of election to fill such vacancies.

A governor does not have the discretion to refrain from filling a vacancy.[12] (Compare this provision with provision for vacancies in Senate, which confers certain powers on State legislatures. *See* Amendment XVII, ¶2.)

¶5. The House of Representatives shall choose their Speaker and other officers, and shall have the sole power of impeachment.

The powers of the Speaker have varied greatly at different times. They depend altogether upon the rules of the House.

The subject of impeachment is dealt with at the end of the next section.

SECTION III

The Senate, a Continuing Body

¶1. The Senate of the United States shall be composed of two Senators from each State, chosen by the legislature thereof, for six years; and each Senator shall have one vote.

This paragraph has been superseded by Amendment XVII.

¶2. Immediately after they shall be assembled in consequence of the first election, they shall be divided as equally as may be into three classes. The seats of the Senators of the first class shall be vacated at the expiration of the second year, of the second class, at the expiration of the fourth year, and of the third class, at the expiration of the sixth year, so that one-third may be

[10] *New York Times*, Feb. 11, 1940. The source of the penalties referred to by the President in his proclamation was the Act of June 18, 1929, 46 *Stat.* 21 (1929).

[11] 1970 *Cong. Quart. Almanac* 527.

[12] Jackson *v.* Ogilvie, 426 F. 2d. 1333 (1970). The Massachusetts Supreme Judicial Court recently held that in filling a vacancy the applicable boundaries of the district would be those in effect at the last regular election if these boundaries had been changed in an intervening reapportionment statute. Opinion of Justices, 282 N.E. 2d. 629 (1972).

chosen every second year; and if vacancies happen by resignation or otherwise during the recess of the legislature of any State, the executive thereof may make temporary appointments until the next meeting of the legislature, which shall then fill such vacancies.

This paragraph explains how it came about that one-third of the Senators retire every two years, as well as why the Senate is a continuing body.[1] While there have been 95 Congresses to date, there has been only one Senate, and this will apparently be the case till the crack of doom.

As applied to a candidate for the United States Senate, an Ohio law prohibiting the candidacy for political office of persons who failed to file a report of campaign contributions within 45 days after their last election was held to be constitutional by a Federal District Court.[2] The three-judge court specifically stated that the law complied "with both the letter and spirit" of Sections III and IV of Article I. (See corresponding case with reference to the House, p. 10.)

The final clause of this paragraph also has been superseded by Amendment XVII.

¶3. No person shall be a Senator who shall not have attained to the age of thirty years, and been nine years a citizen of the United States, and who shall not, when elected, be an inhabitant of that State for which he shall be chosen.

Following the precedent set in the case of Henry Clay, mentioned above, it is not necessary for a person to possess these qualifications when he is chosen Senator; it is sufficient if he has them when he takes the oath of office and enters upon his official duties.[3]

¶4. The Vice-President of the United States shall be President of the Senate, but shall have no vote, unless they be equally divided.

This is the source of the "casting vote" of the Vice-President, which has been decisive on more than one critical occasion. Indeed, John Adams, our first Vice-President, thus turned the scales in the Senate some twenty times, one of them being the occasion when the President was first conceded the power to remove important executive officers of the United States without consulting the Senate, with whose "advice and consent" they are appointed.[4] All other

The "Casting Vote" of the Vice-President

---

[1] McGrain *v*. Daugherty, 273 U.S. 135, 181-182 (1927).

[2] Lukens *v*. Brown, 368 F.Supp. 1340 (1974).

[3] *See* 79 *Cong. Rec.* 5915-5917, 9650-9657, 9749-9778, 9824-9842 (1935). Senator Biden, Jr., of Delaware was elected at age 29 but turned 30 prior to taking office.

[4] Charles Francis Adams (ed.), *Life and Works of John Adams*, I (Boston, 1856), 448-450.

powers of the Vice-President as presiding officer depend upon the
rules of the Senate, or his own initiative. In early days they were
considerably broader than today.

¶5. The Senate shall choose their other officers, and also a President *pro tempore* in the absence of the Vice-President, or when
he shall exercise the office of President of the United States.

(*See* Amendment XXV.)

¶6. The Senate shall have the sole power to try all impeachments.
When sitting for that purpose, they shall be on oath or affirmation. When the President of the United States is tried, the Chief
Justice shall preside: and no person shall be convicted without
the concurrence of two-thirds of the members present.

The Im-
peachment
Power

Because the Constitution deals with impeachment in two separate articles, the discussion of impeachment is treated in two parts,
each deemed appropriate to the separate provisions. Consequently, pages 201-203 should be read in conjunction with what
follows here.

Impeachments are charges of misconduct in office, and are comparable to presentments or indictments by grand jury. They are
voted by the House of Representatives by a majority vote, that is, a
majority of a quorum (*see* Section V, ¶1).

The persons subject to impeachment are "civil officers of the
United States" (*see* Article II, Section IV), which term does not include members of the House or the Senate (*see* Article I, Section
VI, ¶2), who, however, are subject to discipline and expulsion by
their respective houses (*see* Section V, ¶2).

The charge of misconduct must amount to a charge of "treason,
bribery, or other high crimes and misdemeanors" (*see* Article II,
Section IV); but the term "high crimes and misdemeanors" is used
in a broad sense, being equivalent presumably to lack of that "good
behavior" which is specifically required of judges (*see* Article III,
Section I). It is for the House of Representatives to judge in the
first instance and for the Senate to judge finally whether alleged
misconduct on the part of a civil officer of the United States falls
within the terms "high crimes and misdemeanors," and from this
decision there is no appeal.

In 1803 District Judge Pickering was removed from office by the
process of impeachment on account of drunkenness and other unseemly conduct on the bench. The defense of insanity was urged in
his behalf, but unsuccessfully. One hundred and ten years later
Judge Archbald of the Commerce Court was similarly removed for
soliciting for himself and friends valuable favors from railroad
companies, some of which were at the time litigants in his court;
and in 1936 Judge Ritter of the Florida District Court was removed

for conduct in connection with a receivership case which raised serious question of his integrity, although on the specific charges against him he was acquitted.[5]

When trying an impeachment the Senate sits as a court, but has full power in determining its procedure and is not required to disqualify its members for alleged prejudice or interest. However, "when the President of the United States is tried, the Chief Justice shall preside," the idea being no doubt to obviate the possibility of bias and unfairness on the part of the Vice-President, who would succeed to the President's powers if the latter was removed.

The use of the words "try" and "tried" in this provision raises some intriguing questions. The concept of what constitutes due process and a fair trial has received much attention in the last several decades with ever-increasing protections afforded an accused. On the proposition that he who decides must hear the case, would this require that every Senator voting would have to hear all the testimony? What of the Senators' penchant for walking in and out of deliberations? And what of the Senators who in public statements before the impeachment proceeding have shown bias? As to the argument that the Constitution apparently provides that the Senate should decide these matters, what is to be made of the opinion in the *Powell* case (pp. 20-21)? There, the Supreme Court speaking through Chief Justice Warren specifically rejected a contention that the Court could only "declare its lack of jurisdiction to proceed" in the face of among other examples that the Senate's sole power to try impeachments was an explicit grant of "judicial power" to the Senate and was an exception "to the general mandate of Article III that the 'judicial power' shall be vested in the federal courts."[6]

"Two-thirds of the members present" logically implies two-thirds of a quorum at least (*see* Section V, ¶1).

¶7. Judgment in cases of impeachment shall not extend further than to removal from office, and disqualification to hold and enjoy any office of honor, trust, or profit under the United States; but the party convicted shall, nevertheless, be liable and subject to indictment, trial, judgment, and punishment, according to law.

The House has impeached twelve civil officers of the United States, of whom the Senate convicted four. The two most famous cases of impeachment were those of Supreme Court Justice Samuel Chase (1802) and of President Andrew Johnson (1868), both of which failed. All of those who have been convicted were judges of inferior

---

[5] W. S. Carpenter, *Judicial Tenure in the United States* (New Haven, 1918), 145-152; 80 *Cong. Rec.* 5602-5608 (1936).
[6] Powell *v.* McCormack, 395 U.S. 486, 514 (1969).

Federal courts. In several instances, however, Federal officers have
resigned to escape impeachment or trial.[7]

Since conviction upon impeachment does not constitute
"jeopardy of life or limb" (*see* Amendment V), a person ousted
from office by process of impeachment may still be reached by the
ordinary penalties of the law for his offense if it was of a penal
character.[8]

The Court of Appeals for the Seventh Circuit dealt in 1974 with
the interesting question of "whether a court has jurisdiction to try a
federal judge upon an indictment before his removal from office
by the impeachment process."[9] That court's answer was: "On the
basis of the text of the Constitution, its background, its contemporaneous construction, and the pragmatic consequences of its
provisions on impeachment, we are convinced that a federal judge
is subject to indictment and trial before impeachment. . . ."

On account of the cumbersomeness of the impeachment proceeding and the amount of time it is apt to consume, it has been
proposed that a special court should be created to try cases of alleged misbehavior in office, especially of inferior judges of the
United States. There can be little doubt that Congress has power to
establish such a court and to authorize such proceedings.[10]

SECTION IV

Congres-
sional Reg-
ulation of
Elections
¶ 1. The times, places, and manner of holding elections for Senators
and Representatives shall be prescribed in each State by the
legislature thereof; but the Congress may at any time by law
make or alter such regulations, except as to the places of choosing Senators.

This is one of the few clauses of the Constitution to delegate power
to the States. "Legislature" here means the State legislature acting
in its *law making* capacity and consequently subject to the governor's
veto, where this exists under the State constitution,[1] as it does today

---

[7] John D. Feerick, "Impeaching Federal Judges: A Study of the Constitutional
Provisions," 39 *Fordham Law Review*, 1, 25 (1970).

[8] Roger Foster, *Commentaries on the Constitution*, I (Boston, 1895), 505ff. This work,
of which only the first volume was ever published, contains a valuable, although
considerably out-of-date, discussion of the entire subject of impeachment under the
Constitution. *See also* remarks of Senator Joseph D. Tydings in 89th Congress, 2d.
Sess., Senate Committee on the Judiciary, *Hearings*, "Judicial Fitness," February 15,
1966, pp. 3-4. For difficulties in impeaching even corrupt judges, *see* Joseph Borkin,
The Corrupt Judge (New York, 1962), pp. 189-204.

[9] United States *v.* Isaacs, 493 F. 2d. 1124 (1974).

[10] Burke Shartel, "Federal Judges," 28 *Michigan Law Review*, 870-907 (1930);
speech of Senator Wm. G. McAdoo, 80 *Cong. Rec.* 5933-5940 (1936). *See also* Raoul
Berger, "Impeachment of Judges and 'Good Behavior' Tenure," 79 *Yale Law Journal*, 1475, 1530 (1970).

---

[1] Smiley *v.* Holm, 285 U.S. 355 (1932).

in all the States except North Carolina. Until 1842 State regulations of Congressional elections went unaltered by Congress, and Representatives were frequently chosen on State-wide tickets. By an act passed that year Congress imposed the district system on the States, and by one passed in 1911 added further requirements: Representatives must "be elected by districts composed of a compact and contiguous territory and containing as nearly as practicable an equal number of inhabitants." These provisions were omitted from the Act of June 18, 1929 (*see* p. 11).[2] As a result remarkable disparities in population existed at times even as between districts in the same State. The seventh Illinois district, for example, at one time contained over 900,000 inhabitants as against only 112,000 in the fifth Illinois district. Thus a single vote in the latter district counted more than eight votes did in the former in the choice of a Representative. Ultimately the Supreme Court decided that such disparity was unconstitutional on the grounds that Article I, Section II, required that as nearly as practicable "one man's vote in a congressional election is to be worth as much as another's."[3]

Under earlier legislation which the Act of 1929 leaves unimpaired, unless the State constitution specifies some other date—no State constitution does so now—elections for members of the House take place on the Tuesday following the first Monday of November of the even years; and votes must be by written or printed ballot, or by voting machine where this method is authorized by State law.[4]

May Congress, by way of regulating "the manner of holding elections," limit the expenditures of candidates for nomination or election to Congress? In the Newberry case,[5] which concerned a candidate for the Senate, four members of the Supreme Court took the view that the above quoted words referred only to the last formal act whereby the voter registers his choice, and so answered this question, "no"; but a fifth Justice, who with these constituted the majority of the Court on this occasion, expressly confined his opinion to the state of Congress's power before the adoption of the Seventeenth Amendment, when the election of Senators, being by the State legislatures, was much more evidently separable from the preliminary stages of candidacy than it is today. In United States *v.* Classic[6] the Court ruled in 1941 that certain Louisiana election officials who were charged with tampering with ballots cast in a primary election for Representative had been properly indicted under the United States Criminal Code for conspiring to deprive citizens of the United States of a right secured to them by the Constitution, namely, the right to participate in the choice of Representatives in

Party Primaries as "Elections"

---

[2] 46 *Stat.* 20, 26 (1929); Wood *v.* Brown, 287 U.S. 1 (1932).
[3] Wesberry *v.* Sanders, 376 U.S. 1 (1964).
[4] 2 U.S.C. 1 and 9.   [5] Newberry *v.* U.S., 256 U.S. 232 (1921).
[6] 313 U.S. 299.

Congress. This was held to include not only the right of the elector "to cast a ballot and to have it counted at the general election whether for the successful candidate or not," but also his right to have his vote counted in the primary in cases where the State law has made the primary "an integral part of the procedure of choice," or where "the primary effectively controls the choice." Three Justices dissented on a question of statutory interpretation, but took pains to voice their belief that Congress may regulate primaries at which candidates for the Senate and House are selected, a position which is further bolstered by later holdings that the Fifteenth Amendment protects the right to vote in party primaries.[7] Years earlier, moreover, the Court had asserted that the National Government must, simply by virtue of its republican character, possess "power to protect the elections on which its existence depends from violence and corruption," a sentiment which it reiterated and emphasized in 1934 with the *Newberry* case before it.[8]

In recent years Congress has endeavored to protect voters in Federal elections from intimidation, interference, and more subtle forms of voting discrimination in provisions of the Civil Rights Acts of 1957, 1960, 1964, and 1968 and the Voting Rights Acts of 1965 and 1970.[9] The 1957 act was based primarily on Congress's power under Section IV, but the later provisions aimed at vindication of voting rights were based on Congress's power under Amendment XV.[10]

In dealing with constitutional challenges to Congress's legislative efforts to remedy some of the perceived evils disclosed during the Watergate investigations by, among other things, limiting campaign contributions and expenditures, the Supreme Court in Buckley *v.* Valeo reiterated that "The constitutional power of Congress to regulate federal elections is well established."[11] However the Court went on to decide an important aspect of the case, the manner in which the commission to oversee the operation of the law was appointed (*see* p. 314), reasoning that: "There is of course no doubt that Congress has express authority to regulate congressional elections, by virtue of the power conferred in Art. I, §4. This Court has also held that it has very broad authority to prevent corruption in national Presidential elections. . . . But Congress has

[7] Smith *v.* Allwright, 321 U.S. 649 (1944); Terry *v.* Adams, 345 U.S. 461 (1953).
[8] *Ex parte* Yarbrough, 110 U.S. 651 (1884); Burroughs *v.* U.S., 290 U.S. 534 (1934). The right to have a vote counted means the right to have it counted honestly. United States *v.* Mosley, 238 U.S. 383 (1915); United States *v.* Saylor, 322 U.S. 385 (1944).
[9] 71 *Stat.* 634 (1957); 74 *Stat.* 86 (1960); 78 *Stat.* 241 (1964); 79 *Stat.* 437 (1965); 82 *Stat.* 73 (1968); 84 *Stat.* 314 (1970).
[10] U.S., 85th Congress, 1st Sess., House Report 291 (1957); 2 *U.S. Cong. & Adm. News* 1925, 1936 (1960); South Carolina *v.* Katzenbach, 383 U.S. 301 (1966); 2 *U.S. Cong. & Adm. News* 3278 (1970).
[11] Buckley *v.* Valeo, 424 U.S. 1 (1976).

plenary authority in all areas in which it has substantive legislative jurisdiction, . . . so long as the exercise of that authority does not offend some other constitutional restriction. We see no reason to believe that the authority of Congress over federal election practices is of such a wholly different nature from the other grants of authority to Congress that it may be employed in such a manner as to offend well established constitutional restrictions stemming from the separation of powers."

When U.S. Senate candidate Richard L. Roudebush sought a recount of the vote in his close 1970 race with Senator R. Vance Hartke of Indiana, it served as the occasion for the Supreme Court to address the question of the relationship between Article I, Section IV, and Article I, Section V. In 1972, the Court held that: "Unless Congress acts, Art. I, §4, empowers the States to regulate the conduct of senatorial elections. . . . A recount is an integral part of the Indiana electoral process and is within the ambit of the broad powers delegated to the States by Art. I, §4. . . . It is true that a state's verification of the accuracy of election results pursuant to its Art. I, §4 powers, is not totally separable from the Senate's power to judge elections and returns. But a recount can be said to 'usurp' the Senate's function only if it frustrates the Senate's ability to make an independent final judgment. A recount does not prevent the Senate from independently evaluating the election any more than the initial count does. The Senate is free to accept or reject the apparent winner in either count, and, if it chooses, to conduct its own recount."[12]

Further, the 1975 contest over a New Hampshire seat in the U.S. Senate illustrated two things about the provision that "each house shall be the judge of the elections . . . of its own members": One, the highly partisan nature of the contest in Congress[13] and, two, the reluctance of the courts to become involved.[14] Even more, the lengthy contest illustrated that the words do mean what they say, that the house (in this case, the Senate) will be the judge, although in the end it may pass the buck back to the voters.

Additional illustrations of judicial reluctance to settle elections to Congress were provided by the Supreme Court of Illinois and Texas in 1977.[15]

A three-judge Federal district court held in 1972 that a State statute that limited the absentee ballot in *State* and *local* elections to certain classes of voters such as members of the armed forces, students enrolled in colleges away from home, etc., was not unconstitutional.[16] The court did hold, however, that the law did conflict

---

[12] Roudebush v. Hartke, 405 U.S. 15 (1972).

[13] 1975 *Cong. Quart. Weekly Report*, 1409, 1325.

[14] Wyman v. Durkin, 330 A. 2d. 778 (1975).

[15] Young v. Mikva, 363 N.E. 2d. 851 (1977), and Gammage v. Compton, 548 S.W. 2d. 1 (1977).

[16] Prigmore v. Renfro, 356 F.Supp. 427 (1972).

with Federal law regarding *Presidential* elections and that the State must comply with the Federal statute.

See also references to *Storer*, *Alex*, and *Lukens* discussed above under Article I, Sections II and III.

¶2. The Congress shall assemble at least once in every year, and such meeting shall be on the first Monday in December, unless they shall by law appoint a different day.

This provision has been superseded by Amendment XX—the so-called Norris "Lame Duck" Amendment.

SECTION V

Powers of **¶1.** Each house shall be the judge of the elections, returns, and
the Houses   qualifications of its own members, and a majority of each shall
over   constitute a quorum to do business; but a smaller number may
Members   adjourn from day to day, and may be authorized to compel the
                 attendance of absent members, in such manner, and under
                 such penalties, as each house may provide.

The power conferred by this paragraph carries with it authority to take all necessary steps to secure information which may form the basis of intelligent action, including the right to summon witnesses and compel them to answer;[1] as well as the right to delegate such powers to a committee. And whenever either house doubts the qualifications of one claiming membership it may, during investigation, suspend him or even refuse to swear him in.

For a good many years the "qualifications" here referred to did not consist solely of the qualifications prescribed in Sections II and III above for Representatives and Senators, respectively. "Congress," it was said, "may impose disqualifications for reasons that appeal to the common judgment of mankind." In 1900 the House of Representatives excluded a Representative from Utah as "a notorious, demoralizing and audacious violator of State and Federal laws relating to polygamy and its attendant crimes";[2] while in 1928 the Senate refused to seat a Senator-elect from Illinois on the ground that his acceptance of certain sums in promotion of his candidacy had been "contrary to sound policy, harmful to the dignity of the Senate, dangerous to the perpetuity of free government," and had tainted his credentials "with fraud and corruption."[3] But when Adam Clayton Powell was elected to the House for the 90th Congress and was not permitted to take his seat on the grounds that he "had asserted an unwarranted privilege and im-

[1] Barry *v*. U.S., 279 U.S. 597 (1929).
[2] J. A. Woodburn, *The American Republic and Its Government* (New York, 1903), 247.
[3] 69 *Cong. Rec.* 1581-1597, 1665-1672, 1703-1718 (1928). On the privileges and procedure of the House generally, and supporting precedents, *see* Asher C. Hinds, *Precedents of the House of Representatives* (Washington, 1907-1908), 8 vols.

munity from the processes of the courts of New York; that he had wrongfully diverted House funds for the use of others and himself; and that he had made false reports on expenditures of foreign currency to the Committee on House Administration," the Supreme Court decided that "our examination of the relevant historical materials leads us to the conclusion . . . that the Constitution leaves the House without authority to *exclude* any person, duly elected by his constituents, who meets all the requirements for membership expressly prescribed in" Article I, Section II.[4]

Further, in *Buckley* (*see* immediately above), the Supreme Court gave short shrift to the argument that the provisions of Article I, Section V "augmented" Article I, Section IV saying: "The power of each House to judge whether one claiming election as Senator or Representative has met the requisite qualifications cannot reasonably be translated into a power granted to the Congress itself to impose substantive qualifications on the right to hold such office. Whatever power Congress may have to legislate such qualifications must derive from §4 rather than §5, of Article I."[5]

The circumstance that refusal by the Senate to seat one claiming membership must cause a State to lose its equality of representation in that body for a time is a fact of no importance constitutionally, equality of representation being guaranteed merely as against the power to amend the Constitution.[6]

For more on the relationship between this provision and Article I, Section IV, *see* p. 19 above.

¶2. Each house may determine the rules of its proceedings, punish its members for disorderly behavior, and with the concurrence of two-thirds, expel a member.

It is by virtue of its power to "determine the rules of its proceedings" that the Senate has been able to develop that most peculiar institution, the "filibuster." The core of the filibuster is the right of any Senator who can secure recognition from the Chair to talk on any subject that may enter his head, however remote it may be from the business underway, for as long as his legs will hold him up. For a time this unique institution seemed to be losing ground. Indeed, in 1917 the Senate for the first time in its history adopted a mitigated cloture rule. However, in 1948 Senator Vandenburg ruled in his capacity as President *pro tem*, that a motion to change the Senate's rules required the affirmative vote of two-thirds of the entire Senate membership, and this ruling was adopted by the Senate as "Rule 22." Asked for a clarification of this rule in 1957, Vice

---

[4] Powell *v.* McCormack, 395 U.S. 486, 522 (1969). Also instructive on this point is the decision on an exclusion by a State legislature, Bond *v.* Floyd, 385 U.S. 116 (1966).

[5] Buckley *v.* Valeo, 424 U.S. 1, 133 (1976).

[6] Barry *v.* U.S., 279 U.S. 597 (1929).

President Nixon expressed the opinion that it was "unconstitutional," inasmuch as it "denied the membership of the Senate the power to make its own rules." He acknowledged, however, that only the Senate could decide the issue.[7] Efforts to change the rule in recent years have been interesting.[8] The Senate in 1959 agreed that only two-thirds of those present would be enough to invoke cloture even on proposals for rules changes. Vice President Rockefeller was roughly initiated into his duties as presiding officer of the Senate in 1975 with another go-round on the filibuster rule. The outcome of the bitter contest was a modified cloture rule that changed the majority needed to end a filibuster to three-fifths of the *entire* membership. The old rule required two-thirds of all the Senators present and voting.[9]

Paradoxically, by virtue of its power to make its own rules, the Senate has adopted a practice that limits this power.

The Power of Each House over its Proceedings
In the exercise of their constitutional power to determine their rules of proceedings, the Houses of Congress may not "ignore constitutional restraints or violate fundamental rights, and there should be a reasonable relation between the mode or method of proceeding established by the rule and the result which is sought to be attained. But within these limitations all matters of method are open to the determination of the House. . . . The power to make rules is not one which once exercised is exhausted. It is a continuous power, always subject to be exercised by the House, and within the limitations suggested, absolute and beyond the challenge of any other body or tribunal."[10] But when a rule affects private rights, the construction thereof may become a judicial question. In Christoffel v. United States[11] a sharply divided Court upset a conviction for perjury in the district courts of one who had denied under oath before a House Committee any affiliation with Communism. The reversal was based on the ground that, inasmuch as a quorum of the committee, while present at the outset, was not present at the time of the alleged perjury, testimony before it was not before a "competent tribunal" within the sense of the District of Columbia Code. Further the Supreme Court ruled that Congressional committees conducting investigations must abide by their own rules.[12]

Congressional rules pertaining to access to the press galleries came under judicial scrutiny in recent years. In late 1973, in a case that involved denying *Consumer Reports* representatives access to the press galleries of Congress, District Judge Gerhard A. Gesell decided that "The Constitution requires that congressional press galleries remain available to all members of the working press, regardless of their affiliation. Exclusion of a publication can only be

---

[7] 103 *Cong. Rec.* 178 (1957).
[8] For a brief and illuminating history of the cloture rule, *see* U.S., 92d Congress, 1st Sess., Senate Committee on Rules and Administration, *Senate Cloture Rule*.
[9] 1975 *Cong. Quart. Weekly Report*, 545.
[10] U.S. *v.* Ballin, 144 U.S. 1, 5 (1892).   [11] 338 U.S. 84 (1949).
[12] Yellin *v.* U.S., 374 U.S. 109 (1963) and Gojack *v.* U.S., 384 U.S. 702 (1966).

sanctioned under carefully drawn definite rules developed by Congress and specifically required to protect its absolute right of speech and debate or other compelling legislative interest."[13]

The U.S. Court of Appeals for the District of Columbia reversed the decision of District Judge Gerhard A. Gesell holding that the rules pertaining to access to the press galleries were "for Congress to determine as a matter of constitutional power."[14] Despite the seriousness of the contention of *Consumer Reports* that the denial of access to the galleries violated the equal protection, due process and freedom of the press clauses, the court said it was "content to rest our ruling that this cause is not justiciable upon the ground that, performed in good faith, the acts of appellants [The Periodical Correspondents' Association was created to administer the Periodical Press Galleries; its regulations are promulgated by Congress, which retains the right of final approval of applications for admission to the galleries.] were within the spheres of legislative power committed to the Congress and the legislative immunity granted by the Constitution [Article I, 6, 1]."

The Legislative Reorganization Act of 1946 stems in part from the powers here conferred on the houses individually.[15] So far as it purports to limit such powers, the measure would, seemingly, amount to a sort of gentleman's agreement rather than a true law.[16]

¶3. Each house shall keep a journal of its proceedings, and from time to time publish the same, excepting such parts as may in their judgment require secrecy, and the ayes and nays of the members of either house on any question shall, at the desire of one-fifth of those present, be entered on the journal.

The obvious purpose of this paragraph is to make it possible for the people to watch the official conduct of their Representatives and Senators. It may be, and frequently is, circumvented by the "house" resolving itself into "committee of the whole," to whose proceedings the provision is not regarded as applying.[17]

¶4. Neither house, during the session of Congress, shall, without the consent of the other, adjourn for more than three days, nor to any other place than that in which the two houses shall be sitting.

---

[13] Consumers Union of U.S., Inc. *v.* Periodical Corresp. Ass'n, 365 F.Supp. 18 (1973).

[14] 515 F. 2d. 1341 (1975).   [15] 60 *Stat.* 812 (1946).

[16] Some of the provisions of 53 *Stat.* 561 (1939) raised similar questions. 83 *Cong. Rec.* 3547-3484 (1938).

[17] On the availability of the Journal as evidence concerning the presence of a quorum, the passage of an act, and collateral questions, *see* United States *v.* Ballin, 144 U.S. 1, 4 (1892); Field *v.* Clark, 143 U.S. 649 (1892); and Flint *v.* Stone Tracy Co., 220 U.S. 107, 143 (1911).

Legislative   In addition to the powers enumerated above, each house also
Contempts   possesses certain "inherent" powers which are implied in the
fact that it is a deliberative body or which were inherited, *via*
the early State legislatures, from the Parliament of Great Britain.
Each house may pass resolutions, either separately or "concurrently" with the other house, with a view to expressing its opinion
on any subject whatsoever, and may create committees to deal with
the matters which come before it. Also, each house has certain
powers of a judicial character over outsiders. If a stranger rudely
interrupts or physically obstructs the proceedings of one of the
houses, he may be arrested and brought before the bar of the
house involved and punished by the vote of its members "for contempt";[18] but if the punishment takes the form of imprisonment it
terminates with the session of the house imposing it. Also, each
house has full power to authorize investigations by committees
looking to possible action within the scope of its powers or of those
of Congress as a whole, which committees have the right to
examine witnesses and take testimony; and if such witnesses prove
The Investi-   recalcitrant, they too may be punished "for contempt," though in
gatory   this case the punishment is nowadays imposed, under an act of
Power   Congress passed in 1857, by the District Court of the District of Columbia, for "misdemeanor."[19] But it is not within the power of
either house to pry into the purely personal affairs of private individuals, or to investigate them for the purpose of "exposing" them,
or to deprive them of freedom of speech, press, and association;
and whether in a particular investigation a committee of Congress
has attempted to do any of these things rests with the Supreme
Court to say.[20] Indeed, in Watkins *v.* U.S. the Court went so far as
to suggest that it is entitled to rule whether a question put to a person under investigation by a Congressional committee was "relevant."[21] But the Supreme Court has made clear its general reluctance to question the motives of Congress. Justice Harlan speaking

[18] In the noteworthy case, involving Father Groppi's disruption of the Wisconsin
legislature, the Court held in 1972 that: "The past decisions of this Court expressly
recognizing the power of the Houses of Congress to punish contemptuous conduct
leave little question that the Constitution imposes no general barriers to the legislative exercise of such power. . . . We are therefore concerned only with the procedures which the Due Process Clause of the Federal Constitution requires a state
legislature to meet in imposing punishment for contemptuous conduct committed
in its presence." Groppi *v.* Leslie, 404 U.S. 496 (1972).
[19] 11 *Stat.* 155 (1857); for revised version of law, *see* 2 U.S.C. 192.
[20] On this topic, *cf.* Anderson *v.* Dunn, 6 Wheat. 204 (1821); Kilbourn *v.*
Thompson, 103 U.S. 168 (1880); *in re* Chapman, 166 U.S. 661 (1897); Marshall *v.*
Gordon, 243 U.S. 521 (1917); McGrain *v.* Daugherty, 273 U.S. 135 (1927); Jurney *v.*
McCracken, 294 U.S. 125 (1935); 2 U.S.C. 192; United States *v.* Bryan, 339 U.S. 323
(1950); Watkins *v.* United States, 354 U.S. 178 (1957); Barenblatt *v.* U.S., 360 U.S.
109 (1959).
[21] 354 U.S. 178 (1957); *see also* Barenblatt *v.* U.S., 360 U.S. 109 (1959); Wilkinson
v. U.S., 365 U.S. 399 (1961); Braden *v.* U.S., 365 U.S. 431 (1961); Deutch *v.* U.S.,
367 U.S. 456 (1961).

for the Court in Barenblatt *v*. United States said: "Nor can we accept the further contention that this investigation should not be deemed to have been in furtherance of a legislative purpose because the true objections of the Committee and of the Congress was purely 'exposure.' So long as Congress acts in pursuance of its constitutional power, the Judiciary lacks authority to intervene on the basis of motives which spurred the exercise of that power."[22]

For the treatment of the impact of the "executive privilege" on Congress's power to investigate, see pages 183-187.

SECTION VI

¶1. The Senators and Representatives shall receive a compensation for their services, to be ascertained by law and paid out of the Treasury of the United States. They shall, in all cases except treason, felony, and breach of the peace, be privileged from arrest, during their attendance at the session of their respective houses, and in going to and returning from the same; and for any speech or debate in either house they shall not be questioned in any other place.

Privileges and Immunities of Members

Since "treason, felony, and breach of the peace" cover violations of State as well as national laws, the immunity from arrest here conferred applies only to civil suits; it does not include immunity from service of summons in a civil suit; nor, by reasoning and authority, from being required to testify before a Congressional committee.[1] To illustrate, failure to obey a subpoena in a civil case resulted in a thirty-day jail sentence for Congressman Adam Clayton Powell. When appealed, the State appeals court's uneasiness about upholding the decision was manifested in *dicta* and the staying of the sentence to give Powell time to comply. But, nonetheless, the appeals court agreed with the lower court that Section VI was not a bar to sentencing Powell to jail for failure to obey the subpoena.[2]

Despite a like provision of the Illinois Constitution, a state legislator was convicted for speeding while returning home from legislative business. He asserted that he was privileged from such an arrest. An Illinois appellate court found that he had no such privilege asserting that the Framers of like language in the United States Constitution intended to exclude all crimes from coverage of the privilege.[3]

In practice, since the abolition of imprisonment for debt, this particular clause has lost most of its importance.

The provision concerning "speech or debate" not only removes

---

[22] Barenblatt *v*. U.S., 360 U.S. 109, 132 (1959).

[1] *See* Long *v*. Ansell, 293 U.S. 76 (1934), and cases there cited.

[2] James *v*. Powell, 274 N.Y.S. 2d. 192, 195 (1966), *affirmed*, 18 N.Y. 2d. 931 (1966) and 19 N.Y. 2d. 813 (1967).

[3] People *v*. Flinn, 362 N.E. 2d. 3 (1977).

every restriction upon freedom of utterance on the floor of the houses by members thereof except that supplied by their own rules of order, but applies also to reports and resolutions which, though in writing, may be reproduced in speech; and, "in short, to things generally done in a session of the House by one of its members in relation to the business before it."[4] Nor will the claim of an unworthy purpose suffice to destroy the privilege. "One must not expect uncommon courage even in legislators."[5]

A covey of recent highly publicized cases have buttressed broad claims for the immunity privilege as it relates to the "speech or debate" provision.[6] As Chief Justice Warren put it in the *Powell* case: "Although the clause sprang from a fear of seditious libel actions instituted by the Crown to punish unfavorable speeches made in Parliament, we have held that it would be a 'narrow view' to confine the protection of the Speech and Debate Clause to words spoken in debate. Committee reports, resolutions, and the act of voting are equally covered as are 'things generally done in a session of the House by one of its members in relation to the business before it.' "[7] The Court had a short time before explained that the purpose of the clause is "to prevent intimidation [of legislators] by the executive and accountability before a possibly hostile judiciary."[8] But it should be borne in mind that Congressmen can still be held accountable for acts and utterances which cannot be construed as part of their *legitimate* legislative duties. Thomas F. Johnson was ultimately convicted for violations of a conflict of interest statute while he was a Congressman. He was found guilty of accepting payment for attempting to have the Justice Department dismiss a mail fraud indictment against the officers of a savings and loan association.[9] The first time around, the Supreme Court had upheld the court of appeals which had overturned Johnson's original conviction on the grounds that a speech he had given in the House and the preparation for it were part of the evidence used against him.[10] In June 1972, the Supreme Court overturned a district court ruling that former Senator Daniel B. Brewster could not be indicted for alleged bribery to per-

---

[4] Kilbourn v. Thompson, 103 U.S. 168, 203-204 (1880), citing and quoting from Chief Justice Parsons' famous opinion in Coffin v. Coffin, 4 Mass. 1 (1808); Powell v. McCormack, 395 U.S. 486 (1969).

[5] Justice Frankfurter, for the Court in Tenney v. Brandhove, 341 U.S. 367, 377 (1951).

[6] U.S. v. Johnson, 383 U.S. 169 (1966); U.S. v. Johnson, 419 F. 2d. 56 (1969); *cert. denied*, 397 U.S. 1010 (1970); Powell v. McCormack, 395 U.S. 486 (1969); U.S. v. Brewster, 408 U.S. 501 (1972); U.S. v. Doe, 332 F.Supp. 930 (1971), 445 F. 2d. 753 (1972) and 408 U.S. 606 (1972) (cited as Gravel v. U.S.); Stamler v. Willis, 287 F.Supp. 734 (1968).

[7] Powell v. McCormack, 395 U.S. 486, 502 (1969).

[8] U.S. v. Johnson, 383 U.S. 169, 181 (1966).

[9] U.S. v. Johnson, 419 F. 2d. 56 (1969); *cert. denied*, 397 U.S. 1010 (1970).

[10] U.S. v. Johnson, 383 U.S. 169 (1966).

form a legislative act. Chief Justice Burger speaking for the Court insisted that: "Taking a bribe is, obviously, no part of the legislative process or function; it is not a legislative act. It is not, by any conceivable interpretation, an act performed as part of or even incidental to the role of a legislator. . . . When a bribe is taken, it does not matter whether the promise for which the bribe was given was for the performance of a legislative act as here or, as in Johnson, for use of a Congressman's influence with the Executive Branch. And an inquiry into the purpose of a bribe 'does not draw into question the legislative acts of the defendant member of Congress or his motives for performing them.' "[11]

More recently, U.S. District Judge W. Arthur Garrity, Jr., concluded that, although Senator Mike Gravel could with impunity read the Pentagon Papers to his subcommittee and hence into the public record even while publication of the papers was temporarily barred pending a Supreme Court decision, *"Senator Gravel's arranging for private publication of the Pentagon Papers by Beacon Press stands on a different footing and, in the court's opinion, is not embraced by the Speech or Debate Clause. The test is not the public benefit or the political value of such private publication but whether it is a legislative act*"[12] (emphasis supplied). Subsequently, the Supreme Court buttressed this decision. It held that "We have no doubt that Senator Gravel may not be made to answer—either in terms of questions or in defending himself from prosecution—for the events that occurred at the subcommittee meeting. Our decision is made easier by the fact that the United States appears to have abandoned whatever position it took to the contrary in the lower courts."[13] The Court went on "We are convinced also that the Court of Appeals correctly determined that Senator Gravel's alleged arrangement with Beacon Press to publish the Pentagon Papers was not protected speech or debate."

Significantly, Justice Harlan speaking for the Court in *Johnson* suggested an interesting possibility for limiting immunity in the future: "Without intimating any view thereon we expressly leave open for consideration, when the case arises, a prosecution which though possibly entailing inquiry into legislative acts or motivations, is founded upon a narrowly drawn statute passed by Congress in the exercise of its legislative power to regulate the conduct of its members."[14] Congress has not yet accepted Harlan's invitation to pass such a statute.

---

[11] U.S. *v.* Brewster, 408 U.S. 501 (1972). Later, Brewster pleaded no contest to the charge of accepting an illegal gratuity and was fined $10,000. The judge, George L. Hart, Jr., was quoted as saying "I think it's time to say 'enough.' " The proceedings had covered six years. *San Diego Union*, June 26, 1975. A U.S. District Court recently held that a suit against a Congressman alleged to have submitted false travel vouchers was not barred by speech or debate clause. U.S. *ex rel.* Hollander *v.* Clay, 420 F.Supp. 853 (1976).

[12] U.S. *v.* Doe, 332 F.Supp. 930 (1971).

[13] Gravel *v.* U.S., 408 U.S. 606, 616 (1972).   [14] 383 U.S. 169, 185 (1966).

Another interesting question which arose in the Gravel case was the question of the immunity of Congressmen's staffs. The Supreme Court resolved that issue by holding that "We agree with the Court of Appeals that for the purpose of construing the privilege a Member and his aide are to be 'treated as one.' "[15] But the Court was also quick to conclude that "Neither do we perceive any constitutional or other privilege that shields Rodberg [the Senator's aide], any more than any other witness, from grand jury questions relevant to tracing the source of obviously highly classified documents that came into the Senator's possession and are the basic subject matter of inquiry in this case, as long as no legislative act is implicated by the questions." The Court then provided specific guidelines and remanded the case to the court of appeals. Consequently, the way was opened for the Government to seek indictments for the alleged arrangement with Beacon Press to publish the Pentagon Papers.

Following the *Gravel* case, the Supreme Court reaffirmed the broad protections afforded Congressmen-committee members, committee staff, consultant and investigator "for introducing material at committee hearings that identified particular individuals, for referring the Report that included the material to the Speaker of the House, and for voting publication of the report."[16] Justice White, speaking for a divided Court, explained that "Doubtless, also, a published report may, without losing Speech or Debate Clause protection, be distributed to and used for legislative purposes by Members of Congress, congressional committees, and institutional or individual legislative functionaries. . . . But he then went on to add these significant words: "However, the question remains whether the act . . . [of informing the public], simply because authorized by Congress must always be considered 'an integral part of the deliberative and communicative processes by which Members participate in committee and House proceedings' with respect to legislative or other matters before the House. . . . A Member of Congress may not with impunity publish a libel from the speaker's stand in his home district, and clearly the Speech and Debate Clause would not protect such an act even though the libel was read from an official committee report." Consequently, "By the same token, others, such as the Superintendent of Documents or the Public Printer or legislative personnel, who participate in distributions of actionable material beyond the reasonable bounds of the legislative task, enjoy no Speech or Debate Clause immunity."

[15] Gravel *v*. U.S., 408 U.S. 606, 616 (1972). *But see* Powell *v*. McCormack, 395 U.S. 486, 504-505 (1969).
[16] Doe *v*. McMillan, 412 U.S. 306, 311-314 (1973). The controversy over which the case arose is itself noteworthy for the emotions it stirred up. Parents of children in the District of Columbia schools were incensed by the dissemination of a congressional report on the D.C. school system which identified students in derogatory contexts.

In this case the Court also dealt with the doctrine of "official immunity." See page 449 for discussion of that issue.

Later, the extraordinary sweep of the Speech and Debate Clause was reaffirmed by the Supreme Court in an unusual case involving Congress's power to investigate. During a study of the Internal Security Act of 1950, the Senate Subcommittee on Internal Security issued a subpoena to the bank in which a particular servicemen's organization held its account, ordering the bank to produce all records involving that account. In the past, organizations that resisted giving over their records to investigating committees of Congress could simply refuse and then contest the legitimacy of the committee's action in responding to contempt charges in the courts. But here the bank, a third party, apparently was unwilling to risk a contempt citation. Consequently, the only way the servicemen's organization could prevent the implementation of the subpoena was to seek to enjoin the subcommittee collectively and individually from issuing the subpoena. When the case reached the Supreme Court, the Court concluded "that the Speech or Debate Clause provides complete immunity for the Members for issuance of this subpoena."[17] As a prelude to the holding, the Court pointed out that "In determining whether particular activities other than literal speech or debate fall within 'the legitimate legislative sphere' we look to see whether the activities are 'done in a session of the House by one of its members in relation to the business before it.' "

Justice Douglas's dissent was short but pungent: "Under our federal regime that delegates, by the Constitution and Acts of Congress, awesome powers to individuals, that power may not be used to deprive people of their First Amendment or other constitutional rights. It is my view that no official, no matter how high or majestic his or her office, who is within the reach of judicial process, may invoke immunity for his actions for which wrongdoers normally suffer. There may be a few occasions when, on the merits, it would be appropriate to invoke such a remedy. But no regime of law that can rightfully claim that name may make trustees of these vast powers immune from actions brought by people who have been wronged by official action."

Several lower court opinions relating to the Speech and Debate Clause are worthy of mention.

The issue involving the Superintendent of Documents and the Public Printer in Doe *v.* McMillan had been remanded to the United States District Court, D.C. After ascertaining the facts, Judge Pratt concluded that all the actions of those officials "did not exceed the legitimate legislative needs of Congress and thus their action remained within the limits of immunity of the Speech or Debate Clause and the doctrine of official immunity."[18]

[17] Eastland *v.* United States Servicemen's Fund, 421 U.S. 491, 507 (1975).
[18] Doe *v.* McMillan, 374 F.Supp. 1313, 1316 (1974).

When G. Gordon Liddy as defendant in one of the Watergate cases sought to strike the testimony of E. Howard Hunt on the grounds that Hunt's testimony before an executive session of a House subcommittee had not been produced in violation of his rights under the Jencks Act,[19] Judge Gesell held that "judicial efforts to compel production of that document would, under the present circumstances, also violate the Speech and Debate Clause." After denying the motion, Judge Gesell did urge "that the House of Representatives, in accordance with its rules and procedures, produce the subpoenaed testimony for *in camera* inspection by the Court"[20]—but to no avail.

A Texas court rejected the novel contention that "The Federal Constitutional immunity bestowed on national legislators by Article I, Section 6, is applicable to state legislators through the due process clause of the Fourteenth Amendment."[21]

A recent decision of the New Hampshire Supreme Court suggests that legislative immunity under this provision is much broader than has previously been recognized. After the Speaker of the New Hampshire House had ordered a member of the House arrested in order to secure a quorum, the member sued for false arrest and false imprisonment. In reviewing the case, the New Hampshire court explicitly pointed out that the State constitutional provision was the equivalent of Article I, Section VI of the United States Constitution. Citing several U.S. Supreme Court decisions, it asserted that "The language of the constitution must be read broadly to include any act 'generally done in a session of the House by one of its members in relation to the business before it.' "[22] The court then held that the Speaker was protected by the legislative privilege: "as the defendant was acting in the performance of official duties in relation to the business before the house, he must be protected 'not only from the consequences of litigation's results but also from the burden of defending (himself).' "

The U.S. Court of Appeals, District of Columbia, decided that subpoenas issued by a Congressional subcommittee "were not invalid as the fruit of an unlawful search and seizure" even though the materials that served as the basis for the subpoenas had been taken from the home of citizens by State agents in an unlawful search and seizure and turned over to a Senator and his aides.[23] The court allowed as how "it would appear impossible to subpoena

---

[19] The act requires that "after a witness called by the United States has testified on direct examination, the court shall, on motion of the defendant, order the United States to produce any statement . . . of the witness in the possession of the United States which relates to the subject matter as to which the witness testified." 18 U.S.C. §3500.

[20] United States *v.* Ehrlichman, 389 F.Supp. 95, 97 (1974).

[21] Mutscher *v.* State, 514 S.W. 2d. 905, 914 (1974).

[22] Keefe *v.* Roberts, 355 A. 2d. 824 (1976).

[23] McSurely *v.* McClellan, 521 F. 2d. 1024 (1975).

materials relating to an investigation without first obtaining enough information to know to whom, where, and for what the subpoena should be directed." It determined that the acquisition of the materials by the Senator and his aides in this case was for a legislative purpose. The court did caution, however, that "If Congressional investigations are to take advantage of the immunity afforded by the Speech or Debate Clause, . . . they must use lawful investigative means to obtain their information." Specifically, the court said that members or employees of Congress would not be protected from a suit under the Fourth Amendment, if *they themselves* engage in an unlawful search and seizure nor would they be protected by constitutional immunity for dissemination of information outside of Congress. Later, on rehearing *en banc*, the Appeals Court held that the use of the seized materials outside of Congress did not, indeed, meet the test of *Gravel*.[24]

In another interesting and significant Speech or Debate Clause case in the lower courts, a U.S. court of appeals held that in *Federal criminal* prosecutions, a State legislator has a Federal common law speech or debate privilege.[25] In the same case, the court decided that a State legislator who testified before a grand jury had waived his privilege in doing so "Because he was a state legislator, knowledgeable in the workings of the government and represented by competent counsel, his election to testify waived his Speech or Debate Clause privilege." As to a general proposition on waiver under this clause, the court said: "To the extent the inquiry impugns only the personal independence of the legislator and does not call into question the independence of other members of the body, the protection of the speech or debate privilege can be waived."

Also with respect to State legislators, the Pennsylvania Supreme Court found that there was "no basis for distinguishing the scope of the State Constitution speech and debate clause . . . from that of the Federal Constitution's."[26] When a Congressman recently sought a defense in this clause to the charge that he had dismissed a female staff member because of her sex, a U.S. court of appeals decided that "statements" of the Supreme Court "compel the conclusion that representatives are not immune from inquiry into their decisions to dismiss staff members," for "legislators are not legislating when they dismiss staff members."[27]

A research scientist angered by a press release from Senator Proxmire's office awarding him one of the Senator's "Golden Fleece of the Month Awards" filed suit for damages. The U.S. district court held that the Speech and Debate Clause rendered the

[24] McSurely *v.* McClellan, 553 F. 2d. 1277 (1976).
[25] United States *v.* Craig, 528 F. 2d. 773 (1976).
[26] Consumers Education & Pro Ass'n *v.* Nolan, 368 A. 2d. 675 (1977).
[27] Davis *v.* Passman, 544 F. 2d. 865, 880, and 881 (1977).

Senator immune from liability for authorizing the press release.[28]

To Maryland Governor Marvin Mandel's claim to legislative immunity where his duties involved interaction with the legislature, a U.S. District Court held that "the denial of the privilege afforded by the doctrine of legislative immunity will not contravene the purposes behind the privilege."[29]

Disabilities of Members
¶2. No Senator or Representative shall, during the time for which he was elected, be appointed to any civil office under the authority of the United States, which shall have been created, or the emoluments whereof shall have been increased during such time; and no person holding any office under the United States shall be a member of either house during his continuance in office.

Despite this paragraph Presidents have frequently appointed members of the houses as commissioners to act in a diplomatic capacity; but as such posts, whether created by act of Congress or not, carried no emoluments and were only temporary, they were not, it would seem, "offices" in the sense of the Constitution.[30]

The first clause became a subject of discussion in 1937, when Justice Black was appointed to the Supreme Court in face of the fact that Congress had recently improved the financial position of Justices retiring at seventy and the term for which Mr. Black had been elected to the Senate from Alabama in 1932 had still some time to run. The appointment was defended by the argument that inasmuch as Mr. Black was only fifty-one years old at the time and so would be ineligible for the "increased emolument" for nineteen years, it was not *as to him* an increased emolument. Similarly, when in 1909 Senator Knox of Pennsylvania wished to become Secretary of State in President Taft's Cabinet, the salary of which office had been recently increased, Congress accommodatingly repealed the increase for the period which still remained of Mr. Knox's Senatorial term. In other words, a Senator or Representative—and especially a Senator—may, "during the time for which he was elected, be appointed to any civil office under the authority of the United States, . . . the emoluments whereof shall have been increased during such time," *provided only* that the increase in emolument is not available to the appointee "during such time."

Another question concerning the first clause arose when the 91st Congress passed the Federal Salary Act of 1967, which authorized the President to include in his budget message for fiscal 1970 recommendations for an increase for Federal officials including the Secretary of Defense. President-elect Nixon announced his inten-

[28] Hutchinson v. Proxmire, 431 F.Supp. 1311 (1977).
[29] United States v. Mandel, 415 F.Supp. 1025, 1033 (1976).
[30] United States v. Hartwell, 6 Wall. 385, 393 (1867). *Cf.* W. W. Willoughby, *The Constitutional Law of the United States*, I (New York, 1929), 605-607.

tion to appoint Melvin R. Laird, a Representative in the 91st Congress, to the post of Secretary of Defense. Laird asked the Attorney General of the United States for an official opinion as to whether or not the Constitution precluded him from accepting the post. The Attorney General, Ramsey Clark, wrote Laird that: "Assuming that you are, in the normal practice at the beginning of a new administration, nominated, confirmed, and appointed as Secretary of Defense within a few days following the inauguration, *i.e.*, during the period in which it remains uncertain whether Congress may disapprove the Presidential salary recommendations, I believe your appointment will not be precluded by this constitutional clause."[31]

The second clause derives from an act of Parliament passed in 1701, which sought to reduce the royal influence by excluding all "placemen" from the House of Commons. The act, however, so cut the Commons off from direct knowledge of the business of government that it was largely repealed within a few years; and so the way was paved for the British "Cabinet System," wherein the executive power of the realm is placed in the hands of the leaders of the controlling party in the House of Commons. Conversely, the revival of the provision in the Constitution, in conformity with the doctrine of the Separation of Powers, lies at the basis of the American "Presidential System," in which the business of legislation and that of administration proceed largely in *formal*, though not *actual*, independence of each other. (*See*, however, Article II, Section II, ¶1, and Section III.) "Cabinet" versus "Presidential" System

In 1970, a committee of anti-war Armed Forces reservists filed suit in the United States District Court for the District of Columbia to force the expulsion of nine Senators and fifty Representatives from commissioned status as Reserve and National Guard officers on the grounds that such service by Congressmen violated this provision of the Constitution. The District Court of the District of Columbia held that the Constitution did, indeed, render "a member of Congress ineligible to hold a commission in the Armed Forces Reserve during his continuance in office." However, the court did not insist on compliance: "In the absence of an urgent necessity, and none is shown, the Court is loathe to take injunctive action which might prejudice the rights of Congressmen now seated who in some cases have been members of the Reserve for many years and may leave Congress at the end of their present terms. . . . In any event, if the issue of incompatibility is finally determined on appeal consistent with this decision, there is no reason to believe that Congress and the Executive will be unable to accommodate themselves voluntarily. . . ."[32]

---

[31] 42 *Op. Atty. Gen.*, Jan. 3, 1969.
[32] Reservists Committee to Stop the War *v.* Laird, 323 F.Supp. 833 (1971). Rep. McCloskey, Jr., resigned as a Colonel, U.S.M.C. Reserve, following an appeals court decision upholding the lower court. *N.Y. Times*, Dec. 10, 1972. *See also* 40 *George Washington Law Review*, 542, and 50 *Texas Law Review*, 509 (1972).

When the Supreme Court subsequently reviewed the case, it disposed of the issue by holding that those who sought to prohibit the Congressmen from serving as officers in the Armed Forces Reserve did not have standing.[33]

The argument about General Alexander M. Haig's holding his post as Vice Chief of Staff of the Army while serving as President Nixon's White House Chief of Staff did not turn, however, on this constitutional provision. Senator Symington objected on the grounds that the *U.S. Code* provides that no military officer "may hold a civil office by election or appointment" and that "the acceptance of such a civil office or the exercise of its function by such an officer terminates his military appointment." The Defense Department's legal officer contended that this provision did not apply since General Haig was performing his duties under the President's role as Commander in Chief.[34] The argument was cut short when it was announced that General Haig would retire from the Army on August 1, 1973, and be appointed an assistant to the President.[35]

SECTION VII

¶1. All bills for raising revenue shall originate in the House of Representatives; but the Senate may propose or concur with amendments as on other bills.

The House has frequently contended that this provision covers appropriation as well as taxation measures, and also bills for appealing revenue acts.[1] Although in practice most appropriation, as well as *all* taxation, measures do originate in the House the provision is otherwise negligible, inasmuch as the Senate may "amend" any bill from the House by substituting an entirely new measure under the enacting clause.

The Veto Power ¶2. Every bill which shall have passed the House of Representatives and the Senate shall, before it become a law, be presented to the President of the United States; if he approve he shall sign it, but if not he shall return it, with his objections, to that house in which it shall have originated, who shall enter the objections at large on their journal and proceed to reconsider it. If after such reconsideration two-thirds of that house shall agree to pass the bill, it shall be sent, together with the objections, to the other house, by which it shall likewise be reconsidered, and if approved by two-thirds of that house it shall become a law. But in all such cases the votes of both houses shall be determined by yeas and nays, and the names of the persons voting for and

---

[33] Schlesinger *v.* Reservists Committee to Stop the War, 418 U.S. 208 (1974).
[34] *New York Times*, May 27, 1973.   [35] 1973 *Cong. Quart. Weekly Report*, 1445.

[1] Richard F. Fenno, Jr., *The Power of the Purse* (Boston, 1966), 97-98 and 616-678.

against the bill shall be entered on the journal of each house respectively. If any bills shall not be returned by the President within ten days (Sundays excepted) after it shall have been presented to him, the same shall be a law in like manner as if he had signed it, unless the Congress by their adjournment prevent its return, in which case it shall not be a law.

A bill which has been duly passed by the two houses may become law in any one of three ways: first, with the approval of the President, which it has been generally assumed must be given within ten calendar days, Sundays excepted, after the *presentation* of the bill to him—not after its passage; secondly, without the President's approval, if he does not return it with his signature within ten calendar days, Sundays excepted, after such presentations; thirdly, despite his disapproval, if it is repassed by "two-thirds of each house," that is, two-thirds of a quorum of each house[2] (*see* Section V, ¶1).

Bills which have been passed within ten days of the end of a session may be kept from becoming law by a "pocket veto," that is, by the President's failing to return them till an adjournment of Congress has intervened; nor does it make any difference that the adjournment was not a final one for the Congress which passed the bill, but a merely *ad interim* one between sessions.[3] Likewise, the President may effectively sign a bill at any time within ten calendar days of its presentation to him, Sundays excepted, even though Congress has adjourned in the meantime, whether finally or for the session;[4] and, on the other hand, he may return a bill with his objections to the house of its origin, *via* an appropriate officer thereof, while it is in recess in accordance with ¶4 of Section V above.[5]

The fact that the President has ten days from their *presentation* rather than their *passage* within which to sign bills became a matter of great importance when President Wilson went abroad in 1919 to participate in the making of the Treaty of Versailles. Indeed, by a curious combination of circumstances plus a little contriving, the late President Roosevelt was enabled on one occasion to sign a bill no less than twenty-three days after the adjournment of Congress.[6] And in 1964 the Court of Claims held that where President Eisenhower during a trip abroad had determined with congressional acquiescence, that bills from Congress were to be received at the White House only for presentation to him upon his return, the President's veto of a bill more than ten days after delivery to the White House, but less than ten days from his return to the country, was timely.[7]

---

[2] Missouri Pac. Ry. Co. *v.* Kan., 248 U.S. 276 (1919).
[3] Okanogan Indians *v.* U.S., 279 U.S. 655 (1929).
[4] Edwards *v.* U.S., 286 U.S. 482 (1932).   [5] Wright *v.* U.S., 302 U.S. 583 (1938).
[6] *See* L. F. Schmeckebier, "Approval of Bills After Adjournment of Congress," 33 *American Political Science Review*, 52-54 (1939).
[7] Eber Bros. *v.*U.S., 337 F. 2d. 624 (1964); *cert. denied*, 380 U.S. 950 (1965).

The most recent controversy over the use of the pocket veto was interesting but somewhat inconclusive because it involved a very short recess. Senator Kennedy challenged a specific use of the pocket veto in Federal court. District Court Judge Waddy summed up his holding in these words: "All that is determined here is that the *short recess of the Senate in this case*, extending only two days beyond the ten day period the President had to sign or disapprove the bill, did not *prevent* the return of the bill to the Senate in which it originated. It follows therefore that the pocket veto was invalid and . . . [the bill] became a law without the signature of the President."[8] [Emphasis supplied.] The Senate had designated its secretary to receive messages from the President during the adjournment.

However, President Ford did not concede immediately.[9] Following the courts' decisions, he announced that he was pocket-vetoing several measures, but simultaneously he took the precaution of returning them with a veto message. In short, he protected his veto by inviting an attempt to override, but he put on the record the assertion that he did not need to do so. Ultimately, the Ford Administration announced in 1976 that it was giving up.[10] This was done in a brief statement to the U.S. District Court indicating that the Justice Department was dropping its opposition to Senator Kennedy's suit. But the Attorney General stated that an official of Congress would have to be designated to receive the President's vetoes during Congressional recesses.

Before President Jackson's time, it was generally held that the President ought to reserve his veto power for measures which he deemed to be unconstitutional. Today the President exercises this power for any reason that seems good to him.[11] But in no case may a President by executive action repeal a Congressional enactment. As the Supreme Court has said: "No Power was ever vested in the President to repeal an act of Congress."[12]

For a time President Ford's generous use of the veto became an important political issue. Despite the huge majorities the Democrats achieved in both houses of Congress in 1974 and the speculation that this might create a "veto proof" Congress, President Ford's first ten months in office saw him veto 30 public bills.[13] In four attempts to override vetoes of the emergency farm bill, the strip mining bill, the jobs bill and the emergency housing bill, the

---

[8] Kennedy v. Sampson, 364 F.Supp. 1075 (1973), *affirmed*, 511 F. 2d. 430 (1974). *See* 1973 *Cong. Quart. Weekly Report*, 2268. For a later decision on the same issue, *see* Kennedy v. Jones, 412 F.Supp. 353 (1976).

[9] *New York Times*, Nov. 10, 1974, and Jan. 12, 1975.

[10] 1976 *Cong. Quart. Weekly Report*, 887.

[11] For further details concerning the President's veto, *see* Edward S. Corwin, *The President, Office and Powers* (New York, 1957), 277-283.

[12] Confiscation Cases, 20 Wall. 92, 112, 113 (1874); Catano v. Local Board, 298 F.Supp. 1183 (1969).

[13] 1975 *Cong. Quart. Weekly Report*, 1333.

Democrats failed.[14] And by May of 1976, President Ford had vetoed 21 bills in the 94th Congress,[15] only three of which were overridden.

As to the question of when a statute takes effect, the Supreme Court has held: "There is no statute fixing the time when acts of Congress shall take effect, but it is settled that where no other time is prescribed, they take effect from their date."[16]

¶3. Every order, resolution or vote to which the concurrence of the Senate and House of Representatives may be necessary (except on a question of adjournment) shall be presented to the President of the United States; and before the same shall take effect shall be approved by him, or being disapproved by him, shall be repassed by two-thirds of the Senate and House of Representatives, according to the rules and limitations prescribed in the case of a bill.

The "Concurrent Resolution"

"Necessary" here means necessary to give an "order," etc., the force of law.[17] Accordingly "votes" taken in either house preliminary to the final passage of legislation need not be submitted to the President, nor resolutions passed by either house separately or by both houses "concurrently" with a view simply to expressing an opinion or to devising a common program of parliamentary action or to directing the expenditure of money appropriated to the use of the two houses. However, the "concurrent resolution" has been shaped to a different and highly important use. It has been employed as a means of claiming for the houses the power to control or recover powers delegated by Congress to the President. Thus the Reorganization Act of 1939 delegated power to the President to regroup certain executive agencies and functions subject to the condition that his orders to that end might be vetoed within sixty days by a concurrent resolution. Similarly, the Lend-Lease Act of 1941, the First War Powers Act of 1941, the Emergency Price Control Act of 1942, the Stabilization Act of 1942, the War Labor Disputes Act of 1943, all rendered the powers which they delegated subject to repeal sooner or later by "concurrent resolution." Congress has gone a step further in recent Reorganization Acts by stipulating that a majority of *either* house is enough to veto a Presidential order.[18] That Congress may qualify in this way its delegations of powers which it might withhold altogether would seem to be obvious.[19]

[14] *Ibid.*   [15] 1976 *Cong. Quart. Weekly Report*, 1116.

[16] Lapeyre *v.* U.S., 17 Wall. 191, 198 (1872).

[17] U.S., 54th Congress, 2d. Sess., Senate Report 1335 (1897).

[18] William J. Keefe and Morris S. Ogul, *The American Legislative Process* (Englewood Cliffs, N.J., 1968), 442-443; Congressional Quarterly Service, *Congress and the Nation* (Washington, D.C., 1969), II, 658; *U.S. Cong. & Adm. News*, 3487 (1971).

[19] On the "concurrent resolution" *see* Edward S. Corwin, *Total War and the Constitution* (New York, 1947), 45-47; U.S., 54th Congress, 2d. Sess., Senate Report 1335 (1897); Howard White, "The Concurrent Resolution in Congress," 35 *American*

Also, it has been settled by practice, which is generally considered, albeit without sufficient reason, to have been ratified by judicial decision, that resolutions of Congress proposing amendments to the Constitution do not have to be submitted to the President[20] (*see* Article V).

SECTION VIII

The
National
Legislative
Power

This is one of the most important sections of the Constitution since it describes, for the most part, the field within which Congress may exercise its legislative power, which is also the field to which the President and the National Courts are in great part confined.

Congress's legislative powers may be classified as follows: First, its "enumerated" powers, that is, those which are defined rather specifically in ¶s 1 to 17, following; second, certain other powers which also are specifically or impliedly delegated in other parts of the Constitution (*see* Section IV, above; also Articles II, III, IV, and V, *passim*, and Amendments XIII-XX, and XXIII-XXVI); third, its power conferred by ¶18, below, the so-called "coefficient clause" of the Constitution, to pass all laws "necessary and proper" to carry into execution any of the powers of the National Government, or of any department or officer thereof; fourth, certain "inherent" powers, that is, powers which belong to it simply because it is the National Legislature, the outstanding instances of which were listed earlier (*see* p. 6 above).

In studying each of the first seventeen paragraphs of this section, one should always bear in mind ¶18, for this clause furnishes each of the "enumerated" powers of Congress with its second dimension, so to speak.

The Taxing
Power

¶1. The Congress shall have power to lay and collect taxes, duties, imposts and excises, to pay the debts and provide for the common defense and general welfare of the United States; but all duties, imposts and excises shall be uniform throughout the United States;

Complete power of taxation is conferred upon Congress by this paragraph, as well as the largest measure of discretion in the selec-

---

Political Science Review, 886 (1941). Justice Jackson of the Supreme Court, who was President F. D. Roosevelt's Attorney General at the time of the enactment of the Lend-Lease Act, brought to light a memorandum of Roosevelt's in which the latter contended that the provision of the act giving the houses of Congress the right to cancel the measure by a simple concurrent resolution, rather than by legislation subject to Presidential veto, was unconstitutional, notwithstanding which, however, he signed the bill for "political reasons." It would appear that President Roosevelt's constitutional qualms were ill-based. Robert H. Jackson, "Presidential Legal Opinion," 66 *Harvard Law Review*, 1353 (1953).

[20] Hollingsworth *v.* Va., 3 Dall. 378 (1798). The case arose under Amendment XI after it had been approved by the required number of State legislatures. In these circumstances the Court declined to interfere.

tion of purposes for which the national revenues shall be expended. This complete power "to lay and collect taxes" is, however, later curtailed by the provision that no tax shall be levied on exports (*see* Section IX, ¶5). Also, it was ruled by the Supreme Court, shortly after the Civil War, that on principle Congress could not tax the instrumentalities of State government, and that the salary of a State judge, though in his pocket, was to be regarded as such an instrumentality;[1] and the benefits of this doctrine were subsequently extended to the holders of State and municipal bonds,[2] who were thereby exempted to the extent that their income was derived from such securities from paying income taxes to the National Government. It was at first widely believed that the Sixteenth Amendment had removed the grounds of this discrimination, so far as income taxes were concerned,[3] but the Court eventually ruled otherwise.[4] Indeed, at one time it appeared to be bent on seeing how far it could carry the principle of exemption, going to the length of holding that a manufacturer of motorcycles was not subject to the Federal excise tax on sales thereof with respect to sales to a municipality.[5] The Court has since abandoned this position completely. In Graves v. New York, decided early in 1939, Collector v. Day and New York v. Graves (decided early in 1937) were pronounced "overruled so far as they recognize an implied constitutional immunity from income taxation of the salaries of officers or employees of the national or a State government or their instrumentalities";[6] and it appears highly probable that the same rule would be applied, should Congress choose to invoke it, to the non-discriminatory taxation of income from State and municipal bonds. The power of Congress, however, to exempt national instrumentalities from State taxation, by virtue of the "necessary and proper" clause, still stands[7] (*see* pp. 227-228).

In a recent case the Court went further to hold that "express congressional consent" was not necessary for a Federal instrumentality to stave off State taxation. The Supreme Court struck down as unconstitutional a Mississippi State Tax Commission regulation that the Court described as requiring "out-of-state liquor distillers and suppliers to collect from military installations within Mississippi, and remit to the Commission, a tax in the form of a wholesale markup of 17% to 20% on liquor sold to the installations."[8]

[1] Collector v. Day, 11 Wall. 113 (1870).

[2] Pollock v. Farmers Loan and Trust Co., 157 U.S. 429 and 158 U.S. 601 (1895).

[3] *See* the evidence compiled in Edward S. Corwin, "Constitutional Tax Exemption," *Supplement to the National Municipal Review*, XIII, No. 1 (January 1924).

[4] Brushaber v. Un. Pac. R.R. Co., 240 U.S. 1 (1916); Evans v. Gore, 253 U.S. 245 (1920).

[5] Indian Motorcycle Co. v. U.S., 283 U.S. 570 (1931).

[6] Graves v. N.Y., 306 U.S. 466 (1939).

[7] Pittman v. HOLC, 308 U.S. 21 (1939); United States v. Stewart, 311 U.S. 60 (1940). Indeed, the Supreme Court has held that national securities are intrinsically exempt from State taxation. Society for Savings v. Bowers, 349 U.S. 143 (1955).

[8] United States v. State Tax Com'n of the State of Mississippi, 421 U.S. 599 (1975).

The Court held that the principle enunciated by Chief Justice Marshall in McCulloch *v.* Maryland "that possessions, institutions, and activities of the Federal Government itself in the absence of express congressional consent are not subject to any form of state taxation" applied. The Court concluded that the exception provided in the Buck Act of 1940 that no person would be relieved of liability for state taxes "on the ground that the sale or use, with respect to which such tax is levied, occurred in whole or in part within a Federal area" because of the further provision of that act that it "shall not be deemed to authorize the levy or collection of any tax on or from the United States or any instrumentality thereof." In short, the Court found that the legal incidence of the tax fell upon the purchaser, the military, which in the Court's view was an instrumentality of the United States. Also, the Court did not find that the Twenty-First Amendment required a different result. With respect to the relationship of the Commerce Clause and the Twenty-First Amendment, the Court most recently stated "the Twenty-First Amendment does not *pro tanto* repeal the Commerce Clause, but merely requires that each provision 'be considered in the light of the other, and in the context of the issues and interests at stake in any concrete case.' "[9]

In contrast to the treatment of Federal instrumentalities, when a State embarks upon an enterprise which if carried on by private concerns would be taxable, like selling liquor or mineral waters, or holding football exhibitions, such activities—once, but no longer, termed "non-governmental"—are subject to a non-discriminatory imposition of applicable national taxes.[10]

Collection of Taxes
In an important 1977 Supreme Court case, it was argued that "there is a broad exception to the Fourth Amendment that allows warrantless intrusions into privacy in the enforcement of tax laws." The Court replied "We recognize that the 'Power to lay and collect Taxes' is a specifically enunciated power of the Federal Government, and that the First Congress, which proposed the adoption of the Bill of Rights, also provided that certain taxes could be levied by distress and sale of goods of the person or persons refusing or neglecting to pay. This, however, relates to warrantless seizures rather than to warrantless searches. It is one thing to seize without a warrant property resting in an open area or seizable by levy without an intrusion into privacy, and it is quite another thing to effect a warrantless seizure of property, even that owned by a corporation, situated on private premises to which access is not otherwise available for the seizing officer." The Court concluded: "We do not find in the cited materials anything approaching the clear evidence that would be required to create so great an exception to the Fourth

[9] Craig *v.* Boren, 97 S.Ct. 451, 461 (1976).
[10] South Carolina *v.* U.S., 199 U.S. 437 (1905); Allen *v.* Regents, 30 U.S. 439 (1938); New York and Saratoga Springs Com'n *v.* U.S., 326 U.S. 572 (1946); Wilmette Park Dist. *v.* Campbell, 338 U.S. 411 (1949).

Amendment's protections against warrantless intrusions into privacy."[11]

Again, Congress must levy its taxes in one of two ways: all "duties, imposts and excises" must be "uniform throughout the United States," that is, the rule of liability to the tax must take no account of geography;[12] while on the other hand, the burden of "direct taxes" must be imposed upon the States in proportion to population (*see* Section II, ¶3, and Section IX, ¶4).

"Duties" are customs duties. If a certain article imported from abroad is taxed five percent at New York it must be taxed at the same rate at San Francisco, etc.

"Excises" are taxes upon the production, sale, or use of articles; also taxes upon certain privileges and procedures of a business nature. Congress has for years taxed the privilege of doing business as a corporation, and the Social Security Act of 1935 levies a tax on payrolls.[13]

"Imposts" is a general term comprehending both duties and excises.

From the time of the Carriage Tax case,[14] decided in 1796, to the Income Tax cases of 1895,[15] the Court proceeded on the theory that the "direct tax" clauses should be confined to land taxes and capitation taxes and should not be extended to taxes which were not easily apportionable on the basis of population. But in 1895, convinced by Mr. Joseph H. Choate that the country was about to go Socialistic, a narrowly divided Bench, one Justice—Justice Gray apparently—changing his mind at the last moment, ruled that a tax on incomes derived from property was a "direct tax" and one, therefore, that must be apportioned according to population; also, that incomes derived from State and municipal bonds might not be taxed at all by the National Government. This decision, which put most of the taxable wealth of the country out of the reach of the National Government, led in 1913 to the adoption of the Sixteenth Amendment.

"Direct" Taxes

Nor has the Court, since 1895, invoked its definition of "direct tax" except once in order to overturn a national tax measure, and that was in the Stock Dividend case of 1920[16] (*see* p. 540). At other times it has been satisfied to sustain challenged taxes on historical grounds as "excises," saying in this connection that "a page of history is worth a volume of logic."[17] Today inheritance taxes are so classified, as are also estate taxes and taxes on gifts, with the result

[11] G. M. Leasing Corp. *v.* U.S., 429 U.S. 338, 354-355 (1977).

[12] Florida *v.* Mellon, 273 U.S. 12 (1927).

[13] Flint *v.* Stone Tracy Co., 220 U.S. 107 (1911); Steward Mach. Co. *v.* Davis, 301 U.S. 548 (1937).

[14] Hylton *v.* U.S., 3 Dall. 171 (1796).

[15] Pollock *v.* Farmers Loan and Trust Co., 157 U.S. 429 and 158 U.S. 601 (1895).

[16] Eisner *v.* Macomber, 252 U.S. 189 (1920). But for a subsequent view of the Court, *see* Helvering *v.* Griffiths, 318 U.S. 371, 404 (1943).

[17] New York Trust Co. *v.* Eisner, 256 U.S. 345, 249 (1921).

that it is sufficient if they are "uniform throughout the United
States" in the geographical sense.[18]

Regulation
by
Taxation

While the raising of revenue is the primary purpose of taxation it
does not have to be its only purpose, as the history of the protective
tariff suffices to demonstrate. And in the field of excise taxation, if
Congress is entitled to regulate a matter, it may do so by taxing it.[19]
Also, Congress may use its power to tax to require gamblers and
marijuana sellers to identify themselves by purchasing tax stamps
and/or paying a special occupational tax. But in so doing, Congress
must be careful that the legislation does not permit violations of the
privilege against self-incrimination for the Court has again and
again in recent years held that "a timely and proper assertion of the
privilege" is "a complete defense to prosecution" under such measures.[20] As the Court explained in *Marchetti*: "The Constitution of
course obliges this Court to give full recognition to the taxing powers and to measures reasonably incidental to their exercise. But we
are equally obliged to give full effect to the constitutional restrictions which attend the exercise of those powers.[21] (*See* discussion of
self-incrimination clause pp. 373-384.) Furthermore, there are
some businesses which Congress may tax so heavily as to drive
them out of existence, one example being the production of white
sulphur matches, another the sale of oleomargarine colored to look
like butter, another the dealing of sawed-off shotguns.[22] On the
other hand, the Court some years ago held void a special tax on the
profits of concerns employing child labor, on the ground that the
act was not a *bona fide* attempt to raise revenue, but represented an
effort by Congress to bring within its control matters reserved to
the States;[23] and later it set aside a special tax on liquor dealers
conducting business in violation of State law, as being a "penalty"
and "an invasion of the police power inherent in the States."[24] That
such attempts to "psychoanalyze" Congress, as the late Justice Cardozo derisively characterized them,[25] would be repeated today,
seems at least doubtful.[26]

[18] *Ibid.*; Knowlton *v.* Moore, 178 U.S. 41 (1900); Bromley *v.* McCaughn, 280 U.S.
124 (1929).
[19] Veazie Bank *v.* Fenno, 8 Wall. 533 (1869); Mulford *v.* Smith, 307 U.S. 38
(1939).
[20] Leary *v.* U.S., 395 U.S. 6, 27 (1969). *See also* U.S. *v.* Covington, 395 U.S. 57
(1969); Marchetti *v.* U.S., 390 U.S. 39 (1968); Grosso *v.* U.S., 390 U.S. 62 (1968);
U.S. *v.* Freed, 401 U.S. 601 (1971).
[21] Marchetti *v.* U.S., 390 U.S. 39, 58 (1968).
[22] McCray *v.* U.S., 195 U.S. 27 (1904); Sonzinsky *v.* U.S., 300 U.S. 506 (1937);
United States *v.* Sanchez, 340 U.S. 42, 44 (1950).
[23] Bailey *v.* Drexel Furniture Co., 259 U.S. 20 (1922).
[24] United States *v.* Constantine, 296 U.S. 287 (1935). For other examples of earlier Supreme Court decisions finding that particular laws purported to be so were
not really revenue laws, *see* U.S. *v.* Norton, 91 U.S. 566 (1875) and Twin City Bank
v. Nebeker, 167 U.S. 196 (1897).
[25] United States *v.* Constantine, 296 U.S. 287 (1936).
[26] *See especially* Mulford *v.* Smith, 307 U.S. 38 (1939) and United States *v.* Darby,

A recent Supreme Court decision with respect to a city's tax is instructive on the subject of regulation by taxation. The city of Pittsburgh, to help solve its traffic problems, imposed a "20% tax on the gross receipts obtained from all transactions involving the parking or storing of a motor vehicle at a non-residential parking place in return for a consideration." The Pennsylvania Supreme Court found the tax to be "an uncompensated taking of property contrary to the Due Process Clause of the Fourteenth Amendment." The Supreme Court reversed saying: "The Court held [in a previous case] that 'the due process of law clause contained in the Fifth Amendment is not a limitation upon the taxing power conferred upon Congress,' that no different rule should be applied to the States, and that a tax within the lawful power of a State should not 'be judicially stricken down under the due process clause simply because its enforcement may or will result in restricting or even destroying particular occupations or businesses."[27]

The money which it raises by taxation Congress may expend "to pay the debts and provide for the common defense and general welfare of the United States." The important term here is "general welfare of the United States." Madison contended that Congress was empowered by it to tax and spend only to the extent necessary to carry into execution the *other* powers granted by the Constitution to the United States. Hamilton contended that the phrase should be read literally, and that the taxing-spending power was *in addition* to the other powers.[28] Time has vindicated Hamilton. Not only has Congress from the first frequently acted on his view, but the Court has gone out of its way to endorse it. This occurred in the case of United States *v.* Butler,[29] in which, nevertheless, the Court overturned the AAA on the ground that in requiring agriculturists to sign contracts agreeing to curtail production as a condition to their receiving certain payments under it, the act "coerced" said agriculturists in an attempt to "regulate" a matter, namely production, which was reserved to the States. Three Justices dissented on the ground that Congress was entitled when spending the national revenues for "the general welfare" to see to it that the country got its money's worth of "general welfare," and that the condemned contracts were "necessary and proper" to that end. Later cases, moreover, uphold the power of the National Government to spend money in support of unemployment insurance, to provide old-age pensions, to loan money to municipalities to enable them to erect their own electric plants; and, generally, to subsidize by so-called

The Spending Power

Social Security

312 U.S. 100 (1941). *But see* Marchetti *v.* U.S., 390 U.S. 39, 58-59 (1968) and Leary *v.* U.S., 395 U.S. 6, 21-25 (1969).

[27] City of Pittsburgh *v.* Alco Parking Corp., *et al.*, 417 U.S. 369, 374 (1974).

[28] On the general subject *see* Edward S. Corwin, "The Spending Power of Congress," 36 *Harvard Law Review*, 548-582 (1923). *Also* Charles Warren, *Congress as Santa Claus* (Charlottesville, Va., 1932).

[29] United States *v.* Butler, 297 U.S. 1 (1936).

"grants-in-aid" all sorts of welfare programs carried on by the States.[30]

With respect to Congress's spending power, the Supreme Court made some significant observations in a case involving the denial of social security insurance benefits to widows and stepchildren who had been wife and children of the deceased for less than nine months prior to his death. The Court concluded that "The administrative difficulties of individual eligibility determinations are without doubt matters which Congress may consider when determining whether to rely on rules which sweep more broadly than the evils with which they seek to deal. In this sense, the duration-of-relationship requirement represents not merely a substantive policy determination that benefits should be awarded only on the basis of genuine marital relationships, but also a substantive policy determination that limited resources would not be well spent in making individual determinations. It is an expression of Congress's policy choice that the Social Security System, and its millions of beneficiaries, would be best served by a prophylactic rule which bars claims arising from the bulk of sham marriages which are actually entered, which discourages such marriages from ever taking place, and which is also objective and easily administered.

"The Constitution does not preclude such policy choices as a price for conducting programs for the distribution of social insurance benefits."[31]

The Federal Government's practice of providing matching funds for public assistance programs was attacked in a case decided in the United States Court of Appeals, Second Circuit, in early 1973. The City of New York, Mayor Lindsay, and several other city officials contended that the Social Security Act *mandates* the State (and, under the New York State plan, the city) to share in responsibility for public assistance. They argued that the public assistance problem is national in scope and that only Congress has the power to provide for the general welfare under the Constitution. Further, to require States and cities to provide funds for public assistance deprived them of funds to pay the cost of purely local concerns like police and educational services. Since these functions are reserved to the states by the Tenth Amendment, it was argued that to make it impossible to perform them is unconstitutional. The court was patently unimpressed by that line of argument.[32]

The view has been advanced at times that the clause "provide for the . . . general welfare of the United States" is much more than a mere grant of power to tax and spend for the general welfare, and

[30] Steward Mach. Co. *v*. Davis, 301 U.S. 548 (1937); Helvering *v*. Davis, 301 U.S. 619 (1937); Alabama Power Co. *v*. Ickes, 302 U.S. 464 (1938). On Federal Grants-in-Aid, *see* pp. 145-147 below.

[31] Weinberger *v*. Salfi, 422 U.S. 749, 784 (1975).

[32] City of New York *v*. Richardson, 473 F. 2d. 923, 928 (1973).

authorizes Congress to legislate generally for that purpose.[33] This view, however, which would render the succeeding enumeration of powers largely tautological, has never so far been directly countenanced by the Court.

In a novel attempt to have the Vietnam conflict declared unconstitutional, Professor Lawrence B. Velvel filed suit contending among other things that, in taxing and spending for the war, Congress was exceeding its power in that the effort in Vietnam could not be construed as paying the debts or providing for the common defense and general welfare of the United States. The United States Court of Appeals deciding the case on appeal held: "Since congressional appropriations for the war are made under authority of the powers 'to raise and support Armies' and 'to provide and maintain a Navy' such expenditures are not exercises of the power to spend for the general welfare, but rather represent exercises of power under later enumerated powers, powers which are separate and distinct from the grant of authority to tax and spend for the general welfare."[34]

¶2. To borrow money on the credit of the United States;

Logically this power would seem to be limited to borrowing money to provide for "the common defense and general welfare of the United States." In practice it is limited only by "the credit of the United States," which today appears to be without limits, inasmuch as the Gross National Debt now tops 700 billions of dollars, a sum more than fifteen times the size of the debt in 1940. But Congress may not, by any of its powers, alter the terms of outstanding obligations of the United States without providing for compensation to the holders of such obligations for "actual loss";[35] but this, unfortunately, does not signify that, by pursuing inflationary fiscal policies, it may not render such obligations practically worthless without being required to compensate the holders thereof for their loss, which is held to be "incidental" or "consequential" merely, and not a "taking" of property in the sense of Amendment V.[36] May Congress authorize "forced loans" under this clause? Not if history counts for anything. Such a "loan" would not be a loan at all, the element of negotiation being absent from the transaction; it would be either a supplementary income tax, or if it took more than "income," would be a capital levy which, to be constitutional, would have to be apportioned among the States.

The above clauses and clauses 5 and 6 following comprise what

The Borrowing Power

---

[33] Corwin, "The Spending Power of Congress," *Harvard Law Review*, 548, 550-552; J. F. Lawson, *The General Welfare Clause* (Washington, D.C., 1926).

[34] Velvel *v.* Nixon, 415 F. 2d. 236 (1969); *cert. denied*, 396 U.S. 1042 (1970).

[35] Perry *v.* U.S., 294 U.S. 330 (1935). *See also* Lynch *v.* U.S., 292 U.S. 571 (1934).

[36] Knox *v.* Lee, 12 Wall. 457 (1871); Norman *v.* Balt. & O. R.R. Co., 294 U.S. 240 (1935). *See also* Omnia Com'l Co. *v.* U.S., 261 U.S. 502 (1923).

Other Fiscal
Powers
may be called the fiscal powers of the National Government. By virtue of these, taken along with the necessary and proper clause, Congress has the power to charter national banks, to put their functions beyond the reach of the taxing power of the States, to alter the metal content and value of the coinage of the United States, to issue paper money and confer upon it the quality of legal tender for debts, to invalidate private contracts of debt which call for payment in something other than legal tender, to tax the notes of issue of State banks out of existence, to confer on national banks the powers of trust companies, to establish a "Federal Reserve System," a "Farm Loan Bank," etc.[37] (*See also* ¶5 of this Section.)

¶3. To regulate commerce with foreign nations, and among the several States, and with the Indian tribes;

The
Commerce
Clause
"Commerce" is *traffic*, that is, the buying and selling of commodities, and includes as an important incident the *transportation* of such commodities from seller to buyer. But the term has also been defined much more broadly. In the famous case of Gibbons *v.* Ogden,[38] which was decided in 1824, Chief Justice Marshall said: "Commerce undoubtedly is traffic, but it is something more—it is intercourse"; and on the basis of this definition the Supreme Court has held that the mere passage of people from one State to another, as well as the sending of intelligence by telegraph—stock quotations, for instance—from one State to another, is "commerce among the States." Likewise radio broadcasting is "commerce" within this definition, and hence subject to regulation by Congress; as are also the activities of a holding company and its subsidiaries in control and direction of gas and electric companies which are scattered through several States and make continuous use of the mails and the instrumentalities of interstate commerce; also, transactions in insurance which involve two or more States; as well as the gathering of news by a press association and its transmission to client newspapers.[39]

Despite contentions that Congress's power to regulate with respect to foreign commerce differed to some degree from its power with respect to interstate commerce,[40] Chief Justice Taney stated

[37] McCulloch *v.* Md., 4 Wheat. 316 (1819); Knox *v.* Lee, 12 Wall. 457 (1871); Veazie Bank *v.* Fenno, 8 Wall. 533 (1869); Smith *v.* Kansas City T. and T. Co., 255 U.S. 180 (1921); Norman *v.* Balt. & O. R.R. Co., 294 U.S. 240 (1935); Holyoke Water Co. *v.* Am. Writing Paper Co., 300 U.S. 324 (1937); Smyth *v.* U.S., 302 U.S. 329 (1937).

[38] 9 Wheat. 1 (1824).

[39] Pensacola Tel. Co. *v.* Western Un. Tel .Co., 96 U.S. 1 (1877); Western Un. Tel. Co. *v.* Pendleton, 122 U.S. 347 (1887); Covington Bridge Co. *v.* Ky., 154 U.S. 204 (1894); International Text Book Co. *v.* Pigg, 217 U.S. 91 (1910); Western Un. Tel. Co. *v.* Foster, 247 U.S. 105 (1918); Federal Radio Com'n *v.* Nelson Bros., 289 U.S. 266 (1933); Electric Bond and Share Co. *v.* SEC, 303 U.S. 419 (1938); United States *v.* South-Eastern Underwriters Assoc., 322 U.S. 533 (1944); Associated Press *v.* U.S., 326 U.S. 1 (1945).

[40] Lottery Case, 188 U.S. 321, 373-374 (1903).

the view which has prevailed: "The power to regulate commerce among the several States is granted to Congress in the same clause, and by the same words, as the power to regulate commerce with foreign nations and is co-extensive with it."[41]

"Among the States," that is, to employ Chief Justice Marshall's words, "that commerce which concerns more States than one," and not "the exclusively internal commerce of a State"; or to use more modern phraseology, *interstate*, in contrast to *intrastate* or *local* commerce.[42]

The power "to regulate" is the power to govern, that is, the power to restrain, to prohibit, to protect, to encourage, to promote, in the furtherance of any public purpose whatsoever, *provided* the constitutional rights of persons be not transgressed. The restrictive aspects of this power have, nevertheless, within recent times been subject, so far as *interstate* commerce is concerned, to an indefinite veto power of the Court, but one which appears today to be in abeyance.

Justice Black, speaking for the Court in 1944, concisely summarized the foregoing: "The power granted Congress is a positive power. It is the power to legislate concerning transactions which, reaching across state boundaries, affect the people of more states than one;—to govern affairs which the individual states, with their limited territorial jurisdictions, are not fully capable of governing."[43] It is within this broad framework that the Supreme Court has been able to uphold efforts to eliminate discrimination through the commerce clause in recent years. The Court upheld the public accommodations provisions of the Civil Rights Act of 1964 as applied against a motel and a family-owned restaurant, businesses which surely would have been regarded in earlier years as local businesses not subject to Congressional regulation under the commerce clause.[44]

In the face of the contention that the application of pay-raise limitations to State employees under the Economic Stabilization Act of 1970 interfered with sovereign State functions protected by the Tenth Amendment (*see* discussion on p. 446), the Supreme Court held that "Even activity that is purely intrastate in character may be regulated by Congress, where the activity, combined with like conduct by others similarly situated, affects commerce among the States or with foreign nations. . . . There is little difficulty in concluding that such an effect could well result from large wage increases to 65,000 employees in Ohio and similar numbers in other states, *e.g.* general raises to state employees could inject millions of dollars of purchasing power into the economy and might exert

[41] License Cases, 5 How. 504, 578 (1847).
[42] *Cf.* however, Bob-Lo Excursion Co. *v.* Michigan, 333 U.S. 28 (1947).
[43] U.S. *v.* South-Eastern Underwriters Assoc., 322 U.S. 533, 552 (1944).
[44] Heart of Atlanta Motel, Inc. *v.* U.S., 379 U.S. 241 (1964); Katzenbach *v.* McClung, 379 U.S. 294 (1964).

pressure on other segments of the work force to demand comparable increases."[45] But the Court quickly made clear that its decision
in this case, *Fry*, could not be extended to its logical limits.

In a *tour de force*, the Supreme Court in June 1976 both declared
an act of Congress unconstitutional and overruled a landmark Supreme Court decision. In 1974 Congress had broadened the Fair
Labor Standards Act by extending the minimum wage and
maximum hours provisions to employees of "the government of a
state or political subdivision thereof." Justice Rehnquist speaking
for the Court said that: "This exercise of congressional authority
does not comport with the federal system of government embodied
in the Constitution. We hold that insofar as the challenged
amendments operate to directly displace the States' freedom to
structure integral operations in areas of traditional governmental
functions, they are not within the authority granted Congress by
Art. I, §8, cl. 3."[46] The Court took great pains to distinguish this
decision from its decision in *Fry*. It explained that "the degree of
intrusion upon the area of state sovereignty" was much less in that
case and it dealt only with a *temporary* freeze on wages of employees.
But, when it came to the *Wirtz* case,[47] the Court felt it must do more
than distinguish: "While there are obvious differences between
schools and hospitals involved in *Wirtz*, and the fire and police departments affected here, each provides an integral portion of those
governmental services which the States and their political subdivisions have traditionally afforded their citizens. We are therefore
persuaded that *Wirtz* must be overruled." Some may see some irony
in Justice Rehnquist's nod to former Justice Douglas in his statement: "We agree that such assertions of power, if unchecked,
would indeed, as Mr. Justice Douglas cautioned in his dissent in
Wirtz, allow 'the National Government [to] devour the essentials of
state sovereignty.' "

As might be expected with such a sweeping decision, there was a
bitter dissent by Justice Brennan joined by Justices White and Marshall. They found it "surprising" that their brethren "should
choose the Bicentennial year . . . to repudiate principles governing
judicial interpretation of our Constitution settled since the time of
Chief Justice Marshall, discarding his postulate that the Constitution contemplates that restraints upon exercise by Congress of its
plenary commerce power lie in the political process and not in the
judicial process."

Some additional striking assertions as to what can be legitimately
encompassed by the commerce clause have currency. The Supreme Court of Arkansas ruled against the contention that the
55-mile-an-hour speed limit on highways set by Congress was not a
regulation of interstate commerce. The court pointed out that

[45] Fry *v.* U.S., 421 U.S. 542, 547, 1795 (1975).
[46] National League of Cities *et al. v.* Usery, 426 U.S. 833 (1976).
[47] Maryland *v.* Wirtz, 392 U.S. 183 (1968).

"Congress established speed limits to be used on public highways, but the States had the right to accept or reject the recommended speed limit subject to certain penalties."[48]

In 1968 Congress passed a law making it a crime for anyone "who travels in interstate or foreign commerce . . . to organize, promote, encourage, participate in, or carry on a riot. . . ."[49] In the course of the hectic cases dealing with the "Chicago Seven," the U.S. Court of Appeals for the Seventh Circuit by a 2-1 vote held the act constitutional.[50] Subsequently, the Supreme Court denied *certiorari*, thus permitting the appeals court decision to stand.[51] Also, the courts have upheld the constitutionality of the Travel Act, which makes it a crime to travel in interstate commerce with intent to promote, manage or carry on "any unlawful activity."[52]

A United States district court has held that Congress had a rational basis for finding that air pollution affected commerce.[53] That decision recalls a startling proposition conjured up a few years ago by the Chief of the Environmental Health Branch of HEW. In discussing pollution control, he wrote: "The validity of the exercise of such power by Congress must therefore hinge on the determination that the movement of such pollution is *itself* commerce."[54] But the Supreme Court has relied on other concepts to uphold Congressional efforts to rid the nation of pollution. One, the idea that Congress has the power to outlaw "obstructions" (broadly interpreted) in interstate or navigable waters.[55] Two, the idea that "It is a fair and reasonable demand on the part of the sovereign that the air over its territory should not be polluted on a great scale. . . ."[56] Lower courts have taken this guidance from the Supreme Court seriously. In 1974, District Judge Ben Krentzman stated that "It is beyond question that water pollution has a serious effect on interstate commerce and that Congress has the power to regulate activities such as dredging and filling which cause such pollution. . . . Congress and the courts have become aware of the lethal effect pollution has on all organisms. Weakening any of the life support systems bodes disaster for the rest of the interrelated life forms. To recognize this and yet hold that pollution does not affect interstate commerce unless committed in navigable waters below the mean water line would be contrary to reason. Congress is not limited by

[48] Neikirk *v.* State, 542 S.W. 2d. 282 (1976).
[49] 18 U.S.C. 2101.
[50] Dellinger *et al. v.* United States, 472 F. 2d. 340 (1972).
[51] *Ibid.*, 410 U.S. 970 (1973).
[52] For listing of cases upholding the Travel Act, see United States *v.* Bergdoll, 412 F.Supp. 1308 (1976).
[53] U.S. *v.* Bishop Processing Co., 287 F.Supp. 624 (1968).
[54] Sidney Edelman, "Federal Air and Water Control . . . ," *George Washington Law Review*, 1067, 1071-1072 (1965).
[55] U.S. *v.* Standard Oil Co., 384 U.S. 224 (1966); Illinois *v.* City of Milwaukee, 406 U.S. 91 (1972).
[56] Illinois *v.* City of Milwaukee, 406 U.S. 91, 104 (1972).

the 'navigable waters' test in its authority to control pollution under the Commerce Clause."[57]

In a parallel case involving the Federal Water Pollution Control Act Amendments of 1972 the U.S. Court of Appeals, Sixth Circuit, seemed to exert itself to rationalize law that was patently "good" (to prohibit pollution of nonnavigable tributaries to navigable rivers and streams) as a legitimate exercise of Congress's power to regulate interstate commerce. The court said: "Obviously water pollution is a health threat to the water supply of the nation. It endangers our agriculture by rendering water unfit for irrigation. It can end the public use and enjoyment of our magnificent rivers and lakes for fishing, for boating, and for swimming. These health and welfare concerns are, of course, proper subjects for Congressional attention *because of their many impacts upon interstate commerce generally.* But water pollution is also a direct threat to navigation—the first interstate commerce system in this country's history and still a very important one." (Emphasis supplied.)[58]

In contrast to these decisions, the U.S. Court of Appeals, Fourth Circuit, said the Supreme Court " 'has always recognized that the power to regulate commerce, though broad indeed, has limits.' "[59] That court held that the Environmental Protection Agency had exceeded its authority under the Clean Air Act in requiring the State of Maryland to establish certain antipollution programs, saying: "If the national legislature may not revise, negative or annul a law of a state legislature, how an Act of Congress may be construed to permit an agency of the United States to direct a state legislature to legislate is difficult to understand." Further, the court said: "it is one thing to strike down a state law under the supremacy clause, or to decide that a state which chooses to engage in activities which Congress has a right to control must do so in Congress's terms, or to hold that Congress may induce a state to act by offering favors or exacting financial penalties if it does not, but it is quite another thing to extract from a state a most fundmental attribute of its sovereignty."

To the contention that the application of the Organized Crime Control Act only to those states where gambling is illegal violates the commerce clause, a U.S. court of appeals answered that "While this argument is intriguing, to say the least, it carries little weight."[60] Citing a number of Supreme Court decisions, the appeals court held that "The law is clear that there is no requirement of national uniformity when Congress exercises its power under the commerce clause." Also, the court said that "The Constitution is not violated when a federal statute incorporates the laws of the states."

[57] United States *v.* Holland, 373 F.Supp. 665, 673 (1974).

[58] United States *v.* Ashland Oil and Transportation Co., 504 F. 2d. 1317, 1325 (1974).

[59] State of Md. *v.* Environmental Protection Ag., 530 F. 2d. 215 (1975).

[60] United States *v.* Hawes, 529 F. 2d. 472 (1976).

Historically, until the early Thirties, Congress had exercised its powers over interstate commerce, for the most part, only over interstate *transportation*, and especially transportation by rail. Since the power to regulate is the power to promote, it was determined early that Congress could build railways and bridges, or charter corporations and authorize them to build railways and bridges; and it could vest such corporations with the power of eminent domain and render their franchises immune from State taxation.[61] For the like reason the Court, in the Adamson Act case of 1916,[62] recognized that Congress had very wide discretion in dealing with an emergency which threatened to stop interstate transportation. When, however, Congress sought in 1933 to invoke the same principle in behalf of the commerce in the sense of *traffic*, in the enactment of the NIRA, the Court declined to give any weight to the emergency justification.[63] Later decisions eliminated this difference between Congress's power over "commerce" in the sense of *transportation* and commerce in the sense of *traffic*. {Commerce as Transportation}

Again, Congress may regulate the rates of transportation from one State to another, or authorize an agent like the Interstate Commerce Commission, to do so.[64] But the rates set must yield a "fair return" to the carrier on the "value" of its property, the theory being that since this property is being used in the service of the public, to compel its public use without just compensation would amount to confiscation.[65] (*See* the "private property" clause of Amendment V.) {Requisites of Rate Regulation}

But just how is such "value" to be ascertained? For many years two formulas competed for the Court's favor. One, "reproduction less depreciation," implied that "fair value" should be deemed the equivalent of what it would cost to reproduce the road at current prices, minus an allowance for the road's depreciation. The other, the "historical cost" or "original prudent investment" formula, suggested that the company was entitled to get a fair return on what it had actually put into the road in dollars and cents, less again allowance for deterioration. The former theory, which until the 1940's was favored by the Court, was considerate of the casual investor's interest in an era of rising prices, but by the same token supplied to shifting a basis for rate-making as to be administratively impracticable.[66] The latter theory escaped this disadvantage, and was also a logical corollary of the legal doctrine upon which rate

[61] California v. Cent. Pac. R.R. Co., 127 U.S. 1 (1888); Luxton v. No. River B. Co., 153 U.S. 525 (1894).

[62] Wilson v. New, 243 U.S. 332 (1917).

[63] Schechter Bros. Corp. v. U.S., 295 U.S. 495 (1935).

[64] For a remarkable argument against the power of Congress to regulate rates, based on extreme *laissez-faire* principles, *see* the speech of Senator William M. Evarts of New York in the course of the debate on the bill to establish the Interstate Commerce Commission. 18 *Cong. Rec.* 603-604 (1887).

[65] Smyth v. Ames, 169 U.S. 466 (1898).

[66] *See* briefs and opinions in St. Louis and O'Fallon R. Co. v. U. S., 279 U.S. 461 (1929), and cases there cited.

regulation originally rested, namely, that the property of a common carrier, or other public utility, was "impressed with a public use" and its business "affected with a public interest" *from the very outset*, and that investors were forewarned of this fact. However, the Court has since the 1940's been disposed to leave the whole business to the regulatory authority, *provided* it affords a fair opportunity to be heard to the interests affected.[67] It had become clear to the Court by that time that the determination of "fair value" was a more complicated matter than it had thought in earlier times. Actually there were more than just the two aforementioned theories being pressed on the Court.[68] Where the Court had found in 1890 that "The question of reasonableness of a rate . . . is eminently a question for *judicial* investigation, requiring due process of law for its determination"[69] (emphasis supplied), the Court conceded in 1944: "It is not theory but the impact of the rate order which counts. If the total effect of the rate order cannot be said to be unjust and unreasonable, judicial inquiry under the Act is at an end. The fact that the method employed to reach that result may contain infirmities is not then important. Moreover, the Commission's order does not become suspect by reason of the fact that it is challenged. It is the product of expert judgment which carries a presumption of validity. And he who would upset the rate order under the Act carries the heavy burden of making a convincing showing that it is invalid because it is unjust and unreasonable in its consequences."[70]

In 1974 the Supreme Court reaffirmed its position in ratemaking, saying "he who would upset . . . [a] rate order . . . carries 'the heavy burden of making a convincing showing that it is invalid because it is unjust and unreasonable in its consequences.' "[71] This was buttressed by another decision a year later. Students Challenging Regulatory Agency Procedures (SCRAP) lost an important round in their effort to prevent railroad rate increases that they contended would result in "the nonuse of recyclable goods" and thus harm the environment. The Supreme Court, reversing the district court, upheld the ICC action that the Court described as "a decision—entirely nonfinal with respect to particular rates—not to declare unlawful a *percentage increase* which on its face limited the increase permitted on other recyclables."[72] (In another proceeding investigating the entire freight rate structure, the ICC is giving

---

[67] *See* Driscoll *v.* Edison Light and P. Co., 307 U.S. 104 (1939); Federal Power Com'n *v.* Natural Gas Pipeline Co., 315 U.S. 575 (1942); Federal Power Com'n *v.* Hope Natural Gas Co., 320 U.S. 591 (1944); Colorado Interstate Gas Co. *v.* FPC, 324 U.S. 581 (1945).

[68] For a concise description of theories available *see* U.S., 88th Cong., 1st Sess., Senate Document 39 (1964), pp. 1117-1120.

[69] Chicago, Milwaukee and St. Paul Railway Co. *v.* Minnesota, 134 U.S. 418, 458 (1890).

[70] Federal Power Com'n *v.* Hope Natural Gas Co., 320 U.S. 591, 602 (1944).

[71] FPC *v.* Texaco, Inc., *et al.*, 417 U.S. 380, 389 (1974).

[72] As the Court explained, "recyclables" at least in the context of their opinion

further and presumably more comprehensive study to environmental issues.)

The Court was satisfied that the ICC had sufficiently considered the environmental issues for the limited decision the ICC had rendered. Justice Douglas was not satisfied! He blistered the ICC: "This litigation presents a history of foot-dragging by the ICC, as other parties to proceedings before it, including other federal agencies, have attempted to prod it into compliance with the National Environmental Policy Act (NEPA). The 'final impact statement' that the Court holds adequate presents a melange of statistics that purport to show that an increase in the transportation rates of recyclable materials will not have a significant adverse impact on the environment. The Commission's 'analysis' has been thoroughly discredited by the comments of other federal agencies, including not only the Environmental Protection Agency and the Council on Environmental Quality, whose principal concerns are environmental, but also the Department of Commerce and the General Services Administration. The Commission has responded to the adverse comments by papering over the defects they identify, rather than dealing with the substance of the deficiencies."

The most important observation about the relevance of this litigation to the Constitution and rate-making is the unquestioned assumption that the requirement of the National Environmental Policy Act that agencies of the Federal government use "a systematic interdisciplinary approach . . . in decision making which may have an impact on man's environment" applies to the rate-makers.

In the Shreveport case,[73] decided in 1914, the Court ruled that "wherever the interstate and intrastate transactions of carriers are so related that the government of the one involves the control of the other," Congress is entitled to regulate both classes of transactions. In other words, whenever circumstances make it "necessary and proper" for Congress to regulate *local* transportation in order to make its control of *interstate* transportation really effective, it may do so—a principle to which the Transportation Act of 1920 gave new application and extension.[74] Similarly, Congress, in protecting interstate telephone messages, may prohibit the disclosure of intercepted intrastate messages;[75] and in sustaining the Fair Labor Standards Act of 1938[76] the Court reached even more striking results. (*See* pp. 65-66 below.)

Furthermore, Congress may regulate the *instruments* and *agents*

National
Supremacy

---

means "products which have already been put to one commercial use—for example, iron or steel obtained from a junked automobile." United States *v.* SCRAP, 422 U.S. 289, 295 (1975).

[73] 234 U.S. 342.

[74] 49 U.S.C. 13 (4); Wisconsin *v.* C.B. & A. R.R. Co., 257 U.S. 563 (1922). But a determination of the I.C.C. superseding a local rate set by a State commission may be set aside by the Supreme Court as being in excess of the I.C.C.'s power under the Act of 1920, Illinois Com. Com'n *v.* Thomson, 318 U.S. 675 (1943); Alabama *v.* U.S., 325 U.S. 535 (1945).

[75] Weiss *v.* U.S., 308 U.S. 321 (1939).   [76] 29 U.S.C. 201-219.

Instruments
and Agents
of Trans-
portation

of interstate transportation; and hence may protect them from injury from any source, whether *interstate* or *local* in character. Thus, when cars engaged in local transportation are hauled as part of a train along with cars which are engaged in interstate transportation, the former as well as the latter must be provided with the safety appliances which are required by the Federal Safety Appliance Act, otherwise they might impede or endanger the interstate transportation.[77] And it is on an extension of this principle that the Federal Employers' Liability Act of 1908 rests, which modified the rules of the common law of the States for determining the liability of railways engaged in interstate commerce to those of their employees who are injured while employed in connection with such commerce.[78]

When, however, Congress, in 1934, passed an act requiring railway carriers to contribute to a pension fund for superannuated employees, the Court, five Justices to four, held the act void both as violative of the "due process" clause of the Fifth Amendment and as not falling within the power to regulate interstate commerce.[79] The measure, Justice Roberts said, had "no relation to the promotion of efficiency . . . by separating the unfit from the industry." Chief Justice Hughes, on the other hand, speaking for the minority, denied that Congress's power to regulate commerce and to "make all laws which shall be necessary and proper" to that end was limited merely to securing efficiency. "The fundamental consideration which supports this type of legislation," said he, "is that industry should take care of its human wastage, whether that is due to accident or age";[80] and it followed that Congress could require interstate carriers to live up to this obligation. Subsequently, when Congress passed legislation very similar to that rejected by the Court in 1935, its constitutionality was not seriously questioned.[81]

The fact that in an earlier time Congressional regulation of interstate transportation focused on railroads was not of legal consequence. It was just that other modes of transportation were developed later. It was established early that other modes and instrumentalities of interstate transportation like trucking, airlines, and pipelines were as subject to regulation by Congress as railroads.[82] But it was not until New Deal days that Congress moved to regulate comprehensively in these other areas of transportation

[77] Southern Ry. Co. *v.* U.S., 222 U.S. 20 (1911). For a parallel case, involving bills of lading considered as instruments of interstate commerce, *see* United States *v.* Ferger, 250 U.S. 199 (1919).

[78] 45 U.S.C. ch. 2; Second Employers' Liability Cases, 223 U.S. 1 (1912).

[79] Railroad Retirement Bd. *v.* Alton R.R. Co., 295 U.S. 330 (1935).

[80] *Ibid.*, at 384.

[81] 45 U.S.C. 228, 261-273; 351-367; *see* Railroad Board *v.* Duquesne Co., 326 U.S. 446 (1946); and Mandeville Farms *v.* Sugar Co., 334 U.S. 219, 230 (1948).

[82] The Pipeline Cases, 234 U.S. 548 (1914); Buck *v.* Kukendall, 267 U.S. 307 (1925).

(Federal Communications Act of 1934; Federal Motor Carrier Act of 1935; Civil Aeronautics Act of 1938).

Navigation, too, is a branch of transportation and so of commerce, and the power to regulate it includes the power to protect navigable streams from obstruction and to improve their navigability, as by the erection of dams.[83] Furthermore, as was held in 1940, in the case of United States *v.* Appalachian Electric Power Co., this power does not stop with the needs of *navigation*, but embraces also flood control, watershed development, and the production of electric power by the erection of dams in "navigable streams." Nor is the term "navigable streams" any longer confined by the Court, as once it was, to streams which are "navigable in their natural condition," but also includes, under the holding just mentioned, those which may be rendered navigable by "reasonable improvements."[84] And any electrical power developed at such a dam is "property belonging to the United States" (*see* Article IV, Section III, ¶2), in disposing of which, it was held in the TVA case,[85] the United States may, in order to reach a distant market, purchase transmission lines from a private company. Indeed, the Court will not intervene to prevent the Government from attempting to create a market for its electrical power by staking potential customers, as by authorizing loans to municipalities to enable them to go into the business of furnishing their residents power which they would purchase from the United States.[86] However convincing the argument may be for allowing the sale of electrical power developed as a consequence of building dams, the argument that Congress can authorize TVA to build steam plants (which obviously do not come as a result of damming) to generate electricity for sale under its power to regulate commerce is less convincing. Yet two Federal courts had no difficulty finding that TVA's "Paradise Steam Plant and the transmission lines connecting it with the TVA system are parts of an integrated system of multi-purpose dams, steam plants, and transmission lines, which together improve navigation, help control floods, produce power, and serve generally to develop the Tennessee River watershed and are authorized by the commerce clause of the Constitution. . . ."[87]

[83] United States *v.* Chandler-Dunbar Co., 229 U.S. 53 (1913); and cases there reviewed.

[84] United States *v.* Appalachian Elec. P. Co., 311 U.S. 377 (1940); Oklahoma *ex rel* Phillips *v.* Atkinson Co., 313 U.S. 508, 523-534 *passim* (1941). For the earlier view, *cf. The Daniel Ball*, 10 Wall. 557 (1870).

[85] Ashwander *v.* TVA, 297 U.S. 288 (1935).

[86] Alabama Power Co. *v.* Ickes, 302 U.S. 464 (1938).

[87] U.S. *v.* An Easement and Right-of-Way, 246 F.Supp. 263, 270 (1965); *affirmed* 375 F. 2d. 120 (1967). In answer to our query in January 1972, the General Counsel of TVA wrote: "Based on our current docket we do not expect the question of TVA's constitutional and statutory authority to build and operate steam plants to be before the Supreme Court in the foreseeable future."

A case that challenged the validity of a Virginia statute prohibiting Federally licensed vessels owned by non-residents from fishing in Chesapeake Bay and prohibiting ships owned by citizens of other states from catching fish anywhere in Virginia provided the Supreme Court with an opportunity to observe that "while appellant may be correct in arguing that at earlier times in our history, there was some doubt whether Congress had power under the Commerce Clause to regulate the taking of fish in state waters, there can be no question today that such power exists where there is some effect on interstate commerce." The Court concluded "The movement of vessels from one State to another in search of fish, and back again to processing plants, is certainly activity which Congress could conclude affects interstate commerce. Accordingly, we hold that, at least, when Congress re-enacted the license form in 1936 using language, which, according to *Gibbons*, gave licensees 'all the right which the grantor can transfer,' it necessarily extended the license to cover the taking of fish in state waters, subject to valid state conservation regulations."[88]

An intriguing and novel case dealt with a dispute over efforts to draw off water feeding an underground pool which had been designated a National Monument in an effort to preserve a unique species of desert fish. The Supreme Court spoke to what it termed the "Reserved Rights Doctrine," saying: "This Court has long held that when the Federal Government withdraws its land from the public domain and reserves it for a federal purpose, the Government by implication, reserves appurtenant water then unappropriated to the extent needed to accomplish the purpose of the reservation. In so doing the United States acquires a reserved right in unappropriated water which vests on the date of the reservation and is superior to the rights of future appropriators. Reservation of water rights is empowered by the Commerce Clause, Art. I, §8, which permits federal regulation of navigable streams, and the Property Clause, Art. IV, §3, which permits federal regulation of federal lands."[89]

The U.S. Court of Claims decided that a hunting club was entitled to recover damages for the permanent flooding of part of its privately owned hunting area resulting from the construction of a dam by the Federal Government.[90] After pointing out that "Under the commerce clause of the Constitution, the Federal Government has the power to improve navigable waters in the interest of navigation; and if such an improvement on a navigable stream raises the water level in the stream and thereby damages privately owned property situated within the bed of the stream, the Government is not liable for the ensuing damages." However, the claims court added: "On the other hand, the navigational servitude of the Gov-

[88] Douglas *v.* Seacoast Products, Inc., 431 U.S. 265, 282 (1977).
[89] Cappaert *v* United States, 426 U.S. 128 (1976).
[90] Goose Creek Hunting Club, Inc. *v.* United States, 518 F. 2d. 579 (1975).

ernment does not extend beyond the beds of navigable streams; and if an action taken by the Government to improve the navigability of a navigable stream raises the water level in the stream and thereby causes it to overflow or otherwise damage property situated outside the bed of such a stream, the Government is liable for the ensuing damages." The basic reason for such a distinction, the claims court explained, was that "privately owned property situated within the bed of a navigable stream is always subject to the Government's dominant servitude in the interest of navigation."

When conservation groups brought an action against the Secretary of the Army, the Army Corps of Engineers and the Environmental Protection Agency complaining of the defendants' interpretation of the Federal Water Pollution Control Act Amendments of 1972, a Federal district court declared that Congress's definition, " 'the waters of the United States, including the territorial seas,' asserted federal jurisdiction over the nation's waters to the maximum extent permissible under the Commerce Clause of the Constitution. Accordingly, as used in the Water Act, the term is not limited to the traditional tests of navigability."[91]

Also relevant to the discussion of Congress's power to regulate navigation are the cases discussed earlier on pages 49-50.

But, as was indicated above, the primitive subject-matter of Congress's power of regulation is *traffic*, that is, the purchase and sale of commodities among the States. This is indicated by the etymology of the word: L. *cum merce*, "with merchandise." The first important piece of legislation to govern interstate commerce in this sense was the Sherman Anti-Trust Act of 1890,[92] the opening section of which declares "illegal" "every contract, combination in the form of trust or otherwise, or conspiracy in restraint of trade or commerce among the several States, or with foreign nations." The main purpose of the act was to check the development of industrial trusts; but in the first important case to arise under it, the Sugar Trust case of 1895,[93] the Court held that its provisions could not be constitutionally applied to a combination which was admitted to manufacture ninety-eight per cent of the refined sugar used in the United States, inasmuch as manufacture and commerce were distinct and the control of the former belonged solely to the States. Any effect of a contract with respect to manufacturing or production upon commerce among the States, the Court asserted, "would

Commerce as Traffic

The Sherman Act and later Acts Regulating Traffic

---

[91] Natural Resources Defense Council, Inc. *v.* Callaway, 392 F.Supp. 685 (1975).
[92] 15 U.S.C. ch. 1.
[93] United States *v.* E. C. Knight Co., 156 U.S. 1 (1895). As Justice Harlan contended, in his notable dissenting opinion, the doctrine of the case boiled down to the proposition that commerce was transportation simply. Actually, however, he pointed out, "both the Court and counsel recognized buying and selling or barter as *included in commerce*." His conclusion was that "whatever a State may do to protect its completely interior traffic or trade against unlawful restraints, the general government is empowered to do for the protection of the people of all the states." *Ibid.* 22-42 *passim*.

be an indirect result, however inevitable and whatever its extent," and hence would be beyond the power of Congress. Only the States, therefore, could deal with industrial monopolies.

The effect of this holding was to put the Anti-Trust Act to sleep for a decade, during which period most of the great industrial trusts of today got their start. But in the Swift case,[94] ten years later, the Court largely abandoned this mode of approach for the view that where the facts show "an established course of business" which involves "a current of commerce" among the States in a certain commodity, Congress is entitled to govern the local incidents of such current. Thus the Anti-Trust Act was formally held to reach labor combinations interruptive of commerce among the States,[95] and while the Court later largely retracted this construction of the act, it did not do so on constitutional grounds.[96] And meantime, in sustaining in 1922 the Packers and Stockyards Act[97] of the previous year the Court, speaking by Chief Justice Taft, had asserted broadly: "Whatever amounts to a more or less constant practice, and threatens to obstruct or unduly to burden the freedom of interstate commerce is within the regulatory power of Congress under the commerce clause, and it is primarily for Congress to consider and decide the fact of the danger and meet it. This Court will certainly not substitute its judgment for that of Congress in such a matter unless the relation of the subject to interstate commerce and its effects upon it are clearly nonexistent."[98]

The "current of commerce" idea was recently reaffirmed when, in 1975, the Supreme Court held that "The cotton exchange, like the live stock marketing regime involved in Swift Co. *v.* United States . . . and in Stafford *v.* Wallace . . . has federal protection under the Commerce Clause." The Court noted that after arrangements are made between buyer and seller, the cotton "enters a long interstate pipeline. That pipeline ultimately terminates at mills across the country or indeed around the world, after a complex sorting and matching process designed to provide each mill with the particular grade of cotton which the mill is equipped to process."[99]

This was not a case involving a state tax but rather the question of whether or not an out-of-state corporation could seek enforcement of a contract in the Mississippi courts without a certificate to do business in the state.[100] The Court in a careful, narrow decision

[94] Swift and Co. *v.* U.S., 196 U.S. 375 (1905).

[95] Bedford Cut Stone Co. *v.* Journeymen, 274 U.S. 37 (1927), and cases there reviewed.

[96] *See* especially Apex Hosiery Co. *v.* Leader, 310 U.S. 469 (1940); and United States *v.* Hutcheson, 312 U.S. 219 (1941).

[97] 7 U.S.C. ch. 9.

[98] Stafford *v.* Wallace, 258 U.S. 495 at 521 (1922). The statement is repeated in Board of Trade *v.* Olsen, 262 U.S. 137 (1923). *See also* 259 U.S. at 408.

[99] Allenberg Cotton Co. Inc. *v.* Pittman, 419 U.S. 20, 24, 29 (1974).

[100] Mississippi law does not permit foreign corporations to maintain actions in the State's courts without requisite certificate.

held only: "appellant's contacts with Mississippi do not exhibit the sort of localization or intrastate character which we have required in situations where a state seeks to require a foreign corporation to qualify to do business. Whether there were local tax incidents of those contacts which can be reached is a different question on which we express no opinion. Whether the course of dealing would subject appellant to suits in Mississippi is likewise a different question on which we express no view. We hold only that Mississippi's refusal to honor and enforce contracts made for interstate or foreign commerce is repugnant to the Commerce Clause."[101]

To return for a moment to the Sherman Act—a decision in 1944, supported however by only a bare majority of the seven Justices participating in it, held that it applied to fire insurance transactions carried on across State lines, although when the act was passed, and for long afterwards, it was the doctrine of the Court that the business of insurance was not "commerce" in the sense of the Constitution.[102] And later the act was projected into the amusement field— to football; to the promotion of boxing on a multiple scale, coupled with sale of television, broadcast and film rights; to the business of booking and presenting theatrical attractions (plays, musicals and operettas).[103]

In a celebrated case, the Supreme Court held that the "minimum fee schedule for lawyers published by the Fairfax County Bar Association and enforced by the Virginia State Bar" violated the Sherman Anti-Trust Act. The Court rejected arguments (1) that Congress intended to include the learned professions within the terms "trade or commerce" in the act and (2) that the fee schedule was within the ambit of the Court's earlier decision in Parker *v.* Brown, 317 U.S. 341 (1943), which held that "an anticompetitive marketing program 'which derived its authority and efficacy from the legislative command of the state' was not a violation of the Sherman Act because the Act was intended to regulate private practices and not to prohibit a state from imposing a restraint as an act of government."[104] The Court's conclusion was careful: "We recognize that the States have a compelling interest in the practice

---

[101] 419 U.S. 20, 33 (1975).

[102] United States *v.* South-Eastern Underwriters Assoc., 322 U.S. 533 (1944). The earlier cases holding the business of insurance not to be "commerce" are reviewed in Justice Black's opinion. They are headed by Paul *v.* Va., 8 Wall. 168 (1868).

[103] Radovich *v.* National Football League, 352 U.S. 445 (1957); United States *v.* Boxing Club of New York, 348 U.S. 236 (1955); United States *v.* Shubert, 348 U.S. 222 (1955). Baseball continues to be treated as an exception. In 1972 the Supreme Court held that although "Professional baseball is a business and it is engaged in interstate commerce. . . . We continue to be loathe, fifty years after *Federal Baseball* and almost two decades after *Toolson*, to overturn those cases judicially when Congress, by its positive inaction has allowed those decisions to stand for so long and, far beyond mere inference and implication, has clearly evinced a desire not to disapprove them legislatively." Flood *v.* Kuhn, 407 U.S. 258, 283 (1972). *See* Haviland *v.* Butz, 543 F. 2d. 169, 175 (1976).

[104] Goldfarb *et al. v.* Virginia Bar *et al.*, 421 U.S. 773, 788 (1975).

of professions within their boundaries, and that as part of their power to protect the public health, safety, and other valid interests they have broad power to establish standards for licensing practitioners and regulating the practice of professions. We also recognize that in some instances the State may decide that 'forms of competition usual in the business world may be demoralizing to the ethical standards of a profession.' . . . The interest of the states in regulating lawyers is especially great since lawyers are essential to the primary governmental function of administering justice, and have been 'officers of the courts.' In holding that certain anticompetitive conduct by lawyers is within the reach of the Sherman Act we intend no diminution of the authority of the State to regulate its professions." Within a few years the Court struck down an Arizona law that restricted advertising by lawyers, holding that "the *Parker* exemption also bars the instant Sherman Act claim." The Court distinguished this case from *Goldfarb*: "In *Goldfarb* we held that . . . the Sherman Act was violated by the publication of a minimum-fee schedule by a county bar association and by its enforcement by the State Bar. The schedule and its enforcement mechanism operated to create a rigid price floor for services and thus constituted a classic example of price fixing. Both bar associations argued that their activity was shielded by the state-action exception. This Court concluded that the action was not protected, emphasizing that 'we need not inquire further into the state-action question because it cannot fairly be said that the State of Virginia through its Supreme Court Rules required the anticompetitive activities of either respondent.' In the instant case, by contrast, the challenged restraint is the affirmative command of the Arizona Supreme Court under its Rules. . . . That Court is the ultimate body wielding the State's power over the practice of law . . . and, thus, the restraint is 'compelled by direction of the State acting as sovereign.' "[105] In the end, the Court held on First Amendment grounds that the State may not "prevent the publication in a newspaper . . . truthful advertisement concerning the availability and terms of routine legal services."

Other interesting anti-trust cases have been decided by the Supreme Court recently. In one, the Court held that the system of fixed commission rates used by the New York Stock Exchange and the American Stock Exchange for transactions of less than $500,000 did not violate the Sherman Act.[106] As the Court saw it: "The Securities Exchange Act was intended by the Congress to leave the supervision of the fixing of reasonable rates of commission to the SEC. Interposition of the anti-trust laws, which would bar fixed commission rates as *per se* violations of the Sherman Act, in the face of positive SEC action, would preclude and prevent the

[105] Bates *v*. State Bar of Arizona, 433 U.S. 350 (1977).
[106] Gordon *v*. New York Stock Exchange, Inc., 422 U.S. 659 (1975).

operation of the Exchange Act as intended by Congress and as effectuated through SEC regulatory activity. Implied repeal of the anti-trust laws is, in fact, necessary to make the Exchange Act work as it was intended; failure to imply repeal would render nugatory the legislative provision for regulatory agency supervision of exchange commission rates."

Likewise, in a second case, the Court held that "certain sales and distribution practices employed in marketing securities of open-end management companies, popularly referred to as 'mutual funds,' are immune from antitrust liability."[107] Justice White speaking for himself and Justices Douglas, Brennan, and Marshall bitterly complained that "The majority repeats the principle so often applied by this Court that 'implied antitrust immunity is not favored, and can be justified only by a convincing showing of clear repugnancy between the antitrust laws and the regulatory system.' . . . That fundamental rule, though invoked again and again in our decisions, retained its vitality because in the many instances of its evocation it was given life and meaning by a close analysis of the legislation and facts involved in the particular case, an analysis inspired by the 'felt indispensable role of antitrust policy in the maintenance of a free economy. . . .' Absent that inspiration the principle becomes an archaism at best, and no longer reflects the tense interplay of differing and at times conflicting public policies." Justice White added that under the majority's holding in the context of this case "implied antitrust immunity becomes the rule where a regulatory agency has authority to approve business conduct whether or not the agency is directed to consider antitrust factors in making its regulatory decisions and whether or not there is other evidence that Congress intended to displace judicial with administrative antitrust enforcement."

In a third complicated case, the Supreme Court held 6-3 that establishment of *de facto* branch banks in Atlanta's suburbs by the Citizens and Southern National Bank did not violate or constitute unreasonable restraints of trade under the anti-trust laws.[108] The decision was bottomed on the conclusion that "By providing new banking options, to suburban Atlanta customers, while eliminating no existing options, the *de facto* branching program of C & S has plainly been procompetitive."

Finally, in a case dealing with the contention that the acquisition by one of the largest suppliers of janitorial services in the country of two other such firms violated the provision of the Clayton Act, which provides that "No corporation engaged in commerce shall acquire . . . the stock or other share capital . . . of another corporation engaged in commerce, where in any line of commerce in any

[107] United States *v.* National Association of Securities Dealers, 422 U.S. 694 (1975).
[108] United States *v.* Citizens and Southern National Bank, 422 U.S. 86 (1975).

section of the country, the effect of such acquisition may be to lessen competition, or to tend to create a monopoly," the Supreme Court held 6-3 that the companies "did not participate directly in the sale, purchase, or distribution of goods or services in interstate commerce, they were not 'engaged in commerce' within the meaning . . . of the Clayton Act."[109] Previously, the Court had explained in its opinion that "we hold that the phrase 'engaged in commerce' as used in . . . the Clayton Act means engaged in the flow of interstate commerce, and was not intended to reach all corporations engaged in activities subject to the federal commerce power."

The "New Deal" Constitutional Revolution
In June 1933, Congress enacted that nine-day wonder, the National Industrial Recovery Act (NIRA), which, among other things, attempted to govern hours of labor and wages in productive industry, on the theory, in part, that in the circumstances of the then existing emergency they affected commerce among the States. The act, however, was set aside by the Court in the *Poultry* ("*Sick Chicken*") case, largely on the basis of the doctrine of the old *Sugar Trust* case; and in the spring of 1936 the same doctrine was reiterated by the Court in setting aside the Guffey Coal Conservation Act of 1935, although the trial court had found that as a matter of fact interstate commerce in soft coal had been repeatedly interrupted for long periods by disputes between owners and workers on questions of hours of labor and of wages.[110]

This extremely artificial view of the subject has since been abandoned. In the *Jones-Laughlin* case and attendant cases,[111] decided on April 12, 1937, a five-to-four Court, speaking by Chief Justice Hughes, declined longer "to deal with the question of direct and indirect effects in an intellectual vacuum," and held that the question whether incidents of the employer-employee relationship in productive industries affected interstate commerce was one of fact and degree; and on this ground held that the Wagner Labor Relations Act of 1935, which requires employers to permit their employees freely to organize and to bargain with them collectively, was constitutionally applicable to certain manufacturing companies seeking an interstate market for their products. But the doctrine of the case applies also to "natural" products, to coal mined, to stone quarried, to fruit and vegetables grown;[112] nor is it restricted "by the smallness of the volume of the commerce affected in any particular case."[113]

Also Congress—subject no doubt to the due process clause of Amendment V—may regulate the prices of commodities sold in interstate commerce, and even the local prices of commodities which

---

[109] United States *v*. American Building Industries, 422 U.S. 271 (1975).
[110] Schechter Bros. *v*. U.S., 295 U.S. 49: (1935); Carter *v*. Carter Coal Co., 298 U.S. 238 (1936).
[111] National Labor Relations Bd. *v*. Jones & L. Steel Corp., 301 U.S. 1 (1937).
[112] Santa Cruz Fruit Packing Co. *v*. NLRB, 303 U.S. 453 (1938).
[113] National Labor Relations Bd. *v*. Fainblatt, 306 U.S. 601 (1939).

affect the interstate prices thereof.[114] Indeed, the power to regulate rates of transportation sometimes carries with it the power to regulate the price of the commodity transported, as in the case of gas and electric power.[115]

It was assumed by the Framers of the Constitution that the power to regulate commerce included the power to prohibit it at the will of the regulatory body. Proof of this is afforded by the provision of Article I, Section IX, which forbade Congress to put a stop to the slave trade until 1808; and one of the constitutional amendments which were suggested early in 1861 for the purpose of settling the slavery question would have forbidden Congress to prohibit the interstate slave trade. As to commerce with foreign nations, moreover, this doctrine has been frequently illustrated from an early date, as in the case of tariff and embargo legislation.[116] As to commerce among the States, on the other hand, the doctrine had come to be established after 1900 that Congress was not ordinarily entitled to prohibit such commerce if its doing so would enable it to control matters which were in the past regulated by the States when they were regulated at all.[117]

Yet, even during the period just referred to, the Court repeatedly recognized that the welfare of interstate commerce as a whole might require that certain portions of it be prohibited, as, for instance, the shipment of high explosives, except under stringent regulations. Indeed it presently went much farther, and laid down this doctrine: "Congress can certainly regulate interstate commerce to the extent of forbidding and punishing the use of such commerce as an agency to promote immorality, dishonesty, or the spread of any evil or harm to the people of other States from the State of origin. In doing this, it is merely exercising the police power, for the benefit of the public, within the field of interstate commerce."[118] And proceeding on this basis, Congress has prohibited the knowing transportation of lottery tickets from one State to another; of impure or falsely branded foods; of "filled" milk; of women for immoral purposes; of liquor; of stolen automobiles; of stolen goods in general; while by the so-called "Lindbergh Law" of

Prohibitions of Commerce

Prohibition as National Police Power

---

[114] United States *v*. Rock Royal Co-op, 307 U.S. 533 (1939).

[115] *See* Public Utilities Com'n *v*. Attleboro Steam and Elec. Co., 273 U.S. 83 (1927); Sunshine Anthracite Coal Co. *v*. Adkins, 310 U.S. 381 (1940); Federal Power Com'n *v*. Natural Gas Pipeline Co., 315 U.S. 575 (1942); Federal Power Com'n *v*. Hope Natural Gas Co., 320 U.S. 591 (1944); Colorado Interstate Gas Co. *v*. F.P.C., 324 U.S. 581 (1945); Federal Power Com'n *v*. East Ohio Gas Co., 338 U.S. 464 (1950).

[116] Hampton, Jr. & Co. *v*. U.S., 276 U.S. 394 (1928); University of Illinois *v*. U.S., 289 U.S. 48 (1933); United States *v*. Curtiss-Wright Export Corp., 299 U.S. 304 (1936).

[117] *See* Edward S. Corwin, *The Commerce Power versus States Rights* (Princeton, 1936), chs. II and III; and "The Power of Congress to Prohibit Commerce," Douglas B. Maggs (ed.), *Selected Essays on Constitutional Law*, III (Chicago, 1938), 103-129.

[118] Brooks *v*. U.S., 267 U.S. 432, 436 (1925). *See* United States *v*. Houston, 547 F. 2d. 104, 107 (1976).

1932 it has made kidnapping, when the victim is taken across State lines, a crime against the United States; and all these measures have been duly sustained by the Court, or their validity has not been challenged before it.[119]

Over the past few years there have been court challenges to the constitutionality of section 1955 of the Organized Crime Act passed by Congress in 1970. That section provides: "Whoever conducts, finances, manages, supervises, directs, or owns all or part of an illegal gambling business shall be fined not more than $20,000 or imprisoned not more than five years, or both." Seven circuit courts have upheld its constitutionality. As one such court put it: "We . . . conclude that Congress acted well within the bounds of the Commerce Clause. . . ."[120]

In a case involving a challenge to the constitutionality of a particular application of the Endangered Species Act of 1973—an application aimed at protecting whales—a Federal district court held that the act did not violate the Fifth Amendment.[121] Citing a number of Supreme Court decisions, the court observed that the Supreme Court "has consistently upheld the power of Congress under the Commerce Clause to exclude from the channels of interstate commerce those products whose movements between the states the congress deems harmful to the national welfare." Further, the court said "Once it is found that the means chosen are appropriate to a permissible end and are neither arbitrary nor patently discriminatory, there is little scope for the operation of the due process clause."

Nevertheless, when in 1916 Congress endeavored to break up a widespread traffic in child-made goods, by forbidding the transportation of such goods outside the State where produced, it was informed, in the case of Hammer v. Dagenhart,[122] by a closely divided Court, that it was not regulating commerce among the States but was invading "the reserved powers of the States," meaning thereby the power of the States over the employer-employee relationship in productive industry. But as Justice Holmes pointed out in his celebrated dissenting opinion, while a State is free to permit production for its own local market to take place under any conditions whatever, so far as national power is concerned, when it seeks a market outside its boundaries for its products it is no longer within its rights, but enters a field where before the Constitution was adopted it could have been met by the prohibitions of sister

[119] 18 U.S.C. 1201; Champion v. Ames, 188 U.S. 321 (1903); Hippolite Egg Co. v. U.S., 220 U.S. 45 (1911); Hoke v. U.S., 227 U.S. 308 (1913); Clark Distilling Co. v. W. Md. Ry., 242 U.S. 311 (1917); Brooks v. U.S., 267 U.S. 432 (1925); Gooch v. U.S., 297 U.S. 124 (1936); United States v. Carolene Products Co., 304 U.S. 144 (1938). But see U.S. v. Bass, 404 U.S. 336 (1971).

[120] United States v. Smaldone, 485 F. 2d. 1333, 1338, 1343 (1973), and United States v. Sacco, 491 F. 2d. 995 (1974).

[121] Delbay Pharmaceuticals v. Department of Commerce, 409 F.Supp. 637 (1976).

[122] 247 U.S. 251 (1918).

States, and where under the Constitution Congress is entitled to govern. What is more, as the decisions stood at that date, *both* Congress and the States were forbidden to prohibit the free flow of the products of child labor from one State to another—the former on the ground that it would be usurping power reserved to the States; the latter on the ground that they would be usurping Congress's power to regulate commerce![123]

This gap in governmental authority in this country was soon closed. In the notable case of United States *v.* Darby[124] the Court gave a clean bill-of-health to the Fair Labor Standards Act of 1938, which not only prohibits interstate transportation of goods produced by labor whose hours of work and wages do not conform to the standards imposed under the act, but even interdicts the production of such goods "for commerce." The decision, which explicitly overrules Hammer *v.* Dagenhart, invokes both the commerce clause and the necessary and proper clause. Subsequently the Court has held that the caretakers of a 22-story building in New York City were covered by the act, heat being essential to warm the fingers of the seamstresses employed by a clothing manufacturer who rented space in the building and who sold goods across State lines,[125] likewise, the maintenance employees of the central office building of a manufacturing corporation engaging in interstate commerce in a product coming from plants located elsewhere;[126] also the employees of a window-cleaning company, the greater part of whose work was done on the windows of industrial plants producing goods for interstate commerce;[127] etc., etc. In the second of the above cases Chief Justice Stone and Justice Roberts had indeed protested, albeit unavailingly, against the "house-that-Jack-built chain of causation" whereby "the sweep of the statute" was extended to "the ultimate *causa causarum* which result in the production of goods for commerce."[128] Quite justifiably Justice Roberts remarked in his Holmes Lectures for 1951, that the Fair Labor Standards Act today places "the whole matter of wages and hours of persons employed in the United States, with slight exceptions, under a single federal regulatory scheme and in this way . . . supersedes state exercise of the police power in this field."[129]

And in Wickard *v.* Filburn, decided some months after the *Darby* case, a still deeper penetration by Congress into the field of production was sustained. As amended by the act of 1941, the Agricultural Adjustment Act of 1938[130] regulates production even when

The "New Deal" Constitutional Revolution Completed

[123] *See* Edward S. Corwin, *The Twilight of the Supreme Court* (New Haven, 1934), 26-37.

[124] 312 U.S. 100 (1941).　　　[125] Kirschbaum *v.* Walling, 316 U.S. 517 (1942).

[126] Borden Co. *v.* Borella, 325 U.S. 679 (1945).

[127] Martino *v.* Mich. Window Cleaning Co., 327 U.S. 173 (1946).

[128] 325 U.S. 679, 685.

[129] Owen J. Roberts, *The Court and the Constitution* (Cambridge, Mass., 1951), 56. *See* Mitchell *v.* H. B. Zachry Co., 362 U.S. 310 (1960).

[130] 52 *Stat.* 31.

not intended for commerce but wholly for consumption on the producer's farm. Sustaining this extension of the act, the Court pointed out that the effect of the statute was to support the market. It said: "It can hardly be denied that a factor of such volume and variability as home-consumed wheat would have a substantial influence on price and market conditions. This may arise because being in marketable condition such wheat overhangs the market and, if induced by rising prices, tends to flow into the market and check price increases. But if we assume that it is never marketed, it supplies a need of the man who grew it which would otherwise be reflected by purchases in the open market. Home-grown wheat in this sense competes with wheat in commerce. The stimulation of commerce is a use of the regulatory function quite as definitely as prohibitions or restrictions thereon. This record leaves us in no doubt that Congress may properly have considered that wheat consumed on the farm where grown, if wholly outside the scheme of regulation, would have a substantial effect in defeating and obstructing its purpose to stimulate trade therein at increased prices." And it elsewhere stated: "Questions of the power of Congress are not to be decided by reference to any formula which would give controlling force to nomenclature such as 'production' and 'indirect' and foreclose consideration of the actual effects of the activity in question upon interstate commerce. . . . The Court's recognition of the relevance of the economic effects in the application of the Commerce Clause, . . . has made the mechanical application of legal formulas no longer feasible."[131] The limits to which the decision could be carried may well have been demonstrated by this holding of a U.S. court of appeals: "We hold that the clearing of land for the purpose of growing grapes is a business which affects interstate commerce."[132]

It was also in reliance on its power to prohibit interstate commerce and to exert like power over the mails that Congress enacted the Securities Exchange Act of 1934 and the Public Utility Holding Company Act ("Wheeler-Rayburn Act") of 1935.[133] The former authorized the Securities and Exchange Commission, which it created, to lay down regulations designed to keep dealing in securities honest and above-board and closed the channels of interstate commerce and the mails to dealers refusing to register under the act. The latter required, by sections 4 (a) and 5, the companies which are governed by it to register with the Securities and Exchange Commission and to inform it concerning their business, organization and financial structure, all on pain of being prohibited use of the facilities of interstate commerce and the mails; while by section 11, the so-called "death sentence" clause, the same act

[131] Wickard *v.* Filburn, 317 U.S. 111, 128-129 (1942).
[132] Godwin *v.* Occupational Saf. & Health Rev. Com'n, 540 F. 2d. 1013, 1016 (1976).
[133] 48 *Stat.* 881 (1934); 49 *Stat.* 803 (1935).

closed after a certain date the channels of interstate communication to certain types of public utility companies whose operations, Congress found, were calculated chiefly to exploit the investing and consuming public. All of the above provisions were sustained.[134]

The commerce clause comprises, however, not only the direct source of the most important peace-time powers of the National Government; it is also, except for the due process of law clause of Amendment XIV, the most important basis for judicial review in limitation of State power. The latter, or restrictive, operation of the clause was, in fact, long the more important one from the point of view of Constitutional Law. Of the approximately 1400 cases which reached the Supreme Court under the clause prior to 1900, the overwhelming proportion stemmed from State legislation.[135] It resulted that, except for the great case of Gibbons v. Ogden, which was dealt with above, the guiding lines in construction of the clause were initially laid down by the Court from the point of view of its operation as a curb on State power, rather than of its operation as a source of national power; and the consequence of this was that the word "commerce," as designating the thing to be protected against State interference, long came to dominate the clause, while the potential word "regulate" remained in the background. The correction of this bias was the very essence of "the Constitutional Revolution" which culminated in United States v. Darby.

The Commerce Clause as a Restraint on the States

Unquestionably, one of the great advantages anticipated from the grant to Congress of power over commerce was that State interferences with trade, which had become a source of sharp discontent under the Articles of Confederation, would be thereby brought to an end. As Webster stated in his argument for appellant in Gibbons v. Ogden: "The prevailing motive was to regulate commerce; to rescue it from the embarrassing and destructive consequences, resulting from the legislation of so many different States, and to place it under the protection of a uniform law." In other words, the constitutional grant was itself a regulation of commerce in the interests of uniformity. Justice Johnson's testimony in his concurring opinion in the same case is to like effect: "There was not a State in the Union, in which there did not, at that time, exist a variety of commercial regulations; . . . By common consent, those laws dropped lifeless from their statute books, for want of sustaining power that had been relinquished to Congress";[136] and Madison's assertion, late in life, that power had been granted Congress

---

[134] Electric Bond and Share Co. v. S.E.C., 303 U.S. 419 (1938); North American Co. v. S.E.C., 327 U.S. 686 (1946); American Power and Light Co. v. S.E.C., 329 U.S. 90 (1946).

[135] E. Parmalee Prentice and John G. Egan, *The Commerce Clause and the Federal Constitution* (Chicago, 1898), 14. The balance began to be adjusted with the enactment of the Interstate Commerce Act in 1887.

[136] 9 Wheat. 1, 226 (1824).

over interstate commerce mainly as "a negative and preventive provision against injustice among the States,"[137] carries a like implication.

State
Taxation
Affecting
Commerce

The first case in which the clause was treated by the Court as a *limitation* on State power was Brown *v.* Maryland,[138] decided in 1827. Here Marshall laid down the double rule that a State may not tax goods imported *from abroad* so long as they remained in the "original package" *in the hands of the importer*; and that the right to import includes the right to sell. This doctrine still remains the basic law on the subject, a unique instance of longevity in this general field, which may be described as a graveyard of discarded concepts. (But *see* p. 142.)

The
Court's
Problem
Today

Practically, foreign commerce is one thing, interstate commerce, a quite different thing. The latter is conducted in the interior of the country by persons and corporations that are ordinarily engaged also in local business; its usual incidents are acts which, if unconnected with commerce among the States, would fall within the State's powers of police and taxation; while the things it deals in and the instruments by which it is carried on comprise the most ordinary subject matter of State power. In this field the Court has, consequently, been unable to rely upon sweeping solutions. To the contrary, its judgments have often been fluctuating and tentative, even contradictory; and this is particularly the case as respects the infringement of the State taxing power on interstate commerce. In the words of Justice Frankfurter: "The power of the States to tax and the limitations upon that power imposed by the Commerce Clause have necessitated a long, continuous process of judicial adjustment. The need for such adjustment is inherent in a Federal Government like ours, where the same transaction has aspects that may concern the interests and involve the authority of both the central government and the constituent States. The history of this problem is spread over hundreds of volumes of our Reports. To attempt to harmonize all that has been said in the past would neither clarify what has gone before nor guide the future. Suffice it to say that especially in this field opinions must be read in the setting of the particular cases and as the product of preoccupation with their special facts."[139]

The "Police
Power"
vis-à-vis
Commerce

But while Justice Frankfurter was speaking primarily with the State's taxing power in mind, his words apply also to the Court's work in endeavoring to draw the line between the commercial interest and the State's police power. In this field the great leading case prior to the Civil War, one which is still invoked by the Court was Cooley *v.* Board of Wardens of the Port of Philadelphia,[140] de-

[137] James Madison, *Letters and Other Writings,* IV (Philadelphia, 1865), 14-15.
[138] 12 Wheat. 419 (1827). The benefits of this holding were extended as recently as 1945 to certain imports from the Philippine Islands. Hooven and Allison Co. *v.* Evatt, 324 U.S. 652 (1945).
[139] Freeman *v.* Hewit, 329 U.S. 249, 251 (1946).   [140] 12 How. 299 (1851).

cided in 1851. The question at issue was the validity of a Pennsylvania pilotage act so far as it applied to vessels engaged in foreign commerce and the coastwise trade. The Court, speaking through Justice Curtis, sustained the act on the basis of a distinction, which was earlier advanced by Webster in Gibbons *v.* Ogden, between those subjects of commerce which "imperatively demand a single uniform rule" operating throughout the country and those which "as imperatively" demand "that diversity which alone can meet the local necessities of navigation," that is to say, of commerce. As to the former, the Court held Congress's power to be "exclusive"; as to the latter it held that the States enjoyed a power of "concurrent legislation." These general propositions are still good law.[141] But they were (and are) too general to resolve all the complicated cases which arose when States exercised their "concurrent" power. Consequently, following the Civil War, other formulas emerged from the judicial smithy, several of which were brought together into something like a doctrinal system, in Justice Hughes's comprehensive opinion for the Court in the Minnesota Rate cases[142] decided in 1913. "Direct" regulation of foreign or interstate commerce by a State was held to be out of the question. At the same time, it was held that the States have their police and taxing powers and may use them as their own views of sound public policy may dictate, even though interstate commerce may be "incidentally" or "indirectly" regulated, it being understood that such "incidental" or "indirect" effects are always subject to Congressional disallowance. "Our system of government," Justice Hughes reflects, "is a practical adjustment by which the National authority as conferred by the Constitution is maintained in its full scope without unnecessary loss of local efficiency."

In more concrete terms, the varied formulas which characterize this branch of our Constitutional Law have been devised by the Court from time to time in an endeavor to effect "a practical adjustment" between two great interests, the maintenance of freedom of commerce *except so far as Congress may choose to restrain it*, and the maintenance in the States of efficient local governments. Thus, while formulas may serve to steady and guide its judgment, the Court's real function in this area of judicial review is essentially that of an arbitral or quasi-legislative body. As the Court speaking through Justice Black summed it up in 1944: ". . . there is a wide range of business and other activities which, though subject to federal regulation, are so intimately related to local welfare that, in the absence of Congressional action, they may be regulated or taxed by the states. In marking out these activities the primary test applied by the Court is not a mechanical one of whether the particular ac-

The Court's Arbitral Role

[141] Florida Avocado Growers *v.* Paul, 373 U.S. 132, 143 (1963); Colorado Com'n *v.* Continental, 372 U.S. 714, 718 (1963); Toye Bros. Yellow Cab Co. *v.* Irby, 437 F. 2d. 806, 809 (1971).

[412] Simpson *v.* Shepard, 230 U.S. 352, 402 (1913).

Holdings
in re State
Taxation
Affecting
Commerce

tivity affected by the state regulation is part of interstate commerce, but rather whether, in each case, the competing demands of the state and national interests involved can be accommodated."[143]

The following situations and the results reached by the Court in treating them are illustrative of its work in the field of State taxation affecting interstate commerce. While the "original package" doctrine does not protect goods imported from sister States from non-discriminatory taxation,[144] goods in transit from one State to another are removed from the taxable wealth of the State of origin from the beginning of their journey,[145] and are not taxable by the State of destination until "they have come to rest there for final sale or disposal."[146] Local sales of goods brought from another State are, however, subject to non-discriminatory taxation.[147] At one time the negotiation of sales to be filled by importations from another State was regarded as "interstate commerce" which could not be taxed. This doctrine, which was first laid down in 1887, in the famous case of Robbins *v.* Shelby Taxing District,[148] was for a time extended to cover deliveries of goods attended by many "local incidents";[149] but later, due primarily to the Depression, this attitude of concession to the commercial interest was considerably curtailed. It was held early in 1937 that States which have sales taxes—at that time the principal defense against bankruptcy in many States—might levy "compensating taxes" upon the use within their territory of articles brought in from other States.[150]

[143] U.S. *v.* South-Eastern Underwriters Assoc., 322 U.S. 533, 548-549 (1944); F.D.G. Ribble's *State and National Power Over Commerce* (Columbia University Press, 1937) is an excellent study both of the Court's formulas and of the arbitral character of its task in this field of Constitutional Law. On the latter point, *see especially* chs. X and XII. *See also* Noel Dowling, "Interstate Commerce and State Power," 27 *Virginia Law Review*, 1 (1940). Chief Justice Stone took repeated occasion to stress the "balancing" and "adjusting" role of the Court when applying the commerce clause in relation to State power. *See* his words in South Carolina State Highway Dept. *v.* Barnwell Bros., 303 U.S. 177, 184-192 (1938); California *v.* Thompson, 313 U.S. 109, 113-116 (1941); Parker *v.* Brown, 317 U.S. 341, 362-363 (1943); and Southern Pacific Co. *v.* Ariz., 325 U.S. 761, 766-770 (1945). For a good recent discussion of "balancing," *see* Dixie Dairy Co. *v.* City of Chicago, 538 F. 2d. 1303 (1976).

[144] Woodruff *v.* Parham, 8 Wall. 123 (1868); Sonneborn Bros. *v.* Cureton, 262 U.S. 506 (1923); Ingels *v.* Morf, 300 U.S. 290 (1937).

[145] State Freight Tax Case, 15 Wall. 232 (1873); Coe *v.* Errol, 116 U.S. 517 (1886).

[146] Brown *v.* Houston, 114 U.S. 622 (1885); Youngstown Co. *v.* Bowers, 358 U.S. 534 (1959).

[147] Emert *v.* Mo., 156 U.S. 296 (1895); Wagner *v.* Covington, 251 U.S. 95 (1919); Eastern Air Transport, Inc. *v.* S.C. Tax Com'n, 285 U.S. 147 (1932). *Cf.* Welton *v.* State of Missouri, 91 U.S 275 (1875), where a tax discriminating against goods from other States was overturned.

[148] 120 U.S. 489 (1887).

[149] *See* Caldwell *v.* N.C., 187 U.S. 622 (1903); Norfolk W. R. Co. *v.* Sims, 191 U.S. 441 (1903); Rearick *v.* Pa., 203 U.S. 507 (1906); Dozier *v.* Ala., 218 U.S. 124 (1910).

[150] Henneford *v.* Silas Mason Co., 300 U.S. 577 (1937). In a case decided in 1969, the Supreme Court held that servicemen who were stationed in Connecticut who were residents or domiciliaries of other States were not exempted from use taxes imposed by Connecticut. Sullivan *v.* U.S., 395 U.S. 169 (1969).

Later, the Court decided that out-of-state corporations could be required to *collect* the use tax if there was a "nexus," that is "some definite link, some minimum connection, between a state and the person, property or transaction it seeks to tax."[151] And in 1977, when the National Geographic Society, a non-profit corporation of the District of Columbia, objected to a use tax collection liability levied by California on sales of its magazine to California residents, the Supreme Court concluded that "the Society's continuous presence in California in offices that solicit advertising for its Magazine provides a sufficient nexus to justify that State's imposition upon the Society of the duty to act as collector of the use tax."[152]

A sale of goods intended for shipment to another State may not be taxed,[153] though their production may be,[154] and the line is not always an easy one to plot.[155]

The decision in Robbins *v.* Shelby Taxing District retained its precedential vitality longest with respect to "license" and "occupation" taxes. As late as 1946 on the authority of that decision, the Court struck down a municipal ordinance which among other things imposed an annual license tax on solicitors from out of state.[156] However, more recently, the Supreme Court did not find a privilege tax imposed by the State of Washington upon the privilege of engaging in business activities within the State and as applied against an out-of-state corporation, "constitutionally impermissible."[157] The Court reasoned: "Although mere entry into a

[151] Miller Bros. Co. *v.* Maryland, 347 U.S. 340, 344-345 (1954); Scripto *v.* Carson, 362 U.S. 207, 210-211 (1960). *Cf.* National Bellas Hess *v.* Dept. of Revenue, 386 U.S. 753 (1967). *Cf.* Halliburton Oil Well Co. *v.* Retly, 373 U.S. 64 (1963).

[152] Nat. Geographic Soc. *v.* Cal. Bd. of Equal., 430 U.S. 551, 552, 562 (1977). This decision contrasts with one the Supreme Court rendered several years earlier. Although it was not a case involving a State tax but rather a question of whether or not an out-of-state corporation could seek enforcement of a contract in Mississippi courts without a certificate to do business in the State. The Court in a careful, narrow decision held only: "appellant's contacts with Mississippi do not exhibit the sort of localization or intrastate character which we have required in situations where a State seeks to require a foreign corporation to qualify to do business. Whether there were local tax incidents of those contacts which can be reached is a different question on which we express no opinion. Whether the course of dealing would subject appellant to suits in Mississippi is likewise a different question on which we express no view. We hold only that Mississippi's refusal to honor and enforce contracts made for interstate or foreign commerce is repugnant to the Commerce Clause." Allenberg Cotton Co. *v.* Pittman, 419 U.S. 20, 24, 29 (1974).

[153] Dahnke-Walker Milling Co. *v.* Bondurant, 257 U.S. 282 (1921). *Cf.* however, Minnesota *v.* Blasius, 290 U.S. 1 (1933).

[154] Oliver Iron Co. *v.* Lord, 262 U.S. 172 (1923), and cases there cited. *See also* Alaska *v.* Arctic Maid, 366 U.S. 199 (1961).

[155] Eureka Pipe Line Co. *v.* Hallanan, 257 U.S. 265 (1921); Utah Power and Light Co. *v.* Pfost, 286 U.S. 165 (1932); Toomer *v.* Witsell, 334 U.S. 385 (1948).

[156] Nippert *v.* Richmond, 327 U.S. 416 (1946). *See also* Spector Motor Service *v.* O'Connor, 340 U.S. 602 (1951) and Freeman *v.* Hewit, 329 U.S. 249 (1946), *but cf.* discussion of these cases in Complete Auto Transit, Inc. *v.* Brady, 97 S.Ct. 1076 (1977).

[157] General Motors *v.* Washington, 377 U.S. 436, 448 (1964).

State does not take from a corporation the right to continue to do an interstate business with tax immunity, it does not follow that the corporation can channel its operations through such a maze of local connections as does General Motors, and take advantage of its gain on domesticity, and still maintain that same degree of immunity." When in 1965 the Supreme Court dismissed an appeal (for want of a substantial Federal question) of a lower court decision upholding a licensing tax, Justice Douglas complained: "Our decisions have heretofore precluded a State from exacting a license of a firm doing an exclusively interstate business as a condition of entry into the State" but to no avail.[158]

"Once again we are presented with 'the perennial problem of the validity of a state tax for the privilege of carrying on within a state, certain activities' relating to a corporation's operation of an interstate business," Justice Blackmun lamented, writing for the Court in 1977. "We now reject the rule of Spector Motor Service, Inc. v. O'Connor (340 U.S. 602 [1951]), that a state tax on the 'privilege of doing business' is *per se* unconstitutional when it is applied to interstate commerce, and that case is overruled."[159] Since the objection to the Mississippi tax raised in the case was only that it taxed the "privilege of doing business" that is interstate, the Court upheld the assessment. Had there been proof of discrimination, of an undue burden on interstate commerce, or of an insufficient nexus with the State, there was a suggestion that the outcome might have been different, particularly in view of the Court's affirmative references to Colonial Pipeline v. Traigle. In that case the Court ruefully provided the statistics for the "perennial problem" description indicating that the Court had handed down some "three hundred full dress opinions" on the matter by 1959.[160] *Colonial* involved a Delaware corporation that has 258 miles of pipeline in Louisiana. The firm maintains a small work force to inspect and maintain the line in that state; however, it has no administrative office or personnel in the state nor does intrastate business there in petroleum products. The corporation sought to recover Louisiana franchise taxes it paid under protest. To overcome constitutional difficulties that befell a previous tax provision imposing a tax on the corporation for the *privilege of carrying on or doing business*, Louisiana amended its laws to provide for the imposition of taxes on domestic and foreign corporations qualified "to carry on or do business in this state or the actual doing of business within this state in a corporate form." The Court held that "Since appellant, a foreign corporation qualified to carry on its business in corporate form, and

[158] Fairfax Family Fund v. California, 382 U.S. 1, 2 (1965). *See also* Rabren v. Pullman Co., 254 So. 2d. 324 (1971); United Air Lines, Inc. v. Porterfield, 276 N.E. 2d. 629 (1971).
[159] Complete Auto Transit, Inc. v. Brady, 430 U.S. 274, 288, 289 (1977).
[160] Colonial Pipeline Company v. Traigle, 421 U.S. 100, 101 (1975).

doing business in Louisiana in the corporate form, thereby gained benefits and protections from Louisiana of value and importance to its business, the application of that State's fairly apportioned and undiscriminatory levy to appellant does not offend the Commerce Clause. The tax cannot be said to be imposed upon appellant merely or solely for the privilege of doing interstate business in Louisiana. It is rather a fairly apportioned and nondiscriminatory means of requiring appellant to pay its just share of the cost of state government upon which appellant necessarily relies and by which it is furnished protection and benefits."

While concurring, Justice Blackmun joined by Justice Rehnquist complained that the Court's decisions in these matters over the past 30 years have failed "to provide what taxpayers and other lawyers who advise them have a right to expect, namely a firm and solid basis of differentiation between that which runs afoul of the Commerce Clause, and that which is consistent with that Clause. It makes little constitutional sense—and certainly no practical sense—to say that a State may not impose a fairly apportioned, nondiscriminatory franchise tax with an adequate nexus upon the conduct of business in interstate commerce, but that it may impose that same tax on the conduct of business in interstate commerce 'in a corporate form' or, for that matter, in partnership or individual form. . . . Certainly to the lay mind, or to any mind other than the purely legal, these are distinctions with little substantive difference and this is taxation by semantics." Justice Stewart was even more critical in dissent: "All agree that the petitioner is engaged *exclusively* in interstate commerce. Yet the Court says that Louisiana can nonetheless impose this franchise tax upon the petitioner because it is for the privilege of engaging in interstate commerce 'in the corporate form.' . . . The fact is that Louisiana has imposed a franchise tax upon the petitioner for the privilege of carrying on an exclusively interstate business. Under our established precedents, such a tax is constitutionally impermissible."

A State may, however, tax the property that is within its borders (and presumably receiving its protection) of a company which engaged in interstate commerce. "The State must be allowed to tax the property and to tax it at its actual value as a going concern."[161] Further, such taxes may take into account the "augmentation of value from the commerce in which it is engaged. . . . So it has been held that a tax on the property and business of a railroad operated within the State might be estimated *prima facie* by gross income, computed by adding to the income derived from business within the State the proportion of interstate business equal to the propor-

[161] Justice Holmes's language in Galveston, Harrisburg, & S.A. R.R. Co. *v.* Texas, 210 U.S. 217, 225, 227 (1908). *See also* Cudahy Packing Co. *v.* Minn., 246 U.S. 450 (1918); Pullman Co. *v.* Richardson, 261 U.S. 330 (1923); and Virginia *v.* Imperial Coal Sales Co., 293 U.S. 15 (1834).

tion between the road over which the business was carried within the State to the total length of the road over which it was carried."[162] This is the concept of an "apportioned" tax, or the "unit of use" rule, the Court's main reliance till 1938 in this area of Constitutional Law. Cases cited below illustrate its application.[163] Likewise, taxation by a State of the gross receipts of companies engaged in interstate commerce within its borders must be "fairly apportioned," at least ordinarily.[164] By an earlier rule a State was entitled also to levy indefinite so-called "franchise taxes" upon companies chartered by it, but this label appears nowadays to possess little or no specific saving quality of its own.[165] In 1938 Justice Stone, speaking for the Court, advanced what has been called the "multiple taxation" test. The question it poses is, what would happen to the interstate commerce affected by it if everybody—that is, every "State which the commerce touches"—did the same?[166] Some of the Justices hastily concluded that the new rubric might safely replace the "apportionment" rule, with all its difficulties and uncertainties, but later holdings dashed this hope.[167]

As the Court summed it up in 1964: "A careful analysis of the cases in this field teaches that the validity of a tax rests upon whether the State is exacting a constitutionally fair demand for that aspect of interstate commerce to which it bears a special relation. For our purposes the decisive issue turns on the operating incidence of the tax. In other words, the question is whether the State has exerted its power in proper proportion to appellant's consequent enjoyment of opportunities and protections which the State has afforded."[168] This summary was further validated in 1972, when the Supreme Court upheld the constitutionality of State and municipal charges of "$1 per commercial airline passenger to help defray the costs of airport construction and maintenance."[169]

[162] *Ibid.*

[163] The foundations of the rule were laid in Western Un. Tel. Co. *v.* Mass., 125 U.S. 530 (1888); Pullman's Palace Car Co. *v.* Pa., 141 U.S. 18 (1891); *and* Adams Express Co. *v.* Ohio, 165 U.S. 194 and 166 U.S. 185 (1897). *See also* Ott *v.* Miss. Barge Line Co., 336 U.S. 169 (1949).

[164] *See* Freeman *v.* Hewit, 329 U.S. 249, 265-266, note 13 (1946), citing cases. *Cf.* Evco Designs *v.* Jones, 41 *LW* 4037 (1972).

[165] Maine *v.* Grand Trunk R. Co., 142 U.S. 217 (1891), was the leading case. *Cf.* Galveston, Harrisburg & San Antonio R. Co. *v.* Tex., 210 U.S. 217 (1908). *See also* Interstate Pipe Line Co. *v.* Stone, 337 U.S. 662 (1949), for an extensive review of the cases.

[166] Western Live Stock *v.* Bureau of Revenue, 303 U.S. 250, 255-256 (1938).

[167] *See* Joseph *v.* Carter and Weekes Stevedoring Co., 330 U.S. 422, 433 (1947); Braniff Airways *v.* Nebraska Board, 347 U.S. 590 (1954); Northwestern Cement Co. *v.* Minn., 358 U.S. 450 (1959).

[168] General Motors *v.* Washington, 377 U.S. 436, 440-441 (1964).

[169] Evansville-Vanderburgh A.A. Dist. *v.* Delta Airlines, Inc., 405 U.S. 707 (1972). The Supreme Court of Hawaii recently decided that application of a general excise tax to commissions received by travel agents "From solicitation and sale of interstate and foreign transportation, hotel accommodations, and sight-seeing tours does not

That the Supreme Court will continued to be plagued in its arbitral role by difficult tax cases was manifested by three cases it decided in the 1970's. One of the cases dealt with South Carolina's assessing a tax on an out-of-state liquor-producing corporation for the income derived from the sale of its goods in South Carolina.[170] Basically, the corporation's transactions in South Carolina appeared to be precisely those covered in a statute enacted by Congress in 1959 which provided that no state can impose "a net income tax on the income derived within such State by any person from interstate commerce," if the business activities within the State constituted only the solicitation of orders which "are sent outside the State for approval or rejection, and, if approved are filled by shipment or delivery from a point outside the State."[171] However, South Carolina law requires that, to do business in the State, liquor producers must have a resident representative to whom the shipments of liquor into the State must go before being passed on to licensed wholesalers. Consequently, South Carolina could and did contend that Heublein, Inc., the liquor producer, was, by virtue of its required representative's performing his required functions, doing more than just soliciting business in the State. Heublein, understandably, argued that a State should not be able to evade the purpose of the Federal law by *requiring* "a firm to do more than solicit business within the State and then taxing the firm for engaging in this compelled additional activity." The Court held "the requirement that, before engaging in the liquor business in South Carolina, a manufacturer do more than merely solicit sales there, is an appropriate element in the State's system of regulating the sale of liquor. The regulation in question here is therefore valid, and . . . [the Federal statute] does not apply." In so holding, the Court stressed that, under the Twenty-First Amendment, the State is "unconfined by traditional Commerce Clause limitations when it restricts the importation of intoxicants destined for use, distribution, or consumption within its borders."

A second case dealt with New Mexico's emergency school and gross receipts tax on a New Mexico corporation which creates and designs instructional programs. This generally involves developing products such as camera-ready copies of programmed textbooks or audio tapes which are delivered to out-of-state customers who reproduce them. The issue in the case boiled down to whether the tax on the proceeds from selling the reproducible originals was a tax on *services performed within the State* or a tax on *tangible property in another State*. The Supreme Court pointed out that, by its previous

contravene the Commerce Clause. . . ." Ramsay Travel, Inc. *v.* Kondo, 495 P. 2d. 1172 (1972). *See also* Kennecott Copper Corp. *v.* State Tax Com'n, 493 P. 2d. 632 (1972) *and* Sinclair Refining Co. *v.* Department of Revenue, 277 N.E. 2d. 858 (1972).

[170] Heublein, Inc. *v.* South Carolina Tax Com'n, 409 U.S. 275 (1972).
[171] 15 U.S.C. 381.

decisions, States were permitted to tax services performed within the State, but that "a tax levied on the gross receipts from the sales of tangible personal property in another State is an impermissible burden on commerce."[172] Since the New Mexico Court of Appeals had "found in effect that the reproducible originals were the *sine qua non* of the contract and that it was a sale of that tangible property in another State that New Mexico had taxed," the Supreme Court held that the tax was not constitutionally permissible.

A third case involved a New York statute imposing a "transfer tax" on securities transactions, if part of the transaction takes place in the State. The law taxed out-of-state sales more heavily than most sales within the State. The Supreme Court concluded by saying "Our decision today does not prevent the States from structuring their tax systems to encourage the growth and development of intrastate commerce and industry. Nor do we hold that a State may not compete with other States for a share of interstate commerce; such competition lies at the heart of a free trade policy. We hold only that in the process of competition no State may discriminatorily tax the products manufactured or the business operations performed in any other State."[173]

With respect to State taxation and the Commerce Clause, there have been three recent noteworthy lower court decisions. The New York Court of Appeals held that vessels and supplies used by a marine dredging company could be assessed sales and use taxes.[174] As the court saw it: "That the work was performed upon interstate waterways is not a dispositive factor." Rather, the court suggested the situation was like that in several other cases where it decided that the "activities in general were a taxable local event, separate and distinct from interstate commerce." Likewise, the Court of Special Appeals of Maryland held that a county ordinance that levied a tax in the form of a percentage of rental fees collected by dock owners from boatowners did not violate the Commerce Clause, saying: "In sum, the subject ordinance does not impose restrictions upon movement upon navigable waters; or impair the entry of vessels into ports or restrain or impede interstate commerce. Rather, it is imposed only upon boat owners who use physical facilities within Anne Arundel County that have been provided for their service and convenience."[175]

By contrast, a New York judge held that New York could not assess alcoholic beverage, cigarette, and sales taxes on companies that sell those items at the border to people going to Canada. The judge reasoned that there was no incident occurring in New York subject

---

[172] Evco *v*. Jones, 409 U.S. 91, 93 (1972).

[173] Boston Stock Exch. *v*. State Tax Com'n, 429 U.S. 318, 336 (1977).

[174] Great Lakes Dredge & Dock Co. *v*. Dept. of Tax and Finance, 382 N.Y.S. 2d. 958.

[175] Reinhardt *v*. Anne Arundel County, 356 A. 2d. 917 (1976).

to an excise tax nor was there a "sale for use within New York."[176]

State courts in recent years have been supportive of State efforts to subject corporations doing interstate business to a variety of State taxes that did not go beyond what struck the courts as a fair share.[177]

As was said before, the States have also their so-called "police power"; that is, the power "to promote the health, safety, morals and general welfare." Laws passed in exercise of this power may often affect commerce incidentally, but if the resultant burden is found by the Court to be on the whole justified by the local interest involved, such laws will be sustained. In other words, the Court's function in the handling of this type of case is, even more emphatically than in the taxation field, that of an arbitral, rather than of a strictly judicial, body. Thus in 1943 it held that a State is entitled to authorize, in the interest of maintaining producers' prices, a scheme imposing restrictions on the sale within the State of a crop ninety-five per cent of which eventually enters interstate and foreign commerce, there being no act of Congress with which the State act was found to conflict.[178] But this holding does not necessarily disturb an earlier one that a State has no right to promote its own "economic welfare" at the expense of the rest of the country, by prohibiting the entrance within its borders or the exit from them of "legitimate articles of commerce," the Constitution having been "framed upon the theory that the people of the several States must sink or swim together, and that in the long run prosperity and salvation are in union and not division."[179]

Similarly, a State may require all engineers operating within its borders, even those driving through-trains, to be tested for color-blindness; but it may not limit the length of trains, nor apply a Jim Crow law to interstate bus passengers.[180] Nor may a State regulate rates of transportation in the case of goods being brought from or carried to points outside the State; and while it may regulate rates

Holdings in re the "Police Power"

---

[176] Ammex Warehouse Co. Inc. v. Procaccino, 378 N.Y.S. 2d. 848 (1975).

[177] Public Utility Dist. No. 2 of Grant County v. State, 510 P. 2d. 206 (1973); Union Pacific Railroad Co. v. Heckers, 509 P. 2d. 1255 (1973); General Motors Corp. v. State, 509 P. 2d. 1260 (1973); Upper Mo. River Corp. v. Board of Rev., Woodbury County, 210 N.W. 2d. 828 (1973); National Liberty Life Ins. Co. v. State, 215 N.W. 2d. 26 (1974); Colonial Pipeline Co. v. Agerton, 289 So. 2d. 93 (1974); Tennessee Blacktop, Inc. v. Benson, 494 S.W. 2d. 760 (1973); Texas Gas Trans. Corp. v. Board of Ed. of Ballard Cty., 502 S.W. 2d. 82 (1973); Union Pacific R. Co. v. City & County of Denver, 511 P. 2d. 497 (1973). *But cf.* Federal Paper Board Co. v. Kosydar, 306 N.E. 2d. 416 (1974).

[178] Parker v. Brown, 317 U.S. 341 (1943).

[179] Baldwin v. Seelig, 294 U.S. 511, 523 (1935).

[180] Smith v. Ala., 124 U.S. 465 (1888); Southern Pacific Co. v. Ariz., 325 U.S. 761 (1945); Morgan v. Va., 328 U.S. 373 (1946). The survey of such cases in Justice Hughes's opinion for the Court in the Minnesota Rate Cases, 230 U.S. at pp. 402-412 (1913), and that by Chief Justice Stone in the just cited Arizona case are very informative. The latter opinion is also a model of hard-hitting factual criticism.

for goods bound simply from one point to another within its own borders, yet even such rates are subject to be set aside by national authority if they discriminate against or burden interstate commerce.[181]

In recent years, the Court has seemed more willing than previously to allow for the exercise of the State police power. For example, the Court upheld as constitutional the application of a Detroit Smoke Abatement Code, forbidding ships to blow their stacks in the harbor, against ships operating in interstate commerce and in accordance with a comprehensive system of regulation devised by Congress.[182] And the Court also held that a Colorado commission's order requiring that an airline refrain from racial discrimination in its hiring of pilots did not unduly burden interstate commerce.[183] Justice Stewart provided the present posture of the Court in these matters this way: "Although the criteria for determining the validity of state statutes affecting interstate commerce have been variously stated, the general rule that emerges can be phrased as follows: Where the statute regulates evenhandedly to effectuate a legitimate local public interest, and its effects on interstate commerce are only incidental, it will be upheld unless the burden imposed on such commerce is clearly excessive in relation to the putative local benefits. If a legitimate local purpose is found, then the question becomes one of degree. And the extent of the burden that will be tolerated will of course depend on the nature of the local interest involved, and on whether it could be promoted as well with a lesser impact on interstate activities."[184]

A covey of recent Supreme Court decisions illustrate how the Court has endeavored to apply Justice Stewart's statement of the rule.

On the last day of the Term in 1976, the Supreme Court decided a case in which it parsed the 1943 Parker *v.* Brown[185] decision to a fare-thee-well. The issue as described by Justice Stevens for the Court was: "In Parker *v.* Brown, the Court held that the Sherman Act was not violated by state action displacing competition in the marketing of raisins. In this case we must decide whether the *Parker* rationale immunizes private action which has been approved by a State and which must be continued while the state approval remains effective."[186] The Court concluded that "The mere possi-

---

[181] Wabash Ry. Co. *v.* Ill., 118 U.S. 557 (1886); the Shreveport Case, 234 U.S. 342 (1914). State-imposed rates, no less than nationally imposed rates, must yield the carrier a "fair return" on the "value" of its property. Smyth *v.* Ames, 169 U.S. 466 (1898).

[182] Portland Huron Cement Co. *v.* Detroit, 362 U.S. 440 (1960).

[183] Colorado Com'n *v.* Continental Airlines, 372 U.S. 714 (1963). *Cf.* Pike *v.* Bruce Church, Inc., 397 U.S. 137 (1970).

[184] *Ibid.* at 142. *But see* the unusual decision of a New Jersey court, State *v.* Comfort Cab, Inc., 286 A. 2d. 742 (1972) and the novel contention in West *v.* Broderick & Bascom Rope Co., 197 N.W. 202, 214 (1972).

[185] 317 U.S. 341.   [186] Cantor *v.* Detroit Edison Co., 428 U.S. 579 (1976).

bility of conflict between state regulatory policy and federal anti-trust policy is an insufficient basis for implying an exemption from the federal antitrust laws. Congress could hardly have intended state regulatory agencies to have broader power than federal agencies to exempt private conduct from the antitrust laws. Therefore, assuming that there are situations in which the existence of state regulation should give rise to an implied exemption, the standards for ascertaining the existence and scope of such an exemption surely must be at least as severe as those applied to federal regulatory legislation."

In a separate opinion, Justice Blackmun hoped "that consideration will be given on remand to allowing a defense against damages wherever the conduct on which such damages would be based was required by state law." He felt that a defendant should not "be held 'responsible' in damages for conduct as to which he had no choice."

In answer to the challenge to a regulation promulgated by the Mississippi State Board of Health that milk and milk products from another state could be sold in Mississippi provided that the regulatory agency of the other state accepted milk and milk products produced and processed in Mississippi on a reciprocal basis, the Supreme Court held that "The mandatory character of the reciprocity requirement . . . unduly burdens the free flow of interstate commerce and cannot be justified as a permissible exercise of any state power."[187] The Court derisively asserted that "Mississippi's contention that the reciprocity clause serves its vital interests in maintaining the State's health standards borders on the frivolous. The clause clearly does not do so in the sense of furthering Mississippi's established milk quality standards."

In an effort to rid the State of the problem of abandoned automobiles, Maryland evolved an elaborate plan for giving bounties to licensed scrap processors who would then destroy them. In 1974, Maryland amended its law to require an out-of-state processor of Maryland cars to submit more elaborate title documentation. As Justice Powell phrased it, the case that eventually got to the Supreme Court involved a "two-pronged constitutional attack" on the recent Maryland amendment, that it violated the Commerce Clause and equal protection of the laws. The Supreme Court held that no violence was done to the Commerce Clause.[188] Speaking for the Court, Justice Powell came on remarkably strongly for State power. "But no trade barrier of the type forbidden by the Commerce Clause, and involved in previous cases, impedes their [the hulks] movement out of state. They remain within Maryland in response to market forces, including that exerted by money from the State. Nothing in the purposes animating the Commerce Clause forbids a State, in the absence of congressional action, from par-

---

[187] Great Atlantic & Pac. Tea Co., Inc. *v.* Cottrell, 424 U.S. 366 (1976).
[188] Hughes *v.* Alexandria Scrap Corp., 426 U.S. 794 (1976).

ticipating in the market and exercising the right to favor its own citizens over others."

With respect to the enforcement of a California statute and regulation pertaining to the labeling by weight of packaged goods, the Supreme Court concluded that, "with respect to the millers' flour," enforcement would prevent "the accomplishment and execution of the full purposes and objectives of Congress in passing the FPLA [Fair Packaging and Labeling Act]. Under the Constitution, that result is impermissible, and the state law must yield to the federal."[189] Earlier in its opinion, the Court had stated the principle that when Congress has "unmistakably ordained that its enactments alone are to regulate a part of commerce, state laws regulating that aspect of commerce must fall."

The Supreme Court also held that a North Carolina law "which required, *inter alia*, all closed containers of apples sold, offered for sale or shipped into the state to bear no grade other than the applicable U.S. grade or standard" was unconstitutional.[190] The Court suggested that there were "nondiscriminatory alternatives to the outright ban of Washington State grades" on apples: "For example, North Carolina could effectuate its goal by permitting out-of-state growers to utilize state grades only if they also marked their shipments with the applicable U.S.D.A. label."

The lower courts also have had recent opportunities to continue to prick the line between what was and what was not a proper exercise of the States' police power against a claim that the exercise unduly burdened interstate commerce.

The New Jersey Supreme Court upheld a State statute and administrative regulations aimed.at excluding from New Jersey solid waste coming from out of the state.[191] The court explained: "We do not mean to be understood as saying that every assertion of a state's quasi-sovereign right to protect its environment, ecological values and natural and human resources will be sustained regardless of the impact upon interstate commerce. Clearly this is not so. But where the effect upon trade and commerce is relatively slight, as is here the case, and where at the same time the values sought to be protected by the state legislation are as crucial to the welfare of its citizens as is here true, we have no hesitancy in sustaining the state action."

With respect to a Dade County, Florida, ordinance requiring among other things that consumer reporting agencies furnish a consumer with a copy of a report about him, where the case stipulated that the reports do move in interstate commerce, a Federal district court held that "requiring a consumer reporting agency to furnish a copy of a consumer report prepared on that consumer is

---

[189] Jones *v.* Rath Packing Co., 430 U.S. 519, 543 (1977).

[190] Hunt *v.* Washington State Apple Advertising Com'n, 432 U.S. 333, 336, 354 (1977).

[191] Hackensack Mead. Dev. Com'n *v.* Municipal San. L.A., 348 A. 2d. 505 (1975).

not a burden on interstate commerce so as to warrant preclusion based on the Commerce Clause."[192]

A U.S. court of appeals in early 1975 upheld as constitutional a Chicago city ordinance banning the use of detergents containing phosphates.[193] In its interesting opinion the court made the following significant distinction: "we are not confronted with a situation in which legislation has reduced the effectiveness of a means of transportation itself. In this context the ordinance is not a burden on interstate commerce, but is merely a 'burden' on a company which happens to have interstate distribution facilities. The effect of the ordinance is that the particular interstate systems of distribution used by Procter and Gamble and other detergent companies before the passage of the ordinance can no longer be used. . . . There is no impairment of the ultimate ability to transport in interstate commerce in the most efficient and economical manner possible. While this factor might necessitate a change in certain production facilities, it does not rise to the level of an unconstitutional burden on interstate commerce." This, the court held, was particularly so where "the objective . . . of this legislation is legitimate," i.e. the elimination and prevention of nuisance algae in the Illinois waterway.[194]

In a decision that created a political furor and drew extensive national media coverage, Federal District Judge Miles Lord enjoined the Reserve Mining Company from discharging taconite tailings into Lake Superior on the grounds that the discharge of the tailings violated the Federal Water Pollution Control Act and constituted a common-law nuisance.[195]

A Federal district court upheld a local ordinance prohibiting take-offs and landings at an airport if the noise level was high. The court emphasized that, with regard to this particular airfield, the ordinance created only an "incidental" burden on interstate commerce.[196]

An interesting question was posed when damages were sought from a non-governmental agency on the grounds that the defendants had put a burden upon interstate commerce. A U.S. district court explained "[the Commerce Clause] is a limitation upon the power of the state. It does not create any implied cause of action and the defendants engaged in private activities, not state action."[197]

It should be stressed that the Court's *quasi*-arbitral function is not

[192] Retail Credit Company v. Dade County, Florida, 393 F.Supp. 577 (1975).
[193] Procter and Gamble Company v. City of Chicago, 509 F. 2d. 69 (1975).
[194] *Ibid.*, 80.
[195] United States v. Reserve Mining Co., 380 F.Supp. 11 (1974). See also circuit court decision at 498 F. 2d. 1073 (1974) and Supreme Court's action, 419 U.S. 802 (1974) and 420 U.S. 1000 (1975). *See also* United States v. Reserve Mining Co., 412 F.Supp. 705 (1976).
[196] National Aviation v. City of Haywood, Cal., 418 F.Supp. 417 (1976).
[197] Ve-Ri-Tas v. Advertising R.C. of Metro. Denver, 411 F.Supp. 1012 (1976).

When
National
and State
Laws
Overlap

confined to the question whether State legislation has unconstitutionally invaded the field of power which the commerce clause is thought to reserve to Congress exclusively. It is also brought into requisition, and with the extension of national power into the industrial field more and more so, in determining whether certain State legislation conflicts with a certain act or acts of Congress. If such is the case, then of course the State legislation must be treated as void so long as the conflicting national legislation remains on the statute books, *provided* it is constitutional; and the Court will not ordinarily be keen to discover such a conflict.[198] For example, the Court sustained the Federal Motor Carriers Act, which precludes a State from suspending the right of an interstate carrier to use the State's highways for interstate goods because of repeated violation of certain state regulations. The State's remedy, the Court said, lay in an appeal to the Interstate Commerce Commission.[199]

Nor, in fact, does Congress always *subtract* from the powers of the States affecting commerce—sometimes it *adds* to them. Thus, the serious confusion that would otherwise have resulted from the Court's decision in 1944 in the South-Eastern Underwriters case (*see* p. 59) was obviated by the passage early in 1945 of the McCarran Act, which provides that the insurance business shall continue to be subject to the laws of the several States except as Congress may specifically decree otherwise,[200] and years ago Congress, by the Webb-Kenyon Act of 1916, subjected interstate shipments of intoxicants to regulation by the State of destination, thereby in effect delegating power over such interstate commerce to the States. And in both these instances Congress was sustained by the Court.[201]

A parsing of the cases in which the Court has performed in its arbitral role invites the observation that this is a very difficult role for the Court to play well and suggests that Justices Black, Frankfurter, and Douglas may have had a valid point when, in a dissent some years ago, they wrote: "Judicial control of national commerce—unlike legislative regulations—must from inherent limitations of the judicial process treat the subject by the hit-and-

[198] Parker *v.* Brown, 317 U.S. 341, 351 (1943). *See also* Allen-Bradley Local No. 1111 *et al. v.* Wisconsin Employment Rels. Bd., 315 U.S. 740 (1912); Penn Dairies *v.* Milk Control Com'n, 318 U.S. 261 (1943); Hill *v.* Fla., 325 U.S. 538 (1945). *See also Jones* case discussed above, p. 80.

[199] Castle *v.* Hayes Freight Lines, Inc., 348 U.S. 61 (1954).

[200] 59 *Stat.* 33 (1945).

[201] *See* Prudential Ins. Co. *v.* Benjamin, 328 U.S. 408 (1946); and Clark Distilling Co. *v.* W. Md. Ry., 242 U.S. 311 (1917). The Supreme Court has never forgotten the lesson administered to it by the act of Congress of August 31, 1852, which pronounced the Wheeling Bridge "a lawful structure," thereby setting aside the Court's determination to the contrary earlier the same year. *See* Pennsylvania *v.* Wheeling and Belmont Bridge, 13 How. 518 (1852); 18 How. 421 (1856). This lesson, stated in the Court's own language thirty years later, was, "It is Congress, and not the Judicial Department, to which the Constitution has given the power to regulate commerce. . . ." Transportation Co. *v.* Parkersburg, 107 U.S. 691, 701 (1883).

miss method of deciding single local controversies upon evidence and information limited by the narrow rules of litigation. Spasmodic and unrelated instances of litigation cannot afford an adequate basis for the creation of integrated national rules which alone can afford that full protection for interstate commerce intended by the Constitution."[202]

Back in 1886, the Supreme Court took a limited view of the meaning of commerce with the Indian tribes. For the power to regulate Indian matters other than commerce, the Court relied on the concept of sovereignty: "The power of the federal government over these remnants of a race once powerful, now weak and diminished in numbers, is necessary to their protection, as well as to the safety of those among whom they dwell. *It must exist in that government*, because it never existed anywhere else. . . ."[203] (Emphasis supplied.)

To Regulate Commerce with the Indian Tribes

Over the years there has been substantial slippage from this position. In 1973, in a highly significant footnote to a case involving Indians, Justice Marshall speaking for the Court observed: "The source of federal authority over Indian matters has been the subject of some confusion, but it is now generally recognized that the power derives from federal responsibility for regulating commerce with Indian tribes and for treaty making."[204]

Again, in 1974, in deciding a case involving Indians, the Supreme Court reaffirmed "the unique legal status of Indian tribes under federal law and upon the plenary power of Congress, based on a history of treaties and the assumption of a 'guardian-ward' status to legislate on behalf of federally-recognized Indian tribes. The plenary power of Congress to deal with special problems of Indians is drawn both explicitly and implicitly from the Constitution itself."[205] Thus, despite the slippage, the courts have not felt compelled to bottom Congress's power to regulate Indian affairs exclusively on the Commerce Clause. Consequently, several recent, important decisions regarding Indians have been made which on their face seem to have little to do with the clause.

On the question of whether a tribal court or the courts of Montana had jurisdiction in an adoption proceeding where all the parties were Indians and residents of a reservation, the Court decided that "The right of the Northern Cheyenne Tribe to govern itself independently of state law has been consistently protected by federal statute" and that State court jurisdiction "plainly would interfere with the powers of self-government."[206]

A 1926 Federal act established the Northern Cheyenne Reserva-

---

[202] McCarroll *v*. Dixie Lines, 309 U.S. 176, 188-189 (1940).

[203] United States *v*. Kagama, 118 U.S. 375, 384 (1886).

[204] McClanahan *v*. Arizona Tax Com'n, 411 U.S. 164 (1973). *But see* Robinson *v*. Wolff, 349 F.Supp. 514, 521 (1972).

[205] Morton *v*. Mancari, 417 U.S. 535, 551 (1974).

[206] Fisher *v*. Dist. Court of Sixteenth Jud. Dist., 424 U.S. 382 (1976).

tion. Among other things, the act provided that title to the mineral deposits was to pass to those who had been allotted the land or their heirs in 50 years. There was a provision in the law under which until the 50 years were up the mineral rights were "reserved for the benefit of the tribe and may be leased. . . ." When the energy crisis considerably increased the value of coal reserves under the land, Congress hastened in 1968 to terminate the grant in order to insure what they conceived as a fairer distribution of the benefits to be derived from the mineral rights by reserving them "in perpetuity for the benefit of the Tribe." The question that then came to the Court was: could Congress terminate the grant "without rendering the United States constitutionally liable to pay the allottees just compensation?"[207] The Court's answer was yes: "The Court has consistently recognized the wide-ranging congressional power to alter allotment plans until those plans are executed."

In a case involving Indian hunting and fishing rights in the State of Washington with respect to an 1891 agreement, the U.S. Supreme Court held that: "Congress exercised its plenary constitutional powers to legislate those federally protected rights into law in enacting the implementing statutes that ratified the Agreement [which provided that "the right to hunt and fish in common with all other persons on lands not allotted to said Indians shall not be taken away or in anywise abridged"]. No congressional purpose to subject the preserved rights to state regulation is to be found in the acts or their legislative history. Rather, the implementing statutes unqualifiedly, 'carr[ied] into effect' and 'ratif[ied]' the explicit and unqualified provision . . . that 'the right to hunt and fish . . . shall not be taken away or in anywise abridged.' State qualification of the rights is therefore precluded by force of the Supremacy Clause, and neither an express provision precluding state qualification nor the consent of the State was required to achieve that result."[208] However, the Court wound up its opinion with these words, "The United States as *amicus curiae*, invites the Court to announce that state restrictions 'cannot abridge the Indians' federally protected rights without [the state] demonstrating a compelling need' in the interest of conservation. . . . We have no occasion in this case to address this question."

As Justice Brennan described it, another case involving Indians presented the question of whether the grant of civil jurisdiction to the States conferred by the Civil Rights Act of 1968 "is a congressional grant of power to the States to tax reservation Indians insofar as taxation is expressly excluded by the terms of the statute."[209] The Court held that the law did not give the States authority to tax reservation Indians reasoning that "if Congress in enacting . . . [the law] had intended to confer upon the states general

---

[207] Northern Cheyenne Tribe *v.* Hollowbreast, 425 U.S. 649 (1976).
[208] Antoine *v.* Washington, 420 U.S. 194, 205 (1975).
[209] Bryan *v.* Itasca Cty., Minnesota, 426 U.S. 373 (1976).

civil regulatory powers, including taxation, over reservation Indians, it would have expressly said so."

Also, in a case dealing with the role of the Federal judiciary with respect to Congressional authority over Indians, a Federal district court held: "Congress has also exclusive authority vis-à-vis the federal judiciary with respect to the *status* of Indians. The status of Indians, therefore, has been considered a nonjusticiable political question."[210] And the North Dakota Supreme Court held that neither income earned nor purchases made by Indians on reservations were subject to State taxation.[211]

There have been nonetheless several important cases where the connection with the Commerce Clause is clear. In one, the Court held that under its power to regulate commerce with the Indian tribes, Congress could prohibit or regulate the introduction of alcoholic beverages into *Indian country* "even though the lands were held in fee by non-Indians, and even though the persons regulated were non-Indians."[212]

The Court speaking through Justice Rehnquist struggled to define "Indian country," a term used in pertinent statutes. They did not supply a precise answer, but, in deciding this particular case, they relied on the location of the bar that was at the center of the controversy and on the nature of the surrounding population. For example, they said: "The evidence showed that the bar was located on the outskirts of Fort Washakie, Wyoming, an unincorporated village bearing the name of the man who was Chief of the Shoshones during the early years on the Wind River Reservation. . . . The evidence also showed that the 212 families living within a 20-square-mile area roughly centered on The Blue Bull [the bar], 170 were Indian families, 41 were non-Indians, and one was mixed."

For a discussion of the delegation problem dealt with in the case, see p. 8.

In another case, the Supreme Court held that, although Montana could not collect cigarette sales taxes on reservation sales by Indians to Indians, the State could require Indian retailers on the reservation to add the sales tax in sales to non-Indians.[213] Justice Rehnquist speaking for the Court averred: "The State's requirement that the Indian tribal seller collect a tax validly imposed on non-Indians is a minimal burden designed to avoid the likelihood that . . . non-Indians . . . will avoid payment of a concededly lawful tax."

In its most recent decision with respect to Indians, the Supreme Court cited Congress's power to regulate commerce with the Indian tribes to demonstrate that "classifications expressly singling

---

[210] National Indian Youth Council *v.* Bruce, 366 F.Supp. 313 (1973).
[211] White Eagle *v.* Dorgan, 209 N.W. 2d. 621 (1973).
[212] United States *v.* Mazurie, 419 U.S. 544, 554 (1975).
[213] Moe *v.* Confederated Salish & Kootenai Tribes, Etc., 425 U.S. 463 (1976).

out Indian tribes as subjects of legislation are expressly provided for in the Constitution."[214] The Court was asked to answer the question: Do "federal criminal statutes violate the Due Process Clause of the Fifth Amendment by subjecting individuals to federal prosecution by virtue of their status as Indians"? The Court concluded that the respondents were not subjected to Federal criminal jurisdiction because they are of the Indian race but because they were enrolled members of the Coeur d'Alene Tribe. "We therefore conclude that federal criminal statutes enforced here are based neither in whole nor in part upon impermissible racial classifications." Nor did the Court accept an equal protection argument as valid, pointing out that "Under our federal system, the National Government does not violate equal protection when its own body of law is evenhanded, regardless of the laws of States with respect to the same subject matter."

¶4. To establish an uniform rule of naturalization, and uniform laws on the subject of bankruptcies throughout the United States;

There seems to be no good reason why two such entirely different subjects should be dealt with in the same clause other than that legislation regarding each has to be "uniform."

Naturalization and Citizenship   Some are born citizens; some achieve citizenship, some have citizenship thrust upon them. The first category fall into two groups. First, those who are born in the United States, "subject to the jurisdiction thereof," are pronounced "citizens of the United States and of the State wherein they reside" by the opening clause of Amendment XIV, which derives from the principle of *jus soli* ("the law of the soil") of the English common law, and further back still from the feudal law. As rather improvidently interpreted by the Court in the Wong Kim Ark case,[215] this clause endows with American citizenship even the children of temporary residents in the United States, provided they do not have diplomatic status. The second group of "citizens at birth" owe their citizenship to Congressional legislation which applies the *jus sanguinis* ("the law of blood relationship") of the Roman civil law, and embraces with certain qualifications persons born outside the United States and its outlying possessions to parents one or both of whom are citizens of the United States.[216]

Those who achieve citizenship are persons who were born aliens but who have become "naturalized" in conformance with the laws of Congress. Formerly this privilege was confined to "white persons and persons of African nativity or descent," but was extended by the Act of December 17, 1943, to "descendants of races indigenous

[214] United States *v.* Antelope, 430 U.S. 641, 642, 647, 649 (1977).
[215] United States *v.* Wong Kim Ark, 169 U.S. 649 (1898).
[216] 8 U.S.C. 1401.

to the Western Hemisphere and Chinese persons or persons of Chinese descent."[217] And in 1952 the law was amended to read: "The right of a person to become a naturalized citizen . . . shall not be denied or abridged because of race or sex or because such person is married."[218] But naturalization is by no means a favor for the asking by those who are qualified. No person may be naturalized who advocates or belongs to a group which advocates "opposition to all organized government" or who "believes in" or belongs to a group which "believes in," "the overthrow by force or violence of the Government of the United States or of all forms of law,"[219] and any person petitioning for naturalization must "before being admitted to citizenship, take an oath in open court . . . to renounce and abjure absolutely . . . all allegiance and fidelity to any foreign prince" or state "of whom or which the petitioner was before a subject or citizen"; "to support and defend the Constitution and laws of the United States against all enemies, foreign and domestic"; and "to bear full faith and allegiance to the same."[220] Prior to a Supreme Court decision in 1946, these provisions were interpreted as requiring a petitioner to swear a willingness to bear arms for the United States. As a consequence of that decision, the law on the matter, drawn up in 1952, specifically permits the petitioner the options of promising to bear arms or to performing "noncombatant service in the Armed Forces" or "work of national importance under civilian direction" when it is required by law.[221] In view of several lower court decisions, it is doubtful that a conscientious objector can be denied naturalization solely for refusing to promise to accept any of the options.[222] But any naturalized person who takes this oath with mental reservations or conceals beliefs and affiliations which under the statute disqualify one for naturalization, is subject, upon these facts being conclusively shown in a proper proceeding, to have his certificate of naturalization cancelled for "fraud." However, as the Court has admonished: "The Government carries a heavy burden of proof in a proceeding to divest a naturalized citizen of his citizenship."[223] In all other respects, however, the naturalized citizen stands "under the Constitution . . . on an equal footing with the native citizen" save as regards

[217] 57 *Stat.* 600 (1943).   [218] 8 U.S.C. 1422.

[219] 8 U.S.C. 1424. These restrictive provisions are, moreover, by the Act of June 27, 1952, "applicable to any applicant for naturalization who at any time within a period of ten years immediately preceding the filing of the petition for naturalization or after such filing and before taking the final oath of citizenship is, or has been found to be within any of the classes enumerated within this section, notwithstanding that at the time the petition is filed he may not be included within such classes." 8 U.S.C. 1424C.

[220] U.S. *v.* Schwimmer, 279 U.S. 644 (1929); U.S. *v.* Macintosh, 283 U.S. 605 (1931); Girouard *v.* U.S., 328 U.S. 61 (1946).

[221] 8 U.S.C. 1448.

[222] *In re* Weitzman, 426 F. 2d. 439 (1970); *In re* Pisciattano, 308 F.Supp. 818 (1970).

[223] Costello *v.* U.S., 365 U.S. 265, 269 (1961); 8 U.S.C. 1451.

eligibility to the Presidency.[224] He enjoys, therefore, the same freedom of speech and publication, the same right to criticize public men and measures, whether informedly or foolishly, the same right to assemble to petition the government, in short, the same civil rights as do citizens from birth. Nevertheless, the naturalized citizen's vulnerability to charges of having obtained citizenship through fraud does raise a question about "equal footing," in spite of Justice Douglas's admonition years ago: "To hold otherwise would be an anomaly. It would mean in effect that where a person . . . perpetrated a fraud on the naturalization court, the United States would be remediless to correct the wrong."[225]

Illustrative of persons who have had citizenship thrust upon them are members of an Indian "or other aboriginal tribe" who, by the Act of 1887 and succeeding legislation, are declared "to be citizens of the United States" if they were born within the United States;[226] and by the Act of June 27, 1952, certain categories of persons born in the Canal Zone, Panama, Puerto Rico, Alaska, Hawaii, the Virgin Islands, and Guam, on or after certain stated dates.[227]

Congress's Inherent Power over Citizenship and Expatriation The interesting question arises whether Congress, when it extends American citizenship to certain categories "at birth," does so by virtue of the constitutional clause here under discussion or by virtue of an "inherent" power ascribable to it in its quality as the national legislature. While the point has never been adjudicated, the dictionary definition of "naturalize" "*to adopt, as a foreigner, into a nation or state*,"[228] tends to confirm the latter theory, as does also the fact that in the pioneer Act of 1855, dealing with the matter, Congress "declared" children born abroad of American citizens to be citizens. Even more clearly does Congress's power to deal with the subject of expatriation seem to require some such explanation. At the common law the *jus soli* was accompanied by the principle of "indelible allegiance," out of which stemmed, for instance, Great Britain's claim of right in early days to impress naturalized American seamen of British birth; and even as far down as 1868 American courts often implicitly accepted this principle. Our Secretaries of State, on the other hand, usually asserted the doctrine of expatriation in their negotiations with other governments respecting the rights abroad of American citizens by naturalization, and on July 27, 1868, Congress passed an act declaring the latter doctrine to be a fundamental principle of this Government, one not to be ques-

---

[224] Osborn *v.* Bk. of U.S., 9 Wheat. 738 at 827 (1824); Luria *v.* U.S., 231 U.S. 9 (1913); Knauer *v.* U.S., 328 U.S. 654 (1946).

[225] Knauer *v.* U.S., 328 U.S. 654, 673-674 (1946).

[226] 8 U.S.C. 1401.

[227] 8 U.S.C. 1402-1407. *See also*, on Collective Naturalization, Boyd *v.* Neb., 143 U.S. 135, 162 (1892).

[228] *See also* Chief Justice Taney's *dictum* in the Dred Scott case that the naturalization clause applies only to "persons born in a foreign country, under a foreign government." 19 How. 393, 417, 419 (1857).

tioned by any of its officers in any of their opinions, orders, decisions.[229] Then by an act passed in 1907, although since repealed in this respect, Congress enacted that any woman marrying a foreigner should take the nationality of her husband. To the contention that this provision deprived American citizens of their constitutional right to that status, the Court replied that the maintenance of "the ancient principle of the identity of husband and wife" was a reasonable requirement of international policy, a field in which the National Government was "invested with all the attributes of sovereignty." While Congress, said the Court, may not "arbitrarily impose a renunciation of citizenship," yet marriage with a foreigner was "tantamount to voluntary expatriation."[230] And for like reasons Congress may provide that naturalized citizens shall lose their acquired status under certain conditions by protracted residence abroad, although their minor children born in the United States, not sharing the parent's intention in the eyes of the law, do not share his fate.[231]

Law presently on the statute books spells out ten ways in which "a national of the United States whether by birth or naturalization, shall lose his nationality." These range from "obtaining naturalization in a foreign state upon his own application" to "departing from or remaining outside the jurisdiction of the United States in time of war or . . . national emergency for the purpose of evading . . . service. . . ."[232] But the Supreme Court has been deeply perplexed and divided on the problem of whether or not these provisions are constitutional.[233] In a sweeping decision, albeit by a five-four majority, the Court in 1967, speaking through Justice Black, held that a citizen had "a constitutional right to remain a citizen in a free country unless he voluntarily relinquishes that citizenship."[234] And apparently voluntariness must not be implied, for the Court said:

---

[229] 15 *Stat.* 223-224; and *see* generally John Bassett Moore, *Digest of International Law*, III (Washington, 1906).

[230] Mackenzie *v.* Hare, 239 U.S. 299, 311-312 (1915); *cf.* United States *v.* Wong Kim Ark, 169 U.S. 649, 703 (1898).

[231] Perkins *v.* Elg, 307 U.S. 325 (1939); Rogers *v.* Bellei, 401 U.S. 815 (1971). Congress's power over naturalization is an exclusive power. A State cannot denationalize a foreign subject who has not complied with Federal naturalization law and constitute him a citizen of the United States, or of the State, so as to deprive the Federal courts of jurisdiction over a controversy between him and a citizen of a State. Chirac *v.* Chirac, 2 Wheat. 259, 269 (1817). But power to naturalize aliens may be, and early was, devolved by Congress upon State courts having a common law jurisdiction. Holmgren *v.* U.S., 217 U.S. 509 (1910), where it is also held that Congress may provide for the punishment of false swearing in such proceedings. *Ibid.* 520. Also, States may confer the right of suffrage upon resident aliens who have declared their intention to become citizens, and have frequently done so. Spragius *v.* Houghton, 3 Ill. 377 (1840); Stewart *v.* Foster, 2 Binney (Pa.) 110 (1800).

[232] 8 U.S.C. 1481.

[233] Perez *v.* Brownell, 356 U.S. 44 (1958); Nishikawa *v.* Dulles, 356 U.S. 129 (1958); Trop *v.* Dulles, 356 U.S. 86 (1958); Kennedy *v.* Mendoza-Martinez, 372 U.S. 144 (1963); Afroyim *v.* Rusk, 387 U.S. 253 (1967).

[234] Afroyim *v.* Rusk, 387 U.S. 253, 268 (1967).

"To uphold Congress' power to take away a man's citizenship because he voted in a foreign election in violation of . . . [law] would be equivalent to holding that Congress has the power to . . . 'take . . . away' citizenship. Because the Fourteenth Amendment prevents Congress from doing any of these things, we agree with the Chief Justice's dissent in the *Perez* case that the Government is without power to rob a citizen of his citizenship. . . ."[235] Since only one member of that majority (Brennan) remains on the Court, it does not seem too hazardous to predict that the current Court might narrow or reverse that decision, given the occasion.[236]

Congress's Inherent Power to Exclude Aliens

Merging with its delegated power over the subject of naturalization is the inherent power of Congress to exclude aliens from the United States. This is absolute. In the words of the Court: "That the government of the United States, through the action of the legislative department, can exclude aliens from its territory is a proposition which we do not think open to controversy. Jurisdiction over its own territory to that extent is an incident of every independent nation. It is a part of its independence. If it could not exclude aliens, it would be to that extent subject to the control of another power. . . . The United States, in their relation to foreign countries and their subjects or citizens are one nation, invested with powers which belong to independent nations, the exercise of which can be invoked for the maintenance of its absolute independence and security throughout its entire territory."[237] The Immigration and Nationality Act of June 27, 1952, excludes some thirty-one categories of aliens from the United States, including "aliens who are, or at any time have been, members . . . of or affiliated with any organization that advocates or teaches . . . the overthrow by force, violence, or other unconstitutional means of the Government of the United States. . . ."[238]

In 1972, the Supreme Court upheld the action of the Attorney General in refusing to allow an alien scholar, a self-acknowledged "revolutionary Marxist" to enter the country to attend academic meetings, stating that he "as an unadmitted and nonresident alien, had no constitutional right of entry to this country as a nonimmigrant or otherwise." To the contention that refusal to admit the scholar trenched on the First Amendment rights of those who desired to hear what he had to say, the Supreme Court gave short shrift: "We hold that when the Executive exercises this power [Congressional delegation of power] negatively on the basis of a facially legitimate and bona fide reason, the courts will neither look behind the exercise of that discretion, nor test it by balancing its justifica-

[235] *Ibid.* at 267.   [236] Rogers *v.* Bellei, 401 U.S. 815 (1971).
[237] Chinese Exclusion case, 130 U.S. 581, 603, 604 (1889); *see also* Fong Yue Ting *v.* U.S., 149 U.S. 698, 705 (1893); Japanese Immigrant case, 189 U.S. 86 (1903); Turner *v.* Williams, 194 U.S. 279 (1904); Bugajewitz *v.* Adams, 228 U.S. 585 (1913); Hines *v.* Davidowitz, 312 U.S. 52 (1941); Hsieh *v.* Civil Service Commission of City of Seattle, 488 P. 2d. 515, 519 (1971).
[238] 66 *Stat.* 163, tit. 2 § 212 (1952).

tion against the First Amendment interests of those who seek personal communication with the applicant."[239]

With the power of exclusion goes, moreover, the power to assert a considerable degree of control over aliens after their admission to the country. By the Alien Registration Act of 1940[240] it was provided that all aliens in the United States, fourteen years of age and over, should submit to registration and finger printing, and willful failure to do so was made a criminal offense against the United States. The Act of June 27, 1952, repeats these requirements, and Supreme Court decisions, which ascribe to the Executive certain inherent powers in the same field, enlarge them.[241] In theory, however, they are all reasonable concomitants of the exclusion power, and do not embrace the right to lay down a special code of conduct for alien residents of the United States to govern private relations with them.[242] This is not to suggest, however, that aliens are accorded the same deference in law accorded citizens. Several examples suffice to demonstrate that they are not.

The Supreme Court was called upon in 1973 to determine whether or not an employer could discriminate in hiring against all aliens in the face of the provision of the Civil Rights Act of 1964 which makes it "an unlawful employment practice for an employer . . . to fail or refuse to hire . . . any individual . . . because of such individual's race, color, religion, sex or national origin." The Court held that "Certainly it would be unlawful for an employer to discriminate against aliens because of race, color, religion, sex or national origin—for example, by hiring aliens of Anglo-Saxon background but refusing to hire those of Mexican or Spanish ancestry. Aliens are protected from illegal discrimination under the Act, *but nothing in the Act makes it illegal to discriminate on the basis of citizenship or alienage.*"[243] (Emphasis supplied.)

In 1976, a U.S. district court held that aliens could be excluded from employment as New York State troopers.[244] To the contention of resident aliens of Cuban origin that they were deprived, in a Federal case, of their Sixth Amendment rights because the grand and petit juries involved in their indictment and conviction did not include resident aliens despite the fact that they comprise 30 per cent of the population of Miami, where the trial took place, a U.S. court of appeals held that Congress may validly exclude aliens from jury service.[245] The Court reasoned that: "Although Congress may not single out aliens for discriminatory treatment in mat-

---

[239] Kliendienst v. Mandel, 408 U.S. 753, 770 (1972).

[240] 54 *Stat.* 670; sustained in Hines v. Davidowitz, 312 U.S. 52, 69-70 (1941).

[241] Knauff v. Shaughnessy, 338 U.S. 537 (1950); Carlson v. Landon, 342 U.S. 524 (1952); Harisiades v. Shaughnessy, 342 U.S. 580, 587 (1952); United States v. Specter, 343 U.S. 169 (1952).

[242] Keller v. U.S., 213 U.S. 138 (1909).

[243] Espinoza v. Farah Manufacturing Company, Inc., 414 U.S. 86, 95 (1973).

[244] Foley v. Connelie, 419 F.Supp. 889 (1976).

[245] United States v. Gordon-Nikkar, 518 F. 2d. 972 (1975).

ters not related to the furtherance of its naturalization responsibilities, Congress has the power to define reasonable prerequisites to an alien's exercise of the rights and duties of citizenship. We believe that preventing resident aliens from serving as jurors is rationally related to Congress's legitimate power to define the extent of resident aliens' rights prior to obtaining citizenship."

President Carter's 1977 proposals for dealing with aliens contained the proverbial good and bad news for aliens. He proposed an "adjustment of status" to permit aliens who have been in the United States illegally for some time to stay and work. They would not be eligible immediately for citizenship, Medicaid, or food stamps.[246] He also proposed penalties for employers who hired aliens who were not registered.

Deportation of Aliens   For a good part of our history, deportation of aliens has been a vexing issue. The issue was stated succinctly by Justice Frankfurter some years ago: "The power of Congress over the admission of aliens and their right to remain is necessarily very broad, touching as it does basic aspects of national sovereignty, more particularly our foreign relations and the national security. Nevertheless, considering what it means to deport an alien who legally became part of the American community, and the extent to which, since he is a 'person,' an alien has the same protection for his life, liberty and property under the Due Process Clause as is afforded to a citizen, deportation without permitting the alien to prove that he was unaware of the Communist Party's advocacy of violence strikes one with a sense of harsh incongruity. If due process bars Congress from enactments that shock the sense of fair play—which is the essence of due process—one is entitled to ask whether it is not beyond the power of Congress to deport an alien who was duped into joining the Communist Party, particularly when his conduct antedated the enactment of the legislation under which his deportation is sought. And this because deportation may . . . deprive a man of all that makes life worth living; and deportation is a drastic measure and at times the equivalent of banishment or exile."[247] He went on to say, however: "In light of the expansion of the concept of substantive due process as a limitation upon all powers of Congress, even the war power, . . . much could be said for the view, were we writing on a clean slate, that the Due Process Clause qualifies the scope of political discretion heretofore recognized as belonging to Congress in regulating the entry and deportation of aliens. And since the intrinsic consequences of deportation are so close to punishment for crime, it might fairly be said also that the *ex post facto* Clause, even though applicable only to punitive legislation, should be applied to deportation."[248] However, he then con

[246] 1977 *Cong. Quart. Weekly Report*, 1671. *See also U.S. News & World Report*, Aug. 15, 1977, p. 19.
[247] Galvan *v*. Press, 347 U.S. 522, 530 (1954).
[248] *Ibid*. at 530-531.

cluded: "But the slate is not clean. As to the extent of the power of
Congress under review, there is not merely a page of history, . . .
but a whole volume. Policies pertaining to the entry of aliens and
their right to remain here are peculiarly concerned with the political conduct of government. In the enforcement of these policies,
the Executive Branch of the Government must respect the procedural safeguards of due process. But that the formulation of
these policies is entrusted exclusively to Congress has become
about as firmly imbedded in the legislative and judicial tissues of
our body politic as any aspect of our government. And whatever
might have been said at an earlier date for applying the *ex post facto*
Clause, it has been the unbroken rule of this Court that it has no
application to deportation."[249] Subsequently, the Court endeavored to soften the impact of this decision by statutory interpretation, but it left unchallenged Frankfurter's description of Congressional power.[250]

Congress's power in the field of bankruptcy legislation has been a
steadily growing power. In the words of Justice Cardozo, sum-
marizing Mr. Warren's volume on the subject: "The history is one
of an expanding concept," but of "an expanding concept that has
had to fight its way. Almost every change has been hotly denounced in its beginning as a usurpation of power. Only time or
judicial decision has had capacity to silence opposition. At the
adoption of the Constitution the English and Colonial bankruptcy
laws were limited to traders and to involuntary proceedings. An act
of Congress passed in 1800 added bankers, brokers, factors, and
underwriters. Doubt was expressed as to the validity of the extension, which established itself, however, with the passing of the
years. Other classes were brought in later, through the Bankruptcy
Act of 1841 and its successors, until now practically all classes of
persons and corporations are included."[251] And where bankruptcy
legislation was originally framed solely from the point of view of
the immediate reimbursement of creditors, it is today designed also
as a relief to debtors and as a mode of putting them back on their
feet ("voluntary bankruptcy"). Yet the creditor's interest has not
been lost sight of, since it is usually better secured, especially in
times of financial depression, by conservation of the debtor's resources than by their sale and distribution.

To be sure, a closely divided Court held in 1936 that Congress
could not extend the benefits of voluntary bankruptcy proceedings
to municipalities and other political subdivisions of the States, since
to do so would be to invade the rights of the States even though the
act required that they first give their consent to such proceedings;

*The
Bankruptcy
Power*

---

[249] *Ibid.* at 531.

[250] Rowoldt *v.* Perfetto, 355 U.S. 115 (1957); Gastelum-Quinones *v.* Kennedy, 374
U.S. 469 (1963).

[251] Ashton *v.* Cameron County, 298 U.S. 513, 535-536 (1936); Charles Warren,
Bankruptcy in United States History (Boston, 1935), 9.

but this decision was speedily superseded by one to the contrary effect, which is now the law of the land.[252]

While Congress is not forbidden to impair "the obligation of contracts" (*see* Article I, Section X, ¶1), in legislating regarding bankruptcies it may not, under the Fifth Amendment, unduly invade the property rights of creditors, which, however, is just what, in the opinion of a unanimous Court, it attempted to do by the Frazier-Lemke Farm Moratorium Act of 1933. A revised act, designed to meet the Court's objections, was in due course challenged and sustained.[253]

Unlike the situation with respect to the commerce clause, it was settled early that States could legislate with respect to bankruptcies if Congress had not acted. In 1819, the Supreme Court held: "The omission of Congress to legislate, amounts to a declaration, that they do not think a *uniform* system is necessary; and they, therefore, leave the States to legislate upon the subject, whenever they think it proper and expedient to do so."[254] When Congress does act, however, it preempts or supersedes State law, but only if there is "a clear collision."[255]

Several recent decisions on the bankruptcy clause are instructive. By a 5-4 decision, the Supreme Court held in 1973 that a filing-fee requirement for bankruptcy did not deny an indigent equal protection of the laws. In so holding, the majority speaking through Justice Blackmun made these important observations: (1) "There is no constitutional right to obtain a discharge of one's debts in bankruptcy"; (2) "the rational basis for the fee requirement is readily apparent"; (3) "congressional power over bankruptcy, of course, is plenary and exclusive."[256]

In an interesting 1974 case, the Supreme Court decided that an income tax refund was "property" within the meaning of the Federal Bankruptcy Act.[257]

In passing on the constitutionality of the Regional Rail Reorganization Act of 1973 (p. 402) the Supreme Court had occasion to parse the meaning of the "uniformity requirement" of the bankruptcy clause.[258] Considering the argument that "the uniformity required by the Constitution is geographic" and that "since the Rail Act operates only in a single statutory defined region, the Act is geographically non-uniform," the Court allowed as how "The argument has a certain surface appeal but is without merit because it overlooks the flexibility inherent in the constitutional provision." The Court went on: "The uniformity provision does not deny Congress power to take into account differences that exist between

---

[252] The case just cited; and United States *v.* Bekins, 304 U.S. 27 (1938).
[253] Louisville Joint Stock Land Bank *v.* Radford, 295 U.S. 555 (1935); Wright *v.* Vinton Branch, 300 U.S. 440 (1937).
[254] Sturges *v.* Crowningshield, 17 U.S. 122,176 (1819).
[255] Kesler *v.* Department of Public Safety, 369 U.S. 153 (1962).
[256] United States *v.* Kras, 409 U.S. 434, 448 (1973).
[257] Kokoszka *v.* Belford, 417 U.S. 642 (1974).
[258] Blanchette *v.* Connecticut General Insurance Corps., 419 U.S. 102 (1974).

different parts of the country, and to fashion legislation to resolve geographically isolated problems."

A district court held that a 1797 Congressional enactment providing that insolvent persons and estates of deceased persons must satisfy debts due to the United States first conformed with Congress's power under the Bankruptcy Clause and that "the claims of the United States are prior to those of any secured creditor of . . . [a bankrupt] unless it can establish a choate [nothing more need to be done to make it enforceable], specific and perfected lien designed to divest the debtor of either title or possession of its property prior to bankruptcy."[259]

When the Connecticut Commissioner of Finance and Control appealed a U.S. district court ruling that a debt owed by a bankrupt to the State for treatment at a state psychiatric hospital was dischargeable in bankruptcy (i.e. debtor was released from obligation), a U.S. court of appeals held that "The Constitution specifically grants Congress the power to enact bankruptcy laws" and that the law Congress enacted "intended to make debts owed to the state and federal governments dischargeable."[260] The court went on to add: "Any exception for a particular kind of state debt should come from Congress, not from us."

Significantly, a U.S. district court cautioned that "While this power of Congress is plenary, it is, like other substantive powers of that governmental body, subject to constitutional guarantees set forth in the Fifth Amendment."[261]

¶5. To coin money, regulate the value thereof, and of foreign coin, and fix the standard of weights and measures;

The Framers of the Constitution apparently assumed a bimetallic currency, and the power to regulate "the value thereof" was probably thought of chiefly as the power to regulate the value of lesser coins in relation to the dollar and the metallic content of the two kinds of dollars with a view to keeping both gold and silver in circulation. As a result of Civil War legislation, however, Congress established its power to authorize paper money with the quality of legal tender in the payment of debts, both past and future; while by the Gold Clause cases of 1934 it is recognized as possessing the power to lower the metal content of the dollar in order to stimulate prices. In short, "the value thereof" comes to mean "value" in the sense of *purchasing power*. Nor may private parties, by resort to the "gold clause" device, contract themselves out of the reach of Congress's power thus to lower the purchasing power of the dollar.[262] (*See also* ¶2, above.)

The Currency Power

[259] *In re* Airport Machinery Corporation, 371 F.Supp. 1262, 1266 (1973).
[260] Matter of Crisp, 521 F. 2d. 172 (1975).
[261] United States *v*. Rome, 414 F.Supp. 517, 519 (1976).
[262] Phanor J. Eder, "The Gold Clause Cases in the Light of History," 23 *Georgetown Law Journal*, 359-388 and 722-760 (1935). *Cf.* Perry *v*. U.S., 294 U.S. 330 (1935). *See* Allen *v*. Craig, 564 P. 2d. 552 (1977).

¶6. To provide for the punishment of counterfeiting the securities and current coin of the United States;

This clause of the Constitution is superfluous. Congress would have had this power without it, under the "co-efficient clause."[263] (*See* ¶18, below.)

¶7. To establish post offices and post roads;

The Postal Clause   In earlier times narrow constructionists advanced the theory that these words did not confer upon Congress the right to *build* post offices and post roads, but only the power to *designate* from existing places and routes those which should serve as post offices and post routes.[264] The debate on the subject was terminated in 1876 by the decision in Kohl *v*. United States[265] sustaining a proceeding by the United States to appropriate a parcel of land in Cincinnati as a site for a post office and courthouse.

It is from this clause also that Congress derives its power to carry the mails, which power comprehends the power to protect them and assure their quick and efficient distribution;[266] also the power to prevent the postal facilities from being abused for purposes of fraud and exploitation, or for the distribution of legitimately forbidden matter.[267] Indeed, it may close the mails to induce conformity with regulations within its power to enact.[268] But all restraints on the use of the mails are in general subject to judicial review because of the close connection between the subject and First Amendment freedoms. In 1965, the Supreme Court held that an act which required the Postmaster General to detain and deliver only upon request of the addressee unsealed foreign mailings of "communist political propaganda" as construed and applied in that case was unconstitutional "because it requires an official act (*viz*., returning the reply card) as a limitation on the unfettered exercise of the addressee's First Amendment rights."[269]

In a complicated case involving a violation of the Federal statute prohibiting the mailing of obscene materials, the Supreme Court in 1977 treated several important issues with respect to Congress's power. First, it reaffirmed Congress's power to exclude obscene materials from the mails. Second, it found that "The fact that the mailings in this case were wholly intrastate is immaterial to a prosecution" under the Federal statute. Third, it instructed that

[263] *See e.g.* United States *v*. Marigold, 9 How. 560, 568 (1850); Fox *v*. Ohio, 5 How. 410 (1847); Baender *v*. Barnett, 255 U.S. 224 (1921).
[264] United States *v*. Railroad Bridge Co., Fed. Cas. No. 16, 114 (1855).
[265] 91 U.S. 367 (1875).   [266] *In re* Debs, 158 U.S. 564 (1895).
[267] *In re* Rapier, 143 U.S. 110 (1892); Public Clearing House *v*. Coyne, 194 U.S. 497 (1904); Lewis Pub. Co. *v*. Morgan, 229 U.S. 288 (1913); Hennegan *v*. Esquire, Inc., 327 U.S. 146 (1946); Donaldson *v*. Read Magazine, 333 U.S. 178 (1948).
[268] Electric Bond and Share Co. *v*. S.E.C., 303 U.S. 419 (1938).
[269] Lamont *v*. Postmaster General, 381 U.S. 301, 305 (1965).

"Just as the individual's right to possess obscene material in the privacy of his home, however, did not create a correlative right to receive, transport, or distribute the material, the State's right to abolish all regulation of obscene material does not create a correlative right to force the Federal government to allow the mails or the channels of interstate or foreign commerce to be used for the purpose of sending obscene material into the permissive State."[270]

The lower courts have had occasion in recent years to deal with post office questions. The Supreme Court of Vermont was faced with the question of whether or not a postmaster was holding an "office of profit or trust under the authority of Congress" in light of the Postal Reorganization Act of 1971.[271] The Vermont Constitution forbids those who do from holding certain State offices simultaneously. In a case involving an effort to make a man give up his postmastership while he served as town selectman, the Vermont Supreme Court found that "Even though the legislation makes the Postal Service an 'independent executive agency,' it is still 'created' by congressional enactment" and "Congress has reserved the entire power to alter, amend, or repeal any or all of the Postal Service law." Further, it is "uncertain whether the pay of a postmaster consists of an emolument provided from the Treasury of the United States." Because of its professed uncertainty about whether or not the State constitution proscribed this combination of posts, the court decided to resolve doubts in favor of the individual and held that the State constitution does not "make the office of postmaster as presently established under Chapter 39 of the United States Code Annotated a position incompatible with that of selectman."

A Federal district court found that, under the circumstances of the case, postal regulations precluding door-to-door delivery service for some people constituted "a reasonable exercise of the Postal Service's rule-making power," which had been delegated to it by Congress under its power to establish post offices.[272] And another district court found a criminal statute prohibiting private express for conveyance of letters constitutional.[273]

When a Connecticut corporation rigged a hook to rural mailboxes to enable it to distribute, without using the mails, its advertising journal to recipients willing to have the hooks installed, a United States court of appeals found that postal regulations invoked to forbid such a practice were constitutional. Those regulations prescribed that rural mailboxes "shall be used exclusively for mail" and that "mailable matter . . . deposited in such receptacles must bear postage at the applicable rate and a proper address."[274]

[270] Smith *v*. U.S., 431 U.S. 291, 305-307 (1977).
[271] Baker *v*. Hazen, 341 A. 2d. 707 (1975).
[272] Parsons *v*. U.S. Postal Service, 380 F.Supp. 815 (1974).
[273] U.S. *v*. Black, 418 F.Supp. 378 (1976).
[274] Rockville Reminder, Inc. *v*. U.S. Postal Service, 480 F. 2d. 4 (1973).

¶8. To promote the progress of science and useful arts by securing
for limited times to authors and inventors the exclusive right to
their respective writings and discoveries;

Patents and   Congress may exercise the power conferred by this clause by either
Copyrights   general or special acts, but the provision has reference only to writings and discoveries which are the result of intellectual labor and
exhibit novelty[275] and which "add to the sum of useful knowledge."[276] Nor is Congress authorized by the clause to grant
monopolies in the guise of patents or copyrights, and the rights
which the present statutes confer are subject to the Anti-Trust
Act.[277] Also, patented articles are subject to the police power and
the taxing power of the States, but must not be discriminated
against as such,[278] and a State may tax royalties from patents or
copyrights as so much income, a decision to the contrary effect in
1928 having been later overruled.[279] But as the Court has cautioned: "Just as a State cannot encroach upon federal patent laws
directly, it cannot, under some other law, such as that forbidding
unfair competition, give protection of a kind that clashes with the
objectives of the federal patent laws."[280] The term "writings" has
been given an expanded meaning, and covers photographs and
photographic films.[281] On the other hand, it was held in the
Trade-Mark cases[282] that a trademark is neither a "writing" nor
"discovery" within the sense of the clause, with the result that Congress could validly legislate for their protection only as they were
instruments of foreign or interstate commerce and at that time the
Court had a very restrictive view of Congress's power to regulate
commerce.[283] Not improbably, however, recently established views

[275] Higgins v. Keuffel, 140 U.S. 428 (1891); Cuno Engineering Corp. v. Automatic Devices Corp., 314 U.S. 84 (1941); E. Burke Inlow, *The Patent Grant* (Baltimore, 1950), ch. VI. For discussion of difference in requirements for copyrights as
distinguished from patents, *see* Imperial Homes Corp. v. Lamont, 458 F. 2d. 895
(1972).
[276] "Innovation, advancement, and things which add to the sum of useful knowledge are inherent requisites in a patent system which by constitutional command
must 'promote the Progress of . . . useful Arts,' " Graham v. John Deere Co., 383
U.S. 1, 6 (1966); Anderson's-Black Rock v. Pavement Co., 396 U.S. 57 (1969). Re
computer programs, *see* Gottschalk v. Benson, 41 *LW* 4015 (1972).
[277] *See* Motion Picture Patents Co. v. Universal Film Mfg. Co., 243 U.S. 502
(1917); Morton Salt Co. v. G. S. Suppiger Co., 314 U.S. 488 (1942); United States v.
Masonite Corp., 316 U.S. 265 (1942); United States v. New Wrinkle, Inc., 342 U.S.
371 (1952); Inlow, *Patent Grant*, ch. V.
[278] Patterson v. Ky., 97 U.S. 501 (1878); Webber v. Va., 103 U.S. 344 (1880). *See
also* Watson v. Buck, 313 U.S. 387 (1941).
[279] The cases referred to are Long v. Rockwood, 277 U.S. 142 (1928); and Fox
Film Co. v. Doyal, 286 U.S. 123 (1932).
[280] Sears, Roebuck & Co. v. Stiffel Co., 376 U.S. 225, 231 (1964).
[281] Burrows-Giles Lithographic Co. v. Sarony, 111 U.S. 53 (1884). *See also* Mazer
v. Stein, 347 U.S. 201 (1954); CBS v. DeCosta, 377 F. 2d. 315 (1967); *cert. denied,* 389
U.S. 1007 (1967).
[282] 100 U.S. 82 (1879).
[283] ". . . there still remains a very large amount of commerce, perhaps the largest,

of Congress's protective power over commerce and its instruments would today vindicate the kind of act which was overturned in 1879. As the Court held most recently, "the direction of Art. I is that *Congress* shall have the power to promote the progress of science and the useful arts. When, as here, the constitution is permissive, the sign of how far Congress has chosen to go can come only from Congress."[284] The international agreements on the subject of patents and copyrights to which the United States is party were entered into under authority conferred by Congress under this clause.

It is worth noting in passing that courts have found litigation in patent cases inordinately difficult. As Justice White recently observed: "We are also aware that some courts have frankly stated that patent litigation can present issues so complex that legal minds, without appropriate grounding in science and technology, may have difficulty in reaching decision."[285] Some recent cases illustrate the kind of issues that make these decisions difficult.

The Supreme Court, in upholding by a 5-4 vote a California law which made it a misdemeanor to "pirate" recordings and tapes, reasoned that "the Constitution neither explicitly precludes the States from granting copyrights nor grants such authority exclusively to the Federal government. The subject matter to which the copyright clause is addressed may at times be of purely local concern. No conflict will necessarily arise from a lack of uniform state regulation, nor will the interest of one State be significantly prejudiced by the actions of another. No reason exists why Congress must take affirmative action either to authorize protection of all categories of writings or to free them from all restraint. We therefore conclude that, under the Constitution, the States have not relinquished all power to grant authors 'the exclusive Right to their respective Writings.' "[286] The Court went on to hold that California "has exercised a power which it retained under the Constitution, and that the challenged statute, as applied in this case, does not intrude into an area which Congress has up to now pre-empted." (Significantly, Congress had, in 1971, passed legislation providing protection of sound recordings from "piracy" after February 15, 1972. The acts of "piracy" involved in this case, however, took place before the Congressional action.)

Building on this decision a year later, the Supreme Court upheld an Ohio trade secret law which provided that "No person, having

---

which being trade or traffic between citizens of the same State, is beyond the control of Congress." *Ibid.*, at 96.

[284] Deepsouth Packing Co. *v.* Laitram Corp., 406 U.S. 518, 530 (1972). In this case, the Supreme Court held that *the statute* which proscribed the making of any patented invention within the United States, did not preclude a manufacturer from exporting abroad the parts of someone else's patented item.

[285] Blonder-Tongue Lab. Inc. *v.* University of Illinois Found., 402 U.S. 313 (1971); *see* note 32 therein. Gottschalk *v.* Benson, 409 U.S. 253 (1972).

[286] Goldstein *v.* California, 412 U.S. 546, 560 (1973).

obtained possession of an article representing a trade secret or access thereto with the owner's consent, shall convert such article to his own use or that of another person, or thereafter without the owner's consent make or cause to be made a copy of such article, or exhibit such article to another." The Court held that "Just as the States may exercise regulatory power over writings so may the States regulate with respect to discoveries. . . . The only limitation on the States is that in regulating the area of patents and copyrights they do not conflict with the operation of the laws in this area passed by Congress. . . ."[287]

The Court of Claims handed down an important decision for this, the Xerox Age in 1973. That court held that, at least in the well-defined circumstances of that case, library photocopying of journal articles was "fair use."[288] But the court's uneasiness about its decision was manifest in its words "Hopefully, the result in the present case will be but a 'holding operation' in the interim period before Congress enacts its preferred solution." And in 1976 Congress gave "statutory recognition" to "the judicial doctrine of fair use."[289]

The copyright owner of a popular song that had been played on the radio and was piped into a fast-food service shop sued the restaurant owner, George Aiken, for copyright infringement. The case ultimately came to the Supreme Court, which saw the issue in these terms: "The question presented by this case is whether the reception of a radio broadcast of a copyrighted musical composition can constitute copyright infringement, when the copyright owner has licensed the broadcaster to perform the composition publicly for profit."[290]

Six justices had no difficulty disposing of the case largely on the grounds of "practicality" and without lengthy comment. They wrote: "To hold in this case that the respondent Aiken 'performed' the petitioners' copyrighted works would thus require us to overrule two very recent decisions of this Court. But such a holding would more than offend the principles of *stare decisis*; it would result in a regime of copyright law that would be wholly unenforcible and highly inequitable.

"The practical enforcibility of a ruling that all of those in Aiken's position are copyright infringers is self-evident."

In a notable dissent Chief Justice Burger joined by Justice Douglas urged that it was up to Congress to resolve the issue, that the Court's decision might ultimately prove to be simplistic rather than practical.

In a fascinating case involving plagiarism of a popular child psy-

[287] Kewanee Oil Co. *v.* Bicron Corp., 422 U.S. 470 (1974).
[288] Williams & Wilkins Co. *v.* U.S., 487 F. 2d. 1345 (1973); *affirmed* (by a 4-4 vote with no opinions), 95 S.Ct. 1344 (1975).
[289] 1976 *U.S. Cong. & Adm. News* 5678. *See* 90 *Stat.* 2541, 2546.
[290] Twentieth Century Music Corp. *v.* Aiken, 422 U.S. 151 (1975).

chology textbook, a U.S. district court elaborated the meaning of "fair use" of copyrighted material. Judge Richard Owen concluded that "three factors should be considered: (1) the competitive effect and function of the usage, (2) the quantity of the materials used, and (3) the purpose of the selections made."[291] Considering these factors, the judge had no difficulty in finding that the obvious and outrageous plagiarism in this case clearly exceeded "fair use."

In response to the contention that the United States is constitutionally barred from undercutting patent rights by treaty or statute by the patent provisions of clause 8, a Federal district court held that "The constitutional provision [clause 8] is not self-executing. It empowers but does not command the Congress to grant patent rights, and the source of any specific patent is the statute which defines the nature and extent of the patent right granted."[292] Judge John F. Dooling, Jr., went on to say that "the patent law must not be so interpreted as to impair the treaty-making capacity of the nation or to clog its power to regulate foreign commerce (since that would make patent grants a surrender *pro tanto* of 'sovereignty' to private persons . . .) and that, hence, unless the language of the patent statute plainly compels it, the statute must not be taken to grant rights in terms so broad that existing or later treaties must necessarily constitute a 'taking' of some part of the patentee's grant."

United States patent law provides that a person shall be entitled to a patent unless, before the applicant's invention, the invention was made by another "who had not abandoned, suppressed, or concealed it."[293] A U.S. court of appeals recently dealt with the question of what protection an inventor has if he markets his invention without disclosing a patent (the practice is technically called a putting to a "noninforming public use").[294] The court held that "it is appropriate to conclude that a public use of an invention forecloses a finding of suppression or concealment even though the use does not disclose the discovery." The court reasoned that "If the new idea is permitted to have its impact in the marketplace, and thus to 'promote the Progress of Science and useful Arts,' it has surely not been suppressed in an economic sense."

A Federal district court held that the President could not determine by executive order the rights to inventions made by a government employee during working hours or with the contribution of government facilities.[295] The court pointed out that Congress had not acted and that the petitioner in the case challenged the President's authority to take such action in light of Article I, Section

[291] Meredith Corporation *v.* Harper & Row, Publishers, Inc., 378 F.Supp. 686, 689 (1974).
[292] Cali *v.* Japan Airlines, Inc., 380 F.Supp. 1120 (1974).
[293] 35 U.S.C. § 102.
[294] Dunlop Holdings Limited *v.* Ram Golf Corp., 524 F. 2d. 33 (1975).
[295] Kaplan *v.* Johnson, 409 F.Supp. 190 (1976).

VIII, Clause 8. The court remonstrated: "Whatever one's feelings might be about our patent system, it is certain that it is not the function of the judicial or the executive branch to bring about wholesale changes in the system. There can be no doubt that article I, section 8, clause 8 of the Constitution leaves that task solely in the hands of Congress."

Most recently, in a case involving a copyright "for an artistic design of a lighting fixture," a district court solemnly declared that the "term 'art' is not confined to traditional forms."[296]

After many years of effort to come up with legislation to clear up the ambiguities, Congress in 1976 provided for a general revision of the United States Copyright Law.[297] The House Report accompanying the bill made clear that there were still unresolved questions.[298]

¶9. To constitute tribunals inferior to the Supreme Court; (*See* Article III, Section I.)

¶10. To define and punish piracies and felonies committed on the high seas and offenses against the law of nations;

Congress and International Law

In Chancellor Kent's words: "When the United States ceased to be a part of the British empire, and assumed the character of an independent nation, they became subject to that system of rules which reason, morality, and custom had established among civilized nations of Europe, as their public law. . . . The faithful observance of this law is essential to national character. . . ."[299] The power here conferred has been broadly construed. Thus, taking the position that the Law of Nations casts upon every government the duty to prevent a wrong being done within its own dominion to another nation with which it is at peace, or to the people thereof, the Court sustained Congress in making the counterfeiting within the United States of notes, bonds and other securities of a foreign government an offense against the United States.[300]

It is under this provision that the Supreme Court has held that Congress may set up a military commission "as it had previously existed in United States Army practice, as an appropriate tribunal for the trial and punishment of offenses against the law of war."[301]

¶11. To declare war, grant letters of marque and reprisal, and make rules concerning captures on land and water;

This paragraph, together with paragraphs 12, 13, 14, 15, 16 and 18 following, and paragraph 1 of Section II of Article II, comprise the

---

[296] Esquire, Inc. *v.* Ringer, 414 F.Supp. 939 (1976).
[297] 90 *Stat.* 2541.   [298] 1976 *U.S. Cong. & Adm. News* 5659, 5663.
[299] *See* James Kent, *Commentaries on American Law*, I (Boston, 1826), 1-2.
[300] United States *v.* Arjona, 120 U.S. 479 (1887).
[301] *In re* Yamashita, 327 U.S. 1, 7 (1946); *Ex parte* Quirin, 317 U.S. 1 (1942).

"War Power" of the United States, but are not, necessarily, the whole of it. Three different views of the source and scope of the power found expression in the early years of the Constitution and have continued to vie for supremacy for more than a century and a half. In *The Federalist*, Hamilton advanced the theory that the power is an aggregate of particular powers—those listed above.[302] In 1795 the theory was elaborated, on the basis of the fact that even before the Constitution was adopted the American people had asserted their right to wage war as a unit, and to act in regard to all their foreign relations as a unit, that these powers were an attribute of sovereignty; and hence not dependent upon the affirmative grants of the Constitution.[303] A third view was adumbrated by Chief Justice Marshall, who in McCulloch *v.* Maryland listed the power "to declare *and conduct* a war" as one of the "enumerated powers" from which the power of the National Government to charter the Bank of the United States was deducible.[304] During the Civil War the two latter theories were both given countenance by the Supreme Court.[305] Then, following World War I, the Court, speaking by Justice Sutherland, plumped squarely for the "attribute of sovereignty" theory. Said he: "The power to declare and wage war, to conclude peace, to make treaties, to maintain diplomatic relations with other sovereignties, if they had never been mentioned in the Constitution, would have vested in the Federal Government as necessary concomitants of nationality";[306] and although the Court, in 1948, lent its sanction, perhaps somewhat casually, to the "enumerated powers" theory,[307] there can be no doubt that the attribute of "sovereignty theory" does fullest justice to the actual holdings of the Court, and especially to those rendered in the course of, or in consequence of, World War II.

"When we are at war, we are not in revolution," the late Chief Justice Hughes once declared.[308] The fact is, nonetheless, that certain major characteristics of the Constitution as it operates in

---

[302] *The Federalist*, No. 23.   [303] Penhallow *v.* Doane, 3 Dall. 54 (1795).

[304] 4 Wheat. 316, 407 (1819) (emphasis supplied).

[305] *Ex parte* Milligan, 4 Wall. 2,139 (1866) (dissenting opinion); Hamilton *v.* Dillin, 21 Wall. 73, 86 (1875). *See also* 58 *Cong. Globe*, app. 1 (1861); Miller *v.* U.S., 11 Wall. 268, 305 (1871); and United States *v.* Macintosh, 283 U.S. 605, 622 (1931).

[306] United States *v.* Curtiss-Wright Export Corp., 299 U.S. 304, 316, 318 (1936). *See also* the same Justice's sweeping opinion for the Court on the scope of the War Power in relation to private rights, in United States *v.* Macintosh, 283 U.S. 605, 622 (1931).

[307] Lichter *v.* U.S., 334 U.S. 742, 755, 757-758 (1948).

[308] Address before the American Bar Association at Saratoga, September 1917. Merlo Pusey, *Charles Evans Hughes*, I (N.Y., 1951), 369. In his opinion for the Court in 1934, in the Minnesota Moratorium case, Chief Justice Hughes said: "The war power of the Federal Government is a power to wage war successfully, and thus permits the harnessing of the entire energies of the people in a supreme cooperative effort to preserve the Nation." 290 U.S. 398, 426. Fourteen years earlier, with the facts of World War I before him, Mr. Hughes raised the question "whether constitutional government as hitherto maintained in this Republic could survive another great war, even victoriously waged." *New York Times*, June 22, 1920.

peacetime recede into the background in wartime. Under the doctrine of "enumerated powers," silence on the part of the Constitution is a *denial* of power to Congress; in wartime it is an *affirmance* of power.[309] Nor is the principle of Dual Sovereignty an ingredient of the War Power. As against it there are no States Rights; to the contrary, an active duty rests on the States to cooperate with the National Government in the prosecution of the war on the home front.[310] Likewise, in wartime the constitutional ban on the delegation by Congress of its powers to the President is in almost complete abeyance. What are termed the "cognate powers" of the two departments may be merged by Congress substantially at will.[311]

The War Power and the Bill of Rights   Probably the thing that Mr. Hughes had foremost in mind were the restraints which are imposed by the Bill of Rights in behalf of private rights, and especially the due process clause of Amendment V: "nor shall any person be deprived of life, liberty, or property without due process of law"—that is, without what the Supreme Court finds to be justifying circumstances (*see* pp. 386-390). But Total War is itself a highly justifying, not to say compulsive circumstance, in the presence of which judicial review is apt to properly self-distrustful, and proportionately ineffective. Witness, for example, the vast powers which by authorization of Congress the War Production Board (WPB) exercised in control of the distribution of materials and facilities, and of industrial production and output during World War II, and the almost equally great powers which the Office of Price Administration (OPA) exercised in rationing supplies and controlling prices, rents, and wages, without any restraint by the courts—almost, in fact, without their exercise of power being challenged in court.[312]

And what Total War can do to personal rights despite the due process clause, and despite its chosen instrument judicial review, is shown by the measures which the National Government adopted

[309] This is a generalization from the cases reviewed below.

[310] *See* note 308 above; *also* University of Illinois *v.* U.S., 289 U.S. 48 (1933); Gilbert *v.* Minn., 254 U.S. 325 (1920). In World War II the Office of Civilian Defense (OCD) was dependent entirely on the local authorities for the enforcement of its "directives" whenever the patriotic impulses of the public proved an insufficient reliance. Mr. Byrnes's curfew "request" of February 28, 1945, issued in his capacity as Director of War Mobilization, was similarly circumstanced, with the result of producing a sharp controversy between Mr. Byrnes and Mayor LaGuardia over the question of closing-time for New York City's restaurants. *See* Mr. Byrnes's statement in the *New York Times*, March 20, 1945.

[311] *See* opinion cited in note 306 above at pp. 320-329; *also* Lichter *v.* U.S., 334 U.S. 742, 778-779, 782-783 (1948).

[312] As to WPB's powers, *see* 56 *Stat.* 351 (1942). Steuart & Bro., Inc. *v.* Bowles, 322 U.S. 398 (1944); John Lord O'Brian and Manly Fleischmann, "The War Production Board, Administrative Policies and Procedures," 13 *George Washington Law Review* (1944). On OPA's powers, *see* 56 *Stat.* 23 (1942). Yakus *v.* U.S., 321 U.S. 414 (1944); Bowles *v.* Willingham, 321 U.S. 503 (1944); Case *v.* Bowles, 327 U.S. 92 (1946). Against enemies of the United States, the War Power is constitutionally unlimited. Brown *v.* U.S., 8 Cr. 110 (1814); Miller *v.* U.S., 11 Wall. 268 (1870).

early in World War II respecting Japanese residents on the West Coast. What, in brief, these measures accomplished was the removal of 112,000 Japanese, two-thirds of them citizens of the United States by birth, from their homes and properties, and their temporary segregation in "assembly centers," later in "relocation centers." No such wholesale or drastic invasion of the rights of citizens of the United States by their own Government had ever before occurred in the history of the country. Nevertheless, taking judicial notice of what they perceived as the facts of the dubious state of our defenses on the West Coast and of the reasonable apprehension of invasion following the attack on Pearl Harbor, of the manifest sympathy of many Japanese residents for Japan and the consequent danger of "Fifth Column" activities, and of certain other more or less speculative possibilities, and asserting the broad scope of the blended powers of Congress and the President in wartime, the Court said, "We cannot say that these facts and circumstances, considered in the particular war setting, could afford no ground for differentiating citizens of Japanese ancestry from other groups in the United States." The measures in question were therefore pronounced valid, but with the later stipulation by the Court that they must be construed and applied strictly as anti-espionage and anti-sabotage measures, not as concessions to community hostility toward the Japanese. A Japanese citizen, accordingly, whose loyalty the Government did not challenge was held to be entitled at any time to unconditional release from a relocation center. At the same time it was clearly implied that the privilege of the writ of *habeas corpus* was always available in like cases unless suspended for reasons deemed by the Constitution to be sufficient.[313]

Perhaps chastened by the recognition of the injustice done to Americans of Japanese ancestry under the War Power, the Supreme Court took the occasion in 1967 in striking down a statute aimed at keeping communists from working in defense facilities to say: "The Government seeks to defend the statute on the ground that it was passed pursuant to Congress' war power. . . . However, the phrase 'war power' cannot be invoked as a talismanic incanta-

The Impact of Total War on Private Rights: the West Coast Japanese

---

[313] Hirabayashi *v.* U.S., 320 U.S. 81 (1943); Korematsu *v.* U.S., 323 U.S. 214 (1944); *ex parte* Endo, 323 U.S. 283 (1944). Hindsight makes it clear that there was no necessity for the Japanese segregation measures. Certainly, chronology supports such skepticism. The Japanese attack on Pearl Harbor occurred December 7, 1941. Yet it was not until February 19 that this policy was inaugurated by the President's order, nor until March 21 that Congress acted, and the Civilian Exclusion Order did not come till May 3—five months after Pearl Harbor! What was the real cause, then, of the segregation measures—increased danger of Japanese invasion, to be aided by sabotage in the United States, or increased pressure from interested and/or hysterical groups of West Coast citizens? Had the authorities stopped short with a curfew order, enforcible by the police, they would have taken ample precaution. *Not one single Japanese, citizen or otherwise, either in continental United States or in Hawaii, was found guilty of one single effort at sabotage or espionage.* Harold W. Chase, *Security and Liberty* (New York, 1954), 20-23.

tion to support any exercise of congressional power which can be brought within its ambit. Even the war power does not remove constitutional limitations safeguarding essential liberties."[314] Despite this recent decision rendered during a time of less than all-out war, the question arises whether, the *habeas corpus* privilege aside, the Constitution permits the possibility of its own suspension in any other respect in time of war or other serious crisis. In the Milligan case, which was decided shortly after the Civil War, a majority of the Court took pains to stigmatize any such idea in the strongest terms. "No doctrine," said Justice Davis, "involving more pernicious consequences, was ever invented by the wit of man than that any of its [the Constitution's] provisions can be suspended during any of the great exigencies of government."[315] Unfortunately, this strongly worded assertion is contradicted by the very decision in justification of which it was pronounced, for the decision held Milligan to have been deprived of his constitutional rights. The Court, however, went on to explain that "during the late Rebellion it [martial law] could have been enforced in Virginia, where the national authority was overturned and the courts driven out, it does not follow that it should obtain in Indiana, where that authority was never disputed, and justice was always administered. And so in the case of a foreign invasion, martial rule may become a necessity in one state, when in another it would be 'mere lawless violence.' " *Milligan* and many such cases grew out of President Lincoln's policy of denying rights on the theory that the entire country was a theater of military operations. It may well be that Lincoln's policy may have been a material factor in the war's outcome.

Far different from the *Milligan* decision was the outlook of President Roosevelt's message to Congress of September 7, 1942, in which he proclaimed his intention and his constitutional right to disregard certain provisions of the Emergency Price Control Act unless Congress repealed them by the following October 1. "The American people," said he, "can be sure that I will use my powers with a full sense of my responsibility to the Constitution and to my country.... When the war is won, the powers under which I act will automatically revert to the people—to whom they belong." While the situation which the President foreshadowed did not materialize, thanks to Congress's compliance with his demand, albeit a day late, yet any candid person must admit the possibility of conditions arising in which the safety of the republic would require the waiving of constitutional methods. When Mr. Hughes uttered his dictum [p. 103] the atomic bomb had not been invented, or used against civilian populations. The circumstances of nuclear warfare would, not improbably, bring about the total supplantation for an indefinite period of the forms of constitutional government by the drastic procedures of military government.

[314] U.S. *v.* Robel, 389 U.S. 258, 263-264 (1967).   [315] 4 Wall. 2, 121 (1866).

Can the Constitution Be Suspended in Wartime?

To some indeterminate extent the power to wage war includes the power to prevent it. It was on this ground in part that, following World War I, the Court sustained TVA as a legitimate governmental enterprise.[316] But the outstanding example of legislation adopted at a time when no actual "shooting war" was in progress, with the object of providing for the national defense, is the Atomic Energy Act of 1946 which has been several times amended. That law establishes an Atomic Energy Commission of five members which is empowered to conduct through its own facilities, or by contracts with or loans to private persons, research and developmental activities relating to nuclear processes, the theory and production of atomic energy, and the utilization of fissionable and radioactive materials for medical, industrial, and other purposes. The act further provides that the Commission shall be the exclusive owner of all facilities (with minor exceptions) for the production of fissionable materials; that all fissionable material produced shall become its property; that it shall allocate such materials for research and developmental activities, and shall license all transfers of source materials. The Commission is charged with the duty of producing atomic bombs, bomb parts, and other atomic military weapons at the direction of the President. Patents relating to fissionable materials must be filed with the Commission, the "just compensation" payable to the owners to be determined by a Patent Compensation Board designated by the Commission from among its employees.[317]

The Power to Prepare for War: The Atomic Energy Act

Again, the War Power "is not limited to victories in the field. It carries with it inherently the power to guard against the immediate renewal of the conflict, and to remedy the evils which have arisen from its rise and progress."[318] So spoke the Court in Reconstruction days. Yet this power cannot be without metes and bounds. For, as the Court has recognized, "if the war power can be used in days of peace to treat all the wounds which war inflicts on our society, it may not only swallow up all other powers of Congress but largely obliterate the Ninth and Tenth Amendments."[319] The issue thus adumbrated is not susceptible to cut-and-dried solutions.[320]

Despite their apparent simplicity and clarity, the words "The Congress shall have power . . . to declare war" have been a source of consternation throughout our history. (*See* pp. 157-158 for brief historical development.) As we have come to learn, war comes in many shapes and a variety of ways. The Marquis of Queensberry rules do not apply. We have learned that we can be attacked without warning, and that we can slowly move one small step after another into a genuine shooting war before we fully realize what

The Power to Declare War

[316] Ashwander *v*. TVA, 297 U.S. 288, 327-328 (1936).　　[317] 23 U.S.C. 2011.
[318] Stewart *v*. Kahn, 11 Wall. 493, 507 (1871).
[319] Woods *v*. Miller, 333 U.S. 138, 144 (1948).
[320] *Cf.* Chastleton *v*. Sinclair, 264 U.S. 543 (1924); Ludecke *v*. Watkins, 335 U.S. 160, 170 (1948).

has happened. It is not always possible for a prudent President to wait for a Congressional declaration before he acts. As the Supreme Court pointed out in the Prize cases in 1863: "This greatest of civil wars was not gradually developed by popular commotion, tumultuous assemblies, or local unorganized insurrections. However long may have been its previous conception, it nevertheless sprung forth suddenly from the parent brain, a Minerva in the full panoply of *war*. The President was bound to meet it in the shape it presented itself, without waiting for Congress to baptize it with a name; and no name given it by him or them could change the fact."[321]

In contrast to the situation the Court described, there have been situations where Presidential initiatives toward involving the nation in warfare seemed unwarranted because there was time for the President to seek a Congressional declaration of war and he chose not to. Certainly, there are many who would contend that that was the case with respect to hostilities in Korea and Vietnam. However, when opportunities arose for the Supreme Court to review a challenge of the constitutionality of the Vietnam war, it refused to do so.[322] But Justices Stewart and Douglas wrote pithy dissents in one case worthy of close study. They thought that "the Court should squarely face" the questions: "I. Is the present United States military activity in Vietnam a 'war' within the meaning of Article I, Section 8, Clause 11 of the Constitution? II. If so, may the Executive constitutionally order the petitioners to participate in that military activity, when no war has been declared by the Congress?"

Frustrated and unhappy with the war in Vietnam, Congressmen sought ways to reassert what they regarded as their constitutional duty. Outraged by the bombing in Cambodia, Congress sought to force the President to end it. After a monumental effort, including a foray into the courts,[323] Congress passed a rider to an appropriations bill cutting off all funds for the bombing. President Nixon promptly vetoed the bill, and the House, 35 votes short, failed to override.[324] A substantial number of Congressmen continued to press on, however, and the President agreed to a compromise to end the bombing by August 15, 1973, saying that he would seek Congressional help if further action became necessary "to win the peace."[325] In the meantime, the courts considered a suit filed by 13

---

[321] Prize Cases, 67 U.S. 635, 688-689 (1863).

[322] Mora *v.* McNamara, 389 U.S. 934 (1967); Orlando *v.* Laird, 443 F. 2d. 1039 (1971); *cert. denied*, 404 U.S. 869 (1971); Massachusetts *v.* Laird, 400 U.S. 886 (1970), but *see* Justice Douglas's dissent. *See also* Da Costa *v.* Laird, 448 F. 2d. 1368 (1971); *cert. denied*, 405 U.S. 979 (1972). *See also* 471 F. 2d. 1146 (1973).

[323] Mitchell *v.* Laird, 476 F. 2d. 533 (1973). *Cf.* Holtzman *v.* Schlesinger, 414 U.S. 1304 (1973).

[324] *New York Times*, June 28, 1973. (Contains text of the veto message.)

[325] *New York Times*, July 2, 1973. The President signed the Social Security bill, which contained a rider cutting off funds for United States combat activities in Indochina.

members of Congress to enjoin the President and the Secretaries of Defense, Army, Navy, and Air Force from prosecuting the war in Indochina unless, within 60 days from the date the injunction became effective, Congress explicitly authorized continuation. After withdrawing its earlier reported opinion, apparently to allow Judge MacKinnon to add a separate statement as to why he and two other judges would have granted rehearing *en banc*,[326] the U.S. Court of Appeals, District of Columbia, reissued its opinion in Mitchell *v*. Laird. As to the complaint of the thirteen Congressmen the Court upheld the District Court's judgment of dismissal, explaining that "In short, we are faced with what has traditionally been called a 'political question' which is beyond the judicial power conferred by Article III of the United States Constitution."[327]

In sharp contrast, U.S. District Judge Orrin G. Judd found that "there is no Congressional authorization to fight in Cambodia after the withdrawal of American troops and the release of American prisoners of war. . . ."[328] He enjoined the Secretary of Defense, the acting Secretary of the Air Force, and the Deputy Secretary of Defense from continuing U.S. air operations over Cambodia, delaying the effective time to give the defendants time to appeal to the U.S. Court of Appeals for the Second Circuit. That appeal set in motion a series of unusual judicial actions. The Court of Appeals granted the stay requested by the Government. On August 1, 1973, the petitioners appealed to Justice Marshall of the Supreme Court in his capacity as Circuit Justice to vacate the stay. He wrote: ". . . if the decision were mine alone, I might well conclude on the merits that continued American military operations in Cambodia are unconstitutional. But the Supreme Court is a collegial institution, and its decisions reflect the views of a majority of the sitting Justices. It follows that when I sit in my capacity as Circuit Justice, I act not for myself alone, but as a surrogate for the entire Court, from whence my ultimate authority in these matters derives. A Circuit Judge therefore bears a heavy responsibility to conscientiously reflect the views of his brethren as best he perceives them . . . and this responsibility is particularly pressing when as now, the Court is not in session."[329] From this perspective, Justice Marshall felt that he would be exceeding his authority were he alone to vacate the stay. Immediately, the petitioners appealed to Justice Douglas, who on August 4 vacated the stay.[330] As Justice Douglas pointed out, "Application for stay denied by one Justice may be made to another." However, on the same day, Justice Marshall again acting as Circuit Justice upon petition of the Solicitor General again stayed the District Court decision. He indicated that he had contacted all the other

---

[326] "Cases Reported," 476 F. 2d. XXVIII.
[327] Mitchell *v*. Laird, 488 F. 2d. 611 (1973). *See also* Drinan *v*. Nixon, 364 F.Supp. 854 (1973).
[328] Holtzman *v*. Schlesinger, 361 F.Supp. 553, 565 (1973).
[329] Holtzman *v*. Schlesinger, 414 U.S. 1304 (1973).   [330] *Ibid*., 1316.

members of the Court and all but Douglas agreed with his action.[331] In the end, the Supreme Court denied *certiorari*.[332]

Congress capped its efforts to reassert its power to declare war by passing over the President's veto, November 7, 1973, the War Powers Resolution. Congress's determination to circumscribe the President's use of the Armed Forces is made clear in its statement of purpose: "to fulfill the intent of the framers of the Constitution of the United States and insure that the collective judgment of both Congress and the President will apply to the introduction of United States Armed Forces into hostilities, or into situations where imminent involvement in hostilities is clearly indicated by the circumstances, and to the continued use of such forces in hostilities or in such situations."[333] To fulfill that purpose the resolution requires, among other things that (1) the President consult with Congress "in every possible instance" before committing forces, and (2) the President remove forces that are engaged in hostilities outside the United States without a declaration of war or statutory authorization "if the Congress so directs by concurrent resolution." Significantly, this legislation seems to take into account the realities suggested by the Court in the Prize cases, that sometimes hostilities break out before thoughtful deliberation is possible. Clearly such legislation did not require a constitutional amendment, since it only spells out how a power already granted to Congress is to be exercised. Conceivably, a President could assert that such a law would be an unconstitutional limitation on his powers as chief executive and Commander-in-Chief. What the Supreme Court would do in such a case is conjectural, of course, but on the basis of the precedent of the *Steel Seizure* case[334] discussed below (pp. 198-201) it is probable that the Court would uphold the act of Congress.

In evaluating any proposal to reassert Congress's power to declare war, a consideration suggested by former President Lyndon B. Johnson in his memoirs is worth some thought: If it is in the national interest to conduct a limited war, would it be possible to keep a declared war from becoming an all-out war?[335] Also, the discussion (p. 203) of the bill of impeachment voted on by the House Judiciary Committee in the case of President Nixon is pertinent to the question of the President's use of the Armed Forces.

Letters of Marque and Reprisal   "Letters of marque and reprisal" were formerly issued to privateers, sometimes for the purpose of enabling their grantees to wage a species of private war upon some state against which they had a grievance. Because of the ban which International Law has

---

[331] *Ibid.*, 1321.   [332] 416 U.S. 936 (1974).

[333] 87 *Stat.* 555 (1973).

[334] Youngstown Co. *v.* Sawyer, 343 U.S. 579 (1952).

[335] Mr. Johnson explained that the reason he did not go to Congress and ask for great sums of money, call up the reserves, and go on a war footing was that he deliberately wanted to keep the war a limited one. Lyndon B. Johnson, *Vantage Point* (New York, 1971), p. 149.

put upon privateering increasingly since the Declaration of Paris of 1856, this power of Congress must today be deemed obsolete.

¶12. To raise and support armies, but no appropriation of money to that use shall be for a longer term than two years;

¶13. To provide and maintain a navy;

The office of these clauses is to assign the powers which they define and which are part of the War Power, to *Congress*, since otherwise they might have been claimed, by analogy to the British constitution, for the President.[336] When Congress, by the National Security Act of 1947, set up the Air Force as a separate service not mentioned in the Constitution, its constitutional power to do so was conceded.[337]

The Air Force

The only type of standing army known to the Framers was a mercenary, volunteer force, and the only compulsory type of military service known to them was service in the militia, which was confined to local and limited purposes, as it had been in medieval England, and as it still is in clause 15 below. Conscription was first employed to raise an army for service abroad in World War I,[338] and the first peacetime conscription was that authorized by the Selective Training and Service Act of September 16, 1940, which as enacted forbade the sending of selectees outside the Western Hemisphere except to possessions of the United States and the Philippine Islands.[339] Following Pearl Harbor this restriction was quickly suspended for the duration.[340] Conscription for recruitment of the Navy rests on a more ancient precedent, namely, impressment into the British Navy, which, although confined to seamen, antedated 1789.

Development of Conscription

From the first time the compulsory draft was employed after the enactment of the Thirteenth Amendment, it was a natural for those who were opposed to being drafted to see it as "involuntary servitude" of a type forbidden by that amendment. But from the first, the Supreme Court has not seen it that way.[341]

[336] Story, *Commentaries*, § 1187.

[337] A California member of the House introduced a resolution looking to a constitutional amendment authorizing the establishment of an air force (H. J. Res. 298, 80th Cong., 2nd Sess.), but nothing happened to it.

[338] The act was sustained in the Selective Draft cases, 245 U.S. 366 (1918). The same Act of June 15, 1917, gave the President sweeping powers to commandeer shipbuilding plants and facilities. Commenting on this feature of the act in United States *v.* Bethlehem Steel Corp., 315 U.S. 289 (1942), the Court said: "Under the Constitutional authority to raise and support armies, to provide and maintain a navy, and to make all laws necessary and proper to carry these powers into execution, the power of Congress to draft business organizations is not less than its power to draft men for battle service." *Ibid.* 305.

[339] 54 *Stat.* 885, 886 (1940).   [340] 55 *Stat.* 799 (1941).

[341] Butler *v.* Perry, 240 U.S. 328 (1916); Selective Draft Law cases, 245 U.S. 316 (1918). As late as 1968, the Supreme Court cited the Selective Draft cases with ap-

A more compelling argument can be made against forced military service for those who can claim that such service runs against their religious scruples and, consequently, denies them the religious freedom safeguarded by the First Amendment. But such an argument is rendered academic by the fact that Congress has long provided exemptions from military service for conscientious objectors.[342] Significantly, courts have upheld Congress's power to require alternative types of service for conscientious objectors and have not regarded them as "involuntary servitude" or invasions of religious freedom.[343]

The plethora of interesting draft cases reaching the Supreme Court in recent years have all turned on the question of who may truly claim to be a conscientious objector under the statute. The Court gave us a good capsule description of where it now stands in the attention-getting case involving the heavyweight boxing champion Muhammad Ali: "In order to qualify for classification as a conscientious objector, a registrant must satisfy three basic tests. He must show that he is conscientiously opposed to war in any form. He must show that this opposition is based upon religious training and belief, as the term has been construed in our decisions. And he must show that this objection is sincere."[344] But the issue is not as cut and dried as the Court suggests. As Justice Douglas pointed out in another recent case, the Court's decisions in this matter "leave considerable latitude for administrative findings."[345]

Limitation of appropriations for the Army to two years reflects the American fear of standing armies. For the Navy and Air Force, on the other hand, building programs may be laid down to run over several years.[346]

The power to create an Army, Navy, and Air Force involves, naturally, the power to adopt measures designed to safeguard the health, welfare, and morale of their personnel, and such measures are enforcible within the States. Thus, for example, Congress may

---

proval. U.S. *v.* O'Brien, 391 U.S. 367, 376 (1968). In deciding that he should not disqualify himself as judge in a draft case because of alleged personal bias, District Judge Edward Dumbauld issued a provocative, noteworthy opinion dealing with the issues that inhere in draft cases. It had been alleged that the judge imposed severe sentences in draft cases and was often reversed. United States *v.* Nehas, 368 F.Supp. 435 (1973).

[342] The current law, The Military Service Act of 1967, provides exemption from military service for any person "who, by reason of religious training and belief, is conscientiously opposed to participation in war in any form." 50 App. U.S.C. 456 (j).

[343] Roodenko *v.* U.S. 147 F. 2d. 752 (1945); *cert. denied*, 324 U.S. 860 (1945); Heflin *v.* Sanford, 142 F. 2d. 798 (1944).

[344] Clay *v.* U.S., 403 U.S. 698, 700 (1971). To support these points, the Court cited the following cases: Gillette *v.* U.S., 401 U.S. 437 (1971); U.S. *v.* Seeger, 380 U.S. 163 (1965); Welsh *v.* U.S., 398 U.S. 333 (1970); Witmer *v.* U.S., 348 U.S. 375 (1955). For a summary of more recent draft cases, *see* Fein *v.* Selective Service, 405 U.S. 365 (1972) and cases cited therein.

[345] Ehlert *v.* U.S., 402 U.S. 99, 112 (1971).   [346] 40 *Op. Atty. Gen.* 555 (1948).

authorize the suppression of houses of ill-fame in the vicinity of places where military personnel are stationed.[347] And the Supreme Court said of a particular Congressional investigation "Inquiry into the sources of funds used to carry on activities suspected by a Subcommittee of Congress to have a potential for undermining the morale of the armed forces is within the legitimate legislative sphere. Indeed, the complaint here tells us that . . . [the organization] operated on or near military and naval bases, and that its facilities became 'the focus of dissent' to declared national policy. Whether . . . [the organization's] activities violated any statute is not relevant; the inquiry was intended to inform Congress in an area where legislation may be had."[348]

¶14. To make rules for the government and regulation of the land and naval forces;

It is by virtue of this paragraph that Congress has enacted the Code of Military Justice, which constitutes the basis of discipline in the Armed Forces.

In view of the sweep of the two clauses preceding, this clause is superfluous except for the purpose of vesting Congress with a power which might be otherwise claimed exclusively for the Commander-in-Chief.[349]

Until the 1950's Congress exercised this power extensively without a serious challenge by the Supreme Court. In 1858 the Court held that: "Congress has the power to provide for the trial of military and naval offenses in the manner then and now practiced by civilized nations; and that the power to do so is given without any connection between it and the 3rd article of the Constitution defining the judicial power of the United States."[350] Nor in an earlier day did the Court find the Bill of Rights a limiting factor at least with reference to those attached to "the army, or navy, or militia in actual service." As the Court explained in 1866: "The sixth amendment affirms that 'in all criminal prosecutions the accused shall enjoy the right to a speedy and public trial by an impartial jury,' language broad enough to embrace all persons and cases; but the fifth, recognizing the necessity of an indictment, or presentment, before any one can be held to answer for high crime, '*excepts* cases arising in the land, or naval forces, or in the militia, when in actual service, in time of war or public danger'; and the framers of the Constitution, doubtless, meant to limit the right of trial by jury,

---

[347] McKinley *v*. U.S., 249 U.S. 397 (1919). *See also* Wissner *v*. Wissner, 338 U.S. 655, 660 (1950).

[348] Eastland *v*. U.S. Servicemen's Fund, 421 U.S. 491, 506 (1975).

[349] In a case involving the West Point honor code, a United States district court held that "So long as the military rules prescribed by the President are not inconsistent with congressional statutes they are within the scope of his authority as commander in chief." Ringgold *v*. United states, 420 F.Supp. 698, 702 (1976).

[350] Dynes *v*. Hoover, 20 How. 65, 75 (1858).

in the sixth amendment, to those persons who were subject to indictment or presentment in the fifth."[351]

Much later, the courts acquiesced in the denial of important constitutional rights to servicemen. The celebrated *Levy* case made its way to a resolution in the Supreme Court in 1974. Dr. Howard Levy was the Army Captain who, while on active duty, admittedly urged enlisted men to refuse to fight in Vietnam. He challenged two of the charges against him on the grounds that they were overbroad and also violated his First Amendment rights. One charge was under an article of the Uniform Code of Military Justice forbidding "conduct unbecoming an officer and gentleman"; the second proscribes "all disorders and neglect to the prejudice of good order and discipline in the armed forces." Justice Rehnquist, speaking for the majority of a sharply divided Court, said: "Because of the factors differentiating military society from civilian society, we hold that the proper standard of review for a vagueness challenge to the Articles of the U.C.M.J. is the standard which applied to criminal statutes regulating economic affairs. Clearly, that standard is met here. . . ." As to the First Amendment, Rehnquist wrote: "While members of the military are not excluded from the protection granted by the First Amendment, the different character of the military community and of the military mission require a different application of those protections."[352]

In 1975, the Supreme Court attempted to resolve important ambiguities inherent in Article 76 of the Uniform Code of Military Justice. That article provides among other things that "the proceedings, findings, and sentences of courts-martial as approved, reviewed, or affirmed . . . are final and conclusive" and "all action taken pursuant to those proceedings [is] binding upon all . . . courts . . . of the United States."[353] Military authorities contended before the Supreme Court (1) that Article 76 repealed other statutes that gave district courts jurisdiction in civil actions[354] and (2) that the legislative history of the article demonstrated "that Congress intended to limit collateral attack in civilian courts on court-martial convictions to proceedings for writs of habeas corpus."

The Court disposed of the issue in the following way: "We have declined to decide this question in the past. We now conclude that although the article [Article 76] is highly relevant to the proper scope of collateral attack on court-martial convictions and to the propriety of equitable intervention into pending court-martial pro-

---

[351] *Ex parte* Milligan, 4 Wall. 2, 123 (1866). *See also* opinion of the Chief Justice, *ibid.*, at 138-139.

[352] Parker *v.* Levy, 417 U.S. 733 (1974). Later, the Supreme Court upheld, on the basis of the decision of *Levy*, the conviction of a Marine who prepared a statement critical of United States involvement in Vietnam. *See* Secretary of the Navy *v.* Avrech, 418 U.S. 676 (1974).

[353] Schlesinger *v.* Councilman, 420 U.S. 738, 745 (1975).

[354] One of the issues before the Court involved the civil action brought to a district court moving for a temporary restraining order and a preliminary injunction to prevent an impending court-martial.

ceedings, it does not have the jurisdictional consequences petitioners ascribe to it." In short, as the Court put it: Article 76 "does not stand as a jurisdictional bar to . . . [a] suit." *However*, the Court took pains to explain that its holding that the district court had subject matter jurisdiction did not warrant the further conclusion that the district court could properly reach the merits in a particular case or issue an injunction to halt an impending court-martial. Indeed, the Court held "that when a serviceman charged with crimes by military authorities can show no harm other than that attendant to resolution of his case in the military court system, the federal district courts must refrain from intervention, by way of injunction or otherwise."

In one of several court cases involving William L. Calley, Jr., of My Lai notoriety, a U.S. court of appeals addressed the issue of "the extent to which a federal court is empowered to review courtmartial convictions on petitions for habeas corpus."[355] After pointing out that Federal courts generally should not intervene in basically military matters, that the Constitution gave great responsibilities to the Congress and President in military affairs, the court summed up the matter this way: "To summarize, the scope of review may be stated as follows: Military court-martial convictions are subject to collateral review by federal civil courts on petitions for writs of habeas corpus where it is asserted that the court-martial acted without jurisdiction, or that substantial constitutional rights have been violated, or that exceptional circumstances have been presented which are so fundamentally defective as to result in a miscarriage of justice. Consideration by the military of such issues will not preclude judicial review for the military must accord to its personnel the protections of basic constitutional rights essential to a fair trial and the guarantee of due process of law. The scope of review for violations of constitutional rights, however, is more narrow than in civil cases. Thus federal courts should differentiate between questions of fact and law and review only questions of law which present substantial constitutional issues. Accordingly, they may not retry the facts or reevaluate the evidence, their function in this regard being limited to determining whether the military has fully and fairly considered contested factual issues. Moreover, military law is a jurisprudence which exists separate and apart from the law governing civilian society so that what is permissible within the military may be constitutionally impermissible outside it. Therefore, when the military courts have determined that factors peculiar to the military require a different application of constitutional standards, federal courts are reluctant to set aside such decisions."

It is not surprising that Justices deeply committed to civil liberties in the 1950's found the Congressional grant of jurisdiction to military courts over certain civilians unconstitutional.[356] And, as Justice Douglas described it, the Court "held in a series of decisions that

---

[355] Calley *v.* Callaway, 519 F. 2d. 184 (1975). *Cert. denied* 425 U.S. 911 (1976).
[356] Toth *v.* Quarles, 350 U.S. 11, 17-18 (1955).

court-martial jurisdiction cannot be extended to reach any person
not a member of the Armed Forces at the times of both the offense
and the trial. Thus, discharged soldiers cannot be court-martialed
for offenses committed while in service. Similarly, neither civilian
employees of the Armed Forces overseas, nor civilian dependents
of military personnel accompanying them overseas, may be tried by
court-martial."[357]

The matter was not allowed to rest there. Even though Congress
has over the years made great efforts to provide men in the service
with a better brand of justice, the Court operating under the premise that "Determining the scope of the constitutional power of
Congress to authorize trial by court-martial presents another instance calling for limitation to *the least possible power adequate to the
end proposed,*' "[358] has decided that a "crime to be under military
jurisdiction must be service connected."[359] But the meaning of
"service connected" apparently does not mean that a serviceman
committing a crime in the civilian community must be tried in a
civilian court. Although it asserted that "the case presents no occasion for resolution of the merits of . . . [the] service-connection
claim,"[360] the Court by implication and words seemed to broaden
the concept of "service connection." The case involved an Army
Captain who allegedly sold, transferred, and possessed marijuana
while off post, off duty and not in uniform—a set of circumstances
that seems to preclude a "service connection," yet the Court in arriving at its decision in the case had this to say: "We see no injustice
in requiring respondent to submit to a system established by Congress and carefully designed to protect not only military interests
but his legitimate interests as well. Of course, if the offenses with
which he is charged are not 'service-connected,' the military courts
will have had no power to impose any punishment whatever. *But
that issue turns in major part on gauging the impact of an offense on military discipline and effectiveness, on determining whether the military interest in deterring the offense is distinct from and greater than that of civilian
society, and on whether the distinct military interest can be vindicated
adequately in civilian courts. These are matters of judgment that often will
turn on the precise set of facts in which the offense occurred. . . . More importantly, they are matters as to which the expertise of military courts is singularly relevant, and their judgments indispensable to inform any eventual
review in Art. III courts.*" (Emphasis supplied.)

Two recent, lower court decisions cast interesting light on the
construction to be given the holding in O'Callahan *v.* Parker with

[357] O'Callahan *v.* Parker, 395 U.S. 258, 267 (1969). The cases cited by Justice
Douglas were: Toth *v.* Quarles, 350 U.S. 11 (1955); McElroy *v.* Guagliardo, 361 U.S.
281 (1960); Grisham *v.* Hagen, 361 U.S. 278 (1960); Kinsella *v.* Singleton, 361 U.S.
234 (1960). Reid *v.* Covert, 354 U.S. 1 (1957).
[358] O'Callahan *v.* Parker, 395 U.S. 258, 265 (1969).
[359] *Ibid.*, at 272. For a detailed listing of commentaries on the O'Callahan case, *see*
Relford *v.* U.S. Disciplinary Commandant, 401 U.S. 355 (1971).
[360] Schlesinger *v.* Councilman, 420 U.S. 738, 759-760 (1975).

regard to "service connection." In one, the U.S. Court of Appeals, Third Circuit, held that a Federal court should not enjoin a court-martial convened to try an Army Sergeant in whose off-post house-trailer was found a quantity of amphetamines and marijuana: "Accordingly, we conclude that it was error for the district court to have made the fact findings in the first instance, to have decided the *O'Callahan* issue, and to have issued the injunction pursuant to a decision on the merits. The district court should have required the appellee to exhaust remedies in the military court system and not have interfered with its orderly process."[361] In the other decision, another circuit court held that *O'Callahan* "does not extend to the jurisdiction of courts-martial in peace time to try non-service offenses committed by servicemen against foreign persons in foreign lands."[362]

Apparently, encouraged by what they perceive as a growing concern for civil liberties generally in the United States, servicemen have recently taken to challenging service regulations and actions on First Amendment grounds. A group of Army bandsmen who were ordered transferred because they arranged or sanctioned an incident in which a fiancée and wives attempted to march with the band in a public parade while carrying signs protesting the Vietnam war contended that the transfers had a chilling effect on their First Amendment rights. The District Court upheld them but was reversed by the Court of Appeals, which said: "We do not say that a case would never arise where a transfer order could be invalidated by a civilian court on such a basis. But any such judicial intrusion into the area broadly confided by the Constitution to the President as Commander-in-Chief and his authorized subordinates must await a stronger case than this one."[363] Airmen objecting to enforcement of an Air Force regulation prohibiting them from wearing uniforms at a public anti-war meeting were told that they must first exhaust the available military remedies before seeking relief in civilian courts.[364]

For a time the courts were beleaguered with cases involving protests of Reserves and National Guardsmen about haircut regulations. The results in the courts were mixed.[365] Apparently, the Supreme Court's decision in 1976 which upheld a county's hair regulation for its police officers has ended the controversy, for it seems a fair inference that the Court would view military hair regulations in the same light.[366]

---

[361] Sedivy v. Richardson, 485 F. 2d. 1115, 1121 (1973).

[362] Williams v. Froehlke, 490 F. 2d. 998, 1001 (1974).

[363] Cortright v. Resor, 447 F. 2d. 245, 246 (1971). For the District Court decision *see* 325 F.Supp. 797 (1971).

[364] Locks v. Laird, 441 F. 2d. 479 (1971); *cert. denied*, 404 U.S. 986 (1971)—cited as Bright *et al. v.* Laird.

[365] Wallace v. Chafee, 451 F. 2d. 1374, 1380 (1971); *also*, 323 F.Supp. 902 (1971). *See* Whitis v. U.S., 368 F.Supp. 822 (1974) and cases cited therein.

[366] Kelley v. Johnson, 425 U.S. 238 (1976).

When some enlisted men went to court over being denied re-enlistment bonuses, a U.S. court of appeals sympathetically declared "And although Congress may constitutionally impair existing contract rights in the exercise of a paramount governmental power such as the 'War Powers,' Congress is 'without power to *reduce* expenditures by abrogating contractual obligations of the United States.' "[367] But a U.S. district court was less sympathetic to the claim that NROTC scholarships for women were too few to accord equality. The court held that Congressional classification of men and women into two categories for service in combat vessels violated no equal protection rights. Significantly, the court in explaining why it considered the case made the point that courts may impose restrictions on Executive and Congressional decisions in the exercise of war powers.[368]

National Purposes of the Militia ¶15. To provide for calling forth the militia to execute the laws of the Union, suppress insurrections, and repel invasions;

Congress passed such an act in 1795, which basically still remains on the statute books. It leaves with the President the right to decide whether an insurrection exists or an invasion threatens.[369]

¶16. To provide for organizing, arming and disciplining the militia, and for governing such part of them as may be employed in the service of the United States, reserving to the States respectively the appointment of the officers, and the authority of training the militia according to the discipline prescribed by Congress;

Who Constitute the Militia The militia was long regarded as a purely State affair, but in the National Defense Act of June 3, 1916, "the militia of the United States" was defined as consisting "of all able-bodied male citizens of the United States" and all similar declarants between the ages of 18 and 45. The same act also provided for the nationalization of the National Guard, which was recognized as constituting a part of the militia of the United States, and provided for its being drafted into the military service of the United States in certain contingencies.[370] The act rested on the principle that the right of the States to maintain a militia is always subordinate to the power of Congress "to raise and support armies," a doctrine which has received the sanction of the Supreme Court.[371] Subsequent legislation has reinforced these provisions and lowered the age for inclusion in the militia to 17.[372] (*See also* Section X, ¶3.)

[367] Larionoff *v.* U.S., 533 F. 2d. 1167, 1179 (1976). *Cf.* Jones *v.* Watkins, 422 F.Supp. 1268 (1976).
[368] Kovach *v.* Middendorf, 424 F.Supp. 72, 77 (1976).
[369] Martin *v.* Mott, 12 Wheat. 19 (1827); 10 U.S.C. 3500 and 8500.
[370] 39 *Stat.* 166 (1916).
[371] Selective Draft cases, 245 U.S. 366 (1918); Cox *v.* Wood, 247 U.S. 3 (1918).
[372] 10 U.S.C. 311, 3500-3501; 32 U.S.C. 302, 303, 307, 313.

In an unusual case growing out of the tragedy at Kent State University in 1970, the Supreme Court in 1973 decided that "The relief sought . . . requiring initial judicial review and continuing surveillance by a federal court over the training, weaponing and orders of the Guard would . . . embrace critical areas of responsibility vested by the Constitution in the Legislative and Executive branches of the Government."[373] It went on to state, however, that "it should be clear that we neither hold nor imply that the conduct of the National Guard is always beyond judicial review or that there may not be accountability in a judicial forum for violations of law or for specific unlawful conduct by military personnel."

In the wake of Gilligan *v.* Morgan lower Federal courts have held (1) that a particular procedure for reducing the number of jet pilots in the Oregon Air National Guard was not subject to judicial review,[374] and (2) that a requirement that Air National Guard technicians wear a military uniform while performing military duties during the work week as well as during weekend drills did not violate the due process clause of the Fifth Amendment.[375]

¶17. To exercise exclusive legislation in all cases whatsoever over such district (not exceeding ten miles square) as may, by cession of particular States and the acceptance of Congress, become the seat of the Government of the United States, and to exercise like authority over all places purchased by the consent of the legislature of the State in which the same shall be, for the erection of forts, magazines, arsenals, dockyards, and other needful buildings; and

This paragraph is, of course, the source of Congress's power to govern the District of Columbia. Congress itself, however, is not required to exercise this power, but may at any time create a government for the District and vest in it the same range of lawmaking power as it has always customarily vested in territories of the United States. In 1871 it did, in fact, do so; and while this government was later (1874) abolished and the commission form of government was instituted, certain of its legislative acts forbidding discrimination by restaurants against Negroes remained in force.[376] The system set up in 1874 provided for an executive board of three commissioners with limited governmental powers, with Congress retaining the power to legislate for the District. This system was extensively overhauled in 1967 in a Reorganization Plan intended, in President Johnson's words: "to bring Twentieth Century government to the Capital of this Nation." But, he added, the plan would not "in any way detract from the powers which the

The District of Columbia

[373] Gilligan *v.* Morgan, 413 U.S. 1, 7, 11 (1973).
[374] Covington *v.* Anderson, 487 F. 2d. 660 (1973).
[375] Bruton *v.* Schnipke, 370 F.Supp. 1157 (1974).
[376] District of Columbia *v.* Thompson Co., 346 U.S. 100 (1953).

Congress exercises with respect to the District." He conceded that the reorganization "is in no way a substitute for home rule."[377]

In 1975, the District of Columbia installed its first elected mayor and city council in more than 100 years. A Home Rule Charter had been approved in May 1974.[378]

Challenges to Congress's power to legislate for the District have been singularly unsuccessful in the courts.[379]

Places Purchased from State   At an early time it was thought that a State's consent to surrender of jurisdiction under this paragraph had to be substantially unqualified; but later decisions held that a State may concede and Congress accept a qualified jurisdiction. Nor is the power of a State to concede and of the United States to receive and exercise jurisdiction, over places purchased by the latter within the boundaries of the former, limited by this paragraph. In fact, the paragraph is today largely superfluous.[380] Yet, a host of questions about States' powers with respect to Federal installations within their borders have found their way to the courts in recent years.

When the Attorney General of Kentucky sought declaratory and injunctive relief requiring Federal installations to obtain State permits before operating air contaminant sources, the Supreme Court observed that "Neither the Supremacy Clause nor the Plenary Powers Clause [this clause] bars all state regulation which may touch the activities of the Federal Government."[381] But in this case, the Court found that "The permit requirement is not intended simply to regulate the amount of pollutants which the federal installations may discharge. Without a permit, an air contaminant source is forbidden to operate even if it is in compliance with every other state measure respecting air pollution control and abatement." The Court stated that it was unconvinced that Congress intended to subject Federal agencies to State permits, even though Congress in the Clean Air Act required Federal facilities to meet State air quality standards. The Court concluded that the act did not contain "any clear and unambiguous declaration by the Con-

---

[377] 5 App. U.S.C. 401-442.

[378] 1974 *Cong. Quart. Weekly Report*, 2544. *Minneapolis Tribune*, Jan. 3, 1975.

[379] *See* Hobson v. Tobriner, 255 F.Supp. 295 (1966) and cases cited therein; Palmore v. U.S., 290 A. 2d. 573 (1972). Federal Judge David L. Bazelon writing for the U.S. Court of Appeals, D.C., expounded on the meaning of Congress's power to legislate for the District of Columbia in this way: "Congress, in legislating for the District, has all the powers of a *state legislature*, and Congress may delegate to the District government that 'full legislative power, subject of course to constitutional limitations to which all lawmaking is subservient and subject also to the power of Congress at any time to revise, alter, or revoke the authority granted.' " (Emphasis supplied.) Firemen's Ins. Co. of Washington, D.C. v. Washington, 483 F. 2d. 1323 (1973).

[380] James v. Dravo Contracting Co., 302 U.S. 134 (1937); Collins v. Yosemite Park & Curry Co., 304 U.S. 518 (1938); Stewart & Co. v. Sandrakula, 309 U.S. 94 (1940); S.R.A., Inc. v. Minnesota, 327 U.S. 558 (1946); United States v. Brown, 552 F. 2d. 817 (1977); State v. Dykes, 562 P. 2d. 1090 (1977).

[381] Hancock v. Train, 426 U.S. 167 (1976).

gress that federal installations may not perform their activities unless a state official issues a permit."

In a case involving the question of which government has jurisdiction over land purchased with a disbursement of trust funds held by the United States, the Mississippi Supreme Court decided that this land was not "Indian country" (*see* p. 85) and that the Federal courts do not have "exclusive jurisdiction of Mississippi Indian citizens simply because they are being aided by the federal government.[382] The State of Mississippi has not relinquished jurisdiction over the acquired territory or its citizens."

To the contention that equal protection required that any criminal defendant tried in the U.S. District Court for the District of Columbia must receive the same treatment he would get in a Federal court elsewhere, the U.S. Court of Appeals, District of Columbia, responded: "The situation is analogous to that which obtains in all of the 50 states, i.e., a person indicted under the criminal laws of a state may be tried in a state court under evidentiary rules different from those employed by the federal courts within that state in the trial of U.S. Code offenses. No one has ever suggested that that violates the Constitution. In any event, for purposes of the exclusive jurisdiction over certain D.C. Code crimes temporarily vested in the District Court during the transitional period, the District Court is functioning as a 'state' court."[383]

A U.S. district court held that a Pennsylvania school district could impose and collect occupation and per capita taxes on employees residing at the Lewisburg Federal Penitentiary, a Federal enclave. The court said the "Clause 17 contains no express requirement that a cession of land must be made without reservations by the ceding state and such a requirement is not to be implied. . . . Pennsylvania's power to tax in the Lewisburg enclave was abated only with respect to lands and buildings but not with respect to individuals who may take up residence on the ceded land."[384]

In a case involving the question of whether or not District of Columbia acts or Federal law applied in a labor relations dispute, a Federal district court made the noteworthy observation that Congress's power under Article I, Section VIII, ¶17 is "separate and distinct from Congress' power to legislate for the entire nation. In passing the two acts relied upon by plaintiff, Congress performed a function much like a state legislature's in passing state legislation."[385]

---

[382] Tubby *v.* State, 327 So. 2d. 272 (1976).

[383] United States *v.* Belt, 514 F. 2d. 837 (1975). The District of Columbia Court Reform and Criminal Procedure Act of 1970 provides for creation of an independent judiciary to be responsible for local matters and to free the Federal courts of the District from that responsibility. The transfer of jurisdiction "was achieved in carefully phased steps."

[384] United States *v.* Lewisburg A. Sch. D., Union Cty, Pa., 398 F.Supp. 948 (1975). *Cf.* Board of Sup'rs of Fairfax County, Va. *v.* U.S., 408 F.Supp. 556 (1976).

[385] Papadopoulos *v.* Sheraton Park Hotel, 410 F.Supp. 217 (1976).

The U.S. Court of Appeals, Eighth Circuit, held that when the United States deeded over some of its land, reserving only the right to use it in an emergency declared by the President or Congress, the United States terminated its "exclusive jurisdiction" as set forth in clause 17.[386] And the Supreme Court of Connecticut held that where the property was not under the exclusive jurisdiction of the United States, a credit union office building must be built in compliance with the town building code and zoning ordinances.[387]

¶18. To make all laws which shall be necessary and proper for carrying into execution the foregoing powers, and all other powers vested by this Constitution in the Government of the United States, or in any department or officer thereof.

"The Co-efficient Clause" What is a "necessary and proper" law under this paragraph? This question arose in 1819, in the great case of McCulloch *v.* Maryland, and was answered by Chief Justice Marshall thus: "Let the end be legitimate, let it be within the scope of the Constitution, and all means which are appropriate, which are plainly adapted to that end, which are not prohibited, but consist with the letter and spirit of the Constitution, are constitutional."[388]

The basis of this declaration was furnished by three ideas: First, that the Constitution was ordained by the people and so was intended for their benefit; secondly, that it was "intended to endure for ages to come and, consequently, to be adapted to the various crises of human affairs"; and thirdly, that while the National Government is one of enumerated powers—a proposition which is today unqualifiedly applicable only to its internal powers—it is sovereign as to those powers. Marshall's view was opposed by the theory that the Constitution was a compact of sovereign States and so should be strictly construed, in the interest of safeguarding the powers of said States. From this point of view the necessary and proper clause was urged to be a limitation on Congress's powers, and was interpreted as meaning, in substance, that Congress could pass no laws except those which were "absolutely necessary" to carry into effect the powers of the General Government.

Broadly speaking, Marshall's doctrine has prevailed with the Court since the Civil War. It is true that certain of its decisions touching the New Deal legislation narrowed Congress's discretion in the choice of measures for the effective exercise of national power by subordinating it to certain powers of the States; but subsequent decisions indicate that this trend was only temporary. In the *Darby* case,[389] referred to earlier, Justice Stone, speaking for the

[386] United States *v.* Boings, 504 F. 2d. 809 (1974).
[387] DuPuis *v.* Submarine Base Credit Union, Inc., 365 A. 2d. 1093 (1976).
[388] 4 Wheat. 316, 421. *See also ibid.*, 415.
[389] 312 U.S. 100 (1941); followed in Fernandez *v.* Wiener, 326 U.S. 340 (1945); and Case *v.* Bowles, 327 U.S. 92 (1946).

Court, asserted that Congress's powers under the necessary and proper clause are no more limited by the reserved powers of the States than are its more specific powers. (*Cf.* Article VI, ¶2, and Amendment X.)

Most recently, in Buckley *v.* Valeo, the Supreme Court took the occasion to comment on the necessary and proper clause, pointing out how the clause enhanced Congress's power to spend for the general welfare and, then, saying: "Whether the chosen means appear, 'bad,' 'unwise,' or 'unworkable' to us is irrelevant; Congress has concluded that the means are 'necessary and proper' to promote the general welfare, and we thus decline to find this legislation without the grant of power in Art. I, §8."[390]

The "co-efficient clause" is further important because of the control which it gives Congress over the powers of the other departments of government, but in this connection the doctrines of the Supreme Court at times confront the clause with certain "inherent" executive and judicial powers, of which the Court itself is the final determinator.[391]

On an earlier page were listed certain "inherent" powers of the National Government, claimed for it as "concomitants of nationality," as "inherent in sovereignty," or simply from the necessity of the case.[392] In the words of the Court, "it is not lightly to be assumed that in matters requiring national action, a power which must belong to and somewhere reside in every civilized government is not to be found."[393] Moreover, "even constitutional power may be established by usage," both in the case of Congress and in that of the President.[394]

Inherent Powers of the National Government

The foregoing may have created the impression that today there is precious little that Congress cannot do under the Constitution as it has been interpreted by the Supreme Court. This would be a false impression. For legislation to pass muster in the Supreme Court, there must still be a reasonable basis in the Constitution for the exercise of power and, above all, the exercise must not arbitrarily abridge constitutionally protected rights such as First Amendment rights. Despite the enormity of the power which Congress has exercised with the acquiescence of the Court, the Court still finds occasion to declare acts of Congress unconstitutional. The fact that there have been relatively few in recent years may as well be evidence of prudence on the part of Congress as evidence of permis-

[390] Buckley *v.* Valeo, 424 U.S. 1, 91 (1976).
[391] *Cf. ex parte* Grossman, 267 U.S. 87 (1925); and Myers *v.* U.S., 272 U.S. 52 (1926).
[392] *See* p. 6 above.
[393] Missouri *v.* Holland, 252 U.S. 416, 433 (1920), quoting Andrews *v.* Andrews, 188 U.S. 14, 33 (1903).
[394] Inland Waterways Corp. *v.* Young, 309 U.S. 517 (1940); United States *v.* Midwest Oil Co., 236 U.S. 459 (1915).

siveness by the Court or Congressional fears of having its actions upset by the Court.[395]

SECTION IX

The purpose of this section is to impose certain limitations on the powers of Congress.

¶1. The migration or importation of such persons as any of the States now existing shall think proper to admit shall not be prohibited by the Congress prior to the year one thousand eight hundred and eight, but a tax or duty may be imposed on such importation, not exceeding ten dollars for each person.

This paragraph referred to the African slave trade and is, of course, now obsolete. It is still interesting, nevertheless, for the evidence it affords of the belief of the Framers of the Constitution that, "under the power to regulate commerce, Congress would be authorized to abridge it in favor of the great principles of humanity and justice"[1] and of the belief of the Framers that "such persons" were not "citizens" in a constitutional sense.[2]

¶2. The privilege of the writ of *habeas corpus* shall not be suspended, unless when in cases of rebellion or invasion the Public safety may require it.

The Writ of *Habeas Corpus* The writ of *habeas corpus* is the most important single safeguard of personal liberty known to Anglo-American law. Often traced to Magna Carta itself, it dates from, at latest, the seventeenth century, and it is interesting to note that the Constitution simply assumes that, of course, it will be a part of the law of the land. The importance of the writ is that it enables anybody who has been put under personal restraint to secure immediate inquiry by a court into the cause of his detention and, if he is not detained for good cause, his liberty.[3] While the writ may not be used as a substitute for appeal, it provides a remedy for jurisdictional and constitutional errors without limit as to time, and may be used to correct such errors by military as well as by civil courts.[4]

Early in the Civil War, President Lincoln, without authorization by

---

[395] For a listing of acts held unconstitutional *see* U.S., 88 Cong., 1st Sess., Senate, Document 39 (1964), 1387-1402.

[1] United States *v. The William*, 28 Fed. Cas. No. 16700 (1808).
[2] Scott *v.* Sandford, 19 How. 393, 411 (1857).
[3] Edward Jenks, *Short History of English Law* (Boston, 1913), 333-335; David Hutchinson, *Foundations of the Constitution* (New York, 1928), 137-139; Zechariah Chafee, "The Most Important Human Right in the Constitution," 32 *Boston Univ. Law Review*, 143 (1947).
[4] United States *v.* Smith, 331 U.S. 469, 475 (1947); Gusik *v.* Schiller, 340 U.S. 128 (1950).

Congress, temporarily suspended the privilege of the writ for the line of transit for troops en route to Washington, thereby giving rise to the famous case of *ex parte* Merryman,[5] in which Chief Justice Taney, after vainly attempting to serve the writ, filed an opinion denouncing the President's course as violative of the Constitution. Whether the President or the Chief Justice was in the right seems to depend on whether the district for which the writ was suspended was properly to be regarded as within the field of military operations at this time, for, if it was, the President's power as Commander-in-Chief had full sway. Subsequently Congress passed an act declaring the President "authorized" to suspend the writ "whenever, in his judgment, the public safety may require it," though whether "authorized" by the act or by the Constitution itself was not made clear.[6]

In recent years, the writ has been invoked most conspicuously to protect in Federal courts those who were apparently incarcerated unjustly in State jurisdictions. The basis for doing so was laid back in 1867 when, according to Justice Brennan, Congress anticipating resistance to its Reconstruction measures had passed legislation which provided that a State prisoner should not have to "abide state court determination of his constitutional defense—the necessary predicate of direct review by this Court—before resorting to federal *habeas corpus*. Rather, a remedy almost in the nature of *removal* from the state to the federal courts of prisoners' constitutional contentions seems to have been envisaged."[7] A 1948 law currently on the books states that an application for a writ in Federal courts "in behalf of a person in custody pursuant to the judgment of a State court shall not be granted unless it appears that the applicant has exhausted the remedies available in the courts of the State, or that there is either an absence of available State corrective process or *the existence of circumstances rendering such process ineffective to protect the rights of the prisoner*"[8] (emphasis supplied).

The Supreme Court held in 1962 that "The language of Congress, the history of the writ, the decisions of this Court, all make clear that the power of inquiry on federal *habeas corpus* is plenary. Therefore, where an applicant for a writ of *habeas corpus* alleges facts which, if proved, would entitle him to relief, the federal court to which the application is made has the power to receive evidence and try the facts."[9] In view of the above, it is not surprising that the Federal courts' *habeas corpus* business has increased,[10] particularly since the Court has also determined that one who believes he is about to be inducted into the Armed Forces unjustly may also avail

[5] 17 Fed. Cas. 145 (1861).
[6] Edward S. Corwin, *The President, Office and Powers* (New York, 1957), 144-145.
[7] Fay *v.* Noia, 372 U.S. 391, 416 (1963).   [8] 28 U.S.C. 2254.
[9] Townsend *v.* Sain, 372 U.S. 293, 312 (1963).
[10] Key decisions include Fay *v.* Noia, 372 U.S. 391 (1963); Townsend *v.* Sain, 372 U.S. 293 (1963); Harris *v.* Nelson, 394 U.S. 286 (1969); Kaufman *v.* U.S., 394 U.S. 217 (1969).

himself of the writ in Federal court.[11] (*See* pp. 239-240 for further discussion.)

In 1977 the Supreme Court highlighted the provision of Federal law that Federal courts shall not entertain applications for the writ from prisoners in Federal custody, "if it appears that the applicant has failed to apply for relief, by motion, to the court which sentenced him, or that such court has denied him relief, unless it also appears that the remedy by motion is inadequate or ineffective to test the legality of his detention."[12] The Court held that such a provision was valid, stating that "the only constitutional question presented is whether the substitution of a new collateral remedy which is both adequate and effective should be regarded as a suspension of the Great Writ within the meaning of the Constitution." The Court went on to hold "that the substitution of a collateral remedy which is neither inadequate nor ineffective to test the legality of a person's detention does not constitute a suspension of the writ of habeas corpus."[13]

On another complicated issue the Supreme Court held in 1973 that "when a state prisoner is challenging the very fact or duration of his physical imprisonment, and the relief he seeks is a determination that he is entitled to immediate or more speedy release from that imprisonment, his sole federal remedy is a writ of habeas corpus."[14] This holding came out of a case where several New York State prisoners challenged the cancellation of their good-behavior-time credits (toward reduction of maximum sentence), invoking the Civil Rights Act as well as making a *habeas corpus* claim. As the Supreme Court saw it: "The question before us is whether state prisoners seeking such redress may obtain equitable relief under the Civil Rights Act, even though the federal habeas corpus statute . . . clearly provides a specific federal remedy." Further, the Court said that the case presented "an unresolved and important problem in the administration of federal justice," a problem involving the interrelationship of two important Federal laws. In short, if the Civil Rights Act prevailed, the prisoners could bring their suits to a Federal court "so as to avoid the necessity of first seeking relief in a state forum." If the *habeas corpus* laws prevailed, then the exhaustion of adequate State remedies was required before the invocation of Federal judicial relief. The Court reasoned that "Congress has determined that habeas corpus is the appropriate remedy for state prisoners attacking the validity of the fact or length of their confinement, and that specific determination must override the general terms of . . . [the Civil Rights Act]."

[11] Oestereich v. Selective Service Bd., 393 U.S. 233 (1968); Parisi v. Davidson, 405 U.S. 34 (1972). For use of *habeas corpus* by a Reservist who was held in service beyond his contract time *see* Scaggs v. Larson, 396 U.S. 1206 (1969).

[12] 28 U.S.C. 2255. Swain v. Pressley, 97 S.Ct. 1224 (1977). The case dealt with a law respecting the Superior Court of the District of Columbia which is comparable to 28 U.S.C. 2255 to which the Court spoke.

[13] Swain v. Pressley, 97 S.Ct. 1224, 1229-1230 (1977).

[14] Preiser v. Rodriguez, 411 U.S. 475 (1973).

A closely split Supreme Court in 1976 held that the provision of the U.S. Code which specified that the United States should pay fees for transcripts for those seeking a *habeas corpus in forma pauperis* only "if the trial judge certifies that the suit or appeal is not frivolous and the transcript is needed to decide the issue presented by the suit or appeal" was not a suspension of the writ of *habeas corpus* in violation of Article I, Section IX, ¶2.[15] The Court said that the argument that it does violate the Constitution "presupposes, *inter alia*, that a right to a free transcript is a necessary concomitant of the writ which the founders declared could not be suspended. This is obviously not the case. The writ of habeas corpus operated until 1944 with no provision for free transcripts for indigents. Congress, when in that year it authorized free transcripts for the first time, could certainly have limited the authorization to non-frivolous cases where a need had to be shown. If Congress could have thus limited the writ directly without 'suspending' it, it follows that it may do so indirectly" (presumably, that means by having trial judge certify).

After discussing at length the long and complicated history of the Court's efforts to "define the substantive reach of the writ" of *habeas corpus*, the Supreme Court in 1976 held "that where the State has provided an opportunity for full and fair litigation of a Fourth Amendment claim, the Constitution does not require that a state prisoner be granted federal habeas corpus relief on the ground that evidence obtained in an unconstitutional search or seizure was introduced at his trial."[16] The Court reasoned that application of the exclusionary rule in Fourth Amendment cases "deflects the truthfinding process and often frees the guilty. The disparity in particular cases between the error committed by the police officer and the windfall afforded a guilty defendant by application of the rule is contrary to the idea of proportionality that is essential to the concept of justice. Thus, although the rule is thought to deter unlawful police activity in part through nurturing of respect for Fourth Amendment values, if applied indiscriminately it may well have the opposite effect of generating disrespect for the law and administration of justice. These long-recognized costs of the rule persist when a criminal conviction is sought to be overturned on collateral review on the ground that a search-and-seizure claim was erroneously rejected by two or more tiers of state courts."[17] To the dissenters' concern that this decision laid the groundwork for a "drastic withdrawal of federal habeas corpus jurisdiction," the Court responded: "With all respect, the hyperbole of the dissenting

[15] United States *v*. MacCollom, 426 U.S. 317 (1976).

[16] Stone *v*. Powell, 428 U.S. 465 (1976).

[17] The Court took pains to show that earlier decisions distinguished Fourth Amendment violations from denials of Fifth or Sixth Amendment rights in that "claims of illegal search and seizure do not 'impugn the integrity of the fact-finding process or challenge evidence as inherently unreliable; rather, the exclusion of illegally seized evidence is singly a prophylactic device intended to generally deter Fourth Amendment violations by law enforcement officers.' "

opinions is misdirected. Our decision today is *not* concerned with the scope of the habeas corpus statute as authority for litigating constitutional claims generally. We do reaffirm that the exclusionary rule is a judicially created remedy rather than a personal constitutional right, and we emphasize the minimal utility of the rule when sought to be applied to Fourth Amendment claims in a habeas corpus proceeding."[18]

¶3. No bill of attainder or *ex post facto* law shall be passed.

By this clause Congress is forbidden to pass bills of attainder and *ex post facto* laws. In the following section a similar prohibition is laid upon the States. It will be convenient to proceed as if both clauses were before us at this point.

"Bills of Attainder"   In English history, a "bill of attainder" was an act of Parliament charging somebody with treason and pronouncing upon him the penalty of death and the confiscation of his estates; but following our Civil War a divided Court held in the famous *Test Oath* cases[19] that the clause ruled out any legislative act "which inflicts punishment without a judicial trial"; and on this ground set aside certain statutes which, by requiring persons who followed certain callings to take an oath declaring they had never borne arms against the United States, excluded former members of the Confederate forces from the pursuit of their chosen professions. And in 1946 the Court, in reliance on these precedents, held void under this same clause a "rider" to a Congressional appropriation act which forbade the payment after a certain date of any compensation to three *named* persons then holding office by executive appointment, unless prior to that date they had been reappointed by the President with the advice and consent of the Senate. The Court took notice of the fact, which does not appear in the rider itself, that the three persons had been found by a House sub-committee to have engaged in "subversive activities," as the sub-committee defined this term; it also construed the rider as intended to bar its victims from government service.[20]

So, from being a protection of life against legislative wrath, the "bills of attainder" clause has become a protection of livelihood, and even a protection of livelihood at public expense. That the rider in the above case might have been held void as an attempt by Congress to usurp the executive power of removal seems obvious, the fact being notorious that—"dollar-a-year" men aside—people do not often serve government gratuitously. A general provision aimed at officials advocating certain doctrines presents a different question, as indicated by the Supreme Court's decision that the provision of the Subversive Activities Control Act of 1950 requir-

[18] 428 U.S. 465, 495 fn. 37 (1976).
[19] *Ex parte* Garland, 4 Wall. 333 (1867). *See also* Cummings *v.* Mo., 4 Wall. 277.
[20] United States *v.* Lovett, 328 U.S. 303 (1946). On June 13, 1940, the House passed a bill, later dropped, ordering the Secretary of Labor to deport Harry Bridges to Australia, his own country.

ing "Communist-action" organizations to register was not a bill of attainder.[21] However, the Court later held that a statute which made it a crime for a member of the Communist Party to serve as an officer of a labor union was a bill of attainder, hence unconstitutional.[22]

In recent years there have been some unusual claims as to what constitutes a bill of attainder. In the landmark Presidential tapes case, it was argued in Nixon's behalf that the Presidential Recordings and Materials Preservation Act constituted a bill of attainder because "Congress acted on the premise that he had engaged in 'misconduct,' and was an 'unreliable custodian' of his own documents, and generally was deserving of a 'legislative judgment of blameworthiness.' " The Supreme Court made short shrift of this contention: "In short, appellant constituted a legitimate class of one, and this provides a basis for Congress' decision to proceed with dispatch with respect to his materials while accepting the status of his predecessors' papers and ordering the further consideration of generalized standards to govern his successors."[23] The Court went on to instruct that "even if the specificity element were deemed to be satisfied here, the Bill of Attainder Clause would not automatically be implicated" for "burdensome consequences" cannot be equated to "inflicted punishment."

A U.S. court of appeals held that the Federal conflict-of-interest statute was not a bill of attainder, even though it was argued that it punished government employees by restricting "their practice of law or similar activity after leaving the government so as to exclude representation of others in government matters in which the particular employee participated personally and substantially when he was an employee."[24] Also, a California court found that the legislature's exclusion of the faculties of the State university and colleges from an across-the-board salary increase granted to all other State employees did not constitute a bill of attainder.[25] But a Federal district court held that Arizona statutes which disenfranchised the Communist Party and its affiliates were bills of attainder.[26]

Although it was undoubtedly the belief of many of the Framers of the Constitution that the ban here placed on *ex post facto* laws and its counterpart in Section X would henceforth rule out all retroactive legislation, and particularly all special acts interfering with "vested rights,"[27] the Court in the early case of Calder *v.* Bull[28]

"Ex Post Facto Laws"

---

[21] Communist Party *v.* Subversive Activities Control Board, 367 U.S. 1 (1961).

[22] U.S. *v.* Brown, 381 U.S. 437 (1965). The opinion provides a good historical summary and a review of pertinent cases on the subject. Significantly, it was a five-four decision with a forceful dissenting opinion.

[23] Nixon *v.* Administrator of General Services, 433 U.S. 425, 472 (1977).

[24] United States *v.* Nasser, 476 F. 2d. 1111 (1973).

[25] California State Employees Ass'n *v.* Flournoy, 108 Cal. Rptr. 251 (1973).

[26] Blawis *v.* Bolin, 358 F.Supp. 349 (1973).

[27] Story, *Commentaries*, § 1345; note appended to Justice Johnson's opinion in Satterlee *v.* Matthewson, 2 Pet. 380, 681 ff. (1829).

[28] 3 Dall. 386 (1798).

confined the prohibition to retroactive *penal* legislation. An "*ex post facto* law" today is a law which imposes penalties retroactively, that is, upon acts already done, or which increases the penalty for such acts; but laws which might seem at first glance to do these things have been frequently sustained as within State legislative power. Thus a New York statute which forbade physicians who had been convicted of certain offenses to continue in the practice of the medical profession was held not to be an "*ex post facto* law" as to one who prior to the passage of the act had been convicted of such an offense. The Court held that since the statute merely laid down a thoroughly justifiable test of fitness for the practice of medicine, and was entirely devoid of any punitive intention, it was well within the State's police power.[29] Likewise, laws which impose heavier penalties on old than on first offenders for the same offense are not considered to add an additional penalty to the old offender's previous crimes, but merely to punish more suitably and effectively his latest crime.[30] And it is now well settled that "statutory changes in the mode of trial or the rules of evidence, which do not deprive the accused of a defense and which operate only in a limited and unsubstantial manner to his disadvantage, are not prohibited by the *ex post facto* clause . . . and this includes statutes which change the 'rules of evidence . . . so as to render admissible against the accused evidence previously held inadmissible.' "[31] But the U.S. Court of Appeals, D.C., determined that a statute that mandated admission into evidence of certain prior convictions of defendants applied retroactively was an *ex post facto* law. The court labored to reconcile its holding with Supreme Court precedents that seem to cut the other way and then went on to say: "Whether the retrospective application of the new impeachment statute worked a deprivation of a substantial right depends upon the nature and degree of the disadvantage to the accused imposed by the substitution of a fixed legislative judgment for a judge's informed discretion on this issue. We conclude that the particularized consideration which this claim of an accused has heretofore received is a protection of the magnitude necessary to involve the *ex post facto* clause."[32]

As to a change in State law from a statute providing for the death penalty unless the jury recommended mercy to one giving the jury only the right to an advisory opinion, the Supreme Court concluded that "the changes in the law are procedural, and on the whole ameliorative, and that there is no *ex post facto* violation."[33]

Curiously, the Supreme Court has held that neither deportation

---

[29] Hawker *v.* N.Y., 170 U.S. 189 (1898); *ex parte* Scott, 471 S.W. 2d. 54 (1971); Schmidt *v.* Masters, 490 P. 2d. 1029 (1971).

[30] Graham *v.* W. Va., 224 U.S. 616 (1912).

[31] Dixon *v.* U.S., 287 A. 2d. 89 (1972) citing Thompson *v.* Missouri, 299 U.S. 167, 170-171 (1925). *See also* Todd *v.* State, 187 S.E. 2d. 835 (1972).

[32] United States *v.* Henson, 486 F. 2d. 1292, 1307 (1973).

[33] Dobbert *v.* Florida, 97 S.Ct. 2290, 2297 (1977).

nor termination of old age benefits constitutes punishment in a legal sense; consequently, it has upheld legislation which permitted both for Communist affiliation prior to enactment of the legislation.[34] But a three-judge district court in 1972 struck down as an *ex post facto* law, the Hiss Act, which forbids Government pension payments to those who before enactment of the act concealed material facts concerning affiliation or support of the Communist Party in a Federal employment application or who were convicted of perjury under a Federal statute in connection with a matter involving national security.[35]

While Congress may not pass *ex post facto* laws, the President is not thus hampered in his capacity as Commander-in-Chief in wartime of our forces in the field. Otherwise, Presidents Roosevelt and Truman would be chargeable with violating the Constitution in agreeing at Yalta and Potsdam to the creation of the Nuremberg Court for the trial of leading Nazis on the charge of plotting war, a crime not previously punishable under either International Law or any other law.[36]

The Supreme Court in 1977 held that the clause "is a limitation upon the powers of the legislature and does not of its own force apply to the Judicial Branch of government."[37] The Court added: "But the principle on which the clause is based—the notion that persons have a right to fair warning of that conduct which will give rise to criminal penalties—is fundamental to our concept of constitutional liberty. As such, that right is protected against judicial action by the Due Process Clause of the Fifth Amendment." Consequently, in a case that dealt with jury instructions in an obscenity case the Court decided that "the Due Process Clause precludes the application to petitioners of the standards announced in *Miller v. California* [1973] to the extent that those standards may impose criminal liability for conduct not punishable under *Memoirs* [1966].

[34] Galvan *v*. Press, 347 U.S. 522 (1954); Flemming *v*. Nestor, 363 U.S. 603 (1960). *See also* Keefer *v*. Al Johnson Construction Co., 193 N.W. 2d. 305 (1971).

[35] Hiss *v*. Hampton, 338 F.Supp. 1141 (1972). The Court held: "We think disabilities imposed upon the plaintiffs by the Hiss Act are punitive and not regulatory. Neither Hiss nor Strasburger was a federal employee at the time the Act was passed and we do not understand how the conduct of federal employees could be regulated or their moral standards elevated by imposing a financial penalty for their prior conduct upon men who were not federal employees or likely ever again to become federal employees. Retroactive punishment of former employees for their past misdoings has no reasonable bearing upon regulation of the conduct of those presently employed. The proper function of regulation is to guide and control present and future conduct, not to penalize former employees for acts done long ago."

[36] *Cf. in re* Yamashita, 327 U.S. 1, 26 (1946), for Justice Murphy's dissenting opinion; and Hirota *v*. MacArthur, 338 U.S. 197, 198 (1948), for concurring opinion of Justice Douglas. *See also* the article by Leo Gross on "The Criminality of Aggressive War," 41 *American Political Science Review*, 205 (1947).

[37] Marks *v*. U.S., 430 U.S. 188, 191 (1977). *See also* United States *v*. Wasserman, 504 F. 2d. 1012, 1015 (1974); United States *v*. Sherpix, Inc., 512 F. 2d. 1361 (1975); United States *v*. B & H Dist. Corp., 375 F.Supp. 136 (1974); and Morales *v*. Hamilton, 391 F.Supp 85 (1975).

Specifically, since the petitioners were indicted for conduct occurring prior to our decision in *Miller*, they are entitled to jury instructions to acquit . . . [in accordance with standards laid down in *Memoirs*]."[38] But, interestingly enough, in another obscenity case the same year the Supreme Court rejected the petitioner's contention that the instructions to the jury were "given pursuant to a statute enacted *after* the conduct for which he was prosecuted."[39] The Court explained that the particular section, "however, does not create any new substantive offense, but merely declares what type of evidence may be received and considered in deciding whether the matter in question was 'utterly without redeeming social importance.' " The Court took pains to point out that the petitioner's *ex post facto* argument was based on the premise that an earlier California Supreme Court decision would have precluded the use of evidence against him except for enactment of the new law. The Court accepted the interpretation of the California Court of Appeal that that was a wrong reading of the California Supreme Court's decision. Consequently, the United States Supreme Court found it unnecessary to determine whether, if the *statute itself* "had permitted the introduction of evidence which would have been previously excluded under California law, petitioner would have had a tenable claim under the *ex post facto* clause of the United States Constitution."[40]

For a discussion of the other issues inhering in obscenity cases see p. 321.

A recent decision of a U.S. court of appeals suggests a way to limit the protection of the *ex post facto* clause. Five persons who had been convicted of, among other things, a conspiracy to conduct a pattern of racketeering activity appealed their conviction in part on the grounds that the conviction was based largely on acts done prior to the effective date of the statute being employed.[41] The appeals court concluded that the statute had been drafted to avoid the problem of unconstitutionality. "This was done by defining 'pattern of racketeering activity' to require one act of racketeering activity after the effective date of the chapter."

¶4. No capitation or other direct tax shall be laid, unless in proportion to the census or enumeration hereinbefore directed to be taken.

A "capitation tax" is a poll tax. The requirement that such taxes should be apportioned grew, in part at least, out of the fear that otherwise Congress might endeavor by a heavy tax on negro slaves *per* poll, to drive "the peculiar institution" out of existence.[42] In

---

[38] *Ibid.*, 995. *See also* Justice Black's dissent in Ginzburg *v.* U.S., 383 U.S. 463, 477 (1966).
[39] Splawn *v.* California, 431 U.S. 595, 599 (1977).
[40] *Ibid.*   [41] United States *v.* Campanale, 518 F. 2d. 352 (1975).
[42] Ware *v.* Hylton, 3 Dall. 171 (1796).

other words, the Framers were of the opinion, later voiced by Marshall, that "the power to tax involves the power to destroy," and may be used for that purpose.

"Direct tax" was defined under Section VIII, ¶1. (*See* p. 41 above.)

¶5. No tax or duty shall be laid on articles exported from any State.

"Exported" means exported to a foreign country.[43] This provision has been held applicable even to general imposts with respect to goods in process of being sold for exportation.[44] Although the conditions in light of which this provision was framed have long since disappeared, it is good to be informed that there is still something which Congress cannot clamp a tax on.

¶6. No preference shall be given by any regulation of commerce or revenue to the ports of one State over those of another; nor shall vessels bound to or from one State be obliged to enter, clear or pay duties in another.

The Supreme Court summarized the meaning of this provision in 1931: "The specified limitations on the power of Congress were set to prevent preference as between States in respect of their ports or the entry and clearance of vessels. It does not forbid . . . discriminations as between ports. Congress, acting under the commerce clause, causes many things to be done that greatly benefit particular ports in the same or neighboring states. The establishing of ports of entry, erection and operation of lighthouses, improvement of rivers and harbors and the providing of structures for the convenient and economical handling of traffic are examples."[45]

¶7. No money shall be drawn from the Treasury but in consequence of appropriations made by laws; and a regular statement and account of the receipts and expenditures of all public money shall be published from time to time.

Appropriations and Expenditures

This paragraph is obviously addressed to the Executive, whose power is thus assumed to embrace that of expenditure. Throughout our history Congress has had occasion to make large lump-sum grants for such things as public works and relief, not to mention the sweeping terms in which appropriations are made in war time for the use of the Armed Services. It seems clear that such grants to an executive agency do not violate the maxim against delegation of legislative power, first, because the function of expenditure is historically an executive function; second, because appropriation acts

[43] Woodruff *v.* Parham, 8 Wall. 123 (1868).
[44] Spalding and Bros. *v.* Edwards, 262 U.S. 66 (1923). *Cf.* Peck & Co. *v.* Lowe, 247 U.S. 165 (1918).
[45] Commission *v.* Texas & N.O.R. Co., 284 U.S. 125, 131 (1931); Alabama G.S.R. Co. *v.* U.S., 340 U.S. 216 (1951).

are not "laws" in the true sense of the term, inasmuch as they do not lay down general rules of action for society at large. Rather, they are administrative regulations, and may go into detail or not, as the appropriating body—Congress—may choose.[46]

The above clause was once violated by none other than Abraham Lincoln, who early in the Civil War paid out two millions of dollars from unappropriated funds in the Treasury to persons unauthorized to receive them, for confidential services deemed by him to be of the utmost necessity at the time.[47] But this exception does not dispose of the fact that the clause is the most important single curb in the Constitution on Presidential power. The President can always veto Congressional measures intended to curb him directly, and his veto will be effective nine times out of ten. But a President cannot do much very long without funds, and these Congress can withhold from him simply by inaction.[48]

The Legislative "Rider"   The question has sometimes arisen whether Congress by attaching provisos or "riders" to its appropriations is constitutionally entitled to lay down conditions by which the President becomes bound if he accepts the appropriation, even though otherwise Congress could not have controlled his discretion, as for example, in deploying the Army and Navy. A logically conclusive argument can be made on either side of this question which, being of a "political" nature, appears to have been left to be determined by the tussle of political forces.

Congressmen in recent years have been perturbed when the President has refused to spend funds which Congress has appropriated. For example, in 1967, when President Johnson impounded several billions of Federal-aid highway funds which had been apportioned to the States, his lawyer, the Attorney General, said he had the power, at least in that particular fact situation.[49] And, later, Senators McGovern and Humphrey "assailed . . . the Nixon Administration for withholding $202-million in spending for the food stamp program."[50]

Continual Presidential impoundment of funds appropriated by Congress provoked a bitter battle in 1973. President Nixon, euphoric over the 1972 election results and before developments in

[46] Edward S. Corwin, "Constitutional Aspects of Federal Housing," 84 *University of Pennsylvnia Law Review*, 131-156 (1935); *also* Cincinnati Soap *v.* U.S., 301 U.S. 308, 321 (1937).

[47] James D. Richardson, *Messages and Papers of the President*, VI (Washington, 1909), 77-79.

[48] Of course, the major problems involving government spending are complex, but not constitutional issues. *See* Aaron Wildavsky, *The Politics of the Budgetary Process* (Boston,1964); Charles L. Schultze, *The Politics and Economics of Public Spending* (Washington, D.C., 1968); David J. Ott and Attiat F. Ott, *Federal Budget Policy* (Washington, D.C., 1969).

[49] 42 *Op. Atty. Gen.*, Feb. 25, 1967.

[50] *New York Times*, Jan. 13, 1972. The struggle goes on, *see* Sen. Humphrey's remarks, 118 *Cong. Rec.* No. 165, S18039ff. (1972).

the Watergate Affair, cut a great swath through Congressional appropriations. The White House put the total of impoundments at $8.7 billion for Fiscal 1973, but critics suggested that the figure was much higher. Representative Joe L. Evins, chairman of the Appropriations public works sub-committee suggested that the proper figure was at least $12.2 billion.[51]

Incensed Congressmen fought back in both the legislative and judicial arenas. When the State Highway Commission of Missouri sued for the release to it of impounded highway funds, 14 of the Senate's 17 committee chairmen intervened as friends of the court. Speaking for the chairmen, an angry Senator Sam J. Ervin, Jr. said, "This practice of impoundment is contemptuous of the role of Congress in our tripartite system. The power of the purse belongs exclusively to Congress under the Constitution."[52] To the argument of the Secretary of Transportation (the defendant in the case) that the executive power to control the rate of expenditure was a political question, the Court of Appeals for the Eighth Circuit answered: "We disagree. The only issue before the district court and this court is the question of statutory construction, i.e., whether the Secretary of Transportation, pursuant to his delegated duties under the Federal Highway Act, can withhold from the State of Missouri, for the reasons he stated, the authority to obligate funds duly apportioned to the State under the Act. Surely such a determination is within the competence of the courts."[53] On the merits, the court held that the act did not authorize the Secretary to withhold the funds.

The Administration continued to lose a series of impoundment cases in the lower courts. The U.S. Court of Appeals, Fourth Circuit, succinctly summed up the situation as it now exists: "The power to spend rests primarily with Congress under the Constitution; the executive, on the other hand, has the constitutional duty to execute the law in accordance with the legislative purpose so expressed. When the executive exercises its responsibility under appropriate legislation in such a manner as to frustrate the Congressional purpose, either by absolute refusal to spend or by a withholding of so substantial an amount of the appropriation as to make impossible the attainment of the legislative goals, the executive trespasses beyond the range of its legal discretion and presents an issue of constitutional dimensions which is obviously open to judicial review."[54]

[51] 1973 *Cong. Quart. Weekly Report*, 270.   [52] *Ibid.*, 3.
[53] State Highway Com'n of Missouri *v*. Volpe, 479 F. 2d. 1099 (1973).
[54] Campaign Clean Water, Inc. *v*. Train, 489 F. 2d. 492 (1973). *See also* State Highway Com'n of Mo. *v*. Volpe, 479 F. 2d. 1099 (1973); Local 2677, Amer. Fed. of Gov't Employees *v*. Phillips, 358 F.Supp. 60 (1973); City of New York *v*. Ruckelshaus, 358 F.Supp. 669 (1973), *remanded* 489 F. 2d. 492 (1973); Oklahoma *v*. Weinberger, 360 F.Supp. 724 (1973); Pennsylvania *v*. Lynn, 362 F.Supp. 1363 (1973); Community Action Programs Executive Directors Ass'n of New Jersey, Inc. *v*. Ash,

Ultimately, the Supreme Court became involved when in early 1975 it decided a case involving the holding back of several billions of dollars that had been appropriated by Congress for Federal assistance toward the cost of municipal sewers and sewer treatment works. The funds had been held back on the order of the President (Nixon). In a letter to the Administrator of the Environmental Protection Agency, who was tasked by the law to allot the funds, the President told the Administrator to allot "no more" than a specified amount, an amount far below Congress's figure. The Supreme Court unanimously decided the case on the grounds that the Congressional act that provided for the funds at issue did not permit the Administrator to allot less than the entire amounts authorized. Importantly, the Solicitor General conducting the case for the Administrator made no claim that the President had inherent power to use discretion in allotting funds contrary to the expressed intention of Congress. In the course of arriving at its decision, the Court made two points. One, this particular case did not involve the Congressional Budget and Impoundment Control Act of 1974, since the events took place before its enactment (and the act itself contained a provision saying that the act should not affect "in any way the claims or defenses of any party to litigation"). Second, the Court expressly cautioned that "no issues as to the reach or coverage of the Impoundment Act are before us."[55]

In the meantime, Congress moved ahead and passed the Congressional Budget and Impoundment Act of 1974.[56] Among other things the act requires that "Whenever the President determines that all or part of any budget authority will not be required . . . the President shall transmit to both Houses of Congress a special message" that gives particulars as to amounts and as to reasons. Further, the law requires that the amounts rescinded would be made available *unless* within a 45-day period "Congress has completed action on a rescission bill rescinding all or part of the amount proposed to be rescinded or that is to be reserved." In the face of Congress's constitutional power to spend and the statute, it would be difficult now for a President to assert successfully that he had a constitutional power to impound funds unilaterally. Whether or not this development is wise as well as constitutional remains to be seen. In a system of government that extols checks and balances, the President's ability to check Congressional spending has been reduced, although he still, of course, has the enormous power to veto appropriation bills. In any event, the new law received an auspicious start when President Ford displayed a remarkably cooperative spirit by sending Congress in September

365 F.Supp. 1355 (1973); Sioux Valley Empire Electric Ass'n Inc. *v.* Butz, 367 F.Supp. 686 (1973); Louisiana *v.* Weinberger, 369 F.Supp. 850 (1973); People *v.* Weinberger, 368 F.Supp. 721 (1973); Nat'l Treasury Employees Union *v.* Nixon, 492 F. 2d. 587 (1974).

[55] Train *v.* City of New York, 95 S.Ct. 839, 843 (1975).   [56] 88 *Stat.* 297.

1974 a $20-million list of proposed recisions and deferrals. He wrote "Reasonable men frequently differ on interpretation of law. The law to which this message pertains is no exception. It is particularly important that the executive and legislative branches develop a common understanding as to its operation. Such an understanding is both in keeping with the spirit of the partnership implicit in the law and essential for its effective use. As we begin the management of the Federal Budget under this new statute, I would appreciate further guidance from Congress."[57]

It is noteworthy that when several taxpayers and Congressmen sought to enjoin officers of the executive branch from making shipment of military ordnance to southeast Asia on the grounds that the expenditures were prohibited by statute, a Federal district court held that the questions presented were political and consequently beyond the scope of judicial inquiry or decision.[58] Also, when an effort was made to force the Secretary of HEW to use appropriated funds for abortions contrary to law, a Federal district court simply said that the Constitution and the law makes clear that "no officer may pay an obligation of the United States without an appropriation for that purpose, and no mandamus may issue to that end.[59]

¶8. No title of nobility shall be granted by the United States; and no person holding any office of profit or trust under them shall, without the consent of the Congress, accept of any present, emolument, office or title of any kind whatever from any king, prince or foreign State.

This provision has almost never served as the basis for litigation. A New York court not so long ago held that an American-born citizen was not entitled under this provision to add "von" to his surname.[60] And the Comptroller General has advised that certain retired enlisted servicemen could not take posts with foreign governments and still claim retired pay.[61] Amusingly, a U.S. court of appeals in a case involving the inheritance rights of a child born out of wedlock saw fit to invoke this provision, albeit in a footnote, in the following way: "The rationale behind the prohibition against the grant of any title of nobility by the United States equally would prohibit the United States from attacking any badge of ignobility to a citizen at birth."[62]

Aware of the penchant of foreign officials to give presents and decorations, Congress has passed legislation "consenting" to employees' (defined to include all officials and, specifically, the Presi-

[57] 1974 *Cong. Quart. Weekly Report*, 2622-2623.
[58] Harrington *v*. Schlesinger, 373 F.Supp. 1138 (1974).
[59] Doe *v*. Mathews, 420 F.Supp. 865 (1976).
[60] Application of Jama, 272 N.Y.S. 2d. 677 (1966).
[61] 44 *Comp. Gen.* 130, 227 (1964).
[62] Eskra *v*. Morton, 524 F. 2d. 9, 13 (1975).

dent) accepting and retaining gifts of "minimal value tendered . . . as a souvenir or mark of courtesy" and accepting gifts of "more than minimal value when it appears that to refuse the gift would be likely to cause offense or embarrassment. . . . However, a gift of more than minimal value is deemed to have been accepted on behalf of the United States and shall be deposited by the donee for use and disposal as property of the United States."[63] The President is delegated the power under the Act of 1967 to prescribe regulations to carry out its purposes. President Johnson delegated that power to the Secretary of State by Executive Order.[64] Undoubtedly, not every gift of more than "minimal value" is turned over to the Government. Clearly, that requirement is most difficult to police.

SECTION X

Restraints on the States

¶1. No State shall enter into any treaty, alliance or confederation; grant letters of marque and reprisal; coin money, emit bills of credit; make anything but gold and silver coin a tender in payment of debts; pass any bill of attainder, *ex post facto* law or law impairing the obligation of contracts, or grant any title of nobility.

Because of the restrictions imposed on them by this paragraph and ¶3 below, as well as those which result from the powers of the National Government, the States of the Union retain only a very limited capacity at International Law and may exercise that only by allowance of Congress.[1]

In an earlier day, the Supreme Court found that on the basis of this provision, the Confederation cannot "be regarded in this Court as having any legal existence."[2]

As the context shows, the kind of "treaty" here referred to is one whose purpose is the setting up of an arrangement of a distinctly political nature. (*See* ¶3, below.)

"Bills of credit" are bills based on the credit of the State. Banks chartered by a State may issue notes of small denomination despite this provision, although, of course, they cannot be given the quality of legal tender; and since 1866 such notes have been subject to such a heavy tax by the United States as to render them unprofitable.[3] (*See* Article I, Section VIII, ¶2.)

In a case of interest in this credit-card era, a Texas court rejected

---

[63] 5 U.S.C. 7342.   [64] *Ibid.*

---

[1] Zschernig v. Miller, 389 U.S. 429 (1968); Chief Justice Taney's opinion in Holmes v. Jennison, 14 Pet. 540 (1841); Skiriotes v. Fla., 313 U.S. 69 (1941); United States v. Calif., 332 U.S. 19 (1947).

[2] Williams v. Bruffy, 96 U.S. 176, 182 (1878).

[3] Briscoe v. Bank of Ky., 11 Pet. 257 (1837); Veazie Bank v. Fenno, 8 Wall. 533 (1869). Although States are denied the power to make anything but gold and silver legal tender, Congress "is free of the constitutional restriction imposed upon the States." Rush v. Casco Bank & Trust Company, 348 A. 2d. 237 (1975). *See also* Allen v. Craig, 564 P. 2d. 552 (1977).

the appellant's argument that credit restrictions in a private club set by the Texas Liquor Control Board which did not permit guests to pay in cash put the State of Texas "in a position of prohibiting a club from accepting legal tender in contravention of [this provision of the Constitution and the Federal Code]."[4]

A "law impairing the obligation of contracts" is a law materially weakening the commitments of one of the parties thereto, or making its enforcement unduly difficult, as by the repeal of essential supporting legislation.[5]

"The Obligation of Contracts" Clause

The clause was framed primarily for the purpose of preventing the States from passing laws to relieve debtors of their legal obligation to pay their debts, the power to afford such relief having been transferred to the National Government[6] (*see* Section VIII, ¶4). Later, the Supreme Court under Chief Justice Marshall, in an effort to offset the narrow construction given the ban on *ex post facto* legislation in Calder *v.* Bull (*see* p. 129 above), extended the protection of the clause first to public grants of land; then to exemptions from taxation; then, in the celebrated *Dartmouth College* case, to charters of corporations.[7]

Yet even with this extension the clause nowadays no longer interferes seriously with the power of the States to protect the public health, safety, and morals, or even that larger interest which is called the "general welfare," for the simple reason that a State has no right to bargain away this power.[8] Moreover, "nothing passes by implication in public grants," which are accordingly construed in favor of the State whenever possible.[9] Thus the mere fact that a corporation has a charter enabling it to manufacture intoxicating beverages will not protect it from the operation of a prohibition enactment.[10] Similarly, a contract between two persons by which they agree to buy and sell intoxicating beverages would be immediately cancelled by a prohibition law going into effect.[11] And in modern times the Court has relaxed its standards in cases affecting private contracts. In the *Minnesota Moratorium* case, the Court held that a State could, in the midst of an industrial depression, enable debtors to postpone meeting their obligations for a "reasonable" period.[12]

[4] Attic Club Inc. *v.* Texas Liquor Control Board, 450 S.W. 2d. 149, 153 (1970).

[5] Home Building and Loan Asso. *v.* Blaisdell, 290 U.S. 398, 431, 435 (1934); Von Hoffman *v.* Quincy, 4 Wall. 535, 552 (1867).

[6] Sturges *v.* Crowninshield, 4 Wheat. 122 (1819).

[7] Fletcher *v.* Peck, 6 Cranch 87 (1810); New Jersey *v.* Wilson, 7 Cranch 164 (1812); Dartmouth College *v.* Woodward, 4 Wheat. 518 (1819); U.S. Trust Co. of New York *v.* New Jersey, 431 U.S. 1, 17 (1977).

[8] Stone *v.* Miss., 101 U.S. 814 (1879); Levine *v.* L.I.R.R. Co., 331 N.Y.S. 2d. 451 (1972). *But see* People *v.* Northwestern U., 281 N.E. 2d. 334 (1972).

[9] Charles River Bridge Co. *v.* Warren Bridge Co., 11 Pet. 420, 545-554 (1837); Blair *v.* Chicago, 201 U.S. 400 (1906).

[10] Boston Beer Co. *v.* Mass., 97 U.S. 25 (1877).

[11] Manigault *v.* Springs, 199 U.S. 473 (1905).

[12] 290 U.S. 398 (1934). *Cf.* Bronson *v.* Kinzie, 1 How. 311 (1843); McCracken *v.* Hayward, 2 How. 608 (1844).

The   Generally speaking, the protection afforded by this clause does
"Police   not today go much, if at all, beyond that afforded by Section I of
Power"   the Fourteenth Amendment. In the words of the Court: "It is settled that neither the 'contract' clause nor the 'due process' clause
has the effect of overriding the power of the State to establish all
regulations that are reasonably necessary to secure the health,
safety, good order, comfort, or general welfare of the community"[13]—in short, its police power. And what *is* reasonably
necessary" for these purposes is today a question ultimately for the
Supreme Court; and the present disposition of the Court is to put
the burden of proof upon any person who challenges State action
as *not* "reasonably necessary."[14]

Until after the Civil War, the "obligation of contracts" clause was
the principal source of cases challenging the validity of State legislation. Today the clause is much less important. But as a 1977 Supreme Court decision makes plain, it would be premature to issue
the clause's death certificate. Justice Blackmun described the issue
this way: "The case presents a challenge to a New Jersey statute . . .
as violative of the Contract Clause. . . . That statute, together with a
concurrent and parallel New York statute . . . repealed a statutory
covenant made by the two States in 1962 that had limited the ability
of The Port Authority of New York and New Jersey to subsidize
rail passenger transportation from revenues and reserves."[15] The
Court held that the contract clause "prohibits the retroactive repeal
of the 1962 covenant." The Court reasoned that the clause "is not
an absolute bar to subsequent modification of a State's own financial obligations. As with laws impairing the obligations of private
contracts, an impairment may be constitutional if it is reasonable
and necessary to serve an important public purpose. In applying
this standard, however, complete deference to a legislative assessment of reasonableness and necessity is not appropriate because
the State's self-interest is at stake." And the Court went on to say
that on the facts of the case "we cannot conclude that the repeal was reasonable in the light of changed circumstances."

The vitality of the contract clause has been further demonstrated
by a host of lower court decisions in recent years. The Wisconsin
Supreme Court held that enforcement of a statute that required

[13] Atlantic Coast Line Co. *v.* Goldsboro, 232 U.S. 548 (1914); Totten *v.* Saionz,
327 N.Y.S. 2d. 55 (1971); Schmidt *v.* Masters, 490 P. 2d. 1029 (1971). *But see* Opinion of the Justices, 283 A. 2d. 832 (1971).

[14] El Paso *v.* Simmons, 379 U.S. 497, 508 (1965); Thorpe *v.* Housing Authority,
393 U.S. 268, 280 (1969). *See also* Helvering *v.* Northwest Steel Rolling Mills, 311
U.S. 46 (1940); and Gelfert *v.* National City Bk., 313 U.S. 221 (1941). In Higgin-
botham *v.* Baton Rouge, 306 U.S. 535 (1939), it was held that the "obligation of contracts" clause does not protect a right to office. The same result had been reached
nearly a century earlier in Butler *v.* Pa., 10 How. 402 (1851). For a statistical survey
of the rise and decline of the obligation clause as a restraint on State power, *see* Benjamin F. Wright's *Contract Clause of the Constitution* (Cambridge, Mass., 1938), ch. IV.

[15] United States Trust Co. of New York *v.* New Jersey, 431 U.S. 1, 3 (1977).

landlords to pass on to tenants property tax relief was an unconstitutional impairment of obligation of contract if the landlord was
forced to collect less rent than a lease called for.[16] The Supreme
Judicial Court of Massachusetts ruled that the State legislature
could not authorize the city of Revere to use for school purposes
land it received as a gift with the condition it would be used as a
public park.[17] Several other decisions held (1) that a Youngstown,
Ohio, Civil Service Commission rule requiring residency of ten-
ured civil service employees applied to those in the service before
the rule was adopted was unconstitutional (because it impaired the
obligation of contracts);[18] (2) that proposed legislation that would
raise the contribution of government (State) employees to a government retirement plan without any increase in benefits would be
invalid as an impairment of contract;[19] and (3) that a State statute
giving counties the opportunity to purchase State lands that had
been leased to private parties with option to buy was an unconstitutional impairment.[20] In contrast, a New York State court decided
that a statute eliminating a *public* employee's obligation to bargain
collectively over retirement benefits in the face of a previous
agreement that allowed for it was constitutional,[21] and a Federal
district court found that an amendment to the Massachusetts Constitution requiring State judges to retire at 70 was not an unconstitutional impairment of contract even as applied to judges already
on the bench.[22] Also a U.S. district court upheld the New York no-
fault law, which required automatic renewal of most auto insurance
policies, saying "the public need for these extensions had been sufficiently demonstrated. Regulation of the insurance industry, in
order to provide adequate protection of the public, is surely a
proper subject for the state's exercise of its police power."[23] Predictably, the seeking of remedies for New York City's financial
woes raised contract clause problems.[24]

Other noteworthy contract clause decisions made the following
points: (1) that the marriage relationship was "something other
than a constitutionally protected contract";[25] (2) that "the impairment of contracts is not violated by a *judicial* determination";[26] (3)

[16] State *ex rel.* Building Owners, Etc. *v.* Adarnany, 219 N.W. 2d. 274 (1974).
[17] Opinion of the Justices to the Senate, 338 N.E. 2d. 806 (1975).
[18] Fraternal Order of Police, Etc. *v.* Hunter, 303 N.E. 2d. 103 (1973).
[19] Commonwealth *v.* Gilchrest, 303 N.E. 2d. 331 (1973); Miller *v.* State, 557 P. 2d.
970 (1977); *cf.* Miles *v.* The Tennessee Consolidated Retirement System, 548 S.W.
2d. 299 (1977).
[20] Aerojet-General Corp. *v.* Askew, 366 F.Supp. 901 (1973).
[21] Security Unit Employees, Etc. *v.* Rockefeller, 351 N.Y.S. 2d. 348 (1974).
[22] Kingston *v.* McLaughlin, 359 F.Supp. 25 (1972).
[23] County-Wide Ins. Co. *v.* Hartnett, 426 F.Supp. 1030 (1977); Guest *v.* Fitzpatrick, 409 F.Supp. 818 (1976).
[24] Flushing Nat. Bank *v.* Mun. Ass't. Corp., 379 N.Y.S. 2d. 978 (1975), and 358
N.E. 2d. (1976); Quirk *v.* Mun. Ass't. Corp., 363 N.E. 2d. 549 (1977).
[25] Flora *v.* Flora, 337 N.E. 2d. 846 (1975).
[26] Mariniello *v.* Shell Oil Company, 511 F. 2d. 853 (1975).

that the contract clause only lies against States and not the United States.[27]

¶2. No State shall, without the consent of Congress, lay any imposts or duties on imports or exports, except what may be absolutely necessary for executing its inspection laws; and the net produce of all duties and imposts, laid by any State on imports or exports, shall be for the use of the Treasury of the United States; and all such laws shall be subject to the revision and control of the Congress.

"Imports" and "exports" refer only to goods brought from or destined to foreign countries.[28] For a long time in our history, all taxes on imports still in the original package and in the hands of the importer were prohibited by this clause.[29] But in 1959 the Court upheld particular State *ad valorem* taxes, on imported ores and bundles of veneers in their "original packages" because, the Court said, "Breaking the original package is only one of the ways by which packaged goods that have been imported for use in manufacturing may lose their distinctive character as imports. Another way is by putting them 'to the use for which they were imported.' "[30]

More recently, the Supreme Court affirmed a decision of the Georgia Supreme Court that held that in the particular circumstances of the case a Georgia *ad valorem* tax on imported tires was constitutional.[31] After a long and careful review of the Framers' intent, the Court concluded that "Nothing in the history of the Import-Export Clause even remotely suggests that a nondiscriminatory ad valorem property tax which is also imposed on imported goods that are no longer in import transit was the type of exaction that was regarded objectionable by the Framers of the Constitution." As to the particular facts of this case, the Court stated that "Petitioner's tires in this case were no longer in transit. They were stored in a distribution warehouse from which petitioner operated a wholesale operation, taking orders from fran-

[27] Jackson Sawmill Co. *v*. United States, 428 F.Supp. 555 (1977).

[28] Woodruff *v*. Parham, 8 Wall. 123 (1868); Sonneborn Bros. *v*. Cureton, 262 U.S. 506 (1923). *Cf.* however, Baldwin *v*. Seelig, 294 U.S. 511 (1935), where a different view was advanced, but quite unnecessarily for the decision of the case, and probably inadvertently.

[29] Brown *v*. Md., 12 Wheat. 419 (1827). Hooven & Allison Co. *v*. Evatt, 324 U.S. 652 (1945).

[30] Youngstown *v*. Bowers, 358 U.S. 534, 549 (1959); American Smelting & Refin. Co. *v*. County of Contra Costa, 77 Cal. Rptr. 570 (1969); *appeal dismissed*, 396 U.S. 273 (1970); Nestle Co. *v*. Porterfield, 277 N.E. 2d. 222 (1971); Halo Sales Corp. *v*. City and County of San Francisco, 98 Cal. Rptr. 473 (1971); Detroit *v*. Klockener, 173 N.W. 2d. 214 (1970); Thyssen Steel Corp. *v*. Mich. Tax Com'n, 196 N.W. 2d. 325 (1972); Volkswagen Pacific Inc. *v*. Los Angeles, 496 P. 2d. 1237 (1972); *in re* Asheville Citizen-Times Pub. Co., 188 S.E. 2d. 310 (1972); Citroen Cars Corp *v*. City of N.Y., 283 N.E. 2d. 758 (1972).

[31] Michelin Tire Corp. *v*. Wages, 423 U.S. 276 (1976).

chised dealers and filling them from a constantly replenished inventory. The warehouse was operated no differently than would a distribution warehouse utilized by a wholesaler dealing solely in domestic goods, and we therefore hold that the nondiscriminatory property tax levied on petitioner's inventory of imported tires was not interdicted by the Import-Export Clause of the Constitution." The Court had reasoned earlier in the opinion that "such taxation is the *quid pro quo* for benefits actually conferred by the taxing state. There is no reason why local taxpayers should subsidize the services used by the importer; ultimate consumers should pay for such services as police and fire protection accorded the goods just as much as they should pay transportation costs associated with those goods."

Significantly, a Texas court held that "Merchandise brought into one of the United States from Puerto Rico would be 'imports' under the Export-Import Clause of the U.S. Constitution and entitled to the immunity from taxation as goods from a foreign country."[32] The court observed that it did not believe that "Puerto Rico is a part of the United States in the sense that it is subject to and enjoys the benefits or protection of the Constitution as do the States which are united under the Constitution."

State courts have been endeavoring to determine precisely *when* imported goods are actually being put to the "use for which they were imported" and can be legitimately taxed by the States. The trouble comes in deciding what part of an inventory can be said to have been put to use. For that purpose a phrase and a formula has found favor with State jurists. The phrase is "current operational needs" and the formula is: "current operational needs" of a company equals the number of days the company needs to replenish its stock, multiplied by the daily average of the amount of stock used.[33]

The practice of shippers palletizing shipments of goods has created headaches for State tax collectors and judges. What is the "original package" of palletized items? One State court held that, on the facts in a particular case, "the entire shipment is not the 'original package' and that the original package has not been broken by selling any one package or pallet out of the shipment." Citing other decisions, the court concluded that "the sorting and stockpiling of imported items in preparation for sale does not, by itself, cause the goods to lose their exempt status."[34]

Regarding the taxing of exports, the Supreme Court a few years ago decided a case involving a challenge of the National Cash Register Company of a State property tax assessment on cash registers and other machines built to specifications of foreign buyers and

[32] City of Farmers Branch *v.* Matushita Elec. Corp., 527 S.W. 2d. 768 (1975).

[33] Production Steel Strip Corp. *v.* City of Detroit, 202 N.W. 2d. 719 (1972) and cases cited therein.

[34] Wilson *v.* County of Wake, 199 S.E. 2d. 665 (1973).

awaiting shipment. The grounds were that since the machines could only be used abroad they were clearly "exports" within the meaning of this article. The Supreme Court held otherwise.[35] Speaking for the Court, Justice Stewart said: "The basic principle of *Coe v. Errol* is a simple one—the exemption from taxation in the Import-Export Clause 'attaches to the export and not to the article before its exportation.' This Court has adhered to that principle in the almost 90 years since *Coe* was decided, and the essential problem in cases involving the constitutional prohibition against taxation of exports has therefore been to decide whether a sufficient commencement of the process of exportation has occurred so as to immunize the article at issue from state taxation. Of necessity the inquiry has usually been a factual one."

¶3. No State shall, without the consent of Congress, lay any duty of tonnage, keep troops or ships of war in time of peace, enter into any agreement or compact with another State or with a foreign power, or engage in war, unless actually invaded or in such imminent danger as will not admit of delay.

The full possibilities of securing cooperation among States by means of "agreement or compact" sanctioned by Congress have only begun to be realized within the last forty-five years.[36] In 1834 New York and New Jersey entered into such a compact "for fixing and determining the rights and obligations of the two States in and about the waters" between them; and in 1921, by a further agreement, they created the "Port of New York District" and established the "Port of New York Authority," which is "a body both corporate and politic," for the comprehensive development of the port. Two years later Congress was asked to sanction an agreement among seven western States which had for its purpose the reclamation of a vast stretch of arid land in the great Colorado River basin. Then in May, 1934, seven northeastern States signed a compact looking to the establishment within their respective jurisdictions of minimum wages for women and minors; while by an act passed June 6 of the same year, Congress gave its consent in general terms "to any two or more States to enter into agreements or compacts for cooperative effort and mutual assistance in the prevention of crime and in the enforcement of their criminal laws and policies."[37] Subsequently Congress authorized, on varying conditions, compacts touching the produc-

[35] Kosydar *v.* Nat'l Cash Register Co., 417 U.S. 62, 67 (1973). A Louisiana court later held that the exemption from State taxes applies where there is certainty that the goods are headed to sea and that the process of exportation has started but in the end the evidence must support "an invincible claim to the exemption." Ortiz *v.* Agerton, 329 So. 2d. 238 (1976).

[36] Richard H. Leach and Redding S. Sugg, Jr., *The Administration of Interstate Compacts* (Baton Rouge, 1959); W. Brooke Graves, *American Intergovernmental Relations* (New York, 1964), ch. XVII.

[37] 48 *Stat.* 909 (1934).

tion of tobacco, the conservation of natural gas, the regulation of fishing in inland waters, the furtherance of flood and pollution control, and other matters.[38] Moreover, since 1935 all the states, beginning with New Jersey, have set up permanent commissions for interstate cooperation, which have led to the formation of a Council of State Governments ("Cosgo" for short), the creation of special commissions for the study of the crime problem, the problem of highway safety, the trailer problem, problems created by social security legislation, etc., and the framing of uniform State legislation for dealing with some of these.

One of a series of such statutes drawn up in 1935 gives State officers in "fresh pursuit" of a criminal the right to ignore State lines; another expedites the process of interstate extradition (*see* Article IV, Section II, ¶2); while a third provides for the extradition of material witnesses. Many States have already adopted all these measures. The interstate compact device, supplemented by commissions on interstate cooperation and by uniform legislation, is today producing cooperation among the States on a grand scale even if it has not fulfilled all of its promise.[39]

The question arises whether the assent of Congress is constitutionally essential to any and all agreements among two or more States. Apparently Chief Justice Taney thought so in 1840;[40] but a half century later the Court indicated the opinion that such assent was not required to agreements having no tendency to increase the political powers of the States or to encroach on the just supremacy of the National Government.[41]

As to what form and to what timing Congress must adhere, the Supreme Court has been most permissive: "Congress may give its approval after the fact or permit the States wide discretion in implementing details, and its approval may even be inferred by circumstance."[42] This permissiveness is indicated in the observation of two highly regarded experts in the field that "Congress plays a merely formal role with regard to most compacts, however, simply granting its consent to compacts already drawn and agreed to by the party states. As a matter of fact, some compacts have gone into effect without benefit of consent legislation passed by Congress."[43]

From a comparatively early date the National Government has systematically entered into compacts with newly admitted States whereby, in return for a grant of lands for educational purposes, and other concessions, such States have pledged themselves to re-

Federal Grants-in-Aid: Social Security

---

[38] 7 U.S.C. 515; 15 U.S.C. 717j; 16 U.S.C. 552 and 667a; 33 U.S.C. 11 and 567-567b.

[39] Leach and Sugg, *Interstate Compacts.*

[40] *See* his opinion in Holmes *v.* Jennison, 14 Pet. 540, 570-572 (1840).

[41] Virginia *v.* Tenn., 148 U.S. 503, 518 (1893).

[42] Virginia *v.* Tenn., 148 U.S. 503 (1893); Virginia *v.* West Virginia, 11 Wall. 39 (1871); Wharton *v.* Wise, 153 U.S. 155 (1894); Deveau *v.* Braisted, 363 U.S. 144 (1960).

[43] Leach and Sugg, *Interstate Compacts,* pp. 15-16.

frain from taxing for a term of years lands sold by the National Government to settlers.[44] And since 1911, through so-called "Federal Grants-in-Aid," a quasi-contractual relationship between the National Government and the States has developed on a much more extensive scale. Thus Congress has voted money to subsidize forest protection, education in agricultural and industrial subjects and in home economics, vocational rehabilitation and education, the maintenance of nautical schools, experimentation in reforestation, highway construction, etc., in the States; in return for which cooperating States have appropriated equal sums for the same purposes, and have brought their further powers to the support thereof along lines laid down by Congress.[45] The Social Security Act of August 14, 1935, is illustrative of this type of National-State cooperation. It brought the national taxing-spending power to the support of such States as desired to cooperate in the maintenance of old-age pensions, unemployment insurance, maternal welfare work, vocational rehabilitation, and public health work, and in financial assistance to the impoverished aged, dependent children, and the blind. Such legislation is, as we have seen, within the national taxing-spending power (*see* p. 43) but what of the objection that it "coerces" complying States into "abdicating" their powers? Speaking to this point in the Social Security Act cases, the Court said: "The . . . contention confuses motive with coercion. . . . To hold that motive or temptation is equivalent to coercion is to plunge the law in endless difficulties." And again: "The United States and the state of Alabama are not alien governments. They coexist within the same territory. Unemployment is their common concern. Together the two statutes before us [the Act of Congress and the Alabama Act] embody a cooperative legislative effort by State and National Governments, for carrying out a public purpose common to both, which neither could fully achieve without the cooperation of the other. The Constitution does not prohibit such cooperation."[46]

In short, expansion of national power within recent years has been matched by *increased* governmental activity on the part of the States also, sometimes in cooperation with each other, sometimes in cooperation with the National Government, sometimes in cooperation with both.

In entering upon a compact to which Congress has given its consent a State accepts obligations of a legal character which the Court and/or Congress possess ample powers to enforce.[47] Nor will it

[44] Stearns *v.* Minn., 179 U.S. 223 (1900).

[45] U.S., Advisory Commission on Intergovernmental Relations, *Fiscal Balance in the American Federal System* (Washington, D.C., 1967), ch. V.

[46] Steward Mach. Co. *v.* Davis, 301 U.S. 548 (1937); Carmichael *v.* So. Coal and Coke Co., 301 U.S. 495, 526 (1937).

[47] Virginia *v.* West Virginia, 246 U.S. 565 (1918). United States *v.* Groomes, 520 F. 2d. 830 (1975).

avail a State to endeavor to read itself out of its obligations by pleading that it had no constitutional power to enter upon such an arrangement and has none to fulfill its duties thereunder.[48]

A 1976 Supreme Court decision and its aftermath provided further instruction about the meaning of the compact clause. The State of New Hampshire contended that a proposed consent decree in a boundary dispute between New Hampshire and Maine, a decree that invoked a 1740 decree fixing the boundary, should not be accepted "without an independent determination by the Court as to the legal principles on which it is based." To do so, New Hampshire contended, "would be a circumvention of the Compact Clause." The Supreme Court held that "The premise of this argument is that the proposed settlement is an 'Agreement or Compact' within the meaning of the Clause and thus requires the consent of Congress to be effective. We disagree."[49] Harking back to Virgina *v.* Tennessee (*see* p. 145), the Court said that "Whether a particular agreement respecting boundaries is within the Clause will depend on whether 'the establishment of the boundary line may lead or not to the increase of the political power or influence of the states affected.' " The Court concluded that the proposed consent decree fell outside the compact clause because the 1740 decree fixed the boundary and that the "consent decree is directed simply to locating precisely this already existing boundary." Later, when the New Hampshire legislature attempted to modify the consent decree, the New Hampshire Supreme Court chided the legislature saying that our system of government "cannot tolerate attempts by states to annul the judgments of the Supreme Court."[50]

With respect to an unusual claim made under the clause, a Federal district court held that New Jersey and Pennsylvania had waived their sovereign immunity under the Eleventh Amendment with respect to suits against the Delaware River Port Authority, when they entered into an interstate compact sanctioned by Congress. The Court emphasized that the compact contained a "sue and be sued" clause.[51]

[48] West Virginia *v.* Sims, 341 U.S. 22 (1951).
[49] New Hampshire *v.* Maine, 426 U.S. 363 (1976).
[50] Opinion of the Justices, 373 A. 2d. 647 (1977).
[51] Yancoskie *v.* Delaware River Port Authority, 385 F.Supp. 1170 (1974).

ARTICLE II

This article makes provision for the executive power of the United States, which it vests in a single individual, the President.

SECTION I

¶1. The executive power shall be vested in a President of the United States of America. He shall hold his office during the term of four years, and together with the Vice-President, chosen for the same term, be elected as follows:

"Executive Power" What, precisely, does the opening clause of this paragraph do? Does it confer on the President his power, or merely his title? If the former, then the remaining provisions of this article exist only to emphasize or to qualify "the executive power," as, for instance, where they provide for the participation of the Senate in the appointing and treaty-making powers. If the latter, then the President has only such powers as are conferred on him in more specific terms by these same remaining provisions.

The question is one which has been debated from the adoption of the Constitution. The first occasion was in 1789, when Congress, in the absence of a specific constitutional provision regarding the power of removal, conceded the power in the case of the heads of the executive departments to the President alone.[1] Then in 1793 Hamilton and Madison renewed the debate with reference to Washington's Neutrality Proclamation of that year. No provision either of the Constitution or of an act of Congress gave the President the power to issue such a proclamation, but Hamilton defended it, nevertheless, as within the "executive power"; while Madison, reversing his position in the debate of four years earlier, urged the opposed view.[2]

Today the honors of war rest distinctly with the "power" theory of the clause. Especially is this so when one consults the views and practices of some incumbents of the Presidency. The first Roosevelt classified all Presidents as of either the Buchanan or the Lincoln type. Mr. Taft was a Buchanan President, sticking as close as bark to a tree to the letter of the Constitution and the statutes in interpreting his powers. T. R., on the other hand, was the Lincoln type, taking the position that the President was a "steward of the people," and as such entrusted with the duty of doing "anything that the needs of the Nation demanded unless such action was forbidden by the Constitution and the laws."[3] Although in his book on the Presidency *Professor* Taft denounced this view as making the

[1] Edward S. Corwin, *The President's Removal Power* (New York, 1927), 10-23.
[2] Corwin, *The President, Office and Powers*, 179-181.
[3] Theodore Roosevelt, *Autobiography* (New York, 1913), 388-389.

President "a universal Providence,"[4] *Chief Justice* Taft in his opinion for the Court in the Oregon Postmaster case supplied the constitutional basis for it when he invoked the opening clause of Article II.[5] For the second Roosevelt's conception of his powers one turns not to the "stewardship theory," but the Stuart theory, which is summed up by John Locke in his second *Treatise on Civil Government* in his description of "Prerogative" as "the power to act according to discretion for the public good, without the prescription of the law and sometimes even against it." Mr. Roosevelt's incumbency was marked by a succession of emergencies, and in meeting them he did not always keep to the path of constitutional or legal prescription. In handing over to Great Britain in the late summer of 1940 fifty reconditioned naval craft the President violated several statutes and appropriated to himself temporarily Congress's power to "dispose of property of the United States" (*see* Article IV, Section III).[6] Yet that this was done with the general approval of the American people there can be no reasonable doubt—thus confirming Locke's further remark that "the people are very seldom or never scrupulous or nice in the point of questioning the prerogative whilst it is in any tolerable degree employed for the use it was meant—that is, the good of the people and not manifestly against it." It is true that the Court's decision in the *Steel Seizure* case has been interpreted by some as marking a definite setback for strong theories of Presidential power, but this diagnosis hardly survives examination of the opinions of the Justices accompanying the case. (*See* pp. 199-200 below.)

The President's term of four years, prior to the adoption of the Twentieth, Norris "Lame Duck," Amendment, began on March 4 of the year following each leap-year. This happened for two reasons. In the first place, the old Congress of the Confederation set the first Wednesday in March 1789, which chanced to be March 4, as the date on which the Constitution should go into effect. Actually Washington did not take the oath of office until April 30 of that year. Nevertheless, disregarding this fact, the first Congress, by an act which Washington himself approved on March 1, 1792, provided that "the term of four years for which a President and Vice-President shall be elected, shall, in all cases, commence on the fourth day of March next succeeding the day on which the votes of the election shall have been given." Thus Washington's first term was in effect, if not technically, shortened by act of Congress nearly two months; while that of President F. D. Roosevelt was similarly curtailed by the going into effect of the Twentieth Amendment.

The
President's
Term

Although the original Constitution made no provision regarding the re-election of a President, there can be no doubt that the pre-

[4] William H. Taft, *Our Chief Magistrate and His Powers* (New York, 1916), 114.
[5] Myers *v.* U.S., 272 U.S. 52 (1926).
[6] *See* Edward S. Corwin, *New York Times*, Oct. 13, 1940.

vailing sentiment of the Philadelphia Convention favored his indefinite reeligibility. It was Jefferson (who was not at the Convention) who raised the objection that indefinite eligibility would in fact be for life and degenerate into an inheritance. Prior to 1940 the idea that no President should hold for more than two terms was generally thought to be a fixed tradition, although some quibbles had been raised as to the meaning of the word "term." President Roosevelt's violation of the tradition led to the proposal by Congress on March 24, 1947, of an amendment to the Constitution to rescue the tradition by embodying it in the Constitutional Document. The proposal became a part of the Constitution on February 27, 1951, in consequence of its adoption by the necessary thirty-sixth State, which was Minnesota.[7]

The "Electoral College"   ¶2. Each State shall appoint, in such manner as the legislature thereof may direct, a number of electors, equal to the whole number of Senators and Representatives to which the State may be entitled in the Congress; but no Senator or Representative, or person holding an office of trust or profit under the United States, shall be appointed an elector.

This and the following paragraph provide for the so-called "Electoral College," or Colleges. It was supposed that the members of these bodies would exercise their individual judgments in their choice of a President and Vice-President, but since 1796 the Electors have been no more than party dummies.

The word "appoint" in this section is used, the Court has said, "as conveying the broadest power of determination." Electors have consequently been chosen, first and last, in the most diverse ways: "by the legislature itself on joint ballot; by the legislature through a concurrent vote of the two houses; by vote of the people for a general ticket; by vote of the people in districts; by choice partly by the people in districts and partly by the legislature; by choice by the legislature from candidates voted for by the people; and in other ways. . . ."[8]

Although Madison testified that the district system was the one contemplated by the Framers, Electors are today universally chosen by popular vote on State-wide tickets. The result is that the successful candidate may have considerably less than a majority, or even than a plurality, of the popular vote cast. Thus, suppose that New York and Pennsylvania were the only two States in the Union, and that New York with forty-one electoral votes went Democratic by a narrow margin, while Pennsylvania with twenty-seven electoral votes and with a somewhat smaller population than New York went overwhelmingly Republican. The Democratic candidate

[7] On the anti-third term tradition, see Corwin, The President, Office and Powers, 34-38, 331-334.
[8] McPherson v.Blacker, 146 U.S. 1, 27, 29 (1892).

would be elected, although the Republican candidate would have the larger popular vote.

In fact, both Lincoln in 1860 and Wilson in 1912, while carrying much less than a majority of the popular vote in the country at large, had sweeping majorities in the "Electoral College." This was because the defeated party was split in those particular elections. Should, however, a strong third party arise which drew about equally from the two old-line parties, the probable result would be to throw successive elections into the House of Representatives, where the constitutional method of choice would give Nevada equal weight with New York in choosing from the persons, "not exceeding three," having the highest votes in the College. (*See* Amendment XII, p. 452 below.) For this reason, and some others, Senator Norris urged an amendment to the Constitution abolishing the College and requiring that the electoral vote of each State be divided among its principal parties in proportion to their strength at the polls; and early in 1949 the Senate adopted such a proposal, which, however, was rejected by the House.[9]

"Minority Presidents"

The elections of 1948, 1960, and 1968 have served to feed the fears of a Presidential election being decided by the House. In those elections Presidents Truman, Kennedy, and Nixon failed to receive a majority of the votes cast even though they ended up with substantial majorities in the Electoral College. In 1969 the House passed a resolution for a proposed constitutional amendment to abolish the Electoral College. After a great deal of fireworks, the proposal died a victim of filibusters by Southern and small-State Senators.[10] But Electoral College reform is a hardy perennial. In 1977 Congress was still contemplating what to do about it.[11]

Although the Court has characterized Electors as "State officers,"[12] the truth of the matter is that they are not "officers" at all, by the usual tests of office.[13] They have neither tenure nor salary and, having performed their single function, they cease to exist as Electors. This function is, moreover, "a federal function,"[14] their capacity to perform which results from no power which was originally resident in the States, but springs directly from the Constitution of the United States.[15] In the face, therefore, of the proposition that Electors are State officers, the Court has upheld the power of Con-

---

[9] S. J. Res. 2, 81st Cong., 1st Sess., was introduced by Senator Lodge and others, legislative day January 4, 1949, and passed February 1 (same legislative day); reported to the House, March 29, 1950; rejected July 17, 1950. *See* Lucius Wilmerding, Jr. on "Reforming the Electoral System," 64 *Political Science Quarterly*, 1 (1949), for well-documented criticism of the proposal; *also* 32 *Congressional Digest*, Nos. 8-9 (1953).

[10] 1969 *Cong. Quart. Almanac* 895-901; 1970 *Cong. Quart. Almanac* 840-845.

[11] 1977 *Cong. Quart Weekly Report* 1295.

[12] *In re* Green, 134 U.S. 377, 379-380 (1890).

[13] United States *v.* Hartwell, 6 Wall. 385, 393 (1868).

[14] Hawke *v.* Smith, 253 U.S. 221 (1920).

[15] Burroughs *v.* U.S., 290 U.S. 534, 545 (1934).

gress to protect the right of all citizens who are entitled to vote to lend aid and support in any legal manner to the election of any legally qualified person as a Presidential Elector;[16] and its power to protect the choice of Electors from fraud or corruption. "If this government," said the Court, "is anything more than a mere aggregation of delegated agents of other States and governments, each of which is superior to the general government, it must have the power to protect the elections on which its existence depends from violence and corruption. If it has not this power it is left helpless before the two great natural and historical enemies of all republics, open violence and insidious corruption."[17] The conception of Electors as State officers is still, nevertheless, of some importance, as was shown in the case of Ray v. Blair,[18] which is dealt with in connection with Amendment XII.

To recent predictable challenges that the Electoral College was a "variation" from the "one man-one vote" criterion, the courts have not been sympathetic. As one district court put it: "Obviously, it cannot be questioned constitutionally since the Electoral College is established in the Constitution." The court went on to liken the situation constitutionally to that of the Senate where each state "has two senators irrespective of population."[19]

In recent years there have been a number of lower court cases involving the States' power to pass laws regulating the selection of Electors. Generally, the decisions have affirmed the States' power with the proviso set forth in one U.S. district court decision that in doing so they could not impose burdens on the right to vote, "where such burdens are expressly prohibited in other Constitutional provisions."[20]

---

[16] *Ex Parte* Yarbrough, 110 U.S. 651 (1884). *See* the interesting decision of the Alabama Supreme Court, Opinion of the Justices, 217 So. 2d. 53 (1968).

[17] Burroughs v. U.S., 290 U.S. 534, 546 (1934).

[18] 343 U.S. 214 (1952). During World War II Congress laid claim in the Act of September 16, 1942, to the power "in time of war" to secure to every member of the Armed Forces the right to vote for Members of Congress and Presidential Electors, notwithstanding any provisions of State law relating to the registration of qualified voters or any poll tax requirement under State law. The constitutional validity of this act at that time was open to serious question and by the Act of April 1, 1944, was abandoned. The latter act established a War Ballot Commission, which was directed to prepare an adequate number of official war ballots, whereby the servicemen would be enabled in certain contingencies to vote for Members of Congress and Presidential Electors; but the validity of such ballots was left to be determined by State election officials under State laws. 58 *Stat.* 140, 146 (1944). All of which is, perhaps, a point in favor of the "State officer" idea. In an act passed in 1956, a serviceman, "notwithstanding any State law relating to the registration of voters," absent from his home in time of war was entitled to vote for Electors if he was eligible to register and vote except for his absence. He was in that situation exempted from any requirement to pay a poll tax, 70 A *Stat.* 82 (1956). Curiously, these provisions were repealed in 1958, 72 *Stat.* 1570.

[19] Irish v. Democratic-Farm-Labor Party of Minnesota, 287 F.Supp. 794 (1968); *affirmed* 399 F. 2d. 119 (1968); Williams v. Virginia State Board, 288 F.Supp. 622 (1968).

[20] Raza Unida Party v. Bullock, 349 F.Supp. 1272 (1972); McClendon v. Slater,

When the Ripon Society challenged the formula used by the Republican Party for allocating delegates to the national convention as constituting a denial of equal protection, a U.S. court of appeals suggested that "the justification for electoral college apportionment carries within it much of the justification" for the formula used in allocating delegates, since 72 per cent are allocated according to the Electoral College vote of the States.[21] As the court pointed out in earlier decisions, it had upheld the parties' practice of apportioning delegates according to Electoral College strength. As to giving a "bonus" to states that had turned in Republican victories, the court felt that it served the purpose of improving the party's chances for victory. And, as the court saw it: "The Equal Protection Clause, assuming it is applicable, does not require the representation in presidential nominating conventions of some defined constituency on a one person, one vote basis. It is satisfied if the representational scheme and each of its elements rationally advance some legitimate interest of the party in winning elections or otherwise achieving its political goals."

It may come as a surprise that in 1975 a statute still prohibited United States citizens who reside in Puerto Rico from voting for President and Vice-President. Judge Luther Youngdahl, a Federal district judge, held that regrettably the constitutional challenge to the law "is plainly without merit." He pointed out that "the Constitution does not, by its terms grant citizens the right to vote [for President], but leaves the matter entirely to the *States*."[22]

¶3. The electors shall meet in their respective States and vote by ballot for two persons, of whom one at least shall not be an inhabitant of the same State with themselves. And they shall make a list of all the persons voted for, and of the number of votes for each; which list they shall sign and certify, and transmit sealed to the seat of government of the United States, directed to the President of the Senate. The President of the Senate shall, in the presence of the Senate and House of Representatives, open all the certificates, and the votes shall then be counted. The person having the greatest number of votes shall be the President, if such number be a majority of the whole number of electors appointed; and if there be more than one who have such majority, and have an equal number of votes, then the House of Representatives shall immediately choose by ballot one of them for President; and if no person have a majority, then from the five highest on the list the said House shall in like manner choose the President. But in choos-

---

554 P. 2d. 774 (1976); *cf.* McCarthy *v.* Exon, 424 F.Supp. 1143 (1976), and McCarthy *v.* Tribbitt, 421 F.Supp. 1193 (1976).

[21] Ripon Society *v.* National Republican Party, 525 F. 2d. 567 (1975). *Cert. denied,* 96 S. Ct. 1147 (1976).

[22] Sanchez *v.* U.S., 376 F.Supp. 239 (1974).

ing the President the votes shall be taken by States, the representation from each State having one vote; a quorum for this purpose shall consist of a member or members from two-thirds of the States, and a majority of all the States shall be necessary to a choice. In every case, after the choice of the President, the person having the greatest number of votes of the electors shall be the Vice-President. But if there should remain two or more who have equal votes, the Senate shall choose from them by ballot the Vice-President.

This provision was early superseded by Amendment XII.

¶4. The Congress may determine the time of choosing the electors and the day on which they shall give their votes, which day shall be the same throughout the United States.

Under the Act of March 1, 1792, previously mentioned, the Electors are chosen on the Tuesday following the first Monday in November of every fourth year; while by the Act of June 5, 1934, enacted to give effect to the Twentieth Amendment, the Electors of each State meet and give their votes on the first Monday after the second Wednesday in December, following the November election, and the two houses meet to count the votes in the hall of the House of Representatives on the ensuing January 6, at 1 p.m.[23] (*See also* Article I, Section IV, ¶2.)

A question which has plagued us for some time is, what can be done about an Elector who casts his ballot contrary to the choice indicated by the voters? Apparently, under the present arrangement of law and custom, there are no sanctions available other than possible public opprobrium.[24] The courts, however, might well regard the matter differently, if a Presidential contest were decided by defecting Electors. That to date has never happened, although there were some fears that it might in 1968.

¶5. No person except a natural-born citizen, or citizen of the United States at the time of the adoption of this Constitution, shall be eligible to the office of President; neither shall any person be eligible to that office who shall not have attained to the age of thirty-five years, and been fourteen years a resident within the United States.

All Presidents since, and including Martin Van Buren, except his immediate successor, William Henry Harrison, having been born in the United States subsequently to the Declaration of Independence, have been "natural-born" citizens of the United States, the earlier ones having been born subjects of the King of Great Britain. The question, however, has been frequently mooted, whether a

---

[23] 3 U.S.C. 7 and 15.   [24] State *v*. Albritton, 37 So. 2d. 640 (1948).

child born abroad of American parents is "a natural-born citizen" in the sense of this clause. Although the courts have never been called upon to decide the question, there is a substantial body of authoritative opinion supporting the position that they are.[25] It should be borne in mind that the term used is "natural-born" and not "native-born."

Does "fourteen years a resident within the United States" mean residence immediately preceding election to office? This question would seem to have been answered in the negative in the case of President Hoover.

¶6. In case of the removal of the President from office, or of his death, resignation, or inability to discharge the powers and duties of the said office, the same shall devolve on the Vice-President, and the Congress may by law provide for the case of removal, death, resignation, or inability, both of the President and Vice-President, declaring what officer shall then act as President, and such officer shall act accordingly until the disability be removed or a President shall be elected.

This provision has been superseded by Amendment XXV ratified in 1967. Its historical significance is discussed below, pp. 552-555.

¶7. The President shall, at stated times, receive for his services a compensation, which shall neither be increased nor diminished during the period for which he shall have been elected, and he shall not receive within that period any other emolument from the United States or any of them.

Earlier decisions exempting Federal judicial salaries from taxation under a general income tax having been overruled, doubtless the President's salary is subject to the same kind of exaction. A special tax on the President's salary would be void on the face of it.[26] (*See* p. 213 for discussion of "diminished.")

¶8. Before he enter on the execution of his office he shall take the following oath or affirmation:

"I do solemnly swear (or affirm) that I will faithfully execute the office of President of the United States, and will to the best of my ability preserve, protect and defend the Constitution of the United States." The President's Oath of Office

[25] Warren Freedman, "Presidential Timber: Foreign Born Children of American Parents," 35 *Cornell Law Quarterly*, 357 (1950). When George Romney announced his candidacy for the Presidency in 1967, he said the question had been studied by several law firms and there was no question that as the son of Americans he was a "natural born" American even though born in Mexico. *New York Times*, Nov. 19, 1967.

[26] *See* O'Mally v. Woodrough, 307 U.S. 277 (1939), overruling Evans v. Gore, 253 U.S. 245 (1920), and Miles v. Graham, 268 U.S. 501 (1925).

What is the time relationship between a President's assumption of office and his taking the oath? Apparently the former comes first. This answer seems to be required by the language of the clause itself, and is further supported by the fact that, while the act of March 1, 1792, assumes that Washington became President March 4, 1789, he did not take the oath till April 30. Also, in the parallel case of the coronation oath of the British monarch, its taking has been at times postponed for years after the heir's succession.

Why then did President Johnson within recent memory make such haste to take the oath? His answer: "Attorney General Kennedy said he would look into the matter and report to me on whether the oath should be administered immediately or after we returned to Washington. . . . He said [later] that the oath of office should be administered immediately."[27]

The fact that the President takes an oath "to preserve and protect" the Constitution does not authorize him to exceed his own powers under the Constitution on the pretext of preserving and protecting it. The President may veto a bill on the ground that in his opinion it violates the Constitution, but if the bill is passed over his veto, he must, by the great weight of authority, ordinarily regard it as law until it is set aside by judicial decision, since the power of interpreting the law, except as it is delegated by the law itself, is not an attribute of "executive power."[28]

It may be, nevertheless, that in an extreme case the President would be morally justified in defying an act of Congress which he regarded as depriving him of his constitutional powers, until there could be an appeal to the courts or to the people, and in point of fact such defiances have in a few instances occurred.[29]

SECTION II

¶1. The President shall be Commander-in-Chief of the Army and Navy of the United States, and of the militia of the several States when called into the actual service of the United States; he may require the opinion, in writing, of the principal officer in each of the executive departments, upon any subject relating to the duties of their respective offices, and he shall have power to grant reprieves and pardons for offenses against the United States, except in cases of impeachment.

[27] Johnson, *Vantage Point*, p. 13.

[28] For an illustration of Presidential interpretation of the Constitution that did not "come off," *see* the final draft of Jefferson's message to Congress of December 8, 1801. A. J. Beveridge, *Life of John Marshall*, III (Boston, 1919), 605-606. The supposition that Jackson "asserted a right not to carry out a court decision when acting in an executive capacity" is denied by Mr. Charles Warren in his *Supreme Court in United States History*, II (Boston, 1926), 222-224; *see also ibid.* 205 ff.

[29] *See* the speeches of Curtis, Groesbeck and Stanbery in President Johnson's behalf, U.S. Congress, *Trial of Andrew Johnson* (Washington, 1868), I, 377; II, 189 and 359; also Corwin, *The President, Office and Powers*, 62-66.

The purely military aspects of the Commander-in-Chiefship were those which were originally stressed. Hamilton said the office "would amount to nothing more than the supreme command and direction of the military and naval forces, as first general and admiral of the confederacy."[1] Story wrote to the same effect in his *Commentaries*;[2] and in 1850 the Court, speaking by Chief Justice Taney, asserted: "His [the President's] duty and power are purely military."[3]

The modern expanded conception of "the power of Commander-in-Chief in wartime" stems in the first instance from Lincoln, who brought the clause to the support of his duty "to take care that the laws be faithfully executed" in proceeding against an insurrection which be treated as public war. Claiming on these premises "the War Power," he declared, following the attack on Fort Sumter in April, 1861, a blockade of Southern ports, raised a large force of volunteers, increased the Army and Navy, took over the railroad between Washington and Baltimore, and declared a suspension of the writ of *habeas corpus* along the line, eventually as far as Boston. In 1862 he established a temporary draft and suspended the writ of *habeas corpus* in the case of persons suspected of "disloyal practices." At the outset of 1863 he issued the Emancipation Proclamation.[4]

"Commander-in-Chief in Wartime": Lincoln and F.D.R.

In the *Prize* cases[5] the Supreme Court, by a narrow majority, ratified his conception of "the greatest civil war in history" as "public war," and hence as vesting the President with the full powers of a supreme military commander against the persons and property of the enemy. Substantially all his acts were, on his suggestion, sooner or later ratified by Congress, or were replaced with legislation designed to accomplish the same ends.[6] Early in 1866, in the famous *Milligan* case,[7] certain military trials ordered or sanctioned by him were overruled, but four of the Justices held that Congress could have authorized them, had it deemed such action necessary for the successful prosecution of the war or for the safety of the Armed Forces.

Controversy over American involvement in the fighting in Vietnam provided more grist for determining the President's powers as Commander-in-Chief. When President Nixon's directive ordering

Vietnam

---

[1] *The Federalist*, No. 69.   [2] § 1492.

[3] Fleming *v*. Page, 9 How. 603, 615, 618 (1850).

[4] On Lincoln's view of his powers as Commander-in-Chief in wartime *see* J. G. Randall, *Constitutional Problems Under Lincoln* (New York, 1926). Randall deals with the legal basis of the Emancipation Proclamation at pp. 372-385. *See also* Lincoln's famous message to Congress of July 4, 1861. Richardson, *Messages and Papers*, VI, 20ff.

[5] 2 Black 635 (1863). *See also* Martin *v*. Mott, 12 Wheat. 19, 32-33 (1827), asserting the finality of the President's judgment of the existence of a state of facts requiring his exercise of the powers conferred by the early acts of Congress authorizing the calling forth of the militia and the employment of the Army and Navy in repressing unruly combinations. 1 *Stat*. 424 (1795); 2 *Stat*. 443 (1807).

[6] *See* 12 *Stat*. 326 (1861).   [7] *Ex parte* Milligan, 4 Wall. 2 (1866).

the mining of the ports and harbors of North Vietnam and the continuation of air and naval strikes against North Vietnamese military targets was challenged, the U.S. Court of Appeals, Second Circuit, handled the issues with all the care attributed to porcupines making love. The court narrowed the contention in the case, saying: "We do not understand appellant to argue that every tactical decision made by the President is subject to challenge under the theory advanced in this case. Any such contention would necessarily be unpersuasive in light of the Constitution's specific textual commitment of decision-making responsibility in the area of military operations in a theatre of war to the President, in his capacity as Commander in Chief. What is unique about the President's action, according to . . . [the appellant] is the 'unilateral escalation' involved in the decision. With this characterization in hand, the appellant draws on language . . . [from one of our previous decisions] where we said, 'if the Executive were now escalating the prolonged struggle instead of decreasing it, additional supporting action by the Legislative Branch over what is presently afforded, might well be required' . . . and argues that the 'escalation' represented by the order to mine North Vietnam's harbors is illegal because unsupported by additional congressional authorization."[8] The court then held: "Thus it is our judgment that this Court is without power to resolve the issue narrowly presented in this case. Having previously determined, in accordance with our duty, that the Vietnamese war has been constitutionally authorized by the mutual participation of Congress and the President, we must recognize that those two coordinate branches of government—the Executive by military action and the Congress, by not cutting off appropriations that are the wherewithal for such action—have taken a position that is not within our power, even if it were our wish, to alter by judicial decree."

There were other efforts in courts to stay the President's unilateral military actions in Vietnam on the grounds that Congress's power to declare war and limitations on the spending power precluded his doing so. Courts generally were as reluctant as the U.S. Court of Appeals, Second Circuit, cited in the text above, "to alter by judicial decree" actions by the President for which Congress did not choose to cut off funds.[9] *See* pages 107-110.

Presidential
Legislation:
"Indirect
Sanctions"

In World War II Mr. Roosevelt quite frankly avowed the belief that as "Commander-in-Chief in wartime" he possessed powers *other* than those of military command, powers which, if claimable at all by the National Government in peacetime, would have first to be

---

[8] DaCosta *v.* Laird, 471 F. 2d. 1146, 1154-1155 (1973).

[9] Harrington *v.* Schlesinger, 373 F.Supp. 1138 (1974); Mitchell *v.* Laird, 488 F. 2d. 611 (1973);' Drinan *v.* Nixon, 364 F.Supp. 854 (1973); Holtzman *v.* Schlesinger, 361 F.Supp. 553 (1973), 484 F. 2d. 1307 (1973), *cert. denied*, 416 U.S. 936 (1974). *But see* Justice Douglas's views, 414 U.S. 1316 (1973) and in Massachusetts *v.* Laird, 400 U.S. 886 (1970).

put in operation by Congressional legislation, and then enforced through the usual peacetime agencies in conformity with such legislation. Thus, to take the most conspicuous exemplification of the President's theory, industrial relations were governed in the main throughout the war under an agreement between the President and certain representatives of employers and employees which was entered into shortly after Pearl Harbor. By this agreement labor was pledged not to strike for the duration and ownership was pledged not to resort to the lockout; and all disputes between employers and employees were referred to the War Labor Board, a body which was without legal status and whose decisions were only "advisory." Suppose, however, its advice was not accepted by one of the parties to a dispute; what then? At this point the President stepped in, and brought to bear upon the recalcitrants such "indirect sanctions" as were available from various acts of Congress, most of which were certainly not enacted with any anticipation that the powers they conferred would be utilized for such purpose. Thus non-compliant workers who happened to be subject to conscription were confronted with induction into the Armed Forces, or employers holding war contracts were ordered not to employ such workers; and non-compliant employers might be denied "priorities," or have their plants seized by the Government under legislation authorizing this to be done when "necessary production" lagged. But in the case of Montgomery Ward, which claimed to be engaged not in "production" but in "distribution" only, the applicability of the legislation just referred to was challenged by a non-compliant company, with the result of raising the question whether the President as "Commander-in-Chief in wartime" was vested by the Constitution itself with the power to make such a seizure. That a military commander has the right to requisition private property to meet an impelling military necessity, subject to the requirement that the property be paid for in due course, is well established; but the taking over of the Ward properties clearly fell outside the precedents. It has to be acknowledged, however, that just as the permeation of the North with disloyal opinions and activities during the Civil War made it difficult to set definite boundaries to the theater of military operations, so do the facts of Total War, which is as much of an industrial operation as it is a military one, make it difficult to maintain a hard and fast line between civilian and military activities and between the governmental powers which are respectively applicable to each. Total War has completely destroyed International Law so far as it formerly attempted to set limits to methods of warfare. Its effect on constitutional limitations could be equally disastrous.[10] Some solace may be derived

---

[10] On the above paragraph *see* Judge Sullivan's informative opinion dismissing the Government's petition for an injunction and declaratory opinion against Montgomery Ward & Co., U.S. *v.* Montgomery Ward, 58 F.Supp. 408 (1945); *reversed* 150 F. 2d. 369 (1945); judgment of the Circuit Court was vacated and the cause remanded

from the knowledge that the Court is quite prepared to limit the Commander-in-Chief in these matters when the warfare is less than total. During the Korean hostilities, the Court held with respect to President Truman's seizure of steel mills: "Even though 'theater of war' be an expanding concept, we cannot with faithfulness to our constitutional system hold that the Commander in Chief of the Armed Forces has the ultimate power as such to take possession of private property in order to keep labor disputes from stopping production. This is a job for the Nation's lawmakers, not for its military authorities."[11]

Military Powers of the President   While the President customarily delegates supreme command of the forces in active service, there is no constitutional reason why he should do so; and he has been known to resolve personally important questions of military policy. Lincoln early in 1862 issued orders for a general advance in the hope of stimulating McClellan to action; Wilson in 1918 settled the question of an independent American command on the Western Front; Truman in 1945 ordered that the bomb be dropped on Hiroshima and Nagasaki. As against an enemy in the field the President possesses all the powers which are accorded by International Law to any supreme commander. "He may invade the hostile country, and subject it to the sovereignty and authority of the United States."[12] In the absence of attempts by Congress to limit his power, he may establish and prescribe the jurisdiction and procedure of military commissions, and of tribunals in the nature of such commissions, in terrritory occupied by Armed Forces of the United States, and his authority to do this sometimes survives cessation of hostilities.[13] He may employ secret agents to enter the enemy's lines and obtain information as to its strength, resources, and movements.[14] He may, at least with the assent of Congress, authorize intercourse with the enemy.[15] He may also requisition property and compel services from American citizens and friendly aliens who are situated within the theatre of military operations when necessity requires, thereby incurring for

to the District Court with directions to dismiss the cause as moot, 326 U.S. 690 (1945). Presumably, the Administration had decided discretion was the better part of valor and chose not to persist in the matter. Executive Order 9370, 8 *Fed. Reg.*, 164 (1943); Employers Group of Motor Freight Carriers, Inc. *v*. NWLB, 143 F. 2d. 145 (1944); Steuart and Bro., Inc. *v*. Bowles, 322 U.S. 398 (1944); John Lord O'Brian and Manly Fleischman, "The War Production Board, Administrative Policies and Procedures," 13 *George Washington Law Review*, 1 (1944); Thomas J. Graves, "The Enforcement of Priorities, Conservation and Limitation Orders of the War Production Board, 1942-1944" (Princeton University Ph.D. thesis); *also* United States *v*. Macintosh, 283 U.S. 605, 622 (1931).

[11] Youngstown Co. *v*. Sawyer, 343 U.S. 579, 587 (1952); *cf*. dissent of Chief Justice Vinson, *ibid*. 683-700.

[12] Fleming *v*. Page, 9 How. 603, 615 (1850).

[13] Madsen *v*. Kinsella, 343 U.S. 341, 348 (1952). *See also* Johnson *v*. Eisentrager, 339 U.S. 763, 789 (1950).

[14] Totten *v*. U.S., 92 U.S. 105 (1876).

[15] Hamilton *v*. Dillin, 21 Wall. 73 (1875).

the United States the obligation to render "just compensation."[16] By the same warrant he may bring hostilities to a conclusion by arranging an armistice, stipulating conditions which may determine to a great extent the ensuing peace.[17] He may not, however, effect a permanent acquisition of territory,[18] though he may govern recently acquired territory until Congress sets up a more permanent regime.[19] He is the ultimate tribunal for the enforcement of the rules and regulations which Congress adopts for the government of the forces, and which are enforced through courts-martial.[20] Indeed, until 1830, courts-martial were convened solely on his authority as Commander-in-Chief.[21] Such rules and regulations are, moreover, it would seem, subject in wartime to his amendment at discretion.[22] Similarly, the power of Congress to "make rules for the government and regulation of the law and naval forces" (Art. I, §8, cl. 14) did not prevent President Lincoln from promulgating in April 1863 a code of rules to govern the conduct in the field of the armies of the United States which was prepared at his instance by a commission headed by Francis Lieber and which later became the basis of all similar codifications both here and abroad.[23] All of which notwithstanding, the Commander-in-Chief remains in the contemplation of the Constitution a civilian official.[24]

The Supreme Court invoked the Commander-in-Chief clause to

[16] Mitchell *v.* Harmony, 13 How. 115 (1852); United States *v.* Russell, 13 Wall. 623 (1871); Totten *v.* U.S., note 14 above; 40 *Op. Atty. Gen.* 251-253 (1942).

[17] *Cf.* the Protocol of August 12, 1898, which largely foreshadowed the Peace of Paris; *and* President Wilson's Fourteen Points, which were incorporated in the Armistice of November 11, 1918.

[18] Fleming *v.* Page, 9 How. 603, 615 (1850).

[19] Santiago *v.* Nogueras, 214 U.S. 260 (1909). As to temporarily occupied territory, *see* Dooley *v.* U.S., 182 U.S. 222, 230-231 (1901).

[20] Swaim *v.* U.S., 165 U.S. 553 (1897); and cases there reviewed. *See also* Givens *v.* Zerbst, 255 U.S. 11 (1921). Nonetheless, in a case in which a *habeas corpus* petition was sought to annul a court-martial murder conviction, the Supreme Court, while denying the writ, said: "the constitutional guarantee of due process is meaningful enough, and sufficiently adaptable, to protect soldiers—as well as civilians—from crude injustices of a trial so conducted that it becomes bent on fixing guilt by dispensing with rudimentary fairness rather than finding truth through adherence to those basic guarantees which have long been recognized and honored by the military courts as well as the civil courts." Burns *v.* Wilson, 346 U.S. 137, 142-143 (1953). Also, with respect to the Selective Service Act, a Federal court recently held that "the only 'lawmakers' who could explicitly authorize denial of counsel in hearings before the local draft boards are Congress, not the President. . . ." U.S. *v.* Weller, 309 F.Supp. 50 (1969).

[21] On the President's authority over courts-martial and military commissions, *see* Clinton Rossiter, *The Supreme Court and the Commander-in-Chief* (Ithaca, 1951), 102-120; *also* Burns *v.* Wilson, 346 U.S. 137 (1953).

[22] *Ex parte* Quirin, 317 U.S. 1, 28-29 (1942).

[23] General Orders, No. 100, *Official Records, War of Rebellion*, ser. III, vol. III; April 24, 1863.

[24] Interesting in this connection is the holding of the Surrogate's Court of Dutchess County, New York, that the estate of Franklin D. Roosevelt was not entitled to certain tax benefits that are extended by statute to persons dying in the military service of the United States, *New York Times*, July 26, 1950, 27.

support the assertion that "One of the very purposes for which the Constitution was ordained and established was to 'provide for the common defense' " as it decided that "it is consequently the business of a military installation like Fort Dix to train soldiers, not to provide a public forum."[25] Accordingly, the Court upheld the specific regulations of Fort Dix limiting political speechmaking and the distribution of literature on the base as applied in the case. (For further discussion, *see* p. 334.)

Lower courts recently have also dealt with the clause in a variety of cases. A U.S. district court, dealing with the issue of whether or not the Secretary of Defense had made a "full" report to Congress as required by law before closing a military installation, found that "the Constitution vests authority over decisions concerning the deployment of national military resources, and thus the continued operation or closure of individual military bases, in the Executive and Congress, but not the Judiciary."[26] (The court made clear that its reference to "Executive" stemmed from the Commander-in-Chief clause.) The court eschewed a decision on the adequacy of the report, saying that if the Congress intends for the courts to do so, "Congress may so instruct the courts."

With respect to an action aimed at halting the construction of a support facility for the Trident submarine program on the claim that the decision to undertake the construction had not complied with provisions of the National Environment Protection Act, a Federal district court held that "There is a 'textually demonstrable constitutional commitment' of the conduct of national defense to Congress in Article I, §8, and the President in Article II, §2."[27] Spelling out the reasons why courts "are not the proper forum for debate on national security and defense issues," the court concluded that "the substantive decision to choose one alternative of national defense over another lies with the political branches and not with the courts."

Likewise, a U.S. court of appeals observed in the *Calley* case (p. 115) that Federal courts should be slow to intervene in basically military matters because Congress and the President have been accorded "great powers and responsibilities in military affairs."[28]

Legally, the President is limited in choosing his principal military subordinates, whose grades and qualifications are determined by Congress and whose appointment is ordinarily made by and with the advice and consent of the Senate, though undoubtedly Congress could if it wished vest their appointment in "the President alone."[29] Also, the President's power to dismiss an officer from the

---

[25] Greer *v.* Spock, 424 U.S. 828 (1976).
[26] National Ass'n of Govern. Emp., Inc. *v.* Schlesinger, 397 F.Supp. 894 (1975).
[27] Concerned About Trident *v.* Schlesinger, 400 F.Supp. 454 (1975).
[28] Calley *v.* Callaway, 519 F. 2d. 184, 201 (1975).
[29] *See* e.g., Mimmack *v.* U.S., 97 U.S. 426, 437 (1878); United States *v.* Corson, 114 U.S. 619 (1885). However, in practice the President does pick them and Senate approval is virtually automatic. This is not to imply that the President plays a lone

service, once unlimited, is today confined by statute to require a trial by court-martial if the officer contends that "he has been wrongfully dismissed" and requests one in writing.[30] But the provision is not regarded by the Court as preventing the President from displacing an officer of the Army or Navy by appointing with the advice and consent of the Senate another person in his place.[31] The President's power of dismissal in time of war Congress has never attempted to limit.

As to the President's constitutional power to relieve a military commander, there should have been no question. But when President Truman relieved General MacArthur in April 1951, there were great cries of outrage and anguish from certain quarters in Congress. Ultimately, a Joint Senate Committee on Armed Services and Foreign Relations after a searching inquiry was unanimous in the view that the President clearly had the power, although some of them felt he had exercised it unwisely.[32]

In recent years a naval officer who had been summarily removed from command of a ship by his superiors afforded a Federal court the opportunity to hold that: "military decisions concerning internal duty assignments and promotions must be left, absent Congressional regulation to the contrary, to the judgment of the chain of command under the President as Commander-in-Chief. If reviewable at all by the federal court, the only possible question would be whether . . . certain procedural Navy Regulations were violated."[33]

"The principal officers" "of the executive departments" have, since Washington's day, composed the President's Cabinet, a body utterly unknown to the Constitution. They are customarily of the President's own party, and loyalty to the President is usually an indispensable qualification which, however, has been at times exhibited in very curious ways; and, of course, such loyalty may not be carried to the extent of violating the law.[34] This fact was demonstrated in the conviction of former Attorney General Richard G. Kleindienst in 1974. He pleaded guilty to the charge that he failed to testify fully to the Senate Judiciary Committee about the settlement of anti-trust charges against the International Telephone and Telegraph Corporation.[35]

The President's Cabinet

---

hand in selection. Normally, he consults and accepts the advice of civilian and military leaders in the Defense establishment. There have been occasions, however, when Presidents have made selections for heads of Services or other important assignments that were very personal choices. Past practice, of course, does not preclude the Senate's playing a stronger role by virtue of its consent power if it so chooses.

[30] 10 U.S.C. 804.

[31] Mullan *v.* U.S., 140 U.S. 240 (1891); Wallace *v.* U.S., 257 U.S. 541 (1922).

[32] For good accounts of the fascinating story, *see* Richard Lowitt, ed., *The Truman-MacArthur Controversy* (Chicago, 1967), and John Spanier, *The Truman-MacArthur Controversy and the Korean War* (Cambridge, 1959).

[33] Arnheiter *v.* Ignatius, 292 F.Supp. 911 (1968); *affirmed*, 435 F. 2d. 691 (1970).

[34] *See* generally Richard F. Fenno, Jr., *The President's Cabinet* (Cambridge, 1959).

[35] 1974 *Cong. Quart. Weekly Report* 1265, 1467.

It has been frequently suggested, twice indeed by committees of Congress, that the members of the Cabinet should be given seats on the floors of Congress, and permitted to speak there.[36] There is obviously nothing in the Constitution which stands in the way of this being done at any time.

Nor, for that matter, is there anything to prevent the President from making his Cabinet up out of the chairmen of the principal committees of the House of Representatives or the Senate, for a Cabinet post is not *as such* a "civil office under the authority of the United States"; nor does a member of the Cabinet *as such* "hold any office under the United States" (*see* p. 32). At a time when there is a great deal of soul-searching for ways to involve Congress more in the making of foreign policy and in the disposition of the Armed Forces there is much to recommend such a proposal.[37] Such a step might eventually lead to something akin to the British system of Cabinet government.

As a practical matter, the extent to which Presidents have employed the principal officers of the executive departments as a Cabinet has varied widely in accordance with the style and ideas of particular Presidents. Like some other Presidents, President Eisenhower made extensive use of Cabinet meetings; President Kennedy, on the other hand, like some other Presidents and as the Cuban Missile Crisis attests, relied instead on ad hoc gatherings of selected advisers chosen on the basis of what expertise they could contribute irrespective of the offices they held.

President Nixon in early 1973 designated three department heads "to serve simultaneously as Counsellors to the President with coordinating responsibilities in these three broad areas of concern.

"Earl L. Butz, Secretary of Agriculture will take on the additional post of Counsellor for Natural Resources. Caspar Weinberger, Secretary-designate of Health, Education and Welfare, will become Counsellor for Human Resources. James Lynn, Secretary-designate of Housing and Urban Development, will become Counsellor for Community Development."[38]

Two aspects of the President's action were particularly noteworthy. The President explicitly stated that "The individual department heads and the Counsellors will routinely report to me via the appropriate Assistant to the President, but will continue to work directly with me on important matters." On the face of it, such a practice would seem to diminish the importance of department heads as Presidential advisers at least vis-à-vis the "appropriate Assistant." Second, the President took the action after Congress had not acted upon his request in 1971 for legislation to accomplish the same objective. The President explained: "Though the actual integration

[36] *See* generally Stephen Horn, *The Cabinet and Congress* (New York, 1960).
[37] For a detailed discussion of the proposal and its merits, *see* Edward S. Corwin, "Wanted: A New Type of Cabinet," *New York Times Magazine*, Oct. 10, 1948, p. 14.
[38] 1973 *Cong. Quart. Weekly Report*, 35-39.

of fragmented departmental operations must wait on Congressional action, the broadening of policy perspectives on the part of top managers and advisers can be achieved at once. . . . I am therefore taking the first of a series of steps aimed at increasing the management effectiveness of both the Cabinet and White House staff, by reordering the time-worn and in many cases obsolete relationships among top staff and line officials to the full extent of my legal authority to do so."

The only constitutional question which has arisen concerning the Cabinet is whether or not it can meet on the call of the Secretary of State in the President's absence. It is an interesting footnote to history that President Wilson strenuously objected on constitutional grounds when his Secretary of State Lansing called a meeting in his absence. With all deference to that great constitutional scholar-President, as vexing as it might have been to have a subordinate take liberties, it does not seem at that stage of the power struggle a *constitutional* issue.[39]

A "reprieve" suspends the penalties of the law; a "pardon" remits them.

"Offenses against the United States" are offenses against the national laws, not State laws. The term also includes acts of so-called "criminal contempt," in defiance of the national courts or their processes.[40]

The Pardoning Power

Pardons may be absolute or conditional and may be conferred upon specific individuals or upon classes of offenders, as by amnesty.

It was formerly supposed that a special pardon, to be effective, must be accepted by the person to whom it was proffered.[41] In 1927, however, in sustaining the right of the President to commute a sentence of death to one of life imprisonment, against the professed will of the prisoner, the Court abandoned this view. "A pardon in our days," it said, "is not a private act of grace from an individual happening to possess power. It is a part of the constitutional scheme. When granted it is the determination of the ultimate authority that the public welfare will be better served by inflicting less than what the judgment fixed."[42]

In 1973, the United States Court of Appeals, D.C., held that President Eisenhower's commutation of a death sentence to imprisonment for life with the understanding that the individual would never be paroled was within his power and "may not be reviewed by a court, and is not to be undone twelve years later upon the basis of *ex post facto* hypothesis and rationalization."[43] The Su-

---

[39] Corwin, *The President, Office and Powers*, 3rd. ed., 402. (The description of this event is not found in the 4th. ed.)

[40] *Ex parte* Grossman, 267 U.S. 87 (1925). Note that the constitutional provision itself excepts "cases of impeachment."

[41] United States *v.* Wilson, 7 Pet. 150 (1833); Burdick *v.* U.S., 236 U.S. 79 (1915).

[42] Biddle *v.* Perovich, 274 U.S. 480, 486 (1927).

[43] Schick *v.* Reed, 483 F. 2d. 1266, 1270 (1973).

preme Court affirmed that decision[44] adding "We are not moved by petitioner's argument that it is somehow 'unfair' that he be treated differently from persons whose death sentences were pending at the time that *Furman* [*see* p. 433] was decided.[[45]] Individual acts of clemency inherently call for discriminating choices because no two cases are the same. Indeed, . . . petitioner's life was undoubtedly spared by President Eisenhower's commutation order of March 25, 1960. Nor is petitioner without further remedy since he may, of course, apply to the present or future Presidents for a complete pardon, commutation to time served, or relief from the no-parole condition. We hold only that the conditional commutation of his death sentence was lawful when made and that intervening events have not altered its validity."

In passing, the Court stated that "even if Furman *v*. Georgia applies to the military, a matter which we need not and do not decide it could not affect a conditional commutation which was granted 12 years earlier."

Pardons may issue at any time after the offense pardoned has been actually committed but not before then, for that would be to give the President a power to set the laws aside, that is, a dispensing power,[46] for asserting the like of which James II lost his throne.

It is sometimes said that a pardon "blots out of existence the guilt" of the offender, but such a view, although applicable in the case of one who was pardoned *before* conviction, is extreme as to one whose offense was established by due process of law. A pardon cannot qualify such a man for a post of trust from which those convicted of crime are by law excluded. In such case the pardoned man is in precisely the same situation as a man who had served his sentence. The law will punish him no further for his past offense, but neither will it ignore altogether the fact that he committed it.[47] But a pardon is efficacious to restore a convicted person's civil rights even when completion of his sentence would not have been.

In a case dealing with the rights of a convicted draft evader who had been pardoned by the President, a U.S. court of appeals concluded that "a presidential pardon restores state as well as federal civil rights."[48] The court reasoned that "The power to punish for a conviction which has been pardoned is the power to vitiate and destroy a presidential pardon."

---

[44] Schick *v*. Reed, 419 U.S. 379 (1974). Earlier, a district court dealt with the issue of a conditional commutation in a noteworthy case, Hoffa *v*. Saxbe, 378 F.Supp. 1221 (1974).

[45] As the Court put it "the essence" of the petitioner's case is that he could not foresee the Court's holding in *Furman* and that he had accepted a "bad bargain." *But see* dissenter's rejoinder on this point, 419 U.S. 379, 388 (1974).

[46] 1 *Op. Atty. Gen.* 342 (1820); United States *v*. Wilson, cited above; *ex parte* Garland, 4 Wall. 333 (1867); United States *v*. Klein, 13 Wall. 128 (1872).

[47] *See* Samuel Williston, "Does a Pardon Blot Out Guilt?" 28 *Harvard Law Review*, 647-663 (1915); *also* Carlesi *v*. New York, 233 U.S. 51 (1914); Reed Cozart, "The Benefits of Executive Clemency," 32 *Federal Probation*, No. 2, p. 33 (1968).

[48] Bjerkin *v*. U.S., 529 F. 2d. 125 (1975).

Perhaps it was as inevitable as it was quixotic that someone would go to court to challenge President Ford's pardon of President Nixon in the face of the ancient precedent that the President's pardoning power is *unlimited* except in cases of impeachment.[49] F. Gregory Murphy, a Michigan attorney brought an action in a U.S. district court seeking a declaration that the President's pardon of former President Nixon was void on the grounds (1) that a pardon could not be granted to one who had not been indicted nor convicted (2) that this pardon constituted unequal enforcement of the law.[50] Judge Fox dismissed the case, but some of the dicta were exceptionally provocative. He wrote "Evidence now available suggests a strong probability that the Nixon Administration was conducting a covert assault on American liberty and *an insurrection and rebellion* against constitutional government itself." (Emphasis supplied.) And as Judge Fox saw it: "By pardoning Richard Nixon, who many believed was the leader of a conspiratorial insurrection and rebellion . . . President Ford was taking steps, in the words of Alexander Hamilton in the Federalist, to '*restore the tranquility of the commonwealth*' by a 'well-timed offer of pardon' to the putative rebel leader."

Although Congress may not interfere with the President's exercise of the pardoning power, it may itself, under the "necessary and proper" clause, enact amnesty laws remitting penalties incurred under the national statutes.[51] *Congressional Amnesties*

For several years Congress talked about granting amnesty for draft evaders, but ultimately it was President Ford who took the initiative.[52] In September 1974, he issued a proclamation saying "pursuant to my powers under Article II, Sections 1, 2, and 3 of the Constitution, [I] do hereby proclaim a program to commence immediately to afford reconciliation to Vietnam era draft evaders and military deserters." The program the President initiated granted relief from prosecution and punishment in return for swearing allegiance to the United States and performing up to 24 months of low-paid alternative service.[53]

Shortly after taking office, President Carter granted a blanket pardon to all Vietnam draft evaders who had not been involved in a violent act.[54] Military deserters were not included, but a study of

[49] *Ex parte* Garland, 4 Wall. 333 (1867).

[50] Murphy v. Ford, 390 F.Supp. 1372 (1975).

[51] Brown v. Walker, 161 U.S. 591 (1896).

[52] Edward B. Fiske, "To Forgive or Not To Forgive Dissenters?" *New York Times*, Feb. 20, 1972; 117 *Cong. Rec.*, No. 196, S21588 (1971). *Also see* Louis Lusky, "Amnesty: Question Isn't If, but How and When?" *Washington Post*, Jan. 16, 1972.

[53] 1974 *Cong. Quart. Weekly Report*, 2532ff. and 2563. Of interest is a district court decision on a challenge to the administration of the President's program. Although the court held that the matter was a political question, not subject to judicial review, it did range over some of the substantive issues by way of dicta. Vincent v. Schlesinger, 388 F.Supp. 370 (1975).

[54] 1977 *Cong. Quart. Weekly Report* 104. For text of Proclamation and Executive Order, *see ibid.*, 177.

their cases was ordered as well as a study of upgrading less than honorable discharges. Implementation of the program to review over 400,000 less than honorable discharges has, of course, been much more difficult than simply granting a blanket pardon to draft evaders.[55]

In a plucky campaign appearance before the American Legion Convention President Carter stressed what he saw as a difference between pardon and amnesty. He told the Legionnaires in no uncertain terms that he was for a pardon: "Amnesty means what you did was right. A pardon means that what you did, right or wrong, is forgiven. So pardon, yes, amnesty, no."[56]

The Treaty-Making Power
¶2. Clause 1. He shall have power, by and with the advice and consent of the Senate, to make treaties, provided two-thirds of the Senators present concur;

It is usual to regard the process of treaty-making as falling into two parts, negotiation and ratification, and to assign the former to the President exclusively and the latter exclusively to the Senate. In fact, it will be observed, the Constitution makes no such division of the subject, but the President and the Senate are associated throughout the entire process of "making" treaties. Originally, indeed, Washington tried to take counsel with the Senate even regarding the negotiation of treaties, but he early abandoned this method of procedure as unsatisfactory.[57] Thus what was intended to be *one* authority consisting of two closely collaborating organs became split into *two*, usually rival and often antagonistic, authorities, performing sharply differentiated functions. In consequence, in 1816, the Senate created the Committee on Foreign Relations as a standing committee, and through this medium most Presidents have managed to keep more or less in touch with Senatorial sentiment regarding pending negotiations, but not always with the result of conciliating it.[58] Today the actual initiation and negotiation of treaties is, by the vast weight of both practice and opinion the President's alone.[59]

Although it is popularly thought that the Senate ratifies treaties, ratification also belongs to the President alone. But he may not ratify a treaty with the result of *making* it, unless the Senate by a two-thirds vote of the members present, there being at least a quorum, advises such ratification and consents to it.[60] And since

[55] 1977 *Cong. Quart. Weekly Report* 817 and Jack Calhoun, "Vietnam Pardon, Stage II," *The Nation*, May 14, 1977, p. 594.
[56] *New York Times*, Aug. 26, 1976.
[57] Corwin, *The President, Office and Powers*, 255-257.
[58] Edward S. Corwin, *The Constitution and World Organization* (Princeton, 1944), ch. III.
[59] United States *v.* Curtiss-Wright Corp., 299 U.S. 304, 319 (1936).
[60] The statement that consent of the Senate must be given by a two-thirds vote of a *quorum of the Senate* has apparently not always been true. Senator H. Alexander

the Senate may or may not consent, it may consent conditionally, stating its conditions in the form of amendments to the proposed treaty or of reservations to the proposed act of ratification, the difference between the two being, that whereas amendments, if accepted by the President and the other party or parties to the treaty, change it for all parties, reservations merely limit the obligations of the United States thereunder. Amendments are accordingly resorted to in the case of bilateral treaties, and reservations in the case of general international treaties, like the Hague Conventions or the United Nations Charter.

Of course, if the President is dissatisfied with the conditions laid down by the Senate to ratification he may refuse to proceed further with the matter, as may also the other party or parties to the proposed treaty.[61] With well over 1000 treaties submitted by Presidents to the Senate from 1789 through 1971, it is a good calculation that the Senate amended about 14 per cent, and rejected or so tampered with about 12 per cent that either the President or the other contracting party declined to go on with them.[62]

The power to make treaties is bestowed upon the United States in general terms and extends to all proper subjects of negotiation between nations. It should be noted, however, that a treaty to which the United States is party is not only an international compact but also "law of the land," in which latter respect it may not override the higher law of the Constitution. Therefore, it may not change the character of the government which is established by the Constitution nor require an organ of that government to relinquish its constitutional powers.[63]

The Scope of the Power

Smith of New Jersey, a member of the Foreign Relations Committee, wrote to Edward S. Corwin August 14, 1957, as follows: "Replying to your letter of August 11th with regard to the making of treaties—a few years ago we were very lax in this matter and treaties were frequently ratified by voice vote. We adopted the rule then, however, that there must be a full quorum present, and two-thirds of the Senators present must concur. This means two-thirds of a quorum, of course. Under the present practice we have a quorum call first, and then a roll call vote, with the vote announced and a statement from the chair that two-thirds of a quorum being present and having voted, etc., the treaty is agreed to."

[61] "Obviously the treaty must contain the whole contract between the parties, and the power of the Senate is limited to a ratification of such terms as have already been agreed upon between the President, acting for the United States, and the commissioners of the other contracting power. The Senate has no right to ratify the treaty and introduce new terms into it, which shall be obligatory upon the other power, although it may refuse its ratification, or make such ratifications conditional upon the adoption of amendments to the treaty." Fourteen Diamond Rings v. U.S., 183 U.S. 176, 183 (1901).

[62] Charles H. McLaughlin, "The Scope of the Treaty Power," 43 *Minnesota Law Review*, 651, 659-678 (1959). McLaughlin's figures were updated by information provided to the editors by the Department of State. For the tabulation, see 13th edition of this work, p. 131.

[63] *See* e.g., Geofroy v. Riggs, 133 U.S. 258, 267 (1890); Doe v. Braden, 16 How. 635, 657 (1853); The Cherokee Tobacco, 11 Wall. 616, 620-621 (1870); United States v. Minn., 270 U.S. 181, 207-208 (1926).

How broad the scope of the treaty-making power is, is well illustrated by the treaty of 1916 between the United States and Canada providing for the reciprocal protection of migratory birds which make seasonal flights from the one country to the other. Congress passed a law putting this treaty into effect and authorizing the Secretary of Agriculture to draw up regulations to govern the hunting of such birds, any violation of these regulations to be subject to certain penalties; and, in the case of Missouri v. Holland,[64] the treaty and the law were sustained by the Supreme Court, the latter as a law "necessary and proper" to put the treaty into effect.

With respect to the treaty-making power, two significant observations were made by courts. First, the Supreme Court observed that, at least in part, Federal authority over Indian matters extends from the treaty-making power. *See* page 83. Second, a Federal district court held that the New York Domestic Relations Law, which grants to citizens of a foreign country (Canada) the same procedural remedies in New York courts as the foreign state grants to our citizens, "is not a compact with a foreign country, and does not violate Article II, Section 2 (2) of the Constitution."[65]

The Supremacy of Treaties over States Rights   In the 1950's, the decision in Missouri v. Holland was vehemently assailed as putting the treaty-making power beyond all constitutional metes and bounds, but more especially as invading States Rights; and various constitutional amendments were proposed (including the famed Bricker Amendment) in the tenor of the one proposed by the American Bar Association in 1952 that "A provision of a treaty which conflicts with any provision of this Constitution shall not be of any force or effect. . . ."[66]

Actually, Justice Holmes's opinion for the Court in Missouri v. Holland did not bear out the more sweeping charge. It is true that at one point the Justice indulged in some speculation as to whether "authority of the United States means more than the formal acts prescribed to make the convention," but he straightway added: "We do not mean that there are no qualifications to the treaty-making power," and pointed out that the convention before the Court did "not contravene any directly prohibitory words of the Constitution"; also that it dealt with "a national interest of very nearly the first magnitude," and one that could "be protected only by national action in concert with that of another power."[67] In short, it was made *bona fide*, and not for the purpose of aggrandizing the powers of the National Government.

On the other hand, the argument that the treaty impaired States Rights the Justice disparaged, and quite warrantably in view of the unambiguous terms of the supremacy clause. In this respect, in-

[64] 252 U.S. 416 (1920).
[65] Blovin v. Dembritz, 367 F.Supp. 415, 417 (1973).
[66] For further discussion and analysis of these proposals *see* the superb articles by McLaughlin, "The Scope of the Treaty Power in the United States," 42 *Minnesota Law Review*, 705 (1958), and 43 *Minnesota Law Review*, 651 (1959), especially the latter, pp. 704-715.
[67] 252 U.S. 416, 433-435 (1920).

deed, the case only confirmed familiar doctrine and practice. From the time of the Jay Treaty (1794) down to the present, the National Government has entered into many treaties extending to the nationals of other governments the right to inherit, hold, and dispose of real property in the States, although the tenure of such property and its modes of disposition were conceded to be otherwise within the exclusive jurisdiction of the States.[68] Missouri v. Holland simply follows the pattern of these precedents.

In other words, it was proposed in the attempts at constitutional amendment to strip the treaty-making power of the right to enter into conventions of a kind which have thereafter furnished the ordinary grist of the treaty-making process—conventions extending to the nationals of other countries the right to engage in certain businesses in the States, to hold property there, to enjoy access to the courts thereof on terms of equality with American citizens, and so on, all in return for like concessions to our nationals residing abroad. More than that, however, it was proposed that that whole area of power which today rests, in the cases, on the mutual support that the treaty-making power and the power of Congress under the "necessary and proper" clause lend one another, shall be expunged from the map of national power. Thus the right of Congress to accord judicial powers to foreign consuls in the United States[69] would have become at least doubtful; so also would have its right to confer judicial powers upon American consuls abroad;[70] its right to provide for the extradition of fugitives from justice;[71] its right to penalize acts of violence within a State against aliens;[72] and so on and so forth.[73] The treaty-making power would have been demoted from the rank of a substantive power of the United States to that of a mere auxiliary power to the other delegated powers. Consequently, it is surprising that the Bricker Amendment was only one vote short of two-thirds approval by the U.S. Senate when it was voted on in 1954.

How is a treaty enforced? Being "law of the land" the provisions of a treaty may, if they do not intrude upon Congress's domain and it was the design of the treaty-making body to put them into effect without reference to Congress, be enforced in court like any other law when private claims are based upon them; and by the President, when the other contracting sovereignty bases a claim upon them. An example of the former case would be where an alien claimed the right to own land in the United States or to engage in business under a provision of a treaty, of the kind above mentioned, between the United States and his home country.[74] An in-

How Treaties Are Enforced

---

[68] *See* McCormick v. Sullivant, 10 Wheat. 192, 202 (1825); United States v. Fox, 94 U.S. 315, 320 (1876); *cf.* Hauenstein v. Lynham, 100 U.S. 483 (1879).

[69] 22 U.S.C. 256.   [70] *In re* Ross, 140 U.S. 453 (1891).

[71] 18 U.S.C., 3181-3195.   [72] Baldwin v. Franks, 120 U.S. 678, 683 (1887).

[73] *See* Neely v. Henkel, 180 U.S. 109, 121 (1901).

[74] Hauenstein v. Lynham, 100 U.S. 483 (1879); Jordan v. Tashiro, 278 U.S. 123 (1928); Nielson v. Johnson, 279 U.S. 47 (1929); Kolovrat v. Oregon, 366 U.S. 187 (1961); Zschernig v. Miller, 389 U.S. 429 (1968).

stance of the latter would be a request by a party to the consultative pact which issued from the Inter-American Conference for Peace at Buenos Aires in December, 1936, for a further conference regarding inter-American relations. To agree to such a conference would be well within the President's diplomatic powers.

The Power of Congress over Treaties

But it frequently happens that treaty provisions contemplate supplementary action by Congress, as did the treaty with Canada above referred to; and this is necessarily the case where money is needed to carry a treaty into effect (*see* Article I, Section IX, ¶7). Does, however, the same rule apply generally in the case of treaty provisions the enforcement of which involves executive and/or judicial action in the area of *Congress's enumerated powers*, its power for instance to declare war, its power to regulate foreign commerce, etc.? While there are a few judicial *dicta* which assert that the maxim "*leges posteriores priores contrarias abrogant* (later laws repeal earlier contradictory ones)" operates reciprocally as between treaties and acts of Congress, and hence carry the implication that the treaty-making power is capable of imparting to its engagements the quality of "law of the land" enforceable by the courts *within the area of Congress's powers*, yet only in one instance has a treaty provision ever been found to effect such a repeal.[75] Moreover, the trend of practice has been from an early date toward an affirmative answer to the above question, a development which is registered in the United Nations Participation Act of 1945. By this measure the steps to be taken to fulfill our engagements under the United Nations Charter in the matter of furnishing armed forces for use at the behest of the Security Council were all to be subject to the approval of Congress.[76] The frustration of this mode of procedure by the circumstances of our involvement in Korea in 1950 is dealt with later. (*See* p. 197.)

It is also by act of Congress that officers and employees of the United Nations have been accorded various diplomatic immunities, and their incomes exempted from taxation.[77]

But is Congress *obliged* to carry out a treaty which it alone may carry out? The answer would seem to be that it is not *legally* obliged to do so, since the Constitution generally leaves it full discretion as to whether or not it shall exercise its powers. But morally it would be obliged to carry out the pledges of the United States duly entered into unless in the specific situation before it an honorable nation would be morally justified in breaking its word.

The Termination of Treaties

Treaties of the United States may be terminated in accordance with their own provisions or by agreement with the other contracting party; or as "law of the land" they may be repealed by act of

---

[75] *See* e.g. Whitney *v.* Robertson, 124 U.S. 190 (1888); United States *v.* Lee Yen Tai, 185 U.S. 213 (1902); Pigeon River Improvement, etc. Co. *v.* Cox, 291 U.S. 138 (1934); *and* Cook *v.* U.S., 288 U.S. 102 (1933)—which is the exceptional and exceptionable—holding.

[76] 59 *Stat.* 613 (1945).   [77] 59 *Stat.* 669 (1945).

Congress, or denounced by the President or the President and Senate; but any such one-sided procedure still leaves the question of their international obligation outstanding.[78] The United States has the same right as any other nation has, and no more, to determine the scope of its obligations under International Law.

Besides treaties proper, the President frequently negotiates agreements with other governments which are not referred to the Senate for its advice and consent. These are of two kinds: those which he is authorized by Congress to make, or which he lays before Congress for approval and implementation; and those which he enters into by virtue simply of his diplomatic powers and powers as Commander-in-Chief.[79] As early as 1792 Congress authorized the Postmaster-General to enter into postal conventions; in 1934 it authorized the President to enter into foreign-trade agreements and to lower customs rates as much as fifty per cent on imports from the other contracting countries in return for equivalent concessions. Present law reflecting more concern about increasing rates still authorizes the President to make agreements.[80] Similarly, the Lend-Lease Act of March 11, 1941, was the fountainhead of the numerous agreements with our allies and associates in World War II under which our government first and last furnished them more than forty billions worth of munitions of war and other supplies. Nor is the validity of such agreements and compacts today open to serious question in view of repeated decisions of the Court.[81]

Executive Agreements by Authorization of Congress

Instances of "treaty making" by the President without the aid or consent of either Congress or the Senate are much fewer in number but some of them have dealt with issues of considerable magnitude. One was the exchange of notes in 1817 between the British Minister Bagot and Secretary of State Rush for the limita-

Executive Agreements Pure and Simple

[78] Head Money cases, 112 U.S. 580 (1884). *See also* The Cherokee Tobacco, 11 Wall. 616 (1871); United States *v.* Forty-Three Gallons of Whiskey, 108 U.S. 491, 496 (1883); Botiller *v.* Dominguez, 130 U.S. 238 (1889); Chae Chan Ping *v.* U.S., 130 U.S. 581, 600 (1889); Whitney *v.* Robertson, 124 U.S. 190, 194 (1888); Fong Yue Ting *v.* U.S., 149 U.S. 698, 721 (1893); "Congress by legislation, and so far as the people and authorities of the United States are concerned, could abrogate a treaty made between this country and another country which had been negotiated by the President and approved by the Senate." La Abra Silver Mining Co. *v.* U.S., 175 U.S. 423, 460 (1899). *Cf.* Reichart *v.* Felps, 6 Wall. 160, 165-166 (1868), where it is stated obiter that "Congress is bound to regard the public treaties, and it had no power . . . to nullify [Indian] titles confirmed many years before. . . ."

[79] *See* Corwin, *The President, Office and Powers*, 259-264; McLaughlin, 42 *Minnesota Law Review*, 764-771, and 43 *Minnesota Law Review*, 678-693, 720-755. For the period 1938-1957, McLaughlin reports that 160 of 2,687 executive agreements (about 5.9%) were neither authorized nor approved; virtually all the other executive agreements in that period were authorized in advance by treaty or statute, 43 *Minnesota Law Review*, 721. For these figures and a Department of State update through 1968, *see* 13th edition of this work, p. 136.

[80] 19 U.S.C. 1351.

[81] The leading cases are Field *v.* Clark, 143 U.S. 649 (1892); and Hampton, Jr. & Co. *v.* U.S., 276 U.S. 394 (1928). For Lend-Lease, *see* 55 *Stat.* 31 (1941).

tion of naval forces on the Great Lakes. Not till a year later was it submitted to the Senate, which promptly ratified it. Of like character was the protocol of August 12, 1898, between the United States and Spain, by which the latter agreed to relinquish all title to Cuba and cede Puerto Rico and her other West Indian possessions to the United States; the exchange of notes between the State Department and various European governments in 1899 and 1900 with reference to the "Open Door" in China; the exchange in 1908 of so-called "identic notes" with Japan concerning the maintenance of the integrity of China; the "Gentlemen's Agreement," first drawn in 1907, by which Japanese immigration to this country was long regulated; the *modus vivendi* by which after the termination of the Treaty of Washington in 1885 American fishing rights off the coast of Canada and Newfoundland were defined for more than a quarter of a century; the protocol for ending the Boxer Rebellion in 1901; the notorious Lansing-Ishii agreement of November 2, 1917, recognizing Japan to have "special rights" in China; the armistice of November 11, 1918—to say nothing of the entire complexus of conventions and understandings by which our relations with our "Associates" in World War I and our "Allies" in World War II were determined, of the latter of which those labelled "Yalta" and "Potsdam" have come to achieve special notoriety. More recently, President Nixon revived and renewed an executive agreement with Portugal allowing the United States to refuel military planes in the Azores and granting $435 million in economic aid to Portugal without consulting Congress.[82] But the demise of the Thieu government in 1975 brought on a controversy over the assurances that President Nixon had given President Thieu in the course of reaching the Paris peace accords several years earlier. Senator Jackson charged that there had been "secret agreements" and that the Ford administration had suggested that Congress had reneged on "commitments" and "obligations."[83] In Jackson's words: "The fact is that Congress is being accused of violating commitments and obligations it never heard of. . . . I call upon the President now to make public and to provide to Congress all documents embodying or reflecting these secret agreements. . . . We in Congress cannot play our constitutional role in constructing a coherent foreign policy so long as information to which we are entitled is kept from us."

President Ford did not press the claim that the assurances of President Nixon constituted an executive agreement *requiring* Congressional support. In any case, Congress was in no mood to accept it as such and patently did not.

Significantly, President Nixon evidently did not regard his assurances as an executive agreement for he did not report them to

[82] *New York Times* (editorial), Dec. 26, 1971.
[83] 1974 *Cong. Quart. Weekly Report*, 845ff. and 728ff. For reference to Case Act, *see* 1972 *Cong. Quart. Almanac*, 619.

Congress as such, as he is required to do under the Case Act of 1972, which calls upon the executive branch to report to Congress the substance of executive agreements that have been made.

Another rhubarb erupted when the Vietnamese claimed that President Nixon had promised $3.25 billion in postwar economic aid to the North Vietnamese. Kissinger who, as Secretary of State, had been party to the agreement indignantly asserted that "It would be absurd to claim that the Vietnamese have the right to economic aid after having brutally violated every provision of the 1973 peace agreement."[84] The House of Representatives voted 2-1 to ban the use of any funds in the 1978 State Department authorization bill for payment to Hanoi. Patently, the fact that Hanoi had violated the agreement made it unnecessary for Congress to deal with the question of the nation's obligation to provide funds on the basis of the President's commitment.

Interestingly enough there is a special category of executive agreements involving Indians. As the United States Court of Appeals, Ninth Circuit, explained: "In 1871 Congress banned any further use of the treaty power in dealing with Indians. After the period of treaty-making, much of the responsibility for reserving parts of the public domain for Indian use shifted from Congress to the Executive. Although Indian reservations had been created by executive order as early as 1855 . . . the authority of the President and the nature of the Indians' rights with respect to such reservations were matters of doubt in the 1870's and 1880's.

"Most of these doubts have now been resolved. The Supreme Court has held that Congress delegated to the President the power to reserve public lands from disposition under the public land laws for Indians or for other purposes by long-continued acquiescence in the exercise of that power."[85]

Obviously, the line between executive agreements and treaties which have to be submitted to the Senate for its approval is not an easily definable one. So when the Senate refused in 1905 to ratify a treaty which the first Roosevelt had entered into with the government of Santo Domingo for putting its customs houses under United States control, the President simply changed the "treaty" into an "agreement" and proceeded to carry out its terms, with the result that a year or so later the Senate capitulated and ratified the "agreement," thereby converting it once more into a "treaty." Furthermore, by recent decisions of the Supreme Court, an "executive agreement" within the power of the President to make is law of the land which the courts must give effect to, any State law or judicial policy to the contrary notwithstanding.[86] This, undoubtedly, is going rather far. It would be more accordant with American ideas

Executive Agreements Involving Indians

Presidential and Congressional Inroads on the Treaty Power

[84] 1977 *Cong. Quart. Weekly Report* 884.
[85] United States *v.* Southern Pacific Transp. Co., 543 F. 2d. 676, 686 (1976).
[86] United States *v.* Belmont, 301 U.S. 324 (1937); United States *v.* Pink, 315 U.S. 203 (1942).

of government by law to require, before a purely executive agreement be applied in the field of private rights, that it be supplemented by a sanctioning act of Congress. And that Congress, which can repeal any treaty as "law of the land or authorization," can do the same to executive agreements, would seem to be obvious. Yet, significance must be attached to the fact that when constitutional amendments were being prepared in the 1950's to limit the President's power to make executive agreements, they were rejected.[87] However, the Senate later manifested renewed interest in finding ways to require Congressioal consideration of executive agreements.[88]

Nor is the "executive agreement," whether made with or without the sanction of Congress, the only inroad which practice under the Constitution has made upon the original role of the Senate in treaty-making. Not only, as was pointed out above, is the business of negotiation today within the President's exclusive province, but Congress has come into possession of a quite indefinite power to legislate with respect to external affairs. The annexation of Texas in 1845 by joint resolution is the leading precedent. The example thus set was followed a half century later in the case of Hawaii; and of similar import are the Joint Resolution of July 2, 1921, by which war with the Central Powers was brought to a close, and the Joint Resolution of June 19, 1934, by which the President was enabled to accept membership for the United States in the International Labor Organization.[89] Such precedents make it difficult to state any limit to the power of the President and Congress, acting jointly, to implement effectively any foreign policy upon which they agree, no matter how "the recalcitrant third-plus-one-man" of the Senate may feel about the matter. Nonetheless, the Supreme Court has held that a Status of Forces Agreement (i.e. an agreement authorized by treaty made with a country in which U.S. troops are based) could not be used to sustain implementing legislation which abridged constitutional guarantees of the Bill of Rights.[90]

The National Executive Establishment

¶2. Clauses 2 and 3. And he shall nominate, and, by and with the advice and consent of the Senate, shall appoint ambassadors, other public ministers and consuls, judges of the Supreme Court and all other officers of the United States, whose appointments are not herein otherwise provided for, and which shall be established by law; but the Congress may by law vest

---

[87] McLaughlin, 43 *Minnesota Law Review*, 715-718.

[88] 1972 *Cong. Quart. Weekly Report*, 219, 1006, 1220. On March, 3, 1972, the Senate passed a resolution stating that "any agreement with Portugal or Bahrain for military bases or foreign assistance should be submitted as a treaty to the Senate for advice and consent." Subsequent efforts to reverse that resolution were defeated in the Senate. 118 *Cong. Rec.* No. 99, S9639ff. (1972).

[89] 42 *Stat.* 105; 49 *Stat.* 2741.

[90] Reid *v.* Covert, 354 U.S. 1 (1957); *but see* Wilson *v.* Girard, 354 U.S. 524 (1957).

the appointment of such inferior officers, as they think proper, in the President alone, in the courts of law, or in the heads of departments.

Evidently, the Framers of the Constitution assumed that all officials of the United States would be appointive and fall into two classes: the so-called "Presidential officers" and "inferior officers." They, of course, had no way of knowing, and, indeed probably would have been astounded that one day there would be a Federal bureaucracy of well over two million people. The total population in the country at that time was less than four million. Consequently, constitutional provisions for only those two classes were not adequate for the long haul of history. Eventually, Congress by law provided for officials whose appointments were not made in accordance with Section II. In 1879, the Supreme Court held that an official who is not appointed in the manner prescribed in the Constitution "is not an *officer*, though he may be an agent or employé working for the government and paid by it, as nine-tenths of the persons rendering service to the government undoubtedly are, without thereby becoming its officers."[91] What the Court said in effect is that Congress could provide for appointment of officials in a manner inconsistent with the appointment provisions of the Constitution and those who were so appointed by definition were not "officers." Current law on the subject reflects the distinction made by the Court. "Officers" are defined as those "required by law to be appointed in the civil service by one of the following acting in an official capacity—(A) the President; (B) a court of the United States; (C) the head of an Executive agency; or (D) the Secretary of a military department." An "employee" is defined as one appointed by other specified officials as well as the President when he is appointing "in an official capacity" but not in pursuance of a requirement by law.[92] In sum, this constitutional provision has been interpreted to conform with the realities of the need for a large bureaucracy operating under some kind of merit system.

One other crucial distinction should be made at this point. The term "Civil Service" consists "of all appointive positions in the executive, judicial and legislative branches"; the terms "Competitive Service" and "Classified Service" indicate those who are covered by the merit system, including its job protection. Those outside the merit system are in the "Excepted Service"; or "Unclas-

[91] U.S. *v.* Germaine, 99 U.S. 508, 509 (1879).
[92] 5 U.S.C. 2104 and 2105. In an interesting opinion rendered in 1907, the Attorney General stated that "A fortiori it would seem clear that the recognition in a Federal statute of a person in public employ as an officer of the United States constitutes the person such officer. . . . If it be assumed, argumenti gratia, that the method of their appointment would be unconstitutional if they are officers, it does not seem that this fact constitutes any bar to their classification, so long as they continue to be recognized as officers de facto." 26 *Op. Atty. Gen.* 364, 370 (1907).

sified Civil Service." These include, most importantly, the so-called "Political officers" like Secretaries, Under Secretaries, and Assistant Secretaries who are appointed by the President with the advice and consent of the Senate, who do not have to take Civil Service examinations and who do not have the job protections of those in the "Competitive Service."

The steps of appointment provided for in the first clause are, first, their nomination by the President; second, their appointment "by and with the advice and consent of the Senate," the latter of which may not be, as in the case of treaties, qualified by conditions;[93] third, their commissioning, which is also by the President[94] (*see* Section III). As recent monumental battles over Supreme Court appointments suggest, obtaining the consent of the Senate is not always a *pro forma* matter.[95]

The offices of "ambassador," "public minister" and "consul" being recognized by the Law of Nations, it was at first thought that the President might nominate to them as occasion arose in our intercourse with foreign nations, but since 1855 Congress has asserted its right to restrict such appointments, which it is able to do through its control of the purse.

Besides "ambassadors" and "public ministers" there has sprung up in the course of time a class of "personal agents" of the President, in whose appointment the Senate does not participate. Theoretically these do not usually have diplomatic quality, but if their identity is known they will be ordinarily accorded it in the countries to which they are sent.[96]

In part, as a tactical maneuver in the controversy over the impoundment of funds in 1973, Congress passed a bill requiring Senate confirmation of the director and deputy director of the Office of Management and Budget. When Congress had created the old Bureau of the Budget in 1921 (predecessor of OMB) the prevailing theory was that these offices as well as other staff offices were personal to the President and should not require Senate confirmation. The Senate Committee reporting the bill stated that OMB now "has developed into a major governmental agency with enormous policy-making and operational functions, responsibilities and authority" and as such requires that Congress play a role in the appointment of its chief officers. Ultimately, the President vetoed the bill and the House failed to override the veto. Undaunted, the Senate in June 1973 passed a bill which would require confirmation of *future* nominees for those high offices as well as several others.[97]

The situation would have been different were this the case of

[93] 3 *Op. Atty. Gen.* 188 (1837); Story, *Commentaries*, II, §1531; Gaillard Hunt, ed., *Writings of James Madison* (New York, 1900-1910), IX, 111-113.

[94] Marbury *v*. Madison, 1 Cr. 137 (1803).

[95] For a detailed description of the appointing process generally *see* Harold W. Chase, *Federal Judges, The Appointing Process* (Minneapolis, 1972).

[96] Corwin, *The President, Office and Powers*, 251-253.

[97] 1973 *Cong Quart. Weekly Report*, 39.

Congress setting up new offices providing for Senate confirmation. Then the President would have had to worry that a veto would have the effect of preventing the offices from being established. But here legislation already permitted the President to appoint without confirmation, and his veto had the effect of maintaining the status quo. Ultimately Congress prevailed.[98]

In this context, some words written by Vice President Mondale are provocative: "We should bolster this legislation [establishing a statutory basis for key White House Office jobs] with the requirement that heads of the Domestic Council and National Security Council be subjected to Senate confirmation. . . . Confirmation of additional key White House aides—similar to the confirmation of the heads of Office of Management and Budget and the Council on International Economic Policy now written into law—would give Congress a greater ability to probe the activities and attitudes of the principal advisers within the White House."[99]

In his statement explaining the government reorganization he initiated in early 1973, President Nixon said that "Through a combination of Presidential directives, reorganization plans, and budgetary changes, I shall assign or propose reassignment of most of the activities currently carried on by a number of organizations within the Executive Office of the President, to appropriate line departments and agencies." Although present law requires that executive reorganization plans be submitted to the Congress and that Congress have the opportunity to scuttle them by a resolution of either house,[100] the President apparently believed that he had the legal power to make changes unilaterally within the Executive Office but needed the approval of Congress for changes in the rest of the executive branch. The concluding words of his statement support such an observation: "I hope the Congress will accept this practical proof and join me in adopting throughout the executive branch the same concepts on which I am now patterning my own staff and Executive Office."[101]

"Shall be established by law": All civil offices of the United States except those of President, Vice-President, Ambassadors, Public Ministers and Consuls, and possibly of Justices of the Supreme Court, are supposed to be the creations of Congress. The great majority, however, of the alphabetical agencies, like WPB, WLB, WMC, ODT, and so on, through which World War II was conducted on the home front, were created by the President as ramifications of the OEM (Office of Emergency Management), also his creation; but most of them eventually received Congress's blessing

The War Agencies

[98] 88 *Stat.* 11 (1974). President Nixon signed the bill. *See* 30 *Cong. Quart. Almanac*, 671 (1974).

[99] Walter F. Mondale, *The Accountability of Power* (New York, 1975), p. 152.

[100] 1973 *Cong. Quart. Weekly Report*, 250, 313, 1330-1331.

[101] *New York Times*, June 26, 1973. In June a Federal judge ruled that Howard J. Phillips was acting as the head of OEO illegally becuse his name had not been submitted to the Senate for approval. President Nixon directly nominated a new di-

and approval in the shape of appropriations or in legislation aug-
menting or regulating their powers. OPA (successor to Presiden-
tially created OPACS) was brought into existence by Congress.

When Congress creates offices it does so by virtue of its powers
under the "necessary and proper" clause; and by the same authorization it may also stipulate what qualifications appointees to them
shall have.[102]

Congres-
sional
Regulation
of Offices
and Officers

Furthermore, Congress has very broad power to regulate the
conduct in office, especially regarding their political activities, of
officers and employees of the United States. All such persons, and
members of Congress as well, are forbidden to receive or solicit any
contribution to be used for a political purpose.[103] By the Hatch Act
of 1939[104] all persons in the executive branch of the Government,
or any department or agency thereof, except the President and
Vice-President and certain "policy determining" officers, are forbidden to "take an active part in political management or political
campaigns," although they are still permitted to "express their
opinions on all political subjects and candidates"; and by the Hatch
Act of 1940[105] these regulations were extended to employees of
State and local governments who were engaged in activities financed in whole or part by national funds. Although Justice Douglas and two other dissenters saw the Hatch Act as a limitation on
government employees' "right to speak, to propose, to publish, to
petition government, to assemble," a majority had no difficulty finding that "neither the First Amendment nor any other provision of
the Constitution invalidates a law barring . . . partisan political conduct by federal employees."[106]

Would the Court take the same view with a law which renders a
person ineligible for a position with the Federal Government if he
is convicted for "inciting, organizing, promoting, encouraging, or
participating in a riot or civil disorder"?[107] A lower court has struck
down as unconstitutional, a statute which denies Federal employment to an individual who among other things advocates overthrow of the Government or "asserts the right to strike against the
Government."[108] But the law in that case did not require a conviction.

Power to
Remove as
an Incident
of the
Power to
Appoint

Also, Congress may, and usually does, limit the term for which
an appointment to office may be made; while as to those officers
who are instruments and agents only of the constitutional powers
of Congress, the latter may limit drastically their removability during such terms. If, however, an officer *is an agent of the President in
the exercise of any of his powers*—whether constitutional or statu-

---

rector. *New York Times*, June 27, 1973. The case is reported in Williams *v.* Phillips,
360 F.Supp. 1363 (1973).

[102] *Ibid.*, 363-365.   [103] 18 U.S.C. 602.

[104] 53 *Stat.* 1147.   [105] 54 *Stat.* 767-772.

[106] United States C. Serv. Com'n *v.* National Ass'n of Let. Car., 413 U.S. 548, 556
(1973).

[107] 5 U.S.C. 7313.   [108] Stewart *v.* Washington, 301 F.Supp. 610 (1969).

tory—such officer is for that reason removable at the will of the President.[109]

Chief Justice Taft, a former President not known for his assertions of Presidential power while in that office, speaking for the majority in the celebrated *Myers* case asserted that "The power to remove superior officers, is an incident of the power to appoint them, and is in its nature an executive power."[110] For about a decade following that decision it was thought that the President's power to remove was more sweeping than it turned out to be. In another celebrated case decided in 1935, the Court held: "Whether the power of the President to remove an officer shall prevail over the authority of Congress to condition the power by fixing a definite term and precluding a removal except for cause, will depend upon the character of the office; the *Myers* decision, affirming the power of the President alone to make the removal, is confined to purely executive officers" and that a Federal Trade Commissioner was not such an officer.[111] Later, it was determined that a War Claims Commissioner was not "an Executive Officer."[112] These decisions do not alter the fact that all non-judicial officers of the United States are subject to disciplinary removal by the President for good cause, by virtue of his duty to "take care that the laws be faithfully executed."[113]

On the other hand, Presidents have more than once had occasion to stand in a protective relation to their subordinates, assuming their defense in litigation brought against them[114] or pressing litigation in their behalf,[115] refusing a call for papers from one of the houses of Congress which might be used, in their absence from the seat of government, to their disadvantage[116] challenging the constitutional validity of legislation which the President deemed detrimental to their interests.[117] There is one matter, moreover, as to which he is able to spread his own official immunity to them. Normally, the courts may not require Presidential assistants to divulge confidential communications from or to the President, that is, communications that they choose to regard as confidential. Until recently, it was thought that the immunity was virtually absolute.[118]

The Power of the President to Protect Subordinates

---

[109] *Cf.* Myers *v.* U.S. ("Oregon Postmaster Case"), 272 U.S. 52 (1926); Humphrey's Executor *v.* U.S., 295 U.S. 602 (1935); Wiener *v.* U.S., 357 U.S. 349 (1958); Kandall *v.* U.S., 186 Ct. Cl. 900 (1969).

[110] 272 U.S. 52 at 161 (1926).

[111] Humphrey's Executor *v.* U.S., 295 U.S. 602, 631-632 (1935).

[112] Wiener *v.* U.S., 357 U.S. 349 (1958).

[113] Corwin, *The President, Office and Powers*, 102-104.

[114] 6 *Op. Atty. Gen.*, 220 (1853); *in re* Neagle, 135 U.S. 1 (1890).

[115] United States *v.* Lovett, 328 U.S. 303 (1946).

[116] Richardson, *Messages and Papers of the Presidents*, II, 847 (January 10, 1825).

[117] *See* U.S. *v.* Lovett, 328 U.S. 303, 313 (1946).

[118] Marbury *v.* Madison, 1 Cr. 137, 144-145 (1803).

A ruling by Attorney General Jackson, dated April 20, 1941, holds that all FBI investigative reports are confidential documents that the President is entitled in the public interest to withhold from Congressional investigating committees. Early in

But the Supreme Court's recent decision in United States *v*. Nixon has made clear that it is not.[119] The Court held 8-0 (Justice Rehnquist not participating) that there was, indeed, an executive privilege and that it was important to support it, but it could not be absolute as the President claimed for there were other important values to be considered. As the Court explained: "In this case we must weigh the importance of the general privilege of confidentiality of presidential communications in performance of his responsibilities against the inroads of such a privilege on the fair administration of criminal justice. The interest in preserving confidentility is *weighty indeed and entitled to great respect*. However, we cannot conclude that advisors will be moved to temper the candor of their remarks by the infrequent occasions of disclosure because of the possibility that such conversations will be called for in the context of a *criminal prosecution*." (Emphasis supplied.)

It is significant that the Court emphasized two points in its opinion. It took pains to say, "*Absent a claim of need to protect military, diplomatic, or sensitive national security secrets*, we find it difficult to accept the argument that even the very important interest in confidentiality of presidential communications is significantly diminished by production of such material for *in camera* inspection with all the protection that a district court will be obliged to provide." (Emphasis supplied.) The Court was also painstaking in saying several times that the need for the subpoena at issue was in connection with a criminal trial, i.e., "The generalized assertion of the privilege must yield to the demonstrated specific need for evidence in a pending criminal trial."

Left for speculation, then, are the questions: (1) What if a claim were made for the privilege on the grounds of the need to safeguard national security secrets? (2) What if a Congressional committee, rather than a court, seeks information against a claim of the privilege?

Finally, the Court gave specific directions to the district court as to how careful it must be in examining the material and deciding what could be used as evidence, saying "it is obvious that the District Court has a very heavy responsibility to see to it that presidential conversations which are either not relevant or not admissible, are accorded that high degree of respect due the President of the United States."

Following the decision of the Court, the President issued a state-

---

1944 an administrative assistant to the President refused to answer questions put to him by a Senate sub-committee, but later yielded on the President's order to do so. *New York Times*, February 29 and March 1, 5, and 10, 1944. *And see* generally Charles Warren, "Presidential Declarations of Independence," 10 *Boston University Law Review*, 1 (1930); *also* Attorney General Brownell's Memorandun, *New York Times*, May 18, 1954.

[119] United States *v*. Nixon, 418 U.S. 683 (1974).

ment which included the words: "While I am of course disappointed in the result, I respect and accept the Court's decision, and I have instructed Mr. St. Clair to take whatever measures are necessary to comply with that decision in all respects."[120]

What if a Congressional committee, rather than a court, seeks information against a claim of executive privilege?

There seems to be a substantial basis for asserting that the "separation of powers" principle precludes compelling a President to testify and that it also covers those who would be asked to testify about what the President said or wrote to them on a confidential basis. But this opens up the broader issue involved with respect to "executive privilege." More and more over the years the executive officers have refused to testify before Congressional committees, usually on the grounds that to do so would endanger national security. Some Congressmen suspect that more often than not the Administration is merely trying to prevent embarrassment through the exposure of misjudgments and inefficiencies. And even if the national security is involved, it can be persuasively argued that in a democratic society Congressmen should be given any information they need to know to legislate intelligently and that it can be done safely in executive session. But before the *Nixon* case it had become conventional wisdom, based in part on the opinions of a succession of Attorneys General, that there was no point in Congressmen trying to settle the matter in the courts.[121] Consequently, a resolution to the issue seemed to have been worked out through the political process. In a carefully staged scenario in 1962 stemming from a dispute over whether or not a Senate sub-committee was entitled to know the names of Defense Department officials who had censored speeches of Generals and Admirals, Secretary of Defense McNamara appeared before the sub-committee and read a letter to him from President Kennedy directing him (McNamara) not to testify about certain matters. Among other things the Kennedy letter stated that "the principle which is at stake here cannot be automatically applied to every request for information. Each case must be judged on its merits. . . ." Senator Stennis, the Chairman of the sub-committee, obviously prepared for the event, "read from prepared notes and annotated transcripts of court decisions and Congressional hearings to justify his ruling" to accept the President's plea.[122] Subsequent events indicated that a precedent had been set. If the President himself indicated in writing that he did not want his subordinate to testify, the Congressional committee would usually let the matter drop there.[123]

The Executive Privilege

[120] *New York Times*, July 25, 1974.

[121] *See* generally the brilliant articles by Raoul Berger, "Executive Privilege *v.* Congressional Inquiry," 12 *U.C.L.A. Law Review*, 1044 and 1288 (1965). He argues persuasively that the conventional wisdom is wrong.

[122] *New York Times*, Feb. 9, 1962.

[123] 1971 *Cong. Quart. Weekly Report*, 1786 and 1873.

But, during a subsequent donnybrook over the confirmation of Richard G. Kleindienst as Attorney General, when some Senators wanted White House aide Peter Flanigan to testify contrary to President Nixon's wishes, they had (and used) some unusual political leverage. They could and did put pressure on the President by threatening to hold up confirmation unless Flanigan testified.[124] Ultimately, a compromise was effected by which Flanigan would testify only as to certain events. During his testimony, several Senators angrily objected to Flanigan's refusal to answer questions that he thought were beyond the scope of the agreement. In terms of developing the meaning of the Constitution, perhaps the most significant event in the controversy was the Senate Judiciary Committee's refusal to subpoena Flanigan. A motion to that effect was defeated by a 6-6 tie vote and thus precluded a possible court test.[125]

As the mire of the Watergate Affair increasingly threatened to suck in high Administration officials, indeed eventually the President himself, the meaning of the executive privilege with respect to a Congressional investigation was debated with a ferocity which made previous contests seem desultory.[126] To foresall the Senate inquiry, the Administration at first made some extraordinary claims for the privilege. For example, to Senator Muskie's question "Does . . . [the executive privilege] apply to every one of the employees of the executive branch of the federal government of the United States?" the then-Attorney General, Richard G. Kliendienst, answered: "Boy, if a President directed him not to, I think logically I'd have to say that's correct."[127] Later, some backtracking put the Administration more in line with previous claims. The White House issued a statement in May 1973 that "The President desires that the invocation of Executive Privilege be held to a minimum." His guidance was that "Past and present members of the President's staff questioned by the FBI, the Ervin Committee, or a Grand Jury should invoke the privilege only in connection with conversations with the President, conversations among themselves (involving communications with the President) and as to Presidential papers. Presidential papers are all documents produced or received by the President or any member of the White House Staff in connection with his official duties."[128] But, as unfolding events and Presidential counsel Leonard Garment attested, there is no way a President can force an aide to invoke the privilege, if the aide does not want to.[129]

---

[124] Fred P. Graham, "Again the Clash Over Who Should Testify," *New York Times*, April 16, 1972.
[125] 1972 *Cong. Quart. Weekly Report*, 846 and 913; *New York Times*, April 13, 1972.
[126] 1973 *Cong. Quart. Weekly Report*, 181, 184-85, 294-95, 518, 557, 729, 862, 895, 1120, 1203.
[127] *Ibid.*, 862.   [128] *Ibid.*, 1120.
[129] *Ibid.*, 1203.

Refusing to be intimidated by the President or anyone else, and provoked by the revelations unfolding before him, Senator Ervin led his investigating committee to become the first Congressional committee in American history to sue the President to obtain evidence in his control. The President sought to withhold the tapes and other subpoenaed materials in significant part on the executive privilege.[130] In due course, the D.C. Circuit Court of Appeals decided the case. The court held that Presidential communications are "presumptively privileged" and that the assumption can be overcome only by "a showing that the responsibilities of . . . [a governmental institution] cannot responsibly be fulfilled without access to records of the President's deliberations."[131] The court held that under the circumstances of the case, the committee could not make the kind of strong showing of need required. What can be inferred from this decision is that there could be circumstances in which a Congressional committee could legally obtain Presidential materials even against the claim of executive privilege. Any attempt to assess this outcome should include a review of another earlier attempt to subpoena a President.

As an *ex*-President, Harry S Truman in 1953 declined to answer a subpoena served on him by the House Un-American Activities Committee, which was inquiring into the charge that Harry Dexter White (who had been promoted from Assistant Secretary of the Treasury to Executive Director of the International Monetary Fund) "was known to be a Communist spy by the very people who appointed him to the most sensitive and important position he ever held in government service." In a detailed letter to the committee citing sixteen precedents, Mr. Truman explained that "I feel constrained by my duty to the people of the United States to decline to comply with the subpoena."[132] President Eisenhower, who had been very critical of his predecessor's general performance in office, nonetheless publicly lent his support to Mr. Truman in this matter.[133]

When Congress passed the Presidential Recordings and Materials Preservation Act of 1974, which provided in part for the Administrator of General Services to promulgate regulations governing public access to tape recordings and other Presidential materials subject to oversight by Congress, it raised yet another question about the reach of executive privilege. The Court held that Mr. Nixon "may legitimately assert the Presidential privilege, of course, only to those materials whose contents fall within the scope of the privilege recognized in *United States v. Nixon*" i.e., to communications "in performance of [a President's] responsibilities," "of his office" and made "in the process of shaping policies and making

"Public Access" to Presidential Materials

---

[130] For a detailed and fascinating account of these events, *see* James Hamilton, *The Power to Probe* (1976).

[131] Senate Select Committee *v*. Nixon, 498 F. 2d. 725 (1974).

[132] *New York Times*, Nov. 13, 1953.   [133] *New York Times*, Nov. 12, 1953.

decisions."[134] Then the Court went on to say that "there is no reason to believe that the restriction on public access ultimately established by regulation will not be adequate to preserve executive confidentiality. An absolute barrier to all outside disclosure is not practically or constitutionally necessary." Carefully, the Court concluded "that the screening process contemplated by the Act will not constitute a more severe intrusion than the *in camera* inspection by the District Court approved in *United States v. Nixon*. We must of course presume that the Administrator and the career archivists concerned will carry out the duties assigned to them by the Act. Thus, there is no basis for appellant's claim that the Act 'reverses' the presumption in favor of confidentiality of Presidential papers recognized in *United States v. Nixon*. Appellant's right to assert the privilege is specifically preserved by the Act. The guideline provisions on their face are as broad as the privilege itself. If the broadly written protections of the Act should nevertheless prove inadequate to safeguard appellant's rights or to prevent usurpation of executive powers, there will be time enough to consider that problem in a specific factual context. For the present, we hold in agreement with the District Court, that the Act on its face does not violate the Presidential privilege."

Two other noteworthy points were made by the Court. First, the Court observed that this was a case involving an "assertion of the privilege against the very Executive Branch in whose name the privilege is invoked." The relevance of this observation apparently is only that it gives support to the contention that only an incumbent President can assert the privilege. As to that point, the Court explicitly adopted the view of the Solicitor General's brief that "the privilege survives the individual President's tenure."[135]

Also, two recent lower court decisions are instructive. The court of claims held that the executive privilege did not bar discovery of a former President's papers in a civil suit. The court held that "a court concludes whether or not there is an enforceable privilege in a given case by examining the motion papers, or affidavits of the parties concerning a claim of privilege. . . . Since a President is not absolutely immune from court process, a former President can claim no greater immunity, and the Court must determine whether his claim of privilege, assuming his right to assert it, is overcome by a plaintiff's need in litigation."[136] In this case the court held that the plaintiff's need prevailed.

When former President Nixon sought to avoid giving a deposition in the case of Halperin *v.* Kissinger by invoking what the court called "presidential confidentiality—a form of executive privilege," a U.S. district court decided against him on the condition that the deposition be taken at or near his home.[137] After indicating that it

[134] Nixon *v.* Administrator of General Services, 433 U.S. 425, 449, 450 (1977).
[135] *Ibid.*, 450-452   [136] Sun Oil Co. *v.* U.S., 514 F. 2d. 1020 (1975).
[137] Halperin *v.* Kissinger, 401 F.Supp. 272 (1975).

was questionable that the privilege is retained by an *ex*-President, the court pointed out that, assuming *arguendo* a privilege was involved, in accordance with the Supreme Court's decision in United States *v.* Nixon[138] it was necessary to resolve the issue by balancing the "competing interests of presidential privilege and the legitimate needs of the judicial process." The court went on to conclude that such a weighing entitled the plaintiffs to obtain a deposition from Mr. Nixon.

"Inferior officers" are evidently officers subordinate to the heads of departments or the courts of law, but many classes of such officers are still appointed by the President with the advice and consent of the Senate because Congress has never vested their appointment elsewhere. Also, there is good reason for believing that the Federal court judges other than the Supreme Court justices are "inferior officers."[139] "Inferior Officers"

By the Oregon Postmaster case, one who is vested under this clause with the power to appoint an inferior officer is at the same time vested with the power to remove him, the power of removal being a part of the appointing power.

The challenge to the constitutionality of the Federal Election Campaign Act of 1971, as amended in 1974, required the Supreme Court to review carefully the meaning of the constitutional provisions respecting the President's appointment power.[140] The act created a Federal Elections Commission with important responsibilities for effectuating the purposes of the act. The commission comprised two members who were nominated by the President and whose appointment required confirmation by *both* houses of Congress, and four members appointed by the President *pro tempore* of the Senate and by the Speaker of the House. The Court quickly concluded that members of the commission were "officers of the United States" saying that "We think its fair import is that any appointee exercising significant authority pursuant to the laws of the United States is an Officer of the United States, and must, therefore, be appointed in the manner prescribed by [Article II]." The Court then went on to point out that requiring confirmation by both houses and giving appointive power to the Speaker and the President *pro tempore* did not come within the "language" of the constitutional provision whether the commissioners were "officers" or "inferior officers."[141] The Court gave short shrift to the argu-

---

[138] 418 U.S. 683 (1974). *See* p. 183.

[139] Article III, Section I speaks of "inferior courts." For further discussion of this point *see* Chase, *Federal Judges: The Appointing Process*, p. 5.

[140] Buckley *v.* Valeo, 96 S. Ct. 612 (1976).

[141] The Court evidently did not feel that it was imperative for them to decide what kind of officers the commissioners were in this case for they put it this way: "If a Postmaster first class . . . and the Clerk of a District Court . . . are inferior officers . . . within the meaning of the Appointments Clause, as they are, surely the Commissioners before us are at the very least such 'inferior Officers' within the meaning of that Clause."

ment that Congress "had ample authority under the Necessary and Proper Clause of Art. I to effectuate this result" (tied with Congress's power under Article I, §§IV and V). The Court said: "The proper inquiry when considering the Necessary and Proper Clause is not the authority of Congress to create an office or a commission, which is broad indeed, but rather its authority to provide that its own officers may appoint to such office or commission." Ultimately the Court held "that these provisions of the Act, vesting in the Commission primary responsibility for conducting civil litigation in the courts of the United States for vindicating public rights, violate Art. II, cl. 2, §2 of the Constitution. Such functions may be discharged only by persons who are 'Officers of the United States' within the language of that section." Significantly, the Court took pains to say that "Insofar as the powers confided in the Commission are essentially of an investigative and informative nature, falling in the same category as those powers which Congress might delegate to one of its own committees, there can be no question that the Commission as presently constituted may exercise them."[142]

A U.S. district court held that the appointment by district courts of special prosecuting officers when the Attorney General or the U.S. Attorney refuses to prosecute after the court refuses dismissal of an indictment was bottomed on the proposition that, in providing for such a possibility in legislation, Congress "implemented Article 2, Section 2, Clause 2."[143] To the argument that the appointment of special prosecutors was within the Presidential responsibility "to take care that the laws be faithfully executed," the court answered: "To read the Article II powers of the President as providing the Justice Department with absolute discretion to refuse to prosecute a criminal indictment on no more than the bare claim that 'a bargain had been made' and that 'it would be in the interest of justice' would upset the constitutional balance of powers and would 'gravely impair the role of the courts under Art. III.' " Although a U.S. Court of Appeals reversed the district court on the grounds that it had exceeded the bounds of its discretion in denying the government's motion to dismiss, the appeals court explicitly stated that it was not considering the propriety of the appointment of special prosecutors.[144] In short, the appeals court held only that the district court "was undoubtedly clothed with a discretion to determine whether the dismissal of these charges was clearly contrary to the public interest" but that, upon an "appraisal of all the relevant factors," the trial court had "committed a clear error of judgment in the conclusion it reached." Significantly, in its opinion, the Court of Appeals distinguished between the power of a court to di-

[142] For a State case spawned by the *Buckley* decision *see* Guidry *v.* Roberts, 331 So. 2d. 44 (1976). A Louisiana appeals court dealt with the governor's appointment power under the State constitution and the State law which had been modeled on the Federal law.
[143] United States *v.* Cowan, 396 F.Supp. 803 (1974).
[144] United States *v.* Cowan, 524 F. 2d. 504 (1975).

rect the commencement of a prosecution as against the "termination of a prosecution in being." As to the former, the court said the "absolute power and discretion of the Attorney General or his subordinates to institute prosecution is conceded." (*See* p. 192.)

¶3. The President shall have power to fill up all vacancies that may happen during the recess of the Senate, by granting commissions which shall expire at the end of their next session.

There has been considerable argument throughout our history as to what the word "happen" means in this context. Some have argued that the President could fill any vacancy which happened to *exist* during recess; others have contended that he could only fill those which happened to *occur* during the recess.[145] In practice Presidents have tended to take the broader view. This practice received judicial sanction in 1962 from the United States Court of Appeals for the Second Circuit.[146] It was pointed out that if a vacancy existed on account of inaction in the Senate it would have to continue throughout the recess, and in this way the work of government might be greatly impeded. The power to make recess appointments gives the President an advantage in a contest with the Senate over an appointment. Once someone is in a post, even temporarily, it is more difficult to oppose confirmation.[147] Consequently, Congress as early as 1863 sought to discourage Presidents from making frequent use of the recess appointment by enacting a provision reading: "nor shall any money be paid out of the Treasury of the United States, as salary, to any person appointed during the recess of the Senate, to fill a vacancy in any existing office . . . until such appointee shall have been confirmed by the Senate."[148] Current law on the subject is more carefully drawn to withhold salary payment, with some exceptions, from a recess appointee who was picked to fill a vacancy which "existed while the Senate was in session and was by law required to be filled by and with the advice and consent of the Senate,[149] until such appointee has been confirmed by the Senate. . . ." Thus there is financial risk in accepting an appointment to a vacancy which *existed while the Senate was in session.*[150]

SECTION III

¶He shall from time to time give to the Congress information of the state of the Union, and recommend to their consideration such measures as he shall judge necessary and expedient; he may, on

[145] Joseph Harris, *The Advice and Consent of the Senate* (New York, 1953), 255-257.
[146] U.S. *v.* Alloco, 395 F. 2d. 704 (1962); *cert. denied*, 371 U.S. 964 (1963).
[147] For further elaboration, *see* Chase, *Federal Judges: The Appointing Process*, pp. 14-16.
[148] 12 *Stat.* 646 (1863).   [149] 5 U.S.C. 5503.
[150] 41 *Op. Atty. Gen.* 463 (1960).

extraordinary occasions, convene both houses, or either of them, and in case of disagreement between them with respect to the time of adjournment, he may adjourn them to such time as he shall think proper; he shall receive ambassadors and other public ministers; he shall take care that the laws be faithfully executed, and shall commission all the officers of the United States.

Legislative
Leadership
of the
President

Prior even to recent Administrations, the duty conferred by the opening clause of this section had come to be, at the hands of outstanding Presidents like Washington, Jefferson, Theodore Roosevelt, and Wilson a tremendous power of legislative leadership.[1] The President is not, on the other hand, obliged by this clause to impart information which, in his judgment, the public interest requires should be kept secret.[2]

The President has frequently summoned Congress into what is known as "special session." His power to adjourn the houses has never been exercised.

The power to "receive ambassadors and other public ministers" includes the power to dismiss them for sufficient cause; and the exercise of the latter power may, as in the case of Count Bernstorff early in 1917, result in a breach of diplomatic relations leading eventually to hostilities. The same power also carries with it the power to recognize new governments or to refuse them recognition, also a very important power sometimes, as was shown by President Wilson's success in thus bringing about the downfall of President Huerta of Mexico in 1916.

Finally, it may be said that it is the President's power under this clause, taken together with his power in connection with treaty-making and with the appointment of the diplomatic representatives of the United States, that gives him his large initiative in determining the foreign policies of the United States. In the words of Jefferson, although, characteristically, he did not always choose to abide by their consequences, "the transaction of business with foreign nations is executive altogether."[3] Moreover, as Chief Executive the President is protector of American rights and interests abroad, a capacity which has become progressively more and more difficult to demark *vis-à-vis* Congress's power "to declare war."

It is worth noting in passing, at a time when it has become common for self-appointed negotiators to seek rapprochement with Cuba and Vietnam, there has been legislation (the Logan Act) on the books since 1798 which makes it a crime for "any citizen" without authority of the United States to carry on "any correspondence or intercourse with any foreign government or of any officer or

---

[1] Louis W. Koenig, *The Chief Executive* (New York, 1968), ch. 6, and Joseph E. Kallenbach, *The American Chief Executive* (New York, 1966), chs. 10 and 11.

[2] *See* pp. 183-187 above.

[3] "Opinion on the Question Whether the Senate Has the Right," etc., April 24, 1790, Saul K. Padover, *The Complete Jefferson* (New York, 1943), 138.

agent thereof in relation to any disputes or controversies with the United States."[4]

The President, be it noted, does not enforce the laws himself, but sees to it that they are enforced, and this is so even in the case of those laws which confer powers upon the President directly rather than upon some head of department or bureau.[5] But a circuit court has held that "the function of initiating a judicial proceeding for the enforcement of a legislative enactment is not the exercise of a prerogative exclusively reserved to the President" and that administrative bodies, such as the Interstate Commerce Commission could do so without violating the Constitution.[6]

Frequently, of course, statutes give power to specific officers to perform certain duties. This raises the question of what the President may do if he does not believe that an officer is executing a law faithfully. Ultimately, that answer must ride on the President's removal power. Whomever he can remove, he can force to do his bidding or replace him. With those he cannot remove, he can only contest. (*See* p. 181 and the cases cited therein.) Commonly Presidents have been exercised about actions of chairmen of the Board of the Federal Reserve System, for example; none has found a means for bringing them to heel except persuasion.

Because of his duty "to take care that the laws be faithfully executed," the President has the right to take any necessary measures which are not forbidden by statute to protect against impending danger those great interests which are entrusted by the Constitution to the National Government. He may order a marshal to protect a Justice of the Supreme Court whose life has been threatened, and his order will be treated by the courts as having the force of law.[7] He may dispatch troops to points at which the free movement of the mails and of interstate commerce is being impeded by private combinations, or through the Department of Justice he may turn to the courts and ask them to employ the powers which the statutes regulating their jurisdiction afford them to forbid such combinations.[8] And, generally, from an early date he has been authorized by statute to employ available military forces against "combinations too powerful to be suppressed by the ordinary course of judicial proceedings or by the power vested in the marshals."[9]

It was under such statutes that President Eisenhower ordered troops to Arkansas in 1957, and President Kennedy to Mississippi and Alabama in 1962 and 1963.[10] However, these statutes require that "Whenever the President considers it necessary to use the

Presidential Powers in Law Enforcement

---

[4] For the current law, *see* 18 U.S.C. 953.

[5] Williams *v.* U.S., 1 How. 290 (1843), and cases there cited.

[6] I.C.C. *v.* Chatsworth Cooperative Marketing Ass'n, 347 F. 2d. 821, 822 (1965); *cert. denied*, 382 U.S. 938 (1965).

[7] *In re* Neagle, 135 U.S. 1 (1890).

[8] *In re* Debs, 158 U.S. 564 (1895); United States *v.* U.M.W., 330 U.S. 258 (1947), 61 *Stat.* 136, 155-156 (1947); the "Taft-Hartley Act."

[9] 1 *Stat.* 264, 424 (1795); 2 *Stat.* 443 (1807).   [10] 10 U.S.C. 332, 333, 334.

militia or the armed forces under this chapter, he shall, by proclamation, immediately order the insurgents to disperse and retire
peaceably to their abodes within a limited time." For that reason we
queried the Justice Department as to why President Nixon did not
do so during the May Day confrontation of 1971. We quote from
the reply: "No proclamation was issued by the President. However,
as you know, the admitted purpose of the May Day demonstrations
was to halt the functioning of the federal government. The President has the inherent power and the duty under the Constitution
as Chief Executive to insure the continued functioning of the government and to protect government property. The troops were
used to insure that federal employees had access to their places of
employment so that they could carry on the government's work
and to protect the government's property."

Some recent lower court decisions are enlightening as to the
powers that inhere in the Presidency as a result of the constitutional instruction that "he shall take care that the laws be faithfully
executed."

In 1976, the U.S. Court of Appeals, Ninth Circuit, reminded that
"It has long been recognized that the Executive Branch of government 'has exclusive authority and absolute discretion to decide
whether to prosecute a case' " and that "This power has its roots in
the Executive's constitutional duty to take care that the laws of the
United States be faithfully executed."[11] (*See* p. 189.)

Another U.S. appeals court held that an executive order and its
implementing directive requiring government agencies to evaluate
the inflationary impact of proposed regulations was "intended
primarily as a managerial tool for implementing the President's
personal economic policies and not as a legal framework enforceable by private civil action."[12] The court instructed that the President's power to execute the laws does not *alone* give an executive
order "the force and effect of law." There must be, the court insisted, "a statutory mandate or a delegation of authority from Congress" for Presidential proclamations and orders to have the force
and effect of laws.

In a case arising from an effort by the U.S. Attorney General to
enjoin certain practices and policies of the Maryland health administrators, which he charged violated the constitutional rights of
the mentally retarded, a Federal district court stated that the clause
was circumscribed in the manner described by Justice Frankfurter
in the *Steel Seizure* case. The court concluded there was no
emergency justifying the Attorney General's action: "Thus, this
court concludes that the executive's severe burden to justify independent action in the face of Congressional disapproval of such action has not been met."[13]

[11] United States *v.* Alessio, 528 F. 2d. 1079 (1976).
[12] Independent Meat Packers Ass'n *v.* Butz, 526 F. 2d. 228 (1975).
[13] United States *v.* Solomon, 419 F.Supp. 358, 372 (1976).

In cases of "necessity," the President, or his subordinates at the scene of action, may proclaim martial law, of which two grades are today recognized—*preventive* and *punitive*. The latter, which is equivalent to *military government* is not, by the *Milligan* case,[14] allowable when the civil courts are open and properly functioning, nor in the presence of merely "threatened invasion. The necessity must be actual and present; the invasion real." And it was by applying this test literally that a divided Court held in 1946 that the President had had no constitutional power to institute military government in the Territory of Hawaii following the Japanese assault on Pearl Harbor, or to continue it after that date.[15] The Achilles' heel of the decision consists in the fact that it was not rendered till after the war was over and the danger past. For Total War, when "home front" activities are only an extension of the battlefront and when crippling and demoralizing attacks by air may be launched from bases hundreds of miles away, the test set by the above-quoted dictum is inadequate.

Under "preventive martial law," so-called because it authorizes "preventive" arrests and detentions, the military acts as an adjunct of the civil authorities but not necessarily subject to their orders. It may be established whenever the executive organ, State or national, deems it to be necessary for the restoration of good order. The concept, being of judicial origin, is of course for judicial application, and ultimately for application by the Supreme Court, in enforcement of the "due process" clauses.[16] (*See also*, Section III of this Article, and Article IV, Section IV.)

Another way in which the President's executive powers have been enlarged in recent years is by the growing practice by Congress of passing laws in broad, general terms, which have to be supplemented by regulations drawn up by a head of department under the direction of the President. Under legislation which Con-

Two Kinds of Martial Law

Delegations of Legislative Power to the President

---

[14] 4 Wall. 2 (1866).

[15] Duncan *v.* Kahanamoku and White *v.* Steer, 327 U.S. 304 (1946).

[16] Moyer *v.* Peabody, 212 U.S. 78 (1909); Sterling *v.* Constantin, 287 U.S. 378 (1932). The Great Depression produced an epidemic of declarations of "martial law" in some ill-defined sense of the term, by governors of States. "The records of the War Department show that in the fiscal year 1934, twenty-seven States mobilized the Guard for emergency duty, and in the next year the number reached thirty-two. The occasions have often been small, even trivial in compass." Charles Fairman, "Law of Martial Rule and the National Emergency," 55 *Harvard Law Review*, 1253 (1942), at p. 1275. In recent years, the calling out of the Guard has again reached epidemic proportions. When Governor Faubus of Arkansas called out the Guard to maintain the peace in Little Rock and prevented black children from attending a school which had been ordered to integrate, the occasion was afforded the Supreme Court to decide an important constitutional issue. The Court held that "law and order are not here to be preserved by depriving the Negro children of their constitutional rights." Cooper *v.* Aaron, 358 U.S. 1, 16 (1958). In short, courts will not usually challenge the governor's judgment in calling out the Guard, but they will require that when he does so, he must use it to uphold the exercise of constitutional rights. *See* Wilson and Company *v.* Freeman, 179 F.Supp. 520 (1959). (Note in that case the Court did challenge the governor's judgment.)

gress passed during World War I, the following powers, among others, were vested in the President: to control absolutely the transportation and distribution of foodstuffs; to fix prices; to license importation, exportation, manufacture, storage, and distribution of the necessaries of life; to operate the railroads; to issue passports; to control cable and telegraph lines; to declare embargoes; to determine priority of shipments; to loan money to foreign governments; to enforce Prohibition; to redistribute and regroup the executive bureaus; and in carrying these powers into effect the President's authorized agents put in operation a huge number of executive regulations having the force of law; and the two War Powers Acts and other legislation repeated this pattern in World War II.[17]

Meantime, however, the Court had held that Congress in enacting the NIRA in 1933 had parted with its own powers somewhat too lavishly, and for the first time in the history of the country an act of Congress was set aside, in the "Hot Oil" cases of 1934,[18] as violative of the maxim that "the legislature may not delegate its powers." Congress, the Court argued, had failed to lay down sufficient "standards" to guide executive action, and without doubt it had acted with unnecessary haste. Even so, subsequent decisions upholding broad delegations of power to various administrative agencies of the Government make it plain that, as the sphere of national power expands and the problems confronting the National Government become more complex, Congress will encounter ever lessening judicial resistance to its developing policy of leaving the details of legislative projects to be filled in by such agencies, which are able to carry on constant researches in their respective fields and to adapt their measures to changing conditions with comparative ease.[19] For example, in the early 1970's we lived under a Presidential wage and price freeze stemming from a statute which reads: "The President is authorized to issue such orders and regulations as he may deem appropriate to stabilize prices, rents, wages, and salaries at levels not less than those prevailing on May 25, 1970. Such orders and regulations may provide for the making of such adjustments as may be necessary to prevent gross inequities."[20] Shades of NIRA!

Moreover, in United States *v.* Curtiss-Wright Export Corpora-

[17] *See* especially Yakus *v.* U.S., 321 U.S. 414 (1944), in which the Emergency Price Control Act of January 30, 1942, was sustained against the objection that it delegated legislative power unconstitutionally to OPA.

[18] Panama Refining Co. *v.* Ryan, 293 U.S. 388 (1935). *See also* Schechter Bros. *v.* U.S., 295 U.S. 495 (1935).

[19] *See* especially Justice Roberts's dissenting opinion in Hood & Sons *v.* U.S., 307 U.S. 588, 603 (1939); Opp Cotton Mills *v.* Administrator, etc., 312 U.S. 126 (1941); and the Yakus case, cited above.

[20] 84 *Stat.* 799 (1970). *See* Executive Order No. 11627 promulgated Oct. 16, 1971, 36 *Fed. Reg.* 20139. Subsequently, the Economic Stabilization Program was terminated by Executive Order No. 11788, 39 *Fed. Reg.* 22113 (1974).

tion,[21] the Court, speaking by Justice Sutherland, used language implying that there is virtually no constitutional limit to Congress's power to delegate to the President authority which is "cognate" to his own constitutional powers, and especially his powers in the diplomatic field. The Lend-Lease Act,[22] while we were still formally at peace, authorized the President for a stated period (it was afterward renewed) to manufacture or "otherwise procure" to the extent of available funds "defense articles" (i.e., anything judged by him to be such), and lease, lend, exchange, or "otherwise dispose" of them, on terms "satisfactory" to himself, to any government, if he deemed that in so doing he was aiding the defense of the United States.

In 1976 the Supreme Court further demonstrated that the doctrine of non-delegation of Congressional powers as a judicially enforceable constitutional limitation has suffered enfeeblement. (*See* p. 7.) The Trade Expansion Act of 1962 as amended by the Trade Act of 1974 provides that, if the Secretary of the Treasury finds that an "article is being imported into the United States in such quantities or under such circumstances as to threaten to impair the national security," the President is authorized to take such action to "adjust the imports . . . so that . . . [they] will not impair the national security." In a challenge to a Presidential action that, among other things, raised the license fees on imported oil, the Supreme Court decided that "Taken as a whole then, the legislative history . . . belies any suggestion that Congress, despite its use of broad language in the statute itself, intended to limit the President's authority to the imposition of quotas and to bar the President from imposing a license fee system like the one challenged here. To the contrary [the history] lead[s] to the conclusion that . . . [the act] does in fact authorize the actions of the President challenged here. Accordingly, the judgment of the Court of Appeals to the contrary cannot stand."[23] But the Court did warn in conclusion that the "holding today is a limited one," that the act "in no way compels the further conclusion that *any* action the President might take, as long as it has even a remote impact on imports, is also so authorized."

In brief, the President's duty "to take care that the laws be faithfully executed" becomes often a power to make the laws. Furthermore, as was pointed out earlier, his duty also embraces the defense of American rights and interests abroad, since he is, *vis-à-vis* other governments, the Chief Executive of its treaties and of International Law. The function is one the discharge of which it sometimes becomes difficult to demark from the war-making power of Congress. Nor was this unforeseen by the Framers.

Thus when it was proposed in the Federal Convention, on August 17, 1787, to authorize Congress "to make war," Madison and

Presidential War-Making

---

[21] 299 U.S. 304, 327 (1936).   [22] 55 *Stat.* 31 (1941).
[23] Federal Energy Administration *v.* Algonquin SNG, Inc., 426 U.S. 548 (1976).

Gerry "moved to insert 'declare,' striking out 'make' war, leaving to the Executive the power to repel sudden attacks," and the motion carried.[24] Early in Jefferson's first administration, the question arose whether the President had the right to employ naval forces to protect American shipping against the Tripolitan pirates. The President himself was so doubtful on the point that he instructed his commander, that if he took any prisoners he should release them; also, that while he could disarm captured vessels in self-defense, he must release those too. These scruples excited the derision of Hamilton, who advanced the contention that if we were attacked we were *ipso facto* at war willy-nilly, and that Congress's prerogative was exclusive only when it came to putting the country into a state of war *ab initio*.[25] At the time Jefferson's view prevailed, Congress formally voting him war powers against the Bey of Tripoli.[26] Later developments have favored Hamilton's thesis. Commenting on the action of Lieutenant Hollins in 1854 in ordering the bombardment of Greytown, Nicaragua, in default of reparations from the local authorities for an attack by a mob on the United States consul stationed there, Justice Nelson, on circuit, said: "As respects the interposition of the Executive abroad for the protection of the lives or property of the citizen, the duty must, of necessity rest in the discretion of the President . . . under our system of government the citizen abroad is as much entitled to protection as the citizen at home,"[27] words which were endorsed by the Supreme Court in 1890. The President's duty, said Justice Miller, is not limited "to the enforcement of acts of Congress or of treaties of the United States according to their express terms," but includes "the rights, duties and obligations growing out of the Constitution itself, our international relations, and all the protection implied by the nature of the Government under the Constitution."[28]

In his small volume on *World Policing and the Constitution*[29] Mr. James Grafton Rogers listed 149 episodes similar to the Greytown affair, stretching between the undeclared war with France in 1798 and Pearl Harbor. While inviting some pruning, the list demonstrates beyond peradventure that Presidents as Chief Executives and Commanders-in-Chief, have for a long time exercised the power to judge whether a situation requires the use of available forces to protect American rights of persons and property outside

[24] Max Farrand, ed., *The Records of the Federal Constitution of 1787*, II (New Haven, 1937), 318-319.
[25] Corwin, *The President, Office and Powers*, 242-243.
[26] Act of February 6, 1802.
[27] Durand *v*. Hollins, 4 Blatch. 451, 454 (1860).
[28] *In re* Neagle, 135 U.S. 1, 64.
[29] (Boston, 1945.) *See also*, for the period 1811 to 1934, J. Reuben Clark's Memorandum as Solicitor of the Department of State entitled *Right to Protect Citizens in Foreign Countries by Landing Forces* (Washington, D.C., 1934). The great majority of the landings were for "the simple protection of American citizens in disturbed areas," and only about a third involved belligerent action.

the United States and to take action in harmony with that decision. Such employment of the forces has, it is true, been usually justified as acts of self-defense rather than acts of war, but the countries where they occurred were entitled to treat them as acts of war nevertheless, although they were generally too feeble to assert their prerogative in this respect, and sometimes actually chose to turn the other cheek. Thus when in 1900 President McKinley, without consulting Congress, contributed a sizeable contingent to the joint forces that went to the relief of the foreign legations in Peking, the Chinese Imperial Government agreed that this action had not constituted war.[30]

And Article V of the North Atlantic Treaty was built on such precedents. The novel feature was its enlarged conception of defensible American interests abroad. In the words of the published abstract of the Report of the Committee on Foreign Relations on the Pact, "Article 5 records what is a fact, namely, that an armed attack within the meaning of the treaty would in the present-day world constitute an attack upon the entire community comprising the parties to the treaty, including the United States. Apparently, the President and the Congress, each within their sphere of assigned constitutional responsibilities, were expected to take all action necessary and appropriate to protect the United States against the consequences and dangers of an armed attack committed against any party to the treaty."[31] And from the very nature of things, the discharge of this obligation against overt force would ordinarily have rested with the President in the first instance, just as had the discharge in the past of the like obligation in the protection of American rights abroad. Furthermore, in the discharge of this obligation the President would be expected to use force and perform acts of war. Such was the verdict of history, a verdict which was confirmed by our intervention in Korea under the auspices of the United Nations.

President and Congress and the Atlantic Pact

That Congress has attempted to reverse that verdict during the Vietnam conflict and its aftermath is clear.[32] *See* pages 107-111. On the face of the War Powers Resolution, it would seem that Congress has been successful. Hopefully, the test will never come. But as indicated in those earlier pages, there is no guarantee that a future President will not challenge the constitutionality of the Resolution. Also, there is no guarantee that the facts in a given situation may provide the President with ample public support in such an in-

[30] Moore, *International Law Digest*, V, 478-510, *passim*.
[31] U.S., 81st Congress, 1st Sess., Senate, Document 123 (1949). 63 *Stat.* 2244. *Note also* Article IV of the Southeast Asia Collective Defense Treaty. 6 UST 82, 83 (1954).
[32] *See* the "Yale Paper," "Indo-China: The Constitutional Crisis" Part I in 116 *Cong. Rec.* S7117-S7123 (daily ed. May 13, 1970); Part II in 116 *Cong. Rec.* S7591-S7593 (May 21, 1970). For view upholding President's power, *see* William H. Rehnquist's remarks in Lockhart, Kamisar, Choper, *Constitutional Law Supplement 1971* (St. Paul, 1971), 20-25.

stance. In that connection the *Mayaguez* incident may provide some guidance.[33]

"The aggregate of powers" available to the President in the absence of controlling legislation is impressive, a fact which was dramatically advertised when, in April 1952, President Truman, in order to avert a nationwide strike of steel workers, directed the Secretary of Commerce to seize and operate most of the steel mills of the country.[34] The President cited no specific statutory warrant for this step, but urged the requirements of national defense at home and of our allies abroad, and cited generally "the authority vested in me by the Constitution and laws of the United States." Before he could execute the order, the Secretary was stopped by an injunction which, in due course, the Supreme Court affirmed.[35]

The pivotal proposition of "the opinion of the Court" by Justice Black was that, inasmuch as Congress could have ordered the seizure of the mills, the President lacked power to do so without its authorization. In support of this position, which purported to have the endorsement of four other members of the Court, Justice Black invoked the principle of the Separation of Powers, but otherwise adduced no proof from previous decisions or from governmental practice. The opinion bears, in fact, the earmarks of hasty improvisation, and is unquestionably contradicted by a considerable record of Presidential pioneering in territory that was eventually occupied by Congress.

Thus Washington in 1793 issued the first Neutrality Proclamation. The year following Congress, at the President's suggestion, enacted the first neutrality statute.[36] In 1799 the elder Adams extradited the first fugitive from justice under the Jay Treaty, and was successfully defended by Marshall in the House of Representatives for his course.[37] Not till 1848 did Congress provide another method.[38] Also in 1799, an American naval vessel seized a Danish craft trading in the West Indies. Although it disallowed the seizure as violative of an act of Congress, the Court, by Chief Justice Marshall, voiced the opinion that but for the act, the President could in the circumstances have ordered it by virtue of his duty "to take care that the laws be faithfully executed" and of his power as commander of the forces.[39] That the President may, in the absence of legislation by Congress, control the landing of foreign cables in the United States and the passage of foreign troops through American

The *Steel Seizure Case of 1952*

Presidential Pioneering in the Legislative Field

---

[33] For discussion of Congressional reaction to *Mayaguez* incident, *see* 1975 *Cong. Quart. Weekly Report*, 1008.

[34] Executive Order 10340, 17 *Fed. Reg.* 3139.

[35] Youngstown Sheet & Tube Co. *v*. Sawyer, 343 U.S. 579 (1952).

[36] 1 *Stat.* 381 (1794). For Washington's suggestion, *see* his Message of December 5, 1793, Richardson, *Messages and Papers of the President*, I, 139.

[37] 343 U.S. 579, 684 (1952), citing 10 *Annals of Congress* 619.

[38] *Rev. Stat.* §§5270-5279 (1878).

[39] Little *v*. Barreme, 2 Cr. 170, 177 (1804).

territory, has been shown repeatedly.[40] Likewise, until Congress
acts, he may govern conquered territory[41] and, "in the absence of
attempts by Congress to limit his power," may set up military commissions in territory occupied by the Armed Forces of the United
States.[42] That during the Civil War Lincoln's suspensions of the
writ of *habeas corpus* paved the way to authorizing legislation was
pointed out above (*see* p. 125). Similarly, Lincoln's action in seizing
the railroad and telegraph lines between Washington and Baltimore in 1861 was followed early in 1862 by an act of Congress generally authorizing such seizures when dictated by military necessity.[43]

On the specific issue of seizures of industrial property, Justice
Frankfurter incorporated much pertinent data in an appendix to
his concurring opinion.[44] Of statutes authorizing such seizures he
listed eighteen between 1916 and 1951; and of Presidential seizures without specific statutory authorization he listed eight for the
World War I period and eleven for the World War II period, several of which occurred before the outbreak of hostilities. In the
War Labor Disputes Act of June 25, 1943,[45] such seizures were put
on a statutory basis; and in United States *v.* Pewee Coal Co., Inc.,[46]
they were, in implication, sustained as having been validly made.[47]

In consequence of the evident belief of at least four of the Justices who concurred in the judgment in Youngstown that Congress
had exercised its powers in the premises of the case in opposition to
seizure, by the procedures which it had laid down in the Taft-
Hartley Act, the lesson of the case is somewhat blurred. But that
the President does possess, in the absence of restrictive legislation,
a residual or resultant power above, or in consequence of his
granted powers, to deal with emergencies which he regards as
threatening the national security, is explicitly asserted by Justice
Clark,[48] and was evidently held, with certain qualifications, by Justices Frankfurter and Jackson, and was the essence of the position
of the dissenting Justices.[49] The lesson of the case, therefore, if it

Presidential
Seizures of
Property

[40] 22 *Op. Atty. Gen.* 13 (1898); Tucker *v.* Alexandroff, 183 U.S. 424, 435 (1902).
An act passed May 27, 1921, 42 *Stat.* 8, requires Presidential license for the landing
and operation of cables connecting the United States with foreign countries. Quincy
Wright, *The Control of American Foreign Relations* (New York, 1922), p. 302 n. 75.

[41] Santiago *v.* Nogueras, 214 U.S. 260 (1909).

[42] Madsen *v.* Kinsella, 343 U.S. 341 (1952).   [43] 12 *Stat.* 334.

[44] 343 U.S. 579, 615-626 (1952).   [45] 57 *Stat.* 163.

[46] 341 U.S. 114 (1951).

[47] This is because damages were awarded in the Pewee case, implying the Court's
acceptance of the idea that the seizure had been a governmental act. *See* Hooe *v.*
United States, 218 U.S. 322, 335-336 (1910); United States *v.* North American Co.,
253 U.S. 330, 333 (1920). *Cf.* Larson *v.* Domestic and Foreign Corp., 337 U.S. 682,
701-702 (1949).

[48] 343 U.S. at 662-663.

[49] A notable feature of Chief Justice Vinson's opinion for himself and Justices
Reed and Minton is a long passage extracted from the Government's brief in United

has a lesson, is that escape from Presidential autocracy today must be sought along the legislative route rather than that of judicial review.[50] But any impression that the American President has become a modern incarnation of Caesar, as has been alleged from time to time, does not conform to reality, despite the President's enormous legal powers described above. A distinction should be recognized and acknowledged between a President's power with respect to foreign affairs and domestic affairs. The President's role in foreign affairs is much more conclusive than his role in domestic affairs. In a television interview in which President Kennedy discussed his first two years in office, he described at length the inordinate difficulty a President, any President, has in getting a program through Congress. He concluded by saying: "So that they are two separate offices and two separate powers, the Congress and the Presidency, there is bound to be conflict, but they must cooperate to the degree that is possible. But that is why no President's program is *ever* put in. *The only time a President's program is put in quickly and easily is when the program is insignificant. But* if it is significant and affects important interests and is controversial, therefore, then there is a fight, and the President is never wholly successful (emphasis supplied)."[51] The best explanation for why this is so was provided by Professor James M. Burns: "We have been too much entranced by the Madisonian model of government. . . . This model was the product of the gifted men who gathered in Philadelphia over 175 years ago, and it deserves much of the admiration and veneration we have accorded it. But this is also the system of checks and balances and interlocked gears of government that requires the consensus of many groups and leaders before the nation can act; and it is a system that exacts the heavy price of delay and devitalization that I have noted."[52] In addition, Professor Richard Neustadt has provided a graphic account of just how difficult it is for a President in practice to have his wishes translated into action on the home front.[53]

For those disenchanted with the American system in the 1970's, seeking solutions to the problems of war, civil rights, pollution,

States *v.* Midwest Oil Co., 236 U.S. 459 (1915). It emphasizes and illustrates the proposition that there "are fields [of power] which are common to both [Congress and the President] in the sense that the Executive may move within them until they shall have been occupied by legislative action." 343 U.S. 574, 691 (1952). The authors of the brief were Solicitor General John W. Davis and Assistant Attorney General Knaebel. The former, ironically, was Youngstown's principal counsel.

[50] This conclusion is emphasized by the division of the Court in the case of Cole *v.* Young, 351 U.S. 536 (1956) and by the care with which the Court safeguarded the executive privilege (albeit a non-absolute one) in United States *v.* Nixon, 418 U.S. 683. *See* p. 182.

[51] Harold W. Chase and Allen H. Lerman, *Kennedy and the Press* (New York, 1965), 353.

[52] James M. Burns, *The Deadlock of Democracy* (Englewood Cliffs, N.J., 1963), 6.

[53] Richard E. Neustadt, *Presidential Power: The Politics of Leadership* (New York, 1960).

poverty, safety in the streets among others, the answers may well lie in finding ways to reduce the checks and balances with respect to domestic action and finding some with respect to the conduct of foreign affairs.

SECTION IV

¶The President, Vice-President and all civil officers of the United States shall be removed from office on impeachment for and conviction of treason, bribery, or other high crimes and misdemeanors.

As indicated earlier, pp. 14-15, there have been important impeachments in our history, but as former Senator Joseph D. Tydings has so eloquently pointed out: "Even in the early years of the Republic the inadequacy of this process was recognized. As early as 1819, Thomas Jefferson said: 'Experience has already shown that the impeachment the Constitution has provided is not even a scarecrow. It is a cumbersome, archaic process. . . .' "[1]

As to the meaning of "conviction of treason, bribery, or other high crimes and misdemeanors," constitutional scholar Raoul Berger enlightens us with these words: "Parliament, it is true, asserted virtually unlimited power; but the Framers had no intention of conferring such power upon Congress. Untrammeled declarations of treason in any form were made impossible by a tight definition of treason. And the Framers adopted 'high crimes and misdemeanors' because they thought the words had a 'limited,' 'technical' meaning. Whether they misconceived the actual scope of the words is of no moment if they acted upon that view, as the records of the Convention show they did." He continued, "For special reasons, the Founders conceived that the President would be impeachable for 'great offenses' such as corruption, perfidy."[2]

Because of his duty "to take care that the laws be faithfully executed (Section III, ¶s 6 and 7), the President's principal subordinates are answerable to him, since as the law has stood from the beginning of the National Government, except for a brief period after the Civil War, he has had a practically unrestricted power of removal; but Congress may qualify this power in the case of agencies whose powers are derived solely from Congress, and especially is this true as to agencies like the Interstate Commerce Commission, the Federal Trade Commission, and so on, which are often required to proceed in a semi-judicial manner.[3] *The Legal Responsibility of Inferior Officers*

Furthermore, all officers below the President, including such "independent commissions," are responsible to the courts in vari-

[1] U.S., 89th Congress, 2d. Sess., Senate, Committee on the Judiciary, *Hearing*, "Judicial Fitness," Feb. 15, 1966, pp. 3-4.

[2] Raoul Berger, *Impeachment: The Constitutional Problems* (Cambridge, 1973), p. 298. *See also* Charles L. Black, Jr., *Impeachment: A Handbook* (New Haven, 1974).

[3] Humphrey's Executor *v.* U.S., 295 U.S. 602 (1935); Wiener *v.* U.S., 357 U.S. 349 (1958).

ous ways. Indeed, an order of the President himself not in accordance with law will be set aside by the courts if a case involving it comes before them.[4] Also, while the President may not be prohibited by writ of injunction from doing a threatened illegal act, or be compelled by writ of mandamus to perform a duty definitely required by law,[5] his subordinates do not share his immunity, suits against them being usually brought in the United States District Court for the District of Columbia.[6] Also, by common law principles, a subordinate executive officer is personally liable under the ordinary law for any act done in excess of authority.[7] Indeed, district courts of the United States are bound to entertain suits for damages arising out of alleged violation of plaintiff's constitutional rights, even though as the law now stands the court is often times powerless to award damages.[8] But Congress may, in certain cases, exonerate the officer by a so-called act of indemnity;[9] while as the law stands at present, any officer of the United States who is charged with a crime under the laws of a State for an act done "under the authority of the United States" is entitled to have his case transferred to the national courts.[10]

The extent of the President's own liability under the ordinary law, while he is clothed with official authority, is a matter of some doubt. Impeachment aside, his principal responsibility seems to be simply his accountability, as Chief Justice Marshall expressed it, "to his country in his political character, and to his own conscience."[11]

It is safe to predict that the invocation of the impeachment process to force President Nixon out of office will be debated endlessly among practitioners in the political process and students and scholars of the Constitution as to the meaning and the effectiveness of the impeachment process set forth in the Constitution. As to effectiveness, there undoubtedly will be those who will hold that it was the threat of impeachment that forced Nixon to resign. On the other hand, there will be those who will argue that Jefferson was right that "the impeachment the Constitution has provided is not even a scarecrow," that it was only the highly unusual and bizarre circumstances where the President was virtually caught with the "smoking gun" in hand that impeachment became a real possibility. And for that to happen chance had to play an enormous role. What

[4] Kendall v. U.S., 12 Pet. 524 (1838); United States v. Lee, 106 U.S. 196 (1882).

[5] Mississippi v. Johnson, 4 Wall. 475 (1866).

[6] United States v. Schurz, 102 U.S. 378 (1880); United States v. Black, 128 U.S. 40 (1888); Riverside Oil Co. v. Hitchcock, 190 U.S. 316 (1903).

[7] Little v. Barreme, 2 Cr. 170 (1804); United States v. Lee, cited above; Spalding v. Vilas, 161 U.S. 483 (1896).

[8] Bell v. Hood, 327 U.S. 678 (1946). 28 U.S.C. 2331 and 28 U.S.C. 2680. See particularly Bivens v. Six Unknown Named Agents of Fed. Bur. of Narc., 409 F. 2d. 718 (1969), cert. denied, 397 U.S. 928 (1970).

[9] Mitchell v. Clark, 110 U.S. 633 (1884).

[10] 28 U.S.C. 1442; Willingham v. Morgan, 395 U.S. 402 (1969).

[11] Marbury v. Madison, 1 Cr. 137, 166-167 (1803).

if the Watergate break-in had not been bungled? What if there had been no tapes? What if—?

More solid stuff emerges from the experience with respect to the meaning of the impeachment provisions. The House Judiciary Committee debated and rendered its decision about what it considered to be impeachable offenses, and surely its conclusions will have some precedential value. Further, the proceedings were covered by television and a good portion of the sovereign people followed them with interest. Presumably that should give the Judiciary Committee's determinations additonal impact for the future. In that context, what the committee rejected may in the long run have greater significance than what it approved. The articles constituting the bill of impeachment dealt with (1) the President's alleged obstruction of justice, (2) the President's alleged violation of the constitutional rights of citizens, and (3) the President's alleged failure to comply with subpoenas issued by the committee. Most significantly, as indicated earlier (p. 110), the committee rejected an article that dealt with the alleged secret bombing of Cambodia. What can be reasonably inferred from this rejection about the President's powers as Commander-in-Chief and chief organ in foreign affairs? Is it a fair inference that the explicit rejection of this article has broadened and legitimized the exercise of those powers of the President? One could argue that President Ford was inhibited by the impeachment effort from endeavoring to go it alone and try to intervene militarily to prevent the collapse of South Vietnam. But then how does one explain his willingness to commit Marines to the rescue effort of the crew of the *Mayaguez* and the generally favorable Congressional reaction?[12]

[12] For text of articles *see* 1974 *Cong. Quart. Weekly Report*, 2020-2021. For discussion of Congressional reaction to *Mayaguez* incident, *see* 1975 *Cong. Quart. Weekly Report*, 1008.

ARTICLE III

This article completes the framework of the National Government by providing for "the judicial power of the United States."

SECTION I

¶ The judicial power of the United States shall be vested in one Supreme Court, and in such inferior courts as the Congress may from time to time ordain and establish. The judges, both of the Supreme and inferior courts, shall hold their offices during good behavior, and shall, at stated times, receive for their services a compensation which shall not be diminished during their continuance in office.

Inherent Elements of "Judicial Power"

"Judicial power" is the power to decide "cases" and "controversies" in conformity with law and by the methods established by the usages and principles of law.[1] It should not be confused with "jurisdiction," which is the authority of a court to exercise "judicial power" in a particular case. The Constitution vests the "judicial power" in the courts; Congress cannot, of course, change that, short of a constitutional amendment. But as shown below, Congress has considerable power under the Constitution to define the "jurisdiction" of the courts.

Like "legislative" and "executive power" under the Constitution, "judicial power," too, is thought to connote certain incidental or "inherent" attributes. One of these is the ability to interpret the standing law, whether the Constitution, acts of Congress, or judicial precedents, with an authority to which both the other departments are constitutionally obliged to defer.[2] But "political questions" often afford an exception to this general rule,[3] as also do so-called "questions of fact," which are often left to administrative bodies, although their determination may affect the scope of the authority of such bodies very materially.[4] And closely related to this attribute of judicial power is another, which may be termed power of "finality of decision." The underlying idea is that when a court of the United States is entrusted with the determination of any question *whether* of law or of fact, its decision of such question cannot

[1] Prentis *v*. Atl. Coast Line Co., 211 U.S. 210, 226 (1908). *See also* Muskrat *v*. U.S., 219 U.S. 346, 361 (1911); Securities & Exc. Com'n *v*. Medical Com. For Human Rights, 404 U.S. 403 (1972).

[2] *See* e.g., Federal Power Com'n *v*. Pacific Power and L. Co., 307 U.S. 156 (1939).

[3] On "political questions," *see* p. 219 below.

[4] Apparently, both Congress and the Supreme Court do not feel that leaving "questions of fact" primarily to administrative agencies and broadening the concept of what is a "question of fact" as opposed to a "question of law" is an abrogation of "judicial power." Consolo *v*. Federal Maritime Commission, 383 U.S. 607 (1966); Universal Camera Corp. *v*. Labor Board, 340 U.S. 474 (1951); 5 U.S.C. 706. For a thorough explication of this issue *see* Kenneth C. Davis, *Administrative Law Treatise* (St. Paul, 1958) and Supplement (St. Paul, 1970), ch. 30 in both.

constitutionally be made reviewable except by a higher *court*, that is, cannot be made reviewable by either of the other two departments, or any agency thereof.[5] Thus, so long as the decisions of the Court of Claims as to amounts due claimants against the Government were subject to disallowance by the Secretary of the Treasury, it was held not to be a "court," with the result that the Supreme Court could not take appeals from it.[6] But the principle is not an altogether rigid one, for the Court of Claims is today regarded as a true court, stemming from Article III, Section I, of the Constitution, despite the fact that its judgments have to be satisfied out of sums which only Congress can appropriate.[7] Also, the courts of the United States are today generally required to serve as adjuncts in the work of such administrative bodies as the Interstate Commerce Commission, the Federal Trade Commission, the National Labor Relations Board, etc., by backing up the valid findings of such tribunals with orders which those to whom they are addressed must obey if they do not want to go to jail for "contempt of court."[8]

Which calls attention to a third "inherent" judicial attribute, namely, the power of a court to vindicate its dignity and authority in the way just mentioned. This power was defined in general terms in the Judiciary Act of 1789 and further restricted by the Act of 1831, which limited punishable contempt to disobedience to any judicial process or decree and to misbehavior in the presence of the court, "or so near thereto as to obstruct the administration of justice."[9] The purpose of the last clause was to get rid of a doctrine of the common law which, although it has the sanction of Blackstone, is otherwise of dubious authenticity, that criticism reflecting on the conduct of a judge in a pending case constituted contempt because of its tendency to draw into question the impartiality of the court and to "scandalize justice."[10] Eighty-five years later, nevertheless, the Supreme Court largely restored the discredited doctrine by an enlarged interpretation of the "so near thereto" clause.[11] But not

Contempt
of Court

[5] For the start of this doctrine, *see* Hayburn's case, decided in 1792, 2 Dall. 409, and especially the reporter's notes. However, as the Supreme Court has pointed out "To give due weight to . . . congressional declarations is not of course to compromise the authority or responsibility of this Court as the ultimate expositor of the Constitution." Glidden Company *v.* Zdanok, 370 U.S. 530, 542-543 (1962).

[6] *See* Gordon *v.* U.S., 117 U.S., appendix (1864).

[7] DeGroot *v.* U.S., 5 Wall. 419 (1867); 67 *Stat.* 26 (1953); Glidden Company *v.* Zdanok, 370 U.S. 530 (1962).

[8] The great leading case is Interstate Com. Com'n *v.* Brimson, 154 U.S. 447 (1894). A 1946 decision inferentially sustains the right of Congress to confer the subpoena power upon administrative agencies. Justice Murphy dissented, saying he was "unable to approve the use of non-judicial subpoenas issued by administrative agents," but his protest was based on the great growth of administrative law "in the past few years," and not on the ground that the subpoena power was inherently or exclusively judicial. Oklahoma Press Pub. Co. *v.* Walling, 327 U.S. 186 (1946).

[9] 4 *Stat.* 487 (1831); *ex parte* Robinson, 19 Wall. 505 (1874).

[10] *See* the bibliographical data in Justice Douglas's opinion for the Court in Nye *v.* U.S., 313 U.S. 33 (1941).

[11] Toledo Newspaper Co. *v.* U.S., 247 U.S. 402 (1918).

only was this decision overturned in 1941,[12] but the Court a little later, by a vote of five Justices to four, ruled that for an utterance to be held in contempt simply in reliance on the common law, it must offer an "extremely serious" threat of causing a miscarriage of justice or of obstructing its orderly administration, otherwise the constitutional guaranty of freedom of press would be invaded.[13]

In recent years, the Supreme Court has been sharply divided over another aspect of the contempt power—the extent to which judges are entitled to punish for contempt *summarily*. There is no quarrel with the idea that judges must have the power to *cite* people for contempt. In 1970, the Supreme Court was unanimous in the belief that: "It is essential to the proper administration of criminal justice that dignity, order, and decorum be the hallmarks of all court proceedings in our country. The flagrant disregard in the courtroom of elementary standards of proper conduct should not and cannot be tolerated. We believe trial judges confronted with disruptive, contumacious, stubbornly defiant defendants must be given sufficient discretion to meet the circumstances of each case. No one formula for maintaining the appropriate courtroom atmosphere will be best in all situations. We think there are at least three constitutionally permissible ways for a trial judge to handle an obstreperous defendant . . . (1) bind and gag him, thereby keeping him present; (2) cite him for contempt; (3) take him out of the courtroom until he promises to conduct himself properly."[14] In 1958, Justice Black dissenting and speaking for Chief Justice Warren and Justice Douglas as well as himself bitterly complained: "The power of a judge to inflict punishment for criminal contempt by means of a summary proceeding stands as an anomaly in the law. In my judgment the time has come for a fundamental and searching reconsideration of the validity of this power which has aptly been characterized . . . as, 'perhaps, nearest akin to despotic power of any power existing under our form of government.' Even though this extraordinary authority first slipped into the law as a very limited and insignificant thing, it has relentlessly swollen, at the hands of not unwilling judges, until it has become a drastic and pervasive mode of administering criminal justice usurping our regular constitutional methods of trying those charged with offenses against society."[15] Justice Black ultimately won the day. In 1968, the Court held that the constitutional guarantees of a jury trial extended to "serious" criminal contempts[16] and in 1971 the

---

[12] *See* note 10 above.

[13] Bridges *v.* Calif., 314 U.S. 252 (1941); followed in Pennekamp *v.* Fla., 328 U.S. 331 (1946).

[14] Illinois *v.* Allen, 397 U.S. 337, 343 (1970).

[15] Green *v.* U.S., 356 U.S. 165, 194 (1958).

[16] Bloom *v.* Illinois, 391 U.S. 194 (1968). The Court explicitly refused to set the exact location of the line between petty offenses and "serious crimes" but went on to add "a crime punishable by two years in prison is . . . a serious crime." *Ibid.*, 211. *See* McGowan *v.* State, 258 So. 2d. 801 (1972). *See also* 18 U.S.C. 402 and 2691.

Court held that, in those criminal contempt cases which can still be tried without jury and which involve behavior contemptuous of a judge, due process requires that a defendant "should be given a public trial before a judge other than the one reviled by the contemnor."[17]

The U.S. Court of Appeals, Seventh Circuit, added to the meaning of the 1968 and 1971 Supreme Court decisions on criminal contempts, when it reviewed the contempt convictions emanating from the trial of the Chicago Seven. Judge Hoffman, who presided over the original trial, had sentenced most of the Chicago Seven to several months for *each* act of misbehavior, making the aggregate sentence for them more than six months. The circuit court held that "each appellant whose sentences aggregated more than 6 months was entitled to a jury trial."[18] Further, the circuit court held that the decision in *Mayberry* applies to lawyers as well as others. The court evidently felt compelled to address that issue because the opinion (as distinguished from the judgment) in *Mayberry* suggested that a trial judge *must* disqualify himself *only* if he waits until the conclusion of a trial to act against a contemnor[19] but at the same time indicated that contempts involving lawyers might be another matter. Justice Douglas had written: "Generalizations are difficult. Instant treatment of contempt where lawyers are involved *may* greatly prejudice their clients but it *may* be the only wise course where others are involved. . . . Where, however, he does not act the instant the contempt is committed, but waits until the end of the trial, on balance, *it is generally wise* where the marks of the unseemly conduct have left personal stings to ask a fellow judge to take his place."[20] (Emphasis supplied.) Whatever the true meaning of the *Mayberry* decision, the circuit court decided that "while the possible prejudice to the lawyer's clients may counterbalance the need to preserve order in the court through immediate action, this consideration simply has no bearing on whether the trial judge may himself proceed summarily or must call in another judge to take his place when he has already decided to wait."[21]

Later, the Supreme Court held that, although it could not accept the argument "that a contemnor is entitled to a jury trial whenever a strong possibility exists that he will face a substantial term of imprisonment upon conviction," in this particular case, "where contemnors were sentenced to an aggregate of six months' sentences for three years, three months and 2 years, eight months, respectively, each contemnor was tried for what was equivalent to a seri-

[17] Mayberry *v.* Pennsylvania, 400 U.S. 455 (1971).
[18] *In re* Dellinger, 461 F. 2d. 389, 397 (1972). *See also* United States *v.* Seale, 461 F. 2d. 345 (1972).
[19] *See* Justice Black's cryptic concurring opinion. Mayberry *v.* Pennsylvania, 400 U.S. 466 (1971).
[20] *Ibid.*, pp. 463-464. Compare this language with Justice Douglas's description of the Court's actual judgment as quoted at top of page.
[21] *In re* Dellinger, 461 F. 2d. 389, 395 (1972).

ous offense and was entitled to a jury trial." The Court went on to say that "Neither are we impressed with the contention that today's decision will provoke trial judges to punish summarily during trial rather than awaiting a calmer, more studied proceeding after trial and deliberating 'in the cool reflection of subsequent events.' . . . Summary convictions during trial that are unwarranted by the facts will not be invulnerable to appellate review."[22]

In 1974, in its canvass of Supreme Court opinions with respect to jury trials in contempt cases, the U.S. Court of Appeals, Ninth Circuit, made this significant observation: "Where contemnor is a corporation, association, union or other artificial person and a fine is the ordinary punishment, the rules become obscure. The Court has never said that while a $500 fine marks the contempt as being 'petty' under 18 U.S.C. 1 (3) with no jury required, a fine of $501 labels it as 'serious' with the necessary consequence that a jury must be empaneled. A fine which might under all of the circumstances constitute only a slap on the wrist of one artificial entity might be a 'serious' penalty to another."[23]

Subsequently, the Supreme Court cleared up the question raised by the U.S. Court of Appeals, Ninth Circuit. The Supreme Court held that "we cannot accept the proposition that a contempt must be considered a serious crime under all circumstances where the punishment is a fine of more than $500, unaccompanied by imprisonment. It is one thing to hold that deprivation of an individual's liberty beyond a six-month term should not be imposed without the protections of a jury trial, but it is quite another to suggest that, regardless of circumstances, a jury is required where any fine greater than $500 is contemplated. From the standpoint of determining the seriousness of the risk and the extent of the possible deprivation faced by a contemnor, imprisonment and fines are intrinsically different. It is not difficult to grasp the proposition that six months in jail is a serious matter for any individual, but it is not tenable to argue that the possibility of à $500 fine would be considered a serious risk to a large corporation or labor union."[24]

Another limitation on the contempt power is that it exists for the protection of the processes of the Court, and thereby of justice. "The judge," the Court has said, "must banish the slightest personal impulse to reprisal, but he should not bend backward and impair the authority of the Court by too great leniency."[25] In Sacher v. United States,[26] an outgrowth of the trial of the so-called Eleven Communists, this rule was adhered to. Here counsel for the

[22] Codispoti v. Pa., 418 U.S. 506 (1974). *See also* Taylor v. Hayes, 418 U.S. 488 (1974).

[23] Hoffman v. International Longshoremen's & Warehousemen's Union, Local No. 10, 492 F. 2d. 929, 937 (1974).

[24] Muniz v. Hoffman, 422 U.S. 454 (1975).

[25] Cooke v. U.S., 267 U.S. 517, 539 (1925).

[26] Sacher v. U.S., 343 U.S. 1, 13-14 (1952); Dennis v. U.S., 341 U.S. 494 (1951).

defense engaged in practices designed to break down the judge and break up the trial. In order not to further the latter objective Judge Harold Medina deferred calling them to account until the termination of the proceedings, and was sustained by the Court in so doing.

Two other restraints on the contempt power are, first, the provisions in recent civil rights legislation which grant the right to jury trial in contempt proceedings in situations where the alleged contempt might fall short of being of a "serious" crime.[27] Second, as was mentioned earlier, the President's pardoning power (*see* p. 165).

When an attorney appealed an order by the U.S. District Court for the District of New Jersey disbarring him from the practice of law in that court, the U.S. Court of Appeals, Third Circuit, held that it was an "unquestioned principle" that all Federal courts have the power "both to prescribe requirements for admission to practice before that court and to discipline attorneys who have been admitted to practice before that court."[28] As to Claims of Other Inherent Elements

But, with regard to mandatory sentences laid down by legislatures, the Connecticut Supreme Court recently held that "the judiciary's power to impose a particular sentence is defined by the legislature, and there is no Constitutional requirement that courts be given discretion in imposing a sentence."[29]

Also, it has been contended that legislation permitting non-unanimous jury verdicts intrudes upon "judicial power."[30] Apparently, the Supreme Court regards the contention as being without merit.[31]

In contrast to certain State courts, no court of the United States possesses the power, *in the absence of authorization by Congress*, to suspend the sentence of a convicted offender,[32] clemency being under the Constitution an executive function.

Also, it would seem that the Supreme Court regards itself as having the inherent power to determine whether an appointment to it was constitutionally valid, although such power may be invoked only by one who is able to show that "he has sustained or is in danger of sustaining a direct injury" as a result of the challenged appointment.[33] Varying Size of the Supreme Court

Although *a* Supreme Court is provided for by the Constitution, the organization of the existing Court rests on an act of Congress. The size of the Court is also a matter for legislative determination

---

[27] 42 U.S.C, 1995 and 2000h.

[28] Matter of Abrams, 521 F. 2d. 1094 (1975).

[29] State *v*. Darden, 372 A. 2d. 99 (1976).

[30] State *v*. Jackson, 254 So. 2d. 259 (1971).

[31] Apodaca *v*. Oregon, 406 U.S. 404 (1972); McKay *v*. State, 362 A. 2d. 666 (1976).

[32] *Ex parte* United States, 242 U.S. 27 (1916); Holiday *v*. Johnston, 313 U.S. 342 (1941). Congress has in fact given such authorization, 18 U.S.C. 3651.

[33] *Ex parte* Albert Levitt, Petitioner, 302 U.S. 633 (1937).

at all times, subject to the requirement that existing incumbents shall not be thrown out of office. Originally the Court had six members; today it has nine, any six of whom constitute a quorum.[34] At one time during the Civil War it had ten members, an enlargement which was partly occasioned by the fact that the unfavorable attitude of several of the Justices toward the war was thought to endanger the Government's policies.[35] Again, in 1870, at the time of the decision in Hepburn v. Griswold,[36] setting aside the Legal Tender Act of 1862, the two vacancies then existing in the Court's membership were filled by appointees who were known to disapprove of that decision, and fifteen months later the decision was reversed by the new majority.[37] Though possessing all the formal attributes of a judicial tribunal, the Court today exercises such vast, and such undefined powers, in the censorship of legislation, both national and State, and in interpretation of the former, that the social philosophies of suggested appointees to it are quite legitimately a matter of great concern to the appointing authority, the President and Senate.[38]

The "inferior courts" covered by this section comprise today eleven circuit courts of appeals and 91 district courts, the court of claims, the court of customs and patent appeals and the custom court[39] with over 500 judges serving on them. Since they rest upon act of Congress alone, they may be abolished by Congress at any time; but whether their incumbents may be thus thrown out of office is at least debatable. When in 1802 Congress repealed an act of the previous year creating certain circuit courts of the United States, it also threw their judges out of office; but the Act of 1913,

[34] 28 U.S.C. 1.

[35] C. B. Swisher, *Roger B. Taney* (New York, 1935), 566.

[36] 8 Wall. 603.

[37] Sidney Ratner, "Was the Supreme Court Packed by President Grant?" in 50 *Political Science Quarterly*, 343 (1935); Knox v. Lee, 12 Wall. 457 (1871).

[38] This was well understood by the Senatorial opponents of Mr. Hughes's appointment as Chief Justice. *See New York Times*, February 12-15, 1930; *and see* the data compiled by the late Senator Robinson in his answer to Senator Borah, respecting President Roosevelt's Court Proposal of February 5, 1937. *Ibid.*, March 31, 1937. The avowed utilization of "sociological data" by the Court in the *Desegregation* cases confirms Senator Robinson's argument. In the recent battle over the nomination of William H. Rehnquist, President Nixon and some Senators understood that the issue was a question of social philosophies. Leon Friedman, "Rehnquist: He Was an Elusive Target," *New York Times*, Dec. 12, 1971. *See also* Harold W. Chase, "Review of Abraham's *Justices and Presidents*," *Virginia Quarterly Review*, Autumn 1974.

[39] The Supreme Court in an earlier day held that the latter three courts were Article I courts. In the 1950's, Congress "Pronounced its disagreement by providing as to each that 'such court is hereby declared to be a court established under article III. . . .' " The Supreme Court acquiesced. Glidden Co. v. Zdanok, 370 U.S. 530, 531-532 (1962). For a brief description of these courts, *see* U.S. Cong., House, Committee on the Judiciary, *The United States Courts: Their Jurisdiction and Work* (Washington, 1971). Note that that publication speaks of 93 district courts. However, the judges in the Canal Zone, Guam and the Virgin Islands are not appointed for life. Therefore, we use the figure of 90 plus 1 newly added, *ibid.*, 6-7.

abolishing the commerce court, left its judges still judges of the United States.

The Commission on Revision of the Federal Court Appellate System created by Congress in 1972 issued its final report June 20, 1975. It proposed the establishment of a national court of appeals to be inserted between the Supreme Court and the eleven circuit courts of appeals. The purpose of the proposal is to ease the burden of the Supreme Court by having another court that can issue final, nationally binding decisions subject to review only by the Supreme Court. It was reported that the Supreme Court Justices were split 5-4 on the issue: *for*, Burger, White, Blackmun, Powell, and Rehnquist; *against*, Brennan, Stewart, Marshall, and Douglas.[40] But, at that time, the Democratic Congress was in no hurry to implement a proposal that would create new judicial appointments for a Republican President to fill.

The territorial courts, e.g., those of Guam, the Virgin Islands, and the Canal Zone do not exercise "judicial power of the United States," but a special judicial power conferred upon them by Congress, by virtue of its sovereign power over these places (*see* Article IV, Section III, ¶2). Their judges accordingly have a limited tenure and are removable by the President.[41] As to the question of whether the provision of the 1950 Organic Act of Guam, which provided that the District Court of Guam "shall have such appellate jurisdiction as the [Guam] legislature may determine" authorizes the Legislature of Guam to divest the appellate jurisdiction of the district court to hear appeals from local Guam courts and to transfer that jurisdiction to the newly created Supreme Court of Guam, the Supreme Court said no. The Court explained "We are unwilling to say that Congress made an extraordinary exception in the case of Guam. . . . Moreover, we should hesitate to attribute such a purpose to Congress since a construction that denied litigants access to Art. III courts for appellate review of local court decisions might present constitutional questions."[42]

Also, there are certain courts exercising jurisdiction over a limited class of cases, like the Tax Court of the United States and the Court of Military Appeals, which are regarded as "legislative," *not* "constitutional" courts. The powers of such courts sometimes embrace non-judicial elements, but any purely "judicial" determination by them may be made appealable, if Congress wishes, to the regular national courts. Nevertheless, since they do not participate in "the judicial power of the United States" within the sense of this section, the tenure of their judges rests solely on act of Congress.[43]

"Legislative Courts"

[40] 1975 *Cong. Quart. Weekly Report*, 1364, and John P. MacKenzie, *Washington Post Special*, as reported in *Chicago Sun-Times*, June 21, 1975.

[41] American Ins. Co. *v.* Canter, 1 Pet. 511 (1828) is still the leading case on the constitutional status of territorial courts.

[42] Territory of Guam *v.* Olsen, 431 U.S. 195, 204 (1977).

[43] *Ex parte* Bakelite, 279 U.S. 438 (1929). *See* 10 U.S.C. 867 and 26 U.S.C. 7443; *see also* Palmore *v.* U.S., 290 A. 2d. 573 (1972).

Faced with the proposition "that an Article III judge [lifetime tenure] preside over every proceeding in which charge, claim, or defense is based on an Act of Congress or a law made under its authority," the Supreme Court found that "There is no support for this view in either constitutional text or in constitutional history and practice."[44] Congress could constitutionally, therefore, set up Article I courts to hear and decide criminal cases in the District of Columbia.

An interesting question that has confronted the lower courts in recent years is the extent to which a Federal district court under the Federal Magistrates Act can delegate judicial functions to magistrates without conferring judicial power to decide cases on someone other than an Article III judge.[45] Later, the Supreme Court cleared up an important part of the question. The Court held that previous law was not changed by the Magistrates Act, that the district judges are required *in federal habeas corpus cases* personally to hold evidentiary hearings, saying: "Review by Magistrates of applications for post-trial relief is thus limited to review for the purpose of proposing, not holding, evidentiary hearings. In connection with the preliminary review whether or not to propose that the District Judge hold an evidentiary hearing, we agree that Magistrates may receive the state court record and all affidavits, stipulations and other documents, submitted by the parties. Magistrates are prohibited only from conducting the actual evidentiary hearings."[46]

Despite the Supreme Court decision with respect to the powers of Federal magistrates, the lower Federal courts continue to have to deal with cases which an appeals court described as "an ongoing series of cases designed to judicially establish the perimeters of powers and duties which may be delegated to United States magistrates."[47]

Regarding the referral of cases to magistrates, a U.S. court of appeals allowed as how "on occasion, perhaps when the legal issue is closely balanced and the stakes are not high, or when expedition and expense are dominating factors, parties may prefer prompt decision, through a magistrate, to decision by a judge."[48] But the court insisted "in order that such references not be subtly coerced by a harried court, intentionally or not, district courts should adopt a procedure such as requiring that the parties file with the clerk of the court a letter of consent to have the magistrate render decision in the case, the clerk being bound not to disclose the identity of any who consent or who withhold consent."

[44] Palmore *v.* U.S., 411 U.S. 389 (1973).
[45] Noorlander *v.* Ciccone, 489 F. 2d. 642, 648 (1973).
[46] Wingo *v.* Weeding, 418 U.S. 461, 472 (1974).
[47] National Ethical Pharmaceutical Ass'n *v.* Weinberger, 503 F. 2d. 1051 (1974). *See also* Campbell *v.* U.S. Dist. Ct. for N. Dist. of Cal., 501 F. 2d. 196 (1974); and DeCosta *v.* Columbia Broadcasting System, Inc., 385 F.Supp. 326 (1974).
[48] DeCosta *v.* Columbia Broadcasting System, Inc., 520 F. 2d. 499 (1975).

In July 1977, the Senate Judiciary Committee approved a bill to expand the authority of magistrates to try any civil case, regardless of the amount involved, with the consent of both parties.[49]

With respect to the provision that Federal judges shall "receive for their services a compensation which shall not be diminished during their continuance in office," the Court of Claims recently held that an "economic burden placed nondiscriminatorily upon the public generally afforded judges no cause to complain under the Constitution. Inflation generally experienced by the public is just such a nondiscriminatory burden." Consequently, the court concluded that it "has no power to grant relief on plaintiffs' complaint that inflation without substantial pay increases has diminished the real value of their official salaries, for the Constitution affords no protection from such an indirect, nondiscriminatory lowering of judicial compensation, not involving an assault upon the independence of judges."[50] *See* p. 155.

SECTION II

¶1. The judicial power shall extend to all cases, in law and equity, arising under this Constitution, the laws of the United States, and treaties made, or which shall be made, under their authority; to all cases affecting ambassadors, other public ministers, and consuls; to all cases of admiralty and maritime jurisdiction; to controversies to which the United States shall be a party; to controversies between two or more States; between a State and citizens of another State; between citizens of different States; between citizens of the same State claiming lands under grants of different States, and between a State, or the citizens thereof, and foreign States, citizens, or subjects.

The "cases" and "controversies" here enumerated fall into two categories; first, those over which jurisdiction "depends on the character of the cause," that is to say, the law to be enforced; second, those over which jurisdiction "depends entirely on the character of the parties."[1] In both instances, however, the jurisdiction described is only *potential*, except as to the *original* jurisdiction of the Supreme Court. Thus the lower Federal courts derive *all* their jurisdiction immediately from acts of Congress, and the same is true of the Supreme Court as to its *appellate* jurisdiction.[2] Also, all writs by which jurisdiction is asserted or exercised are authorized by Congress.

Categories of "Cases" and "Controversies"

---

[49] *St. Paul Dispatch*, July 14, 1977.   [50] Atkins *v.* U.S., 556 F. 2d. 1028 (1977).

---

[1] Cohens *v.* Va., 6 Wheat. 264, 378 (1821).

[2] Turner *v.* Bk. of No. Am., 4 Dall. 8 (1798); Kline *v.* Burke Constr. Co., 226 U.S. 266 (1922); Durousseau *v.* U.S., 6 Cr. 307 (1810); *ex parte* McCardle, 7 Wall. 506 (1869); *The Francis Wright*, 105 U.S. 381 (1881); St. Louis and Iron Mountain R.R. *v.* Taylor, 210 U.S. 281 (1908); *also* Robert J. Harris, Jr., *The Judicial Power of the United States* (Baton Rouge, 1940), ch. II, for a review of controversies on this point.

Require-
ments of
Same

    "Controversies" are civil actions or suits;[3] "cases" may be either
civil or criminal. The connotations of these terms are otherwise
substantially the same. Outstanding is the requirement of adverse
litigants presenting an honest and antagonistic assertion of rights.
Thus it was said in an earlier day to be "well settled" that "the Court
will not pass upon the constitutionality of legislation . . . , upon the
complaint of one who fails to show that he is injured by its operation . . ."; also that, "litigants may challenge the constitutionality of
a statute only insofar as it affects them."[4]

    In a recent case involving a boundary dispute between New
Hampshire and Maine, the Supreme Court felt compelled to expound on its "Art. III function and duty."[5] The Special Master
involved in the case found that there was a case and controversy
originally but, now that there was a consent decree, a case or controversy no longer existed in which the Court might apply "principles of law or equity to the facts." Indicating that the Court would
eschew, as it had in the past, taking jurisdiction where a consent
decree required the Court to "police prospectively the conduct of
the parties," for it would then be acting more "in an arbitral rather
than judicial manner," the Court held that this was not the situation
in this case, that the consent decree "proposes a wholly permissible
final resolution of the controversy both as to facts and law."

Standing

    As it has in so many other areas, the Supreme Court in recent
years has done much soul-searching on the question of "standing,"
i.e., who will be permitted to maintain a suit in a Federal court. In
the landmark case, Flast v. Cohen, 1968, the Supreme Court expanded considerably old judicial notions of who could properly
claim standing. Based on a Supreme Court decision of 1923, it was
long assumed, for example, that Federal courts could not entertain
taxpayer suits.[6] Speaking for the Court in 1968, Chief Justice Warren wrote: "Thus, in terms of Article III limitations on federal
court jurisdiction, the question of standing is related only to
whether the dispute sought to be adjudicated will be presented in
an adversary context and in a form historically viewed as capable of
judicial resolution. It is for that reason that the emphasis in standing problems is on whether the party invoking federal court jurisdiction has 'a personal stake in the outcome of the controversy,' . . .
and whether the dispute touches upon 'the legal relations of parties
having adverse legal interests.' . . . A taxpayer may or may not have
the requisite personal stake in the outcome, depending upon the
circumstances of the particular case. Therefore, we find no absolute bar in Article III to suits by federal taxpayers challenging al-

---

    [3] Smith v. Adams, 130 U.S. 167, 173-174 (1889).
    [4] Fleming v. Rhodes, 331 U.S. 100, 104 (1947). *See also* Blackmer v. U.S., 284 U.S.
421, 442 (1932); Virginian R. Co. v. System Federation, 300 U.S. 515 (1937); Carmichael v. Southern Coal & Coke Co., 301 U.S. 495, 513 (1937).
    [5] New Hampshire v. Maine, 426 U.S. 363 (1976).
    [6] Frothingham v. Mellon, 262 U.S. 447 (1923).

legedly unconstitutional federal taxing and spending programs."
He went on to add "We have noted that, in deciding the question of
standing, it is not relevant that the substantive issues in the litigation might be nonjusticiable. However, our decisions establish that,
in ruling on standing, it is both appropriate and necessary to look
to the substantive issues for another purpose, namely, to determine
whether there is a logical nexus between the status asserted and the
claim sought to be adjudicated. For example, standing requirements will vary in First Amendment religion cases depending
upon whether the party raises an Establishment Clause claim or a
claim under the Free Exercise Clause. . . . Such inquiries into the
nexus between the status asserted by the litigant and the claim he
presents are essential to assure that he is a proper and appropriate
party to invoke federal judicial power. Thus, our point of reference in this case is the standing of individuals who assert only the
status of federal taxpayers and who challenge the constitutionality
of a federal spending program. Whether such individuals have
standing to maintain that form of action turns on whether they can
demonstrate the necessary stake as taxpayers in the outcome of the
litigation to satisfy Article III requirements."[7]

The requirement in *Flast* that courts must determine if "there is a
logical nexus between the status asserted and the claim sought to be
adjudicated" placed the courts in the role of arbiter, deciding each
case on its own facts. Consequently, it is not surprising that the Supreme Court over the past few years has been beset with a host of
cases raising difficult questions of standing.[8] For example, in the
most recent Supreme Court case in which standing was an issue, it
was argued that foster parents "have no standing to rely upon a
supposed right of the foster *children* to avoid 'grievous loss,' because
the foster children are independently represented by court-
appointed counsel who has consistently opposed the relief requested . . . [by the foster parents], and denied that the children
have any such right." But, the Court held otherwise, saying "This
argument misunderstands the peculiar circumstance of this lawsuit. Ordinarily, it is true, a party would not have standing to assert
the rights of another, himself a party in the litigation; the third
party himself can decide how best to protect his interests. But children usually lack the capacity to make that sort of a decision, and

---

[7] Flast *v.* Cohen, 392 U.S. 83, 101-102 (1968). To fully appreciate the complexities
of the "standing" issue, this decision deserves to be read in its entirety. Particularly
enlightening is the section on the relationship between "standing" and "justiciability," which is discussed below. *See also* Jenkins *v.* McKeithen, 395 U.S. 411 (1969).

[8] Eisenstadt *v.* Baird, 405 U.S. 438 (1972); Sierra Club *v.* Morton, 407 U.S. 926
(1972); United States *v.* Richardson, 418 U.S. 239 (1974); Schlesinger *v.* Reservists
Committee to Stop the War, 418 U.S. 208 (1974); Warth *v.* Seldin, 422 U.S. 490
(1975); Bigelow *v.* Virginia, 421 U.S. 809 (1975); Rizzo *v.* Goode, 423 U.S. 362
(1976); Buckley *v.* Valeo, 424 U.S. 1 (1976); Simon *v.* Eastern Ky. Welfare Rights
Organization, 426 U.S. 26 (1976); Singleton *v.* Wulff, 428 U.S 106 (1976).

thus their interest is ordinarily represented in litigation by parents or guardians."[9]

Advisory
Opinions
Another element of a "case" or "controversy" formerly much insisted upon is the doctrine that the party initiating it must be asking the Court for a remedy or "execution" not just an advisory opinion. This no longer represents the position of the Court; and by an act passed by Congress on June 14, 1934, courts of the United States were authorized, "in cases of actual controversy," "to declare rights and other legal relations of any interested party petitioning for such declaration, whether or not further relief is or could be requested and such declaration shall have the force and effect of a final judgment or decree and be reviewable as such."[10] But the Supreme Court is extraordinarily careful at times to ensure that declaratory judgments are issued only where there is a real controversy. To illustrate, when some resident alien fishermen wanted to know whether or not, if they left to take temporary work in Alaska, they would be treated as "aliens entering the United States for the first time" under the law, the Supreme Court took a hard-nosed position. Frankfurter wrote for the Court: "Appellants in effect asked the District Court to rule that a statute the sanctions of which had not been set in motion against individuals on whose behalf relief was sought, because an occasion for doing so had not arisen, would not be applied to them if in the future such a contingency should arise. That is not a lawsuit to enforce a right; it is an endeavor to obtain a court's assurance that a statute does not govern hypothetical situations that may or may not make the challenged statute applicable. Determination of the scope and constitutionality of legislation in advance of its immediate adverse effect in the context of a concrete case involves too remote and abstract an inquiry for the proper exercise of the judicial function. . . ."[11] Justice Black's dissent seemed more in accord with reality and compassion: "This looks to me like the very kind of 'case or controversy' courts should decide. With the abstract principles of law relied on by the majority for dismissing the case, I am not in disagreement. Of course federal courts do not pass on the meaning or constitutionality of statutes as they might be thought to govern mere 'hypothetical situations. . . .' Nor should courts entertain such statutory challenges on behalf of persons upon whom adverse statutory effects are 'too remote and abstract an inquiry for the proper exercise of the judicial function.' But as I read the record it shows that judicial action is absolutely essential to save a large

[9] Smith *v.* Organ. of Foster Families for E. & Reform, 431 U.S. 817, 841 fn. 44 (1977). *See also* Craig *v.* Boren, 429 U.S. 190 (1976), and Nyquist *v.* Mauclet, 432 U.S. 1, 6 fn. 7 (1977).
[10] 28 U.S.C. 2201; Aetna Life Ins. Co. *v.* Haworth, 300 U.S. 227 (1937); Alvater *v.* Freeman, 319 U.S. 359 (1943); Alabama State Federation of Labor *v.* McAdory, 325 U.S. 450 (1945).
[11] Longshoremen's Union *v.* Boyd, 347 U.S. 222, 223-224 (1954). *See* Securities & Exch. Com'n *v.* Medical Com. for Human Rights, 404 U.S. 403 (1972).

group of wage earners on whose behalf this action is brought from irreparable harm due to alleged lawless enforcement of a federal statute."[12]

The highly controversial *DeFunis* case provided a good example of the Court's refusal to decide "moot" cases on the grounds that such are not "cases or controversies within the meaning of Article III." The Court held "Because the petitioner will complete his law school studies at the end of the term for which he has now registered regardless of any decision this Court may reach on the merits of this litigation, we conclude that the Court cannot, consistently with the limitations of Article III of the Constitution, consider the substantive constitutional issues tendered by the parties."[13] But this decision should be compared with the Court's decision a week earlier, where it held that, even though a strike had been settled ending the need for an injunction, the litigant may show "the existence of an immediate and definite governmental action or policy that has adversely affected and continues to adversely affect a present interest."[14]

Mootness

In a perplexing but well-reasoned opinion, the supreme court of the State of Washington decided that the U.S. Supreme Court's determination that the *DeFunis* case was moot did not foreclose the State supreme court on remand from deciding the case again.[15] As the Washington court pointed out, "the Supreme Court itself recognized that 'as a matter of Washington state law it appears that this case would be saved from mootness,'" and also, that the Supreme Court had not simply dismissed the appeal on grounds of mootness but had remanded the cause for further proceedings. In any event the Washington court reinstated its original judgment.

Three other recent Supreme Court decisions elucidate on the issues inhering in mootness. As to an action by a wife to have a one-year divorce residency requirement declared unconstitutional, even after she satisfied the requirement and had obtained her divorce elsewhere, the Court held that, since she had brought the suit as a class action, that factor "significantly affects the mootness determination."[16] The Court explained that "We believe that a case such as this, in which, . . . the issue sought to be litigated escapes full appellate review at the behest of any single challenger, does not inexorably become moot by the intervening resolution of the controversy as to the named plaintiffs."

In a decision heralded for upholding the granting of retroactive seniority for those who had been discriminated against in hiring, the Supreme Court had to deal at the threshold of its opinion with the issue of mootness, since the sole representative in one class action could no longer be eligible for hiring relief. The Court pro-

[12] *Ibid.*, 224.   [13] DeFunis *v.* Odegaard, 416 U.S. 312 (1974).
[14] Super Tire Engineering Co. *v.* McCorkle, 416 U.S. 115 (1974).
[15] DeFunis *v.* Odegaard, 529 P. 2d. 438 (1974).
[16] Sosna *v.* Iowa, 419 U.S. 393 (1975).

ceeded on the basis that "The only constitutional mootness question is therefore whether, with regard to seniority issues presented, 'a live controversy [remains] at the time this Court reviews the case.' "[17] The Court concluded that "there is no meaningful sense in which a 'live controversy' reflecting the issues before the Court could be found absent." In 1977 the Court reaffirmed the position that "The fact that it would be convenient for the parties and the public to have promptly decided whether the legislation assailed is valid, cannot justify a departure from these settled rules [of mootness]."[18]

Class Action Suits

The reasoning for permitting class action suits has been spelled out in Rule 23 of the Federal Rules of Civil Procedure as prerequisites: "(1) The class is so numerous that joinder of all members is impracticable, (2) there are questions of law or fact common to the class, (3) the claims or defenses of the representative parties are typical of the claims or defenses of the class, and (4) the representative parties will fairly and adequately protect the interests of the class." In a 1974 decision, the Supreme Court severely limited the ability to file such suits by holding that individual notice to identifiable class members is not a discretionary consideration to be waived in a particular case. It is rather an unambiguous requirement of Rule 23. . . . Accordingly, each class member who can be identified through reasonable effort must be notified that he may request exclusion from the action and thereby preserve his opportunity to press his claim separately or that he may remain in the class and perhaps participate in the management of the action. There is nothing in Rule 23 to suggest that the notice requirements can be tailored to fit the pocketbooks of particular plaintiffs."[19]

In another decision that promises to affect substantially access to the courts, the Supreme Court reversed a court of appeals decision that had awarded attorneys' fees to environmental groups against the Alyeska Pipeline Service Co. "based upon the Court's equitable powers and the theory that respondents were entitled to fees because they were performing the services of a 'private attorney general.' " The Court concluded that it was up to Congress rather than the courts to decide on the allowance of attorneys' fees, saying "it is not for us to invade the legislature's province by redistributing litigation costs."[20]

"Law" versus "Equity"

Whether a case is one "in law" or "in equity" is a mere matter of history, and depends today on the kind of remedy that is asked for. Criminal prosecutions and private actions for damages are cases "in law," since these were early decided in England in the regular law courts. An application for an injunction, on the other hand,

---

[17] Franks v. Bowman Transportation Co. Inc., 424 U.S. 747 (1976). *See also*, Abood v. Detroit Bd. of Education, 431 U.S. 209, 216 fn. 9 (1977).
[18] Kremens v. Bartley, 431 U.S. 119, 136 (1977).
[19] Eisen v. Carlisle & Jacquelin, 417 U.S. 156, 176 (1974).
[20] Alyeska Pipeline Service Co. v. Wilderness Society, 421 U.S. 240, 241 (1975).

was passed upon by the Lord Chancellor, as a matter of grace, and so is a *suit* "in equity." Heretofore the distinction between the two kinds of cases has been maintained in the field of national jurisdiction, as it is in most of the States, although the same courts dispense both "law" and "equity." By the Act of June 19, 1934, however, the Supreme Court was empowered to merge the two procedures "so as to secure one form of civil action . . . for both" in the district courts of the United States and the courts of the District of Columbia, and it has since adopted rules for this purpose.[21]

A case is one "arising under this Constitution, the laws of the United States, and treaties" of the United States, when an interpretation of one or the other of these is required for its final decision.[22] But while the "judicial power" extends to *all* such cases, there is a certain category of them in which the Court does not usually claim full liberty of decision. These are cases involving so-called "political questions," the best example of which is furnished by questions respecting the rights of duties of the United States in relation to other nations. When the "political departments," Congress and the President, have passed upon such questions, the Court will generally accept their determinations as binding on itself in deciding cases. "Political Questions"

Historically, precise understanding of what kinds of questions were political and what the Court actually did with respect to political questions has been lacking. In 1962, the Court endeavored to remedy that situation. Speaking through Justice Brennan, the Court said: "The District Court was uncertain whether our cases withholding federal judicial relief rested upon a lack of federal jurisdiction or upon the inappropriateness of the subject matter for judicial consideration—what we have designated 'nonjusticiability.' The distinction between the two grounds is significant. In the instance of non-justiciability, consideration of the cause is not wholly and immediately foreclosed; rather, the Court's inquiry necessarily proceeds to the point of deciding whether the duty asserted can be judicially identified and its breach judicially determined, and "Non-justi-ciability"

---

[21] 48 *Stat.* 1064 (1934); 28R U.S.C. 1 and 81.

[22] Cohens *v.* Va., 6 Wheat. 264, 379 (1821). Willoughby, *The Constitutional Law of the United States*, III, 1326-1329. The cases fall into several categories, some of which touch the problem of constitutional interpretation more directly than others: (1) Those that raise the issue of what proof is required that a statute has been enacted, or a constitutional amendment ratified; (2) questions arising out of the conduct of foreign relations; (3) the termination of wars, or rebellions; (4) the question of what constitutes a "republican form of government" and the right of a State to protection against invasion or domestic violence; (5) questions arising out of political actions of States in determining the mode of choosing Presidential Electors, State officials, and Congressional reapportionment; (6) suits brought by States to test their sovereign rights. *See* Melville Fuller Weston, "Political Questions," 38 *Harvard Law Review*, 296 (1925). Some outstanding cases are Foster *v.* Neilson, 2 Pet. 253 (1929); Luther *v.* Borden, 7 How. 1 (1849); Georgia *v.* Stanton, 6 Wall. 50 (1868); Coleman *v.* Miller, 307 U.S. 433 (1939); Colegrove *v.* Green, 328 U.S. 549 (1946), with which *cf.* McDougall *v.* Green, 335 U.S. 281 (1948); South *v.* Peters, 339 U.S. 276 (1950); National City Bank *v.* Republic of China, 348 U.S. 356 (1955).

whether protection for the right asserted can be judicially molded. In the instance of lack of jurisdiction the cause either does not 'arise under' the Federal Constitution, laws or treaties (or fall within one of the other enumerated categories of Art. III, §2), or is not a 'case or controversy' within the meaning of that section; or the cause is not one described by any jurisdictional statute."[23] It went on to add later: "We have said that 'In determining whether a question falls within the [political question] category, the appropriateness under our system of government of attributing finality to the action of the political departments and also the lack of satisfactory criteria for a judicial determination are dominant considerations.' . . . The nonjusticiability of a political question is primarily a function of the separation of powers. Much confusion results from the capacity of the 'political question' label to obscure the need for case-by-case inquiry. Deciding whether a matter has in any measure been committed by the Constitution to another branch of government, or whether the action of that branch exceeds whatever authority has been committed, is itself a delicate exercise in constitutional interpretation, and is a responsibility of this Court as ultimate interpreter of the Constitution."[24] Of course, it rests with the Supreme Court to say finally whether a question is "a political question" in this sense. (*See also* Article IV, Section IV.)

In this connection, in an extraordinary proceeding after the Court had recessed for the summer of 1972, the Supreme Court rendered a dramatic decision with respect to the dispute over the seating of delegates at the Democratic National Convention. The Court concluded in a *per curiam* decision that "it cannot in this limited time give to these issues the consideration warranted for final decision on the merits; we therefore take no action on the petitions for certiorari at this time." Nonetheless, the Court said: "We must consider the absence of authority supporting the Court of Appeals in intervening in the internal determinations of a national political party, on the eve of its convention, regarding the seating of delegates. No case is cited to us in which any federal court has undertaken to interject itself into the deliberative processes of a national political convention; no holding of this Court up to now gives support for judicial intervention in the circumstances presented here, involving as they do, relationships of great delicacy and essentially political in nature." And the Court granted the stays of the judgments of the Court of Appeals.[25]

More recently, in judging that it was without power to decide the issue of whether or not the President had exceeded his constitutional powers in ordering the mining of North Vietnamese harbors and stepping up the bombing, the U.S. Court of Appeals, Second Circuit, reviewed succinctly the political question doctrine. Sum-

[23] Baker *v.* Carr, 369 U.S. 186, 198 (1962).   [24] *Ibid.*, 210-211.
[25] O'Brien *v.* Brown, 409 U.S. 1 (1972).

ming up, it observed "Clearly, some of the principles enumerated call for discretionary judgments that will not always require a court to refrain from action. Nevertheless, we are at a loss to understand how a court may decide a question when there are no judicially discoverable or manageable standards for resolving it."[26]

In his capacity as a circuit justice, Mr. Justice Marshall was called upon to determine whether or not the effort of the Socialist Workers Party to enjoin the FBI from monitoring a national convention of their youth organization "raised a justiciable controversy under this Court's decision in Laird v. Tatum, 408 U.S. 1 (1972) [*see* p. 309]."[27] Justice Marshall felt that the allegations were more specific in this case but that "Whether the claimed 'chill' is substantial or not is still subject to question, but that is a matter to be reached on the merits, not as a threshold jurisdictional question." He concluded that "Although applicants have established jurisdiction, they have not, in my view, made a compelling case on the merits."

Cases "arising under this Constitution" are cases in which the validity of an act of Congress or a treaty or of a legislative act or constitutional provision of a State, or of any official act whatsoever which purports to stem directly from the Constitution, is challenged with reference to it. This clause, in alliance with the Supremacy Clause (Article VI, ¶2), furnishes the constitutional warrant for that highly distinctive feature of American Government, judicial review. The initial source of judicial review, however, is much older than the Constitution and indeed of any American constitution. It traces back to the common law, certain principles of which were earlier deemed to be "fundamental" and to comprise a "higher law" which even Parliament could not alter. "And it appears," wrote Chief Justice Coke in 1610, in his famous dictum in Bonham's case, "that when an act of Parliament is against common right and reason . . . the common law will control it and adjudge such act to be void."[28] This idea first commended itself to Americans as offering an available weapon against the pretensions of Parliament in the agitation leading to the Revolution.[29] Thus in 1765 the royal governor of Massachusetts Province wrote his government that the prevailing argument against the Stamp Act was that it contravened "Magna Charta and the natural rights of Englishmen and therefore, according to Lord Coke," was "null and void";[30] and on the eve of the Declaration of Independence Judge William Cushing, later one of Washington's appointees to the original bench of the Supreme Court, charged a Massachusetts jury to ignore certain acts of Parliament as "void and inoperative," and was

"Judicial Review": Its Origin

---

[26] DaCosta v. Laird, 471 F. 2d. 1146, 1153 (1976).
[27] Socialist Workers Party v. Attorney General of U.S., 419 U.S. 1314 (1974).
[28] 8 Reps. 107, 118 (1610).
[29] *See* Josiah Quincy, *Reports of Cases* (Early Massachusetts cases) (Boston, 1865), 469-488.
[30] *Ibid.*, 527

congratulated by John Adams for doing so. In fact, the Cokian doctrine was invoked by the Supreme Court of the United States as late as 1874.[31]

With, however, the establishment of the first written constitutions, a new basis for judicial review was suggested, the argument for which was elaborated by Hamilton, with the pending Federal Constitution in mind, in *The Federalist*, No. 78, as follows: "The interpretation of the laws is the proper and peculiar province of the courts. A constitution is in fact, and must be regarded by the judges as, a fundamental law. It therefore belongs to them to ascertain its meaning as well as the meaning of any particular act proceeding from the legislative body, and, in case of irreconcilable difference between the two, to prefer the will of the people declared in the constitution to that of the legislature as expressed in statute."

The Constitutional Basis of Judicial Review — The attention of the Federal Convention was drawn to judicial review as offering a means for securing the conformity of State laws and constitutional provisions with "the Supreme Law of the Land," comprising "this Constitution and the laws of Congress made in pursuance thereof, and the treaties made . . . under the authority of the United States," of which the State judiciaries were made the first line of defense, with, presumably, a final appeal to the Supreme Court.[32] Nor has judicial review on this basis ever been seriously contested.[33] Judicial review of acts of Congress has had a more difficult row to hoe, although it is clearly predicated in the clause of Article III now under discussion; and at any rate significant debate on the subject was concluded by Marshall's famous ruling in 1803, in Marbury *v.* Madison.[34] Not only has this decision never been disturbed, its influence soon spread into the States, with the result that long before the Civil War judicial review by State courts of local legislation was established under the local constitutions, and usually with far less textual support than the Constitution of the United States affords judicial review of acts of Congress.[35]

Inasmuch as judicial review is exercised only in connection with the decision of *cases* and for the purpose of "finding the law of the case," it is intrinsically subject to the limitations adhering to the judicial function as such (*see* pp. 213-221). Hence the Court will not render advisory opinions at the request of the coordinate departments; and a self-denying ordinance which it adopted in 1793 to

[31] Loan Assoc. *v.* Topeka, 20 Wall. 655, 662 (1874).

[32] *See* Cohens *v.* Va., 6 Wheat. 264 (1821).

[33] The right of the Supreme Court, however, to take appeals from the State judiciaries in cases covered by the supremacy clause was for a time disputed by the Virginia Court of Appeals. *See* preceding note; and Martin *v.* Hunter's Lessee, 1 Wheat. 304 (1816).

[34] 1 Cr. 137 (1803). *But see* Justice Gibson's dissent in Eakin *v.* Raub, Supreme Court of Pennsylvania, 12 S. & R. 330 (1825).

[35] On State judicial review prior to the Civil War, *see* Edward S. Corwin, *Doctrine of Judicial Review* (Princeton, 1914), 75-78.

this effect has, perhaps with one exception, been observed ever since.[36]

Also, the Court has announced from time to time certain other self-restraining maxims which were evoked rather by its recognition of the extraordinary nature of judicial review than by judicial decorum as such. Thus it has said that it will intervene only in "clear cases" and only when the constitutional issue cannot be avoided.[37] The latter doctrine has sometimes led it to construe the challenged statute so narrowly as to impair greatly its intended operation;[38] the former doctrine is frequently equivocal, the application of it turning on the Court's "philosophy." Thus the Court has never exercised its censorship of legislation, whether national or State, more energetically than during the half century between 1887 and 1937, when its thinking was strongly colored by *laissez faire* concepts of the role of government. This point of view, translated into congenial constitutional doctrines, like that of "liberty of contract" and the exclusive right of the States to govern industrial relations, brought hundreds of State laws to grief, as well as an unusual number of Congressional enactments. Two persistent dissenters from this tendency were Justices Holmes and Brandeis, both of whom thrust forward maxims of judicial self-restraint in vain. The Court had converted judicial review, declared Justice Brandeis, into the power of "a super-legislature," while Justice Holmes complained that he could discover "hardly any limit but the sky" to the power claimed by the Court to disallow State acts "which may happen to strike a majority" of its members "as for any reason undesirable."[39] Conversely, the so-called "Constitutional Revolution" of

Maxims Governing Its Exercise

Effect of Laissez Faire on

---

[36] In 1793 the Supreme Court refused to grant the request of President Washington and Secretary of State Jefferson to construe the treaties and laws of the United States pertaining to questions of International Law arising out of the wars of the French Revolution. Warren, *The Supreme Court in United States History*, I, 110-111. For the full correspondence *see* Henry P. Johnston, ed., *Correspondence and Public Papers of John Jay* (New York and London, 1890-1893), III, 486. According to E. F. Albertsworth, "Advisory Functions in Federal Supreme Court," 23 *Georgetown Law Journal*, 643, 644-647 (1935), the Court rendered an advisory opinion to President Monroe in response to a request for legal advice on the power of the Government to appropriate Federal funds for public improvements, by responding that Congress might do so under the war and postal powers. *See also* Chief Justice Hughes's letter to Senator Wheeler *in re* F.D.R.'s "Court packing" plan. Merlo Pusey, *Charles Evans Hughes*, II (New York, 1951), 756-757.

[37] Willoughby, *Constitutional Law*, I, 25-33, *passim*.

[38] *See* in this connection United States *v.* E. C. Knight Co. ("The *Sugar Trust* Case"), 156 U.S. 1 (1895); United States *v.* Delaware and Hudson Co., 213 U.S. 366 (1909); and First Employers' Liability Cases, 207 U.S. 463 (1908). The Court may also treat an act of Congress as "severable" and sustain a part of it, while holding the rest void. Pollock *v.* Farmers' Loan & Trust Co., 157 U.S. 429 (1895). But on one occasion it disregarded a statement, thrice repeated in a statute, that certain sections of it were severable, and thereby contrived to overturn the entire act. Carter *v.* Carter Coal Co., 298 U.S. 238 (1936).

[39] Burns Baking Co. *v.* Bryan, 264 U.S. 504, 534 (1924); Baldwin *v.* Mo., 281 U.S. 586, 595 (1930).

1937 connotes a distinct lightening of judicial censorship in the *economic* realm, based on a new set of constitutional values. When in recent times civil liberties issues came to the forefront on the Supreme Court's docket, there was a revival of judicial activism predicated on the argument that when it came to "preferred freedoms" (those of the First Amendment, particularly), the usual presumptions about constitutionality of legislation could not attach in the face of guarantees of at least the First Amendment. There is further discussion of this development on pp. 304-309 and 317-324.[40] In short, judicial review is at any particular period a "function" of its own product, the constitutional law of the period. Surely, there must be a lesson in the story of Justice Frankfurter, who came on the Court after the 1937 "revolution" hailed by liberals and feared by conservatives because he was an articulate practitioner of judicial self-restraint. Years later, when he retired from the bench, now the *most* articulate practitioner of judicial self-restraint, he was admired by conservatives and denigrated by liberals.

All of which considerations raise the question of the importance of the doctrine of *stare decisis* as an element of Constitutional Law. Story was strongly of the opinion that it was fully operative in that field. Whether, however, because of the difficulty of amending the Constitution or for cautionary reasons, the Court took the position as early as 1851 that it would reverse previous decisions on constitutional issues when convinced that they were "erroneous."[41] An outstanding instance of this nature was the decision in the Legal Tender cases, in 1870, reversing the decision which had been rendered in Hepburn *v.* Griswold fifteen months earlier;[42] and no less shattering to the prestige of *stare decisis* in the constitutional field was the Income Tax decision of 1895,[43] in which the Court, accepting Joseph H. Choate's invitation to "correct a century of error," greatly expanded its interpretation of the "direct tax" clauses.

Stare Decisis in Constitutional Law   The "Constitutional Revolution" of 1937, just alluded to, produced numerous reversals of earlier precedents on the ground of "error," some of them, Congressman James M. Beck complained, without "the decent obsequies of a funeral oration."[44] In 1944 Justice Reed cited fourteen cases decided between March 27, 1937, and June 14, 1943, in which one or more prior constitutional decisions were overturned.[45] On the same occasion Justice Roberts expressed the opinion that adjudications of the Court were rapidly

[40] *See* Harold W. Chase, *Security and Liberty* (New York, 1955), ch. II.
[41] The pioneer case on the point was *The Genessee Chief*, 12 How. 443 (1851) overturning *The Thomas Jefferson*, 10 Wheat. 428 (1825). *See* especially Chief Justice Taney's opinion, 12 How. at p. 456.
[42] 8 Wall. 603 (1869); Knox *v.* Lee, 12 Wall. 457 (1871).
[43] Pollock *v.* Farmers' Loan & Trust Co., 157 U.S. 429 and 158 U.S. 601 (1895).
[44] 78 *Cong. Rec.* 5358 (1934).
[45] Smith *v.* Allwright, 321 U.S. 649, 665 note 10 (1944).

gravitating "into the same class as a restricted railroad ticket, good for this day and train only."[46]

There is much to be said for Chief Justice Stone's dictum that "To give blind adherence to a rule or policy that no decision of this Court is to be overruled would be itself to overrule many decisions of the Court which do not accept that view. But the rule of *stare decisis* embodies a wise policy because it is often more important that a rule be settled than that it be settled right."[47] In rejoinder we have Justice Black's later observation: "Ordinarily it is sound policy to adhere to prior decisions but this practice has quite properly never been a blind, inflexible rule."[48] Note the common denominator between the two points of view—*stare decisis* is "ordinarily" sound policy. Courts do not take lightly the matter of overruling precedent.

Two other doctrinal limitations on judicial review are one which limits the *occasions* for judicial review and one which limits the *effect* of its exercise. The former is the doctrine of political questions, dealt with earlier (*see* p. 219 above). The latter is the doctrine, or theory, of Departmental Construction, which stems from the contention, advanced by Jefferson and Jackson and endorsed by Lincoln, that while the Court is undoubtedly entitled to interpret the Constitution independently in the decision of cases, by the same token the other two "equal" branches of the Government are entitled to the like freedom in the exercise of their respective functions.[49] Actually, this claim was not pushed—some mythology to the contrary notwithstanding—to the logical extreme of exonerating the President from the duty of enforcing the Court's decisions, and ordinarily acts of Congress also, unless and until they have been held by the Court to be "void."[50] Its intention was to assert for the President and Congress in their *legislative* capacity the right to shape new legislation in accordance with their independent views of constitutional requirements, unembarrassed by the judicial gloss. The brittleness of *stare decisis* in the Constitutional Law field goes far to support this contention.

The chief external restraint upon judicial review arises from Congress's unlimited control over the size of the Supreme Court and its equally unlimited control over the Court's appellate jurisdiction, as well as of the total jurisdiction of the lower Federal courts. By virtue of the latter, Congress is in position to restrict the actual exercise of judicial review at times, or even to frustrate it al-

Congressional Restraints on Judicial Review

---

[46] *Ibid.*, 669.   [47] U.S. *v.* Underwriters Ass'n, 322 U.S. 533, 579 (1944).
[48] Green *v.* U.S., 356 U.S. 165, 195 (1958).
[49] The classic statement of the doctrine of Departmental Construction occurs in President Jackson's famous Veto Message of July 10, 1832. Richardson, *Messages and Papers of the President*, II, 582.
[50] Warren, *The Supreme Court in United States History*, II, 221-224, where it is asserted that Andrew Jackson never said, "John Marshall has made his decision, now let him enforce it."

together. Thus in 1869 it prevented the Court from passing on the constitutionality of the Reconstruction Acts by repealing the latter's jurisdiction over a case which had already been argued and was ready for decision,[51] and in World War II it confined the right to challenge the validity of provisions of the Emergency Price Control Act and of orders of the OPA under it to a single Emergency Court of Appeals and to the Supreme Court upon review of that court's judgments and orders.[52] There is good reason to believe that the nearly successful effort in Congress to withdraw certain kinds of cases from the Supreme Court's appellate jurisdiction in the 1950's caused the Court to pull in its horns.[53] In that bitter controversy there was never any real question raised about Congress's power to diminish the Court's appellate jurisdiction, only the wisdom of doing so.

Judicial Review and National Supremacy

It frequently happens that cases "arising under this Constitution, the laws of the United States, and treaties" of the United States are first brought up in a State court, in consequence of a prosecution by the State itself under one of its own laws or of an action by a private plaintiff claiming something under a law of the State. If in such a case the defendant sets up a counter-claim under the Constitution or laws or treaties of the United States, thereupon the case becomes one "arising under this Constitution," etc.[54] By the famous 25th Section of the Judiciary Act of 1789, the substance of which still remains on the statute books, such a case may be appealed to the Supreme Court if the decision of the highest State court to which under the law of the State it can come affirms the claim based on State law,[55] while by an act passed in 1914 the Supreme Court may by writ of *certiorari* bring the kind of case described before itself for final review even if the claim which was based on State law was rejected by the State court in deference to national law.[56]

Further, although Federal law provides that "*Final* judgment or decrees rendered by the highest court of a State in which a decision could be had may be reviewed by the Supreme Court," the Court has demonstrated there are exceptions. Where a State Supreme Court has decided that a State law was unconstitutional and remanded a case to an administrative agency with instructions to reconsider its action "sans" the constitutional question, the Supreme

---

[51] *Ex parte* McCardle, 7 Wall. 506.

[52] 56 *Stat.* 23, 31 and 32 (1942). Lockerty *v.* Phillips, 319 U.S. 182 (1943); Yakus *v.* U.S., 321 U.S. 414 (1944); Bowles *v.* Willingham, 321 U.S. 503 (1944).

[53] Walter F. Murphy, *Congress and the Court* (Chicago, 1962).

[54] Cohens *v.* Va., 6 Wheat. 264 (1821).

[55] 28 U.S.C. 1257; Pope *v.* Atlantic Coast Line Co., 345 U.S. 379, 381-382 (1953); Sibron *v.* N.Y., 392 U.S. 40, 58-59 (1968); Mills *v.* Alabama, 384 U.S. 214, 217-218 (1966); Atlantic Coast Line Co. *v.* Engineers, 398 U.S. 281, 294-296 (1970).

[56] 28 U.S.C. 1257, *see* Historical and Revision Note: Street *v.* N.Y., 394 U.S. 576, 583 (1969).

Court found that "It is . . . important that we treat the judgment in the instant case as 'final,' for we have discovered no way by which [sic] . . . [the administrative agency] has of preserving the constitutional question now ripe for decision."[57] It should be emphasized, however, that in these situations there must be a *Federal* question involved for the Court to review since its mandate rides on the words "arising under this Constitution etc."[58]

"All cases affecting ambassadors, other public ministers, and consuls": The word "all" is used here in a rather Pickwickian sense, as we learn from a case in which the Supreme Court refused to pass on the marital difficulties of the, then, Roumanian vice-consul stationed at Cleveland, Ohio.[59]

"Cases in admiralty and maritime jurisdiction": These largely overlapping terms embody a broader content that they possessed in England,[60] but connote the peculiarities of English admiralty procedure, subject to modification by Congress: to wit, proceedings *in rem*, against the vessel; and the trial of both law and facts by a judge without the aid of a jury. Today this jurisdiction embraces, first, cases involving acts on the high seas or in navigable waters, including prize cases, and torts or other injuries; second, those involving contracts and transactions connected with shipping employed on the high seas or in navigable waters.[61] In the first category the *locality* of the act is the determinative element; in the second, *subject-matter* is the decisive factor.

"Admiralty and Maritime Jurisdiction"

What is meant by "navigable waters" in this connection? The English rule confined the term to the high seas and to rivers as far as the ebb and flow of the tide extended, and in the case of *The Thomas Jefferson*,[62] decided in 1825, the Court, speaking by Justice Story, followed this rule. Twenty-seven years later, in the case of *The Genessee Chief*,[63] the Court, speaking by Chief Justice Taney, overruled this holding, on the ground that it was not adapted to American conditions, and sustained an act of Congress giving the Federal courts jurisdiction over the Great Lakes and connecting waters. Later decisions have brought within the term canals, waters wholly within a single State but forming a connecting link in interstate commerce, waters navigable in their normal condition, and finally waterways capable of being rendered navigable by "reason-

[57] North Dakota St. Bd. of Pharm. *v.* Snyder's Drug Stores, Inc., 414 U.S. 156, 162 (1973).

[58] Fay *v.* Noia, 372 U.S. 391, 428-429 (1963); NAACP *v.* Alabama, 357 U.S. 449 (1958).

[59] Ohio *ex rel.* Popovich *v.* Agler, 280 U.S. 379 (1930); U.S. *v.* Fitzpatrick, 214 F.Supp. 425 (1963); U.S. *v.* Egorov, 222 F.Supp. 106 (1963).

[60] New Jersey Steam Nav. Co. *v.* Merchants' Bk., 6 How. 344 (1848); Erastus C. Benedict, *The Law of American Admiralty, Revised* (New York, 1970), I, 1-7.

[61] Waring *v.* Clarke, 5 How. 441 (1847); *ex parte* Easton, 95 U.S. 68 (1877); North Pacific S.S. Co. *v.* Hall Brothers M. R. & S. Co., 249 U.S. 119 (1919); Grant Smith-Porter Ship Co. *v.* Rohde, 257 U.S. 469 (1922).

[62] 10 Wheat. 428 (1825).   [63] 12 How. 443 (1852).

able improvement."[64] Throughout this development the catalytic effect of the commerce clause clearly appears.

It has reached the point where the United States Court of Appeals, Eighth Circuit, has held that "The operation of a boat on navigable waters, no matter what its size or activity, is a traditional maritime activity to which the admiralty jurisdiction of the federal courts may extend."[65] In short this includes small pleasure craft engaged in non-commercial navigation.

Despite assertions to the contrary in our early history, it was settled in 1874 that Congress may amend the maritime law.[66] Justice Bradley speaking for the Court gave an exceptionally clear explanation of the meaning and operation of maritime law. "But it is hardly necessary to argue that the maritime law is only so far operative as law in any country as it is adopted by the laws and usages of that country. In this respect it is like international law or the laws of war, which have the effect of law in no country any further than they are accepted and received as such; . . . The adoption of the common law by the several States of this Union also presents an analogous case. It is the basis of all the State laws; but is modified as each sees fit. Perhaps the maritime law is more uniformly followed by commercial nations than the civil and common laws are by those who use them. But, like those laws, however fixed, definite, and beneficial the theoretical code of maritime law may be, it can have only so far the effect of law in any country as it is permitted to have. But the actual maritime law can hardly be said to have a fixed and definite form as to all the subjects which may be embraced within its scope. . . . But no nation regards itself as precluded from making occasional modifications suited to its locality and the genius of its own people and institutions, especially in matters that are of merely local and municipal consequence and do not affect other nations. . . ."[67] But Congress wisely has largely left to the Supreme Court "the responsibility for fashioning the controlling rules of admiralty law."[68]

Powers of
Congress
Over

Nor does the Constitution forbid the States to create rights enforcible in Federal admiralty proceedings. In 1940 a Florida statute whereby a cause of action for personal injury due to another's neg-

---

[64] *The Daniel Ball*, 10 Wall. 557 (1871); *ex parte* Boyer, 109 U.S. 629 (1884); United States *v.* Appalachian Elec. P. Co., 311 U.S. 377 (1940); Southern S.S. Co. *v.* N.L.R.B., 316 U.S. 31 (1942). Evidently, there are limits, however. A Federal court recently held that: "We cannot find substance to plaintiff's argument that Conneaut Lake is navigable under the admiralty definition because it was once connected by a feeder channel conveying water from the lake to the Erie Extension Canal. The canal system has been gone for almost a century." Doran *v.* Lee, 287 F.Supp. 807, 812 (1968).

[65] St. Hilaire Moye *v.* Henderson, 496 F. 2d. 973 (1974), *but see* Roberts *v.* Grammer, 432 F.Supp. 16 (1977).

[66] *The Lottawanna*, 88 U.S. 558 (1874).   [67] *Ibid.*, 572-573.

[68] Fitzgerald *v.* U.S., 374 U.S. 16, 20 (1963).

ligence survives the death of the tort-feasor against his estate was enforced in a proceeding *in rem* in a United States district court, and the holding was sustained by the Supreme Court.[69]

Even so, the Court held in 1917, five Justices to four, that a New York Workmen's Compensation statute was unconstitutional when applied to employees engaged in maritime work, being destructive, it said, of "the very uniformity in respect to maritime matters which the Constitution was designed to establish";[70] and three years later it stigmatized an attempt by Congress to save such claimants their rights and remedies under State law as an "unconstitutional delegation of legislative power to the States."[71]

Just *when* "uniformity" is disturbed by this species of legislation is therefore difficult to say. Speaking for the Court in 1942 in sustaining the applicability of a Washington "death act," in an action brought by the widow of a harbor worker who was drowned in a navigable stream, Justice Black hinted that the choice presented the Justices by the precedents was about a 50-50 one.[72] That problem continues to plague the Court, but its latest decisions continue to uphold the application of State wrongful death statutes.[73] Significantly, in late 1971 the Supreme Court held that a suit brought by a longshoreman injured on a dock was governed by State law and not Federal maritime law.[74] But lower courts have recently taken a broader view of the reach of Congress's power under maritime law, extending it to compensation coverage under the Longshoreman's Act to workers in the immediate waterfront area[75] and to ocean bills of lading.[76]

"Controversies to which the United Sttates shall be a party": It is a universally accepted maxim of public law that the sovereign may not be sued except on his own consent. In Chisholm v. Georgia,[77] decided in 1792, the Court held that the States of the United States were not "sovereign" within the sense of this principle—a ruling which was soon "recalled" by the adoption of the Eleventh Amendment (*see* p. 448 below). On the same occasion Chief Justice Jay voiced the opinion that the United States, i.e., the National Government, was "sovereign" in this sense, and this opinion has always been adhered to in theory.

---

[69] Just *v.* Chambers, 312 U.S. 383 (1941).

[70] Southern Pacific Co. *v.* Jensen, 244 U.S. 205, 215-218 (1917).

[71] Knickerbocker Ice Co. *v.* Steward, 253 U.S. 149, 163-166 (1920).

[72] Davis *v.* Dept. of Labor, 317 U.S. 249, 252-253 (1942).

[73] The Tungus *v.* Skovgaard, 358 U.S. 588 (1959); United Pilots Ass'n *v.* Halecki, 358 U.S. 613 (1959); Hess *v.* U.S., 361 U.S. 314 (1960). For related issues *see* Kossick *v.* United Fruit Co., 365 U.S. 731 (1961); Moragne *v.* States Marine Lines, Inc., 398 U.S. 375 (1970); 42 *Op. Atty. Gen.* 25 (1966).

[74] Victory Carriers Inc. *v.* Law, 404 U.S. 202 (1971).

[75] Jacksonville Shipyards, Inc. *v.* Perdue, 539 F. 2d. 533 (1976).

[76] Orient Overseas Line *v.* Globemaster Balti., Inc., 365 A. 2d. 325 (1977).

[77] 2 Dall. 419 (1793).

Suability of   It follows that the "controversies" mentioned above are either
the United   those in which the United States appears as party plaintiff or those
States   in which it has, through Congress, consented to be sued. By the
so-called Tucker Act of 1887 the United States did consent to be
sued, in the Court of Claims at Washington, on all claims founded
upon any contract "express or implied"; while by the Federal Tort
Claims Act of 1946 it consented to be sued for injuries "caused by
the negligent or wrongful act or omission of any employee . . . acting within the scope of his office or employment." Excluded were
claims for damage caused by loss of mails, false imprisonment, operations in wartime of the Armed Forces, etc. These laws have survived.[78] In contrast to these acts of generosity, the United States
may spread its immunity to corporations created by it to act as instrumentalities of its powers, but its intention to do so must be
clear.[79] The Supreme Court has generally given a broad, if at times
uneven interpretation to those entitled to recover under the law.[80]
(*Re* suability of States, *see* p. 450.)

The right of the government in actions against it to withhold evidence alleged to reveal military secrets is very broad.[81] However,
with the Supreme Court leading the way in the highly controversial
Jencks case, a combination of statute and Court decisions have
made government files a lot less sacrosanct.[82]

Suability of   How is it as to suits brought against Federal officials? Under the
Federal   common law an officer of government who acts in excess of his law-
Officers   ful authority loses his official character and becomes legally responsible. Following this rule, the Supreme Court in 1882 held, by a
vote of five to four, in the famous case of United States *v.* Lee,[83]
that ejectment proceedings could be brought against Army officers
whom it found to be in "illegal" possession of the Arlington estate
of the Lee family, under an "unlawful" order of the President. But
the Court was destined to learn that the issue was much too complicated to be serviced by a simple rule. As Justice Frankfurter
pointed out in a notable dissent in 1949, there are really four different kinds of cases which arise in this area: "(1) Cases in which the
plaintiff seeks an interest in property which concededly, even
under the allegation of the complaint, belongs to the government,
or calls for an assertion of what is unquestionably official authority.
(2) Cases in which action to the legal detriment of a plaintiff is taken

---

[78] 28 U.S.C. 1346, 2680, 1481.

[79] Larson *v.* Domestic and Foreign Corp., 337 U.S. 682 (1949).

[80] Indian Towing Co. *v.* U.S., 350 U.S. 61 (1955); U.S. *v.* Muniz, 374 U.S. 150 (1963); Rayonier, Inc. *v.* U.S., 352 U.S. 315 (1957), *cf.* Dalehite *v.* U.S., 346 U.S. 15 (1953).

[81] United States *v.* Reynolds, 345 U.S. 1 (1953).

[82] This fascinating, complicated story is well told by the Court in Palermo *v.* U.S., 360 U.S. 343 (1959); *see also* Rosenberg *v.* U.S., 360 U.S. 367 (1959); Campbell *v.* U.S., 365 U.S. 85 (1961); Clancy *v.* U.S., 365 U.S. 312 (1961); U.S. *v.* Augenblick, 393 U.S. 348 (1969).

[83] 106 U.S. 196, 207-208 (1882).

by an official justifying his action under an unconstitutional statute. (3) Cases in which a plaintiff suffers a legal detriment through action of an officer who has exceeded his statutory authority. (4) Cases in which an officer seeks shelter behind statutory authority or some other sovereign command for the commission of a common-law tort."[84] He concluded his analysis with these words: "The matter boils down to this. The federal courts are not barred from adjudicating a claim against a governmental agent who invokes statutory authority for his action if the constitutional power to give him such a claim of immunity is itself challenged. Sovereign immunity may, however, become relevant because the relief prayed for also entails interference with governmental property or brings the operation of governmental machinery into play. The Government then becomes an indispensable party and without its consent cannot be implicated."[85] And there is much truth to the dictum of Justice Douglas that in this type of case "The question of jurisdiction is dependent on decision on the merits."[86]

In a case discussed earlier under the speech and debate clause (see p. 29), the Supreme Court also dealt with the question of the "official immunity doctrine." The Court concluded that "for the purposes of the judicially fashioned doctrine of immunity, the Printer and the Superintendent of Documents are no more free from suit in the case before us than would be a legislative aide who made copies of the materials at issue and distributed them to the public at the direction of his superiors. . . . The scope of inquiry becomes equivalent to the inquiry in the context of the Speech and Debate Clause, and the answer is the same. The business of Congress is to legislate; congressmen and aides are absolutely immune when they are legislating. But when they act outside the 'sphere of legitimate legislative activity,' . . . they enjoy no special immunity from local laws protecting the good name or the reputation of the ordinary citizen."[87]

In the face of some alleged gross violations of constitutional rights by the director of the White House advance office during a Presidential visit to Pekin, Illinois, a Federal district court held that he had official immunity because he had "sufficiently large responsibilities and potential conflict with the public that he or she should be free to exercise the duties of the office unembarrassed by the fear of damage suits."[88]

The immunity cases involving State officials have been treated under Amendment XI. Where the issue is controlled by common

[84] Larson v. Domestic & Foreign Corp. 337 U.S. 682, 709-710 (1949).

[85] Ibid., 715. See also the opinion of highly regarded Judge Friendly in Knight v. N.Y., 443 F. 2d. 415 (1971).

[86] Land v. Dollar, 330 U.S. 731, 735 (1947); Hawaii v. Gordon, 373 U.S. 57 (1963).

[87] Doe v. McMillan, 412 U.S. 306 (1973).

[88] Gardels v. Murphy, 377 F.Supp. 1389 (1974).

law principles, the courts including the Supreme Court make no
distinctions based on whether the officials involved are Federal or
State. However, differences in the laws of different jurisdictions will
affect the outcome of a particular case if the issue rides on statutory
interpretation.

"Controversies between two or more States": From the outset the
Court has generally construed its jurisdiction in this field liberally.
In earlier years its principal grist comprised State boundary disputes, which were held to be justiciable, not political in nature.[89]
Later arose a succession of suits in which the plaintiff State prayed
that defendant State be enjoined from diverting or polluting the
former's water resources.[90] "A river," said Justice Holmes, "is more
than an amenity, it is a treasure."[91] In 1911, in Virginia v. West
Virginia[92] the Court undertook to determine the proportion of the
public debt of the original State of Virginia which West Virginia
ought to shoulder. Speaking again by Justice Holmes, it said: "The
case is to be considered in the untechnical spirit proper for dealing
with a quasi-international controversy, remembering that there is
no municipal code governing the matter, and that this Court may
be called on to adjust differences that cannot be dealt with by Congress or disposed of by the legislature of either State alone."[93] It
was also at a later stage of these same proceedings that Chief Justice
White, for the Court, asserted with much emphasis that the National Government possessed adequate authority to enforce the
Court's decrees against any State which failed to comply with
them—an announcement which stimulated West Virginia to abandon dilatory tactics and vote the sum which the Court had held to
be due Virginia.[94]

In recent years, where the problem of use of scarce water resources has been much aggravated, the Supreme Court has been
deeply involved, for as the Court has said: ". . . this Court does have
serious responsibility to adjudicate cases where there are actual,
existing controversies over how interstate streams should be apportioned among the States."[95]

Lately the Court has shown itself disinclined to exercise its *original* jurisdiction over "controversies between two or more States" as
a shortcut method whereby the citizens of a State may secure a determination of their alleged rights against the legislative policies of
another State or of the National Government, such as the effort a

---

[89] Rhode Island v. Mass., 12 Pet. 657, 721, 736-737 (1838). On the whole subject
see Charles Warren, *The Supreme Court and Sovereign States* (Princeton, 1924).

[90] Missouri v. Ill. and Sanitary Dist. of Chicago, 180 U.S. 208 (1901); Nebraska v.
Wyo., 325 U.S. 589 (1945).

[91] New Jersey v. N.Y., 283 U.S. 336, 342 (1931).   [92] 220 U.S. 1 (1911).

[93] *Ibid.*, 27.   [94] Virginia v. W. Va., 246 U.S. 565 (1918).

[95] Arizona v. California, 373 U.S. 546 (1963); Arizona v. California, 383 U.S. 268
(1966). Recently, there have been several other interesting cases involving controversies between States, Arkansas v. Tennessee, 397 U.S. 88 (1970) and Ohio v.
Wyandotte Chemicals Corp., 401 U.S. 493 (1971).

few years ago of Massachusetts to have the Supreme Court find the war in Vietnam illegal.[96] Nor may a State make itself a collection agency of debts due its citizens from another State and expect the Supreme Court to further the transaction by its original jurisdiction; but an outright assignment of such debts to the plaintiff State is a horse of another color.[97]

By the terms of the Eleventh Amendment "controversies between a State and citizens of another State" include only such controversies as are commenced by a State. But the restrictive force of this limitation had been in earlier decades greatly broken down by the practice of the United States district courts in entertaining applications for injunctions against State officers, and especially State public utility commissions, forbidding them to attempt to enforce State laws or regulations which were claimed by the applicant to be unconstitutional, with the result often of postponing the actual going into effect of such laws or regulations until—if ever—their constitutionality was sustained by the Supreme Court. Sometimes a period of several years—in one case fifteen years—had elapsed before the State measure involved, although it was finally held to be valid, was allowed to go into operation.[98] Certain statutory restraints have been laid upon this practice from time to time,[99] but even more important in curbing it today are the present Supreme Court's enlarged views of State power in the regulation of public utility rates. (*See* pp. 465-466 below.) Judicial Invasion of State Power

Even so, the grounds upon which such controversies, commenced by the State itself, may be based still remain broad; the Court having recognized repeatedly within recent years the right of a State government to intervene in behalf of important interests of its citizens, or a considerable section of them, and to ask the Court to protect such interests against the tortious acts of outside persons and corporations of other States. Thus, in the leading case the Court granted the petition of Georgia for an injunction against certain copper companies in Tennessee, forbidding them to discharge noxious gases from their works in Tennessee over the adjoining counties of Georgia; and it was on this precedent that Governor Arnall relied chiefly in his successful appeal to the Court in 1945 to concede Georgia's right to maintain before it an original suit under the Sherman Act to enjoin an alleged conspiracy of some twenty railroads to fix discriminatory rates from which, he claimed, Georgia and the South generally suffered grave economic Judicial Protection of State Interests

---

[96] Massachusetts *v.* Laird, 400 U.S. 886 (1970). *See* the Douglas dissent. *See* Hawaii *v.* Standard Oil Co., 405 U.S. 251 (1972) particularly Justice Douglas's dissent. *See also* Alabama *v.* Ariz., 291 U.S. 286 (1934); Massachusetts *v.* Mo., 308 U.S. 1, 17 (1939); Massachusetts *v.* Mellon, 262 U.S. 447 (1923).

[97] *Cf.* New Hampshire *v.* La., 108 U.S. 76 (1883), and South Dakota *v.* N.C., 192 U.S. 286 (1904).

[98] Justice Brandeis, concurring, in St. Joseph Stockyards Co. *v.* U.S., 298 U.S. 38, 90-91 (1936).

[99] For example, *see* 28 U.S.C. 1342 and 2281.

detriment.[100] On the question of merits, however, Georgia eventually lost out in the latter case.[101] But in 1971, the Court declined to exercise its jurisdiction in a case involving Ohio's complaint against companies allegedly polluting Lake Erie, explaining that the issues were bottomed on local law, which Ohio courts are competent to consider.[102]

The Diversity of Citizenship Jurisdiction

The judicial power of the United States is extended to the kinds of controversies already mentioned because there is no other tribunal for such controversies. It is extended to controversies "between citizens of different States" for a quite different reason, namely, to make available a tribunal for such cases which shall be free from local bias. In this field, accordingly, Congress has felt free to leave the States a concurrent jurisdiction, and as the statute now stands, the United States district courts have original jurisdiction of controversies between citizens of different States in which ten thousand dollars or more is involved, while controversies of the same pecuniary importance, if brought by a plaintiff in a court of a State of which defendant is not a resident, may be removed by the latter to the nearest United States district court.[103] It was long the doctrine of the Court that the national courts were free to decide cases of this description in accordance with their own notions of "general principles of common law," but later decisions overrule this view, holding that the substantive law enforced must be that laid down by the courts of the State where the cause of action arose, a rule which applies equally to suits in equity and actions at law.[104]

The word "citizens" in this clause, as well as other clauses of this paragraph, has come practically to include corporations, since the Court, by an extended course of judicial legislation which was completed prior to the Civil War, has established the "jurisdictional fiction" that the stockholders of a corporation are all citizens of the State which chartered it, even when the corporation is being sued by a stockholder from another State.[105]

The Diversity Clause and the D. of C.

On the other hand, the word "State" in the clause was held by the Court, speaking by Chief Justice Marshall, in 1805, to be confined to "the members of the American confederacy," with the consequence that a citizen of the District of Columbia could not sue a citizen of Virginia on the ground of diversity of citizenship.[106] At the same time, the Chief Justice indicated that the subject was one

[100] Georgia v. Tenn. Copper Co., 206 U.S. 230 (1907); Georgia v. Pa. R.R. Co., 324 U.S. 439 (1945).

[101] *See* 340 U.S. 889.

[102] Ohio v. Wyandotte Chemicals Corp., 401 U.S. 493 (1971). *See also* Hawaii v. Standard Oil Co., 405 U.S. 251 (1972).

[103] 28 U.S.C. 1332.

[104] Erie R.R. Co. v. Tompkins, 304 U.S. 64 (1938); Prima Paint v. Flood & Conklin, 388 U.S. 395, 404 (1967). The cases overruled are headed by Swift v. Tyson, 16 Pet. 1, decided in 1842.

[105] Dodge v. Woolsey, 18 How. 331 (1855); Ohio and Miss. R.R. Co. v. Wheeler, 1 Bl. 286 (1861); Ross v. Bernhard, 396 U.S. 531, 534 (1970).

[106] Hepburn v. Ellzey, 2 Cr. 445 (1805).

for "legislative, not for judicial consideration"; and, apparently relying on this dictum, Congress in 1940 adopted an amendment to the Federal Judicial Code to extend the jurisdiction of Federal district courts to civil actions involving no Federal question "between citizens of different States or citizens of the District of Columbia ... and any State or Territory."[107] This act was sustained by five Justices, but for widely different reasons, with the result that while the District of Columbia is still not a "State," its citizens may sue citizens of States in the absence of a Federal question, not on the basis of any statable constitutional principle, but through the grace of what Justice Frankfurter has called "conflicting minorities in combination."[108]

Not surprisingly, the presence within the same territory of two autonomous jurisdictions has produced numerous clashes between them. In the vast majority of such cases the State courts involved have, since the boisterous days of Worcester v. Georgia, come off second best, thanks to the Supreme Court's vigorous application of the principle of National Supremacy. Nor have occasional legislative efforts to protect the local interest proved especially successful. By an act passed in 1793[109] Congress forbade the Federal courts to enjoin proceedings in State courts, but that act is today honeycombed with exceptions. First, it has been held that an injunction will lie against proceedings in a State court to protect the lawfully acquired jurisdiction of a Federal court against impairment or defeat.[110] This exception is notably applicable to cases where the Federal court has taken possession of property which it may protect by injunction from interference by State courts.[111] Second, in order to prevent irreparable damage to persons and property the Federal courts may restrain the legal officers of a State from taking proceedings to State courts to enforce State legislation alleged to be unconstitutional.[112] Also Federal courts may issue injunctions restraining the execution of judgments in State courts obtained by fraud,[113] and restraining proceedings in State courts in cases which have been removed to the Federal courts.[114] And, for a time, Fed-

Clashes between Federal and State Courts

[107] 54 *Stat.* 143; 28 U.S.C. 1332.
[108] National Mutual Ins. Co. v. Tidewater Transfer Co., 337 U.S. 582, 655 (1949); Metlakatla Indians v. Egan, 363 U.S. 555, 558 (1960).
[109] 1 *Stat.* 355 (1793); 28 U.S.C. 2283 and 2281.
[110] Freeman v. Howe, 24 How. 450 (1861); Julian v. Central Trust Co., 193 U.S. 93 (1904); Riverdale Cotton Mills v. Ala. & Ga. Mfg. Co., 198 U.S. 188; (1905); Looney v. Eastern Texas R. Co., 247 U.S. 214 (1918).
[111] Farmers' Loan & Trust Co. v. Lake St. Elev. R. Co., 177 U.S. 51 (1900); Riverdale Cotton Mills v. Ala. & Ga. Mfg. Co., 198 U.S. 188 (1905); Julian v. Central Trust Co., 193 U.S. 93 (1904); Kline v. Burke Construction Co., 260 U.S. 226 (1922). For a discussion of this rule *see* Toucey v. New York Life Ins. Co., 314 U.S. 118, 134-136 (1941).
[112] *Ex parte* Young, 209 U.S. 123 (1908), is the leading case.
[113] Arrowsmith v. Gleason, 129 U.S. 86 (1889); Marshall v. Holmes, 141 U.S. 589 (1891); Simon v. Southern R. Co., 236 U.S. 115 (1915).
[114] French v. Hay, 22 Wall. 231 (1875); Dietzsch v. Huidekoper, 103 U.S. 494 (1881); Madisonville Traction Co. v. St. Bernard Mining Co., 196 U.S. 239 (1905).

eral courts could restrain proceedings in State courts to relitigate issues previously adjudicated and finally settled by decrees of a Federal court.[115] Congressional unhappiness with these decisions led to enactment of the requirement that these kinds of injunctions could only be issued by a three-judge court.[116]

Some special questions about the relationship of Federal and State courts have been addressed by the lower courts in recent years. A Federal district court held that "if jurisdiction is vested in the federal courts, then neither a crowded docket nor the possibility of a more expeditious resolution by the state court nor anything else can deprive litigants of a federal forum."[117]

When an individual charged with spraying red paint on the outside wall of the United Nations headquarters sought to be tried in a Federal rather than a State court, relying on Article III, Section II, a New York court held that the Headquarters Agreement, an international treaty, gave jurisdiction to Federal, State, and local law as to acts done in the Headquarters District "as provided in applicable federal, state and local laws," that, therefore, gave the New York court jurisdiction.[118]

The doctrine of "ancillary jurisdiction" was explained by a U.S. circuit court: "[It] is a limited exception to the rule that federal district courts have only such jurisdiction as is provided, in terms, by the Constitution or a statute. It may be employed when a federal court is presented with issues or parties so closely related to a matter over which it has jurisdiction as to be part of a single Article III 'case.' In such circumstances, and in the interest of judicial economy and complete justice, a federal court can exercise ancillary jurisdiction over such issues or parties."[119]

To say that Federal courts may, and do to this day, step in to restrain proceedings in State courts is not to suggest that they do it often and blithely. Judicial unease over the perceived necessity to do it on occasion was reflected very well in a recent opinion written for the Court by Justice Black:

"Since the beginning of this country's history Congress has, subject to few exceptions, manifested a desire to permit state courts to try state cases free from interference by federal courts. In 1793 an Act unconditionally provided: [N]or shall a writ of injunction be granted to stay proceedings in any court of a state. . . . A comparison of the 1793 Act with its present-day successor, graphically illustrates how few and minor have been the exceptions granted from the flat, prohibitory language of the old Act. During all this lapse of years from 1793 to 1970 the statutory exceptions to the 1793 con-

---

[115] The earlier cases are Root *v*. Woolworth, 150 U.S. 401 (1893); Prout *v*. Starr, 188 U.S. 537 (1903); Julian *v*. Central Trust Co., 193 U.S. 93 (1904).

[116] 18 U.S.C. 2281.

[117] Lincoln Associates *v*. Great Am. Mortg. Investors, 415 F.Supp. 351 (1976).

[118] People *v*. Weiner, 378 N.Y.S. 2d. 966 (1976).

[119] Warren B. Kleban Engineering Corp. *v*. Caldwell, 490 F. 2d. 800, 802 (1974).

gressional enactment have been only three: (1) except as expressly authorized by Act of Congress; (2) where necessary in aid of its jurisdiction; and (3) to protect or effectuate its judgments. In addition, a judicial exception to the longstanding policy evidenced by the statute has been made where a person about to be prosecuted in a state court can show that he will, if the proceeding in the state court can show that he will, if the proceeding in the state court is not enjoined, suffer irreparable damages. *See ex parte* Young, 209 U.S. 123 (1908).

"The precise reasons for this longstanding public policy against federal court interference with state court proceedings have never been specifically identified but the primary sources of the policy are plain. One is the basic doctrine of equity jurisprudence that courts of equity should not act, and particularly should not act to restrain a criminal prosecution, when the moving party has an adequate remedy at law and will not suffer irreparable injury if denied equitable relief. . . . This underlying reason for restraining courts of equity from interfering with criminal prosecutions is reinforced by an even more vital consideration, the notion of 'comity,' that is, a proper respect for state functions, a recognition of the fact that the entire country is made up of a Union of separate state governments, and a continuance of the belief that the National Government will fare best if the States and their institutions are left free to perform their separate functions in their separate ways. . . . The concept does not mean blind deference to 'States' Rights' any more than it means centralization of control over every important issue in our National Government and its courts. The Framers rejected both these courses. What the concept does represent is a system in which there is sensitivity to the legitimate interests of both State and National Governments, and in which the National Government, anxious though it may be to vindicate and protect federal rights and federal interests, always endeavors to do so in ways that will not unduly interfere with the legitimate activities of the States."[120] Yet, in its understandable and commendable zeal to safeguard important civil liberties from violation at the State level, the Supreme Court in the Warren years had made inroads on the inviolability of a doctrine it had long employed, the "abstention doctrine."[121] "Abstention," according to the Warren Court's own description, "is a judge-fashioned vehicle for according appropriate deference of the state and federal court systems. Its recognition of *the role of state courts as the final expositors of state law* implies no disregard for the primacy of the federal judiciary in deciding questions of federal law. Accordingly, we have on several occasions explicitly recognized that abstention 'does not, of course, involve the abdication of federal jurisdiction, but only the postponement of

The
Abstention
Doctrine

---

[120] Younger *v*. Harris, 401 U.S. 37 (1971).

[121] Dombrowski *v*. Pfister, 380 U.S. 479 (1965); England *v*. Medical Examiners, 375 U.S. 411 (1964).

its exercise'" (emphasis supplied).[122] But the spirit of *Younger* seems to prevail these days.

Significantly, in June 1972 the Supreme Court held that the statute which authorizes a suit in equity to redress the deprivation "under color" of State law "of any rights, privileges, or immunities secured by the Constitution" was within the exceptions of the Federal anti-injunction statute which provides among other things that a Federal court may not enjoin State court proceedings "except as expressly authorized by Act of Congress."[123]

In 1975, the Court made clear that Justice Black's paean of praise for "Our Federalism" in *Younger* sounds sweet to a majority of the Court. In a case involving the seizure of the film *Deep Throat* and a complex of resulting actions in State and Federal courts, the Court held that "where state criminal proceedings are begun against federal plaintiffs after the federal complaint is filed but before any proceedings of substance on the merits have taken place in the federal court, the principles of Younger v. Harris should apply in full force. . . . Unless we are to trivialize the principles of Younger v. Harris, the federal complaint should have been dismissed on the state motion absent satisfactory proof of those extraordinary circumstances calling into play one of the limited exceptions to the rule of Younger v. Harris and related cases."[124] The Court, however, in a case decided a week later dealing with an ordinance proscribing topless dancing stated that "The principle underlying *Younger* . . . is that state courts are fully competent to adjudicate constitutional claims, and therefore a federal court should, in all but the most exceptional circumstances, refuse to interfere with an ongoing state criminal proceeding. In the absence of such a proceeding, however, . . . a plaintiff may challenge the constitutionality of the state statute in federal court, assuming he can satisfy the requirements for federal jurisdiction."[125]

In a case involving a court-martial, there were several suggestions in the majority opinion that *Younger* had application.[126] As the Court put it, "While the peculiar demands of federalism are not implicated, the deficiency is supplied by factors equally compelling. The military is 'a specialized society separate from the civilian society.'" Further on, the Court stated that "it must be assumed that the military court system will vindicate servicemen's constitutional rights." The Court went on to hold "that when a serviceman charged with crimes by military authorities can show no harm other than that attendant to resolution of his case in the military court system, the federal district courts must refrain from interven-

---

[122] England v. Medical Examiners, 375 U.S. 411, 415-416 (1964).

[123] Mitchem v. Foster, 407 U.S. 225 (1972). The statutes referred to above are contained in 42 U.S.C. 1983 and 28 U.S.C. 2283, respectively.

[124] Hicks v. Miranda, 422 U.S. 332, 350 (1975).

[125] Doran v. Salem Inn, Inc., 422 U.S. 922 (1975). *See also* Ellis v. Dyson, 421 U.S. 1691 (1975).

[126] Schlesinger v. Councilman, 420 U.S. 738 (1975).

tion, by way of injunction or otherwise." Chief Justice Burger in a concurring opinion stated explicitly that in his view the district court should have dismissed the complaint on the basis of *Younger*.

In yet another case that year, the Supreme Court held that under some circumstances "the principles of Younger are applicable even though the state proceeding is civil in nature."[127]

In 1977 Justice Rehnquist, speaking for the Court, significantly extended the reach of *Younger*, saying, "We now hold, however, that the principles of *Younger* and *Huffman* [Huffman v. Pursue, 420 U.S. 592 (1975)] are not confined solely to the types of state actions which were sought to be enjoined in those cases." Turning to the substantive issue in the case, Rehnquist went on, "These principles apply to a case in which the State's contempt process is involved. . . . Perhaps, it is not quite as important as is the State's interest in the enforcement of its criminal laws, *Younger*, or even of its interest in the maintenance of a quasi-criminal proceeding such as was involved in *Huffman*. But we think it is of sufficiently great import as to require application of the principles of those cases."[128]

As one Federal district court summed it up not long ago "When an individual waits to assert federal rights in federal court until after he is already embroiled in litigation within the state judicial system, the *Younger* sextet and its progeny establish the principle that, absent unusual circumstances, it is then too late for him to invoke his right to a federal forum to vindicate his federal rights, since the existing state forum is presumably fully capable of affording him that opportunity."[129]

From the 1940's until recently, a new source of intervention by Federal courts in the domain of State judicial process emerged in consequence, first, of the impact of the expanding concept of due process upon enforcement by the States of their criminal laws, and, second, of the almost complete freedom claimed by the Supreme Court today "to decline to review decisions which, right or wrong, do not present questions of sufficient gravity." The natural product of these cooperating factors had been a vast increase in the number of petitions filed in Federal district courts for the writ of *habeas corpus*, in the name of persons accused or convicted of crime in the States, in alleged violation of their constitutional rights. In a case decided in 1948 Justice Murphy, while favoring this increased availability of the writ, revealed that in the fiscal years 1944, 1945, and 1946 an average of 451 *habeas corpus* petitions were filed each year in Federal district courts by persons in State custody, although an average of only six per cent resulted in a reversal of the conviction and release of the petitioner.[130] Based on these figures Justice

The *Habeas Corpus* Problem

[127] Huffman v. Pursue, Ltd., 420 U.S. 592 (1975).
[128] Juidice v. Vail, 97 S.Ct. 1211, 1216-1217 (1977).
[129] Hamar Theatres, Inc. v. Cryan, 393 F.Supp. 34 (1975). *See also* Sole v. Grand Jurors of N.J. For Co. of Passaic & Bergen, 393 F.Supp. 1322 (1975).
[130] Wade v. Mayo, 334 U.S. 672, 682 (1948).

Frankfurter observed in 1953 that "the writ has possibilities for evil as well as good," that abuse of it "may undermine the orderly administration of justice," the responsibility for which "rests largely with the States," and in consequence "weakening the forces of authority that are essential for civilization."[131] Imagine how the minds of those two Justices would have boggled to learn that in 1969 there were *12,000* such petitions.[132] (For a substantive discussion of *habeas corpus, see* pp. 124-128.)

Retroactivity of Right to Counsel Decisions
In the wake of its landmark decisions with respect to right to counsel, illegal search and seizures, and involuntary confessions (discussed below under the Bill of Rights), the Warren Court was forced to wrestle with another trying problem respecting judicial review. Once the Court decides that the Constitution requires right to counsel in a criminal case, what happens to all those languishing in jail who had been denied that right? It hardly seems justice to let them remain there. But if we allow them to take steps to freedom, what of the felon who was convicted on the basis of good evidence which was illegally obtained? Once the Court decides to deny the use of such evidence to prevent illegal police activity in the future, does it change the likelihood that those already convicted were guilty? The Court's answer to these questions fashioned in a series of cases is this: "Relying on prior cases, we firmly rejected the idea that all new interpretations of the Constitution must be considered always to have been the law and that prior constructions to the contrary must always be ignored. Since that time, we have held to the course that there is no inflexible constitutional rule requiring in all circumstances either absolute retroactivity or complete prospectivity for decisions construing the broad language of the Bill of Rights. Nor have we accepted as a dividing line the suggested distinction between cases on direct review and those arising on collateral attack. Rather we have proceeded to weigh the merits and demerits in each case by looking to the prior history of the rule in question, its purpose and effect, and whether retrospective operation will further or retard its operation.

"Where the major purpose of new constitutional doctrine is to overcome an aspect of the criminal trial which substantially impairs its truth-finding function and so raises serious questions about the accuracy of guilty verdicts in past trials, the new rule has been given complete retroactive effect. Neither good-faith reliance by state or federal authorities on prior constitutional law or accepted practice, nor severe impact on the administration of justice has sufficed to require prospective application in these circumstances.

"It is quite different where the purpose of the new constitutional standard proscribing the use of certain evidence or a particular

---

[131] Brown *v.* Allen, 344 U.S. 443 (1953). All quoted passages are from Justice Frankfurter's supplementary opinion, *ibid.*, 488-513.

[132] George C. Doub, "The Case Against Modern Federal *Habeas Corpus*," 57 *ABA Journal*, 323, 325 (1971).

mode of trial is not to minimize or avoid arbitrary or unreliable results but to serve other ends. In these situations the new doctrine raises no question about the guilt of defendants convicted in prior trials. Mapp *v.* Ohio cast no doubt on the relevance or probity of illegally seized evidence but excluded it from criminal trials to deter official invasions of individual privacy protected by the Fourth Amendment."[133]

The short of the matter is that the Court has made the right-to-counsel decision retroactive but has refused to do so as a general proposition with respect to "Fourth Amendment cases and new interpretations of the Fifth Amendment's privilege against compelled self-incrimination."[134]

¶2. In all cases affecting ambassadors, other public ministers and consuls, and those in which a State shall be party, the Supreme Court shall have original jurisdiction. In all the other cases before mentioned the Supreme Court shall have appellate jurisdiction, both as to law and fact, with such exceptions and under such regulations as the Congress shall make.

Jurisdiction is either original or appellate. In Marbury *v.* Madison, the case in which the Court first pronounced an act of Congress unconstitutional, it was held that Congress could not extend the original jurisdiction of the Supreme Court to other cases than those specified in the first sentence of this paragraph.[135] But, if a case "in which the State is party" is also one "arising under the Constitution and laws of the United States," it may, if Congress so enacts, be brought elsewhere in the first instance. In face of the express words of Section II, ¶2, of the Constitution this may seem a little surprising but Chief Justice Marshall explained it this way: "The words of the constitution are, 'in all cases affecting ambassadors, other public ministers, and consuls, and those in which a State shall be a party, the Supreme Court shall have original jurisdiction. In all the other cases before mentioned, the Supreme Court shall have appellate jurisdiction.'

"This distinction between original and appellate jurisdiction excludes, we are told, in all cases, the exercise of the one where the other is given.

"The constitution gives the Supreme Court original jurisdiction in certain enumerated cases, and gives it appellate jurisdiction in all others. Among those in which jurisdiction must be exercised in the appellate form are cases arising under the constitution and laws of the United States. These provisions of the constitution are equally

---

[133] Williams *v.* U.S., 401 U.S. 646, 651-653, 1151-1153 (1971).

[134] *Ibid.* , 655 note 7. *See also* Linkletter *v.* Walker, 381 U.S. 618 (1965); Desist *v.* U.S., 394 U.S. 244 (1969); Tehan *v.* U.S., 382 U.S. 406 (1966); Johnson *v.* N.J., 384 U.S. 719 (1966); Mackey *v.* U.S., 401 U.S. 667 (1971).

[135] 1 Cr. 137 (1803). This holding was anticipated by Chief Justice Ellsworth in his opinion in Wiscart *v.* Dauchy, 3 Dall. 321 (1796).

obligatory, and are to be equally respected. If a State be a party, the jurisdiction of this Court is original; if the case arise under a constitution or a law, the jurisdiction is appellate. But a case to which a State is a party may arise under the constitution or a law of the United States. What rule is applicable to such a case? What, then, becomes the duty of the Court? Certainly, we think, so to construe the constitution as to give effect to both provisions, as far as it is possible to reconcile them, and not to permit their seeming repugnancy to destroy each other. We must endeavour so to construe them as to preserve the true intent and meaning of the instrument."[136]

Whatever the intent of the Framers, Justice Douglas, speaking for the Court, explained that "It has long been this Court's philosophy that 'our original jurisdiction should be invoked sparingly' . . . to make it obligatory only in appropriate cases." According to Douglas, what constitutes appropriateness depends upon "the seriousness and dignity of the claim" and "beyond that it necessarily involves the availability of another forum where there is jurisdiction over the named parties, where the issues tendered may be litigated, and where appropriate relief may be had." He further explained: "We incline to a sparing use of our original jurisdiction so that our increasing duties with the appellate docket will not suffer."[137] Even in so important a matter as a complaint against automobile manufacturers alleging a conspiracy "to restrain the development of motor vehicle air pollution control equipment" in which eighteen States were the plaintiffs, the Court refused in 1972 to take original jurisdiction. Admitting that "our jurisdiction over the controversy cannot be disputed," Justice Douglas, speaking for the Court, stated that "corrective remedies for air pollution . . . necessarily must be considered in the context of localized situations," and concluded, therefore, that the cases should first be heard in the appropriate Federal district courts.[138] In assessing the Court's wisdom in this decision, one must bear in mind that in practical terms it may be as much as ten years before the issue is fully litigated.

In response to the attempt of the State of Arizona to invoke the Supreme Court's original jurisdiction in an action against New Mexico's electrical energy tax, the Supreme Court held firm on the proposition that "our original jurisdiction should be invoked sparingly."[139] The Court said that "In the circumstances of this case, we are persuaded that the pending state court action provides an appropriate forum in which the *issues* tendered here may be litigated." The Court pointed out that, if Arizona should not be vindicated in the New Mexico courts, "the issues raised now may be brought to this Court by way of direct appeal."

[136] Cohens *v.* Va., 6 Wheat. 264, 392-393 (1821); Ames *v.* Kan., 111 U.S. 449 (1884); United States *v.* Calif., 297 U.S. 175 (1936).

[137] Illinois *v.* City of Milwaukee, 406 U.S. 91 (1972).

[138] Washington *v.* General Motors Corp., 406 U.S. 109 (1972).

[139] Arizona *v.* New Mexico, 96 S.Ct. 1845 (1970).

The Court's appellate jurisdiction Congress may, as indicated earlier (p. 225), enlarge or diminish at will so long as it does not exceed the catalogue of "cases" and "controversies" given in ¶1, above. The appellate jurisdiction of the Supreme Court as to fact in "cases of law" is much curtailed by Amendment VII. Even so, the Court will always review findings of fact by a State court, or by an administrative agency, to any extent necessary to vindicate rights claimed under the Constitution.[140]

¶3. The trial of all crimes, except in cases of impeachment, shall be by jury; and such trial shall be held in the State where the said crimes shall have been committed; but when not committed within any State, the trial shall be at such place or places as the Congress may by law have directed.

In spite of its mandatory form the opening clause of this paragraph, like the parallel provision on the same subject in Amendment VI, only establishes trial by jury as a privilege of accused persons, which such persons may accordingly waive if they choose[141] and the government consents. The substance of the other two clauses is also covered by that amendment. (*See* p. 404 for discussion.)

But several recent lower court decisions are worthy of mention here because of their specific reference to this paragraph.

Lower courts have had occasion to deal with the issue of whether the penalty provisions of the Occupational Safety and Health Act were criminal or civil in nature, for, if they are criminal, this provision of the Constitution could be invoked. The U.S. Court of Appeals for the Fifth Circuit reviewed the pertinent Supreme Court decisions and held: "That the civil sanction under attack is in the form of a dollar penalty is not a sufficient distinction to deny the power of Congress to prescribe an administrative, as distinguished from a judicial mechanism. To so hold would produce the absurd spectacle of Congress—having full power to prescribe an administrative structure with sanctions of denial or revocation of a life-or-death license—being denied the power to prescribe a money fine of a single dollar or for that matter a single red sou."[142]

In a case in which a campaign worker for Senator Hubert H. Humphrey was found guilty of knowingly causing another to accept or receive an illegal corporate contribution, the question of venue was raised. The United States Court of Appeals, Second Cir-

---

[140] This does not contradict what was said on p. 237. To determine whether or not a determination of facts is supported by "substantial evidence" requires a review of those facts.

[141] Patton *v.* U.S., 281 U.S. 276 (1930); U.S. *v.* Harris, 314 F.Supp. 437 (1970); Goldstein *v.* Pavlikowski, 489 P. 2d. 1159 (1971); *ex parte* Quirin, 317 U.S. 1 (1942); U.S. *v.* National City Lines, 334 U.S. 573 (1948); Reid *v.* Covert, 354 U.S. 1 (1957).

[142] Atlas Roofing Co. *v.* Occupational S. & H. Rev. Com'n, 518 F. 2d. 990 (1975). *See also* Lake Butler Apparel Company *v.* Secretary of Labor, 519 F. 2d. 84 (1975).

cuit, held that "The constitutional standards for venue concern the locality of the substantive offense rather than the location of the offender at the time of the offense."[143] (*See* page 417.)

SECTION III

¶1. Treason against the United States shall consist only in levying war against them, or in adhering to their enemies, giving them aid and comfort. No person shall be convicted of treason unless on the testimony of two witnesses to the same overt act, or on confession in open court.

"Levying war" consists, in the first place, in a combination or conspiracy to effect a change in the laws or the government by force, but a war is not "levied" until the treasonable force is actually assembled.[1]

One "adheres" to the enemies of the United States, "giving them aid and comfort," when he knowingly furnishes them with assistance of any sort.[2]

Vicissitudes of the "Treason" Clause

"Overt act" means simply open act, that is to say, an act which may be testified to, and not a mere state of consciousness. Otherwise, the precise force of this requirement is still a matter of some doubt. At the common law, treason by levying war involved a conspiracy, so that if an overt act of war in pursuance of the conspiracy took place, all the conspirators were equally liable for it at the place where it occurred; and in the *Bollman* case early in 1807 Chief Justice Marshall followed the common law doctrine. A few weeks later, however, while presiding at Richmond over the trial of Aaron Burr for treason, he turned his back on this doctrine completely by holding that Burr must be linked with the conspiracy by an overt act of his own. And in 1945 the Court held, five to four, that in a prosecution for treason by giving "aid and comfort," the overt act or acts testified to must be of themselves sufficient to establish treasonable intent. This holding, based in part on an error of history, has since been abandoned for something more nearly approaching the older doctrine, that a traitor may be convicted on any kind of admissible evidence into which the testimony of two witnesses to an overt act enters.[3]

[143] United States *v*. Chestnut, 533 F. 2d. 40 (1976).

---

[1] *Ex parte* Bollman, 4 Cr. 75 (1807).
[2] Charles Warren, "What is Giving Aid and Comfort to the Enemy?" 27 *Yale Law Journal*, 331 (1918); Tomoya Kawakita *v*. U.S., 343 U.S. 717 (1952).
[3] *Cf.* the *Bollman* case, cited above; Beveridge, *Marshall*, III, 618-626; Willoughby, *Constitutional Law*, II, 1125-1133; Cramer *v*. U.S., 325 U.S. 1 (1945); Haupt *v*. U.S., 330 U.S. 631 (1947). The error referred to was Justice Jackson's mistaken idea that the two-witness requirement originated in the Constitution. It comes from the Treason Trials Act of 1696 (7 and 8 Wm. III, c. 3). David Hutchison, *The Foundations of the Constitution* (New York, 1928), 215.

¶2. The Congress shall have power to declare the punishment of treason, but no attainder of treason shall work corruption of blood or forfeiture except during the life of the person attainted.

Some years ago, the Supreme Court said all that needs to be said on this provision:

"In England, attainders of treason worked corruption of blood and perpetual forfeiture of the estate of the person attainted, to the disinherison of his heirs, or of those who would otherwise be his heirs. Thus innocent children were made to suffer because of the offence of their ancestor. When the Federal Constitution was framed, this was felt to be a great hardship, and even rank injustice. For this reason, it was ordained that no attainder of treason should work corruption of blood or forfeiture, except during the life of the person attainted. No one ever doubted that it was a provision introduced for the benefit of the children and heirs alone; a declaration that the children should not bear the iniquity of the fathers."[4]

[4] Wallick *et al. v.* Van Riswick, 92 U.S. 202, 210 (1875).

ARTICLE IV

This article, sometimes called "the Federal Article," defines in certain important particulars the relations of the States to one another and of the National Government to the States.

SECTION I

¶Full faith and credit shall be given in each State to the public acts, records, and judicial proceedings of every other State. And the Congress may by general laws prescribe the manner in which such acts, records, and proceedings shall be proved, and the effect thereof.

In accordance with what is variously known as Conflict of Laws, Comity, or Private International Law, rights acquired under the laws or through the courts of one country may often receive recognition and enforcement in the courts of another country, and it is the purpose of the above section to guarantee that this shall be the case among the States in certain instances.[1]

Operation of the "Full Faith and Credit" Clause on Judgments

Article IV, Section I, has had its principal operation in relation to judgments. The cases fall into two groups: First, those in which the judgment involved was offered as a basis of proceedings for its own enforcement outside the State where rendered, as for example, when an action for debt is brought in the courts of State B on a judgment for money damages rendered in State A; secondly, those in which the judgment involved was offered in conformance with the principle of *res judicata*, in defense in a new or "collateral" proceeding growing out of the same facts as the original suit, as for example, when a decree of divorce granted in State A is offered as barring a suit for divorce by the other party to the marriage in the courts of State B.

By an act of Congress passed in 1790, and still on the statute books, "the records and judicial proceedings of the Courts of any State . . . shall have such faith and credit given to them in every court within the United States as they have by law or usage in the courts of the State from which they are taken."[2] In the pioneer cases of Mills *v*. Duryee and Hampton *v*. McConnel this language was given literal application by the Marshall Court, and the judgments there involved were held to be entitled in the courts of sister States to the validity of final judgments.[3] In 1839, however, in McElmoyle *v*. Cohen,[4] the Court, then in the grip of States' Rights prepossessions, ruled that the Constitution was not intended "materially to interfere with the essential attributes of the *lex fori*" ("the

---

[1] T. M. Cooley, *Principles of Constitutional Law* (Boston, 1898), 3rd ed., 196-206.
[2] 28 U.S.C. 1738.   [3] 7 Cr. 485 (1813); 3 Wheat. 234.
[4] McElmoyle *v*. Cohen, 13 Pet. 312, 326 (1839).

forum State"); that the act of Congress only established a rule of evidence—of conclusive evidence to be sure, but still of evidence only—and that it was necessary, in order to carry into effect in a State the judgment of a court of a sister State, to institute a fresh action in a court of the former, in strict compliance with its laws; and that consequently, when remedies were sought in support of the rights accruing in another jurisdiction, they were governed by the *lex fori*.

One consequence of this errant nullification of the Act of 1790 was that for a time the Court was occasionally confronted with the contention that a State need not provide a forum for some particular type of judgment from a sister State that it chose to disrelish—a contention which the Court rejected categorically at least by 1945 when it said: "But the Clause does not make a sister State judgment a judgment in another State. The proposal to do so was rejected by the Philadelphia Convention. To give it the force of a judgment in another state, it must be made a judgment there. McElmoyle *v.* Cohen. It can be made a judgment there only if the court purporting to render the original judgment had power to render such a judgment. *A judgment in one State is conclusive upon the merits in every other State*, but only if the court of the first State had power to pass on the merits—had jurisdiction, that is, to render the judgment (emphasis supplied)."[5] The Court has never since that time found occasion to backtrack and other courts accept this statement as the law without question.[6]

The important and lasting consequence of the Court's partial nullification of the Act of 1790 has been the spawn of cases it has bred raising the question whether the judgment for which recognition was being sought under the "full faith and credit" clause was rendered "with jurisdiction," i.e. in accordance with some test or standard alleged not to have been observed by the court rendering it. Foreshadowed in a dissenting opinion in 1813,[7] this doctrine was definitely accepted by the Court in 1850 as to judgments *in personam*,[8] and in 1874 as to judgments *in rem*,[9] and in 1878 was transferred from the shadowy realm of "fundamental principles of justice" to the more solid contours of the "due process clause" of Amendment XIV where it still remains.[10]

The Jurisdictional Question

What the law and doctrine of these cases boils down to is this: A judgment of a State court, in a civil, not a penal, cause within its

[5] Williams *v.* N.C., 325 U.S. 226, 229 (1945).
[6] For examples *see* Western Auto Supply Co. *v.* Dillard, 172 S.E. 2d. 388, 394 (1970); State *ex. rel.* Lynn *v.* Eddy, 163 S.E. 2d. 472 (1968). Contentions to the contrary generally cite cases decided prior to 1945.
[7] *See* Mills *v.* Duryee, 7 Cr. 481, 486-487.
[8] D'Arcy *v.* Ketchum, 11 How. 165 (1850).
[9] Thompson *v.* Whitman, 18 Wall. 457 (1874).
[10] Pennoyer *v.* Neff, 95 U.S. 714 (1878); *see also* Milliken *v.* Meyer, 311 U.S. 457 (1940); International Shoe Co. *v.* Washington, 326 U.S. 310, 316 (1945); McGee *v.* International Life Insurance Co., 355 U.S. 220 (1957).

jurisdiction, and against a defendant lawfully summoned, or against lawfully attached property of an absent defendant, is entitled to as much force and effect against the person summoned or the property attached, when the question is presented for decision in a court in another State, as it has in the State in which it was rendered.[11]

The Court still maintains that with respect to *in personam* judgments, "the consistent constitutional rule has been that a court has no power to adjudicate a personal claim or obligation unless it has jurisdiction over the person of the defendant."[12] But this holding must be read against the backdrop of a previous holding that: "Since *Pennoyer v. Neff*, this Court has held that the Due Process Clause of the Fourteenth Amendment places some limit on the power of state courts to enter binding judgments against persons not served with process within their boundaries. But just where this line of limitation falls has been the subject of prolific controversy, particularly with respect to foreign corporations. In a continuing process of evolution this Court accepted and then abandoned 'consent,' 'doing business,' and 'presence' as the standard for measuring the extent of state judicial power over such corporations. . . . More recently in *International Shoe Co. v. Washington* the Court decided that 'due process requires only that in order to subject a defendant to a judgment *in personam*, if he be not present within the territory of the forum, he have certain minimum contacts with it such that the maintenance of the suit does not offend traditional notions of fair play and substantial justice."[13]

In 1977, the Supreme Court took a long step toward requiring the same test of "fair play and substantial justice" to assertions to jurisdiction *in rem* as to assertions to jurisdiction *in personam.* In determining "The constitutionality of a Delaware statute that allows a court of that State to take jurisdiction of a lawsuit by sequestering any property if the defendant happens to be located in Delaware," the Court decided "The fiction that an assertion of jurisdiction over property is anything but an assertion of jurisdiction over the owner of the property supports an ancient form without substantial modern justification. Its continued acceptance would serve only to allow state court jurisdiction that is fundamentally unfair to the defendant.

"We therefore conclude that all assertions of state court jurisdiction must be evaluated according to the standards as set forth in *International Shoe* and its progeny."[14] In a pregnant footnote the Court said "It would not be fruitful for us to re-examine the facts of cases decided on the rationales of *Pennoyer* . . . [and another case] to determine whether jurisdiction might have been sustained

[11] McGee *v.* International Life Insurance Co., 355 U.S. 220, 223 (1957).
[12] Zenith Corp. *v.* Hazeltine, 395 U.S. 100, 110 (1969).
[13] McGee *v.* International Life Insurance Co., 355 U.S. 220, 222 (1957).
[14] Shaffer *v.* Heitner, 433 U.S. 186, 189-212 (1977).

under the standard we adopt today. To the extent that prior decisions are inconsistent with this standard, they are overruled."

Today, the jurisdictional question comprises the principal grist of cases arising under Article IV, Section I, but is most copiously illustrated in divorce cases, particularly in those in which the respondent to a suit for divorce has offered in defense an earlier divorce from the courts of some sister State, most likely Nevada.

By the almost universally accepted view prior to 1906, a proceeding in divorce was one against the marriage status, i.e. *in rem*, and hence might be validly brought by either party in any State where he or she was *bona fide* domiciled;[15] and, conversely, when the plaintiff did not have a *bona fide* domicile in the State, a court could not render a decree binding in other States even if the nonresident defendant entered a personal appearance.[16] That year, however, the Court discovered, by a vote of five-to-four, a situation in which a divorce proceeding is one *in personam*.

Divorce Cases: a Judicial Tilting Field

The case referred to is Haddock v. Haddock,[17] while the earlier rule is illustrated by Atherton v. Atherton,[18] decided five years previously. In the latter it was held, in the former denied, that a divorce granted a husband without personal service upon the wife, who at the time was residing in another State, was entitled to recognition under the "full faith and credit" clause and the acts of Congress; the difference between the cases consisting solely in the fact that in the *Atherton* case the husband had driven the wife from their joint home by his conduct, while in the *Haddock* case he had deserted her. The court which granted the divorce in Atherton v. Atherton was held to have had jurisdiction of the marriage status, with the result that the proceeding was one *in rem* and hence required only service by publication upon the respondent. Haddock's suit, on the contrary, was held to be as to the wife *in personam*, and so to require personal service upon her, or her voluntary appearance, neither of which had been had; although, notwithstanding this, the decree in the latter case was held to be valid as to the State where obtained on account of the State's inherent power to determine the status of its own citizens. The upshot was a situation in which a man and a woman, when both were in Connecticut, were divorced; and when both were in New York, were married; and when the one was in Connecticut and the other in New York, the former was divorced and the latter married. In Atherton v. Atherton the Court had earlier acknowledged that "a husband without a wife, or a wife without a husband, is unknown to the law."

Nor, in overruling Haddock v. Haddock in 1942, did the Court clarify the situation materially. For while holding that any State is

---

[15] Cheever v. Wilson, 9 Wall. 108 (1870).

[16] Andrews v. Andrews, 188 U.S. 14 (1903). *See also* German Savings Society v. Dormitzer, 192 U.S. 125 (1904).

[17] 201 U.S. 562 (1906). *See also* Thompson v. Thompson, 226 U.S. 551 (1913).

[18] 181 U.S. 155, 162 (1901).

entitled to divorce anybody who is *"bona fide* domiciled" within its borders even though the other spouse, being outside the State, was not personally served, yet it has since handed down another ruling, the logic of which appears to expose to the danger of going to jail anybody who, having left his home State, gets a divorce in another State, remarries, and then returns to State No. 1, or *goes to some third State*, provided a jury of his last place of residence can be persuaded that his residence in the divorcing State lacked "domiciliary intent," that is to say, the intention of remaining there from then on.[19] Quite evidently this contravenes the Act of 1790, the divorce being conceded to be valid in the State where granted.

How can one account for this abrupt backing and filling? At first glance it appears to stem from an ideological quarrel between Justices who set great store by the principle of *res judicata*, as the "full faith and credit" clause itself does, and other Justices who swear by the principle of domicile as a kind of substitute for the due process of law requirement. This, however, would be a superficial account of the matter. A divorce case may involve other questions than that merely of the marital status of the party holding the divorce. It may also involve issues connected with the right of a divorced wife to support, with the custody of the children of the dissolved partnership, with the ownership of property, etc.; and when this happens, first one and then the other of the opposed concepts may appear best adapted to do the tangled situation essential justice.

"Divisible Divorce"   Recognizing this fact, the Court sought to strike a working compromise, as it were, between *res judicata* and domicile. The leading case is Estin *v.* Estin, decided in 1948.[20] Here, while conceding the validity of an *ex parte* Nevada decree obtained by a husband, the Court held that New York had not denied full faith and credit to said decree when, subsequently thereto, it granted the wife a judgment for arrears in alimony founded upon a decree of separation previously awarded to her when both she and her husband were domiciled in New York. The Nevada decree issued to the husband after he had resided there a year, and upon constructive notice to the wife in New York who entered no appearance, was held to be effective to change the marital status of both parties in all States of the Union but ineffective on the issue of alimony. Divorce, in other words, was viewed as being divisible; and Nevada, in the absence of acquiring jurisdiction over the wife, was held incapable of adjudicating the rights of the wife in the prior New York judgment awarding her alimony. Such a result was justified as accommodating the interests of both New York and Nevada in the broken marriage by restricting each State to matters of dominant concern to it, the concern of New York being that of protecting the abandoned wife against impoverishment.

---

[19] Williams *v.* N.C., 317 U.S. 287 (1942); Williams *v.* N.C., 325 U.S. 226 (1945)—"Williams I" and "Williams II."
[20] 334 U.S. 541 (1948).

The doctrine of divisible divorce is now well established.[21] And on that basis it seems safe to assert that an *ex parte* divorce, founded upon acquisition of domicile by one spouse in the State which granted it, is effective to destroy the marital status of both parties in the State of domiciliary origin and probably in all other States and therefore to preclude subsequent prosecutions for bigamy, but not to alter rights as to property, alimony, or custody of children in the State of domiciliary origin of a spouse who was neither served nor personally appeared.[22]

The Court held in 1975 in a case dealing with an Iowa law respecting a one-year residency requirement for divorce that the requirement was justified. Speaking for the Court, Justice Rehnquist distinguished the residency requirement here from those that had been struck down by the Court. In addition to pointing up a state's interest in not becoming a divorce mill, Justice Rehnquist stressed that "Perhaps even more importantly, Iowa's interests extend beyond its borders and include the recognition of its divorce decrees by other States under the Full Faith and Credit Clause. . . . The State's decision to exact a one-year residency requirement as a matter of policy is therefore buttressed by a quite permissible inference that this requirement not only effectuate state substantive policy but likewise provide a greater safeguard against successful collateral attack than would a requirement of bona fide residence alone. This is precisely the sort of determination that a State in the exercise of its domestic relations jurisdiction is entitled to make."[23]

Intriguing and complex questions with respect to the Full Faith and Credit Clause have been considered by the lower courts in recent years.

As to the contention that the law of the Navaho Nation was entitled to receive full faith and credit in the courts of New Mexico, a New Mexico court decided no.[24]

A convicted felon who had been pardoned by the governor of Montana was refused a license as a dealer and manufacturer of firearms, a license required under Federal law. He contended that the refusal to license him constituted a failure to grant full faith and credit. The U.S. Court of Appeals, Seventh Circuit, held otherwise saying "We conclude that in imposing on convicted fel-

[21] Vanderbilt v. Vanderbilt, 354 U.S. 416 (1957) *but see* Justice Harlan's dissent; Simons v. Miami Beach Nat. Bank, 381 U.S. 81 (1965); *see also* Justice Harlan's concurring opinion; Edwards v. Edwards, 481 P. 2d. 432 (1971); *see* Stucky v. Stucky, 185 N.W. 2d. 656, 661 (1971). The Iowa Supreme Court recently ruled that full faith and credit need only be accorded final judgments, saying that "an interlocutory decree does not come within the ambit of the [full faith and credit clause]." Morris v. Morris, 197 N.W. 2d. 357 (1972).

[22] Harold W. Chase, "The Lawyers Need Help with 'the Lawyer's Clause,' " in Gottfried Dietze, ed., *Essays on the American Constitution* (Englewood Cliffs, N.J., 1964), 110-116. *See* Gunther v. Gunther, 478 S.W. 2d. 821 (1972).

[23] Sosna v. Iowa, 419 U.S. 393 (1975).

[24] Jim v. CIT Financial Services Corporation, 527 P. 2d. 1222 (1974). *See also* Lohnes v. Cloud, 254 N.W. 2d. 430 (1977).

ons an otherwise appropriate disqualification from regulated activity, Congress has the power to accord a state pardon differing effects in differing contexts, depending on its objectives in creating the qualification. Neither the inherent nature of a pardon nor full faith and credit require that a state pardon automatically relieve federal disabilities."[25]

The Ohio Supreme Court expressed its judgment that "in determining a full faith and credit question arising out of a custody case, courts must also be cognizant of the fact that the best interests of the child are of primary concern. A change in circumstances subsequent to a custody order may affect those interests and have a direct bearing upon whether to give full faith and credit to a sister state's court order."[26]

An Illinois court held that a husband had not established a *bona fide* domicile in Nevada despite the fact that he had "terminated the lease for his rented room, obtained a Nevada driver's license, opened a bank account, looked for employment and took temporary employment as a taxicab driver." The court was more impressed by the fact "His search for a teaching position, for which he was qualified by experience and education, and which would require him to enter into a contract, was conducted casually through conversations with waitresses and school personnel."[27]

The Michigan Supreme Court held that "plaintiff's award in California does not act as a bar under the full faith and credit clause to proceedings in this state for workmen's compensation benefits arising out of the same injury."[28] However, the court also held that the prior award must be credited against the award received under Michigan's Workmen's Compensation Act.

An Oregon court held that, with respect to divorce decrees, decisions of tribal courts are not "entitled to the same 'full faith and credit' accorded decrees rendered in sister states, the quasi-sovereign nature of the tribe does suggest that judgments rendered by tribal courts are entitled to the same deference shown decisions of foreign nations as a matter of comity."[29]

The Supreme Court of Kentucky decided that the disbarment of a lawyer in Ohio did not mean that he was disbarred or suspended in Kentucky as long as the Ohio disbarment remained in force. The court explained that "the Full Faith and Credit Clause cannot possibly be twisted into giving to the Ohio action an effect it did not purport to have" and that the Ohio court had only ruled that he could not practice in Ohio.[30]

A Federal district court held that the State of South Dakota could require a brand inspection of all cattle transported into the State

[25] Thrall *v.* Wolfe, 503 F. 2d. 313 (1974).
[26] Williams *v.* Williams, 336 N.E. 2d. 426 (1975).
[27] Fink *v.* Fink, 346 N.E. 2d. 415 (1976).
[28] Stanley *v.* Hinchliffe and Kenner, 238 N.W. 2d. 13 (1976).
[29] Red Fox and Red Fox, 542 P. 2d. 918 (1975).
[30] Kentucky Bar Ass'n *v.* Singer, 533 S.W. 2d. 534 (1976).

even though it was protested that such cattle had been branded and inspected under the statutes of sister States.[31] The court reasoned that "Even if this Court were to find that prior foreign state inspections of cattle gave the state of South Dakota constructive notice of the plaintiff's ownership of the cattle, its full faith and credit argument must still fail. It is a well-recognized principle that if the state of South Dakota has a governmental interest which outweighs the governmental interests of the foreign state for whose statute recognition is sought, the refusal of the forum state to give effect to the rights under the foreign statute does not constitute a denial of full faith and credit to that statute."

As to the extrastate protection of rights which have *not matured into final judgments*, the unqualified rule prior to the Civil War was that of the dominance of local policy over the rules of comity.[32] This was stated by Justice Nelson in the Dred Scott case, as follows: "No State, . . . can enact laws to operate beyond its own dominions, . . . Nations, from convenience and comity, . . . , recognizes [*sic*] and administer the laws of other countries. But, of the nature, extent, and utility, of them, respecting property, or the state and condition of persons within her territories, each nation judges for itself. . . ." He added that it was the same as to a State of the Union in relation to another. It followed that even though Scott had become a free man in consequence of his having resided in the "free" State of Illinois, he had nevertheless upon his return to Missouri, which had the same power as Illinois to determine its local policy respecting rights acquired extraterritorially, reverted to servitude under the laws and decisions of that State.[33]

In a case decided in 1887, however, the Court remarked: "Without doubt the constitutional requirement, Art. IV, §1, that 'full faith and credit shall be given in each State to the public acts, records and judicial proceedings of every other State,' implies that the public acts of every State shall be given the same effect by the courts of another State that they have by law and usage at home."[34] And this proposition was later held to extend to State constitutional provisions.[35] Later this doctrine was stated in a much more mitigated form, the Court saying that where statute or policy of the forum State is set up as a defense to a suit brought under the statute of another State or territory, or where a foreign statute is set up as a defense to a suit or proceedings under a local statute, the conflict is to be resolved, not by giving automatic effect to the full faith and credit clause, thereby compelling courts of each State to sub-

Extraterritorial Operation of State Laws

---

[31] Black Hills Packing Co. *v.* S. D. Stockgrowers Ass'n, 397 F.Supp. 622 (1975).

[32] Bank of Augusta *v.* Earle, 13 Pet. 519, 589-596 (1839). *See* Kryger *v.* Wilson, 242 U.S. 171 (1916); Bond *v.* Hume, 243 U.S. 15 (1917).

[33] 19 How. 393, 460 (1857). *Cf.* Bonaparte *v.* Tax Court, 104 U.S. 592 (1882), where it was held that a law exempting from taxation certain bonds of the enacting State did not operate extraterritorially by virtue of the full faith and credit clause.

[34] Chicago & Alton R. Co. *v.* Wiggins Ferry, 119 U.S. 615, 622 (1887).

[35] Smithsonian Institution *v.* St. John, 214 U.S. 19 (1909).

ordinate its own statutes to those of others, but by appraising the
governmental interest of each jurisdiction and deciding accordingly.[36] Obviously this doctrine endows the Court with something
akin to an arbitral function in the decision of cases to which it is
applied, just as does the concept of divided divorce. Take for
example, the *Pearson* case, which attracted so much attention some
years ago.[37] A widow, whose husband had been killed in an
airplane crash in Massachusetts, was granted a $160,000 award by a
jury in a New York court. Although the crash occurred in Massachusetts, the husband had bought the ticket in New York and the
plane had taken off from La Guardia Airport in New York. Since a
Massachusetts statute limited recovery in such cases to $15,000 at
that time and New York's law did not, the airline appealed the decision on the grounds that Massachusetts law should have been controlling in this case. A three-judge panel of the United States Court
of Appeals, Second Circuit, reversed the decision and remanded
the case. When the case came again to the Court of Appeals, the
full court heard the case, explaining that "The issue being one of
great significance—the constitutional power of the states to develop
conflict of laws doctrine—it was ordered upon application by the
plaintiff appellee and the affirmative vote of a majority of the active
judges of this circuit, that the appeal be reheard *en banc*." This time
the court reversed itself. It cited with approval the reasoning of a
lower court in a parallel case: "An air traveler from New York may
in a flight of a few hours' duration pass through several common-
wealths. His plane may meet with disaster in a state he never intended to cross but into which the plane has flown because of bad
weather or other unexpected developments, or an airplane's catastrophic descent may begin in one state and end in another. The
place of injury becomes entirely fortuitous."[38] Eventually the case
was brought to the United States Supreme Court which denied *certiorari*.[39] The case is recalled here not for the outcome on the merits
but rather to make the point that at the late date of 1962, lawyers
and judges were still not quite sure which State's law would apply in
such a situation and the case was not resolved until it went all the
way to the Supreme Court.

It is today "the settled rule" that the defendant in a transitory action is entitled to all the benefits resulting from whatever material
restrictions the statute under which plaintiff's right of action originated sets thereto, except that courts of sister States cannot be thus
prevented from taking jurisdiction in such cases.[40] Nor is it alone to
defendants in transitory actions that the "full faith and credit"

[36] Alaska Packers Asso. *v.* Industrial Acci. Commission, 294 U.S. 532 (1935);
Bradford Electric Light Co. *v.* Clapper, 286 U.S. 145 (1932); Crider *v.* Zurich Ins.
Co., 380 U.S. 39 (1965); D.R.-T. *v.* O.M., 244 So. 2d. 752, 756 (1971); Application of
Schatz, 497 P. 2d. 153 (1972).
[37] Pearson *v.* Northeast Airlines, 309 F. 2d. 553 (1962).
[38] *Ibid.*, 561, note 10.   [39] 372 U.S. 912 (1963).
[40] Northern Pacific R.R. *v.* Babcock, 154 U.S. 190 (1894); Atchison, T. & S.F.
R. Co. *v.* Sowers, 213 U.S. 55, 67 (1909).

The Prob-
lem of Con-
flict of Law

clause is today a shield and a buckler. Some legal relationships are so complex, the Court holds, that the law under which they were formed ought always to govern them as long as they persist.[41] One such relationship is that of a stockholder and his corporation;[42] another is the relationship which is formed when one takes out a policy in a "fraternal benefit society."[43] Stock and mutual insurance companies and mutual building and loan associations, on the other hand, are beings of a different stripe;[44] as to them the *lex fori* controls. Finally, the relationship of employer and employee, so far as the obligations of the one and the rights of the other under workmen's compensation acts are concerned, is, in general, governed by the law of the State under which the relationship was created.[45]

The question arises whether the application to date of the full faith and credit clause can be said to have met the expectations of its Framers. A partial answer is that there are few clauses of the Constitution, the literal possibilities of which have been so little developed as the full faith and credit clause. Congress has the power under the clause to decree the effect that the statutes of one State shall have in other States. This being so, it does not seem extravagant to argue that Congress may under the clause describe a certain type of divorce and say that it shall be granted recognition throughout the Union, and that no other kind shall. Or, to speak in more general terms, Congress has under the clause power to enact standards whereby uniformity of State legislation may be secured as to almost any matter in connection with which interstate recognition of private rights would be useful and valuable.[46]

Unrealized Possibilities of the Clause

SECTION II

¶1. The citizens of each State shall be entitled to all privileges and immunities of citizens in the several States.

This is a compendious, although not especially lucid, redaction of Article IV of the Articles of Confederation. First and last, some four theories have been offered as to its real intention and meaning. The first is that the clause is a guaranty to the citizens of the different States of equal treatment by Congress—is, in other words, a species of equal protection clause binding on the National Government. The second is that the clause is a guaranty to the citizens of each State of all the privileges and immunities of citizenship that are enjoyed in any State by the citizens thereof—a view which, if it had been accepted at the outset, might well have endowed the Su-

Four Theories of the Clause

---

[41] Modern Woodmen of Am. *v.* Mixer, 267 U.S. 544 (1925).

[42] Converse *v.* Hamilton, 224 U.S. 243 (1912); Selif *v.* Hamilton, 234 U.S. 652 (1914).

[43] Royal Arcanum *v.* Green, 237 U.S. 531 (1915), aff'd in Modern Woodmen *v.* Mixer, cited above; Order of Travelers *v.* Wolfe, 331 U.S. 586, 588-589, 637 (1947).

[44] National Mutual Building and Loan Asso. *v.* Braham, 193 U.S. 635 (1904); Pink *v.* A.A.A. Highway Express, 314 U.S. 201, 206-208 (1941).

[45] Bradford Electric Co. *v.* Clapper, 286 U.S. 145, 158 (1932) is the leading case.

[46] Chase, "The Lawyers Need Help With 'the Lawyer's Clause.' "

preme Court with a reviewing power over restrictive State legislation as broad as that which it later came to exercise under the Fourteenth Amendment. The third theory of the clause is that it guarantees to the citizen of any State the rights which he enjoys as such even when sojourning in another State, that is to say, enables him to carry with him his rights of State citizenship throughout the Union, without embarrassment by State lines. Finally, the clause is interpreted as merely forbidding any State to discriminate against citizens of other States in favor of its own. Though the first theory received some recognition in one of the opinions in the Dred Scott case,[1] it is today obsolete. Theories 2 and 3 have been specifically rejected by the Court;[2] the fourth has become a settled doctrine of Constitutional Law.[3]

Yet even this theory is not all-inclusive. For there are certain privileges and immunities for which a State, as *parens patriae*, may require a previous residence, like the right to fish in its streams, to hunt game in its fields and forests, to divert its waters, even to engage in certain businesses of a quasi-public nature, like that of insurance.[4] Furthermore, universal practice has established another exception to which the Court has given approval in the following words: "A State may, by a rule uniform in its operation as to citizens of the several States, require residence within its limits for a given time before a citizen of another State who becomes a resident thereof shall exercise the right of suffrage or become eligible to office."[5]

Nor does the term "citizens" include corporations.[6] Thus a corporation chartered elsewhere may enter a State to engage in local business only on such terms as the State chooses to lay down, provided these do not deprive the corporation of its rights under the Constitution—of its right, for instance, to engage in interstate commerce, or to appeal to the national courts, or, once it has been admitted into a State, to receive equal treatment with corporations chartered by the latter.[7]

Also, while a State may not substantially discriminate between

[1] Scott v. Sandford, 19 How. 393, 527-529 (1857).
[2] McKane v. Durston, 153 U.S. 684, 687 (1894); Detwit v. Osborne, 135 U.S. 492, 498 (1890).
[3] The Slaughter-House cases, 16 Wall. 36, 77 (1873).
[4] McCready v. Va., 94 U.S. 391 (1877); Geer v. Conn., 161 U.S. 519 (1896); Hudson County Water Co. v. McCarter, 209 U.S. 349 (1908); La Tourette v. McMaster, 248 U.S. 465 (1919). In the case of Toomer v. Witsell, 334 U.S. 385, 403 (1948), the Court refused to follow the above rule as to free-swimming fish caught in the three-mile belt off South Carolina. *See also* Mullaney v. Anderson, 342 U.S. 415 (1952) in which the Toomer case was followed. In 1971, a Florida court held that a continued residency requirement for retention of a real estate broker's license was reasonable and constitutional. Hall v. King, 254 So. 2d. 223 (1971).
[5] Blake v. McClung, 172 U.S. 239, 256 (1898).
[6] Paul v. Va., 8 Wall. 168 (1868).
[7] International Paper Co. v. Mass., 246 U.S. 135 (1918); Terral v. Burke Constr. Co., 257 U.S. 529 (1922). *See also* Crutcher v. Ky., 141 U.S. 47 (1891).

residents and non-residents in the exercise of its taxing power,[8] yet what may at first glance appear to be a discrimination may turn out not to be when the entire system of taxation prevailing in the enacting State is considered. Nor are occasional or accidental inequalities to a non-resident taxpayer sufficient to defeat a scheme of taxation whose operation, in the judgment of the Court, is generally equitable.[9]

In an exceptionally important case decided in 1969, the Supreme Court struck down State and District of Columbia laws which denied welfare assistance to persons who had not been resident in the State for one year.[10]

It seemed to be an appropriate case to invoke the privileges and immunities clause of Article IV. However, in spelling out the "right to travel interstate," the Court said that it had no occasion "to ascribe the source of this right . . . to a particular constitutional provision." It pointed out that the privilege and immunities clause of the Fourteenth Amendment and the commerce clause had also been invoked in the past as a basis for the right to travel. In a pregnant footnote, the Court cautioned that this decision was limited to the issues in the case at hand, that "We imply no view of the validity of waiting-period *or* residence requirements determining eligibility to vote, eligibility for tuition-free education, to obtain a license to practice a profession, to hunt or fish, and so forth. Such requirements may promote compelling state interests on the one hand, or, on the other, may not be penalties upon the exercise of the constitutional right of interstate travel."[11] In short, for those who would see this particular provision as a possible vehicle for asserting "rights" not already found to be guaranteed elsewhere in the Constitution, this decision did not hold out much promise. But those who were disappointed that the Court did not use this case as an opportunity to read *more* meaning into Article IV, Section II, ¶1, could ponder the thought expressed by Justice Douglas in a concurring opinion some years ago, that the privileges and immunities safeguarded by the Fourteenth Amendment are *national* whereas those safeguarded under Article IV are *State*. The implication, of course, was that if there was to be an expansion of "rights," it would be more easily done under the Fourteenth Amendment.[12] But in recent years courts have read more meaning into the privileges and immunities clause.

[8] Ward *v*. Md., 12 Wall. 418, 424 (1871); Travis *v*. Yale and Towne Mfg. Co., 252 U.S. 60, 79-80 (1920).

[9] Travelers' Ins. Co. *v*. Conn., 185 U.S. 364, 371 (1902); Maxwell *v*. Bugbee, 250 U.S. 525 (1919).

[10] Shapiro *v*. Thompson, 394 U.S. 618, 630 (1969).

[11] *Ibid*., 638 note 21. *See also* Hall *v*. King, 254 So. 2d. 223 (1971).

[12] Edwards *v*. California, 314 U.S. 160, 180-181 (1941). Recently, in an interesting New York State case, it was held that a statute establishing a procedure for residents' obtaining permits for having weapons but which did not provide a procedure for travelers to do so was not a violation of this clause. People *v*. Percy, 325 N.Y.S. 2d. 183 (1971).

In one of the Abortion Decisions of 1973, the Supreme Court held unconstitutional a Georgia statute limiting abortions performed in the State to Georgia residents: "Just as the Privileges and Immunities Clause . . . protects persons who enter other States to ply their trade . . . so it must protect persons who enter Georgia seeking the medical services that are available there."[13] Also, the Supreme Court struck down the New Hampshire Commuters Income Tax on the grounds that it did violence to the privileges and immunities clause. In the Court's view: "The overwhelming fact, as the State concedes, is that the tax falls exclusively on the incomes of nonresidents; and it is not offset even approximately by other taxes imposed upon residents alone."[14]

The Supreme Court, however, in 1977 declined to decide whether a Massachusetts law prohibiting non-residents from dragging for fish in certain waters violated the privileges and immunities clause because the issue could be decided on the basis that Federal law preempted State law.[15]

Wrestling with the problem of residency requirements, lower courts have in recent years rendered some noteworthy decisions. The Court of Special Appeals of Maryland expounded on the meaning of Shapiro v. Thompson[16] (*see* p. 498). The court concluded that only if there is an "impingement of fundamental constitutional rights" was a State "required to make a showing that the statute is 'necessary to promote *a compelling* government interest.' " The court found that a Maryland requirement, that for a person to qualify under the Unsatisfied Claim and Judgment Fund Law for injuries sustained in an automobile accident, bore a rational relationship to a legitimate State purpose and was, therefore, constitutional.[17]

The Illinois Supreme Court held that a State law giving "preference for employment of Illinois residents on public works projects does not violate the privileges and immunities clause of the Federal Constitution."[18] Interestingly enough, in the same decision, the court held that "preference against employment of resident aliens on public works projects is violative of the equal protection clause of the Federal Constitution."

In contrast to those two decisions, a Massachusetts court decided that a State statute that prohibited non-residents from dragging for

---

[13] Doe v. Bolton, 410 U.S. 179, 200 (1973).
[14] Auston v. New Hampshire, 420 U.S. 656 (1975).
[15] Com. of Mass. v. Westcott, 431 U.S. 322 (1977).
[16] 394 U.S. 618 (1969).
[17] Holly v. Maryland Automobile Insurance Fund, 349 A. 2d. 670 (1975).
[18] People *ex rel.* Holland v. Bleigh Construction Co., 335 N.E. 2d. 469 (1975). The Alaska Supreme Court in 1977 held that it was not a violation of privileges and immunities to give residents a preference in jobs if durational residence requirements were stricken. The court reasoned "It gives state's benefits to those who bear its burdens, without placing any limitation on those who may voluntarily assume those benefits and burdens." Hicklin v. Orbeck, 565 P. 2d. 159 (1977).

fish in Vineyard Sound during the months of July, August and September "violated the Privileges and Immunities Clause."[19]

Also, a Federal district court held that a New York statute that set an 11-month minimum residence requirement for eligibility to vote in a primary election was unconstitutional.[20] Judge Weinfeld concluded that such a requirement was "not necessary to effect the compelling state interest of preventing raiding of primary elections or to promote administrative efficiency." Further, he said, "it impermissibly deprives a substantial number of qualified voters from participating in the primary election of their designated party; it penalizes those persons who have traveled from one place to another to establish a new residence; it discriminates against them in favor of long-time residents of the state by denying them the opportunity to participate in a primary election and to associate with those who share their political views."

¶2. A person charged in any State with treason, felony, or other crime, who shall flee from justice, and be found in another State, shall, on demand of the executive authority of the State from which he fled, be delivered up, to be removed to the State having jurisdiction of the crime.

The word "crime" here includes "every offense forbidden and made punishable by the laws of the State where the offense is committed."[21] The performance of the duty which is cast by this paragraph upon the States was imposed by an act of Congress passed February 12, 1793, upon the governors thereof, but the Supreme Court shortly before the Civil War ruled that, while the duty is a legal duty, it is not one the performance of which can be compelled by writ of mandamus,[22] and in consequence governors of States have often refused compliance with a demand for extradition when in their opinion substantial justice required such refusal. On the other hand, the Act of 1793 does not prevent a State from surrendering one who is not a fugitive within its terms, nor from trying a fugitive for a different offense than the one for which he was surrendered.[23]

Interstate Extradition on a Voluntary Basis

As was pointed out earlier, the deficiences of this clause have been today partly remedied by compacts among the States and by uniform State legislation, as well as by national legislation under the commerce clause. Especially important in the latter connection is the Act of May 18, 1934, which makes it an offense against the

[19] Commonwealth *v.* Westcott, 344 N.E. 2d. 411 (1976). But notice that the U.S. Supreme Court decided the case on other grounds. *Supra.*
[20] Echevarria *v.* Carey, 402 F.Supp. 183 (1975).
[21] Kentucky *v.* Dennison, 24 How. 66, 99 (1861).
[22] *Ibid.*; *cf.* Virginia *v.* W. Va., 246 U.S. 565 (1918).
[23] Lascelles *v.* Ga., 148 U.S. 537 (1893); Innes *v.* Tobin, 240 U.S. 127 (1916). *See* 18 U.S.C. 3182; Ray *v.* Warden, Baltimore City Jail, 281 A. 2d. 125 (1971); Hidaleo *v.* Purcell, 488 P. 2d. 858 (1971).

United States for a person to flee from one State to another in order to avoid prosecution or the giving of testimony in certain cases.[24] But this raises an interesting question about what Federal officials do when they apprehend such a fugitive. In that connection, several years ago a newspaper story regarding extradition caught the authors' eyes. The *New York Times* reported:

". . . With the arrival here of the California warrants, Miss [Angela] Davis and her attorney, John Abt, were summoned once again to the [Federal] Commissioner's office where Mr. Bishop revoked her bail and released her on her own recognizance. Her Federal handcuffs were removed.

"Then Detective Alfred C. Hatalkts of the city's safe and loft squad stepped forward and said, 'Miss Davis, you're under arrest,' and placed her hands in city handcuffs."[25] Curious to know the legal basis for what seemed an unusual performance, we queried the Justice Department. Here is their explanation:

"Miss Davis was arrested in New York City by the Federal Bureau of Investigation on the basis of a federal warrant for unlawful flight to avoid prosecution, Title 18, United States Code, Section 1073. It is our practice to turn over a fugitive to local authorities at the place where the fugitive is apprehended. The statute serves basically as a device to locate and apprehend fugitives from justice. It is not generally used as a substitute for State extradition proceedings nor is it generally used for the purpose of prosecution for the substantive offense."[26]

Several recent lower court decisions invite citation. The supreme court of Arkansas harking back to the Supreme Court's decision in *Kentucky v. Dennison*, 65 U.S. 66 (1860) and citing a batch of lower court cases held unequivocally that "Misdemeanors are definitely extraditable offenses."[27]

Other decisions held the following:

(1) Once a governor's extradition warrant is issued, the accused cannot be admitted to bail by the State of his arrest.[28]

(2) For a grant of extradition, a demonstration of probable cause for arrest in demanding State was not required in asylum state[29]

---

[24] 18 U.S.C. 1073.   [25] *New York Times*, Oct. 15, 1970.

[26] An obliging U.S. Attorney was kind enough to provide a more detailed explanation which read in part: "The conclusions reached in our discussion were admittedly simplistic; however, I am tempted to believe they are sound. It was pointed out that the defendant could not be taken into the custody of either state B or state A officers until dissolution of the federal custody status. Once the defendant posts bond and is released from federal custody, the defendant physically enters the jurisdiction of state B. The defendant's presence in state B is no longer a mere geographical incident; the defendant is subject to the sovereignty of state B. If state B takes the defendant into custody, the federal government can proceed personally against the defendant only by procuring his presence in federal court through a writ of habeas corpus directed against defendant's state B custodian."

[27] *Glover v. State*, 515 S.W. 2d. 641, 644 (1974).

[28] *Matter of Lucas*, 343 A. 2d. 845 (1975).

[29] *Commonwealth ex rel. Marshall v. Gedney*, 352 A. 2d. 528 (1975); *Taylor v. Garrison*, 329 So. 2d. 506 (1976); *Wellington v. State*, 238 N.W. 2d. 499 (1976).

nor could consideration be given to a fugitive's claim of denial of the right to a speedy trial.[30]

(3) "Technical deficiencies in the indictment are not sufficient to interfere with the governor's constitutional duty to extradite."[31]

(4) The Governor of North Carolina should have refused to send an individual back to Mississippi when his parole was revoked in a situation where under *Mississippi* law he had been entitled to hearing that he did not receive and revocation was based on his only being charged with a crime.[32]

But of all the decisions the one that promises to have the greatest impact on public policy was that rendered by the New York Court of Appeals in 1976. That court held that, where it was alleged that a father was in the State of New York at the time he failed to provide support for his children in California, he could not be extradited to California for the crime (failing to support his minor children) with which he was charged in California because, in the absence of evidence of his ability to pay, he could not be convicted under New York law.[33]

¶3. No person held to service or labor in one State, under the laws thereof, escaping into another, shall, in consequence of any law or regulation therein, be discharged from such service or labor, but shall be delivered up on claim of the party to whom such service or labor may be due.

"Person held to service or labor" meant slave or apprentice. The paragraph is now of historical interest only.

SECTION III

¶1. New States may be admitted by the Congress into this Union; but no new State shall be formed or erected within the jurisdiction of any other State; nor any State be formed by the junction of two or more States or parts of States, without the consent of the legislatures of the States concerned as well as of the Congress.

The theory which the Supreme Court has adopted in interpretation of the opening clause of this paragraph is that when new States are admitted into "this Union" they are admitted on a basis of equality with the previous members of the Union. By the Joint Resolution of December 29, 1845, Texas "was admitted into the Union on an equal footing with the original States in all respects whatever."[1] Again and again, in adjudicating the rights and duties

"A Union of Equal States"

---

[30] Application of Jeffries, 548 P. 2d. 594 (1976).
[31] Williams *v*. Wayne County Sheriff, 235 N.W. 2d. 552 (1975).
[32] Ewing *v*. Waldrop, 397 F.Supp. 509 (1975).
[33] People *v*. Hinton, 386 N.Y.S. 2d. 703 (1976).

---

[1] Justice Harlan, speaking for the Court in United States *v*. Tex., 143 U.S. 621,

of States admitted after 1789, the Supreme Court has referred to the condition of equality as if it were an inherent attribute of the Federal Union.[2] In 1911, it invalidated a restriction on the change of location of the State capital, which Congress had imposed as a condition for the admission of Oklahoma, on the ground that Congress may not embrace in an enabling act conditions relating wholly to matters under State control.[3] In an opinion, from which Justice Holmes and McKenna dissented, Justice Lurton argued: "The power is to admit 'new States into *this* Union.' 'This Union' was and is a union of States, equal in power, dignity and authority, each competent to exert that residuum of sovereignty not delegated to the United States by the Constitution itself."

State Proprietorship versus Federal Dominion

Sovereignty is one thing, however, property a different thing. Holding that a "mere agreement in reference to property" involved "no question of equality of status," the Supreme Court upheld, in Stearns *v.* Minnesota,[4] a promise exacted from Minnesota upon its admission to the Union which was interpreted to limit its right to tax lands held by the United States at the time of admission and subsequently granted to a railroad. The "equal footing" doctrine has had an important effect, however, on the property rights of new States to soil under navigable waters. In Pollard *v.* Hagan,[5] the Court held that the original States had reserved to themselves the ownership of the shores of navigable waters and the soils under them, and that under the principle of equality the title to the soils of navigable waters passes to a new State upon admission. This was in 1845. The Court refused, 102 years later, to extend the same rule to the three-mile marginal belt along the coast,[6] and shortly after applied the principle of the Pollard case in reverse, as it were, in United States *v.* Texas.[7] Since the original States had been found not to own the soil under the three-mile belt, Texas, which concededly did own this soil before its annexation to the United States, was held to have surrendered its dominion and sovereignty over it, upon entering the Union on terms of equality with the existing States. To this extent, the earlier rule that, unless otherwise declared by Congress, the title to every species of property owned by a territory passes to the State upon admission has been qualified.[8] However in 1953, Congress passed the Submerged Lands Act of

634 (1892); 9 *Stat.* 108. For an interesting recent affirmation of the doctrine, *see* Cherokee Nation or Tribe of Indians *v.* Oklahoma, 402 F. 2d. 739 (1968).

[2] Permoli *v.* New Orleans, 3 How. 589, 609 (1845); McCabe *v.* Atchison, T. & S.F. R. Co., 235 U.S. 151 (1914); Illinois Central R. Co. *v.* Illinois, 146 U.S. 387, 434 (1892); Knight *v.* United Land Assoc., 142 U.S. 161, 183 (1891); Weber *v.* State Harbor Comrs., 18 Wall. 57, 65 (1873).

[3] Coyle *v.* Smith, 221 U.S. 559, 567 (1911).   [4] 179 U.S. 223, 245 (1900).

[5] 3 How. 212, 223 (1845). *See also* Martin *v.* Waddell, 16 Pet. 367, 410 (1842).

[6] United States *v.* Calif., 332 U.S. 19, 38 (1947); United States *v.* La., 339 U.S. 699 (1950).

[7] 339 U.S. 699, 707, 716 (1950).

[8] Brown *v.* Grant, 116 U.S. 207, 212 (1886).

1953 declaring it to be in the public interest to turn over to the States "title to and ownership of the lands beneath navigable waters within the boundaries of the respective states."[9] By definition in the law this included lands covered by tidal waters up to three miles seaward *"and to the boundary line of each such State where in any case as it existed at the time such State became a member of the Union . . . extends seaward (or into the Gulf of Mexico) beyond three geographical miles."* When the act was challenged in part on the basis that it violated the "equal footing" doctrine, the motions were simply denied by the Court, which said: "The power of Congress to dispose of any kind of property belonging to the United States 'is vested in Congress without limitation.' "[10]

1975 saw the unfolding of another chapter in the saga of the struggle between the Federal government and the coastal States to lay claim to riches under the coastal waters. In upholding the claims of the National Government in four high-stake cases, the Supreme Court made apparent and explicit that it was bound by the previous decisions in United States *v.* California, 332 U.S. 19 (1947), United States *v.* Louisiana, 339 U.S. 699 (1950), and United States *v.* Texas, 339 U.S. 707 (1950). The Court held that "We are quite sure that it would be inappropriate to disturb our prior cases, major legislation, and many years of commercial activity by calling into question, at this date, the constitutional premise of prior decisions. We add only that the Atlantic States, by virtue of the *California*, *Louisiana*, and *Texas* cases, as well as by reason of the Submerged Lands Act, have been on notice of the substantial body of authoritative law, both constitutional and statutory, which is squarely at odds with their claims to the seabed beyond the three-mile marginal sea. Neither the States nor their putative lessees have been in the slightest misled."[11]

¶2. The Congress shall have power to dispose of and make all needful rules and regulations respecting the territory or other property belonging to the United States; and nothing in this Constitution shall be so construed as to prejudice any claims of the United States or of any particular State.

Congress's control of the public lands is derived from this paragraph. The relation of the National Government to such of its public lands as lie within the boundaries of States is not, however, that of simple proprietorship, it is more, for it includes many of the

What Property Congress May Dispose of

---

[9] 43 U.S.C. 1311.

[10] Alabama *v.* Texas, 347 U.S. 272, 273 (1954); *see also*, U.S. *v.* Louisiana, 363 U.S. 1 (1960); U.S. *v.* California, 381 U.S. 139, 184 (1965); Sierra Club *v.* Hickel, 433 F. 2d. 24, 28 (1970); *affirmed*, 405 U.S. 727 (1972).

[11] United States *v.* Maine, 420 U.S. 515, 519, 528 (1975). *See also* United States *v.* Florida, 420 U.S. 531 (1975); United States *v.* Louisiana, 420 U.S. 529 (1975) with Supplemental Decree, 422 U.S. 13 (1975); and United States *v.* Alaska, 422 U.S. 184 (1975).

elements of sovereignty. The States may not tax such lands;[12] and Congress may punish trespassers upon them, "though such legislation may involve the exercise of the police power."[13] Furthermore, in disposing of such lands, Congress may impose conditions on their future alienation or that of the water power thereon which the State where the lands are may not alter.[14]

When ranchers pumped ground water out of Devil's Hole, which had been reserved by the Federal Government as a National Monument, in order to preserve a unique desert fish, the Supreme Court was asked to answer the question of whether the reservation also "reserved federal water rights in unappropriated water." The Court held that reservation of water rights was empowered both by the commerce clause and this provision of the Constitution.[15] The Court said "This Court has long held that when the Federal Government withdraws its land from the public domain and reserves it for a federal purpose, the Government, by implication, reserves appurtenant water then unappropriated to the extent needed to accomplish the purpose of the reservation."

The Supreme Court upheld the Wild Free-Roaming Horses and Burros Act, designed to protect those animals on public lands from "capture, branding, harassment, or death," as a proper exercise of Congressional power under the Property Clause. The Court said "In our view, the 'complete power' that Congress has over public lands necessarily includes the power to regulate and protect the wildlife living there."[16]

A Federal district court held in 1974 that "for the Property Clause to be invoked as a basis for congressional enactment, some actual and substantial property interest of the federal government must be involved."[17] It is not enough that the Federal government partially funds a program.

Although "other property" undoubtedly includes warships, this fact did not, as we saw earlier, deter President Roosevelt from handing over to Great Britain, in September 1940, in return for leases from the latter of certain sites for naval bases in the west Atlantic, fifty newly conditioned destroyers without consulting Congress. But as Congress later appropriated money for the construction of the said bases, it may perhaps be thought to have ratified the arrangement.

The debts of various nations of Europe to the United States are also "property belonging to the United States," so that Congress's

---

[12] Van Brocklin v. Tenn., 117 U.S. 151 (1886). *Cf.* Wilson v. Cook, 327 U.S. 474 (1946).

[13] Camfield v. U.S., 167 U.S. 518 (1897).

[14] United States v. San Francisco, 310 U.S. 16 (1940). This case involved the famous "Hetch-Hetchy" grant by the Raker Act of December 19, 1913.

[15] Cappaert v. U.S., 426 U.S. 128 (1976).

[16] Kleppe v. State of New Mexico, 426 U.S. 529 (1976).

[17] United States v. Brown, 384 F.Supp. 1151 (1974).

ratification had to be obtained to agreements for their settlements after World War I. Likewise, electrical power developed at a dam of the United States is "property belonging to the United States."

But the above clause is also important for another reason—it is the source to which has sometimes been traced the power of the United States to govern territories, though, as we have seen, this and the power to acquire territory can be ascribed simply to the sovereignty inherent in the National Government as such;[18] as is also the power to cede territory to another government, as for example, the Philippine Islands to the Philippine Republic.

And while the United States may, through the treaty-making power acquire territory, its incorporation in the United States ordinarily waits upon action by Congress. Such incorporation may be effected either by admitting the territory into "this Union" as new States or, less completely, by extending the Constitution to it.[19] Until territory is thus incorporated into the United States, persons born therein are not citizens of the United States under the Fourteenth Amendment, though Congress may admit them to citizenship, as in fact it has done in several instances (*see* pp. 86-88); and the power of Congress in legislating for such unincorporated territory is limited only by "fundamental rights" of the individual, of which trial by jury was in an earlier day not one.[20] Incorporation, however, makes the inhabitants of territories citizens of the United States, and extends to them full protection of the Constitution. Consequently, it came as no surprise in 1977, when the Supreme Court said "We should be reluctant without a clear signal from Congress to conclude that it intended the Guam Legislature to foreclose appellate review of Art. III courts, including this Court, of decisions of territorial courts in cases that may turn in questions of federal law."[21] (For a discussion of substantive issue in the case, *see* p. 211.) A lower court decision several years earlier also buttressed Congress's extensive powers with respect to territories. In finding that former residents of the Philippines who are now either residents or citizens of the United States were not denied equal protection or due process by being given only limited veterans' benefits for World War II service, a Federal district court held that, except for fundamental personal rights, "Constitutional guarantees extend to such unincorporated territories *only* as the Congress, exercising its Art. IV, Sec. 3 powers, makes them applicable and

"Incorporated" and "Unincorporated" Territories

---

[18] American Insurance Co. *v.* Canter, 1 Pet. 511, 542 (1928).

The entire subject of the power to acquire and govern territories is comprehensively treated in Willoughby, *Constitutional Law*, I, chs. 23-32.

[19] Downes *v.* Bidwell, 182 U.S. 244 (1901). *Cf.* Duncan *v.* Louisiana, 391 U.S. 145 (1968). *See also*, p. 237 note 5.

[20] Dorr *v.* U.S., 195 U.S. 138 (1904). In view of recent Supreme Court decisions on trial by jury, it is unlikely that today a jury trial would not be regarded as a fundamental right in like circumstances. *See* pp. 343-348. Also *see* 1968 amendment to Guam's Bill of Rights, which expressly provides for jury trial. 48 U.S.C. 1421b.

[21] Territory of Guam *v.* Olsen, 431 U.S. 195, 201 (1977).

'large powers' and 'the widest latitude of discretion' are entrusted to the Congress when dealing with terrritories which are not incorporated in the United States, e.g., the Philippines."[22]

Since Alaska and Hawaii became States, there are no "incorporated" territories in this nomenclature; Guam is an example of an "unincorporated" territory.[23] Puerto Rico has a unique status of "commonwealth"—an experiment decidedly worth study.[24] Conquered territory may be governed temporarily by the President by virtue of his power as Commander-in-Chief of the Army and Navy, but Congress may at any time supplant such government with one of its own creation.[25]

SECTION IV

¶The United States shall guarantee to every State in this Union a republican form of government, and shall protect each of them against invasion, and on application of the legislature, or of the executive (when the legislature cannot be convened), against domestic violence.

"The United States" here means the governing agency created by the Constitution, but especially the President and Congress; for the Court has repeatedly declared that what is a "republican form of government" is "a political question," and one finally for the President and the houses to determine within their respective spheres.[1] Thus Congress may approve of the government of a new State by admitting it into the Union, or the houses of Congress may indicate their approval by seating the Senators and Representatives of the State, or the President may do the same by furnishing a State with military assistance in cases where he is authorized so to act.

National Guarantees to the States: a "Political Question"

Inasmuch as the adoption of the initiative, referendum, and recall by many States some decades back appears not to have imperiled their standing with Congress, it must be concluded that a considerable admixture of direct government does not make a government "unrepublican."[2]

Despite the Supreme Court's stance, Section IV still tempts those who are unhappy with what they regard as an "unrepublican" governmental institution, law, or practice to take their cause to the courts, invariably without success.[3] However, interestingly enough, a United States court of appeals observed in the course of a recent decision: "abrogation of judicial immunity by Congress would de-

[22] Filippino American Vet. & Dep. Ass'n *v.* United States, 391 F.Supp. 1314 (1974).
[23] 48 U.S.C. 1421a.   [24] 48 U.S.C. 731.
[25] Santiago *v.* Nogueras, 214 U.S. 260 (1909).

[1] *See*, for example, Luther *v.* Borden, 7 How. 1 (1849).
[2] Pacific States Tel. and Tel. Co. *v.* Ore., 223 U.S. 118 (1912).
[3] *See*, for example, Kohler *v.* Tugwell, 292 F.Supp. 978 (1968), *affirmed*, 393 U.S. 531 (1969) *and* O'Keefe *v.* Atascadero County Sanitation District, 98 Cal. Rptr. 878 (1971).

stroy the independence of the judiciary in the various States, and consequently deprive them of a republican form of government."[4]

The President is authorized by statute to employ the forces of the United States to discharge the duties of the United States under the second part of this paragraph, in which connection he may in proper cases proclaim martial law.[5] But this does not mean that a President must always await an invitation before employing troops, for this provision does not comprise the whole of the Chief Executive's power to send troops into a State.[6] (*See* pages 191-193 above.)

With respect to regulations adopted by the administration of the Environmental Protection Agency asserting great powers over a State government and its subdivisions, including the authority to enforce an implementing plan under the Clean Air Act when a State has failed to do so, a U.S. court of appeals said: "This severance of spending from taxing at the state level in our view does suggest that the petitioners are not irresponsible when they strongly suggest that the Republican Form of Government of the states would be seriously impaired."[7]

[4] Bauers *v.* Heisel, 361 F. 2d. 581, 588-589 (1966), *cert. denied*, 386 U.S. 1021 (1967).
[5] 10 U.S.C. 331.
[6] *In re* Debs, 158 U.S. 564 (1895). *Cf.* 10 U.S.C. 331 and 10 U.S.C. 332.
[7] Brown *v.* Environmental Protection Agency, 521 F. 2d. 827 (1975).

ARTICLE V

The
Amending
Power ¶The Congress, whenever two-thirds of both houses shall deem it necessary, shall propose amendments to this Constitution, or, on the application of the legislatures of two-thirds of the several States, shall call a convention for proposing amendments, which in either case shall be valid to all intents and purposes as part of this Constitution, when ratified by the legislatures of three-fourths of the several States, or by conventions in three-fourths thereof, as the one or the other mode of ratification may be proposed by the Congress, provided that no amendment which may be made prior to the year one thousand eight hundred and eight shall in any manner affect the first and fourth clauses in the ninth section of the first article; and that no State, without its consent, shall be deprived of its equal suffrage in the Senate.

From the opinions filed in the case of Coleman v. Miller,[1] in 1939, in which certain questions were raised concerning the status of the proposed Child Labor Amendment (pending since 1924), it would seem that the Court today regards all questions relating to the in-
"Political terpretation of this article as "political questions," and hence as ad-
Questions" dressed exclusively to Congress. This is either because all such questions have been in the past effectually determined by Congressional action; or because the Court lacks adequate means of informing itself about them; or because the "judicial power" established by the Constitution does not extend to this part of the Constitution. Nevertheless, certain past decisions of the Court dealing with Article V may still be usefully cited for the light shed by their statement of the actual results, as well as the logical implications, of Congressional action in the past.

"The Congress, whenever . . . both houses shall deem it necessary": The necessity of amendments to the Constitution is a question to be determined by the two houses alone, but not necessarily without suggestion or guidance from the President.[2]

"Two-thirds of both houses" means two-thirds of a quorum in both houses.[3] (See Article I, Section V, ¶1.)

"Legislatures" means the legislative assemblies of the States and does not include their governors, far less their voters. Moreover, when acting upon amendments proposed by Congress, the State legislatures—and doubtless the same is true of conventions within the States—do not act as representatives of the States or the populations thereof, but in performance of a "federal function" imposed upon them by this article of the Constitution.[4]

[1] 307 U.S. 433 (1939).
[2] The National Prohibition Cases, 253 U.S. 350 (1920); Richardson, *Messages and Papers*, I, 53; *ibid.*, II, 447, 518, 557, 605; etc.
[3] *Ibid.*; Missouri Pac. R. Co. v. Kan., 248 U.S. 276 (1919).
[4] Hawke v. Smith, 253 U.S. 221 (1920).

Several recent lower court decisions provide further illumination in the process of ratification. The Supreme Court of Tennessee concluded that the State constitutional provision that "No Convention or General Assembly of this State shall act upon any amendment of the Constitution of the United States proposed by Congress to the several States; unless such Convention or General Assembly shall have been elected after such amendment is submitted" was invalid as "a limitation upon the General Assembly of Tennessee in the exercise of its federally derived power."[5]

Citing Hawke v. Smith (*supra*), the Montana Supreme Court decided that the ratification by the State legislature of the proposed Equal Rights Amendment could not be subjected to a popular referendum.[6] As the Court saw it, it would be a useless act "since the voters cannot constitutionally compel the legislature to rescind its ratification."

Efforts to ratify the Equal Rights Amendment gave rise to another issue. Could the Illinois legislature require a three-fifths majority of each of its houses for ratification? A three-judge district court decided that it could, that the Framers of the Constitution had intended for each State legislature or State convention to decide for itself what would be the necessary vote for ratification.[7]

If a State legislature ratifies a proposed amendment may it later reconsider its vote, the amendment not having yet received the favorable vote of three-fourths of the legislatures? In Coleman v. Miller this question was answered "No," on the basis of Congressional rulings in connection with the adoption of the Fourteenth Amendment.

Apparently the question is not considered closed for, as debate over the ratification of the Equal Rights Amendment continues, there are knowledgeable scholars who judge that State legislatures can rescind their approval despite the decision in *Coleman*.[8]

May a legislature, after rejecting a proposed amendment, reconsider and ratify it? On the same basis, this question was answered "Yes" in Coleman v. Miller. Within what period may a proposal of amendment be effectively ratified? Within any period which Congress chooses to allow either in advance, or by finding that a proposed amendment has been ratified, is again the verdict of Coleman v. Miller.

Of the two methods here laid down for proposing amendments to the Constitution only the first has ever been successfully resorted to, and, prior to the proposal to repeal the Eighteenth Amend-

---

[5] Walker v. Dunn, 498 S.W. 2d. 102 (1972).

[6] State *ex rel.* Hatch v. Murray, 526 P. 2d. 1369 (1974). The North Dakota Supreme Court held likewise. State *ex rel.* Askew v. Meier, 231 N.W. 2d. 821 (1975).

[7] Dyer v. Blair, 390 F.Supp. 1291 (1975).

[8] William L. Dunker, "Constitutional Amendments—The Justiciability of Ratification and Retraction," 41 *Tennessee Law Review*, 93 (1973).

ment, all proposals had been referred to the State legislatures.[9] In that instance, Congress prescribed that ratification should be by popularly elected conventions, chosen for the purpose, but left their summoning, as well as other details, to the several State legislatures. What ordinarily resulted was a popular referendum within each State, the conventions being made up almost entirely of delegates previously pledged to vote for or against the proposed amendment.[10] The term "convention," therefore, it must be presumed, does not today, if it ever did, denote a *deliberative* body; it is sufficient if it is representative of popular sentiment.

The word "successfully" was used advisedly above. For in recent years there have been several attempts to get proposed amendments started through the State legislature route, one of very serious proportions under the aegis of the Council of State Governments. One of the three amendments they sought would have changed the mode of the amending process.[11] Also, Senator Dirksen led an effort to take this route for an amendment which would in effect modify the Court's rulings in reapportionment.[12] But more pertinent to the present discussion is the fact that it was discovered that the State legislature route might actually be much easier to use effectively than previously thought, and it held some strategic advantages for proposers of amendments. Protagonists could quietly make their pitch in the various State legislatures without attracting the attention and concern that a serious effort in Congress would.[13] It is an unfortunate fact of American politics that the work of State legislatures is not as carefully monitored by the press and public as the proceedings of Congress.

The recent efforts to have State legislatures apply to Congress for a convention highlighted another unresolved problem. Would such a convention be limited to consideration of specific amendments or would it be able to consider anything and possibly become, in the popular expression a "run-away" convention?[14]

Chief Justice Marshall characterized the Constitution-amending machinery as "unwieldy and cumbrous." Undoubtedly it is, and the fact has had an important influence upon our institutions. Espe-

---

[9] It was contended in United States *v.* Sprague, 282 U.S. 716 (1931), that, as the Eighteenth Amendment affected the liberties of the people and the rights of the State, it ought to have been submitted to conventions in the States, but the Court rejected the contention.

[10] *See* Everett S. Brown's valuable article on "The Ratification of the Twenty-First Amendment," 29 *American Political Science Review*, 1005 (1935).

[11] Charles L. Black, Jr., "The Proposed Amendment of Article V: A Threatened Disaster," 72 *Yale Law Journal*, 957 (1963). For a measure of how seriously the effort was viewed, *see* report of the speech of Chief Justice Warren, *New York Times*, May 24, 1963.

[12] 1969 *Cong. Quart. Almanac* 1200; 1967 *Cong. Quart. Almanac* 461. The Dirksen effort only needed the approval of one more State legislature.

[13] *New York Times*, April 14, 1963.

[14] Morris D. Forkosch, "The Alternative Amending Clause in Article V: Reflections and Suggestions," 51 *Minnesota Law Review*, 1053, 1074-1077 (1967).

cially has it favored the growth of judicial review, since it has forced us to rely on the Court to keep the Constitution adapted to changing conditions. What is more, this machinery is, *prima facie* at least, highly undemocratic. A proposed amendment can be added to the Constitution by 38 States containing considerably less than half of the population of the country, or can be defeated by 13 States containing less than one-twentieth of the population of the country.

Of the two exceptions to the amending power, the first is today obsolete. This does not signify, however, that the only change that the power which amends the Constitution may not make in the Constitution is to deprive a State without its consent of its "equal suffrage in the Senate." The amending, like all other powers organized in the Constitution, is in form a delegated, and hence a limited power, although this does not imply necessarily that the Supreme Court is vested with authority to determine its limits. The one power known to the Constitution which clearly is not limited by it is that which ordains it—in other words, the original, inalienable power of the people of the United States to determine their own political institutions.

ARTICLE VI

¶ 1. All debts contracted and engagements entered into, before the adoption of this Constitution, shall be as valid against the United States under this Constitution as under the Confederation.

This paragraph, which is now of historical interest only, was intended to put into effect the rule of International Law that when a new government takes the place of an old one it succeeds to the latter's financial obligations.

The Supremacy Clause ¶ 2. This Constitution, and the laws of the United States which shall be made in pursuance thereof, and all treaties made, or which shall be made, under the authority of the United States, shall be the supreme law of the land; and the judges in every State shall be found thereby, anything in the Constitution or laws of any State to the contrary notwithstanding.

This paragraph has been called "the linchpin of the Constitution," and very fittingly, since it combines the National Government and the States into one governmental organization, one Federal State.

It also makes plain the fact that, while the National Government is for the most part one of enumerated powers, as to its powers it is supreme over any conflicting State powers whatsoever.[1] When, accordingly, a collision occurs between national and State law the only question to be answered is, ordinarily, whether the former was within a fair definition of Congress's powers. As Chief Justice Marshall so eloquently put it: "This government is acknowledged by all to be one of enumerated powers. . . . If any one proposition could command the universal assent of mankind, we might expect it would be this—that the government of the Union, though limited in its powers, is supreme within its sphere of action."[2] Notwithstanding which the Court has at various periods proceeded on the view that the Tenth Amendment segregates to the control of the States certain "subjects," production for instance, with the result that the power of the States over such "subjects" constitutes a limitation on the granted powers of Congress. Obviously such a view cannot be logically reconciled with the supremacy clause. (*See* Tenth Amendment, p. 442.)

In applying the supremacy clause to subjects which have been regulated by Congress, the primary task of the Court is to ascertain whether a challenged State law is compatible with the policy expressed in the Federal statute. When Congress condemns an act as unlawful, the extent and nature of the legal consequences of its doing so are Federal questions, the answers to which are to be de-

[1] McCulloch v. Maryland, 4 Wheat. 316 (1819) *and* Gibbons v. Ogden, 9 Wheat. 1 (1824).
[2] McCulloch v. Maryland, 4 Wheat. 316, 405 (1819).

rived from the statute and the policy thereby adopted. To the Federal statute and policy, conflicting State law and policy must yield.[3]

So when the United States performs its functions directly through its own officers and employees, State police regulations clearly are inapplicable. In reversing the conviction of the governor of a national soldiers' home for serving oleomargarine in disregard of State law, the Court said that the Federal officer was not "subject to the jurisdiction of the State in regard to those very matters of administration which are thus approved by Federal authority."[4] An employee of the Post Office Department is not required to submit to examination by State authorities concerning his competence and to pay a license fee before performing his official duty in driving a motor truck for transporting the mail.[5] To Arizona's complaint, in a suit to enjoin the construction of Hoover Dam, that her quasi-sovereignty would be invaded by the building of the dam without first securing approval of the State engineer as required by its laws, Justice Brandeis replied that, "if Congress has power to authorize the construction of the dam and reservoir, Wilbur [Secretary of the Interior] is under no obligation to submit the plans and specifications to the State Engineer for approval."[6]

As to the question of what happens when State and Federal laws appear to conflict, Chief Justice Warren in 1956 provided the criteria used by the Court to decide such cases: "Where . . . Congress has not stated specifically whether a federal statute has occupied a field in which States are otherwise free to legislate, different criteria have furnished touchstones for decision. . . .

"*First*, [t]he scheme of federal regulation is so pervasive as to make reasonable the inference that Congress left no room for the States to supplement it. . . .

"*Second*, the federal statutes 'touch a field in which the federal interest is so dominant that the federal system [must] be assumed to preclude enforcement of state laws on the same subject.' . . .

"*Third*, enforcement of state sedition acts presents a serious danger of conflict with the administration of the federal program."[7] (*See also* discussion under Commerce Clause.)

The Doctrine of Preemption and Supersession

[3] Sola Electric Co. *v.* Jefferson Electric Co., 317 U.S. 173, 176 (1942). *See also* Francis *v.* Southern Pacific Co., 333 U.S. 445 (1948); Testa *v.* Katt, 330 U.S. 386, 391 (1947); Hill *v.* Fla., 325 U.S. 538 (1945); Amalgamated Assoc. *v.* Wis. Emp. Rels. Bd., 340 U.S. 383 (1951); Adams *v.* Md., 347 U.S. 179 (1954).

[4] Ohio *v.* Thomas, 173 U.S. 276, 283 (1899).

[5] Johnson *v.* Md., 254 U.S. 51 (1920).

[6] Arizona *v.* Calif., 283 U.S. 423, 451 (1931); California Commission *v.* U.S., 355 U.S. 534 (1958); U.S. *v.* Georgia Public Service Com'n, 371 U.S. 285 (1963).

[7] Pennsylvania *v.* Nelson, 350 U.S. 497, 501-505 (1956). This decision was highly controversial and became the basis for much Congressional criticism of the Court. *See* Murphy, *Congress and the Court.* Nonetheless, Warren's criteria have been upheld in subsequent cases and followed by the lower courts. *See* for example of the latter, Conant *v.* Hill, 326 F.Supp. 25, 27 (1971) *and* Mobil Oil Corp. *v.* Atty. General, 280 N.E. 2d. 406 (1972). *Also*, "When there is an unavoidable conflict between the Federal and a State Constitution, the supremacy clause, of course, controls." Reynolds *v.* Sims, 377 U.S. 533 (1964).

In recent years, the Supreme Court has been called upon to deal with the supremacy clause on more than a few occasions.

Three important cases were decided in 1973. With respect to a city ordinance prohibiting jet aircraft from taking off at night, the Supreme Court affirmed a court of appeals decision that the ordinance was invalid because Federal regulation of air commerce was pervasive. Justice Douglas writing for the majority acknowledged that "there is to be sure no express provision of pre-emption in the 1972 [Federal Noise Control] Act. That, however, is not decisive. . . . It is the pervasive nature of the scheme of federal regulation of aircraft noise that leads us to conclude that there is pre-emption."[8]

In one of the other cases, the Court demonstrated that it would not be cavalier with State claims in matters arising under the supremacy clause. The majority, again speaking through Justice Douglas, held that it was not to be presumed that Congress in extending the Fair Labor Standards Act to certain State employees intended to take away the constitutional immunity of States from suits in Federal courts involving their own citizens. (The act provides for suits by employees against their employer for damages as well as unpaid minimum wages and overtime.) Justice Douglas concluded: "We are reluctant to believe that Congress in pursuit of a harmonious federalism desired to treat the States so harshly. The policy of the Act so far as the States are concerned is wholly served by allowing the delicate federal-state relationship to be managed through the Secretary of Labor."[9]

The third case involved New York's controversial Work Rules Law, which was designed to get welfare recipients off welfare rolls and into jobs. The Supreme Court reversed a lower court ruling that the Federal work incentive program pre-empts the New York law.[10]

Again in the following Term, the Supreme Court demonstrated a deference to State interests in a challenge invoking the supremacy clause. "This case [according to the Court] presents the question whether certain rules of the New York Stock Exchange, promulgated as self-regulating measures pursuant . . . [to Federal law] and a broker's employee's pledge to abide by those rules, pre-empt avenues of wage relief otherwise available to the employee under state law." The Court's answer to the question was "No," that "In other contexts, pre-emption has been measured by whether the state statute frustrates any part of the purpose of the federal legislation."[11]

In a noteworthy case, the California Supreme Court held that Federal military retirement pay was subject to California commu-

[8] City of Burbank *v.* Lockheed Air Terminal, Inc., 411 S.Ct. 624 (1973).
[9] Employees of Dept. of Public Health & Welf. *v.* Missouri, 411 U.S. 279 (1973).
[10] New York State Dept. of Social Services *v.* Dublino, 413 U.S. 405 (1973).
[11] Merrill Lynch, Pierce, Fenner & Smith, Inc. *v.* Ware, 414 U.S. 117, 119, 140 (1973).

nity property law in face of the contention that it was Congress's intent to let retired servicemen pick their beneficiary for retirement pay.[12]

The Supreme Court in 1975 in justifying judicial abstention with respect to courts-martial wandered into a discussion of the Court's position with respect to equitable intervention into pending State criminal proceedings. The Court reminded us that "under Art. VI of the Constitution, state courts share with federal courts an equivalent responsibility for the enforcement of federal rights, a responsibility one must expect they will fulfill." The significance of the reference is not its novelty but the fact that the Court saw fit to stress it.[13]

Also, in the same Term, the Supreme Court held that "a legislative ratification of an agreement between the executive branch and an Indian tribe is a 'Law of the United States made in Pursuance' of the Constitution and, therefore, like 'all Treaties made,' is made binding upon affected States by the Supremacy Clause."[14]

In 1976, the Court held in one case that California's statute forbidding employers from hiring an alien "who is not entitled to lawful residence in the United States if such employment would have an adverse effect on lawful resident workers" was not pre-empted by the Immigration and Nationality Act.[15] Carefully distinguishing this decision from earlier Supreme Court decisions, the Court said: "to the extent those [earlier] cases were based on the predominance of federal interest in the fields of immigration and foreign affairs, there would not appear to be a similar federal interest in a situation in which the state law is fashioned to remedy local problems, and operates only on local employers, and only with respect to individuals whom the Federal Government has already declared cannot work in this country. Finally, the Pennsylvania statutes in *Hines*[16] and *Nelson*[17] imposed burdens on aliens lawfully within the country that created conflicts with various federal laws."

Arguing that even Indians on a particular reservation "are now so completely integrated with non-Indians . . . that there is no longer any reason to accord them different treatment than other citizens," the State of Montana sought to apply cigarette sales and personal property taxes to reservation Indians. The Supreme Court held that "The personal property tax on personal property located within the reservation; the vendor license fee sought to be applied to a reservation Indian conducting a cigarette business for the Tribe on reservation land; and the cigarette sales tax as applied

[12] *In re* Marriage of Fithian, 517 P. 2d. 449 (1974). *See also* Francis v. Colorado Board of Social Services, 518 P. 2d. 1174 (1974).

[13] Schlesinger v. Councilman, 420 U.S. 738, 756 (1975).

[14] Antoine v. Washington, 420 U.S. 194 (1975). *See also* State v. Coffee, 556 P. 2d. 1185 (1976).

[15] DeCanas v. Bica, 96 S.Ct. 933 (1976).

[16] Hines v. Davidowitz, 312 U.S. 52 (1941).

[17] Pennsylvania v. Nelson, 350 U.S. 497 (1956).

to on-reservation sales by Indians to Indians, conflict with the congressional statutes which pervade the basis for decision with respect to such impositions."[18] The Court, however, held that an Indian tribal seller could be required to collect a tax validly imposed on non-Indians.

Justice White, speaking for the Court, succinctly described the issue in a third case as "whether a State whose federally approved implementation plan forbids an air contaminant source to operate without a state permit may require existing federally owned or operated installations to secure such a permit."[19] Parties to the dispute had agreed that the Federal Clean Air Act obligates Federal installations to conform to State air pollution standards; what was at issue was the State permit requirement. The Court resolved that issue by saying: "we are not convinced that Congress intended to subject federal agencies to state permits." As to why the Court viewed the permit as different from other means of regulation, the Court explained: "Neither the Supremacy Clause nor the Plenary Powers Clause bars all state regulation which may touch the activities of the Federal Government. . . . 'Here, however, the State places a prohibition on the Federal Government.' The permit requirement is not intended simply to regulate the amount of pollutants which the federal installations may discharge. Without a permit, an air contaminant source is forbidden to operate even if it is in compliance with every other state measure respecting air pollution control and abatement. It is clear from the record that prohibiting operation of the air contaminant sources for which the State seeks to require permits is tantamount to prohibiting operation of the federal installations on which they are located."

The Supreme Court has held for years that Congressional intent to "occupy the field" required the invalidation of any State legislation that burdens or conflicts in any manner with any Federal laws or treaties. This has not diminished the frequency with which lower courts have had to decide cases involving conflicting law, for the Supreme Court has also held that "conflicting law absent repealing or exclusivity provisions, should be pre-empted . . . 'only to the extent necessary to protect the achievement of the aims of' the federal law since the proper approach is to reconcile 'the operation of both statutory schemes with one another rather than holding [the State scheme] completely ousted.' "[20] Since the Supreme Court's holdings do not serve as an absolute bar to State law in areas touched by Federal law, it is not surprising that the lower courts each year must, in large numbers of cases involving the supremacy clause, serve as arbiters to determine which State law does prevent "The achievement of the aims of the federal law."

Continuing to address supremacy clause issues in 1977, the Su-

---

[18] Moe *v.* Confederated Salish & Kootenai Tribes, Etc., 425 U.S. 463 (1976).
[19] Hancock *v.* Train, 426 U.S. 167 (1976).
[20] DeCanas *v.* Bica, 424 U.S. 351 fn. 5 (1976).

preme Court held (1) that a California statute regulating the labeling by weight of packaged goods was pre-empted by Federal regulations;[21] (2) that a California use and property tax on possessory interests in improvements in tax-exempt land was not invalid under the supremacy clause even though it was claimed that the tax interfered with a Federal function and discriminated against Federal employees;[22] (3) that persons charged with crimes on Federal military bases or enclaves could not "demand that their federal prosecutors be governed by state law to the extent that state law was more 'lenient' than federal law";[23] (4) that a Viriginia statute forbidding federally licensed vessels owned by non-residents from fishing in Chesapeake Bay and prohibiting ships owned by non-citizens to catch fish anywhere in Virginia was invalid with the supremacy clause.[24]

With the great concern over the quality of the environment, attempts by States to effect standards higher than the Federal government requires have created problems with the supremacy clause. The United States Court of Appeals, Eighth Circuit, recently made plain that the States are limited in what they can do. That court held that the Federal Water Pollution Control Act was pervasive and that the Corps of Engineers could not be required to obtain discharge permits from the State of Minnesota for dredging activities, nor were they required to meet State water pollution standards in those operations.[25]

Not only, however, is the supremacy clause important as a sort of third dimension of national power, thrusting aside all conflicting State powers; it is also of great significance as having been a source of private immunity, particularly from State taxation. Thus, in the famous case of McCulloch v. Maryland,[26] the Court under Chief Justice Marshall held that a State might not tax an "instrumentality" of the National Government on its operations; and it was later held that a State might not reach by a general tax national bonds, national official salaries, incomes from national bonds, or lands owned by the National Government.[27] Then in a case decided in 1928 the Court ruled that a State tax on sales of gasoline might not be validly applied in the case of sales of the commodity to the Na-

Tax Exemption Again; Its Rise and Decline

[21] Jones v. Rath Packing Co., 430 U.S. 519 (1977).

[22] United States v. County of Fresno, 429 U.S. 452 (1977).

[23] United States v. Antelope, 430 U.S. 641, 650 fn. 13 (1977).

[24] Douglas v. Seacoast Products, Inc., 97 S.Ct. 1740 (1977). *See also*, C.D.R. Enterprises v. Bd. of Ed. of City of N.Y., 412 F.Supp. 1164 (1976).

[25] State of Minnesota v. Hoffman, 543 F. 2d. 1198 (1976).

[26] 4 Wheat. 316 (1819). Marshall's initial statement of the principle of national supremacy, however, occurs in United States v. Fisher, 2 Cr. 358 (1805), where is asserted the priority of United States claims to debtor's assets over those of a State. Spokane County v. U.S., 279 U.S. 80, 87 (1929), follows this rule.

[27] Weston v. Charleston, 9 Wheat. 738 (1824); Dobbins v. Coms. of Erie City, 16 Pet. 435 (1842); Pollock v. Farmers' L. and T. Co., 157 U.S. 429 (1895); Van Brocklin v. Tenn., 117 U.S. 151 (1886). For the most recent exemplification of this principle, *see* First Federal Savings, etc. v. Bowers, 349 U.S. 143 (1955).

tional Government for use by its Coast Guard fleet and a Veterans' Hospital,[28] thus prompting the query whether a butcher who sold meat to a Congressman would be subject validly to State taxation on such sales or on the profits thereof! But starting in the late 1930's, the Court has greatly curtailed the operation of the principle of tax exemption not only as a limitation on national power, but as a limitation on State power also, and especially in the field of income taxation. Thus in 1937 it held that a State may impose an occupation tax upon an independent contractor, measured by his gross receipts under contracts with the United States.[29] Previously it had sustained a gross receipts tax levied in lieu of a property tax upon the operator of an automobile stage line, who was engaged in carrying the mails as an independent contractor,[30] and an excise tax on gasoline sold to a contractor with the Federal Government and used to operate machinery in the construction of levees in the Mississippi River.[31] Subsequently it has approved State taxes on the net income of a government contractor,[32] and income[33] and social security[34] taxes on the operators of bathhouses maintained in a national park under a lease from the United States; sales and use taxes on sales of beverages by a concessionaire in a national park;[35] taxes on purchases of materials used by a contractor in the performance of a cost-plus contract with the United States;[36] and a severance tax imposed on a contractor who severed and purchased timber from lands owned by the United States.[37]

Tax Exemption by Congressional Grant   But Congress is still able, by virtue of the necessary and proper and supremacy clauses in conjunction, to exempt instrumentalities of the National Government, or private gains therefrom, from State or local taxation; but any person, natural or corporate, claiming such an exemption must ordinarily be able to point to an explicit stipulation by Congress to that effect. Moreover, Congress is always free to waive such exemptions when it can do so without breach of contract, and any such waiver will generally be liberally construed by the Court in favor of the taxing authority.[38]

[28] Panhandle Oil Co. *v.* Knox, 277 U.S. 218 (1928); *cf.* Union Pac. R.R. Co. *v.* Peniston, 18 Wall. 5 (1873).

[29] James *v.* Dravo Contracting Co., 302 U.S. 134 (1937).

[30] Alward *v.* Johnson, 282 U.S. 509 (1931).

[31] Trinityfarm Const. Co. *v.* Grosjean, 291 U.S. 466 (1934).

[32] Atkinson *v.* Tax Commission, 303 U.S. 20 (1938).

[33] Superior Bath House Co. *v.* McCarroll, 312 U.S. 176 (1941).

[34] Buckstaff Bath House *v.* McKinley, 308 U.S. 358 (1939).

[35] Collins *v.* Yosemite Park & Curry Co., 304 U.S. 518 (1938). *See also* Humble Oil and Refining Co. *v.* Calvert, 478 S.W. 2d. 926 (1972) and Buck Act, 4 U.S.C. 105-110.

[36] Alabama *v.* King & Boozer, 314 U.S. 1 (1941), overruling Panhandle Oil Co. *v.* Knox, 277 U.S. 218 (1928) and Graves *v.* Texas Co., 298 U.S. 393 (1936). *See also* Curry *v.* U.S., 314 U.S. 14 (1941).

[37] Wilson *v.* Cook, 327 U.S. 474 (1946).

[38] Besides the leading case of Graves *v.* N.Y., 306 U.S. 466 (1939), *see also* Pittman *v.* HOLC, 308 U.S. 21 (1939); Tradesmen's National Bank *v.* Okla. Tax Com'n, 309 U.S. 560 (1940); Philadelphia Co. *v.* Dipple, 312 U.S. 168 (1941); and Cleveland *v.* U.S., 323 U.S. 329 (1945). *Cf.* Mayo *v.* U.S., 319 U.S. 441 (1943).

A case illustrative of the Court's stance in this general field was the case in which the Court was confronted with an attempt on the part of Tennessee to apply its tax on the use within the State of goods purchased elsewhere to a private contractor for the Atomic Energy Commission and to vendors of such contractors.[39] This, the Court held, could not be done under Section 9b of the Atomic Energy Commission Act, which provides in part that: "The Commission, and the property, activities, and income of the Commission, are hereby expressly exempted from taxation in any manner or form by any State, county, municipality, or any subdivision thereof."[40] The power of exemption, said the Court, "stems from the power to preserve and protect functions validly authorized— the power to make all laws necessary and proper for carrying into execution the powers vested in Congress." The term, "activities," as used in the act, was held to be nothing less "than all of the functions of the Commission."[41]

In 1928 the Court went so far as to hold that a State could not tax as income royalties for the use of a patent issued by the United States.[42] This proposition was soon overruled in Fox Film Corp. v. Doyal,[43] where a privilege tax based on gross income and applicable to royalties from copyrights was upheld. Likewise a State may lay a franchise tax on corporations, measured by the net income from all sources, including income from copyright royalties.[44]

It would seem elementary that a State court cannot interfere with the functioning of a Federal tribunal. Nevertheless, this proposition has not always gone unchallenged. Shortly before the Civil War, the Supreme Court of Wisconsin, holding the Federal Fugitive Slave Law invalid, ordered a United States marshal to release a prisoner who had been convicted of aiding and abetting the escape of a fugitive slave. In an act of further defiance, the State court instructed its clerk to disregard and refuse obedience to the writ of error issued by the United States Supreme Court. Strongly denouncing this interference with Federal authority, Chief Justice Taney held that when a State court is advised, on the return of a writ of *habeas corpus*, that the prisoner is in custody on authority of the United States, it can proceed no further.[45] To protect the performance of its functions against interference by State tribunals, Congress may constitutionally authorize the removal to a Federal court of a criminal prosecution commenced in a State court against a revenue officer of the United States on account of any act done

Immunity of National Official Action from State Control

---

[39] Carson v. Roane Anderson Co., 342 U.S. 232 (1952).

[40] 60 *Stat.* 765; that law has since been amended to permit payments to the States in lieu of taxes. *See* 42 U.S.C. 2208.

[41] 342 U.S. 232, 234, 236. *See also* Kern-Limerick Inc. v. Scurlock, 347 U.S. 110 (1954).

[42] Long v. Rockwood, 277 U.S. 142 (1928).   [43] 286 U.S. 123 (1932).

[44] Educational Films Corp. v. Ward, 282 U.S. 379 (1931).

[45] Ableman v. Booth, 21 How. 506, 523 (1859). *See also* United States v. Tarble, 13 Wall. 397 (1872). The Court's opinions in both of these cases invoked the doctrine of Dual Federalism as well as that of National Supremacy, but rather inconsistently.

under color of his office.[46] In the celebrated case of *in re* Neagle,[47] a United States marshal who, while assigned to protect Justice Field, killed a man who had been threatening the life of the latter was charged with murder by the State of California. Invoking the supremacy clause, the Supreme Court held that a person could not be guilty of a crime under State law for doing what it was his duty to do as an officer of the United States.

¶3. The Senators and Representatives before mentioned, and the members of the several State legislatures, and all executive and judicial officers, both of the United States and of the several States, shall be bound by oath or affirmation, to support this Constitution; but no religious test shall ever be required as a qualification to any office or public trust under the United States.

Congress may require no other oath of fidelity to the Constitution, but it may superadd to this oath such other oath of office as its wisdom may require.[48] It may not, however, prescribe a test oath as a qualification for holding office, such an act being in effect an *ex post facto* law;[49] and the same rule holds in the case of the States.[50]

In a noteworthy case decided in 1972, the Supreme Court declared constitutional a Massachusetts law requiring that "every person entering the employ of the commonwealth" to affirm an oath which in addition to the words of the usual oath (*see* p. 155) added "and that I will oppose the overthrow of the government of the United States of America or of this Commonwealth by force, violence, or by any illegal or unconstitutional method."[51]

State Aid in National Law Enforcement

Commenting in *The Federalist* No. 27 on the requirement that State officers, as well as members of the State legislatures, shall be bound by oath affirmation to support this Constitution, Hamilton wrote: "Thus the legislatures, courts and magistrates, of the respective members, will be incorporated into the operations of the national government *as far as its just and constitutional authority extends*, and will be rendered auxiliary to the enforcement of its laws." The younger Pinckney had expressed the same idea on the floor of the Philadelphia Convention: "They [the States] are the instruments upon which the Union must frequently depend for the support and execution of their powers. . . ."[52] Indeed, the Constitution itself

[46] Tennessee *v*. Davis, 100 U.S. 257 (1880); *see also* Maryland *v*. Soper, 270 U.S. 36 (1926).

[47] 135 U.S. 1 (1890).

[48] McCulloch *v*. Maryland, 4 Wheat. 316, 416 (1819); Cole *v*. Richardson, 405 U.S. 676 (1972).

[49] *Ex parte* Garland, 4 Wall. 333, 337 (1867).

[50] Cummings *v*. Mo., 4 Wall. 227, 323 (1867).

[51] Cole *v*. Richardson, 405 U.S. 676 (1972).

[52] Max Farrand, ed., *The Records of the Federal Convention of 1787*, I (New Haven, 1937), 404.

lays many duties, both positive and negative, upon the different organs of State government,[53] and Congress may frequently add others, provided it does not require the State authorities to act outside their normal jurisdiction. Early Congressional legislation contains many illustrations of such action by Congress.

The Judiciary Act of 1789[54] left the State courts in sole possession of a large part of the jurisdiction over controversies between citizens of different States and in concurrent possession of the rest. By other sections of the same act State courts were authorized to entertain proceedings by the United States itself to enforce penalties and forfeitures under the revenue laws, while any justice of the peace or other magistrate of any of the States was authorized to cause any offender against the United States to be arrested and imprisoned or bailed under the usual mode of process. Even as late as 1839, Congress authorized all pecuniary penalites and forfeitures under the laws of the United States to be sued for before any court of competent jurisdiction in the State where the cause of action arose or where the offender might be found.[55] Pursuant also of the same idea of treating State governmental organs as available to the National Government for administrative purposes, the act of 1793 entrusted the rendition of fugitive slaves in part to national officials and in part to State officials and the rendition of fugitives from justice from one State to another exclusively to the State executives.[56] Certain later acts empowered State courts to entertain criminal prosecutions for forging paper of the Bank of the United States and for counterfeiting coin of the United States,[57] while still others conferred on State judges authority to admit aliens to national citizenship and provided penalties in case such judges should utter false certificates of naturalization—provisions which are still on the statute books.[58]

With the rise of the doctrine of States Rights and of the equal sovereignty of the States with the National Government, the availability of the former as instruments of the latter in the execution of its power came to be questioned.[59] In Prigg v. Pennsylvania,[60] decided in 1842, the constitutionality of the provision of the act of 1793 making it the duty of State magistrates to act in the return of fugitive slaves was challenged; and in Kentucky v. Dennison,[61] decided on the eve of the Civil War, similar objection was leveled against the provision of the same act which made it "the duty" of

The States Rights Reaction

---

[53] *See* Art. I, Sect. III, Par. 1; Sect. IV, Par. 1; Sect. X; Art. II, Sect. I, Par. 2; Art. III, Sect. II, Par. 2; Art. IV, Sects. I and II; Art. V; Amendments XIII, XIV, XV, XVII, and XIX.

[54] 1 *Stat.* 73 (1789).   [55] 5 *Stat.* 322 (1839).

[56] 1 *Stat.* 303 (1793).   [57] 2 *Stat.* 404 (1806).

[58] *See* Kent, *Commentaries*, II, 64-65; 34 *Stat.* 596, 602 (1906); 8 U.S.C. 1421 and 18 U.S.C. 1426; 18 U.S.C. 471 and 485; *also* Homlgren v. U.S., 217 U.S. 509 (1910).

[59] For the development of opinion especially on the part of State courts, adverse to the validity of the above-mentioned legislation, *see* Kent, *Commentaries*, I, 396-404.

[60] 16 Pet. 539 (1842).   [61] 24 How. 66 (1861).

the Chief Executive of a State to render up a fugitive from justice upon the demand of the Chief Executive of the State from which the fugitive had fled. The Court sustained both provisions, but upon the theory that the cooperation of the State authorities was purely voluntary. In the *Prigg* case the Court, speaking by Justice Story, said: ". . . state magistrates may, if they choose, exercise the authority [conferred by the act], unless prohibited by state legislation."[62] In the *Dennison* case, "the duty" of State executives in the rendition of fugitives from justice was construed to be declaratory of a "moral duty." Said Chief Justice Taney for the Court: "We think it clear, that the Federal Government, under the Constitution, has no power to impose on a State officer, as such, any duty whatever, and compel him to perform it; for if it possessed this power, it might overload the officer with duties which would fill up all his time, and disable him from performing his obligations to the State, and might impose on him duties of a character imcompatible with the rank and dignity to which he was elevated by the State."[63]

Return to Earlier Views   Eighteen years later, in *ex parte* Siebold,[64] the Court sustained the right of Congress, under Article I, Section IV, ¶1 of the Constitution, to impose duties upon State election officials in connection with a Congressional election and to prescribe additional penalties for the violation by such officials of their duties under State law. The outlook of Justice Bradley's opinion for the Court is decidedly nationalistic rather than dualistic, as is shown by the answer made to the contention of counsel "that the nature of sovereignty is such as to preclude the joint cooperation of two sovereigns, even in a matter in which they are mutually concerned." To this Justice Bradley replied: "As a general rule, it is no doubt expedient and wise that the operations of the State and national governments should as far as practicable, be conducted separately, in order to avoid undue jealousies and jars and conflicts of jurisdiction and power. But there is no reason for laying this down as a rule of universal application. It should never be made to override the plain and manifest dictates of the Constitution itself. We cannot yield to such a transcendental view of State sovereignty. The Constitution and laws of the United States are the supreme law of the land, and to these every citizen of every State owes obedience, whether in his individual or official capacity."[65] Three years earlier the Court, speaking also by Justice Bradley, sustained a provision of the Bankruptcy Act of 1867 giving assignees a right to sue in State courts to recover the assets of a bankrupt. Said the Court: "The statutes of the United States are as much the law of the land in any State as are those of the State; and although exclusive jurisdiction for their enforcement may be given to the federal courts, yet where it is not given, either expressly or by necessary implication, the State courts

---

[62] 16 Pet. 539, 622.   [63] 24 How. 66, 107-108.
[64] 100 U.S. 371 (1880).   [65] *Ibid.*, 392.

having competent jurisdiction in other respects, may be resorted to."[66]

The Selective Service Act of 1917[67] was enforced to a great extent through State "employees who functioned under State supervision";[68] and State officials were frequently employed by the National Government in the enforcement of National Prohibition.[69] Nowadays, there is constant cooperation, both in peacetime and in wartime, in many fields between National and State officers and official bodies.[70] This relationship obviously calls for the active fidelity of both categories of officialdom to the Constitution.

A "religious test" is one demanding the avowal or repudiation of A "Reli-certain religious beliefs. No religious test may be required as a qual- gious Test" ification for office under the United States. In 1961, the Supreme Court held that to enforce a State constitutional requirement which required a belief in God as a qualification for office was unconstitutional.[71] However, an indulgence in immoral practices claiming the sanction of religious belief, such as polygamy, may be made a disqualification.[72] Contrariwise, alleged religious beliefs or moral scruples do not furnish ground for evasion of the ordinary duties of citizenship, like the payment of taxes or military service, although, of course, Congress may of its own volition grant exemptions on such grounds. The related subject of "religious freedom" is discussed immediately below.

"Oath or affirmation": This option was provided for the special benefit of Quakers.

[66] Claflin *v.* Houseman, 93 U.S. 130, 136, 137 (1876); followed in Second Employers' Liability Cases, 223 U.S. 1, 55-59 (1912).

[67] 40 *Stat.* 76 (1917).

[68] Jane Perry Clark, *The Rise of a New Federalism* (New York, 1938), 91.

[69] See James Hart in 13 *Virginia Law Review*, 86 (1926) discussing President Coolidge's order of May 8, 1926, for Prohibition enforcement.

[70] W. Brooke Graves, *American Intergovernmental Relations* (New York, 1964); Morton Grodzins, *The American System* (Chicago, 1966).

[71] Torasco *v.* Watkins, 367 U.S. 488 (1961).

[72] Reynolds *v.* U.S., 98 U.S. 145 (1878) *and* Mormon Church *v.* U.S., 136 U.S. 1 (1890), both support this proposition, assuming they are still law of the land.

ARTICLE VII

¶The ratification of the conventions of nine States shall be sufficient for the establishment of this Constitution between the States so ratifying the same.

The Constitution an Act of Revolution

The Articles of Confederation provided for their own amendment only by the unanimous consent of the thirteen States, given through their legislatures. The provision made for the going into effect of the Constitution upon its ratification by *nine* States, given through *conventions* called for the purpose, clearly indicates the establishment of the Constitution to have been, in the legal sense, an act of revolution.

¶Done in convention by the unanimous consent of the States present, the seventeenth day of September, in the year of our Lord one thousand seven hundred and eighty-seven, and of the independence of the United States of America the twelfth.
In witness whereof we have hereunto subscribed our names.

George Washington, President, and Deputy from Virginia.
New Hampshire—John Langdon, Nicholas Gilman.
Massachusetts—Nathaniel Gorham, Rufus King.
Connecticut—William Samuel Johnson, Roger Sherman.
New York—Alexander Hamilton.
New Jersey—William Livingston, David Brearly, William Paterson, Jonathan Dayton.
Pennsylvania—Benjamin Franklin, Thomas Mifflin, Robert Morris, George Clymer, Thomas Fitzsimons, Jared Ingersoll, James Wilson, Gouverneur Morris.
Delaware—George Read, Gunning Bedford, Jr., John Dickinson, Richard Bassett, Jacob Broom.
Maryland—James McHenry, Daniel of St. Thomas Jenifer, Daniel Carroll.
Virginia—John Blair, James Madison, Jr.
North Carolina—William Blount, Richard Dobbs Spaight, Hugh Williamson.
South Carolina—John Rutledge, Charles Cotesworth Pinckney, Charles Pinckney, Pierce Butler.
Georgia—William Few, Abraham Baldwin.

ATTEST: WILLIAM JACKSON, *Secretary*.

AMENDMENTS[1]

The first ten amendments make up the so-called Bill of Rights of the National Constitution. They were designed to quiet the fears of mild opponents of the Constitution in its original form and were proposed to the State legislatures by the first Congress which assembled under the Constitution. They bind only the National Government and in no wise limit the powers of the States of their own independent force;[2] but the rights which they protect against the National Government are, nevertheless, today not infrequently claimable against State authority under the Court's interpretation of the "due process" clause of the Fourteenth Amendment.[3]

Also, the efficacy of the Bill of Rights as a restriction on the National Government is confined to the territorial limits of the United States, including within that term the "incorporated" territories (*see* p. 265), except when "fundamental rights" are involved, it being for the Supreme Court to say what rights are "fundamental" in this sense.[4] The right to trial by jury, an inherited feature of Anglo-American jurisprudence, was at one time not considered to be such a right;[5] immunity from "cruel and unusual punishment" is.[6]

[1] The first ten amendments were proposed in 1789 and adopted in 810 days. The Eleventh Amendment was proposed in 1794 and adopted in 339 days. The Twelfth Amendment was proposed in 1803 and adopted in 229 days. The Thirteenth Amendment was proposed in 1865 and adopted in 309 days. The Fourteenth Amendment was proposed in 1866 and adopted in 768 days. The Fifteenth Amendment was proposed in 1869 and adopted in 356 days. The Sixteenth Amendment was proposed in 1909 and adopted in 1278 days. The Seventeenth Amendment was proposed in 1912 and adopted in 359 days. The Eighteenth Amendment was proposed in 1917 and adopted in 396 days. The Nineteenth Amendment was proposed in 1919 and adopted in 444 days. The Twentieth Amendment was proposed in 1932 and adopted in 327 days. The Twenty-First Amendment was proposed in 1933 and adopted in 286 days. For these statistics, which were compiled by Sen. Everett M. Dirksen of Illinois, *see* the *New York Times*, February 21, 1937. Several of the amendments were, however, the outcome of many years of agitation.

[2] Barron *v.* Balt., 7 Pet. 243 (1833). According to Mr. Warren, "In at least twenty cases between 1877 and 1907, the Court was called upon to rule on this point and to reaffirm Marshall's decision of 1833." "The New 'Liberty' under the Fourteenth Amendment," 39 *Harvard Law Review*, 431, 436 (1926).

[3] *See* Gitlow *v.* N.Y., 268 U.S. 652 (1925); Near *v.* Minn., 283 U.S. 697 (1931); Powell *v.* Ala., 287 U.S. 45 (1932); Palko *v.* Conn., 302 U.S. 319 (1937).

[4] Downes *v.* Bidwell, 182 U.S. 244 (1901).

[5] Dorr *v.* U.S., 195 U.S. 138 (1904). However, in 1968 the Supreme Court held that trial by jury in a criminal case is a fundamental right which is guaranteed as against the States. Duncan *v.* Louisiana, 391 U.S. 145 (1968). *See* p. 409 below. Presumably, that decision by inference guarantees the right to a jury trial in a criminal case in unincorporated territories now and in the future. *See* 1968 amendment to Guam's Bill of Rights, 48 U.S.C. 1421b.

[6] Weems *v.* U.S., 217 U.S. 349 (1910).

AMENDMENT I

Congress shall make no law respecting an establishment of religion, or prohibiting the free exercise thereof; or abridging the freedom of speech or of the press; or the right of the people peaceably to assemble, and to petition the government for a redress of grievances.

Extension of the "Freedoms" of Amendment I to the States

In the case of Gitlow *v.* New York, decided in 1925,[1] the Court, while affirming a conviction for violation of a State statute prohibiting the advocacy of criminal anarchy, declared: "For present purposes we may and do assume that freedom of speech and of the press—which are protected by the First Amendment from abridgment by Congress—are among the fundamental personal rights and 'liberties' protected by the due process clause of the Fourteenth Amendment from impairment by the States."[2] This dictum became, two years later, accepted doctrine when the Court invalidated a State law on the ground that it abridged freedom of speech contrary to the "due process clause" of Amendment XIV.[3] Subsequent decisions have brought the other rights safeguarded by the First Amendment—freedom of religion,[4] freedom of the press,[5] and the right of peaceable assembly[6]—within the protection of the Fourteenth. (*See* pp. 475-481.) In consequence of this development, cases dealing with the safeguarding of these rights against infringement by the States are included in the ensuing discussion of the First Amendment.

Two Views of "Establishment of Religion"

"An establishment of religion": Two theories regarding the meaning and intention of this clause have confronted each other in decisions of the Court. According to one, what the clause bans is the *preferential* treatment of any particular religion or sect by government in the United States. This theory has the support of Story, except for the fact that he regarded Congress as still free to prefer the Christian religion over other religions.[7] It is also supported by Cooley in his *Principles of Constitutional Law*, where it is said that the clause forbids "the setting up or recognition of a state church, or at least the conferring upon one church of special favors and advantages which are denied to others."[8] This conception of the clause is, moreover, foreshadowed in the Northwest Ordinance of 1787, the third article of which reads: "Religion, morality, and knowledge being necessary to good government and the happiness of mankind, schools and the means of education shall forever be encour-

[1] 268 U.S. 652 (1925).   [2] *Ibid.*, 666.
[3] Fiske *v.* Kan., 274 U.S. 380 (1927).
[4] Cantwell *v.* Conn., 310 U.S. 296 (1940).
[5] Near *v.* Minn., 283 U.S. 697 (1931).
[6] DeJonge *v.* Ore., 299 U.S. 353 (1937).
[7] Joseph Story, *Commentaries on the Constitution*, II (Cambridge, Mass., 1833), §§ 1870-1879.
[8] Cooley, *Principles*, 224-225.

aged."[9] In short, religion as such is not excluded from the legitimate concerns of government, but quite the contrary.

The other theory was first voiced by Jefferson in a letter which he wrote a group of Baptists in Danbury, Connecticut, in 1802. Here it is asserted that it was the purpose of the First Amendment to build "a wall of separation between Church and State."[10] Seventy-seven years later Chief Justice Waite, in speaking for the unanimous Court in the first Mormon Church case, in which the right of Congress to forbid polygamy in the territories was sustained, characterized this statement by Jefferson as "almost an authoritative declaration of the scope and effect of the amendment."[11]

For some thirty years, the Court has wrestled with the problem of where to draw the line between constitutionally permissible and impermissible aid to religious schools. As is clear from the discussion that follows, the Court has rejected any simple test in arriving at its conclusions. Rather, the cases and formulae build on one another as the Court looks to the particulars of the assistance program apparent in a given case. *Financial Aid to Religious Schools*

In the first of a series of cases, a sharply divided Court, speaking by Justice Black, sustained, in 1947, the right of local authorities in New Jersey to provide free transportation for children attending parochial schools,[12] but accompanied its holding with these warning words, which appear to have had, at that time, the approval of most of the Justices: "The 'establishment of religion' clause of the First Amendment means at least this: Neither a state nor the Federal Government can set up a church. Neither can pass laws which aid one religion, aid all religions, or prefer one religion over another. Neither can force nor influence a person to go to or to remain away from church against his will or force him to profess a belief or disbelief in any religion. No person can be punished for entertaining or professing religious beliefs or disbeliefs, for church attendance or non-attendance. No tax in any amount, large or small, can be levied to support any religious activities or institutions, whatever they may be called, or whatever form they may adopt to teach or practice religion. Neither a state nor the Federal Government can, openly or secretly, participate in the affairs of any religious organizations or groups and *vice versa*."[13] And a year later a nearly unanimous Court overturned on the above grounds a "released time" arrangement under which the Champaign, Illinois, *"Released Time." Its Ups and Downs*

[9] H. S. Commager, ed., *Documents of American History* (New York, 1947), 128, 131.
[10] Padover, ed., *The Complete Jefferson*, 518-519.
[11] Reynolds *v.* U.S., 98 U.S. 145, 164 (1879). In his second Inaugural Address, Jefferson expressed a very different, and presumably more carefully considered opinion upon the purpose of Amendment I: "In matters of religion, I have considered that its free exercise is placed by the Constitution independent of the powers of the general government." This was said three years after the Danbury letter. Richardson, *Messages and Papers*, I, 379.
[12] Everson *v.* Board of Education, 330 U.S. 1 (1947).   [13] *Ibid.*, 15, 16.

Board of Education agreed that religious instruction should be given in the local schools to pupils whose parents signed "request cards." By this plan the classes were to be conducted during regular school hours in the school building by outside teachers furnished by a religious council representing the various faiths, subject to the approval or supervision of the superintendent of schools. Attendance records were kept and reported to the school authorities in the same way as for other classes; and pupils not attending the religious-instruction classes were required to continue their regular secular studies.[14] Said Justice Black, speaking for the Court: "Here not only are the State's tax-supported public school buildings used for the dissemination of religious doctrines. The State also affords sectarian groups an invaluable aid in that it helps to provide pupils for their religious classes through use of the State's compulsory public school machinery. This is not separation of Church and State."[15]

Justice Frankfurter presented a supplementary, affirming opinion for himself and three other Justices, the purport of which was that public-supported education must be kept secular.[16] In a dissenting opinion, Justice Reed pointed out that "the Congress of the United States has a chaplain for each House who daily invokes divine blessings and guidance for the proceedings. The armed forces have commissioned chaplains from early days. They conduct the public services in accordance with the liturgical requirements of their respective faiths, ashore and afloat, employing for the purpose property belonging to the United States and dedicated to the services of religion. Under the Servicemen's Readjustment Act of 1944, eligible veterans may receive training at government expense for the ministry in denominational schools. The schools of the District of Columbia have opening exercises which 'include a reading from the Bible without note or comment, and the Lord's Prayer.' "[17]

Justice Reed's views were not without effect. In 1952 the Court, six Justices to three, sustained a New York City "released time" program under which religious instruction must take place off the school grounds and numerous other features of the Champaign model were avoided.[18] Speaking for the majority, Justice Douglas said: "We are a religious people whose institutions presuppose a Supreme Being. We guarantee the freedom to worship as one chooses. We make room for as wide a variety of beliefs and creeds as the spiritual needs of man deem necessary. We sponsor an attitude on the part of government that shows no partiality to any one group and that lets each flourish according to the zeal of its adherents and the appeal of its dogma. When the state encourages religious instruction or cooperates with religious authorities by ad-

---

[14] McCollum v. Board of Education, 333 U.S. 203 (1948).
[15] Ibid., 212.   [16] Ibid., 212ff.
[17] Ibid., 253-254.   [18] Zorach v. Clauson, 343 U.S. 306 (1952).

justing the schedule of public events to sectarian needs, it follows the best of our traditions. For it then respects the religious nature of our people and accommodates the public service to their spiritual needs. To hold that it may not would be to find in the Constitution a requirement that the government show a callous indifference to religious groups. That would be preferring those who believe in no religion over those who do believe. We find no constitutional requirement which makes it necessary for government to be hostile to religion and to throw its weight against efforts to widen the effective scope of religious influence."[19]

Farther back, in 1899, the Court held that an agreement between the District of Columbia and the directors of a hospital chartered by Congress for erection of a building and treatment of poor patients at the expense of the District was valid despite the fact that the members of the corporation belonged to a monastic order or sisterhood of a particular church.[20] It has also sustained a contract made at the request of Indians to whom money was due as a matter of right, under a treaty, for the payment of such money by the Commissioner of Indian Affairs for the support of Indian Catholic schools.[21] In 1930 the use of public funds to furnish nonsectarian textbooks to pupils in parochial schools of Louisiana was sustained,[22] and in 1947, as we have seen, the use of public funds for the transportation of pupils attending such schools in New Jersey.[23] In the former case the Court cited the State's interest in secular education even when conducted in religious schools, in the latter its concern for the safety of school children on the highways; and the National School Lunch Act,[24] which aids all school children attending tax-exempt schools, can be similarly justified. (The most notable financial concession to religion, however, is not to be explained in this way—the universal practice of exempting religious property from taxation. This unquestionably traces back to the idea expressed in the Northwest Ordinance that government has an interest in religion as such, as will be seen below.)

In one recent case, the Court held that a New York statute authorizing the loan of textbooks to students attending parochial schools did not offend the establishment clause.[25] Nor did the Court find that the Higher Education Facilities Act of 1963, which provided grants for the construction of academic facilities to religious institutions, generally unconstitutional, although it did strike down one provision of the act which limited to twenty years the recipients' obligation not to use Federally financed facilities for sectarian instruction or religious worship. With respect to that provi-

Concessions to the Religious Interest

[19] *Ibid.*, 313-314. Justices Black, Frankfurter, and Jackson dissented.
[20] Bradfield *v.* Roberts, 175 U.S. 291 (1899).
[21] Quick Bear *v.* Leupp, 210 U.S. 50 (1908).
[22] Cochran *v.* Louisiana State Board of Education, 281 U.S. 370 (1938).
[23] Everson *v.* Board of Education, 330 U.S. 1 (1947).
[24] 60 *Stat.* 230 (1946).
[25] Board of Education *v.* Allen, 392 U.S. 236 (1968).

sion, the Court said "Limiting the prohibition for religious use of the structure to 20 years obviously opens the facility to use for any purpose at the end of that period. It cannot be assumed that a substantial structure has no value after that period and hence the unrestricted use of a valuable property is in effect a contribution of some value to a religious body."[26] At the same time, in a pair of cases decided together the Court struck down a Rhode Island statute providing salary supplements to teachers of secular subjects in non-public schools operated for the benefit of parochial schools and a Pennsylvania statute providing reimbursement to non-public schools for teachers' salaries, textbooks, and instructional materials used in the teaching of secular subjects, because both statutes involved excessive entanglements of State with church in the matter of implementation.[27] As Chief Justice Burger explained it:

"Every analysis in this area must begin with consideration of the cumulative criteria developed by the Court over many years. Three such tests may be gleaned from our cases. First, the statute must have a secular legislative purpose; second, its principal or primary effect must be one that neither advances nor inhibits religion; finally, the statute must not foster 'an excessive government entanglement with religion.' . . .

"This is not to suggest, however, that we are to engage in a legalistic minuet in which precise rules and forms must govern. A true minuet is a matter of pure form and style, the observance of which is itself the substantive end. Here we examine the form of the relationship for the light that it casts on the substance.

"In order to determine whether the government entanglement with religion is excessive we must examine the character and purposes of the institutions that are benefited, the nature of the aid that the State provides, and the resulting relationship between the government and the religious authority. . . . Here we find that both statutes foster an impermissible degree of entanglement."[28]

With respect to taxation of property, the Court found constitutional a New York statute exempting from a real property tax, real estate owned by an association organized and used exclusively for religious purposes, saying: "Few concepts are more deeply embedded in the fabric of our national life, beginning with pre-Revolutionary colonial times, than for the government to exercise at the very least this kind of benevolent neutrality toward churches and religious exercise generally so long as none was favored over others and none suffered interference."[29]

[26] Tilton *v.* Richardson, 403 U.S. 672, 683 (1971). The Missouri Supreme Court held by a 4-3 majority in Americans United *v.* Rogers, 538 S.W. 2d. 711 (1976), that a State plan providing tuition grants directly to students at approved colleges and universities did not run afoul of the establishment clause even though upon receipt most of the students promptly endorsed the checks over to the institutions they were attending. The U.S. Supreme Court denied *certiorari*, 97 S.Ct. 653.
[27] Lemon *v.* Kurtzman and Early *v.* DiCenso, 430 U.S. 602 (1971).
[28] *Ibid.*, 612-615. [29] Walz *v.* Tax Com'n, 397 U.S. 664, 676 (1970).

Following the Supreme Court's 1971 decision in *Lemon*, the Pennsylvania General Assembly passed a new law which provided funds to reimburse parents for a portion of the tuition paid to send their children to private schools. The law was drawn up to avoid the "entanglement problem" on which the law in *Lemon* had run afoul by precluding the administrative authority from involvement in the administration of non-public schools. The Court, however, held that "Pennsylvania's tuition grant scheme violates the constitutional mandate against the 'sponsorship' or 'financial support' of religion or religious institutions."[30] It also struck down provisions of a New York State statute which provided for (1) tuition reimbursements to parents of children in non-public schools; (2) money grants to non-public schools for maintenance and repair of facilities "to ensure the health, welfare and safety of enrolled pupils"; (3) income tax relief to parents who did not qualify for tuition reimbursement. The Court concluded that "Our examination . . . in light of all relevant considerations, compels the judgment that each, as written, has a 'primary effect that advances religion' and offends the constitutional prohibition against laws 'respecting the establishment of religion.' "[31]

On the same day it handed down the aforementioned decisions, the Court upheld a South Carolina act which assists institutions of higher education, primarily through the use of revenue bonds, in constructing facilities except those which might be used for sectarian or religious purposes. The Court concluded that the act and the transactions under it which had come under challenge in the case "confine the scope of assistance to the secular aspects of this liberal arts college and do not foreshadow excessive entanglement between State and religion."[32]

Relying substantially upon the test articulated earlier in Lemon *v.* Kurtzman,[33] the Supreme Court invalidated most of the provisions of two acts passed by the Pennsylvania legislature to aid non-public, church-related, elementary and secondary schools. The Court sustained the loan of secular textbooks to children attending the religious schools, but voided direct aid to those schools in the form of auxiliary services (e.g., counseling, remedial reading, testing, etc.) and instructional aids (e.g., laboratory equipment, tape recorders, projectors, etc.). In a plurality opinion, Justice Stewart upheld that portion of the lower court's judgment barring forms of aid (particularly the tape recorders and projectors) that could be transferred easily to religious instruction purposes, and enlarged

---

[30] Sloan *v.* Lemon, 413 U.S. 825 (1973). Earlier in the Term, the Court had to deal with another problem stemming from the *Lemon* case. A. U.S. district court had permitted the State to reimburse non-public schools for services provided under the State law before the Supreme Court's decision in *Lemon* declared the law invalid. The Supreme Court affirmed the district court's decision. The several opinions in the case include a significant wide-ranging discussion of the issue of retroactivity. Lemon *v.* Kurtzman (*Lemon II*), 411 U.S. 192 (1973).

[31] Committee for Public Education *v.* Nyquist, 413 U.S. 756 (1973).

[32] Hunt *v.* McNair, 413 U.S. 734 (1973).   [33] 403 U.S. 602 (1971).

the ban to include everything but the textbook loan program on grounds that the volume of aid in the aggregate was so large that, even if it were possible to separate clearly the quasi-ideological from the secular aid, the *quantity* of such *direct* aid *per se* transgressed the establishment clause. He also found that the monitoring of the services and equipment, which would be required, risked substantial continued entanglement. Finally, Stewart concluded that the scope of aid envisioned by the acts "provide[d] successive opportunities for political fragmentation and division along religious lines, one of the principal evils against which the Establishment Clause was intended to protect."[34] Justice Brennan, in an opinion signed also by Justices Douglas and Marshall, would have struck down the textbook loan scheme, too, and implicitly overruled Board of Education v. Allen.[35]

Justice Rehnquist, joined by Justice White, dissented, finding the textbook loan program essentially indistinguishable from the other forms of aid and therefore valid under *Allen*. Rehnquist vehemently objected to what he saw as the Court's purely quantitative measure of direct aid and expressed as much concern at "the overtones of the Court's opinion as by its actual holding." Said Rehnquist: "The Court apparently believes that the Establishment Clause of the First Amendment not only mandates religious neutrality on the part of government but also requires that this Court go further and throw its weight on the side of those who believe our society as a whole should be a purely secular one." Chief Justice Burger, dissenting separately, was alarmed at the majority's insensitivity to the free exercise implications of its judgment. The Chief Justice complained: "If the consequence of the Court's holding operated only to penalize *institutions* with a religious affiliation, the result would be grievous enough; nothing in the Religion Clauses of the First Amendment permits governmental power to discriminate *against* or affirmatively stifle religions or religious activity. . . . But this holding does more: it penalizes *children*—children who have the misfortune to have to cope with the learning process under extraordinarily heavy physical and psychological burdens, for the most part congenital. This penalty strikes them not because of any act of theirs but because of their parents' choice of religious exercise."[36]

In other actions, the Supreme Court summarily affirmed, over vigorous dissents, lower Federal court decisions that struck down a California statute providing income tax deductions to taxpayers who sent their children to religious schools,[37] and upheld a Missouri law providing school bus transportation for public school

[34] Meek v. Pittenger, 421 U.S. 349, 372 (1975).   [35] 392 U.S. 236 (1968).
[36] Meek v. Pittenger, 421 U.S. 349, 395, 386 (1975).
[37] Franchise Tax Board of California v. United Americans for Public Schools, 419 U.S. 890 (1974). *See also* Minnesota Civil Liberties Union v. State, 224 N.W. 2d. 344 (1974).

students but not for children attending church-related schools.[38] Consistent with the thrust of his dissent in *Meek*, Chief Justice Burger, joining Justice White, would have set the Missouri case for argument as to whether the free exercise clause mandates that "a State . . . be compelled to provide such transportation."

Once again asked "to police the constitutional boundary between church and state," Justice Blackmun, for the Court, declared, "Maryland, this time, is the alleged trespasser. It has enacted a statute which, as amended, provides for annual noncategorical grants to private colleges, among them religiously affiliated institutions, subject only to the restrictions that the funds not be used for 'sectarian purposes.' "[39] The Court followed closely the three-part test articulated by the Court in 1971 in *Lemon*. The Court was most troubled by the "entanglement test" but finally concluded that "There is no exact science in gauging the entanglement of church and state. The wording of the test, which speaks of '*excessive* entanglement,' itself makes that clear. The relevant factors we have identified are to be considered 'cumulatively' in judging the degree of entanglement. . . . They may cut different ways, as certainly they do here. In reaching the conclusion that it did, the District Court gave dominant importance to the character of the aided institutions and to its finding that they are capable of separating secular and religious functions. For the reasons stated above, we cannot say that the emphasis was misplaced, or the finding erroneous." Three Justices dissented. As Justice Brennan saw it, State money was being used to advance religion no matter how much vigilance was taken to avoid it.

Finally, addressing "still another case presenting the recurrent issue of the limitations imposed by the Establishment Clause . . . on State aid to pupils in church-related elementary and secondary schools," the Court, relying extensively on Meek v. Pittenger, upheld the constitutionality of part of an Ohio program "authorizing the State to provide nonpublic school pupils with books, standardized testing and scoring, diagnostic services, and therapeutic and remedial services" but struck down "those portions relating to instructional materials and equipment and field trip services."[40] The Court sustained the textbook subsidy on the authority of Board of Education v. Allen and upheld the testing and scoring component because "Nonpublic school personnel are not involved in either the drafting or scoring of the tests." The Court also found that the diagnostic and therapeutic services survived constitutional scrutiny: the diagnostic services, while provided in the non-public school, had "little or no educational content," unlike teaching and counseling, and afforded "only limited contact with the child"; the therapeutic and remedial services were furnished by public school

[38] Luetkemeyer v. Kaufmann, 419 U.S. 888 (1974).
[39] Roemer v. Board of Public Works of Maryland, 426 U.S. 737 (1976).
[40] Wolman v. Walter, 97 S.Ct. 2593 (1977).

personnel at sites away from the non-public school premises and thus away from "the pressures of the [religious] environment." On the other hand, the Court found the remaining components of Ohio's $88 million non-public school aid program unconstitutional because, first, although there was a pretense to aiding the student and his family, the instructional material and equipment and field trip components directly aided the non-public school; and, second, there was no way to guarantee such benefits would not be put to use aiding religious instruction without "excessive entanglement" by the State.

Illustrative of many cases involving the establishment clause that have surfaced in the State and lower Federal courts in the past decade was a case decided by the United States Court of Appeals, Tenth Circuit. In that case, the court held that the erection and maintenance on government property of a granite monolith inscribed with the Ten Commandments was "primarily secular, and not religious in character; that neither its purpose or effect tends to establish religious belief."[41] The court had explained prior to the holding that "we cannot say that the monument, as it stands, is more than a depiction of a historically important monument with both secular and sectarian effects."

Bible-Reading and Prayer in Public Schools

Seldom have decisions of the Court produced more criticism and cries of outrage than the Court's decisions in the so-called "prayer" and "Bible-reading" cases.[42] Ultimately, opposition to those decisions led to a serious and prolonged effort at constitutional amendment lasting into the 1970's.[43] In 1962, the Court held that state officials could not constitutionally compose a prayer and require that it be recited each school day, even though the prayer was non-denominational and pupils who did not want to participate would be excused. Then, in 1963 the Court said that to require a reading from the Bible or a recitation of the Lord's Prayer was also constitutionally impermissible. In the uproar over these decisions, critics of the Court seemed to overlook the fact that the Court did not forbid study of the Bible. On the contrary, the Court specifically said: "Nothing we have said here indicates that . . . study of the Bible or religion, when presented objectively as part of a secular program of education, may not be effected consistently with

[41] Anderson v. Salt Lake City Corp., 475 F. 2d. 29 (1973). The decision contains citations and descriptions of a number of like cases. And in an interesting case twice considered by the Oregon Supreme Court, that court likewise upheld, against an establishment clause challenge, the erection with private funds of a veterans' war memorial in the shape of a cross in a municipal park, Eugene Sand and Gravel, Inc. v. City of Eugene, 558 P. 2d. 338 (1976). Nor, held a Federal appeals court, did New Haven's annual St. Patrick's Day parade violate the First Amendment, Curran v. Lee, 484 F. 2d. 1348 (1973).

[42] Engel v. Vitale, 370 U.S. 421 (1962); Abington School District v. Schempp, 374 U.S. 203 (1963).

[43] 1971 *Cong. Quart. Weekly Report*, 2290ff. and 2307. Examples of the continuing resistance to the *Schempp* decision readily appear in Meltzer v. Bd. of Public Instruction of Orange Cty., Fla., 548 F. 2d. 559 (1977).

the First Amendment."[44] Also, overlooked was the fact that in the "prayer" case, what was involved was a prayer written by government officials. Surely, this must have been precisely the kind of action the Framers of the First Amendment wanted to preclude. In the Court's words: "It is neither sacrilegious nor antireligious to say that each separate government in this country should stay out of the business of writing or sanctioning official prayers and leave that purely religious function to the people themselves and to those the people choose to look to for religious guidance."[45]

A case testing a Tennessee law gives a sense of *déjà vu* (the Scopes trial). The Tennessee statute required among other things that any biology textbook used for teaching in the public schools, if it dealt with "theory about origins or creation," must specifically state that it is theory and not scientific fact. A U.S. court of appeals found the statute "patently unconstitutional."[46]

As pointed out earlier (pp. 111-112), the interesting cases in recent years involving conscientious objectors to service in the Armed Forces have been decided primarily on statutory interpretation. However, Justice Harlan in a concurring opinion in 1970 indicated that he, at least, thought there was an establishment question in these cases: "The constitutional question that must be faced . . . is whether a statute that defers to the individual's conscience only when his views emanate from adherence to theistic religious beliefs is within the power of Congress. Congress, of course, could entirely consistent with the requirements of the Constitution, eliminate *all* exemptions for conscientious objectors. . . . However, having chosen to exempt, it cannot draw the line between theistic or nontheistic religious beliefs on the one hand and secular beliefs on the other. Any such distinctions are not, in my view, compatible with the Establishment Clause of the First Amendment."[47] *Conscientious Objectors*

Some four years later, the Court rejected the contention that a draftee accorded conscientious objector status who performed alternate service and who was denied educational benefits under the Veterans' Readjustment Act of 1966 had the free exercise of his religion abridged "by increasing the price he must pay for adherence to his religious beliefs." As the Court saw it: "The withholding of educational benefits involves only an incidental burden upon appellee's free exercise of religion—if, indeed, any burden exists at all."[48]

As helpful as it is to separate out the two religious clauses of the First Amendment for analysis and explication, it may inhibit understanding to do so. As the Supreme Court recently pointed out: *Sunday Closing Laws*

[44] Abington School District *v.* Schempp, 374 U.S. 203, 225 (1963).
[45] Engel *v.* Vitale, 370 U.S. 421, 435 (1962).
[46] Daniel *v.* Waters, 515 F. 2d. 485 (1975).
[47] Welsh *v.* U.S., 398 U.S. 333, 356 (1970). For a more recent dialogue on this point, *see* Justice Douglas's dissent in Wisconsin *v.* Yoder, 406 U.S. 205, 248-249 (1972) and Chief Justice Burger's opinion at 215.
[48] Johnson *v.* Robison, 415 U.S. 361 (1974).

"The Court has struggled to find a neutral course between the two Religion Clauses, both of which are cast in absolute terms, and either of which, if expanded to a logical extreme, would tend to clash with the other. . . .

"The course of constitutional neutrality in this area cannot be an absolutely straight line: rigidity could well defeat the basic purpose of these provisions, which is to insure that no religion be sponsored or favored, none commanded, and none inhibited. The general principle deducible from the First Amendment and all that has been said by the Court is this: that we will not tolerate either governmentally established religion or governmental interference with religion. Short of those expressly proscribed governmental acts there is room for play in the joints productive of a benevolent neutrality which will permit religious exercise to exist without sponsorship and without interference."[49]

This difficulty is exemplified in the so-called "Sunday Closing Laws" cases. Curiously, in view of our history, the Court found that laws proscribing certain business activities on Sundays was not necessarily based on religion and thus were not laws "respecting an establishment of religion."[50] But when Orthodox Jews protested the application of such a law to them on the grounds that they were thus required to be closed for business two days, Sunday and their own Sabbath, the Court came up with what appears less than a Solomon-like judgment that:

"Furthermore, the law's effect does not inconvenience all members of the Orthodox Jewish faith but only those who believe it necessary to work on Sunday. And even these are not faced with as serious a choice as forsaking their religious practices or subjecting themselves to criminal prosecution. Fully recognizing that the alternatives open to appellants and others similarly situated— retaining their present occupations and incurring economic disadvantage or engaging in some other commercial activity which does not call for either Saturday or Sunday labor—may well result in some financial sacrifice in order to observe their religious beliefs, still the option is wholly different than when the legislation attempts to make a religious practice itself unlawful."[51] Yet two years later, the Court decided that a State could not constitutionally deny unemployment compensation benefits to a woman who had refused employment because that employment would have required her to work on Saturday and "from conscientious scruples she would not take Saturday work."[52]

A 1977 case decided by the Court as a matter of *statutory* interpretation cuts the other way. Hardison, an employee of Trans

[49] Walz v. Tax Commissioner, 397 U.S. 664, 669 (1970).

[50] McGowan v. Maryland, 366 U.S. 420 (1961); Two Guys v. McGinley, 366 U.S. 582 (1961).

[51] Braunfeld v. Brown, 366 U.S. 599, 605-606 (1961); Gallagher v. Crown Kosher Market, 366 U.S. 617 (1961).

[52] Sherbert v. Verner, 374 U.S. 398 (1963).

World Airlines, similarly refused to work on Saturday on the grounds that it would conflict with his religious beliefs. His employer tried but could not accommodate him with a different work schedule because it was bound by a collective-bargaining agreement with the union; that agreement provided that employees with the most seniority have first choice for job and shift assignments. As a consequence, Hardison was fired for refusing to work on Saturday. The issue ultimately reached the Supreme Court on the question of whether or not the firing contravened Title VII of the Civil Rights Act of 1964, which makes it unlawful for an employer to discriminate on the basis of religion. At the time Hardison was fired, a guideline from the Equal Employment Opportunity Commission suggested that an employer make "reasonable accommodations" to the religious needs of its employees short of "undue hardship." The Court held that "the paramount concern of Congress in enacting Title VII was the elimination of discrimination in employment. In the absence of clear statutory language or legislative history to the contrary, we will not readily construe the statute to require an employer to discriminate against some employees in order to enable others to observe their Sabbath."[53] Although the petitioners contended that "to construe the statute to require further efforts at accommodation would create an establishment of religion contrary to the First Amendment of the Constitution," the Court did not feel it had to reach that question because of its decision that Title VII was not violated. In dissent, however, Justice Marshall did deal with the question: "If the State does not establish religion over nonreligion by excusing religious practitioners from obligations owed the State, I do not see how the State can be said to establish religion by requiring employees to do the same with respect to obligations owed the employer. Thus, I think it beyond dispute that the Act does—and, consistently with the First Amendment, can—require employees to grant privileges to religious observers as part of the accommodation process."

"Free exercise thereof": The religious freedom here envisaged has two aspects. It "forestalls compulsion by law of the acceptance of any creed or the practice of any form of worship," and conversely it "safeguards the free exercise of the chosen form of religion."[54] But "the free exercise thereof" does not embrace actions which are "in violation of social duties or subversive of good order"; hence it was within Congress's power to prohibit polygamy in the territories.[55] So it was held in 1878, and sixty-two years later the

Limitations upon the "Free Exercise" of Religion

[53] Trans World Airlines, Inc. v. Hardison, 432 U.S. 63, 85 (1977). Legislation has already been proposed by Sen. Jennings Randolph to change the law and wipe out the effect of the Court's decision. Minneapolis *Star*, June 17, 1977. *See also* Johnson v. U.S. Postal Service, 364 F.Supp. 37 (1973).

[54] Justice Roberts for the Court in Cantwell v. Conn., 310 U.S. 296 at 303 (1940).

[55] Reynolds v. U.S., 98 U.S. 145 (1878). *See also* Davis v. Beason, 133 U.S. 333 (1890); and Mormon Church v. U.S., 136 U.S. 1 (1890). It was never intended that the First Amendment to the Constitution "could be invoked as a protection against

Court added these words of qualification to a decision setting aside a State enactment as violative of religious freedom: "Nothing we have said is intended even remotely to imply that, under the cloak of religion, persons may, with impunity, commit frauds upon the public."[56] Yet four years later, when the promoters of a religious sect, whose founder had at different times identified himself as Saint Germain, Jesus, George Washington, and Godfre Ray King, were convicted of using the mails to defraud by obtaining money on the strength of having supernaturally healed hundreds of persons, they found the Court in a softened frame of mind. Although the trial judge, carefully discriminating between the question of the truth of defendants' pretensions and that of their good faith in advancing them, had charged the jury that it could pass on the latter but not the former, this caution did not avail with the Court, which decided on another ground ultimately to upset the verdict of "guilty." Chief Justice Stone, speaking for himself and Justices Roberts and Frankfurter, dissented: "I cannot say that freedom of thought and worship includes freedom to procure money by making knowingly false statements about one's religious experiences."[57]

In 1945, the Supreme Court did not think that it was a violation of religious freedom to deny conscientious objectors the right to practice law.[58] However, the 1961 decision mentioned earlier that struck down as unconstitutional a requirement that a State officer must declare his belief in the existence of God (*see* p. 283) as well as a recent decision finding unconstitutional efforts to deny people the right to practice law because of unpopular beliefs would indicate that the 1945 decision is no longer good law.[59]

In 1972, in its decision holding that the First and Fourteenth Amendments prevented Wisconsin from compelling Amish parents to have their children attend formal high school, the Court declared that ". . . to agree that religiously grounded conduct must often be subject to the broad police power of the State is not to deny that there are areas of conduct protected by the Free Exercise Clause of the First Amendment and thus beyond the power of the

---

legislation for the punishment of acts inimical to the peace, good order, and morals of society." 133 U.S. at 342. *But see* Justice Douglas's dissent in Wisconsin *v.* Yoder, 406 U.S. 205, 247 (1972).

[56] Cantwell *v.* Connecticut, 310 U.S. 296, 306 (1940). Conversely, a Florida court recently held that an ordinance proscribing the sale of non-kosher foods as kosher did not violate either the establishment or free exercise provisions of the First Amendment. The court said "Rather than to prohibit the free exercise of the religion, the ordinance serves to safeguard the observance of its tenets, and to prohibit actions which improperly would interfere therewith." Sossin Systems, Inc. *v.* City of Miami Beach, 262 So. 2d. 28, 29 (1972).

[57] United States *v.* Ballard, 322 U.S. 78 (1944). The interstate transportation of plural wives by polygamous Fundamentalists is punishable under the Mann Act. Cleveland *v.* U.S., 329 U.S. 14 (1946); 18 U.S.C. 2421.

[58] *In re* Summers, 325 U.S. 561 (1945).

[59] Baird *v.* State Bar of Arizona, 401 U.S. 1 (1971).

State to control, even under regulations of general applicability."[60] But, in dissenting in part, Justice Douglas saw the deprivation of religious freedom in this case in a different light: "If the parents in this case are allowed a religious exemption, the inevitable effect is to impose the parents' notions of religious duty upon their children. Where the child is mature enough to express potentially conflicting desires, it would be an invasion of the child's rights to permit such an imposition without canvassing his views." And Justice Douglas concluded that "if an Amish child desires to attend high school, and is mature enough to have that desire respected, the State may well be able to override the parents' religiously motivated objections."[61] But the majority felt that "there is no reason for the Court to consider that point since it is not an issue in the case."[62]

The rift between parental desires and the rights of young people, alluded to by Justice Douglas, widened quickly and often violently in the controversy over the followers of the Rev. Sun Myung Moon. Alleging that their children had been "brainwashed," several irate parents, relying upon conservatorship laws (statutes that allow for a kind of guardianship in cases where people are unable to handle their own affairs due to physical or mental infirmity), had their sons and daughters forcibly seized and held for "deprogramming." The "Moonies," alleging that they had been kidnapped, asserted that such a use of the law violated the free exercise clause of the First Amendment. Without focusing on the constitutional claim, a California appeals court sustained the claims of the young people, who were all over 21 years of age, to remain free of parental control. The court did not agree with a superior court judge that parents have certain prerogatives over their children who have reached adulthood, ruling that all adults are equal under the law and that conservatorships could not be granted unless the individual in question was unable to take care of himself.[63]

Some State court decisions respecting claims for the exercise of religious freedom are most instructive. The Superior Court of Pennsylvania upheld actions aimed at providing blood transfusions to a sixteen-year-old child over the mother's objections based on religious scruples.[64] The Supreme Court of Kansas found that a regulation requiring a medical examination, contrary to applicant's religious beliefs, as a condition for receiving disability benefits was not a violation of freedom of religion.[65] A Connecticut court found

---

[60] Wisconsin v. Yoder, 406 U.S. 205 (1972).   [61] *Ibid.*, 242.

[62] *Ibid.*, 231.   [63] San Francisco *Chronicle*, Apr. 12, 1977.

[64] *In re* Green, 286 A. 2d. 681 (1971). *See also* In Interest of Ivey, 319 So. 2d. 53 (1975). A State court has also held that where a son's death could not be determined without an autopsy, the State's interest in finding the cause of death outweighed the religious scruples of the Jewish Orthodox father, Snyder v. Holy Cross Hospital, 352 A. 2d. 334 (1976).

[65] Powers v. State Department of Social Welfare, 493 P. 2d. 590 (1972).

that the free exercise clause was not a bar to a mandatory sex education course in school, where the statute permitted parents the option of providing equivalent education in the home or in private schools, including parochial schools.[66] The Court of Appeals of New York held that a State statute providing for the placement of a child with adoptive parents of the same religion did not deny prospective adoptive parents their freedom of religion.[67] And a Federal court of appeals in June of 1972 held that compulsory chapel attendance at the U.S. military academies is an unconstitutional violation of the First Amendment's guarantee of religious freedom.[68]

In still other noteworthy decisions, courts have upheld provisions of State constitutions prohibiting clergymen from membership in the legislature[69] and a ban on the wearing of clerical garb in the courtroom by defense counsel who was also a priest.[70] A Federal district court, however, has held that welfare officials cannot require, as a condition of continued assistance, that the children of recipients obtain social security numbers where it was the parents' good-faith belief that such numbers constituted the biblical "mark of the Beast" and would seriously jeopardize their children's spiritual well-being and chance to enter Heaven.[71] The Washington Supreme Court, on the other hand, upheld a three-day suspension imposed upon a State employee who disregarded an order restricting the discussion of religion during working hours.[72] Finally the Tennessee Supreme Court held that the use of poisonous snakes and strychnine as part of religious ceremony could be "perpetually" enjoined. Particularly noteworthy about the decision is the court's explanation of how it labored before concluding "We could find no rational basis for limiting or restricting the practice, and could conceive of no alternative plan or procedure which would be palatable to the membership or permissible from a standpoint of compelling state interest."[73]

Prisoners' Rights

In a noteworthy decision rendered in 1972, the Supreme Court cautioned that prisons must be careful not to trench on the religious freedom of prisoners. The Court said that "Federal Courts sit not to supervise prisons but to enforce the constitutional rights of all 'persons' which include prisoners. We are not unmindful that prison officials must be accorded latitude in the administration of prison affairs, and that prisoners necessarily are subject to appropriate rules and regulations."[74] But the Court went on to stress that persons in prison do have rights. Among those aspects of the free

[66] Hopkins *v.* Hamden Board of Education, 289 A. 2d. 914 (1971).

[67] Dickens *v.* Ernesto, 330 N.Y.S. 2d. 346 (1972).

[68] Anderson *v.* Laird, 466 F. 2d. 283 (1972); *cert. denied*, 409 U.S. 1076 (1972).

[69] Kirkley *v.* Md., 381 F.Supp. 327 (1974); Paty *v.* McDaniel, 547 S.W. 2d. 897 (1977).

[70] LaRocca *v.* Lane, 338 N.E. 2d. 606 (1975).

[71] Stevens *v.* Berger, 428 F.Supp. 896 (1977).

[72] Kallas *v.* Dept. of Motor Vehicles, 560 P. 2d. 709 (1977).

[73] State *ex rel.* Swann *v.* Pack, 527 S.W. 2d. 99 (1975).

[74] Cruz *v.* Beto, 405 U.S. 319 (1972). *But see* Justice Rehnquist's stinging dissent, *ibid.*, 323.

exercise guarantee that courts have held that prison officials must respect are: (1) the right to worship services and religious counseling;[75] (2) the right to have meals prepared in accordance with certain religiously mandated dietary requirements;[76] and (3) the right of an American Indian prisoner to wear long, braided hair as a tenet of his religion.[77] Courts have reiterated that honoring such claims are necessarily bounded by whether they "present a clear and present danger to prison discipline and control of prison safety."[78] One Federal district court, however, took a hard look at what it characterized as the "non-structured, free-form, do-as-you-please philosophy" of one "religion" which, it determined, had as its "sole purpose . . . to cause or encourage disruption of established prison discipline for the sake of disruption."[79]

Over the years a number of cases have come to the Supreme Court involving church disputes, particularly over property. The Court has held strictly to the line that civil courts ought not to determine ecclesiastical questions and has been equally limiting with respect to state legislation touching on doctrine and church governing bodies.[80] However, in a dispute over control of the Serbian Eastern Orthodox Diocese for the United States and Canada, the Supreme Court of the State of Illinois held that some of the proceedings of the church were procedurally and substantively defective under the church's regulations and consequently arbitrary and invalid. The Supreme Court of the United States reversed, holding that "the inquiries made by the Illinois Supreme Court into matters of ecclesiastical cognizance and polity and the court's actions pursuant thereto contravened the First and Fourteenth Amendments."[81] In conclusion, the Court stated that, when "ecclesiastical tribunals are created to decide disputes over the government and direction of subordinate bodies, the Constitution requires that civil courts accept their decisions as binding upon them." And an Illinois appellate court has ruled that a trial court did not traverse the separation of Church and State when it decided a suit, brought by a priest against his bishop, for breach of a contract providing his salary and support for a mission.[82]

Finally, it is worth noting that in the last few years, there have

Church Disputes

---

[75] O'Malley v. Brierley, 477 F. 2d. 785 (1973); Lipp v. Procunier, 395 F.Supp. 871 (1975).

[76] Ross v. Blackledge, 477 F. 2d. 616 (1973); Kahane v. Carlson, 527 F. 2d. 492 (1975); for fuller exploration of issues *see* district court decision, 396 F.Supp. 687 (1975). *Cf.* United States v. Huss, 394 F.Supp. 752 (1975), Cochran v. Sielaff, 405 F.Supp. 1126 (1976).

[77] Teterud v. Burns, 522 F. 2d. 357 (1975).

[78] Lipp v. Procunier, 395 F.Supp. 871 (1975).

[79] Theriault v. Silber, 391 F.Supp. 578, 582 (1975).

[80] Md. & Va. Churches v. Sharpsburg Ch., 396 U.S. 367 (1970); Presbyterian Church v. Hull Church, 393 U.S. 440 (1969); Kedroff v. St. Nicholas Cathedral, 344 U.S. 94 (1952); Kreshik v. St. Nicholas Cathedral, 363 U.S. 190 (1960). *See also* Draskovich v. Pasalich, 280 N.E. 2d. 69 (1972) for a review of pertinent cases.

[81] The Serbian Eastern Orthodox Diocese for the United States of America and Canada v. Dionisije Milivojevich, 426 U.S. 696 (1976).

[82] Bodewes v. Zuroweste, 303 N.W. 2d. 509 (1973).

been a number of actions in the lower courts protesting as violations of both religion clauses the exhibition of religious symbols
and displays by one or another governmental body; the redoubta-
ble Madalyn Murray O'Hair went to court to restrain NASA from
"further directing or permitting religious activities or ceremonies
and especially the reading of the Sectarian Christian religion Bible
and from prayer recitation in space and in relation to all future
space flight activity." Such petitions have not usually met with success.[83]

The Black-
stonian
Conception
of "Free-
dom of
Speech or
of the
Press"
"Freedom of speech or of the press": According to Blackstone,
who was the oracle of the common law when the First Amendment
was framed, "liberty of the press consists in laying no *previous* restraints upon publications, and not in freedom from censure for
criminal matter when published. Every freeman," he asserted, "has
an undoubted right to lay what sentiments he pleases before the
public; to forbid this is to destroy the freedom of the press; but if
he publishes what is improper, mischievous, and illegal, he must
take the consequences of his own temerity. . . . To punish (as the
law does at present) any dangerous or offensive writings, which,
when published, shall on a fair and impartial trial be adjudged of a
pernicious tendency, is necessary for the preservation of peace and
good order, of government and religion, the only solid foundations
of civil liberty."[84] Also, as the law stood at that time, the question
whether a publication or oral utterance was of "a pernicious tendency" was, in a criminal trial, a question not for the jury but for the
judge; nor was the truth of the utterance a defense.

The Doc-
trine of
Seditious
Libel
While it was originally no intention of the authors of Amendment I to revise the common law, as set forth by Blackstone, on the
subject of freedom of the press,[85] there was one feature of it which
early ran afoul of the facts of life in America. This was the common
law of "seditious libel," which operated to put persons in authority
beyond the reach of public criticism. The first step was taken in the
famous, or infamous, Sedition Act of 1798, which admitted the defense of truth in prosecutions brought under it, and submitted the
general issue of defendant's guilt to the jury.[86] But the Act of 1798
still retained the substantive doctrine of "seditious libel," a circumstance which put several critics of President Adams in jail, and
thereby considerably aided Jefferson's election as President in
1800. Once in office, nevertheless, Jefferson himself appealed to
the discredited principle against partisan critics. Writing his friend
Governor McKean of Pennsylvania in 1803 about such critics, Jef-

[83] O'Hair v. Paine, 312 F.Supp. 434 (1969). *See also*, for example, Paul v. Dade
County, 419 F. 2d. 10 (1969), *cert. denied*, 397 U.S. 1065 (1970).
[84] Sir William Blackstone, *Commentaries on the Laws of England*, edited by Warren
Carey Jones, IV (San Francisco, 1916), 151.
[85] *See* Justice Frankfurter's opinion in Dennis v. U.S., 341 U.S. 494, 521-525
(1951); citing Robertson v. Baldwin, 165 U.S. 275, 281 (1897).
[86] These two improvements upon the common law were, in fact, adopted from
Fox's Libel Act, passed by Parliament in 1792.

ferson said: "The federalists having failed in destroying freedom ⟨Jefferson vs.⟩
of the press by their gag-law, seem to have attacked it in an oppo- ⟨Hamilton⟩
site direction; that is by pushing its licentiousness and its lying to ⟨on Freedom⟩
such a degree of prostitution as to deprive it of all credit. . . . This is ⟨of Press⟩
a dangerous state of things, and the press ought to be restored to its
credibility if possible. The restraints provided by the laws of the
States are sufficient for this, if applied. And I have, therefore, long
thought that a few prosecutions of the most prominent offenders
would have a wholesome effect in restoring the integrity of the
presses. Not a general prosecution, for that would look like perse-
cution; but a selected one."[87]

The sober truth is that it was that archenemy of Jefferson and of
democracy, Alexander Hamilton, who made the greatest single
contribution toward rescuing this particular freedom as a political
weapon from the coils and toils of the common law, and that in
connection with one of Jefferson's "selected prosecutions." The
reference is to Hamilton's many-times-quoted formula in the
Croswell case in 1804: "The liberty of the press is the right to publish with impunity, truth, with good motives, for justifiable ends
though reflecting on government, magistracy, or individuals."[88]
Equipped with this brocard, which is today embodied in about half
of the State constitutions, our State courts working in co-operation
with juries, whose attitude usually reflected the robustness of
American political discussion before the Civil War, gradually wrote
into the common law of the States the principle of "qualified
privilege," which is a notification to plaintiffs in libel suits that if
they are unlucky enough to be office holders or office seekers, they
must be prepared to shoulder the almost impossible burden of
showing defendant's "special malice."[89] (See p. 324.)

In 1907 the Court, speaking by Justice Holmes, rejected the con- ⟨Blackstone⟩
tention that the Fourteenth Amendment rendered applicable ⟨Accepted,⟩
against the States "a prohibition similar to that in the First," and at ⟨then⟩
the same time endorsed Blackstone, in words drawn from an early ⟨Rejected⟩
Massachusetts case: "The preliminary freedom [i.e., from censor-
ship] extends as well to the false as to the true; the subsequent
punishment may extend to the true as to the false."[90] Even as late as
1922 Justice Pitney, speaking for the Court, said: "Neither the
Fourteenth Amendment nor any other provision of the Constitution of the United States imposes upon the States any restriction
about 'freedom of speech' or 'liberty of silence.' "[91] Three

[87] Paul L. Ford, *The Writings of Thomas Jefferson*, IX (New York, 1892-1899), 451-
452.
[88] People v. Croswell, 1 N.Y. Common Law Reports 717 (1804).
[89] *See* Edward S. Corwin, *Liberty against Government* (Baton Rouge, 1948), 157-
159n; Cooley, *Constitutional Limitations*, ch. 12; Samuel A. Dawson, *Freedom of the
Press, A Study of the Doctrine of "Qualified Privilege"* (New York, 1924). *See also* New
York Times Co. v. Sullivan, 376 U.S. 254 (1964).
[90] Patterson v. Colo., 205 U.S. 454, 461-462 (1907).
[91] Prudential Life Ins. Co. v. Cheek, 259 U.S. 530, 543 (1922).

years later, the Court abandoned this position in Gitlow *v.* New York.

Meantime the so-called "clear and present danger doctrine" had made its appearance. The original formulation of that doctrine was a simple assertion that before an utterance can be penalized by government it must, ordinarily, have occurred "in such circumstances or have been of such a nature as to create a clear and present danger" that it would bring about "substantive evils" within the power of government to prevent.[92] The question whether these conditions exist is one of law for the courts, and ultimately for the Supreme Court, in enforcement of the First and/or the Fourteenth Amendment,[93] and in exercise of its power of review in these premises the Court is entitled to review broadly findings of facts of lower courts, whether State or Federal.[94]

The formula emerged in the course of a decision in 1919, holding that the circulation of certain documents constituted an "attempt," in the sense of the Espionage Act of 1917, to cause insubordination in the Armed Forces and to obstruct their recruitment.[95] Said Justice Holmes, speaking for the Court: "We admit that in many places and in ordinary times the defendants in saying all that was said in the circular would have been within their constitutional rights. But the character of every act depends upon the circumstances in which it is done. . . . The most stringent protection of free speech would not protect a man in falsely shouting fire in a theatre and causing a panic. It does not even protect a man from an injunction against uttering words that have all the effect of force. . . . The question in every case is whether the words used are used in such circumstances and are of such a nature as to create a clear and present danger that they will bring about the substantive evils that Congress has a right to prevent. It is a question of proximity and degree."[96]

Though "clear and present danger" was the phrase that eventually came to characterize Holmes's formula, it is important to remember that Holmes's approach took into account much more than this single element. In addition, Holmes's formula, as a replication of the doctrine of criminal attempts, though in a constitutional law setting, required that, to sustain government regulation of speech in a given case, a specific intent to bring about certain results must be shown on the part of the speaker as well as, of course, a grave injury to the public.[97]

Whether Justice Holmes actually intended here to add a new dimension to constitutional freedom of speech and press may be

[92] Schenck *v.* United States, 249 U.S. 47 (1919).
[93] *See* Justice Brandeis's concurring opinion in Whitney *v.* Calif., 274 U.S. 357 (1927); and cases reviewed below.
[94] Fiske *v.* Kansas, 274 U.S. 380 (1927).
[95] Note 92 above.   [96] 249 U.S. 47, 52.
[97] Abrams *v.* U.S., 250 U.S. 616 (1919). *See also* Justice Brandeis's concurring opinion in Whitney *v.* Calif., 274 U.S. 357, 372 (1927).

seriously questioned, inasmuch as in two similar cases following shortly after, in which he again spoke for the Court, and in which prosecutions under the Espionage Act were sustained, he did not allude to the formula.[98] Moreover, when a case did arise in which the formula might have made a difference, seven Justices declined to follow it.[99] This time, however, Justice Holmes, accompanied by Justice Brandeis, dissented on the ground that defendants' utterances did not create a clear and present danger of substantive evils. From this time forth in the course of the next twenty years, these two Justices filed numerous opinions, sometimes in dissent, sometimes in affirmation, of rulings of the Court in freedom of speech cases in which the "clear and present danger" test was urged, but without convincing any of their brethren of its soundness.[100] Indeed as if to distinguish further this approach from the often highly conjectural and remote extrapolations of the defendants' behavior undertaken by the conservative majority on the Court, Justice Brandeis later recast the "clear and present danger" component as "clear and *imminent* danger."[101]

The majority employed the "bad tendency" test (that is, "that a state in the exercise of its police power may punish those who abuse this freedom by utterances inimicable to the welfare, tending to corrupt morals, incite to a crime, or disturb the public peace . . ."). As compared with the strict requirements set out in Holmes's approach, Justice Sanford, implementing the "bad tendency" test in *Gitlow*, wrote: "Every presumption is to be indulged in favor of the validity of the statute." And further: "It was not necessary, within the meaning of the statute, that the defendant should have advocated 'some definite or immediate act or acts' of force, violence or unlawfulness. It was sufficient if such acts were advocated in general terms; and it was not essential that their immediate execution should have been advocated. . . . The advocacy need not be addressed to specific persons."[102]

Then suddenly in 1940, the stone rejected by the builders suddenly appeared at the head of the column, and along with it the further tenet that freedom of speech and press occupied "a preferred position" in the scale of constitutional values.[103] The libertarians on the Court reformulated Holmes's method for dealing with First Amendment cases. This approach sought, first, to expand civil liberties protections by reading through the word "liberty" in the due process clause of the Fourteenth Amendment, and

[98] The reference is to Frohwerk v. U.S., 249 U.S. 204 (1919); *and* Debs v. U.S., 249 U.S. 211 (1919).
[99] Abrams v. U.S., 250 U.S. 616 (1919).
[100] *See* Schaefer v. U.S., 251 U.S. 466 (1920); Gitlow v. N.Y., 268 U.S. 652 (1925); Whitney v. Calif., 274 U.S. 357 (1927).
[101] Whitney v. Calif., 274 U.S. 357, 376-377.
[102] Gitlow v. N.Y., 268 U.S. 652, 668, 671-672.
[103] Thornhill v. Ala., 310 U.S. 88 (1940); *and* Cantwell v. Conn., 310 U.S. 296 (1940) are especially referred to. *Cf.* Herndon v. Lowry, 301 U.S. 242 (1937).

thereby also making applicable against State infringement guarantees emanating from certain freedoms in the Bill of Rights.[104] Second, it provided a rigorous three-pronged test to evaluate whether governmental action was, in any given instance, violative of these specially regarded liberties: (1) where legislation on its face abridged a preferred freedom, the presumption would be with unconstitutionality, the burden lying with the Government to convincingly demonstrate the contrary; (2) the Government would have to prove that the exercise of freedom in this context presented a clear and imminent danger; and (3) the Government would have to show that the remedy espoused was confined to the eradication of the immediate evil and was not some scatter-gun approach which imperiled additional liberties by its overbreadth.[105]

The justification for this concept of incorporation and its companion test of infringement lay in what was asserted to be the requisite of certain freedoms to the conduct of the democratic process (especially insofar as this concept protected the articulation of views and demands by minorities in the society) and the maintenance of individual dignity.[106] Recognizing that freedom was the rule and restraint the exception, they had constructed a balancing framework with a built-in bias against governmental interference, one which justified activism to its former critics, and a doctrine which shifted the focus of the Court's policy-making by recognizing that civil liberties, and not economic liberties, were essential to the maintenance of human dignity and the democratic enterprise.

From 1937 through 1948, a majority of the Court applied this method in fourteen cases.[107] In each of these the Court assumed that the governmental action at issue was invalid. This is not to say that in every case the Court assumed that a particular statute was unconstitutional; in some cases the Court assumed that only the particular application of a broadly drawn statute was unconstitutional. This stand of the Court, in each case, compelled the States or their agents to attempt to prove that the exercise of liberty did *in fact* present a "clear and present danger." In the three cases where the Court, after an inquiry into the facts, found that a clear and present danger did exist, it inquired into the appropriateness of the remedy.

In eleven of the fourteen cases, the Court's decision favored the rights of the individual. In one of the cases where the Court decided against the individuals, there was actual violence involved.[108] In another, it was found that child labor *per se* was an evil.[109] The

---

[104] Palko *v.* Conn., 302 U.S. 319 (1937).

[105] Thomas *v.* Collins, 323 U.S. 516 (1945).

[106] United States *v.* Carolene Products Co., 304 U.S. 144, 152 note 4 (1938).

[107] *See* Justice Frankfurter's catalog of the instances where the Court used the preferred freedoms test and his criticisms of the approach in Kovacs *v.* Cooper, 336 U.S. 77, 90-94 (1949).

[108] Milk Drivers Union *v.* Meadowmoor Dairies Inc., 312 U.S. 287 (1941).

[109] Prince *v.* Massachusetts, 321 U.S. 158 (1944).

Court, in a third case, found that, where an ice peddlers' union sought to picket in an effort to force wholesale distributors into an illegal agreement to sell their goods exclusively to union members, there was a danger to the nation in such a use of free speech.[110] That the Court should have found for the individual in eleven out of fourteen cases should not be regarded as surprising or disproportionate, for as James Madison pointed out in *Federalist* No. 10, in a representative government there is more danger of infringement of individual rights by the majority than *vice versa*.

Both the growing concern over the "Communist Problem" and personnel changes on the Court contributed to the demise of clear and present danger as a useful formulation. Had the Court employed the doctrine as method in the case of the "Eleven Communist Leaders" who were convicted in 1949 under the Smith Act, it would have felt compelled to overturn the conviction.[111] That conviction was reviewed first in the appeals court in which the venerable Judge Learned Hand sat. It was he who gave the Court a new approach. Hand had written: "In each case they [the courts] must ask whether the gravity of the 'evil,' discounted by its improbability, justifies such invasion of free speech as is necessary to avoid the danger. We have purposely substituted 'improbability' for 'remoteness,' *because that must be the right interpretation*" (emphasis supplied).[112] When the case came to it, the Supreme Court specifically endorsed the Hand opinion, adding that: "Overthrow of the Government by force and violence is certainly a substantial enough interest for the Government to limit speech. Indeed, this is the ultimate value of our society, for if a society cannot protect its very structure from armed internal attack, it must follow that no subordinate value can be protected."[113]

Clear and Probable Danger Test

From that point on, the Court's majority, whoever has composed it, has refrained from seeking a doctrine or formulation that will cover all free speech cases, evidently leaving it to the dissenters and some professors to do so.[114] Instead, they take each case on its own merits and balance "the competing private and public interests."[115] Needless to say, several of the more libertarian Justices who had been devotés of the clear and present danger doctrine were not happy with this development. Justice Black's attack on the balancing approach is worthy of study.[116] But, interestingly enough, Justices Douglas and Black took the occasion in 1969 to indicate that

The Balancing Approach

[110] Giboney v. Empire Storage, 336 U.S. 490 (1949).
[111] Chase, *Security and Liberty*, ch. 2. *See also* Yates v. U.S., 354 U.S. 298 (1957).
[112] U.S. v. Dennis, 183 F. 2d. 201, 212 (1950).
[113] Dennis v. U.S., 341 U.S. 494 (1951).
[114] For a superb effort of that kind, *see* Thomas I. Emerson, "Toward a General Theory of the First Amendment," 72 *Yale Law Journal*, 877 (1963).
[115] Barenblatt v. U.S., 360 U.S. 109, 126 (1959). For a more recent expression of the balancing process used in First Amendment cases, *see* Wisconsin v. Yoder, 405 U.S. 205, 214 (1972).
[116] *Ibid.*, 140-145.

their objection to the clear and present danger test was that it did not give *enough* protection to individual rights.[117] Because governmental regulation under the clear and present danger test could reach advocacy under extraordinary conditions—indeed, given the tensions of the postwar era and the conservative coloration of the Court, some thought it had come to reach ordinary conditions as well—Justices Black and Douglas thought Holmes's test trenched impermissibly on expression that the First Amendment protected *absolutely*.[118]

A
Pendulum
Effect

In the post-World War II era neither the preferred freedoms nor balancing of interests approach has completely won out. Rather, constitutional interpretation has become subject to a pendulum effect in which each of these schools of thought becomes dominant at one time or another given the changing composition of the Court. From 1942 until the deaths of Justices Murphy and Rutledge in the summer of 1949, for example, the preferred freedoms approach dominated the Court's outlook.[119] With the Truman appointees (particularly Justices Clark and Minton, added to Truman's earlier appointees, Chief Justice Vinson and Justice Burton), the Court again swung back to a balancing orientation until the appointment of Chief Justice Warren in 1953.[120] From then until the retirements of Justices Frankfurter and Whittaker in 1962, the Court alternated between that and a mild activism depending upon the votes of Justices Frankfurter and Harlan.[121] With the appointment of Justice Goldberg, and to a lesser extent White, by President Kennedy, the Court once again swung to a preferred freedoms orientation and sustained that activist outlook until the retirement of Chief Justice Warren and resignation of Justice Fortas in 1969.[122] With the emergence of the Burger Court, the Court has developed a greater affinity for the balancing approach, though the effect has been more marked in some areas of Constitutional Law than others.[123]

What remains to be stated is where the case law on free speech

[117] Brandenburg *v*. Ohio, 395 U.S. 444, 450-457 (1969).
[118] Of the two, Justice Black was the most thoroughgoing advocate of absolute protection for "pure speech" under the First Amendment. *See* his dissenting opinions in Barenblatt *v*. U.S, 360 U.S. 109, 134 (1959), *and* Konigsberg *v*. State Bar of Calif., 366 U.S. 36, 56 (1961); *see also* Hugo L. Black, "The Bill of Rights," 35 *New York University Law Review*, 865 (1960), *and* Hugo Black, *A Constitutional Faith* (New York, 1969).
[119] *See* C. Herman Pritchett, *The Roosevelt Court* (New York, 1948).
[120] *See* C. Herman Pritchett, *The Vinson Court and Civil Liberties* (Chicago, 1954).
[121] *See* Walter Murphy, *Congress and the Court* (Chicago, 1962); and G. Theodore Mitau, *Decade of Decision* (New York, 1967).
[122] *See* Henry J. Abraham, *Freedom and the Court*, 3rd ed. (New York, 1976); Harold W. Chase and Craig R. Ducat, "The Warren Court and the Second Constitutional Revolution," in *Corwin's The Constitution and What It Means Today*, 13th ed. (Princeton, 1973), pp. 238-268; Mitau, *op cit.*
[123] *See* Steven Wasby, *Continuity and Change: From the Warren to the Burger Court* (Pacific Palisades, Calif., 1976), *and* Leonard Levy, *Against the Law* (New York, 1974).

leaves us at this moment. Apparently, one is free to say pretty much what he pleases, provided the speech is not tied in with a call to violent or other illegal action.[124] True, there are situations when it becomes a subjective judgment as to whether or not there has been a call to action.[125] And the Court has not always opted for the libertarian position. But on the whole, the right of free speech *qua* speech as a practical matter seems thoroughly secure.

"Fighting words" have always been thought to be an exception to First Amendment protection. In Justice Murphy's description: "There are certain well-defined and narrowly limited classes of speech the prevention of which have never thought to raise any Constitutional problem. These include the lewd, the obscene, the profane, the libelous, and the insulting or 'fighting' words those which by their very utterance inflict injury or tend to incite an immediate breach of the peace."[126] The concept is still very much alive, although the Court is generally more permissive as to what actually constitute "fighting words."[127] In one such case, the Court struck down a New Orleans ordinance that made it unlawful "wantonly to curse or revile or to use obscene or opprobrious language toward or with reference to any member of the city police while in the actual performance of his duties." The Court said that the ordinance "has a broader sweep than the constitutional definition of 'fighting words.' . . ."[128]

"Fighting Words"

A relatively new expression has found its way into First Amendment cases, free speech cases particularly. Those words "chilling effect" are applied to government actions which inhibit the exercise of First Amendment freedoms. To the extent the "chill" is real, it will render the action unconstitutional.[129] However, in 1972, five of the nine Supreme Court Justices were unsympathetic to a claim that the Army's civilian surveillance program had a "chilling" effect on those who had initially brought the suit.[130] The Court held that

"Chilling Effect"

[124] Yates *v.* U.S., 354 U.S. 298 (1957); Scales *v.* U.S., 367 U.S. 203 (1960); Noto *v.* U.S., 367 U.S. 290; Brandenburg *v.* Ohio, 395 U.S. 444 (1969); Gooding *v.* Wilson, 405 U.S. 518 (1972). *See* State *v.* Cappon, 285 A. 2d. 287 (1971). *See also* Nat'l Socialist Party of America *v.* Village of Skokie, 97 S.Ct. 2205 (1977).

[125] *Ibid., see also* Street *v.* N.Y., 394 U.S. 576 (1969). In this connection, see the interesting court decisions with respect to urging "blockbusting"; State *v.* Wagner, 291 A. 2d. 161 (1972) and Summer *v.* Teaneck, 251 A. 2d. 761 (1969).

[126] Chaplinsky *v.* New Hampshire, 315 U.S. 568 (1942).

[127] Cohen *v.* California, 403 U.S. 15, 20-27 (1971); Gooding *v.* Wilson, 405 U.S. 518 (1972), *see* particularly Justice Blackmun's dissent, *ibid.*, 534; Hess *v.* Ind., 414 U.S. 105 (1973).

[128] Lewis *v.* City of New Orleans, 415 U.S. 130, 132 (1974). *See also* Reese *v.* State, 299 A. 2d. 848 (1973); *and* State *v.* Rosenfeld, 303 A. 2d. 889 (1973).

[129] *See*, for example, Dombrowski *v.* Pfister, 380 U.S. 479, 494 (1965).

[130] Laird *v.* Tatum, 408 U.S. 1 (1972); *but see* report of a district court decision refusing to dismiss a challenge to police surveillance of protest activities, *N.Y. Times*, Oct. 29, 1972. Recently, the American Civil Liberties Union filed a suit challenging the constitutionality of the Bank Secrecy Act which requires disclosure on Treasury order of certain bank transactions. The ACLU contended that this would have a chilling effect on rights of association since it might make people chary of contribut-

"Allegations of a subjective 'chill' are not an adequate substitute for a claim of specific present objective harm or a threat of specific future harm; 'the federal courts . . . do not render advisory opinions.' " The Court spelled out its holding in these words: "We, of course, intimate no view with respect to the propriety or desirability, from a policy standpoint, of the challenged activities of the Department of the Army; our conclusion is a narrow one, namely, that on this record the respondents have not presented a case for resolution by the courts."

In his capacity as Circuit Justice for the Second Circuit, Justice Marshall refused to stay an appeals court order vacating in part a preliminary injunction issued by a U.S. district court that barred certain surveillance activities of the FBI with regard to an upcoming public convention of the Young Socialists Alliance.[131] Marshall rejected the contention of the Socialist Workers Party (the parent body) that monitoring the proceedings by recording the names of individuals in attendance and use of undercover agents and informants would do irreparable damage insofar as it "chilled" plaintiffs' right of association. Given the limited nature of the surveillance, the legality of the government's conduct, and the damage to FBI investigative efforts that could come from unmasking its agents, Marshall held that the party had not made out a compelling case for immediate judicial action.

As the concept has been most readily used, it refers to the inhibiting effect that vaguely drawn or overbroad (not narrowed to delineate specific conduct) statutes or ordinances can have by forcing the individual to guess whether his conduct might violate the law and thus influencing him to hedge and trim his expression to be on the safe side.

A recent Supreme Court decision may be a harbinger of things to come. Justice Blackmun speaking for a majority of the Burger Court in 1977 wrote: "The reason for the special rule in First Amendment cases is apparent: an overbroad statute might serve to chill protected speech. First Amendment interests are fragile interests, and a person who contemplates protected activity might be discouraged by the *in terrorem* effect of the statute. . . . Indeed, such a person might choose not to speak because of uncertainty whether

---

ing to organizations. *New York Times*, July 2, 1972. The Supreme Court sustained the Act against Fourth and Fifth Amendment challenges and found the First Amendment objections premature. California Bankers Ass'n *v.* Shultz, 416 U.S. 21 (1974).

[131] Socialist Workers Party *v.* Att'y Gen. of the U.S., 419 U.S. 1314 (1974). For the district court decision, see Socialist Workers Party *v.* Att'y Gen. of the U.S., 387 F.Supp. 747 (1974). A decision by the California Supreme Court has enjoined police surveillance of classroom discussions and related academic activities at a State university. Police officers were passing as students. *See*, White *v.* Davis, 533 P. 2d. 222 (1975). For an account of government surveillance activities with regard to the 1971 May Day gathering in Washington *see* Paul W. Valentine, "High Level Strategy Used to Contain 'May Day,' "*Washington Post*, Dec. 1, 1974. And as to damages awarded to 1200 demonstrators falsely arrested by Capitol Police, *see* St. Paul *Pioneer Press*, Aug. 7, 1977.

his claim of privilege would prevail if challenged. The use of the overbreadth analysis reflects the conclusion that the possible harm to society from allowing unprotected speech to go unpunished is outweighed by the possibility that protected speech will be muted."[132] Significant for the future was Blackmun's point on the issue of commercial speech presented by the case. He made clear that "chilling effect" would not be used as a magic talisman to preclude a weighing of claims for limiting the freedom: "But the justification for the application of overbreadth analysis applies weakly, if at all, in the ordinary commercial context. . . . [T]here are 'commonsense differences' between commercial speech and other varieties. . . . Since advertising is linked to commercial well-being, it seems unlikely that such speech is particularly susceptible to being crushed by overbroad regulation."

In several cases involving contentions that alleged vague or overbroad legislation "chilled" First Amendment rights of expression and association, lower Federal and State courts have struck down: (1) an ordinance forbidding any individual from sitting or reclining in any office window in a certain section of the city;[133] (2) an ordinance proscribing behavior "recklessly causing inconvenience or alarm to another by making offensively coarse utterances";[134] (3) a statute making it a misdemeanor if any person "behaves in a riotous or disorderly manner";[135] and (4) an ordinance making it an offense to appear in public in clothing of the opposite sex.[136] However, courts have upheld legislation regulating inflammatory speech directed *at specific individuals*[137] and likely to provoke "fistic encounters."[138] And a Federal appeals court has upheld the conviction of an individual for casually remarking to a stewardess in the cockpit of a commercial airliner prior to take-off that he was studying to be a skyjacker and that, "One of these days I'm going to hijack an airplane."[139]

In the early 1940's the Court, according to Justice Frankfurter, Picketing ". . . broadly assimilated peaceful picketing in general to freedom of speech, and as such protected against abridgement by the Fourteenth Amendment."[140] But ultimately, as Justice Douglas complained, the Court came to view picketing as something more than just an exercise of free speech: "State courts and state legislatures cannot fashion blanket prohibitions on all picketing. But . . . State courts and state legislatures are free to decide whether to permit or

---

[132] Bates v. State Bar of Arizona, 97 S.Ct. 2691, 2707 (1977).

[133] City of Fremont v. Beatty, 218 N.W. 2d. 799 (1974).

[134] City of Akron v. Serra, 318 N.E. 2d. 180 (1974).

[135] Squire v. Pace, 380 F.Supp. 269 (1974); *and see* Wiegand v. Seaver, 504 F. 2d. 303 (1974).

[136] City of Columbus v. Rogers, 324 N.E. 2d. 563 (1975).

[137] State v. Brahy, 529 P. 2d. 236 (1974); *and see* Baton Rouge v. Ewing, 308 So. 2d. 776 (1975).

[138] State v. Heck, 307 So. 2d. 332 (1975).

[139] United States v. Irving, 509 F. 2d. 1325 (1975).

[140] Teamsters Union v. Vogt, Inc., 354 U.S. 284 (1957).

suppress any particular picket line for any reason other than a blanket policy against all picketing."[141]

More recently, in a bare majority decision, the Supreme Court, speaking through Justice Rehnquist, upheld injunctive orders of the Alabama courts against six maritime unions whose members were picketing a foreign flag vessel to publicize the adverse impact on American seamen produced by the relatively low wages paid to crewmen on foreign ships. Longshoremen and other dock workers refused to cross the picket line to service the ship. The Supreme Court held that the jurisdiction of the Alabama courts was not pre-empted by the National Labor Relations Act and that the State court action was justified since the picketing, though peaceful, was a wrongful interference with the shipping business.[142] Justice Stewart, speaking for himself and Justices Douglas, Brennan, and Marshall, dissented on the ground that the dispute was one more properly before the National Labor Relations Board.

Of acute importance in recent years has been the question of whether peaceful labor picketing on private property can be enjoined as an invasion of the rights of the property owner. The Supreme Court has come full circle on the issue. Overruling an earlier decision in which it sustained union picketing of a non-union food store on land owned by the proprietors of the shopping center,[143] the Court held that, in a similar case involving labor picketing of a shoe store chain, the private property owner was under no constitutional obligation, even though the business was open to the public, to entitle the picketers to assert First Amendment rights.[144] However, acknowledging that the Supreme Court has never ruled on the matter, the Maryland Court of Appeals has held that the State may not place a total ban on residential picketing.[145]

Symbolic Speech — Like picketing, symbolic speech constitutes "speech plus"; that is, as a form of expression, it combines both speech and nonspeech

---

[141] *Ibid.*, 297.

[142] American Radio Ass'n v. Mobile Steamship Ass'n, 419 U.S. 215 (1974). For a somewhat related case (picketing of a food store ostensibly for refusal to make a contribution to a political cause but which the court determined was a facade to cover the real purpose, to harm business of the store), Moore v. State, 519 S.W. 2d. 604 (1974). For a recent decision of the Supreme Court, not raising First Amendment questions but concerning labor union picketing to compel general contractors to subcontract only with businesses whose employees were members of the union, *see* Connell Construction Co., Inc. v. Plumbers and Steamfitters Local Union No. 100, 421 U.S. 616 (1975).

[143] Amalgamated Food Employees Union v. Logan Valley Plaza, 391 U.S. 308 (1968).

[144] Hudgens v. N.L.R.B., 424 U.S. 507 (1976). The Court's reasoning in *Hudgens* was substantially transferred from its opinion in Lloyd Corp. v. Tanner, 407 U.S. 551 (1972).

[145] State v. Schuller, 372 A. 2d. 1076 (1977). The opinion presents a comprehensive discussion of picketing and the First Amendment. *See also* People Acting through Community Effort v. Doorley, 468 F. 2d. 1143 (1972); *but cf.* Garcia v. Gray, 507 F. 2d. 539 (1974) *and* Tassin v. Local 832, Nat'l Union of Police Officers, AFL-CIO, 311 So. 2d. 591 (1975).

elements. Certain symbolic acts like wearing armbands, will in certain circumstances be regarded as symbolic free speech and as such be entitled to the full protection of the First Amendment.[146] But burning the American flag or a draft card in the face of a statute making it a crime will not be so regarded,[147] for, the Court has said: "We cannot accept the view that an apparently limitless variety of conduct can be labeled 'speech' whenever the person engaging in the conduct intends thereby to express an idea."[148] Those who use the American flag in provocative ways as symbolic expression gained solace in two recent Supreme Court decisions. One, who sewed a small flag to the seat of his pants and was convicted under the Massachusetts flag misuse statute, was spared by the Court's holding that the law was unconstitutionally vague.[149] Another who displayed out of his apartment window a flag with superimposed peace symbols was saved by the Court's holding that the application of the State of Washington's statute that forbids exhibiting the flag with superimposed symbols was unconstitutional, at least on the basis of the facts of the case. The *per curiam* opinion stated: "He displayed it as a flag of his country in a way closely analogous to the manner in which flags have always been used to convey ideas. Moreover, his message was direct, likely to be understood, and within the contours of the First Amendment. Given the protected character of his expression and in light of the fact that no interest the State may have in preserving the physical integrity of a privately-owned flag was significantly impaired on these facts, the conviction must be invalidated."[150] In several "symbolic speech" cases, lower Federal and State courts have held that First Amendment protection does not extend to: (1) the establishment of a "symbolic campsite";[151] (2) the wearing of a peace pin by a VA staff

---

[146] Tinker v. Des Moines School Dist., 393 U.S. 503 (1969). A California court recently held the wearing of a beard a symbolic expression and consequently ruled that a man who lost his job because he refused to give up his beard was entitled to unemployment insurance, where the state did not show how it would be "adversely affected if benefits were granted" and, if it did, it must show that "no conceivable alternatives would preclude the adverse results without 'infringing First Amendment rights.' " King v. Cal. Unemployment Insurance Appeals Bd., 101 Cal. Rptr. 660 (1972).

[147] U.S. v. O'Brien, 391 U.S. 367 (1968) *and see* Warren's dissent in Street v. N.Y., 394 U.S. 576, 594 (1969). In recent years there has been a rash of State cases involving flag desecrations, almost invariably the desecrators have been punished; in one Texas jurisdiction a flag-burner was sentenced to four years in the penitentiary. Deeds v. State, 474 S.W. 2d. 718 (1972). *See* Commonwealth v. Goguen, 279 N.E. 2d. 666 (1972); State v. Zimmelman, 287 A. 2d. 474 (1972); State v. Saulino, 277 N.E. 2d. 580 (1971); People v. Keogh, 329 N.Y.S. 2d. 80 (1972), *but cf.* State v. Hodson, 289 A. 2d. 635 (1972). *See also* Joyce v. U.S., 454 F. 2d. 971 (1971), *cert. den.* 405 U.S. 969 (1972).

[148] U.S. v. O'Brien, 391 U.S. 367, 376 (1968); State v. Saulino, 277 N.E. 2d. 580 (1971).

[149] Smith v. Goguen, 415 U.S. 566 (1974).

[150] Spence v. State of Washington, 418 U.S. 405, 415 (1974).

[151] Vietnam Veterans Against the War/ Winter Soldier Organization v. Morton, 506 F. 2d. 53 (1974).

psychologist while on duty working with emotionally disturbed veterans;[152] and (3) the display of a Confederate Battle Flag in a public school where it fanned racial irritation that resulted in disruption and violence.[153]

However, the Court has been far less receptive to efforts of government to force citizens to participate in acts of symbolic speech, regardless of the merits of the cause. As far back as 1943, Justice Jackson, for the Court, wrote: "If there is any fixed star in our constitutional constellation, it is that no official, high or petty, can prescribe what shall be orthodox in politics, nationalism, religion, or other matters of opinion or force citizens to confess by word or act their faith therein."[154] In that opinion, delivered ironically enough on Flag Day, the Court struck down West Virginia's statute requiring students in the state's schools to salute the flag. This precedent furnished the basis for an order by a New York court invalidating the dismissal of classes by a city board of education in order to accommodate a war protest.[155] And recently, the Court held that this principle extends to protect from criminal sanctions the action of a Jehovah's Witness in covering up the state motto embossed on his license plate.[156]

Loyalty   Despite their doubtful efficacy, some legislatures have for years
Oaths   been enamored of the use of loyalty oaths as a means for combatting subversion.[157] Since some of the oaths require the oath-taker to affirm that he will not *advocate* overthrow of the government, on their face they constitute an abridgment of freedom of speech. Loyalty oaths have had a checkered career before the Supreme Court. That career was recently succinctly described by the Court itself when, in 1972, the Court endeavored to indicate what kinds of oaths were permissible and which impermissible and for what reasons. "We have made clear that neither federal nor state governments may condition employment on taking oaths which impinge rights guaranteed by the First and Fourteenth Amendments respectively, as for examples those relating to political beliefs. . . . Nor may employment be conditioned on an oath that one has not engaged, or will not engage, in protected speech activities such as the following: criticizing institutions of government; discussing political doctrine that approves the overthrow of certain forms of government; and supporting candidates for political office. . . . Employment may not be conditioned on an oath denying past, or abjuring future associational activities within constitutional protection; such protected activities include membership in organizations

[152] Smith *v*. U.S., 502 F. 2d. 512 (1974).

[153] Augustus *v*. School Bd. of Escambia County, Fla., 507 F. 2d. 152 (1975).

[154] West Virginia State Bd. of Educ. *v*. Barnette, 319 U.S. 624, 642 (1943). *See also* Cobb *v*. Beame, 402 F.Supp. 19 (1975).

[155] Nistad *v*. Bd. of Educ. of City of New York, 304 N.Y.S. 2d. 971 (1969).

[156] Wooley *v*. Maynard, 97 S.Ct. 1428 (1977).

[157] Chase, *Security and Liberty*, 60-61; A. W. Griswold, "Loyalty: An Issue of Academic Freedom," *New York Times Magazine*, Dec. 20, 1959, p. 18.

having illegal purposes unless one knows of the purpose and shares a specific intent to promote the illegal purpose. . . . And, finally, an oath may not be so vague that 'men of common intelligence must necessarily guess at its meaning and differ as to its application, [because such an oath] violates the first essential of due process of law.' . . . Several cases recently decided by the Court stand out among our oath cases because they have upheld the constitutionality of oaths, addressed to the future, promising constitutional support in broad terms. These cases have begun with a recognition that the Constitution itself prescribes comparable oaths in two articles [Article II, Section I, cl. 7, and Article VI, cl. 3]. . . ."[158]

First Amendment claims also came to the fore amid recent efforts to effect reform in the wake of several campaign finance scandals. Congress's post-Watergate effort to control campaign spending and contributions in the 1974 amendments to the Federal Election Campaign Act of 1971 by limiting contributions and expenditures was fractured severely by an important Supreme Court decision.[159] In what might first appear a paradox, the Court ruled that the act's contribution provisions are constitutional, but that the expenditure provisions violated the First Amendment. But, the Court explained: "By contrast with a limitation upon expenditures for political expression, a limitation upon the amount that any one person or group may contribute to a candidate or political committee entails only a marginal restriction upon the contributor's ability to engage in free communication. A contribution serves as a general expression of support for the candidate and his views, but does not communicate the underlying basis for the support." The Court then went on to add: "In sum, although the Act's contributions and expenditure limitations both implicate fundamental First Amendment interests, its expenditure ceilings impose significantly more severe restrictions on protected freedoms of political expression and association than do its limitations on financial contributions." In wrapping up its comprehensive decision with respect to the complex law, the Court wrote: "In summary, we sustain the individual contribution limits, the disclosure and reporting provisions and the public financing scheme. We conclude, however, that the limitations on campaign expenditures, on independent expenditures by individuals and groups, and on expenditures by a candidate from his personal funds are constitutionally infirm." (For a further discussion of constitutional dimensions to campaign, election, and patronage practices, *see* pp. 336-338.)

The Supreme Court also turned its attention to another knotty

Campaign Finance Reform and the First Amendment

[158] Cole *v.* Richardson, 405 U.S. 676, 680-681 (1972). *See also* Socialist Labor Party *v.* Gilligan, 406 U.S. 583 (1972).

[159] Buckley *v.* Valeo, 424 U.S. 1 (1976). *See also* Partido Nuevo Progresista *v.* Hernandez Colon, 415 F.Supp. 475 (1976). Federal courts have also upheld campaign disclosure acts against allegations that they infringed the right of privacy, *see* Fortson *v.* Weeks, 208 S.E. 2d. 68 (1974); Stoner *v.* Fortson, 379 F.Supp. 704 (1974); United States *v.* Finance Committee to Re-Elect the President, 507 F. 2d. 1194 (1974).

First Amendment problem, the constitutionality of limitations imposed on communication by mail where inmates of penal institutions are concerned. In striking down certain censorship of prisoner mail regulations issued by the California Department of Corrections, which among other things forbid inmates to "unduly complain" or "magnify grievances" or to "send or receive letters that pertain to criminal activity; are lewd, obscene, or defamatory . . . ," the Court took the occasion to spell out on what basis censorship of prisoner mail is justified. "First, the regulation or practice in question must further an important or substantial governmental interest unrelated to the suppression of expression. . . . Second, the limitation of First Amendment freedoms must be no greater than is necessary or essential to the protection of the particular governmental interest involved. . . ."[160]

Private
Abridg-
ments of
Free Speech
　　　One of the most distressing manifestations of protest on our college and university campuses of recent memory has been the shouting down of speakers and the use of other forms of derision to prevent people from speaking. Clearly, the First Amendment does not itself prohibit private persons from attempting to abridge Free Speech. At the same time, the Constitution does not forbid Government from endeavoring to insure that the freedom can be exercised. For example, a carefully drawn State law making it a crime to prevent any one from exercising his freedom of speech would not only be constitutional but seem highly desirable. In implementing such a law, care would have to be taken not to prevent protesters to a speech from exercising *their* freedom to speak. But this does not seem a hard practical problem, protesters could protest outside a meeting (exercising their freedom) but not inside someone else's meeting.

　　　Those better placed in society are often able to silence those with whom they disagree. Losing one's job because one has expressed certain opinions or because of one's lifestyle is nothing new. The reach of the Constitution to protect freedom of expression is sharply bounded, however, by whether the aggrieved individual is publicly or privately employed. With respect to public employment, the Court stated in Pickering *v.* Board of Education[161] that in each case the right to free speech would have to be balanced against the legitimate interest of government in promoting efficient public services taking into account two broad considerations: the character of the speech involved, and the potential such speech has for

[160] Procunier *v.* Martinez, 416 U.S. 396, 413 (1974). *See also* Hopkins *v.* Collins, 411 F.Supp. 831 (1975).
[161] 391 U.S. 563 (1968). However, as the Court later indicated in Mt. Healthy City School Dist. *v.* Doyle, 97 S.Ct. 568 (1977), the fact that constitutionally protected conduct played a part in the decision not to rehire a teacher does not end the matter. The Court held that the district court should have gone on to determine whether the school board had shown, by a preponderance of the evidence, that it would have reached a negative decision anyway without injection of the plaintiff's speech.

disrupting agency operations. Courts have sustained the free speech claims in numerous instances.[162] However, in one recent Supreme Court case, three Justices (with two others concurring in the result but not the reasoning) held that "in certain situations the discharge of a government employee may be based on his speech without offending guarantees of the First Amendment." The case involved a non-probationary Federal employee who was charged, among other things, with recklessly and publicly stating that one of his superiors had attempted a bribe.[163] A Federal appeals court has also upheld a Civil Service Commission's dismissal of a governmental employee who was a homosexual as proper because "under the facts of this case, the interest of the Government as an employer 'in promoting the efficiency of the public service' outweighed the interest of its employee in exercising his First Amendment rights through publicly flaunting and broadcasting his homosexual activities."[164]

As to private employment, on the other hand, a Federal district court upheld a private employer's action dismissing an employee because of his membership in the Ku Klux Klan.[165] And, as the results of a recent referendum in Dade County, Florida, show, there appeared to be considerable support in some quarters for denying homosexuals equal rights in jobs, housing, and public accommodations.[166]

The Framers of the First Amendment, of course, equated press and the printed word. But as radio, movies, and television became important parts of the so-called "media," the Court has expanded the meaning of "press" to cover them.

Freedom of the Press

By and large, freedom of the press has been co-extensive with freedom of speech. When the Court was using a special test like "bad tendency" or "clear and present danger," it applied it to all First Amendment freedoms. The special application of clear and

---

[162] See Alderman v. Philadelphia Housing Authority, 496 F. 2d. 164 (1974) (employees of a public housing authority); Rampey v. Allen, 501 F. 2d. 1090 (1974) (faculty members); Holodnak v. Avco Corp., 381 F.Supp. 191 (1974) (private employee); Ammond v. McGahn, 390 F.Supp. 655 (1975) (state senator excluded from caucus); Rodriguez v. Percell, 391 F.Supp. 38 (1975) (teachers and principals); Haurilak v. Kelley, 425 F.Supp. 626 (1977). *But see,* Williams v. Civil Service Com'n, 329 A. 2d. 556 (1974) (dog warden); Aycock v. Police Comm. of the Bd. of Aldermen of City of Atlanta, 212 S.E. 2d. 456 (1975) (policeman). Also, with regard to a State commissioner's power to "muzzle" members of his department, *see* Sussman v. Cowan, 376 F.Supp. 1000 (1974).

[163] Arnett v. Kennedy, 416 U.S. 134 (1974).

[164] Singer v. U.S. Civil Service Com'n, 530 F. 2d. 247 (1976).

[165] Bellamy v. Mason's Stores, Inc., 368 F.Supp. 1025 (1973).

[166] See *New York Times,* June 8, 1977. The Miami vote, which ran about 2-1 in favor of repealing an equal rights ordinance for homosexuals was the first referendum on equal rights for homosexuals in any major U.S. city. Interestingly enough, these results contrast sharply with recent Harris Poll data that shows that 54 per cent of a national sample "would favor a law banning 'discrimination against homosexuals in any job for which they are qualified.' Twenty-eight percent would oppose such a law." *Minneapolis Star,* July 18, 1977.

present danger to the press came in a series of cases where the Court upheld members of the press against contempt charges laid on them by irate judges whom they had criticized.[167] There are, however, several constitutional doctrines which have been specially tailored to meet problems peculiar to the operation of a Free Press. The first of these is the doctrine of no prior restraints which basically forbids censorship of the press *previous* to publication. Although there have been instances where the Supreme Court has upheld a previous restraint, it is rare.[168] As recently as the Pentagon Papers case, the Supreme Court took for granted that "any system of prior restraint of expression comes to this Court bearing a heavy presumption against its constitutional validity."[169] Chief Justice Warren has spelled out the special vice of prior censorship in this way: "The censor performs free from all the procedural safeguards afforded litigants in a court of law."[170] The doctrine does not preclude holding members of the press responsible for what they do. Once they do something allegedly illegal, they can be so charged and tried. But in all save unusual circumstances, they must be permitted to publish, exhibit or broadcast.

Prior Restraint   A bevy of recent Supreme Court decisions have dealt with governmental regulation in a variety of circumstances where it was alleged such regulation amounted to prior restraint. The Supreme Court decided in 1973 that the application to a newspaper of the Human Relations Ordinance of the City of Pittsburgh aimed at ending discrimination was constitutional. Emphasizing that they were deciding the case on very narrow grounds, a majority held "that the Commission's [on Human Relations] modified order, narrowly drawn to prohibit placement in sex-designated columns of advertisements for non-exempt job opportunities, does not infringe the First Amendment rights of the Pittsburgh Press."[171] The lineup of the Court in this decision is intriguing. Powell, Brennan, White, Marshall, and Rehnquist constituted the majority; the dissenters were Burger, Douglas, Stewart, and Blackmun. Justice Douglas saw the issue in these terms: "there can be no valid law censoring the press or punishing it for publishing its views or the views of subscribers or customers who express their ideas in letters to the editor or in want ads or other commercial spaces"[172] unless it in someway was "closely brigaded" with illegal action.

[167] Bridges *v.* California, 314 U.S. 252 (1941); Pennekamp *v.* Florida, 328 U.S. 331 (1946); Craig *v.* Harney, 331 U.S. 367 (1947).
[168] Times Film Corp. *v.* Chicago, 365 U.S. 43 (1961).
[169] New York Times Co. *v.* U.S., 403 U.S. 713 (1971).
[170] Times Film Corp. *v.* Chicago, 365 U.S. 43, 68 (1961) As to another kind of censorship problem, the Supreme Court recently held that the city of West Palm Beach could not foreclose the use of its auditorium for a production of "Hair" since the auditorium was used for other productions. Southeastern Productions Ltd. *v.* Conrad, 420 U.S. 546 (1975).
[171] Pittsburgh Press Co. *v.* The Pittsburgh Com'n on Human Relations, 413 U.S. 376, 391 (1973).
[172] *Ibid.*, 398.

In view of the controversy it provoked the following Term, it was surprising that the Supreme Court handed down a *unanimous* decision in the case involving the issue of whether or not "a state statute granting a political candidate a right to equal space to reply to criticism and attacks on his record by a newspaper violates the guarantees of a free press."[173] Chief Justice Burger writing for the Court concluded that: "Even if a newspaper would face no additional costs to comply with a compulsory access law and would not be forced to forego publication of news or opinion by the inclusion of a reply, the Florida statute fails to clear the barriers of the First Amendment because of its intrusion into the function of editors."[174]

To the contention that freedom of the press was abridged by the provision in the California Department of Corrections Manual forbidding face-to-face interviews between press representatives and individual inmates whom they specifically name and request to interview, the Supreme Court answered: "It is one thing to say that a journalist is free to seek out sources of information not available to members of the general public, that he is entitled to some constitutional protection of the confidentiality of such sources, . . . and that government cannot restrain the publication of news emanating from such sources. . . . It is quite another thing to suggest that the Constitution imposes upon government the affirmative duty to make available to journalists sources of information not available to members of the public generally. That proposition finds no support in the words of the Constitution or in any decision of this Court."[175]

In 1975, the Supreme Court decided a case involving the constitutionality of a Jacksonville, Florida, ordinance that placed a total ban on the showing of films with any nudity from exhibition at drive-in movie theaters where the screen might be visible from a public place or street. The Court, by a 6-3 vote, rejected the city's arguments in behalf of the ordinance: (1) as a protection against exposure of offensive materials to unwilling citizens; (2) as an exercise of the police power to protect children; and (3) as a traffic regulation. Speaking for the majority, Justice Powell found the ordinance overbroad in its absolute prohibition of all nudity and not

---

[173] Miami Herald Publishing Co. *v.* Tornillo, 418 U.S. 241, 243 (1974). New York's "Fair Campaign Code," which banned certain speech altogether, such as personal and ethnic slurs, met a similar fate, 401 F.Supp. 87 (1975).

[174] *Ibid.*, 258. In another case along the same lines, the Court held that a city which operates a public transit system and sells advertising space on its vehicles is not required by the First and Fourteenth Amendments to accept paid political advertising on behalf of a candidate for public office. Lehman *v.* City of Shaker Heights, 418 U.S. 298 (1974). *See also* a Federal district court decision upholding the Chicago Transit Authority's refusal to post paid advertisements calling for the impeachment of the President, Impeach Nixon Comm. *v.* Buck, 498 F. 2d. 37 (1974).

[175] Pell, *et al. v.* Procunier, 417 U.S. 817, 834 (1974). *See also* Saxbe *v.* Washington Post Co., 417 U.S. 843 (1974). *See also* KQED, Inc. *v.* Houchins, 546 F. 2d. 284 (1976) and the opinion of Justice Rehnquist as Circuit Justice, 97 S.Ct. 773.

easily subject to a narrower interpretation that might save it constitutionally. Said Justice Powell, "[T]he deterrent effect of this ordinance is both real and substantial. Since it applies specifically to all persons employed by or connected with drive-in theaters, the owners and operators of these theaters are faced with an unwelcome choice: to avoid prosecution of themselves and their employees they must either restrict their movie offerings or construct adequate protective fencing which may be extremely expensive or even physically impracticable."[176] Objecting to the "rigidly simplistic approach" of the majority, Chief Justice Burger, joined by Justice Rehnquist dissented and faulted the decision for its insensitivity to the circumstances at hand, particularly the "highly intrusive and distracting effect" such a display could have on passing motorists. Justice White also dissented, focusing on the offensiveness of nudity to the captive viewer on a public street.[177]

The Court, however, did sustain Detroit zoning ordinances aimed at dispersing "adult" theaters as well as keeping them out of residential areas.[178] Evidently, the Court meant it when it said, "what is ultimately at stake is nothing more than a limitation on the place where adult films may be exhibited," for it went on carefully to say in a footnote: "The situation would be quite different if the ordinance had the effect of suppressing, or greatly restricting access to, lawful speech. Here, however, the District Court specifically found that 'the Ordinances do not affect the operation of existing establishments but only the location of new ones. There are myriad locations in the City of Detroit which must be over 1000 feet from existing establishments. This burden on First Amendment rights is slight.'"

A final case in which the Court addressed allegations of prior restraint involved the validity of a Georgia statute making it an offense to report the name of a victim in a rape case. The statute was questioned in a case where a rape victim's father sought damages for invasion of privacy in a civil suit and asserted that the statute

---

[176] Erznoznik v. Jacksonville, 422 U.S. 205, 217 (1975). (*Cf.* Rabe v. Washington, 405 U.S. 313 [1972].) Without reaching the merits, the Court also sustained an injunction against an ordinance which placed a ban on *all* "topless" dancing. Doran v. Salem Inn, Inc., 422 U.S. 922 (1975). Unlike the narrower prohibition upheld earlier in California v. La Rue, 409 U.S. 109 (1972), where "topless" dancing was prohibited in establishments serving liquor, the Court held that the *total* ban in *Salem Inn* was overbroad.

And, on a related matter, lower courts have had little difficulty in upholding bans on nude bathing at public beaches. *See* Williams v. Kleppe, 539 F. 2d. 803 (1976), *and* Eckl v. Davis, 124 Cal.Rptr. 685 (1975).

[177] *Ibid.*, 218, 224. Justice Douglas concurred in the opinion of the Court, but the problem of the captive viewer, or more accurately the problem of the captive auditor, prompted Justice Douglas over twenty years ago to favor the right of privacy as against upholding the constitutionality of fixed-tuned radio broadcasting on public transportation. *See* Pollak v. Public Utilities Com'n, 343 U.S. 451, 467-469 (1952) (dissenting opinion of Justice Douglas).

[178] Young v. American Mini Theatres, Inc., 427 U.S. 50 (1976). McKinney v. Alabama, 424 U.S. 669 (1976).

represented public policy. Speaking for the Court, Justice White held that the State could not impose sanctions on the accurate publication of a rape victim's name where such information was obtained from public records relevant to a public prosecution and which were open to public inspection on demand.[179]

Two Federal court decisions are worth noting with respect to prior restraint. In an opinion that captures the animosity between the press and the Nixon Administration, a district court held that failure of the Secret Service to devise, publicize, and use narrow, specific, and uniform guidelines for the issuance of White House press passes infringed the First Amendment rights of reporters denied the passes.[180] Further, a district court sitting in Dallas has struck down a Texas statute placing an absolute ban on access of news media not only to "death row" but to the execution chamber itself. The court held that, under the First Amendment, the State was required to permit one television reporter *with his camera* to witness any execution.[181]

The Court, has had considerable difficulty defining what it was that the State and national governments had the right to censor. Obscenity proved a very elusive concept for the Court from the beginning, largely because the Court failed to offer any justification for its suppression (and thus provided no foundation for the standards it enunciated) beyond its superficial conclusion that obscenity is not protected by the First Amendment because, unlike speech, it is without redeeming social importance.[182] The Justices incrementally developed a tripartite standard[183] based upon what they discerned as the elements common to all types of obscenity, an approach which produced the conclusion that the Court, in effect, sought to proscribe only "hard-core pornography."[184] Because of its serious shortcomings, however, this initial tack was modified in favor of a variable approach.[185] Though the Court retained the standards which had evolved, it significantly modified their application by hinging its judgment on two contextual factors: the primary audience to whom the material was directed[186] and the na-

Obscenity

---

[179] Cox Broadcasting Corp. *v.* Cohn, 420 U.S. 469 (1975).

[180] Forcade *v.* Knight, 416 F.Supp. 1025 (1976). Equally revealing were lower court cases that discussed the rights of protesters to demonstrate when the President came to town. *See* Sparrow *v.* Goodman, 361 F.Supp. 566 (1973); Farber *v.* Rizzo, 363 F.Supp. 386 (1973); Butler *v.* U.S., 365 F.Supp. 1035 (1973); Glasson *v.* City of Louisville, 518 F. 2d. 899 (1975). *See also* the *Quaker Action Group* cases cited in *Forcade*.

[181] Garrett *v.* Estelle, 424 F.Supp. 468 (1977).

[182] Roth *v.* U.S., 354 U.S. 476, 484 (1957).

[183] Roth *v.* U.S., 354 U.S. 476 (1957); Manual Ent. *v.* Day, 370 U.S. 478 (1962); Jacobellis *v.* Ohio, 378 U.S. 184 (1964); Memoirs *v.* Atty. Gen., 383 U.S. 413 (1966).

[184] William B. Lockhart and Robert C. McClure, "Censorship of Obscenity: The Developing Constitutional Standards," 45 *Minnesota Law Review*, 5, 58-68 (1960).

[185] For the authoritative discussion of the concepts of "constant" and "variable" obscenity, *see ibid.*, at 68 *et seq.*

[186] Mishkin *v.* N.Y., 383 U.S. 502 (1966); Ginsberg *v.* N.Y., 390 U.S. 629 (1968).

ture of the appeal made to that audience.[187] The Court thus came around to the view, articulated earlier by Chief Justice Warren,[188] that obscenity is a relative concept. Even the application of the Court's variable approach came to be tempered by considerations of place: obscene material possessed privately was beyond the reach of legal sanction.[189]

The Burger Court's rulings of 1973, however, constituted major revisions in the law of obscenity and, some observers thought, brought the Court back to where it stood with *Roth* a decade and a half before. Chief Justice Burger, speaking for the majority in a 5-4 decision, reviewed the "somewhat tortured history" of the Court's obscenity decisions and stated: "This much has been categorically settled by the Court, that obscene material is unprotected by the First Amendment. . . . We acknowledge, however, the inherent dangers of undertaking to regulate any form of expression. State statutes designed to regulate obscene materials must be carefully limited." The Chief Justice then went on to explain what the States could do by way of regulation: "We now confine the permissible scope of such regulation to works which depict or describe *sexual conduct*. That conduct must be specifically defined by the applicable state law as written or authoritatively construed. A state offense must also be limited to works which, taken as a whole, appeal to the prurient interest in sex, which portray sexual conduct in a patently offensive way, and which, *taken as a whole*, do not have serious literary, artistic, political, or scientific value."[190] (Emphasis supplied.) The majority explicitly rejected the "*utterly* without redeeming social value" of Memoirs *v.* Massachusetts, pointing out that "that concept has never commanded the adherence of more than three Justices at one time." As to the guidelines for the triers of fact in obscenity cases, the Court held "that obscenity is to be determined by applying 'contemporary community standards' . . . not national standards.' "[191] In a powerful dissent in one of the cases, Justice Brennan wrote: "In short, while I cannot say the interest of the State—apart from the question of juveniles and unconsenting adults—are trivial or nonexistent, I am compelled to conclude that these interests cannot justify the substantial damage to constitutional rights and to this Nation's judicial machinery that inevitably results from state efforts to bar the distribution even of unprotected material to consenting adults. . . . I would hold, therefore, that at least in the absence of distribution to juveniles or obtrusive

---

[187] Ginzburg *v.* U.S., 383 U.S. 463 (1966). Even following its substantial revision of obscenity standards in 1973, the Court continued to say "evidence of pandering to prurient interests in the creation, promotion, or dissemination of material is relevant in determining whether the material is obscene." Splawn *v.* Calif., 97 S.Ct. 1987 (1977).

[188] Roth *v.* U.S., 354 U.S. 476, 495-496 (1957).

[189] Stanley *v.* Ga., 394 U.S. 557 (1969).

[190] Miller *v.* California, 413 U.S. 15, 23-24 (1973). *See also* Paris Adult Theatre I *v.* Slaton, 413 U.S. 49 (1973); Kaplan *v.* California, 413 U.S. 115 (1973).

[191] *Ibid.*, 24-25.

exposure to unconsenting adults, the First and Fourteenth Amendments prohibit the state and federal governments from attempting wholly to suppress sexually oriented materials on the basis of their allegedly 'obscene' contents. Nothing in this approach precludes those governments from taking action to serve what may be strong and legitimate interests through regulation of the *manner of distribution* of sexually oriented materials."[192] (Emphasis supplied.)

The Court also held that carrying obscene materials in interstate commerce for personal use was not the same as possessing such materials in one's own home and was, consequently, subject to congressional regulations.[193] On the other side of the ledger, the Court held that an allegedly obscene movie could not be seized at a commercial movie house without "a constitutionally sufficient warrant," even where the law officer viewed the film himself. The Court held that such a seizure was unreasonable "because prior restraint of the right of expression, whether by books or films, calls for a higher hurdle in the evaluation of reasonableness."[194]

Following its 1973 decisions on obscenity, the Court was constrained the following Term to elaborate them in two cases. The Court explained that "What *Miller* makes clear is that state juries need not be instructed to apply 'national standards.' . . . *Miller* held that it was constitutionally permissible to permit juries to rely on the understanding of the community from which they came as to contemporary community standards, and the States have considerable latitude in framing statutes under this element of the *Miller* decision. A State may choose to define an obscenity offense in terms of 'contemporary community standards' as defined in *Miller* without further specification, as was done here, or it may choose to define the standards in more precise geographic terms, as was done by California in *Miller*." But the Court went on to warn that in *Miller* "we made it plain under that holding 'no one will be subject to prosecution for the sale or exposure of obscene materials unless these materials depict or describe patently offensive "hard core" sexual conduct. . . .' "[195] The Court also reasserted that the "contemporary community standards formulation applied to federal legislation."[196] As might have been anticipated, the Court has been inundated with appeals testing various State standards, but it has side-stepped many of them, repeatedly invoking the devotion to "Our Federalism" as extolled by Justice Black in Younger *v.* Harris[197] to bar Federal injunctive relief against State criminal proceed-

---

[192] Paris Adult Theatre I *v.* Slaton, 413 U.S. 49, 112-113 (1973).

[193] U.S. *v.* Orito, 413 U.S. 139 (1973) *and* U.S. *v.* 12,200 Ft. Reels, 413 U.S. 123 (1973).

[194] Roaden *v.* Kentucky, 413 U.S. 496 (1973). *Cf.* Heller *v.* New York, 413 U.S. 483 (1973).

[195] Jenkins *v.* Georgia, 418 U.S. 153, 157, 160 (1974).

[196] Hamling *v.* U.S., 418 U.S. 87, 103-106 (1974).

[197] 401 U.S. 37 (1971).

ings unless there are "extraordinary circumstances."[198] Such continuous revision of standards has given rise to problems of fairness and notice for those whose cases were pending when new standards were announced. Speaking to this issue in a very recent case,[199] the Court held that retroactive application of its 1973 decision in *Miller* was precluded by the Fifth Amendment (as a denial of due process) to the extent that the standards announced in that case imposed criminal liability for conduct not punishable under the standards articulated in *Memoirs*.

Libel   Consistent with its general application of the preferred freedoms doctrine to open up discussion in the political system, the Warren Court sought to reduce the chilling effects of State libel laws. It acted initially to broaden what might be considered "fair comment" about a public official by insisting that awards for damage to his reputation be predicated on more than a showing of factual inaccuracy in the statements made. Statutes allowing such compensation would be sustained only if a false statement were made with " 'actual malice'—that is, with knowledge that it was false or with reckless disregard of whether it was false or not."[200] In addition, the Court expanded press immunity in this area by enlarging the concept of public official to include "public figures" who were "involved in issues in which the public has a justified and important interest."[201] Aside from the vagueness inherent in these terms, the Court's expansive holding created severe conflict with the correlative right to privacy.[202]

[198] Huffman v. Pursue, Ltd., 420 U.S. 592 (1975).

[199] Marks v. U.S., 430 U.S. 188 (1977). Specifically, the Court ruled that the defendants were entitled to jury instructions requiring acquittal unless the materials were *utterly* without redeeming social importance. However, the Court added, if the principles announced in *Miller* would benefit the defendants, they were entitled to have those principles applied.

[200] New York Times Co. v. Sullivan, 376 U.S. 254 (1964).

[201] Curtis Pub. Co. v. Butts, 388 U.S. 130, 134 (1967); *see also* Associated Press v. Walker, considered together with the Curtis Publishing case; Rosenblatt v. Baer, 383 U.S. 75 (1966); Time, Inc. v. Hill, 385 U.S. 374 (1967); Pickering v. Bd. of Educ., 391 U.S. 563 (1968).

[202] Time, Inc. v. Hill, 385 U.S. 374 (1967). Though this was an invasion of privacy case and not a libel case, the Court relied heavily on its previous construction of "malice" in *New York Times* to assess whether or not the defendant publisher had knowingly or recklessly fictionalized the story about the Hill family so as to put them in a "false light." In a second "false light" case seven years later, Cantrell v. Forest City Publishing Co., 419 U.S. 245 (1974) in which a suit was brought over the publication of an article that depicted the impact on a West Virginia family from the death of the father in a bridge collapse, the Court upheld a jury award of *compensatory* damages to people about whom "knowing or reckless falsehoods" were published. In doing so, the Court made an important distinction about definitions of "malice" and how they impact on claims for *compensatory* and *punitive* damages in libel suits. According to the Court, there is the definition which the Supreme Court itself developed in the *New York Times* case: "actual malice" is "with knowledge that [a defamatory statement] was false or with reckless disregard of whether it was false or not." This definition, the Court said, "is a term of art, created to provide a convenient shorthand for the standard of liability that must be established before a State may constitutionally permit *public officials* to recover for libel in actions brought

Backing off from a 1971 decision that had taken the *New York Times* rule to the limit of its logic (that is, the rule had been expanded so as to apply the "fair comment" exception to cases involving private individuals caught up in matters of public interest),[203] the Court, in Gertz v. Robert Welch, Inc.,[204] held that the *New York Times* rule regarding fair comment did not extend to individuals who were neither public officials nor public figures. Though the Court's decision allowed such private individuals to collect damages under a standard something less than "actual malice," it did make clear that: (1) states may not allow damages to be recovered without a showing of some kind of fault; and (2) "the private defamation plaintiff who establishes liability under a less demanding standard than that stated by *New York Times* may recover only such damages as are sufficient to compensate him for actual injury" (though the Court left the door open to the collection of punitive damages also but under a much stiffer standard).

The Court also went on to point out that a private individual could become a public figure (and thus bring the *New York Times* rule into play) if: (1) he "achieve[s] such pervasive fame or notoriety that he becomes a public figure for all purposes in all contexts"; or (2) he "voluntarily injects himself or is drawn into a particular public controversy and thereby becomes a public figure for a limited range of issues." Considering Gertz's involvement against this background, the Court, per Justice Powell speaking for a bare majority, concluded: "In this context it is plain that petitioner was not a public figure."[205]

---

against publishers." As such, "it is quite different from the common-law standard of 'malice' generally required under state tort law to support an award of punitive damages. In a false-light case, common law malice, frequently expressed in terms of either personal ill will toward the plaintiff or reckless or wanton disregard of the plaintiff's rights—would focus on the defendant's attitude toward the plaintiff's privacy, not towards the truth or falsity of the material published." (Emphasis supplied.) For a discussion of other privacy cases, see note 205.

[203] Rosenbloom v. Metromedia, 403 U.S. 29.

[204] 418 U.S. 323 (1974).

[205] Is a performer who gives a public performance such a "public figure," and is he thus deprived of any redress if his entire act is recorded by the media and broadcast on a television news program? Answering "no," the Court declared that where the "entire act" (lasting 15 seconds) had been filmed and aired, the plaintiff (who was shot out of a cannon into a net 200 feet away) was deprived of the "right to the publicity value of his performance." Zacchini v. Scripps-Howard Broadcasting Co., 435 U.S. 562 (1977). *See also* Floyd Abrams, "The Press, Privacy and the Constitution," *New York Times Magazine*, Aug. 21, 1977. And, in the final round of the extraordinary *Galella* case involving suit by Jackie Onassis against an intrepid photographer bent on filming her every move, and his countersuit for false arrest, malicious prosecution, and interference with the practice of his trade, a U.S court of appeals has upheld an injunction against his harassment of her, but has markedly reduced the distance between them he was ordered to maintain. Galella v. Onassis, 487 F. 2d. 986 (1973). The courts have also held that corporations are "public figures" for purposes of defamation suits, *see* Martin Marietta Corp. v. Evening Star Newspaper, 417 F.Supp. 947 (1976); *and* Trans World Accounts, Inc. v. Associated Press, 425 F.Supp. 814 (1977).

The Court's most recent libel ruling was Time, Inc. *v.* Firestone.[206] When Mary Alice Firestone won a $100,000 libel judgment against *Time* for reporting that her husband had been granted a divorce on grounds of extreme cruelty and adultery, *Time* took the case to the Supreme Court contending that under the ruling in New York Times Co. *v.* Sullivan it could not be "liable for publishing any falsehood unless it is established that the publication was made 'with actual malice.'" *Time* also contended that Mrs. Firestone was a "public figure." The Supreme Court explicitly rejected these arguments, saying that she was not a public figure simply by virtue of going through judicial proceedings. The Court pointed out that she had to go to court and that she did not "freely choose to publicize issues as to the propriety of her married life." Nor did the Court accept the argument that the *New York Times* privilege should extend to all judicial proceedings. In conclusion the Court said: "And while participants in some litigation may be legitimate 'public figures,' either generally or for the limited purposes of that litigation, the majority will more likely resemble respondent [Mrs. Firestone], drawn into a public forum largely against their will in order to attempt to obtain the only redress available to them or to defend themselves against actions brought by the State or others. There appears little reason why these individuals should substantially forfeit that degree of protection which the law of defamation would otherwise afford them simply by virtue of their being drawn into a courtroom." The Court specifically invoked its previous decision in Gertz *v.* Robert Welch, Inc.

In another case with a defamation issue, the Court held that the circulation of a flyer labeled "active shoplifters" and bearing the picture and name of a man who had been arrested for shoplifting did not do violence to the individual's right to privacy.[207] It pointed out that the weight of previous decisions "establishes no constitutional doctrine converting every defamation by a public official into a deprivation of liberty within the meaning of the Due Process Clauses of Fifth or Fourteenth Amendments." With respect to right to privacy guaranteed by the First, Fourth, Fifth, Ninth and Fourteenth Amendments and the claim that "the State may not publicize a record of an official act such as an arrest," the Court rejoined: "None of our substantive privacy decisions hold this or anything like this, and we decline to enlarge them in this manner."

In several related press-privacy conflict cases lower Federal and State courts upheld published or televised accounts of: (1) the Rosenberg spy trial;[208] (2) the safety hazards and resulting fatalities

[206] 424 U.S. 448 (1976).
[207] Paul *v.* Davis, 424 U.S. 693 (1976). *See also* Tennessean Newspaper, Inc., *v.* Levi, 403 F.Supp. 1318 (1975).
[208] Meeropol *v.* Nizer, 381 F.Supp. 29 (1974). The book, *The Implosion Conspiracy*, was also the subject of a copyright infringement suit, *see* Gardner *v.* Nizer, 391 F.Supp. 940 (1975).

arising from defective products sold by certain crib[209] and furnace[210] manufacturers; and (3) the arrest of a suspect who was taken from his home in the nude.[211] Moreover, a Federal district court has held, in disposing of a libel suit brought against millionaire tycoon Howard Hughes, that the First Amendment absolutely bars the recovery of *punitive* damages in a defamation suit where the plaintiff is a public figure and liability is predicated on actual malice because of the "chilling effect" of such a sanction.[212] Finally, the Delaware Supreme Court decided that a proposed State law requiring that newspaper editorials be signed would constitute an unconstitutional abridgment of freedom of the press.[213]

The Supreme Court in a 1975 decision rejected the proposition that "the First Amendment guarantees of speech and press are inapplicable to paid commercial advertisements."[214] Speaking for the seven-man majority in a case involving the validity of a Virginia statute that made the circulation of advertisements for abortion services a misdemeanor, Justice Blackmun held that the advertisements at issue "did more than simply propose a commercial transaction. It contained factual material of clear 'public interest.' " Insofar, then, as the Virginia law barred advertisements with such informative material, it infringed legitimate First Amendment expression. Justice Blackmun observed: "[A] court may not escape the task of assessing the First Amendment interest at stake and weighing it against the public interest allegedly served by the regulation. The diverse motives, means, and messages of advertising may make 'speech' commercial in widely varying degrees." Justice Rehnquist, joined by Justice White, dissented. Given that "Virginia's interest in this statute lies in preventing commercial exploitation of the health needs of its citizens," he concluded, "the statute in question is a 'reasonable regulation that serves a legitimate public interest.' "

Commercial Speech

Acknowledging that, in its decision in *Bigelow*, "the notion of unprotected 'commercial speech' all but passed from the scene," the Court, in a second Virginia case, took up an attack on the constitutionality of the State's total ban on advertising the prices of prescription drugs. The Court held that the First Amendment protected the communication of price information *alone* without being accompanied by the report of a "newsworthy fact" or "generalized observations even about commercial transactions." The Court concluded: "What is at issue is whether a State may completely sup-

---

[209] American Broadcasting Co. *v.* Smith Cabinet Manufac. Co., 312 N.E. 2d. 85 (1974).

[210] Aafco Heating and Air Conditioning Co. *v.* Northwest Publications, Inc., 321 N.E. 2d. 580 (1974).

[211] Taylor *v.* KTVB, Inc., 525 P. 2d. 984 (1974).

[212] Maheu *v.* Hughes Tool Co., 384 F.Supp. 166 (1974).

[213] *In re* Opinion of the Justices, 324 A. 2d. 211 (1974).

[214] Bigelow *v.* Va., 421 U.S. 809, 822, 826 (1975).

press the dissemination of concededly truthful information about entirely lawful activity, fearful of that information's effect upon its disseminators and its recipients. Reserving other questions, we conclude the answer to this one is in the negative." In an important footnote, the Court stressed that they were expressing "no opinions as to other professions," suggesting that different professions "may require consideration of quite different factors."[215]

The following Term, the Court did indeed consider advertising in one of the "other professions." Relying on the preceding decisions, the Court held that lawyers may constitutionally advertise the prices at which they will perform certain routine services.[216] After considering a half-dozen arguments offered by the State to support a total ban on advertising by attorneys, the Court found none of them sufficient to support Arizona's total proscription of this variety of commercial speech; however, the Court left the door open for more precisely drawn limitations by the State: "[W]e, of course, do not hold that advertising by attorneys may not be regulated in any way."

Congressional Control of the Press

Congress has some special controls with respect to the press by virtue of its control of the mails. Few newspapers or periodicals can profitably circulate except locally unless they enjoy the "second class privilege," that is, the privilege of specially low rates—and this privilege, being a gratuity, is under the nearly absolute control of Congress, notwithstanding which Congress's delegate in the matter, the Postmaster General, may not, in carrying out Congress's expressed will that the privilege be confined to publications "originated and published for the dissemination of information of a public character, or devoted to literature, the sciences, arts, or some special industry," set himself up as a censor, for if he does the Court will overrule him and bring his decrees to naught.[217] Moreover, Congress may banish from the mails altogether, as well as from the channels of interstate commerce, obscene and fraudulent matter.[218] For there can be no right to circulate what there is no right to publish, circulation indeed being only an incident of publication. Nor, as we have seen, is it an invasion of freedom of the press to require a news-gathering agency to treat its employees in the same way as other employers are required to treat theirs; or to subject it to the anti-monopoly provisions of the Sherman Anti-Trust Act.[219]

[215] Va. St. Bd. of Pharm. *v.* Va. Cit. Cons. Council, 425 U.S. 748 (1976).

[216] Bates *v.* State Bar of Ariz., 433 U.S. 350 (1977).

[217] United States *ex rel.* Milwaukee Soc. Dem. Pub. Co. *v.* Burleson, 255 U.S. 407 (1921), and cases there cited; Hannegan *v.* Esquire, Inc., 327 U.S 146 (1946); 39 U.S.C. 4354.

[218] *In re* Rapier, 143 U.S. 110 (1892); Public Clearing House *v.* Coyne, 194 U.S. 497 (1904); Lewis Pub. Co. *v.* Morgan, 229 U.S. 288 (1913). 39 U.S.C. 4001; Ginzburg *v.* U.S., 383 U.S. 463 (1966).

[219] Associated Press *v.* NLRB, 301 U.S. 103 (1937); Associated Press *v.* U.S., 326 U.S. 1 (1945). In 1972, a U.S. court of appeals upheld a provision of the Civil Rights Act prohibiting publishing discriminatory notices regarding sale or rental of hous-

As Justice White, speaking for the Court, explained: "The Federal Communications Commission has for many years imposed on radio and television broadcasters the requirement that discussion of public issues be presented on broadcast stations, and that each side of those issues must be given fair coverage. This is known as the fairness doctrine, which originated very early in the history of broadcasting and has maintained its present outlines for some time. It is an obligation whose content has been defined in a long series of FCC rulings in particular cases, and which is distinct from the statutory requirement of . . . the Communications Act of 1934, 48 Stat. 1081, as amended 47 U.S.C. 301 that equal time be allotted all qualified candidates for public office."[220]

The Constitutionality of the "Equal Time" and the "Fairness" Doctrines

In a challenge to the constitutionality of the "fairness doctrine" in 1969 the Court held: "In view of the scarcity of broadcast frequencies, the Government's role in allocating those frequencies, and the legitimate claims of those unable without governmental assistance to gain access to those frequencies for expression of their views, we hold the regulations and ruling at issue here are both authorized by statute and constitutional."[221] In the course of its opinion, the Court also made clear it held the equal-time requirement constitutional also.[222] Needless to say, implementation of these doctrines is fraught with difficulties, a fact recognized by the Federal Communications Commission. Significantly, on June 11, 1971, the Commission released a Notice of Inquiry "instituting a broad-ranging study of the Fairness Doctrine and related public interest policies" and later ordered that panel discussions be held in Washington, D.C., for a three-day period commencing March 27, 1972, and that oral argument be held "before the Commission 'en banc' on March 30, 1972."[223] On June 22, 1972, the Commission issued its first report providing some guidelines for broadcasters but raising more problems than it resolved and pointing to where Congress might take appropriate action to resolve some of the issues discussed.[224]

In a complicated case involving complaints of the Democratic National Committee and the Business Executives' Move for Vietnam Peace that radio station WTOP of Washington, D.C., would not sell advertising time to them to speak out on issues, the Supreme Court once more spoke on the fairness doctrine. The Court reiterated its position that "under the Fairness Doctrine broadcasters are responsible for providing the listening and viewing public with access to a balanced presentation of information on

---

ing. U.S. *v.* Hunter, 459 F. 2d. 205 (1972). A Federal appeals court has recently directed the FCC to formulate divestiture rules, in addition to the agency's proposed rules, barring a single company from owning both a newspaper and a broadcasting station in the same town unless it is clearly in the public interest. *See* Washington *Post,* Mar. 2, 1977.

[220] Red Lion Broadcasting Co. *v.* FCC, 395 U.S. 367, 369-370 (1969).
[221] *Ibid.,* 400-401.   [222] *Ibid.,* 391.
[223] 37 *Fed. Reg.* 4978 (1972).   [224] 37 *Fed. Reg.* 12744 (1972).

issues of public importance.[225] But the Court held that the doctrine need not be applied to editorial advertising and that the question of a broadcaster's fairness was to be determined, when appropriate to do so, by his overall performance. And in a recent development on the fairness doctrine, the Federal Communications Commission rejected a proposal to require broadcasters to provide air time to listeners who object to commercials: "We do not believe that the fairness doctrine provides an appropriate vehicle for the correction of false advertising." But the FCC could "see no reason" why the doctrine should not apply to commercials that consist of commentary on public issues.[226]

Further, the U.S. Court of Appeals for the District of Columbia, in an important decision interpreting the fairness doctrine as bearing upon "the question of good faith, not news judgment" used by a broadcaster, overturned an FCC ruling requiring NBC to air favorable material on private pension plans to counterbalance alleged bias in a highly critical documentary, "Pensions: The Broken Promise," which it broadcasted in 1972.[227] Asserting the accuracy, good faith and essential constitutional freedoms behind its investigative journalism, the broadcasting company had argued that if all the negative findings it reported on the injustices of many private pension plans were not rebutted by affirmative material, it was because many of the pension problems were clear-cut.[228]

A thoughtful and unusually well-balanced assessment of the fairness doctrine, rich in illustrations, is Fred W. Friendly's *The Good Guys, The Bad Guys and the First Amendment: Free Speech vs. Fairness in Broadcasting*.[229] Published in 1975, it is especially valuable for the insights it offers from a seasoned practitioner.

Finally, in a particularly noteworthy development unrelated to the fairness doctrine but bearing on the FCC's power to supervise the content of television programs, a Federal district court struck down "the family hour," an effort to reduce the level of sex and violence on "prime time" shows.[230] In a revealing and comprehensive 99-page opinion, the district judge wrote: "Indeed the record in this case unmistakably demonstrates that the policy as enacted is so vague that no one can adequately define it." The court went on to hold "that unless the Commission enacts valid regulations giving fair notice to licensees of what is expected, the Commission has no authority to use the licensing process to control the depiction of

[225] Columbia Broadcasting Sys., Inc. *v.* Democratic Nat. Comm., 412 U.S. 94, 112 (1973). The FCC has voted to exclude Presidential and Vice-Presidential candidates from the operation of the rule. *See* Washington *Star*, July 27, 1977.

[226] Minneapolis *Star*, July 3, 1974.

[227] Nat'l Broadcasting Co. *v.* FCC, 516 F. 2d. 1101 (1974), *cert. denied* 424 U.S. 910 (1976).

[228] *See San Diego Union*, Feb. 25, 1975; and Tom Wicker, "Freedom Is The Issue," *New York Times*, Sept. 29, 1974.

[229] (New York: Random House.)

[230] Writers Guild of America, West, Inc. *v.* FCC, 423 F.Supp. 1064, (1976).

violence or the presentation of adult material on television." It concluded: "Particularly when Commissioners make recommendations in areas where formal regulation would be questionable, it is vital that any suggestion of pressure or the appearance of pressure be scrupulously avoided."

In a trio of cases decided together in 1972, the Supreme Court came to grips with an issue long debated and litigated. As the Court recounted it: "Petitioners Branzburg and Pappas and respondent Caldwell press First Amendment claims that may be simply put: that to gather news it is often necessary to agree either not to identify the source of information published or to publish only part of the facts revealed, or both; that if the reporter is nevertheless forced to reveal these confidences to a grand jury, the source so identified and other confidential sources of other reporters will be measurably deterred from furnishing publishable information, all to the detriment of the free flow of information protected by the First Amendment. Although petitioners do not claim an absolute privilege against official interrogation in all circumstances, they assert that the reporter should not be forced either to appear or to testify before a grand jury or at trial until and unless sufficient grounds are shown for believing that the reporter possesses information relevant to a crime the grand jury is investigating, that the information the reporter has is unavailable from other sources, and that the need for the information is sufficiently compelling to override the claimed invasion of First Amendment interests occasioned by the disclosure."[231]

Pointing out that, although some states have provided a statutory privilege to newsmen,[232] most along with the Federal Government have not, the Court said it was being asked to interpret "the First Amendment to grant newsmen a testimonial privilege that other citizens do not enjoy. This we decline to do." But the Court did go on to assert that news-gathering "is not without its First Amendment protections, and grand jury investigations if instituted or conducted other than in good faith, would pose wholly different issues for resolution under the First Amendment." Specifically, the Court suggested that a grand jury proceeding for the purpose of

What of the News-gatherer's Privilege?

[231] Branzburg *v.* Hayes (and companion cases), 408 U.S. 665 (1972). In a noteworthy California case, where an even greater privilege was claimed i.e. that a stolen goods statute interpreted "to prohibit receipt of stolen documents by newsmen for purposes of publication . . . abridges the freedom of the press . . . ," the court citing a host of previous decisions stressed that there was no unrestrained right to gather information. People *v.* Kunkin, 100 Cal. Rptr. 845 (1972). *See* particularly its discussion of New York Times Co. *v.* U.S. (1971), *ibid.*, 862. *See also* Farr *v.* Pitchess, 522 F. 2d. 464, *cert. denied*, 427 U.S. 912 (1976), *and* Rosato *v.* Sup'r Ct., 124 Cal.Rptr. 427, *cert. denied*, 427 U.S. 912 (1976).

[232] Such a privilege enacted by the New Mexico legislature was struck down by the State supreme court as an impermissible intrusion on the responsibility of the judiciary for creating evidentiary rules. *See* Ammerman *v.* Hubbard Broadcasting, Inc., 551 P. 2d. 1354 (1976).

disrupting a reporter's relationship with his news sources "would have no justification."

In yet another controversial case, the Supreme Court refused to review lower Federal court decisions with regard to a contempt citation against Will Lewis, manager of Los Angeles FM station KPFK.[233] The citation was issued for his refusal to answer questions before a grand jury and to honor a subpoena for a document pertaining to the Weathermen Underground's bombing of an office of the State attorney general and a tape recording made by Patricia Hearst ·following her alleged abduction by the Symbianese Liberation Army. Lewis contended that the First Amendment protected the confidentiality of his news sources. The U.S. Court of Appeals for the Ninth Circuit, relying on the Supreme Court's decision in Branzburg v. Hayes,[234] sustained the contempt citation.[235] A second contempt citation against Lewis was predicated on his identical refusals in a matter of the grand jury's investigation into the bombing of Sheraton hotels in both San Francisco and Los Angeles allegedly by the New World Liberation Front.[236] When the Supreme Court rejected his appeal,[237] Lewis surrendered his copy of the taped messages.[238]

For discussion of the Press's claim to a "right to know" and the free press-fair trial issue, *see* pp. 406-408 and 413-416, respectively.

Expansion of the Right to Assemble and to Petition

Historically, the right of petition is the primary right, the right peaceably to assemble a subordinate and instrumental right, as if Amendment I read: "the right of the people peaceably to assemble" *in order to* "petition the government."[239] Today, however, the right of peaceable assembly is the language of the Court, "cognate to those of free speech and free press and is equally fundamental. . . . [It] is one that cannot be denied without violating those fundamental principles of liberty and justice which lie at the base of all civil and political institutions—principles which the Fourteenth Amendment embodies in the general terms of its due process clause. . . . The holding of meetings for peaceable political action cannot be proscribed. Those who assist in the conduct of such meetings cannot be branded as criminals on that score. The question . . . is not as to the auspices under which the meeting is held but as to its purposes; not as to the relations of the speakers, but whether their utterances transcend the bounds of the freedom of speech which the Constitution protects."[240] Even so, the right is not unlimited. Under the common law any assemblage was unlawful which aroused the apprehensions of "men of firm and rational

[233] Lewis v. U.S., 420 U.S. 913 (1975).   [234] 408 U.S. 665 (1972).
[235] Lewis v. U.S, 501 F. 2d. 418 (1974): *see also in re* Lewis, 377 F.Supp. 297 (1974).
[236] *In re* Lewis, 384 F.Supp. 133 (1974). *See also Los Angeles Times*, Feb. 15, 1975.
[237] 420 U.S. 913 (1975).   [238] *New York Times*, Feb. 21, 1975.
[239] United States v. Cruikshank, 92 U.S. 542, 552 (1876).
[240] De Jonge v. Ore., 299 U.S. 353, 364-365 (1937). *See also* Hague v. Com. for Indust'l Organization, 307 U.S. 496 (1939).

minds with families and property there," and it is not unlikely that the First Amendment takes this principle into account.[241]

In recent years, "confrontation politics" has given the Court new and urgent occasion to divine the meaning of the right to assemble and petition. The prevailing view was stated by Justice Goldberg in 1965:

"From these decisions certain clear principles emerge. The rights of free speech and assembly, while fundamental in our democratic society, still do not mean that every one with opinions or beliefs to express may address a group at any public place and at any time. The constitutional guarantee of liberty implies the existence of an organized society maintaining public order, without which liberty itself would be lost in the excesses of anarchy. The control of travel on the streets is a clear example of governmental responsibility to insure this necessary order. A restriction in that relation, designed to promote the public convenience in the interest of all, and not susceptible to abuses of discriminatory application, cannot be disregarded by the attempted exercise of some civil right which, in other circumstances, would be entitled to protection. One would not be justified in ignoring the familiar red light because this was thought to be a means of social protest. Nor could one, contrary to traffic regulations, insist upon a street meeting in the middle of Times Square at the rush hour as a form of freedom of speech or assembly. Governmental authorities have the duty and responsibility to keep their streets open and available for movement. A group of demonstrators could not insist upon the right to cordon off a street, or entrance to a public or private building, and allow no one to pass who did not agree to listen to their exhortations."[242]

But Justice Douglas has made a strong case for permitting petitioners wide latitude in choosing where to assemble and how to petition: "The right to petition for the redress of grievances has an ancient history and is not limited to writing a letter or sending a telegram to a congressman; it is not confined to appearing before the local city council, or writing letters to the President or Governor or Mayor. Conventional methods of petitioning may be, and often have been, shut off to large groups of our citizens. Legislators may turn deaf ears; formal complaints may be routed endlessly through a bureaucratic maze; courts may let the wheels of justice grind very slowly. Those who do not control television and radio, those who cannot afford to advertise in newspapers or circulate elaborate pamphlets may have only a more limited type of access to public officials. Their methods should not be condemned as tactics of obstruction and harassment as long as the assembly and petition

---

[241] People *v.* Kerrick, 261 Pac. Rep. 756 (1927); *and* State *v.* Butterworth, 104 N.J.L. 579 (1928), are two relatively early cases on the subject which were thoroughly argued and carefully decided.

[242] Cox *v.* Louisiana, 379 U.S. 536, 554 (1965).

are peaceable. . . ."[243] The late Justice Black confounded his libertarian supporters by the position he took in such cases. Some thought he was backtracking on his absolutist approach to freedom of speech. Black simply explained his views this way:

"While I have always believed that under the First and Fourteenth Amendments neither the State nor the Federal Government has any authority to censor the content of speech, I have never believed that any person has a right to give speeches or engage in demonstrations where he pleases and when he pleases."[244]

Several very recent cases illustrate that the Court is still having difficulty in determining precisely where and when the exercise of First Amendment freedoms is permissible. Over the dissent of three Justices, the Court decided *per curiam* that a member of the American Friends Service Committee had been wrongly arrested for distributing leaflets on an avenue within the limits of Fort Sam Houston because "The Fort Commander chose not to exclude the public from the street where petitioner was arrested."[245] In short order, with a different set of dissenters, the Court held that arresting a student who failed to leave the scene where a State policeman was issuing a traffic ticket to someone else and who continued to engage the officer in conversation did not violate First Amendment rights. Justice White, speaking for the Court, said "the State has a legitimate interest in enforcing its traffic laws and its officers were entitled to enforce them free from possible interference or interruption from by-standers, even those claiming a third-party interest in the transaction."[246]

More recently, the Supreme Court held that Dr. Benjamin Spock and others "had no generalized constitutional right to make political speeches or distribute leaflets at Fort Dix." The Court went on to say that military authorities are constitutionally free to keep "official military activities free of entanglement with partisan political campaigns of any kind" provided that they do so "objectively and even-handedly."[247] Justice Brennan lamented in a dissent that these two cases "narrow the opportunities for free expression in our society." He pegged his legal argument on the propositon that: "Requiring prior approval of expressive material before it may be distributed on base constitutes a system of prior restraint." But he also argued that it would be good public policy to expose the mili-

[243] Adderley *v.* Florida, 385 U.S. 39, 50-51 (1966).
[244] Tinker *v.* Des Moines School District, 393 U.S. 503, 517 (1969).
[245] Flower *v.* U.S., 407 U.S. 197, 198 (1972).
[246] Colton *v.* Kentucky, 407 U.S. 104, 109 (1972). The California Supreme Court recently made short shrift of the contention that "the operations of a roller skating rink are entitled to First Amendment protection." Sunset Amusement Co. *v.* Bd. of Police Com'rs, 496 P. 2d. 840 (1972).
[247] Greer *v.* Spock, 424 U.S. 828 (1976). On a related matter, lower federal courts have held that members of the Armed Forces could not be prevented from attempting to petition Congressmen but that reasonable regulations could be set for the circulation of petitions; *see* Allen *v.* Monger, 404 F.Supp. 1081 (1975), and Glines *v.* Wade, 401 F.Supp. 127 (1975).

tary "to the moderating influence of other ideas," asserting that "any unnecessary isolation only erodes neutrality and invites the danger that neutrality seeks to avoid."

Just as a military base is not a forum for political candidates, neither is a prison a public forum for prisoners. In 1977,[248] the Court, through Justice Rehnquist, sustained decisions of a State corrections official not to permit face-to-face solicitation among prisoners for purpose of organizing a prisoners' union, union meetings among the inmates, or the receipt of bulk mailings from the union to prisoners. Allowing "prison administrators the full latitude of discretion," the Court found asserted First Amendment rights insufficient to prevail over the interest of effective prison management.

In a six-three decision, the Court directed a lower court to reconsider its decision that a company that operated two retail stores could not forbid solicitations on its parking lots. Justice Powell, speaking for the majority, said "Before an owner of private property can be subjected to the commands of the First and Fourteenth Amendments the privately owned property must assume to some significant degree the functional attributes of public property devoted to public use. The First and Fourteenth Amendments are limitations on state action, not on action by the owner of private property used only for private purposes."[249]

In another case, a majority of five held that the corporate owner of a large shopping center could forbid handbilling in the center. Again, Justice Powell, speaking for the majority, pointed out "It is true that facilities at the Center are used for certain meetings and for various promotional activities. The obvious purpose, recognized widely as legitimate and responsible business activity, is to bring potential shoppers to the Center. . . . There is no open-ended invitation to the public to use the Center for any and all purposes, however incompatible with the interests of both the stores and the shoppers whom they serve."[250]

But what of the right of the private property owner to express himself by posting signs on his property? In a 1977 ruling, the Court held that a township ordinance forbidding the display of "For Sale" and "Sold" signs in an attempt to stem the flight of white homeowners from a racially integrated community violated the First Amendment.[251] As might be anticipated, the prohibition of political signs on private property has likewise been received very negatively by the Federal courts.[252]

All the members of the Court but Justice Douglas upheld as con-

[248] Jones *v*. North Carolina Prisoners' Labor Union, 97 S.Ct. 2532 (1977).
[249] Central Hardware Co. *v*. NLRB, 407 U.S. 539 (1972).
[250] Lloyd Corp. *v*. Tanner, 407 U.S. 551 (1972).
[251] Linmark Associates, Inc. *v*. Township of Willingboro, 97 S.Ct. 1614 (1977).
[252] Farrell *v*. Township of Teaneck, 315 A. 2d. 424 (1974); Baldwin *v*. Redwood City, 540 F. 2d. 1360 (1976); Orazio *v*. Town of North Hempstead, 426 F.Supp. 1144 (1977).

stitutional a city ordinance that read: "No person, while on public or private grounds adjacent to any building in which a school or any class thereof is in session, shall willfully make or assist in the making of any noise or diversion which disturbs or tends to disturb the peace or good order of such school session or class thereof. . . ."[253] However, the Court struck down as unconstitutionally vague a municipal ordinance requiring advance, written notice to the police by "any person desiring to canvass, solicit or call from house to house for a recognized charitable . . . or political campaign or cause."[254]

In a day when it is fashionable in some quarters to speak of how repressive America has become, it is reassuring to see to what great length the governments in the United States actually go to permit people to exercise the constitutional rights to peaceably assemble and petition even in the face of provocation and threatened illegal activity.[255]

Government Employment and Political Participation

In recent years, significant decisions by both the Supreme Court and lower courts have focused on the right to associate possessed by public employees. Although Justice Douglas and two other dissenters saw the Hatch Act as a limitation on government employees' "right to speak, to propose, to publish, to petition government, to assemble," a majority had no difficulty finding that "neither the First Amendment nor any other provision of the Constitution invalidates a law barring . . . partisan political conduct by federal employees."[256] And, in a second decision that may have enormous consequences for the American political system, the Supreme Court held "that the practice of patronage dismissals is unconstitutional under the First and Fourteenth Amendments."[257] The case involved two non-civil-service employees of the Cook County, Illinois, sheriff's office who were discharged or threatened with discharge because they were not Democrats. The Court extensively canvassed the reasons for maintaining a patronage system and concluded that, despite the claims made for it, "patronage dismissals severely restrict political belief and association. Though there is a vital need for government efficiency and effectiveness, such dismissals are on balance not the least restrictive means for fostering that end. . . . More fundamentally, however, any contribution of patronage dismissals to the democratic process does not suffice to

[253] Grayned v. Rockford, 408 U.S. 104 (1972). See U.S. v. Crowthers, 456 F. 2d. 1074 (1972), where a U.S. court of appeals held that Pentagon officials could not discriminate against peace protesters in authorizing use of the Pentagon's concourse for "events."

[254] Hynes v. Mayor and Council of Borough of Oradell, 425 U.S. 610 (1976).

[255] See, for example, preparations for the "May Day" demonstration in Washington, D.C., 1971 Cong. Quart. Weekly Report, 959ff., and 1015ff.

[256] CSC v. Letter Carriers, 413 U.S. 548 (1973). But a Federal district court has ruled that city employees cannot be forbidden from running in nonpartisan elections by city charter provisions that forbade partisan political activity. Magill v. Lynch, 400 F.Supp. 84 (1975).

[257] Elrod v. Burns, 427 U.S. 347 (1976).

override their severe encroachment on First Amendment freedoms." However, the Massachusetts Supreme Judicial Court has upheld police regulations forcing officers who are candidates for elective public office to take a leave from their law enforcement duties.[258]

While some restrictions on political association have survived scrutiny, the courts have reached much more negative evaluations of attempts by government to inhibit speech, or organizing activities by public employees seeking to unionize.[259] Indeed, an interesting case dealing with the rights of those who did not favor unionism in the public sector reached the Supreme Court in 1977. Though the Court sustained the constitutionality of the "agency shop" (an arrangement whereby those who were not members of the union, but were represented by it in collective bargaining, were required by law, as a condition of employment, to pay the union a service fee equal to the amount of union dues), it held that the First Amendment barred union financing of political or ideological causes, unrelated to collective bargaining, from the funds contributed by those who did not support those political positions.[260]

In a covey of recent decisions the Supreme Court has addressed State limitations placed on citizen participation in the electoral process in terms of the impact on the freedom of association. The Supreme Court, 5-4, held that a New York law requiring voters to enroll in the party of their choice before the general election in order to be eligible to vote in the following primary (a period of months) did not violate the right to freely associate.[261] The dissenters made explicit their view that a "less drastic enrollment deadline than the eight or 11 months now imposed" would be more in accord with the Constitution and would be adequate to protect against political party raiding. The following Term, the Court held that the following State statutes ran afoul of the right to associate: (1) an Illinois provision that prohibited a person from voting in the primary election of a political party if he had voted in the primary

Freedom of Association and Electoral Participation

---

[258] Boston Police Patrolmen's Ass'n v. City of Boston, 326 N.E. 2d. 314 (1975); *and see also* O'Hara v. Com'r of Public Safety, 326 N.E. 2d. 308 (1975). A Michigan appeals court, however, has struck down as unconstitutional, sweeping provisions of a city charter barring city employees from contributing money to or active participation in city election campaigns. *See* Phillips v. City of Flint, 225 N.W. 2d. 780 (1975).

[259] *See*, with respect to teachers and policemen, City of Madison Joint School Dist. No. 8 v. Wis. Employment Relations Com'n, 97 S.Ct. 421 (1976); Aurora Educational Ass'n East v. Bd. of Educ. of Aurora Public School Dist. No. 131 of Kane County, Ill., 490 F. 2d. 431 (1973); Police Officers' Guild, Nat'l Union of Police Officers v. Washington, 369 F.Supp. 543 (1973); Vorbeck v. McNeal, 407 F.Supp. 733 (1976). In the same vein, the courts have also had no difficulty striking down vague and sweeping prohibitions on police officers associating with people who have been convicted or are suspected of having committed crimes; *see* Sponick v. City of Detroit Police Dept., 211 N.W. 2d. 674 (1973); *and* Brown v. Bronstein, 389 F.Supp. 1328 (1975).

[260] Abood v. District Bd. of Educ., 97 S.Ct. 1782 (1977).

[261] Rosario v. Rockefeller, 410 U.S. 752 (1973). *See also* Friedland v. State, 374 A. 2d. 60 (1977).

of another party within the preceding 23 months;[262] (2) an Indiana statute requiring political parties to file an oath stating the party does not advocate overthrow of the government in order to get on the ballot;[263] (3) a California statute that required payment of a filing fee for candidates for office without providing any alternative means for indigents.[264] In contrast, the Court upheld: (a) a California statute that denied a place on the ballot to *independent* candidates if they voted in the immediately preceding primary of a qualified party or had been affiliated with it in certain specified ways;[265] (b) most of a Texas statute that set up an elaborate formulation for nominating candidates in a general election and that seemed to disadvantage, but not unduly so, minority party and independent candidates.[266]

And, in a stormy controversy less than a year later, involving a State court contempt citation that grew out of a dispute as to which of two rival Chicago delegations (Daley or anti-Daley) would be seated at the 1972 Democratic National Convention, the Supreme Court, per Justice Brennan, held that a national party convention to select a Presidential ticket serves a paramount interest that outweighs any interest of the State in regulating national convention delegate selection and that State interference in national party affairs violates First Amendment rights of association.[267] (For a discussion of State efforts to clean up the electoral process, which raise questions of prior restraint, *see* p. 319.)

Applicability of the Penumbra Theory: Freedom of Association and Academic Freedom

The application of the penumbra theory to the First Amendment is mentioned below, p. 441. At least two important liberties have been found by the Court in the shadow of the First Amendment. Fifteen years ago the Court held that "It is beyond debate that freedom to engage in association for the advancement of beliefs and ideas is an inseparable aspect of the 'liberty' assured by the Due Process Clause of the Fourteenth Amendment, which embraces freedom of speech [First Amendment]."[268] And a fine scholar assures us with evidence that the Court has accepted Justice Frankfurter's inclusion of academic freedom within the ambit of First Amendment protections.[269] In a *concurring* opinion in 1952 well worth a full reading, Justice Frankfurter asserted "But, in view of the nature of the teacher's relation to the effective exercise of the rights which are safeguarded by the Bill of Rights and by the Fourteenth Amendment, inhibition of freedom of thought, and of action upon thought, in the case of teachers brings the safeguards of those amendments vividly into operation."[270]

[262] Kusper *v.* Pontikes, 414 U.S. 51 (1973).
[263] Communist Party of Indiana *v.* Whitcomb, 414 U.S. 441 (1974).
[264] Lubin *v.* Panish, 415 U.S. 709 (1974).
[265] Storer *v.* Brown, 415 U.S. 724 (1974).
[266] American Party of Texas *v.* White, 415 U.S. 767 (1974).
[267] Cousins *v.* Wigoda, 419 U.S. 477 (1975).
[268] N.A.A.C.P. *v.* Alabama, 357 U.S. 449, 460 (1958).
[269] Milton R. Konvitz, *Expanding Liberties* (New York, 1966), ch. III.
[270] Wieman *v.* Updegraff, 344 U.S. 183, 195 (1952).

With respect to the right of association, the Supreme Court in an important decision in 1972 reversed a lower court decision which had upheld the denial of recognition as a campus organization to a group seeking to establish a chapter of Students for Democratic Society (SDS) at Central Connecticut State College.[271] Justice Powell, speaking for the Court, stated that "At the outset we note that state colleges and universities are not enclaves immune from the sweep of the First Amendment" and that "Among the rights protected by the First Amendment is the right of individuals to associate to further their personal beliefs." But in remanding the case to the lower court, the Supreme Court significantly indicated "that we are unable to conclude that no basis exists upon which nonrecognition might be appropriate." The Court went on to say that if the reason for nonrecognition was based on the organization's activities rather than its philosophy and "were factually supported by the record" it would "provide a basis for considering the propriety of nonrecognition. The critical line heretofore drawn for determining the permissibility of regulation is the line between mere advocacy and advocacy 'directed to inciting or producing imminent lawless action and . . . likely to incite or produce such action.' "

A series of recent Federal and State court decisions make it clear that the First Amendment is to be given wide berth in educational institutions. Relying upon a test to limit governmental interference of whether the activity in question results in a disruption of the educational process[272]—an approach reminiscent of the "clear and present danger" test—the courts have sustained the right of students to publish what administrators think are tasteless newspapers[273] and the right of unpopular minorities to organize on campus.[274] A Federal district court has struck down a college regulation which prohibited political canvassing in dormitories unless two-thirds of the residents had given their approval.[275] Further, a State court has held that police officers posing as students, enrolling at a State university, compiling dossiers and filing reports on professors and students has a "potential chilling effect" on First Amendment rights and can only be sustained by a "compelling"

The First Amendment on Campus

---

[271] Healy v. James, 408 U.S. 169 (1972).

[272] For example, a State court held that a "sit-in" in a school superintendent's office that disrupted the office was not a reasonable exercise of First Amendment freedoms and the criminal trespass statute under which the trespasser was convicted is not unconstitutionally vague or overbroad. State v. Williams, 238 N.W. 2d. 302 (1976). However, a lower Federal court invalidated a provision of the Higher Education Act which terminated funds to any student committing a "serious" crime or found contributing to any "serious disruption" on the campus. Rasche v. Board of Trustees, 353 F.Supp. 973 (1972).

[273] See Cintron v. State Bd. of Educ., 384 F.Supp. 674 (1974); Beyer v. Kinzler, 383 F.Supp. 1164 (1974); Trachtman v. Anker, 426 F.Supp. 198 (1976); Bright v. Los Angeles Unified School Dist., 556 P. 2d. 1090 (1976).

[274] See Gay Students Organization of the University of New Hampshire v. Bonner, 509 F. 2d. 652 (1974); and Gay Alliance of Students v. Matthews, 544 F. 2d. 162 (1976); but cf. Gay Lib v. Univ. of Mo., 416 F.Supp. 1350 (1976).

[275] James v. Nelson, 349 F.Supp. 1061 (1972).

State interest.[276] However, ingenious students who argued that rules prohibiting visitations by persons of opposite sex in university residence halls were a violation of free association were wrong, the court explained, because "it has never been held to apply to the right of one individual to associate with another, and certainly it has never been. construed as an absolute right of association between a man and a woman at any and all places and times."[277] In addition, courts have held that juvenile curfew laws are not an infringement of freedom of association.[278]

AMENDMENT II

A well-regulated militia being necessary to the security of a free
    state, the right of the people to keep and bear arms shall not be
    infringed.

The expression "a free state" is obviously here used in the generic sense, and refers to the United States as a whole rather than to the several states (*see* Article I, Section VIII, ¶s 15 and 16).

"Arms"   The amendment does not cover concealed weapons, the right "to bear arms" being the right simply to bear them openly. Nor will the Court apply it to sawed-off shotguns, being unable to say of its own knowledge that their possession and use furthers in any way the preservation of a "well regulated militia."[1] Moreover, this right, being a right of citizenship rather than of person, may be denied aliens, at least on reasonable grounds.[2] Nor will the amendment prevent a State from making it unlawful for men to associate in a paramilitary organization, or to drill or parade with arms unless authorized by law.[3] Indeed, there are several State court decisions of recent vintage which hold that this amendment, unlike some others in the Bill of Rights, applies only to the National Govern-

---

[276] White *v*. Davis, 120 Cal. Rptr. 94 (1975).
[277] Futrell *v*. Ahrens, 540 P. 2d. 214 (1975).
[278] *See* Bykofsky *v*. Borough of Middletown, 401 F.Supp. 1242 (1975); *and* People *v*. Chambers, 360 N.E. 2d. 55 (1976), *reversing* 335 N.E. 2d. 612 (1975).

---

[1] United States *v*. Miller, 307 U.S. 174 (1939), sustaining the National Firearms Act of June 26, 1934 (26 U.S.C. 5811), which levies a virtually prohibitive tax on the transfer of such weapons and requires their registration. Justice McReynold's opinion for the Court in this case contains interesting historical data regarding the antecedents of Amendment II. For an interesting discussion of coverage of present law, *see* 1960 *U.S. Code Cong. and Adm. News*, 2112ff.

[2] Patsone *v*. Pa., 232 U.S. 139 (1914) deals with a closely analogous point. *See also* Presser *v*. Ill., 116 U.S. 252 (1886). Recent decisions regarding denial of rights to aliens cast some doubt as to whether such a holding would pass muster today. Graham *v*. Richardson, 403 U.S. 365 (1971); Leger *v*. Sailer, 321 F.Supp. 250 (1970).

[3] Presser *v*. Illinois, 116 U.S. 252, 265 (1886).

ment and not to the States,[4] and thus no bar in and of itself to State action.

Recently, Federal and State courts have affirmed that the Second Amendment presents no bar against statutes requiring the registration of firearms,[5] prohibiting the possession of submachine guns,[6] and regulating the right to carry concealable weapons.[7] As the courts have clearly indicated, the amendment guarantees a collective not an individual right to bear arms.[8]

AMENDMENT III

No soldier shall, in time of peace, be quartered in any house without the consent of the owner, nor in time of war, but in a manner to be prescribed by law.

This and the following amendment sprang from certain grievances which contributed to bring about the American Revolution. They recognize the principle of the security of the dwelling which was embodied in the ancient maxim that a man's house is his castle. There has never been an instance of an attempted violation of the prohibition. There was, however, a novel challenge to the Federal Housing and Rent Act of 1947[1] on the grounds that the act "as amended and extended is and always was the incubator and hatchery of swarms of bureaucrats to be quartered as storm troopers upon the people in violation of Amendment III." A Federal district court found the challenge without merit.[2]

AMENDMENT IV

The right of the people to be secure in their persons, houses, papers and effects, against unreasonable searches and seizures, shall not be violated, and no warrants shall issue but upon probable cause, supported by oath or affirmation, and particularly describing the place to be searched, and the persons or things to be seized.

"Unreasonable Searches and Seizures"

This amendment reflected the abhorrence of the times against so-called "general warrants," from which the Colonists had suffered

---

[4] Burton v. Sills, 248 A. 2d. 462 (1967), appeal dismissed, 394 U.S. 812 (1969); Hardison v. State, 437 P. 2d. 868 (1968); Harris v. State, 432 P. 2d. 929 (1967); State v. Amos, 343 So. 2d. 166 (1977).

[5] United States v. Birmley, 529 F. 2d. 103 (1976); United States v. King, 532 F. 2d. 505 (1976).

[6] United States v. Warin, 530 F. 2d. 103 (1976).

[7] Guida v. Dier, 375 N.Y.S. 2d. 826 (1975).

[8] United States v. Warin, 530 F. 2d. 103 (1976); Commonwealth v. Davis, 343 N.E. 2d. 847 (1976).

---

[1] 61 *Stat.* 193 (1947).   [2] U.S. v. Valenzuela, 95 F.Supp. 363 (1951).

more or less.[1] Today it derives its chief importance from the doctrine the beginnings of which were laid down by the Court in 1886 in Boyd *v.* United States,[2] that the above provisions must be read in conjunction with the self-incrimination clause of Amendment V, so that when any seizure of papers or things is "unreasonable" in the sense of the Fourth Amendment, such papers and things may not, under the Fifth Amendment, be received by any court, Federal or State, in evidence against the person from whom they were seized.

Arrest and "Stop" and "Frisk"

For years, the commonly accepted definition of "arrest" was "the taking of a person into custody in order that he may be forthcoming to answer for the commission of an offense."[3] The Supreme Court expanded the concept abruptly and emphatically in 1968: "There is some suggestion in the use of such terms as 'stop' and 'frisk' that such police conduct is outside the purview of the Fourth Amendment because neither action arises to the level of a 'search' or 'seizure' within the meaning of the Constitution. We emphatically reject this notion. It is quite plain that the Fourth Amendment governs 'seizures' of the person which do not eventuate in a trip to the station house and prosecution for crime—'arrests' in traditional terminology. *It must be recognized that whenever a police officer accosts an individual and restrains his freedom to walk away, he has 'seized' that person*"[4] (emphasis supplied).

Probable Cause

The Court's expanded definition of "arrest" would on its face seem thereafter to require an "arrest" warrant. Previously, the Court had held that the Fourth Amendment did not require it.[5] But the Court went on to say in the 1968 decision: "We do not retreat from our holdings that the police must, whenever practicable, obtain advance judicial approval of searches and seizures through the warrant procedure. . . . But we deal here with an entire rubric of police conduct—necessarily swift action predicated upon the on-the-spot observations of the officer on the beat—which historically has not been, and as a practical matter could not be, subjected to the warrant procedure."[6] Consequently, arrests can and continue to be made for "probable cause." As the Court has seen it: "In dealing with probable cause, . . . as the very name implies, we deal with probabilities. These are not technical; they are the factual and practical considerations of everyday life in which reasonable and prudent men, not legal technicians act."[7] Also that probable cause exists where "the facts and circumstances within [the arresting officers'] knowledge and of which they had reasonably trustworthy

---

[1] Hutchinson, *Foundations of the Constitution*, 293-298.

[2] 116 U.S. 616.

[3] Caleb Foote, "The Fourth Amendment: Obstacle or Necessity in the Law of Arrest," 51 *J. Crim., L.C. & P.S.* 402 (1960).

[4] Terry *v.* Ohio, 392 U.S. 1, 16 (1968).

[5] Ker *v.* California, 374 U.S. 23, 41 (1963). *See also* U.S. *v.* Hall, 348 F. 2d. 837, 841-842 (1965); Ford *v.* U.S., 352 F. 2d. 927 (1965).

[6] Terry *v.* Ohio, 392 U.S. 1, 20 (1968).

[7] Brinegar *v.* U.S., 338 U.S. 160, 175 (1919); Draper *v.* U.S., 358 U.S. 307, 313 (1959).

information [are] sufficient in themselves to warrant a man of reasonable caution in the belief that" an offense has been or is being committed.[8] Clearly, "probable cause" is a very subjective judgment which law enforcement officers must sometimes make on the run. But the Court assures us that it is not as bad as it sounds:

"The scheme of the Fourth Amendment becomes meaningful only when it is assured that at some point the conduct of those charged with enforcing the laws can be subjected to the more detached, neutral scrutiny of a judge who must evaluate the reasonableness of a particular search or seizure in light of the particular circumstances. And in making that assessment it is imperative that the facts be judged against an objective standard: would the facts available to the officer at the moment of the seizure or the search warrant a man of reasonable caution in the belief that the action taken was appropriate? Anything less would invite intrusions upon constitutionally guaranteed rights based on nothing more substantial than inarticulate hunches, a result this Court has consistently refused to sanction. And simple 'good faith on the part of the arresting officer is not enough.' . . . If subjective good faith alone were the test, the protections of the Fourth Amendment would evaporate, and the people would be 'secure in their persons, houses, papers, and effects,' only in the discretion of the police."[9]

Predictably, the Court has had great difficulty in etching out a clear picture of what in effect constitutes "probable cause." In a recent round with that concept, as applied to a warrant, the Court was split in several directions.[10] There, Chief Justice Burger reviewed the leading cases on the subject and then said "We cannot conclude that a policeman's knowledge of a suspect's reputation— something that policemen frequently know . . . is not a 'practical consideration of everyday life' upon which an officer (or a magistrate) may properly rely in assessing the reliability of an informant's tip."[11]

But in a more recent case dealing with a Jacksonville, Florida, vagrancy ordinance (see p. 420), the Court inveighed against arrests on suspicion: "We allow our police to make arrests only on 'probable cause.' . . . Arresting a person on suspicion, like arresting a person for investigation, is foreign to our system, even when the arrest is for past criminality."[12] The Court then offered some astounding statistics revealing that the notion that such arrests are "foreign to our system" is more honored in the breach than the observance. In three years, 1968 through 1970, over 300,000 people in the United States were arrested on vagrancy charges and well over 200,000 on suspicion.[13]

[8] Carroll v. U.S., 267 U.S. 132, 162 (1925); Draper v. U.S., 358 U.S. 307, 313 (1959).
[9] Terry v. Ohio, 392 U.S. 1, 21-22 (1968).
[10] U.S. v. Harris, 403 U.S. 573 (1971).   [11] Ibid., 583.
[12] Papachristou v. City of Jacksonville, 405 U.S. 156, 169 (1972).
[13] Ibid.

With respect to the propriety of a law officer frisking someone he has stopped, the Court in the very case where it minted the new broader definition of "arrest" admitted that there is still some difference between stopping someone and arresting him:

"The crux of this case, however, is not the propriety of Officer McFadden's taking steps to investigate petitioner's suspicious behavior, but rather *whether there was justification for McFadden's invasion of Terry's personal security by searching him for weapons in the course of that investigation.* We are now concerned with more than the governmental interest in investigating crime; in addition, there is the more immediate interest of the police officer in taking steps to assure himself that the person with whom he is dealing is not armed with a weapon that could unexpectedly and fatally be used against him. Certainly it would be unreasonable to require that police officers take unnecessary risks in the performance of their duties. American criminals have a long tradition of armed violence, and every year in this country many law enforcement officers are killed in the line of duty, and thousands more are wounded. Virtually all of these deaths and a substantial portion of the injuries are inflicted with guns and knives.

"In view of these facts, we cannot blind ourselves to the need for law enforcement officers to protect themselves and other prospective victims of violence in situations where they may lack probable cause for an arrest. When an officer is justified in believing that the individual whose suspicious behavior he is investigating at close range is armed and presently dangerous to the officer or to others, it would appear to be clearly unreasonable to deny the officer the power to take necessary measures to determine whether the person is in fact carrying a weapon and to neutralize the threat of physical harm.

"We must still consider, however, the nature and quality of the intrusion on individual rights which must be accepted if police officers are to be conceded the right to search for weapons in situations where probable cause to arrest for crime is lacking. Even a limited search of the outer clothing for weapons constitutes a severe, though brief, intrusion upon cherished personal security, and it must surely be an annoying, frightening, and perhaps humiliating experience.

"Our evaluation of the proper balance that has to be struck in this type of case leads us to conclude that there must be a narrowly drawn authority to permit a reasonable search for weapons for the protection of the police officer, where he has reason to believe that he is dealing with an armed and dangerous individual, regardless of whether he has probable cause to arrest the individual for a crime. The officer need not be absolutely certain that the individual is armed; the issue is whether a reasonably prudent man in the circumstances would be warranted in the belief that his safety or that of others was in danger. And in determining whether the officer acted reasonably in such circumstances, due weight must be given, not to inchoate and unparticularized suspicion or 'hunch' but to the specific reasonable inferences which he is entitled to draw from the facts in light of his experience."[14] This view was vigorously reinforced by the Court in June 1972.[15]

In 1972, the Supreme Court had occasion to address the question of *who* could issue arrest warrants. The Charter of the city of Tampa, Florida, authorizes the clerks of the Municipal Court to issue certain arrest warrants. It was contended that the Fourth Amendment requires that a "judicial officer" determine whether or not probable cause exists for issuing a warrant. The Court held that there was no constitutional reason that "all warrant authority must reside exclusively in a judge or lawyer." The Court said that "an issuing magistrate must meet [only] two tests. He must be neutral and detached, and he must be capable of determining whether probable cause exists for the requested arrest or search."[16] In order to guarantee the neutrality and detachment of the judicial officer as overseer of the law enforcement process, he must remain independent and may not issue warrants while also occupying a prosecutorial position in the executive branch.[17] Nor may he be granted compensation on a basis that makes his income hinge on the number of warrants issued.[18]

Just as a warrant is not always required to effect an arrest,[19] neither is one always necessary to search and seize property. Compared with what was in many respects the more rigid approach of bygone days,[20] the legitimacy of warrantless searches has come to

Searches Without a Warrant

---

[14] Terry v. Ohio, 392 U.S. 1, 25-27 (1968). As is evident, Chief Justice Warren's opinion for the Court focused heavily on the reasons for the frisk. Feeling constrained, however, "to fill in a few gaps in [the Court's] opinion" Justice Harlan pointed out that "the officer must first have constitutional grounds to insist on an encounter, to make a *forcible* stop." Said Justice Harlan, "I would make it perfectly clear that the right to frisk in this case depends upon the reasonableness of a forcible stop to investigate a suspected crime." Fleshing out these considerations as to what was the standard for assessing the reasonableness of a forcible stop and the manner in which any attendant search was to be conducted, Harlan continued: "Where such a stop is reasonble . . . the right to frisk must be immediate and automatic if the reason for the stop is, as here, *an articulable suspicion* of a crime of violence. . . . [A] limited frisk incident to a lawful stop must often be rapid and routine." (Emphasis supplied.) *Ibid.*, 31-33. In a dissenting opinion, Justice Douglas took strong exception to anything less than "probable cause" as a basis for a forcible stop; *ibid.*, 35-39. For other classic "stop and frisk" situations, *see* Sibron v. N.Y. *and* Peters v. N.Y., companion cases, 392 U.S. 40 (1968). *See also* People v. DeBour, 352 N.E. 2d. 562 (1976). For a good summary of a suspect's right to defend himself from the use of excessive force by an arresting officer, *see* State v. Ramsdell, 285 A. 2d. 399 (1971).

[15] Adams v. Williams, 407 U.S. 143 (1972). *Cf.* the decision of the California Supreme Court in The People v. The Superior Court, 496 P. 2d. 1205 (1972).

[16] Shadwick v. Tampa, 407 U.S. 345 (1972).

[17] Coolidge v. N.H., 403 U.S. 443 (1971).

[18] Connally v. Ga., 97 S.Ct. 546 (1977).

[19] *See* United States v. Watson, 423 U.S. 411 (1976) in which the Court held that the arrest of an individual in a public place based on probable cause did not require a warrant.

[20] Until overturned by the Court's ruling in Warden v. Hayden, 387 U.S. 294 (1967), the "mere evidence" rule (enunciated in Gouled v. U.S., 255 U.S. 298 [1921])

be judged increasingly on purely procedural grounds. Much of the current debate centers on the degree of procedural flexibility to be permitted law enforcement officers.[21] Though the Burger Court has on occasion[22] reaffirmed the general principle, articulated earlier by the Warren Court,[23] that procuring a warrant is the rule and that warrantless searches are the exception, that, in itself, says very little. The heart of the matter is not the articulation of a general principle but the question of how stringently the exceptions to the general rule will be interpreted, whether additional factors will be taken into account to uphold previously unauthorized search and seizure activity, and what consequences will flow from police failure to follow the rules. Carved in boldest relief, the contour of much of the debate over how to assess the constitutionality of a warrantless search reduces to whether the Court should ask "Was this a reasonable search?" (thus inviting the Court to weigh many variables in reaching an overall judgment)[24] or whether it should inquire "Did the police have a reasonable opportunity to procure a warrant?" (thus heightening the impact of the warrant clause and treating all but recognized, narrowly delineated exceptions as searches which are *per se* unreasonable).[25] The drift of recent Court decisions has clearly been in the direction of the former.[26] Still the Court's analysis in warrantless search cases continues to start with an account of the recognized exceptions.

Consent   To begin with, there are searches undertaken with the suspect's consent. Such consent must be given voluntarily and free from intimidation.[27] But consent to a search need not be preceded by a statement from the officers that the suspect has the right to refuse

---

operated as a *substantive* check on the admissibility of certain evidence, requiring that the government demonstrate a property interest superior to that of the private individual. *See also* Katz v. U.S., 389 U.S. 347 (1967), which modified the grip of certain considerations of the law of trespass in wiretapping and eavesdropping.

[21] *See* Herbert Packer, *The Limits of the Criminal Sanction*, ch. 8 (Stanford, 1968).

[22] *See* United States v. Chadwick, 97 S.Ct. 2476 (1977).

[23] Chimel v. Calif., 395 U.S. 752 (1969).

[24] *See e.g.*, Cardwell v. Lewis, 417 U.S. 583 (1974); Coolidge v. N.H., 403 U.S. 443, 493 (1971) (dissenting opinion of Justice Black); South Dakota v. Opperman, 428 U.S. 364 (1976). Earlier articulations of this approach can be found, for example, in Rabinowitz v. U.S., 339 U.S. 56 (1950) *and* Cooper v. Calif., 386 U.S. 58 (1967).

[25] *See e.g.*, Coolidge v. N.H., 403 U.S. 443 (1971); Cardwell v. Lewis, 417 U.S. 583, 596 (1974) (dissenting opinion of Justice Stewart); Cady v. Dombrowski, 413 U.S. 433, 450 (1973) (dissenting opinion of Justice Brennan).

[26] Despite the Court's recognition of the various exceptions in *Chadwick*, the Court reiterated, "Our fundamental inquiry in considering Fourth Amendment issues is whether or not a search or seizure is reasonable under all circumstances," 97 S.Ct. 2476, 2482. *See* note 24, *supra*.

[27] As the Court said in Schneckloth v. Bustamonte, 412 U.S. 218 (1973), the Fourth Amendment requires that the government "demonstrate that the consent was in fact voluntarily given, and not the result of duress or coercion, express or implied. Voluntariness is a question of fact to be determined from all the circumstances. . . ." The Ninth Circuit Court of Appeals has held that a threat by police officers to procure a search warrant and to guard the premises in the interim amounted to coercion, United States v. Agosto, 502 F. 2d. 612 (1974).

or an explanation of the consequences if the search turns up something incriminating.[28] There is also somewhat of a lingering controversy over who other than the suspect may consent to a search of his property. This has generally been resolved by recognizing that anyone who also exercises ownership or control over the area or property may also legally give consent.[29] The Federal and State courts have recently sustained searches where consent was given by a parent,[30] a girlfriend,[31] an employee,[32] a partner in a law office,[33] and a hospital,[34] but not searches undertaken pursuant to consent given by the lessor of a bus station locker,[35] a baby sitter,[36] or one who pitched a tent in the side yard of a home.[37]

Another exception to the warrant requirement are searches incident to a *valid* arrest. There are two reasons for exempting this kind of search from prior judicial approval: (1) to protect the officer's life by allowing a search for weapons which might be used by the suspect to resist arrest; and (2) to prevent the destruction of evidence by the suspect. Because searches incident to arrest ballooned to become general hunts for evidence when these justifications were first recognized,[38] the Court reduced the parameters of this exception to cover only a search of the suspect and the area within his immediate reach.[39] In a recent decision, however, the Court ruled that "once the defendant is lawfully arrested and is in custody the effects in his possession at the place of detention that were subject to search at the time and place of his arrest may lawfully be searched and seized without a warrant even though a substantial period of time has elapsed between the arrest and subsequent administrative processing on the one hand and the taking of the property for use as evidence on the other. This is true where the clothing or effects are immediately seized upon arrival at the jail, held under the defendant's name in the 'property room' of the

Searches Incident to Arrest

[28] Schneckloth v. Bustamonte, 412 U.S. 218 (1973). A casual "yeah" is enough to give consent, see People v. James, 561 P. 2d. 1135 (1977).
[29] United States v. Matlock, 415 U.S. 164 (1974). See also Stoner v. Calif., 376 U.S. 483 (1964) and Chapman v. U.S., 365 U.S. 610 (1961). Stoner and Chapman respectively held that neither a hotel night clerk nor a landlord could consent for the suspect.
[30] In interest of Salyer, 358 N.E. 2d. 1333 (1977).
[31] United States v. Robinson, 479 F. 2d. 300 (1973); but cf. Holloway v. Wolff, 482 F. 2d. 110 (1973); and Commonwealth v. Platou, 312 A. 2d. 29 (1973).
[32] United States v. Grigsby, 367 F.Supp. 900 (1973).
[33] In re Cornelius, 520 P. 2d. 76 (1974).
[34] State v. Smith, 559 P. 2d. 970 (1977).
[35] People v. Miller, 310 N.E. 2d. 808 (1974).
[36] People v. Litwin, 355 N.Y.S. 2d. 646 (1974).
[37] State v. McGovern, 252 N.W. 2d. 365 (1977).
[38] After this exception had been recognized by the Court in United States v. Rabinowitz, 339 U.S. 56 (1950), the scope of such searches reached a paradoxical point: An individual was generally safer in the privacy of his possessions when he was not at home (since probable cause would have to be established for a warrant to issue) than when he was (since searches incident to arrest had grown to become general hunts for evidence in which the entire house was fair game).
[39] Chimel v. Calif., 395 U.S. 752 (1969).

jail and at a later time searched and taken for use at the subsequent criminal trial."[40] Most of the other decisions by the Court expanding custodial searches deal with automobiles. Though such searches were invariably undertaken following an arrest, the Court has specifically addressed those searches in terms of the motor vehicle exception.

Motor Vehicles   The Court long ago recognized that developments in transportation substantially increased the likelihood that evidence relevant to a crime might be removed from the police officer's jurisdiction before he could go and get a warrant.[41] Because motor vehicles are susceptible to speedy disappearance, the officer may stop an automobile and search it on the spot if he has probable cause. A controversy continues, however, in many of the Court's recent decisions as to whether an automobile is always subject to on the spot search without a warrant or whether its ready mobility is to be taken into account on a case-by-case basis so that this exception has greater or lesser applicability.[42] In 1976, the Court compounded the mobility justification with the added rationale that cars, as compared with houses, furnish much less of an expectation of privacy.[43] The upshot has been that recent cases have relaxed the boundaries of the motor vehicle exception considerably. The Court has upheld the absolute right of police to seize automobiles from public places, such as streets and parking lots, without a warrant.[44] Once vehicles were in custody, the Court sustained a warrantless inspection of a car from which officers took scrapings of paint[45] and, where police had probable cause to search the defendant's car immediately after he had been arrested at the scene for attempting to pass fraudulent checks, probable cause was still held to exist and thus support a warrantless search of the auto at the stationhouse.[46] Because of a diminished expectation of privacy, the Court also held that police can routinely search and inventory contents of impounded cars so as to secure and guard them adequately even if

[40] United States v. Edwards, 415 U.S. 800. *See also* Cupp v. Murphy, 412 U.S. 291 (1973), but there no arrest had yet been effected; fingernail scrapings were taken while the suspect was being detained for questioning.

[41] For the traditional justification, *see* Carroll v. U.S., 267 U.S. 132 (1925); for a discussion of cases, *see* Chambers v. Maroney, 399 U.S. 42 (1970). *See also* Note, "Warrantless Searches and Seizures of Automobiles," 87 *Harvard Law Review*, 835 (1974).

[42] *See e.g.*, Coolidge v. N.H., 403 U.S. 443 (1971); U.S. v. Robinson, 414 U.S. 218 (1974); *and* Cady v. Dombrowski, 413 U.S. 433 (1973). *See also* United States v. Robinson, 533 F. 2d. 578 (1976).

[43] *See* South Dakota v. Opperman, 428 U.S. 364 (1976), which summarizes prior cases and offers the conclusion. The diminished "expectation of privacy" rationale was hotly contested by the dissenters, *ibid.*, 386-388.

[44] G. M. Leasing Corp. v. U.S., 97 S.Ct. 619 (1977); *see also* Cardwell v. Lewis, 417 U.S. 583 (1974).

[45] Cardwell v. Lewis, 417 U.S. 583 (1974).

[46] Texas v. White, 423 U.S. 67 (1976).

the car in the instant case was already locked but where some valuables were visible sitting on the dashboard and rear seat.[47]

Given the tendency of the Court's decisions to widen the motor vehicle exception, questions have inevitably arisen as to the scope of an officer's authority to search incident to stopping automobiles for traffic violations. In a pair of 1974 decisions,[48] the Court upheld a full search of the driver's *person* incident to a *custodial arrest* for a traffic violation. The searches in each case had turned up drugs. The Court asserted that such searches were *per se* reasonable and that the officer's authority to search did not depend upon "any subjective fear" or suspicion "that respondent was armed." Thus, it concluded, "limitations placed by Terry v. Ohio on protective searches conducted in an investigatory stop situation based on less than probable cause are not to be carried over to searches made incident to lawful custodial arrests." Court decisions, however, have struck at using the observance of minor traffic violations as a pretext for full-blown auto searches.[49]

A fourth exception to the warrant requirement is presented by circumstances in which the police are in "hot pursuit" of a suspect. If, in the course of the chase, the suspect runs into a building, the officers need not risk losing him by having to go get a warrant; they may follow him and effect the arrest.[50] Recognizing that this, like several other justifications, presents an emergency exception to the warrant requirement, the more remote in time the sequence of events becomes, the faster this exception fades. A recent case gave the Court occasion to apply this exception.[51] The Court sustained a search by police which occurred after they had caught up to the suspect in the vestibule of her house. In that case, police arrived at the suspect's house after receiving a tip from an undercover agent that she had on her person "marked money" used to make a narcotics "buy." They observed her standing in the doorway holding a brown paper bag, but, when they approached, she retreated into the vestibule. In her struggle to escape from the officers once they caught up to her, several glassine envelopes of heroine dropped to the floor. A search subsequently turned up some of the "marked money." The Court concluded that, by standing in the doorway,

"Hot Pursuit"

[47] South Dakota v. Opperman, 428 U.S. 364 (1976).

[48] United States v. Robinson, 414 U.S. 218 (1974); *and* Gustafson v. Fla., 414 U.S. 260 (1974).

[49] United States v. Cupps, 503 F. 2d. 277 (1974); State v. Jones, 308 So. 2d. 790 (1975); Commonwealth v. Mimms, 370 A. 2d. 1157 (1977). In other cases, courts have characterized "routine traffic checks" of a person's driver's license as an unlawful "stop" and have ruled inadmissible, evidence resulting from searches subsequently undertaken, People v. Ingle, 330 N.E. 2d. 39 (1975), and State v. Ochoa, 544 P. 2d. 1097 (1976); *but cf.*, United States v. Jenkins, 528 F. 2d. 713 (1975) *and also* People v. Mangum, 539 P. 2d. 120 (1975), Wimberly v. Sup'r Ct. of San Bernardino Cty., 547 P. 2d. 417 (1976).

[50] Warden v. Hayden, 387 U.S. 294 (1967).

[51] United States v. Santana, 427 U.S. 38 (1976).

she had made herself visible in a public place and that because the
police had probable cause to arrest her, the arrest did not violate
the Fourth Amendment. Their action following her into the vestibule was "hot pursuit" and the search that turned up the heroin
and "marked money" was incident to a lawful arrest.

Plain   Finally, as with searches executed pursuant to a warrant, where
Sight   the officer stumbles on evidence of a crime by accident or where he
finds it in plain sight, he need not avert his eyes and ignore what is
plainly in front of him.[52] This exception, of course, carries with it a
good faith requirement that the policeman did not expect to find
what he happened upon. And the courts have taken a dim view of
trespassing on private property just so the officer could position
himself in plain view.[53]

Where the Court has emphasized the "reasonable search" standard in which the assessment of constitutionality hangs on a consideration of the circumstances *in toto*, the Court has also accorded
weight to the degree of the intrusion and the manner in which the
search was conducted. In cases where such factors were taken into
account, the Court sustained the taking of fingernail scrapings
from a suspect being questioned[54] and the taking of paint scrapings
from a suspect's car that the police had towed from a commercial
parking lot to an impoundment lot,[55] as pointed out earlier.

Body   Much of the remaining controversy over the ambit of the con-
Searches   stitutional guarantee against unreasonable searches and seizures
can be explored by focusing on specific problem areas. One of
these deals with body searches. The problem presented here goes
beyond that of when "frisks" or "pat down" searches of the suspect
may legitimately occur; instead, the problem relates to what constitutional limits are placed on obtaining evidence from *within* the
suspect's body. Over two decades ago, in a case that presented the
grisly drama of police first attempting to force the defendant to
regurgitate drugs he had swallowed by use of their fingers and finally removing him to a hospital where medical personnel pumped
his stomach, Justice Frankfurter, for the Court, held that such
zealous law enforcement transgressed the Fourth Amendment:
"[T]he proceedings by which this conviction was obtained do more
than offend some fastidious squeamishness or private sentimen-

[52] *See* Chimel *v*. Calif., 395 U.S. 752 (1969); Coolidge *v*. N.H., 403 U.S. 443
(1971).
[53] *See* State *v*. Sauve, 544 P. 2d. 1091 (1976); *and* Olivera *v*. State, 315 So. 2d. 487
(1975); *but cf.* State *v*. Crea, 233 N.W. 2d. 736 (1975). No invasion of privacy resulted, however, from looking in an uncurtained portion of an apartment window.
People *v*. Becker, 533 P. 2d. 494 (1975). *See also* United States *v*. Kim, 415 F.Supp.
1252 (1976); *and* People *v*. Rizzo, 353 N.E. 2d. 841 (1976); *but see also* Nordskog *v*.
Wainwright, 546 F. 2d. 69 (1977).
[54] Cupp *v*. Murphy, 412 U.S. 291 (1973). The factors weighed in admitting the
fingernail scrapings into evidence were "the existence of probable cause, the very
limited intrusion undertaken incident to the station house detention, and the ready
distrustibility of the evidence. . . ."
[55] Cardwell *v*. Lewis, 417 U.S. 583 (1974).

talism about combatting crime too energetically. This is conduct that shocks the conscience."[56] But "the forcible extraction of . . . [the defendant's] stomach's contents" in *Rochin* were distinguished from body searches that came later. The Court had little trouble upholding the forcible extraction of a blood sample from a suspect in a drunken driving case.[57] Apparently, a wide spectrum of body searches is constitutionally acceptable so long as they are conducted under hygienic conditions by qualified personnel and, of course, are supported by probable cause.[58] Recent lower Federal and State court decisions have upheld inspections of forearms by border inspectors,[59] vaginal searches,[60] and surgery to recover a bullet.[61] And a State appeals court has upheld the choking of a defendant to keep him from swallowing evidence in a drug case.[62] A Federal district court, however, has held that customs inspectors did overstep the Fourth Amendment when they subjected a suspected drug smuggler to two rectal probes, two enemas, and the drinking of a liquid laxative.[63]

As indicated in the discussion of the motor vehicle exception to the warrant requirement, one of the growing themes in the Court's analysis of warrantless search situations has been its consideration of whether the aggrieved individual had a legitimate "expectation of privacy." What this may be in any given situation is often hard to predict. The concept appears to have originated as an outgrowth of the Court's effort to escape from the concept of privacy defined as certain "constitutionally protected areas." As the Court said in Katz *v.* U.S., "[T]he Fourth Amendment protects people, not places."[64] And, in a concurring opinion, Justice Harlan sought to elaborate, explaining that "there is a twofold requirement, first that a person

Expectations of Privacy

[56] Rochin *v.* Calif., 342 U.S. 165, 172 (1952).

[57] *See* Breithaupt *v.* Abram, 352 U.S. 432 (1957); *and* Schmerber *v.* Calif., 384 U.S. 757 (1966). A Federal district court has given the nod to extraction of blood samples from selected prisoners suspected of using drugs, Ferguson *v.* Cardwell, 392 F.Supp. 750 (1975).

[58] Blackford *v.* U.S., 247 F. 2d. 745 (1957). The search at issue was a rectal search. And, in an observation that has provoked more than one smile, Judge Barnes, speaking for the panel, wrote: "Blackford was treated civilly throughout."

[59] United States *v.* Murphee, 497 F. 2d. 395 (1974); *see also* United States *v.* Cameron, 538 F. 2d. 254 (1976).

[60] United States *v.* Himmelwright, 406 F. Supp. 889 (1975); United States *v.* Mastberg, 503 F. 2d. 405 (1974); *but see* United States *ex rel.* Guy *v.* McCauley, 385 F.Supp. 193 (1974), where the woman was seven months pregnant and the two examinations were painful.

[61] United States *v.* Crowder, 543 F. 2d. 312 (1976); Haynie *v.* State, 234 So. 2d. 406 (1977).

[62] State *v.* Williams, 560 P. 2d. 1160 (1977); *but cf.* People *v.* Bracamonte, 540 P. 2d. 624 (1975).

[63] United States *v.* Cameron, 538 F. 2d. 254 (1976).

[64] Katz *v.* U.S., 389 U.S. 347, 351 (1967). In many—if not most—of the "expectation" analyses courts undertake, this quip is, at best, a half-truth since most of the circumstances involve expectations *about being in certain places.* For a consideration of the multiple meanings in the privacy concept together with illustrative cases, *see* P. Allan Dionisopoulos and Craig R. Ducat, *The Right to Privacy* (St. Paul, Minn., 1976).

have exhibited an actual (subjective) expectation of privacy and, second, that the expectation be one that society is prepared to recognize as 'reasonable.' "[65]

Apart from its discussion in the auto search case, in which several factors were indicated that established less of an expectation of privacy in a motor vehicle than a house,[66] the Court most recently relied upon the "expectation of privacy" principle in a case dealing with the warrantless inspection of a footlocker.[67] In that case, Federal agents in Boston had been alerted by their counterparts in San Diego that two individuals would arrive in Boston with a footlocker that might contain narcotics. The Boston agents met the two with a dog trained to sniff out drugs, and the dog subsequently signaled that such substances were in the footlocker. The Court noted that the search had taken place more than an hour after the Federal agents had gained exclusive control over the footlocker and well after the defendants were in custody. Pointing out that "on this record the issuance of a warrant by a judicial officer was reasonably predictable," Chief Justice Burger, for the Court, emphasized that "a line must be drawn." He went on to assert that this line was placed by the warrant clause "at the point where the property to be searched comes under the exclusive dominion of police authority." Here, the Court acknowledged, there was no emergency shown to support a warrantless search. And the Chief Justice added: "By placing personal effects inside a double-locked footlocker, respondents manifested an expectation that the contents would remain free from public examination. No less than one who locks the doors of his home against intruders, one who safeguards his personal possessions in this manner is due the protection of the Warrant Clause."

In a second decision, the Court held that the expectation of privacy did not extend to checks, deposit slips, and other records of a defendant's bank account. These were not, the Court said, confidential communications, but commercial transactions voluntarily disclosed to a third party (the bank) and, hence, legitimately subpoenaed.[68] As the Court warned in *Katz*, years earlier, "What a person knowingly exposes to the public . . . is not a subject of Fourth Amendment protection."[69]

A number of search and seizure decisions by lower Federal and State courts turned on the defendant's "reasonable expectation of

---

[65] *Ibid.*, 361.

[66] South Dakota *v.* Opperman, 428 U.S. 364 (1976). Among the factors identified by the Court in *Opperman* warranting less of an expectation of privacy were: (1) that "[a]utomobiles, unlike homes, are subjected to pervasive and continuing governmental regulation and controls, including periodic inspection and licensing requirements"; and (2) that "[t]he expectation of privacy as to autos is further diminished by the obviously public nature of automobile travel."

[67] United States *v.* Chadwick, 97 S.Ct. 2476 (1977).

[68] United States *v.* Miller, 425 U.S. 435 (1976).

[69] Katz *v.* U.S., 389 U.S. 347, 351 (1967).

privacy" in certain places. The courts have held that no such expectation attaches to a jacket placed on a coatrack in the working area of an outer office,[70] to a warehouse in which other persons worked,[71] to trash bags sitting at curbside,[72] or to bodily excrements in one's bedpan.[73] Courts, on the other hand, have found a protectable primary interest in people's use of toilet stalls in public washrooms,[74] in the fitting rooms of clothing stores,[75] in a covered package temporarily placed in a public hallway;[76] in a wastebasket in a private office even after the occupant had left for the day,[77] in a detective's office when a husband and wife had been left alone to talk;[78] and in an object lying on the seat of the defendant's car, which was parked in his own driveway.[79] A marijuana-sniffing dog, however, has been held not to have conducted a "search" of defendant's luggage at an airline terminal when he reacted to the odor emanating from a suitcase.[80] A Federal district court has held that police use of "beepers" attached to the undercarriage of the defendant's auto and to his packages constitutes an unreasonable search and seizure.[81]

Finally, considerable controversy still swirls around the question of whether considerations of a reasonable expectation of privacy extend to the inspection of students' lockers and dormitory rooms by school officials. The courts have split badly on the question of whether Fourth Amendment guarantees apply, and, if they do, what kind of protection is proportional to a lesser expectation of privacy than one has in a house.[82]

School Lockers and Dormitory Rooms

[70] United States v. Alewelt, 532 F. 2d. 1165 (1976).

[71] United States v. Novello, 519 F. 2d. 1078 (1975).

[72] People v. Huddleston, 347 N.E. 2d. 76 (1976); Magda v. Benson, 536 F. 2d. 111 (1976). But cf. a contrary holding in People v. Edwards, 458 P. 2d. 713 (1969), where the trash cans were within a few feet of the back door.

[73] Venner v. State, 354 A. 2d. 483 (1976); aff'd 367 A. 2d. 949 (1977).

[74] Kroehler v. Scott, 391 F.Supp. 1114 (1975); People v. Triggs, 506 P. 2d. 232 (1973), and also cases cited therein.

[75] People v. Diaz, 376 N.Y.S. 2d. 849 (1975), and State v. McDaniel, 337 N.E. 2d. 173 (1975).

[76] United States v. Boswell, 347 A. 2d. 270 (1975). See also United States v. Fluker, 543 F. 2d. 709 (1976).

[77] United States v. Kahan, 350 F.Supp. 784 (1972); see also Ball v. State, 205 N.W. 2d. 353 (1973). But cf. United States v. Mustone, 469 F. 2d. 970 (1972).

[78] North v. Sup. Ct. of Riverside Cty., 502 P. 2d. 1305 (1972).

[79] State v. Sauve, 544 P. 2d. 1091 (1976); see also Olivera v. State, 315 So. 2d. 487 (1975). But cf. State v. Crea, 233 N.W. 2d. 736 (1975). The California Supreme Court has taken the position that warrantless arrests within the home are per se unreasonable as are searches incident to such arrests in the absence of exigent circumstances. People v. Ramey, 545 P. 2d. 1333 (1976).

[80] United States v. Bronstein, 521 F. 2d. 459 (1975), but see with respect to a trailer parked at the rear of a gas station, United States v. Solis, 393 F.Supp. 325 (1975).

[81] United States v. Bobisink, 415 F.Supp. 1334 (1976).

[82] Those recent cases holding Fourth Amendment rights applicable are: City of Athens v. Wolf, 313 N.E. 2d. 405 (1974); Young v. State, 209 S.E. 2d. 96 (1974); State v. Walker, 528 P. 2d. 113 (1974); State v. Mora, 307 So. 2d. 317 (1975); and Picha v. Wieglos, 410 F.Supp. 1214 (1976). Those decisions against the applicability

Regulatory
Searches

For a time certain kinds of administrative inspections encompassed generally in municipal fire, health, and housing inspection programs were regarded as at most touching only at the periphery of the "important interest safeguarded by the Fourteenth Amendment's protection against official intrusion,"[83] and as not requiring a warrant. The landmark case of that genre was expressly overruled in 1967. In that year the Court held that the Fourth Amendment bars prosecution of a person who refused to permit a warrantless code-enforcement inspection of his personal residence.[84] However, in 1971, the Supreme Court held that the home visitation provided for in the New York law in connection with the AFDC program is a reasonable administrative tool which does not violate the Fourth and Fourteenth Amendments.[85] The Court distinguished this case from the one previously mentioned on the grounds that in the earlier case, the Court was dealing with a pending criminal prosecution whereas in this case "The *only* consequence of her refusal [to allow the visit] is that the payment of benefits ceases" (emphasis supplied).

Just as the Court held in its 1967 decision that a search of a private house was presumptively unreasonable in the absence of a warrant, it also held in a companion case[86] that similar Fourth Amendment protection extended to the commercial property of a businessman. However, several years later, the Court held that a health inspector who entered the outdoor premises of a corporation plant without seeking consent in order to observe if smoke

---

of Fourth Amendment rights are: State *v.* Wingerd, 318 N.E. 2d. 866 (1974); and Commonwealth *v.* Davy, 323 A. 2d. 148 (1974). For a decision that finds constitutional rights applicable but acknowledges that since "school is a special kind of place," specially tailored constitutional limitations are appropriate, *see* People *v.* D., 315 N.E. 2d. 466 (1974). "Probable cause" appears to be the standard in People *v.* Bowers, 339 N.Y.S. 2d. 783 (1973); Smyth *v.* Lubbers, 398 F.Supp. 777 (1975); People *v.* Haskins, 369 N.Y.S. 2d. 869 (1975); something less, like "reasonable suspicion," meets the test in *In·re W*, 105 Cal.Rptr. 775 (1973); People *v.* Ward, 233 N.W. 2d. 180 (1975); Doe *v.* State, 540 P. 2d. 827 (1975); Nelson *v.* State, 319 So. 2d. 154 (1975); State *v.* McKinnon, 558 P. 2d. 781 (1977); M. *v.* Bd. of Educ., 429 F.Supp. 288 (1977). The Georgia Supreme Court held that the exclusionary rule did not require suppression of evidence regardless of whether the search violated a student's constitutional rights, *see* State *v.* Young, 216 S.E. 2d. 586 (1975); Morale *v.* Grigel, 422 F.Supp. 988 (1976). *See also* the general discussion in State *v.* Kappes, 550 P. 2d. 121 (1976), a case in which marijuana was discovered in the course of a routine room inspection.

[83] Frank *v.* Maryland, 359 U.S. 360 (1959); Eaton *v.* Price, 364 U.S. 263 (1960).

[84] Camara *v.* Municipal Court, 387 U.S. 523 (1967). *See also* Colonnade Corp. *v.* U.S., 397 U.S. 72 (1970). *Cf.* Bennett *v.* Commonwealth, 188 S.E. 2d. 215 (1972). In a very recent decision, the Ohio Supreme Court ruled that "where a municipal ordinance requires the owner of real property to tender a certificate of housing inspection to a prospective buyer, and such certificate may be obtained only by allowing a warrantless inspection of the property, the imposition of a criminal penalty upon the owner's failure to tender the certificate violates the owner's rights under the Fourth Amendment to the United States Constitution." Wilson *v.* City of Cincinnati, 346 N.E. 2d. 666 (1976).

[85] Wyman *v.* James, 400 U.S. 309 (1971).

[86] See *v.* Seattle, 387 U.S. 541 (1967).

plumes being emitted from the plant's chimneys was not violating the Fourth Amendment. Justice Douglas speaking for a unanimous Court took pains to say that the Court was still adhering to *Camera*, "but we think . . . [it is] not applicable here. The field inspector did not enter the plant or offices. He was not inspecting stacks, boilers, scrubbers, flues, grates, or furnaces; nor was his inspection related to respondent's files or papers. He had sighted what anyone in the city who was near the plant could see in the sky—plumes of smoke."[87] In 1977, a Federal district court ruled that the inspection provisions of the Occupational Safety and Health Act of 1970 ran afoul of the Fourth Amendment.[88] And the Michigan Supreme Court ruled that, where fire officials in the course of fighting a blaze lawfully discovered evidence that established probable cause to issue a warrant for an investigation for arson, a subsequent warrantless search of the premises by fire officials was illegal and hence the evidence turned up was inadmissible.[89]

As recently as 1977, the Court reaffirmed the traditional proposition of law that border searches "were not subject to the warrant provisions of the Fourth Amendment" and were reasonable *per se*. Speaking for the Court, Justice Rehnquist wrote: "That searches made at the border, pursuant to the long-standing right of the sovereign to protect itself by stopping and examining persons and property crossing into this country, are reasonable simply by virtue of the fact that they occur at the border should, by now, require no extended demonstration."[90] A covey of recent Court decisions, however, has focused on the constitutionality of various activities of the border patrol aimed at apprehending aliens entering the country illegally, principally from Mexico. In a 1973 case, Almeida-Sanchez *v.* United States,[91] a sharply divided Supreme Court held that *roving patrols* of the Border Patrol cannot stop and search cars

Searches by the Border Patrol

---

[87] Air Pollution Variance Bd. of the State of Colorado *v.* Western Alfalfa Corp., 416 U.S. 861, 864-865 (1974).

[88] Barlow's, Inc. *v.* Usery, 424 F.Supp. 437 (1976). *See also* 97 S.Ct. 776 (1977).

[89] People *v.* Tyler, 250 N.W. 2d. 467 (1977).

[90] United States *v.* Ramsey, 97 S.Ct. 1972, 1979. *Ramsey* presented a particularly interesting question: whether the Fourth Amendment forbids the opening of incoming first class mail from abroad without a search warrant or probable cause. In this case, customs officials suspected that certain bulky envelopes from Thailand contained narcotics. The Court concluded that such a search was authorized by statute and found the statute consistent with the Constitution because border searches do not require probable cause and because "there is nothing in the border search exception which suggests that the mode of entry will be critical." Further, in response to the argument that opening first class mail implicated First Amendment rights, Justice Rehnquist said "Nor do we agree that, under the circumstances presented by this case, First Amendment considerations dictate a full panoply of Fourth Amendment rights prior to the border search of mailed letters. There is, again, no reason to distinguish between letters mailed into the country, and letters carried on the traveler's person. More fundamentally, however, the existing system of border searches has not been shown to invade protected First Amendment rights, and hence there is no reason to think that the potential presence of correspondence makes the otherwise constitutionally reasonable search 'unreasonable.' "

[91] 413 U.S. 266.

20 miles from the border in an effort to detect the illegal importation of aliens without probable cause or a warrant. The Court distinguished these searches from routine inspections and searches at the border or "its functional equivalent" (airports receiving non-stop passengers from foreign countries), which the Court indicated are legal. Two years later, the Court held that the ruling in *Almeida-Sanchez* was not retroactive, even if Fourth Amendment rights were violated in the search of the car.[92] Two other cases, decided that same Term, are worth noting. In one case, the Court held that vehicle *searches at fixed traffic checkpoints*, removed from the border or its functional equivalent, like searches conducted by roving patrols, must be based on probable cause.[93] In the other, the Court ruled that the roving units of the border patrol are also prohibited from stopping automobiles *to question* occupants about their citizenship or immigration status unless "they are aware of specific articulable facts, together with rational inferences from those facts, that reasonably warrant suspicion that vehicles contain aliens who may be illegally in the country."[94] Concurring in the Court's judgment, Justice Rehnquist pointed out that nothing in the decisions makes a highway stop of a motorist by a police officer to examine his driver's license, a highway roadblock to apprehend a known fugitive, or agricultural inspections constitutionally suspect. Justice Douglas concurred in the judgment, at one point objecting to the adoption of a standard that would permit stopping a car on the basis of reasonable suspicion rather than probable cause. And Chief Justice Burger, who attached a lengthy appendix entitled "The Illegal Alien Problem" to his concurring opinion, wondered if "these decisions will be seen . . . as but another example of a society seemingly impotent to deal with massive lawlessness. In that sense history may view us as prisoners of our own traditional and appropriate concern for individual rights, unable—or unwilling—to apply the concept of reasonableness explicit in the Fourth Amendment in order to develp a rational accommodation between those rights and the literal safety of the country."[95]

Finally, the Court took up the question of "whether a vehicle may be stopped at a fixed checkpoint for brief questioning of its occupants even though there is no reason to believe the particular vehicle contains illegal aliens." It decided that "such stops are consistent with the Fourth Amendment" and also held "that the operation of a fixed checkpoint need not be authorized in advance by a judicial warrant."[96] Once again speaking for the Court, Justice Powell ob-

---

[92] United States *v.* Peltier, 422 U.S. 531 (1975); Bowen *v.* U.S., 422 U.S. 916 (1975).

[93] United States *v.* Ortiz, 422 U.S. 891 (1975).

[94] United States *v.* Brignoni-Ponce, 422 U.S. 873 (1975). A Federal appeals court, sitting in Chicago, has affirmed a district court ruling that searches for illegal aliens cannot proceed without search warrants or "cause." Illinois Migrant Council *v.* Pilliod, 540 F. 2d. 1062 (1976), *affirming* 398 F.Supp. 882.

[95] *Ibid.*, 899.   [96] United States *v.* Martinez-Fuerte, 428 U.S. 543 (1976).

served that the costs of requiring border patrol agents to show reasonable suspicion before a checkpoint stop on major inland routes
"would be impractical because the flow of traffic tends to be too
heavy to allow the particularized study of a given car that would
allow it to be identified as a possible carrier of illegal aliens. In particular, such a requirement would largely eliminate any deterrent
to the conduct of well-disguised smuggling operations, even
though smugglers are known to use these highways regularly."
Moreover, compared with the intrusiveness implicit in a stop by
roving patrols, the Court concluded that, with respect to
checkpoint stops, "the . . . intrusion on Fourth Amendment interests is quite limited," because such stops were much less of a surprise and fright to motorists, were limited to exposing only what
was in plain sight, and, because of their routine character, "involve[d] less discretionary enforcement activity." Characterizing
the majority's decision as a "defacement of Fourth Amendment
protections," Justice Brennan, joined by Justice Marshall, objected
"that motorists without number may be individually stopped, questioned, visually inspected, and then further detained without even
a show of articulable suspicion . . . let alone the heretofore constitutional minimum of reasonable suspicion." And, Justice Brennan
remarked with respect to another dimension of the decision: "Every American citizen of Mexican Ancestry and every Mexican alien
lawfully in this country must know after today's decision that he
travels the fixed checkpoint highways at the risk of being subjected
not only to a stop, but also to detention and interrogation, both
prolonged and to an extent far more than for non-Mexican appearing motorists. . . . That deep resentment will be stirred by a
sense of unfair discrimination is not difficult to foresee."

Airline hijackings, once as alarming because of their frequency
as because of their unpredictability, have become comparatively
rare as searches at airports have become commonplace. Where
searches were at one time undertaken only if the suspect fit the secret "hijacker profile," travelers have become accustomed to having
their baggage searched before boarding a plane or to having it pass
through a machine. Just as use of the hijacker profile passed muster early on,[97] mass boarding searches have generally received con-

Airport
Searches

---

[97] United States v. Bell, 335 F.Supp. 797 (1971) aff'd 464 F. 2d. 667 (1972). The
manner in which the Federal appeals court heard the *Bell* case is, in many ways, as
intriguing as the constitutional validity of the hijacker profile (and the subsequent
search entailed) itself. In 1972, in a highly unusual proceeding, the prestigious United
States Court of Appeals for the Second Circuit heard a challenge to the system behind closed doors. The court was very uneasy about the secrecy, stating that "While
secret proceedings are, of course, odious and smack of ideologies as repugnant to
the founders as they are today, there is precedent for the proposition that limited
exceptions are constitutionally permissible." The court justified the search on the
grounds of the need to protect passengers and justified the secrecy of the profile
used for determining whom to search on the grounds that it would be "relatively
simple for the prospective hijacker to avoid the initial designation were any of the

stitutional approval as *quid pro quo* for the privilege of flying. A substantial body of law has, in fact, grown up concerning airport searches, affirming the constitutional validity of that practice in principle and sustaining the admissibility of evidence gained from such searches.[98] However, several cases in which the fruits of airport searches were held inadmissible, or were otherwise distinguished, suggest limitations on the practice:[99] (1) searches may be initiated only on reasonable suspicion (i.e., fitting the "hijacker profile," tripping the magnetometer, failing to properly identify oneself); (2) searches may extend only to areas continuing to justify suspicion (e.g., containers or enclosures large enough to conceal weapons or explosives); (3) searches yield admissible evidence when the articles are in plain sight; (4) searches must afford warning to passengers that they have the right to avoid the search by not boarding the plane, so that consent is entirely voluntary; and (5) searches not executed as a condition of passenger boarding are justified only under customary "stop and frisk" circumstances.

Searches by Private Citizens   Because constitutional guarantees pertain only to abuses by agents of government, private citizens cannot, within the meaning of the Fourth Amendment, commit an unreasonable search or seizure. When a private citizen, therefore, turns evidence of wrongdoing over to a police officer, the evidence is not regarded as tainted with illegality and has traditionally been judged admissible in court.[100] Perhaps the most frequent context of private searches is the discovery of contraband in passengers' luggage by airline employees. While these private searches have been upheld, courts have taken a very different view where employees at police behest deliberately search for evidence[101] or where a police officer searches in an official capacity even while "moonlighting."[102]

norms employed to become generally known." *See New York Times*, July 9, 1972. *See also* United States *v.* Epperson, 454 F. 2d. 769 (1972).

[98] *See* United States *v.* Mitchell, 352 F.Supp. 38 (1972); People *v.* Botos, 104 Cal. Rptr. 193 (1972); State *v.* Damon, 502 P. 2d. 1360 (1972); United States *v.* Moreno, 475 F. 2d. 44 (1973); United States *v.* Riggs, 474 F. 2d. 699 (1973); People *v.* Boyles, 341 N.Y.S. 2d. 967 (1973); People *v.* Lopez, 342 N.Y.S. 2d. 420 (1973). For a comprehensive survey of airport search developments, *see* United States *v.* Davis, 482 F. 2d. 893 (1973); *see also* United States *v.* Skipwith, 482 F. 2d. 1272 (1973); United States *v.* Moore, 483 F.Supp. 1361 (1973); People *v.* Kuhn, 351 N.Y.S 2d. 649 (1973); United States *v.* Edwards, 498 F. 2d. 496 (1974) and People *v.* Hyde, 524 P. 2d. 830 (1974); *but see* United States *v.* Albarado, 495 F. 2d. 799 (1974).

[99] *See* United States *v.* Allen, 349 F.Supp. 749 (1972); United States *v.* Kroll, 351 F.Supp. 148 (1972); United States *v.* Meulener, 351 F.Supp. 1284 (1972).

[100] United States *v.* Blanton, 479 F. 2d. 327 (1973); United States *v.* Ogden, 485 F. 2d. 536 (1973); State *v.* Lohss, 313 A. 2d. 87 (1973); State *v.* Pearson, 514 P. 2d. 884 (1973); Bell *v.* State, 519 P. 2d. 804 (1974); Commonwealth *v.* Kozak, 336 A. 2d. 387 (1975); Gundlach *v.* Janing, 401 F.Supp. 1089 (1975); Smith *v.* Brookshire Bros., Inc., 519 F. 2d. 93 (1975); State *v.* Morris, 329 N.E. 2d. 85 (1975).

[101] United States *v.* Newton, 510 F. 2d. 1149 (1975) and United States *v.* Krell, 338 F.Supp. 1372 (1975).

[102] State *v.* Roccasecca, 328 A. 2d. 35 (1974). However, evidence seized by a private security guard at a store was not inadmissible even if the seizure was improper, *see* State *v.* Keyser, 369 A. 2d. 224 (1977).

In other noteworthy Fourth Amendment rulings, the Supreme Court held that: (1) "Grand jury questions based on evidence obtained . . . [by an illegal search] involve no independent governmental invasion of one's person, house, papers, or effects, but rather the usual abridgement of personal privacy common to all grand jury questioning. Questions based on illegally-obtained evidence are only a derivative use of the product of a past unlawful search and seizure. They work no Fourth Amendment wrong";[103] and (2) the Bank Secrecy Act, which required banks to maintain records and make certain reports considered useful in criminal, tax or regulatory investigations or proceedings, did not violate the Fourth Amendment.[104] And, other decisions by lower courts have: (1) upheld Denver's "hold and treat" ordinance requiring that prostitutes either take drugs for the treatment of venereal disease or face detention in jail during treatment;[105] (2) invalidated much of the Army's drug abuse prevention program as an unjustifiable intrusion on the privacy of soldiers;[106] and (3) ruled that, while the speech and debate clause will not shield an employee or member of Congress from prosecution or suit stemming from violations of the Fourth Amendment in an attempt to obtain information, a committee of Congress should enjoy at least as much latitude as a grand jury in the use of material that has been unlawfully seized.[107] Finally, two developments appeared to reduce appreciably the legacy of lawlessness and disorder bequeathed by the Nixon Justice Department: (1) Congress voted to repeal laws allowing Federal agents to conduct "no knock" searches;[108] and (2) the U.S. District Court for the District of Columbia held that the break-in at the office of Dr. Lewis Fielding (Daniel Ellsberg's psychiatrist) was unconstitutional insofar as agents of the executive branch entered the office and removed materials without a warrant despite their allegations of national security.[109]

And in 1972, the Court, over a bitter dissent of Justice Douglas, upheld a warrantless search of a gun dealer's locked storeroom during business hours.[110] This kind of search is explicitly authorized under the Gun Control Act of 1968.[111] Justice White, speaking for the Court, explained: "We have little difficulty in concluding

---

[103] United States *v*. Calandra, 414 U.S. 338 (1974).

[104] California Bankers Ass'n *v*. Shultz, 416 U.S. 21 (1974). *See also* United States *v*. Miller, 425 U.S. 435 (1976) where an expectation of privacy was held not to extend to the defendant's checks, deposit slips, or bank records.

[105] Reynolds *v*. McNichols, 488 F. 2d. 1378 (1973).

[106] Comm. for G.I. Rights *v*. Callaway, 370 F.Supp. 934 (1974).

[107] McSurely *v*. McClellan, 521 F. 2d. 1024 (1975).

[108] 1974 *Cong. Quart. Weekly Report*, 2994.

[109] United States *v*. Ehrlichman, 376 F.Supp. 29 (1974); *and* United States *v*. Barker, 514 F. 2d. 208 (1975). For an interesting contrast in views, see those of President Nixon as expressed in the Nixon-Frost interviews, *New York Times*, May 20, 1977.

[110] U.S. *v*. Biswell, 406 U.S. 311 (1972).

[111] *Ibid*., 317. *See also* Justice Douglas's dissent, *ibid*., 317.

that where, as here, regulatory inspections further urgent *federal* interest and the possibilities of abuse and threat to privacy are not of impressive dimensions, the inspection may proceed without a warrant, *where specifically authorized by statute"* (emphasis supplied).[112] There seems to be a suggestion here that the Court will give greater deference to Congressional determinations as to when search warrants can be dispensed with than it will to determinations of local and State officials.

Searches
With
Warrants

As the constitutional provision makes plain, warrants for searches shall be issued only for "probable cause." All that has been said above about "probable cause" with respect to arrest has application here. One troublesome question with respect to search warrants is how quickly must they be executed to meet the constitutional test of reasonableness. The New York Appeals Court recently had occasion to canvass the problem, and it held that the State law which required "forthwith execution . . . does not mean immediately, but is qualified by the practicalities and exigencies that the executing officer faces in the performance of duty."[113]

Surprisingly, in view of the observation made at the outset, that a prominent motivation for the Fourth Amendment was the colonists' outrage over "general warrants," a recent decision of the Supreme Court appears to substantially expand the ambit of searches undertaken with a warrant. In that decision, which also spoke to a significant issue of self-incrimination (*see* p. 385), the Court held that a warrant that authorized the search of an attorney's office for documents bearing on the perpetration of an alleged fraud with respect to a specific piece of real estate was not defective in empowering seizure of those documents "together with other fruits, instrumentalities and evidence of crime at this [time] unknown." The Court also upheld the admissibility of documents not bearing on the lot in question but on another piece of property on grounds that the investigators executing the search might reasonably have thought such papers would illuminate the fraud originally alleged, even if such evidence was used to secure additional charges against the defendant-lawyer.[114] Justices Brennan and Marshall, dissenting, believed the warrant to be "impermissibly general."

The
Exclusionary
Rule

As indicated at the outset of this discussion of the Fourth Amendment, in 1914 the Court barred in a Federal prosecution the use of evidence secured through an illegal search and seizure (the "exclusionary rule").[115] In 1949 when the question was raised as to whether or not States should likewise be barred from using

---

[112] *Ibid.*, 317. The same Fourth Amendment standards of probable cause are applicable to arrests as well as to searches. Commonwealth *v.* Stevens, 283 N.E. 2d. 673 (1972) and cases cited therein.

[113] People *v.* Glen, 331 N.Y.S. 2d. 656 (1972).

[114] Andresen *v.* Md., 427 U.S. 463 (1976).

[115] Weeks *v.* U.S., 232 U.S. 383 (1914).

such evidence, Justice Frankfurter speaking for the Court explained that the earlier decision "was not derived from the explicit requirements of the Fourth Amendment; it was not based on legislation expressing Congressional policy in the enforcement of the Constitution. The decision was a matter of judicial implication. Since then it has been frequently applied and we stoutly adhere to it. . . ."[116] Then in what looked like an invitation for Congress to act on the matter, Frankfurter concluded by saying: "And though we have interpreted the Fourth Amendment to forbid the admission of such evidence, a different question would be presented if Congress under its legislative powers were to pass a statute purporting to negate [the exclusionary] doctrine. We would then be faced with the problem of the respect to be accorded the legislative judgment on an issue as to which, in default of that judgment, we have been forced to depend upon our own. Problems of a converse character, also not before us, would be presented should Congress under §5 of the Fourteenth Amendment undertake to enforce the rights guaranteed by attempting to make the [exclusionary] doctrine binding upon the States."[117]

The arrangement, whereby the Federal jurisdiction used the exclusionary rule and some thirty States did not, created some predictable difficulties. Some Federal law enforcement officials turned over evidence they could not use to State officials if they could use it to establish the commission of a State crime. This practice became common enough to be honored in the "silver-platter doctrine" used by courts to justify the use of such evidence. It also covered the situation where State officials gave Federal officials evidence that the latter could not have used had they obtained it themselves in the manner in which State officials had.[118]

Then in 1961 in a ringing decision the Court held that: "Since the Fourth Amendment's right of privacy has been declared enforceable against the States through the Due Process Clause of the Fourteenth, it is enforceable against them by the same sanction of exclusion as is used against the Federal Government."[119]

One of the fascinating questions of American constitutional law is, *why* an exclusionary rule? Evidence is evidence. A gun found in an illegal search may very well link a defendant to a murder beyond a reasonable doubt. Why not use it? And, if it was procured illegally, punish those who acted illegally, don't discard the evidence, some have said. Protagonists of the rule have argued that

[116] Wolf *v*. Colorado, 338 U.S. 25 (1949).   [117] *Ibid.*, 33.
[118] The zany history of the Silver Platter doctrine is described in a decision that put a stop to it. Elkins *v*. U.S., 364 U.S. 206 (1960).
[119] Mapp *v*. Ohio, 367 U.S. 643 (1961). The New Hampshire Supreme Court has held that where evidence is gained by private individuals acting on their own and not as agents of the police, it is not a violation of the Fourth Amendment, State *v*. Salsman, 290 A. 2d. 618 (1972). Miramontes *v*. Superior Court, 102 Calif.Rptr. 182 (1972); People *v*. Mangiefico, 102 Calif. Rptr. 449 (1972); U.S. *v*. Knox, 458 F. 2d. 612 (1972).

only by excluding the evidence can you get law enforcement officials to behave. Other remedies just do not work.

A notable dissent from Chief Justice Burger in 1971 indicates that the last word may not have been spoken on the exclusionary rule. "I do not question the need for some remedy to give meaning and teeth to the constitutional guarantees against unlawful conduct by government officials. . . . But the hope that this objective could be accomplished by the exclusion of reliable evidence from criminal trials was hardly more than a wistful dream. Although I would hesitate to abandon it until some meaningful substitute is developed, the history of the Suppression Doctrine demonstrates that it is both conceptually sterile and practically ineffective in accomplishing its stated objective. Some clear demonstration of the benefits and effectiveness of the Exclusionary Rule is required to justify it in view of the high price it extracts from society—the release of countless guilty criminals. . . . But there is no empirical evidence to support the claim that the rule actually deters illegal conduct of law enforcement officials."[120]

The
Suppression
Doctrine
Recent developments have cast serious doubts on the future of the exclusionary rule. Indeed, if the pejorative change of name to "the suppression doctrine" is any measure of the Court's dissatisfaction with the exclusionary rule, the prognosis is not encouraging. Two decisions are particularly noteworthy. In one case the Court had occasion to rule on the question of whether "evidence seized by a state criminal law enforcement officer in good faith, but nonetheless unconstitutionally, [is] inadmissible in a civil proceeding by or against the United States." Addressing this question in the context of a Federal civil tax proceeding that occurred sometime following the seizure of a large amount of cash and records in a gambling raid, Justice Blackmun, speaking for the majority, wrote: "Clearly, the enforcement of admittedly valid laws would be hampered by so extending the exclusionary rule, and, as is nearly always the case with the rule, concededly relevant and reliable evidence would be rendered unavailable." The Court's opinion then reviewed extensively studies testing whether or not the exclusionary rule fulfills a deterrent function. Given the high social cost of the rule, the opinion observed, the studies, which were admittedly flawed, were sufficiently unclear as to the deterrent effect of the rule so as, in the majority's view, to argue against extension of the rule—even, perhaps, its retention.[121] In dissent, Justice Stewart wrote: "The Court's failure to heed . . . precedents not only rips a hole in the fabric of the law but leads to a result that cannot even save the valid arguments of those who would eliminate the exclu-

---

[120] Bivens v. Six Unknown Named Agents, 403 U.S. 388, 415 (1971). The Pennsylvania Supreme Court recently held that the State may not introduce at trial the testimony of a witness whose existence was solely come upon as the result of an illegal search. Commonwealth v. Cephas, 291 A. 2d. 106 (1972).

[121] United States v. Janis, 428 U.S. 433 (1976).

sionary rule entirely. For under the Court's ruling, society must not only continue to pay the high cost of the exclusionary rule . . . but it must also forfeit the benefit for which it has paid so dearly."

The Court also markedly curtailed Federal *habeas corpus* relief to be accorded State prisoners, at least where Fourth Amendment violations were alleged. Turning its back on an earlier decision of the Warren Court,[122] the majority ruled that, "where the State has provided an opportunity for free and fair litigation of a Fourth Amendment claim, a state prisoner may not be granted federal habeas corpus relief on the ground that evidence obtained in an unconstitutional search or seizure was introduced at his trial."[123] Justice Powell, speaking for the Court, buttressed this conclusion by observing: "Application of the [exclusionary] rule . . . deflects the truthfinding process and often frees the guilty. The disparity in particular cases between the error committed by the police officer and the windfall afforded a guilty defendant by application of the rule is contrary to the idea of proportionality that is essential to the concept of justice. Thus, although the rule is thought to deter unlawful police activity in part through the nurturing of respect for Fourth Amendment values, if applied indiscriminately it may well have the opposite effect of generating disrespect for the law and administration of justice . . . [T]he additional contribution, if any, of the consideration of search-and-seizure claims of state prisoners on collateral review is small in relation to the costs." In a concurring opinion, Chief Justice Burger, characterizing the majority's criticism of the exclusionary rule over-all as "hesitant" and "[b]y way of dictum," declared: "[I]t seems clear to me that the exclusionary rule has been operative long enough to demonstrate its flaws. The time has come to modify its reach, even if it is retained for a small and limited category of cases." Arguing with Justices Brennan and Marshall in dissent that the majority's decision in this case constituted an unjustified exception to the principles governing general Federal *habeas corpus* relief, Justice White nevertheless felt constrained to announce that he "would join four or more other Justices in substantially limiting the reach of the exclusionary rule as presently administered under the Fourth Amendment in federal and state criminal trials."

(For a discussion of the exclusionary rule and grand jury proceedings, *see* p. 379.)

The history of the Supreme Court's handling of the issue arising from wiretapping and electronic surveillance is as complicated as it is fascinating.[124] The short of the history pertinent here is that from 1928 until the late 1960's, the Court held that the Fourth Amendment did not cover these activities except when electronic

Wiretapping and Electronic Surveillance

---

[122] Kaufman *v.* U.S., 394 U.S. 217 (1969).

[123] Stone *v.* Powell, 428 U.S. 465, 494 (1976).

[124] Justice Clark provided a good short history in his opinion for the Court in Berger *v.* N.Y., 388 U.S. 41 (1967).

snooping was accomplished by a "physical trespass," like putting a foot-long spike with a microphone attached into the heating duct of a house. After 1934, cases involving the old-fashioned type of wiretapping were decided on the basis of the meaning of the Communications Act of 1934,[125] which on its face seemed to prohibit wiretapping, but clumsy wording made it an arguable proposition that only wiretapping *and* divulging the contents was forbidden, not wiretapping alone. But all the subtle distinctions, all the formidable rhetoric ("fruit of the poisonous tree") which emerged from these cases were overtaken by events. In a pair of cases decided in 1967, the Court finally swept away past distinctions and held that both wiretapping and electronic surveillance through a "bug" or other device are now covered by the Fourth Amendment.[126] That does not mean therefore that they cannot be used, for, as we have already seen, searches are permissible if done under a warrant issued for probable cause. Subsequently, Congress passed the Omnibus Crime Control and Safe Streets Act of 1968[127] providing an elaborate procedure under which "the Attorney General, or any Assistant Attorney General specially designated by the Attorney General, may authorize an application to a Federal Judge of competent jurisdiction for and such judge may grant . . . an order authorizing or approving the interception of wire or oral communications by the Federal Bureau of Investigation, or a Federal agency having responsibility for the investigation of an offense as to which application is made. . . ."

While still Attorney General, John Mitchell took the position that, in dealing with the threat of domestic subversion, the government needs and has the inherent power to use wiretaps and other devices to maintain surveillance. Mitchell quickly received a verbal thrashing in the courts. A United States court of appeals said in answer to him: "The government has not pointed to, and we do not find, one written phrase in the Constitution, in the statutory law, or in the case law of the United States, which exempts the President, the Attorney General, or federal law enforcement from the restrictions of the Fourth Amendment in the case at hand: . . . that in dealing with the threat of domestic subversion, the Executive Branch of our government, including the Attorney General and the law enforcement agents of the United States, is subject to the limitations of the Fourth Amendment to the Constitution when undertaking searches and seizures for oral communications by wire."[128] In more restrained language, the Supreme Court itself by a vote of 8-0 (Justice Rehnquist not participating) recently rejected

---

[125] 48 *Stat.* 1102.

[126] Berger *v.* N.Y., 388 U.S. 41 (1967); Katz *v.* U.S., 389 U.S. 347 (1967); U.S. *v.* White, 401 U.S. 745 (1971). U.S. courts of appeals recently have held that wiretaps do not violate the Fourth Amendment "when one party consents but the other party has no knowledge of the phone tap." U.S. *v.* Quintana, 457 F. 2d. 874, 878 (1972) and cases cited therein.

[127] 18 U.S.C. 2510 *et seq.*

[128] U.S. *v.* U.S. District Court for E.D. of Mich., 444 F. 2d. 651, 665-667 (1971).

Mitchell's contention, saying: "Thus, we conclude that the Government's concerns do not justify departure in this case from the customary Fourth Amendment requirement of judicial approval prior to initiation of a search or surveillance. Although some added burden will be imposed upon the Attorney General, this inconvenience is justified in a free society to protect constitutional values. Nor do we think the Government's domestic surveillance powers will be impaired to any significant degree. A prior warrant establishes presumptive validity of the surveillance and will minimize the burden of justification in post-surveillance judicial review. By no means of least importance will be the reassurance of the public generally that indiscriminate wiretapping and bugging of law-abiding citizens cannot occur.

"We emphasize, before concluding this opinion, the scope of our decision. As stated at the outset, this case involves only the domestic aspects of national security. We have not addressed, and express no opinion as to, the issues which may be involved with respect to activities of foreign powers or their agents. Nor does our decision rest on the language of §2511 (3) or any other section of Title III of the Omnibus Crime Control and Safe Streets Act of 1968. That Act does not attempt to define or delineate the powers of the President to meet domestic threats to the national security."[129] A few days later, the Court ruled in a 5-4 decision, with the non-Nixon appointees constituting the majority, that grand jury witnesses could, in an adjudication for civil contempt for refusing to answer questions before a Federal grand jury, invoke as a defense that the interrogation would be based on illegal wiretaps.[130] The majority pointed out that Federal law provides that the contents of wiretapping "may not be received in evidence in any proceeding in or before . . . any grand jury, . . . if disclosure of that information would be in violation of this chapter." Justice Rehnquist, speaking for the dissenters, protested bitterly the majority's interpretation of the statute, asserting that "The Court has at least figuratively stood on its head both the language and the legislative history of this section [of the statute] in order to conclude that it was intended to expand the rights of criminal defendants." Despite its importance, it should be noted that this decision involves statutory and not constitutional interpretation.

Interestingly enough, in an interview following the earlier wiretap decision, Attorney General Kleindienst said that the decision would reduce the Government's intelligence activity into subversive activities "but not to an extent that will damage national security."[131]

In an important wiretapping case involving *statutory* interpreta-

---

[129] U.S. *v*. U.S. District Court, 407 U.S. 297 (1972). For statistics on use of Federal wiretapping *see* Justice Douglas's dissent, *ibid*.

[130] Gelbard *v*. U.S., 408 U.S. 41 (1972).

[131] Fred P. Graham, "Wiretap Ruling Called No Danger to Security," *The Dallas Morning News*, June 24, 1972.

tion, the Supreme Court held that the provision of the Omnibus Crime Control and Safe Streets Act of 1968 requiring that "the Attorney General, or any Assistant Attorney General specifically designated by the Attorney General, may authorize an application to a Federal judge . . . for . . . an order authorizing or approving the interception of wire or oral communications" meant just that. And Attorney General Mitchell's failure to be meticulous and allowing other non-designated subordinate officials to so authorize resulted in the unhappy situation where the government was faced with a myriad of "spoiled" cases.[132] And, in a subsequent case interpreting Title III of the Act, the Court ruled that an application for a warrant to wiretap must name all of the individuals, believed by the government to be committing an offense, who will be overheard. It also held that the government was obligated to furnish the judge issuing the warrant with sufficient information to make the exercise of his discretion meaningful. But, in a conclusion that drew fire from the three dissenters in the case, the Court went on to hold that, in the circumstances of this case, violation of these statutory commands did not necessitate suppression of the intercepted conversations.[133] Finally, in the face of silence by the Supreme Court and holdings by lower courts that warrants are not necessary when wiretapping is done against agents of a foreign power, a recent decision by the U.S. Court of Appeals for the District of Columbia appears to suggest that warrants are required for *all* wiretapping.[134]

The U.S. Court of Appeals, District of Columbia Circuit, has ruled that warrantless electronic surveillance of the Jewish Defense League violated Title III of the Omnibus Crime Control and Safe Streets Act of 1968. Though the surveillance was instituted on order of the President in the name of intelligence gathering for national security, the court concluded that such activities were illegal since the JDL was neither the agent of a foreign power nor engaged in any collaboration with one.[135] Moreover, a Federal district court in the same circuit has held the warrantless Army surveil-

---

[132] United States *v*. Giordano, 416 U.S. 505 (1974), *and* United States *v*. Chavez, 416 U.S. 562 (1974).

[133] United States *v*. Donovan, 97 S.Ct. 658 (1977).

[134] Zweibon *v*. Mitchell, 516 F. 2d. 594, 669 (1975). For example, at the onset of its October 1974 Term, the Supreme Court refused to hear a case focusing on the question of whether Federal agents needed court authorization to wiretap a foreign spy, Ivanov *v*. U.S., 419 U.S. 881 (1974); the appeals court decision is reported at 494 F. 2d. 593.

[135] Zweibon *v*. Mitchell, 516 F. 2d. 594 (1975). Presidential orders to wiretap without a warrant also created liability for some of the defendants in Halperin *v*. Kissinger, 424 F.Supp. 838 (1976). The district court subsequently awarded one dollar in damages from each of the defendants responsible. *New York Times*, Aug. 7, 1977. The activities of President Nixon are also referred to in Art. II §2 of the impeachment resolution adopted by the House Judiciary Committee on July 29, 1974. The Carter Administration is apparently preparing a new policy banning all warrantless wiretapping, searches, and mail opening. *See* Minneapolis *Tribune*, Aug, 9, 1977.

lance of the political activities of Americans overseas contravenes the Fourth Amendment.[136] And, in an extensive opinion vividly describing the infiltration activities of the New York City Police Department's BOSS (Bureau of Special Services) unit in the neighborhoods of the city's lower East Side, a State court excoriated as blatantly unconstitutional the longtime, intrusive, often disruptive, intelligence gathering activities performed by undercover agents.[137]

Mostly on the basis of statutory authority, the courts have readily sustained the determined and independent efforts of telephone companies to track down subscribers who cleverly attempt to evade the tolls on long distance calls.[138] A New York court, however, has struck down as arbitrary and capricious an order of the State public service commission requiring phone companies to notify their subscribers three days in advance of releasing toll records pursuant to any subpoena.[139] Finally, the courts have held that the ban on wiretapping does not extend to surveillance by spouses.[140]

As pointed out earlier (pp. 240-241), recent Supreme Court decisions with respect to the Fourth Amendment are generally not retroactive in application.

Non-retroactivity of Fourth Amendment Decisions

Like other important rights, the rights to be free from unreasonable searches and seizures can be waived. But as the California Supreme Court recently put it, those rights "where reasonably related to the achievement of a proper purpose, may be waived as a condition to gaining some other advantage, but the waiver must appear of record to have been knowingly and intelligently made."[141]

Waiver of Fourth Amendment Rights

In a recent Connecticut court challenge to a compulsory sex education course in school, one of the contentions of the parent-plaintiffs was that they feared that their children would disclose private family activities or conversations which had taken place in their homes. The court held that "Disclosures of this nature are not constitutionally protected and do not constitute an unlawful invasion of privacy under the fourth amendment . . . nor under any other law known to the court."[142]

A Novel Contention Rejected

[136] Berlin Democratic Club v. Rumsfeld, 410 F.Supp. 144 (1976).

[137] People v. Collier, 376 N.Y.S. 2d. 954 (1975).

[138] *See* United States v. Clegg, 509 F. 2d. 605 (1975); United States v. Goldstein, 532 F. 2d. 1305 (1976); United States v. Harvey, 394 F.Supp. 228 (1975); State v. Hruska, 547 P. 2d. 732 (1976); People v. Mahoney, 122 Cal.Rptr. 174 (1975); United States v. Auler, 539 F. 2d. 642 (1976). *But cf.* a case where a doctor, hospital, and nurse monitor the conversations of a patient with her lawyer, Gerrard v. Blackman, 401 F.Supp. 1189 (1975).

[139] City of New York v. Public Service Com'n, 379 N.Y.S. 2d. 987 (1976).

[140] *See* Simpson v. Simpson, 490 F. 2d. 803 (1974); Beaber v. Beaber, 322 N.E. 2d. 910 (1974). But *Simpson* has come in for heavy criticism and the postulated spousal exception to Title III has been severely questioned in United States v. Jones, 542 F. 2d. 661 (1976).

[141] People v. Myers, 494 P. 2d. 684 (1972). *Cf.* Himmage v. State, 496 P. 2d. 763 (1972).

[142] Hopkins v. Hamden Bd. of Ed., 289 A. 2d. 914, 924 (1971). *But see* p. 288, n. 91.

AMENDMENT V

No person shall be held to answer for a capital or otherwise infamous crime, unless on a presentment or indictment of a grand
jury, except in cases arising in the land or naval forces, or in the
militia, when in actual service in time of war or public danger;
nor shall any person be subject for the same offense to be twice
put in jeopardy of life or limb; nor shall be compelled in any
criminal case to be a witness against himself, nor be deprived of
life, liberty or property, without due process of law; nor shall
private property be taken for public use without just compensation.

Amendments IV, V, VI, and VIII constitute a "bill of rights" for
accused persons. For the most part they were compiled from the
Bills of Rights of the early State constitutions, and in more than one
respect they represented a distinct advance upon English law of
that time and indeed for many years afterward.

"Infamous crime" is one rendered so by the penalty attached to
it. Any offense punishable by imprisonment, or loss of civil or political privileges, or hard labor, is, the Court has held, "infamous" in
the sense of the Constitution.[1] But "what punishments shall be considered infamous may be affected by the changes of public opinion
from one age to another. In former times, being put in the stocks
was not considered as necessarily infamous. . . . But at the present
day [it] might be thought an infamous punishment."[2]

"Presentment or indictment": A presentment is returned upon
the initiative of the grand jury; an indictment is returned upon
evidence laid before that body by the public prosecutor.

The "grand jury" here stipulated for is the grand jury as it was
known to the common law, and so consists of at least twelve and not
more than twenty-three persons chosen from the community by a
process prescribed by law. Once constituted it has large powers of
investigation, but its presentments or indictments must have the
support of at least twelve members. Despite the fact that much of
the Bill of Rights has been incorporated into the Fourteenth
Amendment, it has been held that States are not required to employ grand juries as long as the process they employ is a fair one.[3]

The use of grand juries to combat crime and to have the power
to make reports is controversial and interesting but beyond the

---

[1] *Ex parte* Wilson, 114 U.S. 417 (1885); United States *v.* Moreland, 258 U.S. 433
(1922). *But see* Harvin *v.* U.S., 445 F. 2d. 675 (1971).

[2] *Ex parte* Wilson, 114 U.S. 417, 427-428 (1885).

[3] ". . . we are unable to say that the substitution for a presentment or indictment
by a grand jury of the proceeding by information, after examination and commitment by a magistrate, certifying to the probable guilt of the defendant, with the
right on his part to aid of counsel, and to the cross-examination of the witness produced for prosecution, is not due process of law." Hurtado *v.* Cal., 110 U.S. 516, 538
(1884); Alexander *v.* Louisiana, 405 U.S. 625, 633 (1972); Gasaway *v.* Page, 303
F.Supp. 391 (1969); Freeman *v.* Page, 443 F. 2d. 493, 495 (1971).

scope of a discussion of the meaning of this particular constitutional provision. For those interested in pursuing that subject *see* citation below.[4] (A few cases recently decided focus on constitutional
problems of those called to testify before grand juries and are discussed under self-incrimination below.)

"The land and naval forces" are, of course, subject to military
law, administered through the court-martial (*see* Article I, Section
VIII, ¶14). But the exception also for a time served a broader purpose, namely, "to authorize the trial by court-martial of the members of the armed forces for all that class of crimes which under the
Fifth and Sixth Amendments might otherwise have been deemed
triable in the civil courts."[5] The term "land and naval forces" included at one time camp followers as well as enrollees[6] but all that
has been changed by recent decisions as described earlier on pp.
115-117.

The Case
of the
Saboteurs

In the Case of the Saboteurs[7] who landed on our shores in June
1942 from German submarines and were later picked up in civilian
dress in New York City and Chicago by the FBI, the Court declined
to say that it included enemy personnel who were found in disguise
within our lines and so were charged with violating the laws of war.
The Court's position was that such cases had never been deemed to
fall within the guarantees of the amendments, citing in this connection Section 2 of the Act of Congress of April 10, 1806, which, following the Resolution of the Continental Congress of August 21,
1776, imposed the death penalty on alien spies "according to the
law and usage of nations, by sentence of a general court martial."[8]
The trial of the saboteurs by military commission was consequently
held to be within the merged powers of the President and Congress; but inasmuch as they were really conducting a hostile operation against the United States, in a way forbidden by the laws of
war, it would have been reasonable to hold that they were answerable to the President simply in his capacity as Supreme Commander. This, in fact, was the result which was later arrived at by the
Court in General Yamashita's case, the doctrine of which is
summed up by Justice Rutledge, in his dissent, as follows: "That
there is no law restrictive upon these proceedings other than whatever rules and regulations may be prescribed for their government
by the executive authority or the military."[9] The charge against

[4] Senator John L. McClellan, "The Organized Crime Act or Its Critics: Which
Threatens Civil Liberties?" 46 *Notre Dame Lawyer*, 55 (1970). *And see* Paul Cowan,
"Kind of Immunity That Leads to Jail: The New Grand Jury," *New York Times*, Apr.
29, 1973, p. 19.

[5] *Ex parte* Quirin, 317 U.S. 1, 43 (1942).

[6] Charles K. Burdick, *Law of the American Constitution* (New York, 1922), 264, and
cases there cited.

[7] Note 5 above.

[8] 317 U.S. 1, 41. The famouse case of Major André during the Revolution was a
prototype of the Case of the Saboteurs. *Ibid.*, 31, note 9.

[9] *In re* General Yamashita, 327 U.S. 1, 81 (1946). For a latitudinarian view of the

Yamashita was that he had systematically violated the laws of war.

"In time of war or public danger" took on new meaning in 1968 as a result of the important case, O'Callahan v. Parker. There the Court held that "We have concluded that the crime to be under military jurisdiction must be service connected, lest 'cases arising in the land or naval forces, or in the Militia, when in actual service in time of War or public danger,' as used in the Fifth Amendment, be expanded to deprive every member of the Armed services of the benefits of an indictment by a grand jury and a trial by a jury of his peers."[10] Previously, it was assumed that all servicemen on active duty were subject to court-martial *at all times*, as were members of the militia in times of war or public danger.[11] The explicit exception for men in service, makes clear that as to all other persons, the Fifth Amendment is designed for times of war as well as for times of peace. But it is obvious that in order to enforce its provisions, as well as those of the following amendment, the courts must be open and functioning properly.[12] (For further discussion of *O'Callahan* and its progeny, *see* pp. 116-117; for a discussion of vagueness as it pertains to the Uniform Code of Military Justice, *see* p. 114; for a discussion of the right to counsel and summary courts-martial, *see* p. 398.)

When "Jeopardy" Arises

"Twice in jeopardy": For years, because of legal complexities this phrase did not seem to mean the comprehensive protection it appears to mean on its face.[13] Furthermore, it was held for a long time that this provision was not applicable to the States.[14] All that has been changed by recent decisions. The Court in 1968 held that the provision did indeed apply to the States, going on to say: "The fundamental nature of the guarantee against double jeopardy can hardly be doubted. Its origins can be traced back to Greek and Roman times and it became established in the common law of England long before this Nation's independence. . . . As this Court put it in Green v. U.S. . . . (1957), 'the underlying idea . . . is that the State with all its resources and power should not be allowed to

---

jurisdiction of courts-martial, *see* Charles Warren, "Spies and the Power of Congress to Subject Certain Classes of Civilians to Trial by Court Martial," *American Law Review*, 195-228 (March-April, 1919); also Article 106 of the Uniform Code of Military Justice: "Any person who in time of war found lurking or acting as a spy in or about any of the fortifications, posts, quarters, or encampments of any of the armies of the United States, or elsewhere [N.B.] shall be tried by a general court-martial or by a military commission, and shall, on conviction thereof, suffer death." 10 U.S.C. 906.

[10] O'Callahan v. Parker, 395 U.S. 258, 272-273 (1969). The decision in *O'Callahan* is not retroactive, *see* Gosa v. Mayden, 413 U.S. 665 (1973).

[11] Johnson v. Sayre, 158 U.S. 109 (1895); Lee v. Madigan, 358 U.S. 228, 232-235 (1959).

[12] *Ex parte* Milligan, 4 Wall. 2 (1866). The attempt of counsel of the Saboteurs to invoke this case in behalf of their clients was countered by the Court pointing out that Milligan had not surrendered his civilian status.

[13] For extended discussion of one of these complexities, *see* Ashe v. Swenson, 397 U.S. 436 (1970).

[14] Palko v. Conn., 302 U.S. 319 (1937).

make repeated attempts to convict an individual for an alleged offense, thereby subjecting him to embarrassment, expense and ordeal compelling him to live in a continuing state of anxiety and insecurity, as well as enhancing the possibility that even though innocent he may be found guilty.' "[15] In subsequent cases, the Supreme Court has viewed with critical eye any governmental action which smacks of double jeopardy within *one system* of government be it State or Federal.[16] These decisions have caused some observers to wonder about the future survival of previous decisions which permitted successive prosecutions by Federal and State governments for the same crime on the theory that they were separate sovereigns. Thus far the Supreme Court has not had occasion to overrule them.[17]

But when has a single sovereign crossed the line of constitutionality and engaged in a second prosecution of the defendant for the same offense or punished the defendant again for the same crime? As reaffirmed by the Court in 1977,[18] the answer is to be found in its formulation of the *Blockburger* rule, "where the same act or transaction constitutes a violation of two distinct statutory provisions, the test to be applied to determine whether there are two offenses or only one, is whether each provision requires proof of an additional fact which the other does not."[19]

Several other propositions relative to the occurrence of double jeopardy are worth noting. One, if a jury cannot agree, or if it is illegally constituted, there is no trial, and so no jeopardy, under the clause; and the same result follows where a verdict of conviction is set aside on appeal by the accused.[20] (A declaration of mistrials for other reasons is more complicated in present law.[21] As the Court states it: "The trial judge must recognize that lack of preparedness by the government to continue the trial directly implicates policies

[15] Benton v. Maryland, 395 U.S. 784, 795-796 (1969). *See* People v. Rushin, 194 N.W. 2d. 718 (1971). *See also* Simpson v. Florida, 403 U.S. 384 (1971).

[16] Waller v. Florida, 397 U.S. 387 (1970); Ashe v. Swenson, 397 U.S. 436 (1970); Simpson v. Florida, 403 U.S. 384 (1971). In Robinson v. Neil, 409 U.S. 505 (1973), the Court held the decision in *Waller* to be fully retroactive.

[17] *See* Bartkus v. Ill., 359 U.S. 121 (1959); Abbate v. U.S., 359 U.S. 187 (1959).

[18] Brown v. Ohio, 97 S.Ct. 2221 (1977). *See also* Jeffers v. U.S., 97 S.Ct. 2207 (1977), applying the principle enunciated in Iannelli v. U.S., 420 U.S. 770 (1975), with respect to complex statutes.

[19] Blockburger v. U.S., 284 U.S. 299, 304 (1932).

[20] U.S. v. Perez, 9 Wheat. 579 (1824); Trono v. U.S., 199 U.S. 521 (1905). And, in Ludwig v. Mass., 427 U.S. 618 (1976), disposing of an appellant's collateral double jeopardy argument, the Supreme Court held that Massachusetts' two-tier court system did not contravene the Double Jeopardy Clause. The Court reasoned that a defendant who elected to undergo jury trial *de novo* in that system after having been convicted without benefit of jury in the tier below, was not put in a significantly different position from that of a convicted defendant who successfully appeals on the basis of the trial record and an appeals court reverses the conviction and remands the case for a new trial.

[21] *See* U.S. v. Jorn, 400 U.S. 470 (1971); United States v. Martin Linen Supply Co., 97 S.Ct. 1349 (1977).

underpinning both the double jeopardy provision and the speedy trial guarantee. Alternatively, the judge must bear in mind the potential risks of abuse by the defendant of society's unwillingness to unnecessarily subject him to repeated prosecution. Yet in the final analysis, the judge must always temper the decision whether or not to abort a trial by considering the importance to the defendant of being able, once and for all, to conclude his confrontation with society through the verdict of a tribunal he might believe to be favorably disposed to .his fate."[22]) As might, perhaps, be inferred, jeopardy does not attach until the merits have been "put to trial before the trier of facts," be that a judge or jury.[23]

Two, if government seeks to "impose both a civil and criminal sanction in respect to the same act or omission," this is not precluded because the clause refers only to criminal liability.[24]

Three, the judgment of a court-martial rendered with jurisdiction is entitled to the same finality as to the issues involved as the judgment of a civil court in cases within its jurisdiction. Hence a soldier, acquitted of a charge of homicide by a court-martial of competent jurisdiction was not subsequently triable by a civil court exercising authority in the same place.[25]

Four, in an important decision extending further the parameters of rights guaranteed to youthful offenders, the Supreme Court unanimously held: (1) that jeopardy attaches at a juvenile court adjudicatory hearing; (2) that a juvenile offender's retrial in adult court violates the guarantee against double jeopardy; and (3) that the burdens consequently imposed by these rulings on the juvenile court system are not so substantial as to justify a departure from the fundamental protection furnished by the Double Jeopardy Clause.[26]

Another complicated issue with which the Court has had to deal under "double jeopardy" is whether, in the event of a retrial, the sentence in the second trial may be more severe without doing violence to

[22] *Ibid.*, 486. *See also* United States *v.* Dinitz, 424 U.S. 600 (1976); Lee *v.* U.S., 97 S.Ct. 2141 (1977); *also* United States *v.* Wilson, 420 U.S. 332 (1975).
[23] Serfass *v.* U.S., 420 U.S. 377 (1975); Lee *v.* U.S., 97 S.Ct. 2141 (1977). *See also* United States *v.* Jenkins, 420 U.S. 358 (1975). The Court ruled 5-4, in State of Ill. *v.* Somerville, 410 U.S. 458 (1973), that a declaration of a mistrial after the jury was impaneled but before any evidence was taken did not bar another trial under a valid indictment. And the Montana Supreme Court, in State *v.* Cunningham, 535 P. 2d. 186 (1975), has held that the Federal rule with respect to attaching jeopardy to criminal trials in U.S. district courts is not so fundamental that due process fastens such a point of attachment at the State level. The Montana court upheld the attachment of jeopardy from that point on in a criminal proceeding where the first witness is sworn rather than adopt the Federal standard of positing jeopardy with the selection of the jury.
[24] Helvering *v.* Mitchell, 303 U.S. 391 (1938); U.S. *v.* Hees, 317 U.S. 537 (1943); One Lot Emerald Cut Stones *v.* U.S., 409 U.S. 232 (1972); *but see* McKeehan *v.* U.S., 438 F. 2d. 739, 744 (1971).
[25] Grafton *v.* U.S., 206 U.S. 333 (1907). *See also* Hiatt *v.* Brown, 339 U.S. 103 (1950); Johnson *v.* Eisentrager, 339 U.S. 763 (1950); Waller *v.* Florida, 397 U.S. 387, 393-394 (1970).
[26] Breed *v.* Jones, 421 U.S. 519 (1975).

the constitutional provision. The Court's answer: "Due process of law requires that vindictiveness against a defendant for having successfully attacked his first conviction must play no part in the sentence he receives after a new trial. And since the fear of such vindictiveness may unconstitutionally deter a defendant's exercise of the right to appeal or collaterally attack his first conviction, due process also requires that a defendant be freed of apprehension of such a retaliatory motivation on the part of a sentencing judge.

"In order to assure the absence of such a motivation, we have concluded that whenever a judge imposes a more severe sentence upon a defendant after a new trial, the reasons for his doing so must affirmatively appear."[27]

Finally, in a novel decision, the U.S. Court of Appeals, Second Circuit, concluded: "We see no valid reason why a corporation which is a 'person' entitled to both equal protection and due process under the Constitution . . . should not also be entitled to the constitutional guaranty against double jeopardy."[28]

"Life or limb" has come to mean, since drawing and quartering have gone out of style, life or liberty.

"Nor shall be compelled in any criminal case to be a witness against himself":

The source of this clause was the maxim that "no man is bound to accuse himself (*nemo tenetur prodere*—or *accusare—seipsum*)," which was brought forward in England late in the sixteenth century in protest against the inquisitorial methods of the ecclesiastical courts. What the advocates of the maxim meant was merely that a person ought not to be put on trial and compelled to answer questions to his detriment unless he had first been properly accused, i.e., by the grand jury. But the idea once set going gained headway rapidly, especially after 1660, when it came to have attached to it most of its present-day corollaries.[29] *(margin: Source of the Self-Incrimination Clause)*

Under the clause as it is today administered by the Supreme Court, a *witness* in *any* governmental proceeding whatsoever including legislative investigations, in which testimony is legally required may refuse to answer any question, his answer to which might be used against him in a future criminal proceeding, or which might uncover further evidence against him.[30] But the witness must explicitly claim his constitutional immunity or he will be considered *(margin: Its Modern Application)*

[27] North Carolina *v*. Pearce, 395 U.S. 711, 725-726 (1969); Chaffin *v*. Stynchcombe, 412 U.S. 17 (1973). *Cf.* Roberson *v*. State, 258 So. 2d. 257 (1972).

[28] United States *v*. Security Nat'l Bank, 546 F. 2d. 492 (1976).

[29] *See generally* J. H. Wigmore, *Evidence in Trials at Common Law*, IV (Boston, 1923), Section 2250; *also* Edward S. Corwin, "The Supreme Court's Construction of the Self-Incrimination Clause," 29 *Michigan Law Review*, 1-27, 195-207 (1930).

[30] McCarthy *v*. Arndstein, 266 U.S. 34, 40 (1924). *See also* Boyd *v*. U.S., 116 U.S. 616 (1886); Counselman *v*. Hitchcock, 142 U.S. 547 (1892); Brown *v*. Walker, 161 U.S. 591 (1896); U.S. *v*. Kordel, 397 U.S. 1, 6 (1970); California *v*. Byers, 402 U.S. 424, 437 (1971). It was on this ground that one Johnny Dio invoked the Fifth Amendment 140 times in the course of a two-hour appearance before a Senate investigating committee, *New York Times*, August 9, 1957.

to have waived it;[31] and he is not the final judge of the validity of his claim.[32] Moreover, the privilege exists solely for the protection of the witness himself, and may not be claimed for the benefit of third parties.[33] Nor does the clause impair the obligation of a witness to testify if a prosecution against him is barred by lapse of time, by statutory enactment, or by a pardon.[34]

Several times in our history Congress has passed immunity acts which granted an individual immunity from criminal prosecution on the basis of what he said in the compelled testimony. In 1970 Congress passed a sweeping law of this kind: "Whenever a witness refuses, on the basis of the privilege against self-incrimination, to testify or provide other information in a proceeding before or ancillary to—(1) a court or grand jury of the United States, (2) an agency of the United States, or (3) [Congressional Committees] and the person presiding over the proceeding communicates to the witness an order issued under this part, the witness may not refuse to comply with the order on the basis of his privilege against self-incrimination; but no testimony or other information compelled under the order (or any information directly or indirectly derived from such testimony or other information) may be used against the witness in any criminal case, except a prosecution for perjury, giving a false statement, or otherwise failing to comply with the order."[35] There are some procedural safeguards in the law. Court decisions in cases involving earlier immunity statutes make plain that such a statute is constitutional (for Congress under the necessary and proper clause) provided the immunity applies to *both* Federal and State jurisdictions.[36] And so the Court held in 1972 with respect to the present law.[37] In addition the Court resolved a continuing controversy of many years about the *scope* of the immunity that had to be granted. The broad view was that a person could not be prosecuted or subject to any penalty "for or on account of any transaction, matter or thing, concerning which he may testify." The narrow view was the one spelled out in the 1970 statute that "no testimony or other information compelled . . . (or any information directly or indirectly derived from such testimony or other information) may be used. . . ." The Court made the narrow view the law of the land in 1972. The Court reasoned that: "such immunity

[31] Rogers v. U.S., 340 U.S. 367, 370 (1951); United States v. Monia, 317 U.S. 424, 427 (1943); California v. Byers, 402 U.S. 424 (1971).
[32] Hoffman v. U.S., 341 U.S. 479, 486 (1951); Mason v. U.S., 244 U.S. 362, 365 (1917); Mackey v. U.S., 401 U.S. 667, 704-705 (1971); California v. Byers, 402 U.S. 424, 432, 435 (1971).
[33] Rogers v. U.S., 340 U.S. 367, 371 (1951); United States v. Murdock, 284 U.S. 141, 148 (1931); Minor v. U.S., 396 U.S. 87, 93 (1969).
[34] Brown v. Walker, 161 U.S. 591, 598-599 (1896).
[35] 18 U.S.C. 6002.
[36] Ullmann v. U.S., 350 U.S. 422 (1956); Murphy v. N.Y. Waterfront Commission, 378 U.S. 52 (1964).
[37] Kastigar v. U.S., 406 U.S. 441, 444 (1972).

from use and derivative use is coextensive with the scope of the privilege against self-incrimination, and therefore is sufficient to compel testimony over a claim of the privilege. While a grant of immunity must afford protection commensurate with that afforded by the privilege, it need not be broader. Transactional immunity, which accords full immunity from prosecution for the offense to which the compelled testimony related, affords the witness considerably broader protection than does the Fifth Amendment privilege. The privilege has never been construed to mean that one who invokes it cannot subsequently be prosecuted. Its sole concern is to afford protection against being 'forced to give testimony leading to the infliction of penalties affixed to . . . criminal acts.' Immunity from the use of compelled testimony and evidence derived directly or indirectly therefrom affords this protection. It prohibits the prosecutorial authorities from using the compelled testimony in *any* respect, and it therefore insures that the testimony cannot lead to the infliction of criminal penalties on the witness."[38]

As indicated above, the immunity may be waived, but if an accused takes the stand in his own behalf, he must submit to cross-examination;[39] if he does not take the stand, the Court has held that the Fifth Amendment (plus the Fourteenth in State cases) "forbids either comment by the prosecution on the accused's silence or instructions by the court that such silence is evidence of guilt."[40]

One of the continuing, perplexing problems growing out of the privilege against self-incrimination has been the problem of whether or not public employees who invoked the privilege in hearings concerning their performance of duties could constitutionally be dismissed from their jobs for so doing. The guidelines wrought by the Supreme Court through a series of difficult cases are these: "public employees are entitled, like all other persons, to the benefit of the Constitution, including the privilege against self-incrimination. At the same time, . . . public employees, subject themselves to dismissal if they refuse to account for their performance of their public trust, *after proper proceedings, which do not involve an attempt to coerce them to relinquish their constitutional rights*" (empha-

---

[38] *Ibid.*, 453. *But see* Justice Douglas's dissent, *ibid.*, 462. *See also* Zicarelli *v.* N.J. State Com'n, 406 U.S. 472 (1972). Recently, a State court held that under a State immunity statute a person compelled to testify in a civil case could not later be prosecuted in a criminal case on the basis of the compelled testimony. Smith *v.* Superior Court, Pima County, 495 P. 2d. 519 (1972). But the Illinois Supreme Court has held that where an attorney testified at the trial of a judge under a grant of immunity, that testimony could be used as basis for disbarment proceeding. *In re* Schwarz, 282 N.E. 2d. 689 (1972).

[39] United States *v.* Murdock, 284 U.S. 141, 149 (1931).

[40] Griffin *v.* California, 380 U.S. 609, 615 (1965). The Court went on to say that it reserved "decision on whether an accused can require . . . that the jury be instructed that his silence must be disregarded." *Ibid.*, 615, note 6. *But see* Bowles *v.* U.S., 439 F. 2d. 536, 542 (1970) and Commonwealth *v.* Greene, 285 A. 2d. 865, 867 (1971).

sis supplied).[41] But these guidelines defy easy application as cases in this area clearly demonstrate.[42]

With respect to the privilege against self-incrimination, the Supreme Court held unconstitutional a New York statute that permitted the immediate cancellation and precluded for five years the future award of contracts by the State or its subdivisions to persons unwilling to waive immunity when asked to testify regarding State contracts they had been awarded. Citing the cases involving dismissal of public employees, the Court said "we fail to see a difference of constitutional magnitude between the threat of job loss to an employee of the State and a threat of loss of contracts to a contractor."[43] And, citing the same cases four years later, the Court struck down another New York statute that promptly removed from party office and prohibited from holding any other party or public office for five years the holder of any party post who was subpoenaed by a grand jury or other tribunal and who refused to testify about the conduct of the party office he occupied.[44]

Involuntary Confessions   Until 1964, the Supreme Court employed a double standard with respect to involuntary confessions. From 1897 the standard employed with respect to Federal prosecutions was that laid down by the Court in the case, Bram *v.* United States, decided that year. There, the Court held that: "in criminal trials, in the courts of the United States, wherever a question arises whether a confession is incompetent because not voluntary, the issue is controlled by that portion of the Fifth Amendment to the Constitution of the United States commanding that no person 'shall be compelled in any criminal case to be a witness against himself.' "[45] As Justice Brennan pointed out in 1964 such a standard means "The constitutional inquiry is not whether the conduct of . . . officials in obtaining the confession was shocking, but whether the confession was 'free and voluntary; that is, it must not be extracted by any sort of threats or violence, nor obtained by any direct or implied promises, however slight, by the exertion of any improper influence. . . . In other words the person must not have been compelled to incriminate himself. We have held inadmissible even a confession secured by so mild a whip as the refusal, under certain circumstances, to allow a

[41] Sanitation Men *v.* Sanitation Comm'r, 392 U.S. 280 (1968).
[42] For a good résumé of the appropriate cases, *see* decision of the Supreme Court of the State of Washington, Seattle Police Officers' Guild *v.* Seattle, 494 P. 2d. 485 (1972). *See also* Napolitano *v.* Ward, 457 F. 2d. 279 (1972), a case involving a State court judge who was dismissed after invoking the self-incrimination clause before a grand jury. With respect to a parallel problem, a New York court recently held that a driver's license could not be suspended for exercising the privilege where he could have been subject to criminal prosecution. Jackson *v.* Commissioner, 328 N.Y.S. 2d. 547 (1972).
[43] Lefkowitz *v.* Turley, 414 U.S. 70, 83 (1973); *see also* People *v.* Avant, 352 N.Y.S. 2d. 161 (1973).
[44] Lefkowitz *v.* Cunningham, 97 S.Ct. 2132 (1977).
[45] Malloy *v.* Hogan, 373 U.S. 1, 7 (1964).

suspect to call his wife until he confessed."[46] Decisions with respect to the use of involuntary confessions in State prosecutions were rendered under the Due Process Clause, i.e. "inquiring whether the proceedings below met the demands of fundamental fairness which due process embodies."[47] It is true as Justice Brennan pointed out that, even before 1964, there had been a "marked shift to the federal standard in state cases. . . ."[48] But whatever difference there was, it was extinguished by the Court's pronouncement in Malloy v. Hogan (1964): "We hold tody that the Fifth Amendment's exception from compulsory self-incrimination is also protected by the Fourteenth Amendment against abridgment by the States."[49] The conclusion as to whether a given confession was voluntarily given must, of course, be drawn on a case-by-case basis. And, while the Court has never taken the position that police trickery[50] alone trenches on the exercise of the suspect's free choice, some factors can flag police behavior as likely to induce coercion: unreasonable delay in arraignment,[51] the absence of a lawyer once the suspect is in custody,[52] lengthy interrogation,[53] and, certainly, the offer of any *quid pro quo.*[54] Perhaps, the greatest significance of the Court's holding in Malloy v. Hogan is its impact on another important right—right to counsel. If an accused must be protected from all kinds of subtle coercion to incriminate himself then he is going to need a lawyer to protect him even in the early stages of an investigation. That issue is explored below, pp. 423-427.

Three cases decided by the Supreme Court in the 1975-76 Term bear upon the use of statements or, in one case, the absence of statements made by the accused following arrest. Oregon v. Hass[55]

[46] Bram v. U.S., 168 U.S. 532, 542-543 (1897). The test of whether a confession is voluntary is, as the Court explained earlier in Spano v. N.Y., 360 U.S. 315 (1959), a matter of whether it was the product of the suspect's "free and rational choice." As if to underscore the point, the Court in Rogers v. Richmond, 365 U.S. 534 (1961), took particular care to point out that the test was not the *reliability* of the confession: "The attention of the trial judge should have focused, for purposes of the Federal Constitution, on the question whether the behavior of the State's law enforcement officials was such as to overbear petitioner's will to resist and bring about confessions not freely self-determined—a question to be answered with complete disregard of whether or not petitioner in fact spoke the truth."

[47] From Justice Harlan's dissent, Malloy v. Hogan, 373 U.S. 1, 28.

[48] *Ibid.,* 7.   [49] *Ibid.,* 6.

[50] For example, *see* Fred E. Inbau and John F. Reid, *Criminal Interrogations and Confessions,* 2d. ed. (Baltimore, 1967).

[51] *See* Mallory v. U.S., 354 U.S. 449 (1957). The inadmissibility of the confession in this case, however, resulted from the Court's interpretation of Rule 5(a) of the Federal Rules of Criminal Procedure. The Court's ruling, therefore, rested on *statutory* not constitutional grounds.

[52] Massiah v. U.S., 377 U.S. 201 (1964); Escobedo v. Ill., 378 U.S. 478 (1964); Miranda v. Ariz., 384 U.S. 436 (1966).

[53] Ashcraft v. Tenn., 322 U.S. 143 (1944); Watts v. Ind., 338 U.S. 49 (1949).

[54] *See* Spano v. N.Y., 360 U.S. 315 (1959); Lynumn v. Ill., 372 U.S. 528 (1963); Haynes v. Wash., 373 U.S. 503 (1963); State v. Biron, 123 N.W. 2d. 392 (1963).

[55] 420 U.S. 714 (1975).

raised the question of whether statements, which the defendant made to police in the squad car after he had indicated a desire to see a lawyer and was told he could do so once they reached the police station, could be admitted to impeach his credibility as a witness once he took the stand in his own defense and testified contrary to what he had earlier told the officers. The Supreme Court upheld the admissibility of such statements *for impeachment purposes only*. Reaching this conclusion, the six-man majority, per Justice Blackmun, addressed itself to the decision of the Oregon Supreme Court barring the use of the defendant's remarks. Said Justice Blackmun: "Hass suggests that 'when state law is more restrictive against the prosecution than federal law,' this Court has no power 'to compel a state to conform to federal law.' . . . This, apparently, is proffered as a reference to our expressions that a State is free *as a matter of its own law* to impose greater restrictions on police activity than those this Court holds to be necessary upon federal constitutional standards. . . . But, of course, a State may not impose such greater restrictions as a matter of *federal constitutional law* when this Court specifically refrains from imposing them." (Emphasis in original.) The Court held that, in this case, the decision below "did not rest on the Oregon Constitution or state law; neither was cited." Justices Brennan and Marshall dissented and would have remanded the case to the State supreme court for explicit consideration of an independent State ground. Justice Douglas did not participate in the decision.

In another ruling the Court held that the mere giving of the *Miranda* warnings at the time of arrest does not *per se* dissipate the taint of an illegal arrest and render statements made to the police admissible in court.[56] Though the warnings are relevant, they do not automatically break the chain of causation and make the statements entirely voluntary. Each case, the Court held, must be judged separately with the prosecution sustaining the burden of proof as to the voluntariness of the statements made. And in a third decision, where the defendant took the stand in his own defense and presented an alibi, the Supreme Court held that the prosecutor could not cross-examine him as to why he stood silent following a reading of the *Miranda* warnings at the time of arrest. Justice Powell, speaking for the six-man majority, explained: "[E]very post-arrest silence is insolubly ambiguous because of what the State is required to advise the person arrested. . . . Moreover, while it is true that the *Miranda* warnings contain no express assurance that silence will carry no penalty, such assurance is implicit to any person who receives the warnings. In such circumstances, it would be fundamentally unfair and a deprivation of due process to allow the arrested person's silence to be used to impeach an explanation subsequently offered at trial."[57] Dissenting, Justice Stevens con-

[56] Brown v. Ill., 422 U.S. 590 (1975).
[57] Doyle v. Ohio, 426 U.S. 610, 617-618 (1976). The preceding Term, the Court handed down a similar decision based, however, *solely on its supervisory power over Fed-*

cluded: "I think a state court is free to regard the defendant's decision to take the stand as a waiver of his objection to the use of his failure to testify at an earlier proceeding or his failure to offer his version of the events prior to trial."

The Supreme Court of North Carolina held that a coerced confession was obtained where the interrogation of an accused took place in the "police-dominated atmosphere" of a seven-foot by seven-foot room, where police told the defendant "that they knew . . . he had committed the crime . . . that his story had too many holes in it . . . that he was 'lying' and that they did not want to 'fool around,' " and where the police officers considered the defendant "the type of person 'that such a thing would prey heavily upon' and that he would be 'relieved to get it off his chest,' " in turn capping this by a statement that "it would simply be harder on him if he didn't go ahead and cooperate.' "[58] The U.S. Court of Appeals also found a resulting confession to be coerced when a prisoner was held for 53 hours before being taken before a magistrate, subjected to seven and one-half hours of intensive interrogation, compelled to provide police officers with one of his own pubic hairs, and told that the abrasions on his knees established his guilt.[59] In another interesting ruling a State court held that statements made by a defendant after a "concerned citizens group" abducted and then questioned him were nonetheless admissible.[60] And a Michigan appellate court has held that Fifth Amendment rights of a defendant are not compromised when he is asked to submit to examination by the prosecution's psychiatrist contemporaneous with entering an insanity plea.[61]

Combined with the sweep of its investigatory power, much of the controversy surrounding the operation of the grand jury stems from the lack of procedural safeguards comparable to those existing at trial. For example, consistent with the view that "the grand jury has been accorded wide latitude to inquire into violations of criminal law" and that "its operation generally is unrestrained by the technical procedural and evidentiary rules governing the conduct of criminal trials," the Supreme Court held that "allowing a grand jury witness to invoke the exclusionary rule would unduly interfere with the effective and expeditious discharge of the grand jury's duties."[62] And, particularly with respect to the later use of statements made by witnesses called to appear before the grand

Self-Incrimination and the Grand Jury

---

eral law enforcement, United States *v.* Hale, 422 U.S. 171 (1975). In *Doyle*, of course, the Court reached the *constitutional* question.

[58] State *v.* Pruitt, 212 S.E. 2d. 92 (1975).

[59] Grant *v.* Wainwright, 496 F. 2d. 1043 (1974).

[60] Commonwealth *v.* Mahnke, 335 N.E. 2d. 660 (1975).

[61] People *v.* Schrantz, 213 N.W. 2d. 257 (1973); *but cf.* Thomas Szasz, *Law, Liberty, and Psychiatry* (New York, 1963) and *Psychiatric Justice* (New York, 1965).

[62] United States *v.* Calandra, 414 U.S. 338, 343, 350 (1974). Included in the Court's opinion is a good summary of which procedural guarantees bind grand jury inquiries and which do not. The ABA, however, has recommended reforms in the grand jury system, *see Minneapolis Star*, Aug. 10, 1977.

jury, the Court has held that the Fifth Amendment did not mandate the suppression of false statements, made to a grand jury, in a
prosecution for perjury where the defendant—who was the putative defendant in the case at the time he was called to testify before
that body—had not been given the *Miranda* warnings at the outset
of his appearance.[63] Nor, does the guarantee against self-
incrimination require that certain witnesses appearing before the
grand jury be informed that they are potential defendants in a
criminal trial and in danger of being indicted.[64]

The   In view of the Court's posture with respect to compulsory self-
Schmerber   incrimination, it has puzzled many that State "Implied Consent
Distinction   Laws" like this one of California have survived court tests:
and   "Any person who drives a motor vehicle on a highway is deemed
Implied   to have given his consent to a chemical test of his blood, breath, or
Consent   urine to determine the alcoholic content of his blood if lawfully ar-
Laws   rested for any offense allegedly committed while he was driving a
motor vehicle under the influence of intoxicating liquor. The test
must be incidental to a lawful arrest and administered at the direction of a peace officer having reasonable cause to believe the person
was driving while under the influence of intoxicating liquor. The
person arrested may have his choice of whether the test shall be of
his blood, breath, or urine. Where the person is dead, unconscious,
or otherwise in a condition rendering him incapable of refusing the
test, he shall not be deemed to have withdrawn his consent thereto.
If the person arrested refuses to submit to a chemical test, the department of motor vehicles must suspend his driving privilege for a
period of six months after notifying him in writing of the suspension and on providing him, on his written request, with a hearing to
determine whether the peace officer had reasonable cause to believe he had been driving while under the influence of intoxicating
liquor, whether he was placed under arrest, whether he refused to
submit to the test, and whether he had been advised that his driving privilege would be suspended if he refused."[65] In the important case of Schmerber v. California (1966), the Court professed to
see a difference in kind between an involuntary confession and an
involuntary blood test: "We therefore must now decide whether
the withdrawal of blood and admission in evidence of the analysis
involved in this case violated petitioner's privilege against self-
incrimination. We hold that the privilege protects an accused only
from being compelled to testify against himself, or otherwise provide the state with evidence of a testimonial or communicative nature, and that withdrawal of blood and uses of the analysis in ques-

[63] United States v. Mandujano, 425 U.S. 564 (1976).
[64] United States v. Washington, 97 S.Ct. 1814 (1977); United States v. Wong, 97
S.Ct. 1823 (1977).
[65] Cal. Jur. 2d. 372. See also Taft A. McKinstry, "Kentucky's 'Implied Consent'
Statute," 59 Kentucky Law Journal, 536 (1970). See also People v. Superior Court of
Kern County, 493 P. 2d. 1145 (1972).

tion in this case did not involve compulsion to these ends."[66] In response to a complaint in a dissent that the report of the blood test was indeed testimonial in nature, the Court replied: "It is clear that the protection of the privilege reaches an accused's communications, whatever form they might take, and the compulsion of responses which are also communications, for example, compliance with a subpoena to produce one's papers. On the other hand, both federal and state courts have usually held that it offers no protection against compulsion to submit to fingerprinting, photographing, or measurements, to write or speak for identification, to appear in court, to stand, to assume a stance, to walk, or to make a particular gesture."[67] Nor has the Fifth Amendment barred taking impressions of the defendant's bite mark,[68] or X-raying the defendant's stomach.[69] Further, the Supreme Court saw no constitutional violation in grand juries' requiring voice exemplars and handwriting samples.[70] (*See* also the discussion on the personal character of the immunity, p. 384.)

In a decision that signals an important modification on its hitherto total ban on the admissibility of the results of lie detector tests at trial, a bare majority on the Massachusetts Supreme Judicial Court, speaking through Chief Justice Tauro, held: "Although we acknowledge that . . . scientific and legal developments indicate that the polygraph is making progress in a hoped for evolution toward complete evidentiary recognition, we . . . are unwilling to say at this time that . . . polygraph tests results should henceforth be subject to the same rules of evidence applicable to other forms of acceptable expert scientific evidence. We do, however, think that polygraph testing has advanced to the point where it could prove to be of significant value to the criminal trial process if its admissibility initially is limited to carefully defined circumstances designed to protect the proper and effective administration of criminal justice. Accordingly, we hold . . . that if a defendant agrees in advance to the admission of the results of a polygraph test regardless of their outcome, the trial judge, after a close and searching inquiry into the qualifications of the examiner, the fitness of the defendant for such examination, and the methods utilized in conducting the tests,

Lie Detectors

[66] Schmerber *v*. California, 384 U.S. 757, 761 (1966). But a penalty cannot be imposed for a motorist's failure to take a breath test, *see* People *v*. Delaney, 373 N.Y.S. 2d. 477 (1975).

[67] *Ibid.*, 763-764. For some instructive State court decisions in this area, *see* Heichelbach *v*. State, 281 N.E. 2d. 102 (1972); State *v*. Heston, 280 N.E. 2d. 376 (1972); State *v*. Ostrowski, 282 N.E. 2d. 359 (1972); State *v*. Tew, 195 N.W. 2d. 615 (1972). State courts have also held that wiretapping "In the absence of compulsion by the authorities does not bring the right against self-incrimination into play." State *v*. Siegel, 285 A. 2d. 671 (1971); Dudley *v*. State, 186 S.E. 2d. 875 (1972).

[68] People *v*. Milone, 356 N.E. 2d. 1350 (1976).

[69] Weeks *v*. State, 342 So. 2d. 1335 (1977).

[70] United States *v*. Dionisio, 410 U.S. 1 (1973), *and* United States *v*. Mara, 410 U.S. 19 (1973).

may, in the proper exercise of his discretion, admit the results, not as binding or conclusive evidence, but to be considered with all other evidence as to innocence or guilt. As a prerequisite the judge would first make sure that the defendant's constitutional rights are fully protected."[71] The court was also quick to point out that both the defendant and the State were not precluded from vigorously cross-examining the polygraph examiner—a point which the court noted "may serve as an incentive for an examiner to make every effort to assure that his examination is properly and thoroughly conducted." And, in related cases, State courts have held that a judge's inquiry into defendant's willingness to take a lie detector test after taking the stand in his own behalf was not harmless error;[72] and that a prosecutor who made a prior agreement with the defendant to dismiss charges if he passed a polygraph examination could not renege.[73]

Keeping Records and Registering
Government has long required that people keep records, file forms, and register with respect to certain activities. That requirement quite naturally raises the question of whether or not the Government can do that without violating the Self-Incrimination Clause. For example, an individual might argue that if he has acquired income by illicit means, he might expose himself to criminal prosecution by making out an income tax return. In dealing with such a case, some years ago, Justice Holmes said: "He could not draw a conjurer's circle around the whole matter by his own declaration that to write any word on the government blank would bring him in danger of the law."[74] Also, the Court upheld the requirement under the Emergency Price Control Act of 1942 that certain merchants keep records.[75] But in 1968, it struck down a statute which required gamblers to register and to submit monthly detailed information concerning their wagering activities.[76] The Court carefully distinguished these latter decisions from the earlier decision in the case involving the Price Control Act (Shapiro v. U.S.) concluding: "We think that neither *Shapiro* nor the cases upon which it relied are applicable here. . . . Moreover, we find it unnecessary for present purposes to pursue in detail the question, left unanswered in *Shapiro*, of what 'limits . . . the government cannot constitutionally exceed in requiring the keeping of records. . . .' It is enough that there are significant points of difference between the situations here and in *Shapiro* which in this instance preclude, under any formulation, an appropriate application of the 'required

---

[71] Commonwealth v. A Juvenile (No. 1), 313 N.E. 2d. 120, 123-124 (1974).
[72] McDonald v. State, 328 N.E. 2d. 436 (1975). *See also* State v. Kearney, 523 P. 2d. 443 (1974).
[73] People v. Reagan, 235 N.W. 2d. 581 (1975).
[74] U.S. v. Sullivan, 274 U.S. 259, 263-264 (1927).
[75] Shapiro v. U.S., 335 U.S. 1 (1948).
[76] Marchetti v. U.S., 390 U.S. 39 (1968); Grosso v. U.S., 390 U.S. 62 (1968). *See also* Mackey v. U.S., 401 U.S. 667 (1971).

records' doctrine."[77] One of the differences stressed by the Court was that "the requirements at issue in *Shapiro* were imposed in 'an essentially non-criminal and regulatory area of inquiry' while those here are directed to a 'selective group inherently suspect of criminal activities.' "[78] And the Court recently upheld California's "hit and run" statute, which requires the driver of a motor vehicle involved in an accident to stop at the scene and give his name and address, concluding that "the disclosure of inherently illegal activity is inherently risky. . . . But disclosures with respect to automobile accidents simply do not entail the kind of substantial risk involved in [the gamblers' cases]. Furthermore, the statutory purpose is noncriminal and self-reporting is indispensable to its fulfillment."[79]

More recently, the Court has heard challenges to the constitutionality of the Bank Secrecy Act of 1970,[80] a piece of legislation enacted following hearings into the unavailability of financial records of foreign and domestic banks some of whose customers were suspected of illegal activities. The act delegated to the Secretary of the Treasury authority to impose reporting and recordkeeping requirements on banks so as to acquire financial information possessing "a high degree of usefulness in criminal, tax, or regulatory investigations or proceedings." Justice Rehnquist, speaking for a divided Court (Justices Douglas, Brennan, and Marshall dissented), upheld as legitimate the burdens placed on banks to, among other things, maintain records of customers' identities and to microfilm copies of checks and other instruments of financial transactions. The Court sustained these requirements in the face of assertions that they violated the privilege against self-incrimination. The Court held that banks *per se* had no Fifth Amendment privilege, neither had they standing to protect the privilege of their customers, and it termed "premature" any claim to violation of that privilege possessed by bank customers.[81] Disagreeing, Justice Douglas said, "Customers have a constitutionally justifiable expectation of privacy in the documentary details of the financial transactions reflected in their bank accounts. . . . Where [as here] fundamental personal rights are involved . . . the Act should be 'narrowly drawn' to meet the precise evil."

Two years later, in another test of the Bank Secrecy Act, the Court saw no bar to government use of bank records—including microfilms, checks, and deposit slips—in a prosecution for tax fraud. Recapping some of the ground it covered previously, the Court held that the defendant had no "expectation of privacy" in

---

[77] Marchetti *v.* U.S., 390 U.S. 39, 56 (1968). For elaboration of the Marchetti decision *see* Williams *v.* State, 287 A. 2d. 803 (1972) and State *v.* Braun, 495 P. 2d. 1000 (1972).

[78] *Ibid.*, 57.   [79] California *v.* Byers, 402 U.S. 424 (1971).

[80] 84 *Stat.* 1114.   [81] California Bankers Ass'n *v.* Shultz, 416 U.S. 21 (1974).

the bank records since they were not "personal papers" and inasmuch as he had voluntarily conveyed such information to the bank. There was, said Justice Powell, no protectable interest in these third-party records to place any special constraints on the reach of the subpoena.[82] A dissenting opinion by Justice Brennan quoted extensively from a past decision of the California Supreme Court holding as a matter of *State* constitutional law that bank customers had protected privacy interests in the records of financial institutions. The concluding portion of Justice Brennan's dissent highlighted what he saw as "the emerging trend among high state courts of relying upon state constitutional protections of individual liberties—protections pervading counterpart provisions of the United States Constitution, but increasingly being ignored by decisions of this Court."[83] Justice Marshall also dissented, remarking at one point, "I wash my hands of today's extended redundancy by the Court."

Personal Character of the Immunity   The privilege of witnesses is a purely personal one, and hence may not be claimed by an agent or officer of a corporation either in its behalf or in his own behalf as regards books and papers of the corporation;[84] and the same rule holds in the case of the custodian of the records of a labor union;[85] nor does the Communist Party enjoy any immunity as to its books and records.[86] Taken in connection with the interdiction of the Fourth Amendment against unreasonable searches and seizures, the clause protects an individual from the compulsory production of private papers which would incriminate him.[87] The scope of this latter privilege was, however, narrowed by the *Shapiro* decision, in which as pointed out above, the Court held that the privilege against self-incrimination does not extend to books and records which an individual is required to keep to evidence his compliance with lawful regulations.[88]

Two rulings, handed down by the Court in 1976, are particularly significant for what they imply about the continuing vitality of the personal privilege developed in *Boyd* from the confluence of the Fourth and Fifth Amendments. The Court held that the Fifth Amendment does not bar enforcement of a summons directed at a taxpayer's attorney to produce accountant's documents in his possession used in the preparation of the taxpayer's income tax re-

[82] United States *v.* Miller, 425 U.S. 435 (1976).
[83] *Ibid.*, 454-455. *See* especially his footnote 4.
[84] Hale *v.* Henkel, 201 U.S. 43 (1906); Wilson *v.* U.S., 221 U.S. 361 (1911); Oklahoma Press Pub. Co. *v.* Walling, 327 U.S. 186 (1946); McPaul *v.* U.S., 364 U.S. 372 (1960); U.S. *v.* Fleischman, 339 U.S. 349 (1950); *in re* Mal Bros. Contracting Co., 444 F. 2d. 615 (1971); People *v.* Pintozzi, 277 N.E. 2d. 844 (1972). Nor does the immunity extend to prevent an accountant from turning over his client's tax records, Couch *v.* U.S., 409 U.S. 322 (1973).
[85] United States *v.* White, 322 U.S. 694 (1944)
[86] Rogers *v.* U.S., 340 U.S. 367-373 (1951).   [87] *See* pp. 342ff.
[88] Shapiro *v.* U.S., 335 U.S. 1 (1948). *See also* People *v.* Pintozzi, 277 N.E. 2d. 844 (1972).

turns.[89] However incriminating the contents of the documents might be, the Court reasoned that such papers were not "private papers" within the ambit of the Fifth Amendment privilege. Emphasizing that since the papers were not in the nature of a testimonial communication by the defendant-taxpayer, it would have made no difference if the taxpayer himself had the accountant's paper in his own possession. Nor, concluded the Court, was the validity of the summons disturbed by the attorney-client privilege since that privilege extends only to encompass full disclosure to the attorney necessary to obtain competent legal advice. Justice Marshall, concurring in the judgment only, took exception to what he saw as the majority's "technical and somewhat esoteric focus on the testimonial elements of production rather than on the content of the evidence the investigator seeks . . . contrary to the history and traditions of the privilege against self-incrimination. . . ." Justice Brennan also concurred only in the judgment. In an opinion that traced the development of the "private papers" privilege from Boyd v. United States[90] to the present, Justice Brennan wrote: "I do not join the Court's opinion . . . because of the portent in much of what is said of a serious crippling of the protection secured by the privilege against compelled production of one's private books and papers."

The Court also found no contravention of the *Boyd* doctrine when it affirmed the decision to admit into evidence, in a State criminal prosecution for false pretenses, documents seized from a settlement attorney's office. In those documents, which pertained to his perpetration of a real estate fraud, the defendant-lawyer had made several incriminating statements. Speaking for the Court, Justice Blackmun ruled that "[t]his case . . . falls within the principle stated by Mr. Justice Holmes: 'A party is privileged from producing the evidence but not from its production.' . . . This principle recognizes that the protection afforded by the self-incrimination clause of the Fifth Amendment 'adheres basically to the person, not to information that may incriminate him.' "[91] In short, the statements were not testimonial evidence, said the Court, since the defendant "was never required to say or to do anything under penalty of sanction." Justice Brennan dissented: "I can perceive no distinction of meaningful substance between compelling the production of such records through subpoena and seizing such records against the will of the petitioner."

In the ensuing discussion of "due process of law" under the Fifth Amendment, it must be borne in mind that there is also a "due process" clause in the Fourteenth Amendment. The Fifth, of course, applies to the National Government and the Fourteenth to

---

[89] Fisher v. U.S., 425 U.S. 391 (1976).   [90] 116 U.S. 616 (1886).
[91] Andresen v. Md., 427 U.S. 463, 473 (1976), quoting respectively Johnson v. U.S., 228 U.S. 457, 458 (1913), and Couch v. U.S., 409 U.S. 322, 328 (1973).

the State governments. However, in the history of conceptualization of "due process" both clauses were inextricably entwined. Consequently, the story of that history can only be traced by dealing with them jointly. Nonetheless, specific applications of "due process" can be separated out in a meaningful way. Consequently, here we will deal with the conceptualization of due process with primary emphasis on its application to the National Government; its application to the State governments is discussed under the Fourteenth Amendment.

Source and
Development of
"Due
Process
of Law"

The phrase "due process of law" comes from chapter 3 of 28 Edw. III (1335), which reads: "No man of what state or condition he be, shall be put out of his lands or tenements nor taken, nor disinherited, nor put to death, without he be brought to answer by due process of law." This statute, in turn, harks back to the famous chapter 29 of Magna Carta (issue of 1225), where the King promises that "no free man (*nullus liber homo*) shall be taken or imprisoned or deprived of his freehold or his liberties or free customs, or outlawed or exiled, or in any manner destroyed, nor shall we come upon him or send against him, except by a legal judgment of his peers or by the law of the land (*per legem terrae*)."[92] Whichever phraseology is used always occurs in close association with other safeguards of accused persons, just as does the clause here under discussion in Amendment V. As a limitation on legislative power, in short, the due process clause originally operated simply to place certain procedures, and especially the grand jury–petit jury process, beyond its reach, but this has not remained its sole importance, or its principal importance.[93]

The absorptive powers of the law of the land clause, the precursor in the original State constitutions, of the due process clause, was foreshadowed as early as 1819 in a dictum by Justice William Johnson of the United States Supreme Court: "As to the words from Magna Charta . . . after volumes spoken and written with a view to their exposition, the good sense of mankind has at length settled down to this: that they were intended to secure the individual from the arbitrary exercise of the powers of government, unrestrained by the established principles of private rights and distributive justice."[94] Thirty-eight years later the prophecy of these words

[92] *See* Sir Edward Coke, *Institutes of the Laws of England* (1669) (First American Edition, Philadelphia, 1853), Part 2, 50-51.

[93] On the above *see* especially Justice Harlan's dissenting opinion in Hurtado *v.* Calif., 110 U.S. 516, 538 (1884); *also* Den *ex dem.* Murray *v.* Hoboken Land & Improvement Co., 18 How. 272, 280 (1856); Twining *v.* New Jersey, 211 U.S. 78 (1908); Corwin, *Liberty Against Government*, ch. 3.

[94] B'k of Columbia *v.* Okely, 4 Wheat. 235, 244 (1819). *See also* Edward S. Corwin, "Due Process of Law before the Civil War," 24 *Harvard Law Review*, 366, 460 (1911), and Clinton Rossiter, ed., *Higher Law Background of American Constitutional Law* (Ithaca, 1953); C. W. Collins, *The Fourteenth Amendment and the States* (Boston, 1912); R. L. Mott, *Due Process of Law* (Indianapolis, 1926); Willoughby, *Constitutional Law*, III, chs. xci-cv; Benjamin F. Wright, *The Growth of American Constitutional Law* (Boston, 1942); Carl B. Swisher, *American Constitutional Development* (Boston, 1943).

was realized in the famous *Dred Scott* case,[95] in which Section 8 of the Missouri Compromise, whereby slavery was excluded from the territories, was held void under the Fifth Amendment, not on the ground that the procedure for enforcing it was not due process of law, but because the Court regarded it as unjust to forbid people to take their slaves, or other property, into the territories, the common property of all the States.

Meanwhile, the previous year the recently established Court of Appeals of New York had, in the landmark case of *Wynehamer v. People*,[96] set aside a State-wide Prohibition law as comprising, with regard to liquors in existence at the time of its going into effect, an act of destruction of property not within the power of Government to perform "even by the forms of due process of law." The term "due process of law," in short, simply drops out of the clause, which comes to read "no person shall be deprived of property," period. And subsequently two other terms of the clause have undergone a comparable enlargement. At the common law, "property" signified ownership, which was "exercised in its primary and fullest sense over physical objects only, and more especially over land."[97] In Court decisions, it came to cover each and all of the valuable elements of ownership, and moreover tended at times to merge with the more indefinite rights of "liberty." "Liberty" at the common law meant little more than the right not to be physically restrained except for good cause. Whether the cause was good or not would be inquired into by a court, in connection with an application for a writ of *habeas corpus*, or in connection with an action for damages for false imprisonment.[98] About eighty years ago, however, the Court, following the urging of influential members of the American Bar and the lead given by certain of the State courts, adopted the view that the word "liberty" as used here and in the Fourteenth Amendment was intended to protect the "freedom of contract" of adults engaged in the ordinary employments, especially when viewed from the point of view of would-be employers.[99] Then in 1925 the Court took the further step of extending the term as it is used in the Fourteenth Amendment to certain of the rights, described as "fundamental," which were already protected against the National Government by the more specific language of the Bill of Rights, among these being freedom of speech and press.[100] Later,

Expanded Conceptions of "Liberty" and "Property"

[95] Scott *v.* Sandford, 19 How. 393 (1857).   [96] 13 N.Y. 378 (1856).

[97] T. E. Holland, *Elements of Jurisprudence*, 13th ed. (Oxford, 1924), 211; Blackstone, *Commentaries*, VII, ch. 1.

[98] C. E. Shattuck, "The True Meaning of the Term 'Liberty,' " 4 *Harvard Law Review*, 365-392 (1891).

[99] Allgeyer *v.* La., 165 U.S. 578 (1897); Holden *v.* Hardy, 169 U.S. 366 (1898); Lochner *v.* N.Y., 198 U.S. 45 (1905). For the Bar's connection with this development, *see* Benjamin R. Twiss, *Lawyers and the Constitution: How Laissez Faire Came to the Supreme Court* (Princeton, 1942).

[100] *See* Charles Warren, "The New Liberty under the Fourteenth Amendment," 39 *Harvard Law Review*, 431 (1926); also Gitlow *v.* N.Y., 268 U.S. 652 (1925).

the Court, responding to the social teachings of the New Deal, came practically to dismiss the conception of "freedom of contract" as a definition of "liberty" and to substitute for it a special concern for "the rights of labor," its right to organize, and to strike and picket so long as too obvious violence was avoided.

The Heyday of Substantive Due Process   In brief, this clause, for a time (roughly from 1900-1937), was employed frequently to challenge the *substantive* content of legislation, or in other words to require that Congress exercise its powers "reasonably," that is to say, *reasonably in the judgment of the Court*. A similar requirement was laid upon the State legislatures by the Fourteenth Amendment but with two differences which operated to Congress's advantage. In the first place, whereas the "police power" of the States is an indefinite power to provide for "the public health, safety, morals, and general welfare," most of Congress's powers are defined by reference to a specified subject-matter, like "post offices and post roads," "commerce among the States," etc., and this difference is sufficient to invoke in Congress's favor and against the States the rule of legal interpretation that the specific is to be preferred to the general. In the second place, the Fifth Amendment contains no "equal protection" clause, although this does not signify that the Court would not pass upon the soundness of the factual justification urged in support of a specially drastic discrimination by the National Government against a particular class of its citizens, as, for example, that which characterized its policies toward the West Coast Japanese early in World War II. (*See* pp. 104-105.)

Relying upon public policy and its supervisory authority over Federal courts, the Court in the 1940's reached results similar to those arrived at under the Equal Protection Clause of the Fourteenth Amendment, in refusing to enforce restrictive covenants in the District of Columbia,[101] and in reversing a judgment of a Federal district court because of the exclusion of day laborers from the jury panel;[102] and in 1944 the Railway Labor Act was construed to require a collective bargaining representative to act for the benefit of all members of the craft without discrimination on account of race.[103] Chief Justice Stone indicated that any other construction would raise grave constitutional doubts,[104] while in a concurring opinion Justice Murphy asserted unequivocally that the act would be inconsistent with the Fifth Amendment if the bargaining agent, acting under color of Federal authority, were permitted to discriminate against any of the persons he was authorized to represent.[105]

[101] Hurd *v.* Hodge, 334 U.S. 24 (1948).
[102] Thiel *v.* Southern Pacific Co., 328 U.S. 217 (1946).
[103] Steele *v.* L. & N. R. Co., 323 U.S. 192 (1944.).   [104] *Ibid.*, 198, 199.
[105] *Ibid.*, 208-209. *Cf.* the following sentence from the concurring opinion of Justice Jackson in Railway Express Agency, Inc. *v.* New York, 336 U.S. 106, 112 (1949): "I regard it as a salutary doctrine that cities, States and the Federal Government must exercise their powers so as not to discriminate between their inhabitants except upon some reasonable differentiation fairly related to the object of regulation."

In another respect, national and State legislation stood much more nearly on a parity with each other, since in the case of both the Court was apt to have available from its own past decisions two widely different approaches to the question of the "reasonableness" of a challenged legislative measure, and hence of its conformity with the "due process of law" requirement. One approach was furnished by the proposition that a legislative act is presumed to be valid, and, deduced from this, the further one that if facts could exist which would render the legislation before it "reasonable," it must be assumed by the Court that they did exist.[106] The other, on the contrary, invoked the idea that "liberty is the rule and restraint is the exception," and hence demanded that special justification be adduced in support of any new inroad upon previous freedom of action, as almost any law was bound to be.[107]

In other words, under the latter rule the Court did something very like what Congress did in the first place, in balancing the apparent detriments of the statute from the point of view of "liberty" or "property" as against its anticipated benefits from the point of view of "public policy." And it was from this approach that the Court in 1923, being then very much under the influence of *laissez-faire* concepts of governmental power, set aside as "unreasonable" and "arbitrary" an act of Congress establishing a minimum wage for women industrially employed in the District of Columbia[108]—a decision which it overturned in 1937[109] under the influence of the New Deal ideology.[110]

After the New Deal had become ensconced, the Supreme Court came to eschew the role it had assumed during the heyday of substantive due process particularly with respect to economic matters. Justice Black summarized the Court's recent views on the matter in a case in 1963 which dealt with a State statute making it a misdemeanor to engage in the debt adjustment business:

The Demise of Substantive Due Process in Economic Realm

"We refuse to sit as a 'superlegislature to weigh the wisdom of legislation,' and we emphatically refuse to go back to the time when courts used the Due Process Clause 'to strike down state laws, regulatory of business and industrial conditions, because they may be unwise, improvident, or out of harmony with a particular school of thought.' . . . Whether the legislature takes for its textbook Adam Smith, Herbert Spencer, Lord Keynes, or some other is no concern of ours."[111]

There has been a tendency among observers of the Court's work to believe that the concept of substantive due process as a useful judicial doctrine is dead. Granted, it has lost importance with re-

Substantive Due Process Still Lives

[106] Munn v. Ill., 94 U.S. 113, 132 (1876); Powell v. Pa., 127 U.S. 678 (1888). *See also* Justice Stone, in United States v. Carolene Products Co., 304 U.S. 144 (1938).

[107] Adkins v. Children's Hospital, 261 U.S. 525, 546.

[108] *Ibid.*

[109] West Coast Hotel v. Parrish, 300 U.S. 379 (1937).

[110] *See* Swisher, *American Constitutional Development* (Boston, 1943), chs. 34 and 35.

[111] Ferguson v. Skrupa, 372 U.S. 726, 731-732 (1963) and cases cited therein. *See also* City of New Orleans v. Dukes, 427 U.S. 297 (1976).

spect to economic regulation, but it does have vitality still with respect to civil liberties and civil rights.[112] Consider what the Supreme Court did in the companion case to the momentous *Brown* case, in which it found segregation in public schools a violation of "equal protection." Since it could not use "equal protection" with respect to schools in the District of Columbia, the Court was compelled to find another basis for the result it desired to achieve. The Court reasoned: "Although the Court has not assumed to define 'liberty' with great precision, that term is not confined to mere freedom from bodily restraint. Liberty under law extends to the full range of conduct which the individual is free to pursue, and it cannot be restricted except for a proper governmental objective. Segregation in public education is not reasonably related to any proper governmental objective, and thus it imposes on Negro children of the District of Columbia a burden that constitutes an arbitrary deprivation of their liberty in violation of the Due Process Clause."[113] That, surely, is a use of the concept of substantive due process. Also, to the extent that the Court continues to assume that the substantive rights of the First Amendment are safeguarded against the States by the Fourteenth, however that incorporation is justified, it is a manifestation of the continued vitality of the idea of substantive due process. (For additional discussion, *see* p. 475ff.)

Equal Protection as Due Process   Although the Court acknowledged in its companion decision to *Brown* that the concepts of equal protection and due process "are . . . not always interchangeable phrases," the link—that "discrimination may be so unjustifiable as to be violative of due process"[114]— which the Court forged in that decision between the Fifth and Fourteenth Amendments came to have significant and lasting importance for constitutional interpretation well beyond desegregation. Since the Court's ruling in 1954, it has examined countless allegations of discrimination in violation of the Fifth Amendment, discrimination based on gender, ethnicity, age, and wealth, among other factors. Because of the logic of the Court's decision in Bolling *v.* Sharpe, the standards of equal protection analysis are today the same under the Fifth as under the Fourteenth. And so Federal legislation, like State law has been brought within the purview of the Equal Protection Clause. For this reason, the Court's Fifth Amendment "equal protection" decisions are discussed together with the State cases under the Fourteenth Amendment. *See* p. 492ff.

In an important decision rendered in 1972, the Supreme Court held that two State laws permitting conditional sales contracts which "simply provided that upon default the seller 'may take

[112] The current Court may yet reassert a stronger role in "safeguarding" economic rights. In a recent decision Justice Stewart speaking for the Court said, "that the dichotomy between personal liberties and property rights is a false one. Property does not have rights. People have rights. The right to enjoy property without unlawful deprivation, no less than the right to speak or the right to travel is, in truth, a 'personal right. . . .' " Lynch *v.* Household Finance Corp., 405 U.S. 538 (1972).
[113] Bolling *v.* Sharpe, 347 U.S. 497, 499-500 (1954).   [114] *Ibid.*, 499.

back,' 'may retake,' or 'may repossess' merchandise" were uncon- Procedural
stitutional on due process grounds. The Court insisted that, before Require-
a person could be deprived of his property, there must be notice ments with
and a hearing at a "meaningful time" and in a "meaningful man- Respect to
ner." The Court said, "The constitutional right to be heard is a Deprivation
basic aspect of the duty of government to follow a fair process of of Property
decision making when it acts to deprive a person of his possessions.
The purpose of this requirement is not only to ensure abstract fair
play to the individual. Its purpose, more particularly, is to protect
his use and possession of property from arbitrary encroachment, to
minimize substantively unfair or mistaken deprivations of property, a danger that is especially great when the State seizes goods
simply upon the application of and for the benefit of a private
party."[115] As to the exact nature of hearings that would meet the
due process requirement the Court was not very specific. "The nature and form of such prior hearings . . . are legitimately open to
many potential variations and are a subject, at this point, for legislation, not adjudication. Since the essential reason for the requirement of a prior hearing is to prevent unfair and mistaken deprivations of property, however, it is axiomatic that the hearing must
provide a real test."[116]

The slack left in due process requirements bearing on repossess-
sion of property with the Court's decision in Fuentes v. Shevin
became even more apparent in two of the Court's subsequent decisions. In Mitchell v. W. T. Grant Co.,[117] which tested the constitutionality of a provision, contained in the Louisiana Code of Civil
Procedure, that avails creditors of a writ of sequestration to prevent
loss or destruction of encumbered property pending a hearing on
the reversion of the property to the creditor, the Supreme Court,
per Justice White, held that issuance of the writ in an *ex parte*
proceeding without notice or hearing to the debtor did not deny
due process. Where the debtor was afforded ample opportunity to
present his side of the case before the creditor's recovery of the
property was made permanent, the Court found the Louisiana
scheme a valid accommodation of creditor-debtor interests by insuring maintenance of the property by one who can best care for it
prior to its disposition on the merits.

In contrast to its decision in *Mitchell* the Supreme Court breathed
life into Fuentes v. Shevin the following Term. The occasion was
the Court's consideration of the constitutionality of Georgia's garnishment statute. Pending suit, the law allowed a writ of garnishment to be issued by a court clerk based upon an affidavit filed by
the creditor or his agent and stating only "conclusory allegations."
The statute also provided for the filing of a bond as the only

[115] Fuentes v. Shevin, 407 U.S. 67, 80 (1972).   [116] *Ibid.*, 96.
[117] 416 U.S. 600 (1974). A second case the same Term that the Court also distinguished from *Fuentes* was Calero-Toledo v. Pearson Yacht Leasing Co., 416 U.S. 663
(1974).

method by which the debtor could dissolve the garnishment, deprived the debtor of the use of property in the garnishee's hands during litigation, and made no provision for a timely hearing. Though this case involved "parties of equal bargaining power," whereas both *Fuentes* and *Mitchell* "dealt with the application of due process protections to consumers who are victims of contracts of adhesion and who might be irreparably damaged by temporary deprivation of household necessities,"[118] the Court held, "We are no more inclined now than we have been in the past to distinguish among differing kinds of property in applying the Due Process Clause." The Court found the vagaries of Georgia's garnishment process sufficiently close to the constitutional transgressions of Florida's and Pennsylvania's replevin statutes in *Fuentes* to warrant invalidating them as an abridgment of due process. Dissenting, Justice Blackmun, in an opinion joined by Justice Rehnquist, expressed concern over what he saw as the unsettling quality of the majority's decision especially when contrasted with *Mitchell*. Much of the problem Justice Blackmun ascribed to the Court's overeagerness in 1972 to render its bare majority decision in *Fuentes*, while there were still two vacancies on the Court, instead of rescheduling that case for reargument before a full complement of nine justices. Chief Justice Burger joined part of Justice Blackmun's dissent. Earlier in the Term, the Supreme Court, over Justice Douglas's frequent dissent, declined to hear appeals in cases challenging State laws allowing repossession of automobiles without a hearing.[119]

Further, a Federal appeals court has held that seizure of property by hotelkeepers for nonpayment of rent, pursuant to a statutory hotelkeeper's lien and without prior notice or hearing to the tenant lacks the quality of "state action" and hence does not violate the guarantee of due process.[120]

Procedural Requirements with Respect to Law Enforcement   Because the specific procedural rights with respect to law enforcement on the national level are spelled out in other Bill of Rights Amendments, the development of the meaning of due process with respect to law enforcement procedures has chiefly centered on efforts to secure these same rights, right to counsel, protection from unreasonable searches and seizures, trial by jury, etc., against the States by incorporating them into the due process clause of the Fourteenth Amendment. In the course of this development, there has been much soul-searching about the meaning of due process. One classic position on the meaning is described by Justice Frankfurter: "Regard for the requirements of the Due Process Clause 'inescapably imposes upon this Court an exercise of

---

[118] North Georgia Finishing, Inc. *v.* Di-Chem, Inc., 419 U.S. 601, 608 (1975).

[119] *San Diego Union*, Nov, 12, 1974. *See*, e.g., Adams *v.* Southern Calif. First Nat'l Bank, 492 F. 2d. 324 (1974), *cert. denied*, 419 U.S. 1006 (1974).

[120] Anastasia *v.* Cosmopolitan Nat'l Bank of Chicago, 527 F. 2d. 150 (1975); *but cf.* Johnson *v.* Riverside Hotel, Inc., 399 F.Supp. 1138 (1975).

judgment upon the whole course of proceedings [resulting in a conviction] in order to ascertain whether they offend those canons of decency and fairness which express the notions of justice of English-speaking peoples even to those charged with the most heinous offenses.' These standards of justice are not authoritatively formulated anywhere as though they were specifics. Due process of law is a summarized constitutional guarantee of respect for those personal immunities which . . . are 'so rooted in the traditions and conscience of our people as to be ranked as fundamental' or are 'implicit in the concept of ordered liberty.' "[121] In practice, for Frankfurter, this meant that any procedure which "shocks the conscience" violates due process.[122] The opposing position has been best articulated by Justice Black, who argued that due process in the Fourteenth Amendment means *only* the procedural guarantees in the Bill of Rights.[123] As he saw it, the "shock the conscience" test was "a test which depends, not on the language of the Constitution, but solely on the views of a majority of the Court as to what is 'fair' and 'decent.' "[124]

With the expanded reach of the specific procedural guarantees with respect to law enforcement by the National Government, described above and below, plus the fact that the Court has long held that it had an inherent "supervisory authority over the administration of criminal justice in the Federal courts,[125] it is difficult to visualize what kinds of cases could arise in the future which would test the meaning of procedural due process in the *Fifth Amendment* in law enforcement. A recent case suggests some possibilities. With respect to the question whether or not, in a State proceeding with a juvenile "proof beyond a reasonable doubt" was a requirement of due process, the Court decided it was.[126] Such a case could conceivably have arisen within Federal jurisdiction. Also, Congress could conceivably pass laws with respect to procedures which go counter to those established by the Court under its supervisory role, and this would set the basis for a possible test on due process grounds. In this connection, it is worth pondering some words contained in Justice Black's dissent in the case just mentioned: "I admit a strong, persuasive argument can be made for a standard of proof beyond a reasonable doubt in criminal cases—and the majority has made that argument well—but it is not for me as a judge to say that Con-

---

[121] Rochin v. California, 342 U.S. 165, 169 (1952).　　　　[122] *Ibid.*, 172.

[123] His dissent in Adamson v. California, 332 U.S. 46 (1947).

[124] Williams v. Florida, 399 U.S. 78, 107 (1970).

[125] McNabb v. U.S., 318 U.S. 332, 341 (1943). *See also* Mallory v. U.S., 354 U.S. 449 (1957); Ker v. Calif., 374 U.S. 23 (1963).

[126] *In re* Winship, 397 U.S. 358 (1970). In a recent noteworthy case, the Court held that the cognovit, an "ancient legal device by which the debtor consents in advance to the holder's obtaining a judgment without notice or hearing" did not offend due process. The Court said "the due process rights to notice and hearing prior to a civil judgment are subject to waiver." D. H. Overmyer Co., Inc. v. Frick Co., 405 U.S. 174, 185 (1972). *See also* Stanley v. Illinois, 405 U.S. 645 (1972).

gress or the States are without constitutional power to establish another standard that the Constitution does not otherwise forbid. It is quite true that proof beyond a reasonable doubt has long been required in federal criminal trials. It is also true that this requirement is almost universally found in the governing laws of the States. . . . But when, as here, a State through its duly constituted legislative branch decides to apply a different standard, then that standard, unless it is otherwise unconstitutional, must be applied to insure that persons are treated according to 'the law of the land.' The State of New York has made such a decision, and nothing in the Due Process Clause invalidates it."[127]

On the basis of its statutory authority and after 13 years of discussion among the U.S. Judicial Conference, judges, and lawyers, the Supreme Court proposed Federal Rules of Evidence, which Congress subsequently amended and adopted.[128] The effect of the Rules, which provide uniform standards of evidence in Federal courts, is to tip the balance slightly in favor of the prosecution, in comparison with the previously existing state of affairs, by increasing the admissibility of evidence.[129] Perhaps the most controversial feature of the Rules was Congressional action that deleted some nine rules proposed by the Court upholding certain non-constitutional privileges (lawyer-client, husband-wife, doctor-patient, trade secrets, discussions with clergyman, state secrets, political vote, etc.) against divulgence.[130] In their place, Congress enacted Rule 501, which governs the invocation of such privilege "by the principles of the common law as they may be interpreted by the courts of the United States in the light of reason and experience,"[131] in other words, on a case-by-case basis. In civil cases, however, where State law provides a rule of decision with respect to a claim or defense, the State rule regarding non-constitutional privilege will apply.

Apparently, the Court still has work to do in determining the meaning of the Fourteenth Amendment's due process clause with respect to law enforcement procedures in State jurisdictions. In three important decisions on the question in 1972 and one in 1977 the Court held the following as violations of Fourteenth Amendment due process: (1) The holding of a convictee in a mental hospital beyond the time of his sentence, where his original commitment was effected on the basis of an *ex parte* order committing him to observation without the safeguards commensurate with a long-term commitment.[132] (2) The revocation of paroles without a hearing.

---

[127] *Ibid.*, 385-386.
[128] 88 *Stat.* 1926. For a discussion of the prolonged effort that went into generating the Rules as well as the legislative background behind their molding by Congress, *see* 1974 *U.S. Code Congressional and Administrative News*, 7051-7112.
[129] *San Diego Union*, June 29, 1975.
[130] 1974 *U.S. Code Congressional and Administrative News*, 7052-7054.
[131] 28 U.S.C. Appen., Rule 501.
[132] McNeil *v.* Director, Patuxent Institution, 407 U.S. 245 (1972). *Cf.* Murel *v.* Baltimore City Criminal Court, 407 U.S. 355 (1972).

The Court held that "the revocation of parole is not part of a criminal prosecution and the full panoply of rights due a defendant in such proceeding does not apply to parole revocations," but "what is needed [for due process] is an informal hearing structured to assure that the finding of parole violation will be based on verified facts and that the exercise of discretion will be informed by an accurate knowledge of the parolee's behavior."[133] (3) But in the third case, where it was contended that, when the defense moved for disclosure of all written statements taken by the police from any witness, six items were withheld by the State, the Supreme Court (5-4) held that "We know of no constitutional requirement that the prosecution must make a complete and detailed accounting to the defense of all police investigating work on a case."[134] The Court then went on to state its allegiance to the standard of due process set in an earlier case that the prosecution could not suppress evidence "in the face of a defense production request, where the evidence is favorable to the accused and is material either to guilt or to punishment." Clearly, the Court felt that the withheld information in the 1972 case did not fit this description. (4) The imposition of the death sentence, at least in part, on the basis of confidential information, not disclosed to the defendant or his counsel, so that he had no chance to deny or explain.[135]

Police behavior that presents the prospect of entrapment is a hardy perennial among due process issues in law enforcement. In a controversial case decided by the Court in 1973,[136] a Federal narcotics agent supplied some manufacturers of "speed" with an essential ingredient on the condition that he be shown a sample of the drug they were making and the laboratory in which it was produced. Justice Rehnquist, speaking for the majority of five (the Nixon appointees plus Justice White), held that "The law enforcement conduct here stops far short of violating that 'fundamental fairness, shocking to the universal sense of justice,' mandated by the Due Process Clause of the Fifth Amendment."[137] As he saw it, the "narc's" contribution to the "criminal enterprise already in process was scarcely objectionable." The measure of the dissenter's disdain for the majority opinion are these words from Justice Douglas: "Federal agents play a debased role when they become the instigators of the crime, or partners in its commission, or the creative brain behind the illegal scheme." And that was precisely what the case was about according to Justice Douglas.[138] Three

Entrapment

---

[133] Morrissey and Booher v. Brewer, 408 U.S. 471 (1972).

[134] Moore v. Illinois, 408 U.S. 786 (1972). *And see* United States v. Augurs, 427 U.S. 97 (1976).

[135] Gardner v. Fla., 430 U.S. 349 (1977).

[136] United States v. Russell, 411 U.S. 423 (1973).   [137] *Ibid.*, 432.

[138] *Ibid.*, 439. In a notable dissent, Justice Stewart endeavored to fashion a general rule to cover entrapment cases: "Government agents may engage in conduct that is likely, when objectively considered, to afford a person ready and willing to commit the crime an opportunity to do so." In this case he felt that the agent had gone beyond "the mere offering of such an opportunity." *Ibid.*, 445.

years later, the Court held that sale to government agents of heroin, supplied to the defendant by a government informer, did not constitute entrapment, and hence a violation of due process, where the defendant was predisposed to commit the crime.[139] Focusing on the conduct of the police and not on the intent of the defendant, Justice Brennan concluded in dissent that "conviction is barred as a matter of law where the subject of the criminal charge is the sale of contraband provided to the defendant by a government agent."

Due Process in Prison   Rejecting out of hand Nebraska's assertion that "the procedure for disciplining prison inmates for serious misconduct is of no constitutional issue," the Supreme Court held in 1974 that while "Prison disciplinary proceedings are not part of a criminal prosecution, and the full panoply of rights due a defendant in such proceedings does not apply,"[140] nevertheless prisoners do possess certain elementary rights to "liberty" and "property" that cannot be taken from them without minimal regard for the commandments of the due process clause even though "there must be mutual accommodation between institutional needs and objectives and provisions of the Constitution that are of general application." The Court per Justice White, held that where inmates face internal disciplinary proceedings that could deprive them of good time credits, they are entitled to receive written notice of the violation 24 hours before the proceedings, and afterwards a written statement of the findings and the reasons supporting them. Prisoners whose conduct is subject to discipline are also entitled to present evidence and call witnesses in their behalf where it does not jeopardize institutional safety. Inmates, however, are *not* entitled to rights of counsel or cross-examination. The Court pointed out, moreover, that opening a prisoner's mail in his presence to check for contraband is not unconstitutional. Finally, the Court held that prisoners claiming unconstitutional deprivation of good time credit have the right to seek damages under the Civil Rights Statutes and to have legal assistance in the preparation of petitions in such suits. Justices Douglas, Brennan, and Marshall dissented on the grounds that due process in their view demanded nothing less than trial-type hearings with all due process safeguards. Also worth noting is a decision by the U.S. Court of Appeals, Fifth Circuit, sitting *en banc* and dividing 12-4, that due process rights do not extend to proceedings granting or denying parole to a Federal prisoner.[141]

Due Process in Administrative Proceedings   In administrative proceedings, which are today an important feature of government, both State and national, the significance of the term "due process" has been elaborated by the Court. Thus Congress has delegated to the Interstate Commerce Commission the power to set "reasonable rates," and when the Commission orders a carrier to observe a certain rate as "reasonable," the Court

[139] Hampton *v.* U.S., 425 U.S. 484 (1976).
[140] Wolff *v.* McDonnell, 418 U.S. 539, 556 (1974).
[141] Scarpa *v.* U.S. Board of Parole, 477 F. 2d. 278 (1973).

will sustain its order as having been set by "due process of law," provided the Commission did not act "arbitrarily" but gave the carrier an opportunity to be heard, that it observed all the rules of law which the Court has laid down for such cases, and finally that its findings of fact were sustained by "substantial evidence."[142]

Judicial decisions in this field frequently turn on whether the Court regards the question before it to be one "of fact" and so within the power of an administrative body to determine, or one "of law" and so within the power of the Court to determine on review. The same question (as, e.g., whether a given rate is "reasonable") may be of either sort, depending on the angle from which it is viewed. Nowadays the Court seems generally to treat such "mixed questions" as "questions of fact."[143]

Congress, of course, is free at any time to add to the bare constitutional requirements of "due process of law" others which must be observed by administrative agencies, and has done so in its Administrative Procedure Act of 1946.[144] Significantly, persons appearing before administrative agencies are not afforded all the protections they would have in a court proceeding (*see* p. 427).[145] And the imposition of procedural guarantees that attach to trial-type hearings (notice, counsel, written record, witnesses, confrontation, and cross-examination, for example) will be weighed by the Court in proportion to any protected interests of the individual involved.[146] It should be noted, however, that there are certain inherent limitations to judicial review of administrative determinations—those which arise out of the vast bulk of facts which a regulatory agency often brings into court and those which arise from the necessity of getting a case decided. State regulation of public utility rates had been at one period rendered largely farcical by the idea that the courts ought to retry from the ground up administrative findings of fact.[147] Finally, whatever the scope of judicial review, before there is any judicial review the administrative remedy generally must be exhausted.[148]

---

[142] Interstate Comm. Com'n v. Un. P. R. R. Co., 222 U.S. 541 (1912); Interstate Com. Com'n v. L. & N. R. R. Co., 227 U.S. 88 (1913); Consolidated Edison Co. v. NLRB, 305 U.S. 197 (1938); Opp Cotton Mills v. Administrator of Wage and Hr. Div. etc., 312 U.S. 126 (1941); Sniadach v. Family Finance Corp., 395 U.S. 337 (1969); Goldberg v. Kelly, 397 U.S. 254 (1970); Wisconsin v. Constantine, 400 U.S. 433 (1971). For cases involving suspension of drivers' licenses, *see* Bell v. Burson, 402 U.S. 535 (1971); Jennings v. Mahoney, 404 U.S 25 (1971).

[143] *See* pp. 204-205 *supra.*   [144] 5 U.S.C. 551-559.

[145] *See* Gerace v. County of Los Angeles, 100 Cal. Rptr. 917 (1972).

[146] *Cf.* Green v. McElroy, 360 U.S. 474 (1959) *with* Hannah v. Larche, 363 U.S. 420 (1960). *See in re* Gault, 387 U.S. 1 (1967); Goldberg v. Kelly, 397 U.S. 254 (1970); Wisconsin v. Constantineau, 400 U.S. 433 (1971); Paul v. Davis, 424 U.S. 693 (1976).

[147] *See* pp. 51-53 *supra.*

[148] Myers v. Bethlehem Shipbuilding Corp., 303 U.S. 41 (1938); Levers v. Anderson, 326 U.S. 219 (1945); DuBois Clubs of America v. Clark, 389 U.S. 309 (1967); *cf.* Oestereich v. Selective Service Board, 393 U.S. 233 (1968).

The process of balancing procedural guarantees and protected interests is readily apparent in a recent Supreme Court decision. Declining to extend further the holding in Goldberg v. Kelly,[149] which established the right of individuals to a pretermination hearing before welfare payments could be shut off, the Supreme Court ruled that the Constitution did not require a similar evidentiary hearing prior to the discontinuation of disability benefits to recipients under the Social Security Act.[150] Weighing what it saw as the relevant considerations—the private interest at stake, the risk of erroneous deprivation, and the public interest, including fiscal and administrative burdens—the Court found that "present administrative procedures fully comport with due process."

Other noteworthy lower court decisions pertaining to the administrative process held: (1) that tenants in a low-income housing project subsidized and insured under the National Housing Act were not entitled to a hearing before rent increases were approved by the Federal Housing Administration;[151] (2) that a police department need not turn over its personnel files and material relevant to its internal investigations to a State civil rights commission;[152] and (3) that the failure of an IRS agent to warn a taxpayer, not in custody, of the criminal nature of a tax investigation, despite agency regulations mandating such warnings, did not contravene the due process clause of the Fifth Amendment.[153] And, in another development bearing upon the conduct of an administrative agency, the Ohio Supreme Court held that, while the U.S. Constitution's Fifth Amendment protection against self-incrimination applies only to natural persons, an Ohio statute extending such protection to corporations, even though they cannot suffer imprisonment, precludes the State civil rights commission from compelling a private business to answer interrogatories as to racial discrimination in its rental policies.[154]

Finally, with an approach that seemed remarkably similar in

---

[149] 397 U.S. 254 (1970).

[150] Mathews v. Eldridge, 424 U.S. 319 (1976). See also Dillard v. Industrial Com'n of Va., 416 U.S. 783 (1974). For a suit attacking the dual participation of an NLRB official, first as hearing officer and then as representative of the board's general counsel issuing a formal complaint, see I.T.&T. Co. v. Local 134, Int. Brotherhood of Elec. Workers, 419 U.S. 600 (1975). In the context of that labor relations controversy, the Court held that the assigning of both adjudicatory and prosecutorial functions to the same person infringed neither the Administrative Procedure Act nor the due process clause.

[151] Keller v. Romney, 504 F. 2d. 483 (1974); Paulsen v. Coachlight Apartments Co., 507 F. 2d. 401 (1974); Harlib v. Lynn, 511 F. 2d. 51 (1975); Fenner v. Bruce Manor, Inc., 409 F.Supp. 1332 (1976); but cf. Ponce v. Housing Auth'y of Cty. of Tulare, 389 F.Supp. 635 (1975). Courts have held, however, that hearings are essential prior to eviction from governmentally subsidized housing, see Lopez v. Henry Phipps Plaza South, Inc., 498 F. 2d. 937 (1974); Short v. Fulton Redevelopment Co., Inc., 390 F.Supp. 517 (1975); Appel v. Beyer, 114 Cal. Rptr. 336 (1974).

[152] McMillan v. Ohio Civil Rights Com'n, 315 N.E. 2d. 508 (1974).

[153] United States v. Potter, 385 F.Supp. 681 (1974); see also United States v. Wohler, 382 F.Supp. 229 (1973).

[154] Ohio Civil Rights Com'n v. Parklawn Manor, Inc., 322 N.E. 2d. 642 (1975).

striking a balance between individual rights and administrative efficiency, the Supreme Court concluded that a summary court-martial was not a "criminal prosecution" within the meaning of the Sixth Amendment and it held that neither did the denial of counsel in that military context offend the due process clause. Weighing "the interests of the individual and those of the regime to which he is subject," the Court found that none of "the factors militating in favor of counsel at summary courts-martial are so extraordinarily weighty as to overcome the balance struck by Congress." Speaking for the Court, Justice Rehnquist summed up: "In short, presence of counsel will turn a brief, informal hearing which may be quickly convened and rapidly concluded into an attenuated proceeding which consumes the resources of the military to a degree which Congress could properly have felt to be beyond what is warranted by the relative insignificance of the offenses being tried." Justice Rehnquist added that such a requirement would be particularly burdensome to the military "whose time may be better spent than in possibly protracted disputes over the imposition of discipline."[155]

Troubles on the campus and the more vigorous assertion of rights by individuals in recent years ultimately led to Supreme Court decisions in 1972 on the question of whether or not non-tenured teachers were entitled to a hearing prior to a non-renewal of contract. In one such case, the Court decided 5-3 that a teacher hired for one year only was not "deprived of liberty or property protected by the Fourteenth Amendment." Consequently, no hearing was constitutionally required, although the Court hinted it might be good policy to grant one.[156] But in another case, the Court held that a non-tenured professor who had been employed for ten years was another matter.[157] Since the complaining professor "alleged that the college had a *de facto* tenure program, and that he had tenure under that program," the Court held that if he could prove that, he was entitled to a hearing. "Proof of such a property interest would not, of course, entitle him to reinstatement. But such proof would obligate college officials to grant a hearing at his request, where he could be informed of the grounds for his nonretention and challenge their sufficiency." *Hearings For Non-Tenured Teachers Whose Contracts Are Not Renewed*

The power which the government exerts when it "takes private property" for "public use" is called the power of eminent domain. Before the Civil War it was generally denied that the National Government could exercise the power of eminent domain within a State without the consent of the State.[158] (*See* Article I, Section VIII, ¶17.) Today, however, it is well settled that the National Gov- *The Eminent Domain Power of the National Government*

---

[155] Middendorf v. Henry, 425 U.S. 25, 45-46 (1976).
[156] Board of Regents v. Roth, 408 U.S. 564 (1972).
[157] Perry v. Sindermann, 408 U.S. 593 (1972). For a ruling that non-probationary Federal employees are not entitled to a trial-type hearing even though they can only be removed for cause, *see* Arnett v. Kennedy, 416 U.S. 134 (1974).
[158] *See* Edward S. Corwin, *National Supremacy* (New York, 1913), 262-263.

ernment may take property by eminent domain whenever it is "necessary and proper" for it to do so in order to carry out any of the powers of the National Government; and that it may, in proper cases, vest this power in corporations chartered by it.[159]

When Property is "Taken"

Property is "taken," generally speaking, only when title to it is transferred to the Government or the Government takes over or assumes to control its valuable uses, or when, in the case of land, it commits a deliberate and protracted trespass, as by the repeated and persistent discharge of heavy guns across the grounds of a summer resort, with the natural result of frightening off the public; or the frequent flight at low altitudes of military planes over a commercial chicken farm, with the natural result of destroying the value of the property for that use.[160] On the other hand, jet aircraft operations which raise havoc with ordinary home activities but do not make private homes uninhabitable do not constitute a taking of an interest for which compensation must be paid.[161] But the Supreme Court of California created a stir in 1972 when it decided that people could seek damages for injuries alleged to have been suffered in consequence of the operation of an airport on the grounds of nuisance, negligence, and zoning violations but not on the grounds that it constituted "a taking."[162]

Property is not "taken simply because its value declines in consequence of an exertion of lawful power by the Government."[163] Thus, Congress may lower the tariff, cheapen the currency, or declare war, and so forth and so on, without having to compensate those who suffer losses as a result of its action. Nor is the destruction of private property by the Army to prevent its falling into enemy hands a compensable loss.[164]

In a 1973 decision, the Supreme Court held that there was no taking of property under the Fifth Amendment where an individual is detained as a material witness and paid only one dollar a day plus subsistence.[165] It also held that a city charter amendment requiring approval for a zoning change by a 55 per cent vote in a public referendum does not violate the due process rights of a

---

[159] Kohl v. U.S., 91 U.S. 367 (1875); California v. Pac. Cent. R.R. Co., 127 U.S. 1 (1888); Luxton v. No. R. Bridge Co., 153 U.S. 525 (1894).

[160] United States v. Great Falls Mfg. Co., 112 U.S. 645 (1884); Portsmouth Harbor Land & Hotel Co. v. U.S., 260 U.S. 327 (1922); United States v. Causby, 328 U.S. 256 (1946); United States v. Dickinson, 331 U.S. 745 (1947); Aris Gloves Inc. v. U.S., 420 F. 2d. 1386 (1970).

[161] Batten v. U.S., 306 F. 2d. 580 (1962); *cert. denied,* 371 U.S. 955 (1963); *rehearing denied,* 372 U.S. 925 (1963). *See also* Thornburg v. City of Portland, 376 P. 2d. 100 (1962), where *Batten* was strongly questioned by the Oregon Supreme Court.

[162] Nestle v. City of Santa Monica, 101 Cal. Rptr. 568 (1972). "Manager Would Close L.A. Airport if It Is Warranted," *Los Angeles Times,* May 4, 1972; "Los Angeles Seeks Legislation to Keep Airport Open," *Washington Post,* May 5, 1972.

[163] New Haven Inclusion Cases, 399 U.S. 392, 491-493 (1970).

[164] Knox v. Lee, 12 Wall. 457 (1871); Omnia Com'l Co. v. U.S., 261 U.S. 502 (1923); United States v. Caltex, 344 U.S. 149 (1952); YMCA v. U.S., 395 U.S. 85 (1969).

[165] Hurtado v. U.S., 410 U.S. 578 (1973).

landowner applying for the zoning change.[166] And, some interesting lower court decisions have: (1) upheld wage and price controls imposed pursuant to the Economic Stabilization Act of 1970;[167] (2) struck down limits on awards in medical malpractice suits imposed by State statute;[168] (3) held unconstitutional a Denver ordinance prohibiting off-premises outdoor advertising signs;[169] (4) ruled that the Interior Secretary's actions suspending drilling operations in the Santa Barbara Channel following an oil spill did not "take" oil and gas lessees' property.[170]

What is a "public use"? Existing precedents yield a broad definition of this term in connection with both the taxing power and the power of eminent domain, when these are exercised by the States;[171] and in the case of the National Government determination of the issue rests with Congress "unless shown to involve an impossibility."[172]

"Just compensation" must be determined by an impartial body, not necessarily a court or a jury; not necessarily, in the case of land, in advance of the taking, so long as the owner is guaranteed the opportunity of being heard sooner or later, but not too late, on the question of value.[173] Theoretically, what the term signifies is the

[166] City of Eastlake v. Forest City Enterprises, Inc., 426 U.S. 668 (1976).

[167] See Salsburg's Meats, Inc. v. Shultz, 363 F.Supp. 269 (1973); Anderson v. Dunlop, 366 F.Supp. 582 (1973), reversed on appeal, 485 F. 2d. 666 (1974); Local Union No. 11 Internationl Brotherhood of Electrical Workers, AFL-CIO v. Boldt, 481 F. 2d. 1392 (1973); Western States Meat Packers Ass'n, Inc. v. Dunlop, 482 F. 2d. 1401 (1973); League of Voluntary Hospitals and Homes of New York v. Local 1199, Drug and Hospital Union, 490 F. 2d. 1398 (1973). Plaintiffs had argued that the controls in substance and as applied were arbitrary, unreasonable, invidiously discriminatory, and constituted a "taking" of property. See also Fry v. U.S., 421 U.S. 542 (1975).

[168] See Wright v. Central DuPage Hospital Ass'n, 347 N.E. 2d. 736 (1976); Simon v. St. Elizabeth Medical Center, 355 N.E. 2d. 903 (1976).

[169] Combined Communications Corp. v. City and County of Denver, 542 P. 2d. 79 (1975). The court held that neither police or zoning powers enabled the city to prohibit an entire industry—in other words, that the ordinance was per se unreasonable. However, courts have had little difficulty sustaining regulation of outdoor advertising under the Highway Beautification Act of 1965; see, e.g., Yarbrough v. Arkansas State H'wy Com'n, 539 S.W. 2d. 419 (1976). But see as to the compensation to be paid to owners of outdoor advertising signs, Vermont v. Brinegar, 379 F.Supp. 606 (1974).

[170] Union Carbide Co. of Calif. v. Morton, 512 F. 2d. 743 (1975).

[171] The Supreme Court of Michigan upheld a city's taking of property to be resold to private persons for redevelopment saying: "The controlling purpose of the city's plan is to rehabilitate a blighted area. The property is acquired, not for the purpose of redevelopment at a profit to the city or any private developer, but to protect the health, safety, morals and general welfare of the municipality. Since the controlling purpose is public use, the circumstance of a private developer's benefit would not change its character." In re City of Center Line, 196 N.W. 2d. 144 (1972).

[172] Green v. Frazier, 253 U.S. 233 (1920); United States v. Gettysburg Elec. R. Co., 160 U.S. 668 (1896); United States ex rel. TVA v. Welch, 327 U.S. 546, 552 (1946). But see Phillips v. Foster, 211 S.E. 2d. 93 (1975); and Finks v. Maine State Highway Com'n, 328 A. 2d. 791 (1974).

[173] United States v. Great Falls Mfg. Co., 112 U.S. 645 (1884); Bauman v. Ross, 167 U.S. 548 (1897); Bailey v. Anderson, 326 U.S. 203 (1945). Where land is taken by the United States under the eminent domain power without compensation pro-

full and perfect equivalent in money of the real property taken,[174] the measure whereof is the owner's loss, not the Government's gain.[175] More concretely, where the property taken has a determinable "market value," in other words, "what a willing buyer would pay in cash to a willing seller,"[176] that is the measure of recovery,[177] which may reflect not only the use to which the property is currently devoted, but also that to which it may be readily converted.[178] Such is the language of the cases. It cannot be said, however, that the Court has displayed impressive unanimity of opinion in its efforts to apply these principles in cases which grew out of the facts of World War II.[179]

Like the Ghost of Christmas Past, the national rail crisis revisited the Court in the form of an action alleging that certain provisions of the Regional Rail Reorganization Act of 1973 short-changed railroad companies that had filed for reorganization under the Bankruptcy Act by failing to provide adequate compensation in the transfer of their properties to Conrail, a private, for-profit, but government-backed corporation. Specifically, it was alleged that in two respects Penn Central's rail properties were being taken without payment of just compensation, by (1) "conveyance taking" ("because compensation is not in cash but largely in stock of an unproven entity"), and (2) "erosion taking" (because the estate of the railroads will be incrementally depleted during the transition period by being obliged under law not to discontinue present service or abandon unprofitable lines). Justice Brennan, speaking for the Court, pointed out that other laws already on the books, not superseded by the rail act, assured that, should there be "any constitutional shortfall," the complainants would have their day in court. As to the issue of transferring property before a court decision, the Court observed: "Complainants evidence no interest in retaining their property for longer than the Rail Act requires. Indeed, their position is really that they want to be free to dispose of it sooner. Thus, there is no interest asserted in retaining the properties themselves; the only interest is in making sure that creditors receive fair compensation for those properties. On the other hand, the pro-

---

ceedings, the owner may, under the Tucker Act, bring suit for compensation in the Court of Claims or in a district court sitting as a court of claims. United States *v.* Great Falls Co., *supra*; Jacobs *v.* U.S., 290 U.S. 13 (1933).

[174] Monongahela Nav. Co. *v.* U.S., 148 U.S. 312, 326 (1893); Acton *v.* U.S., 401 F. 2d. 896 (1968); *cert. denied*, 395 U.S. 945 (1969).

[175] United States *v.* Chandler-Dunbar Co., 229 U.S. 53 (1913); United States *ex rel.* TVA *v.* Powelson, 319 U.S. 266, 281 (1943).

[176] United States *v.* Miller, 317 U.S. 369, 374 (1943). *Cf.* Kimball Laundry Co. *v.* U.S., 338 U.S. 1 (1949).

[177] United States *v.* Powelson, 319 U.S. 266, 275 (1943).

[178] Boom Co. *v.* Patterson, 98 U.S. 403 (1879); McCandless *v.* U.S., 298 U.S. 342 (1936).

[179] *Cf.* United States *v.* Felin & Co., 334 U.S. 624 (1948); United States *v.* Cors, 337 U.S. 325, 333 (1949); United States *v.* Toronto Nav. Co., 338 U.S. 396 (1949); United States *v.* Commodities Trading Corp., 339 U.S. 121 (1950).

cedural sequence is vital to accomplishing the goals of the Act. If judicial review of the terms of the transfer was required before the conveyance could occur, the conveyance might well come too late to resolve the rail transportation crisis. As long as creditors are assured fair value, with interest, for their properties, the Constitution requires nothing more."[180] Drawing upon considerable expertise in business regulation gained in his early career as SEC Chairman, Justice Douglas dissented in a long and provocative opinion, which he capped by saying: "We are urged to bow to the pressure of events and expedite in the public interest the reorganization of these six rail carriers. An emergency often gives Congress the occasion to act. But I know of no emergency that permits it to disregard the Just Compensation Clause of the Fifth Amendment nor the uniformity requirement of the Bankruptcy Clause of the Constitution." (For a discussion of the relevant issues concerning the bankruptcy clause, *see* p. 94.)

In a second case recently before the Court, a 1926 Federal statute established a reservation, allotted lands to individual tribal members, and gave to each the title, effective 50 years later, to the mineral resources underneath his respective holdings. The Supreme Court unanimously held that Congress, acting before the expiration of the time period and using its "vast" and "unique" powers to protect Indians, could lawfully reserve the mineral rights for the benefit of the tribe *as a whole*.[181] The Court rejected the argument that transfer of the mineral rights constitutionally required payment of just compensation to the individual landholders. Congress had acted out of concern that coal deposits underneath the reservation, greatly increased in value with the onset of the energy crisis, would be exploited to the disadvantage of many reservation inhabitants.

To which branch of the National Government is the duty to render just compensation addressed when the National Government is involved in taking property? Undoubtedly to Congress, since it alone has the power to appropriate money for the purpose. But this does not imply that Congress must in all instances have authorized the taking in the first place. Thus, in passing upon a seizure of American-owned property by an American military commander operating in Mexico during the Mexican War, the Court said, that if the exigencies of war clearly warranted the act, the Government was "bound to make full compensation; but the officer is not a trespasser,"[182] doctrine which it reiterated years later with respect to a similar taking in the course of the Civil War.[183]

Which Department the Clause Binds

---

[180] Blanchette *v.* Conn. General Ins. Corps., 419 U.S. 102, 156 (1974).
[181] Northern Cheyenne Tribe *v.* Hollowbreast, 425 U.S. 649 (1976). *See also* United States *v.* Jim, 409 U.S. 80 (1972).
[182] Mitchell *v.* Harmony, 13 How. 115 (1852).
[183] United States *v.* Russell, 13 Wall. 623 (1871). United States *v.* Pewee Coal Co., 341 U.S. 114 (1951).

AMENDMENT VI

In all criminal prosecutions the accused shall enjoy the right to a speedy and public trial, by an impartial jury of the State and district wherein the crime shall have been committed, which district shall have been previously ascertained by law, and to be informed of the nature and cause of the accusation; to be confronted with the witnesses against him; to have compulsory process for obtaining witnesses in his favor, and to have the assistance of counsel for his defense.

Speedy and
Public
Trial

As a consequence of its decision in 1967 that the Fourteenth Amendment incorporated the right to a "speedy trial," enforceable against the States,[1] the Supreme Court had recent occasion to attempt to spell out what a "speedy trial" meant. The Court supplied some handsome rhetoric but no real guidelines when it said: "The right to a speedy trial is not a theoretical or abstract right but one rooted in hard reality in the need to have charges promptly exposed. If the case for the prosecution calls on the accused to meet charges rather than rest on the infirmities of the prosecution's case, as is the defendant's right, the time to meet them is when the case is fresh. Stale claims have never been favored by the law, and far less so in criminal cares. Although a great many accused persons seek to put off confrontation as long as possible, the right to a prompt inquiry into criminal charges is fundamental and the duty of the charging authority is to provide a prompt trial."[2] But what exactly is a "prompt trial"? State courts have struggled with that question since the Supreme Court's decision.[3] Indeed, the Supreme Court itself in 1972 acknowledged the need "to set out the criteria by which a speedy trial right is to be judged," but ended up in frustration, saying "A balancing test necessarily compels courts to approach speedy-trial cases on an *ad hoc* basis. We can do little more than identify some of the factors which courts should assess in determining whether a particular defendant has been deprived of his right. Though some might express them in different ways, we identify four such factors: Length of delay, the reason for delay, the defendant's assertion of his right, and prejudice to the defendant."[4]

Also, Congress has endeavored to step into the breach. With respect to the Interstate Agreement on Detainers Act of 1970, the Senate Report accompanying the bill tells us what the act provides with respect to detainers: "If the prisoner is not brought to trial

---

[1] Klopfer v. North Carolina, 386 U.S. 213 (1967).

[2] Dickey v. Florida, 398 U.S. 30, 37-38 (1970).

[3] For a particularly enlightening State court decision, *see* the decision of the North Carolina Supreme Court in State v. Harrell, 187 S.E. 2d. 789 (1972). *See also* Tennessee v. McCullough, 470 S.W. 2d. 50 (1971); Commonwealth v. Bunter, 282 A. 2d. 705 (1971); State v. Lawless, 283 A. 2d. 160 (1971); Thompson v. State, 290 A. 2d. 565 (1972).

[4] Barker v. Wingo, 407 U.S. 514 (1972).

within the 180-day limit, the charges are dismissed with prejudice and the detainer is no longer valid. The time limit can be extended for good cause shown in open court with the prisoner or his counsel present."[5]

In response to the long delays that plague the Federal criminal justice process, Congress passed the Speedy Trial Act of 1974.[6] The act imposes declining time limits over a five-year period in moving proceedings through the various stages of the criminal justice process. The goal set by the act is resolution of a criminal proceeding from arrest to trial within 100 days. The act specifies sanctions to take effect in the fifth year allowing the accused to move for dismissal of the charges, with certain exceptions, if the time limits in the act are not met. The act also provides sanctions to deal with stalling tactics by both prosecution and defense attorneys. Additional provisions mandate the creation of plans in each Federal district to meet the act's guidelines and provide funding to facilitate compliance. The Speedy Trial Act is limited in its effect to Federal courts and in no way precludes the raising of future speedy trial challenges under the Sixth Amendment.

Speedy Trial Act

In a ruling releasing from custody two alleged big-time drug smugglers who had not been brought to trial within 90 days of arrest as directed by the Speedy Trial Act of 1974, the U.S. Court of Appeals, Ninth Circuit, took Congress to task for the legislation. Observing that "[r]elease of these two foreign nationals from custody is tantamount to an invitation to flee across the Mexican border, less than 3 hours away," the court added: "In light of these facts, the wisdom of the result Congress has ordered is questionable. We release a man alleged to be the head of a foreign criminal organization dedicated to the smuggling of large quantities of illegal drugs, so that he may quickly cross the border and resume operating his business. We are also releasing his alleged right-hand man, as if to make certain that the enterprise continues to operate at top efficiency. But this result is the only one open to us under the plain terms of the statute. It is discouraging that our highly refined and complex system of criminal justice is suddenly faced with implementing a statute that is so inartfully drawn as this one. But this is the law, and we are bound to give it effect."[7]

Of related concern, the New York Court of Appeals recently ruled that "a prosecutor must not make the right to a speedy trial an item of barter in a plea bargaining situation." Judge Rabin, speaking for the court, continued, "It is possible that an innocent defendant,

---

[5] 1970 *U.S. Cong. & Adm. News*, 4864ff. For the law itself *see ibid.*, 1630.

[6] 88 *Stat.* 2076.

[7] United States v. Tirasso, 532 F. 2d. 1298, 1300-1301 (1976). Chief Justice Burger has agreed with this criticism, *see* 62 *Amer. Bar Ass'n Journal* 992-993 (1976). He had indicated earlier that such reforms require additional judgeships and funds; *see* his "The State of the Judiciary—1975," 61 *Amer. Bar Ass'n Journal*, 439 (1975). For additional criticism of the Act, *see* Alex Kozinski, "That Can of Worms: The Speedy Trial Act," 62 *Amer. Bar Ass'n Journal*, 862 (1976).

faced with a trial that is unfair because unreasonably delayed, may
plead guilty to a reduced charge rather than risk such a trial. Because the criminal justice system should scrupulously avoid the
possibility that a plea of guilty may be tainted with unfairness . . .
and because prosecutors should not be allowed to submerge speedy
trial challenges, and the societal interests they represent, in plea
bargains, we hold that a reduced plea conditioned upon a waiver of
a speedy trial claim must be vacated."[8]

With respect to a "public trial" undoubtedly the framers of this
amendment were impelled by the reasons recited by Justice Black
some years ago: "The traditional Anglo-American distrust for secret trials has been variously ascribed to the notorious use of this
practice by the Spanish Inquisition, to the excesses of the English
Court of Star Chamber, and to the French monarchy's abuse of the
lettre de cachet. . . . Whatever other benefits the guarantee to an accused that his trial be conducted in public may confer upon our society, the guarantee has always been recognized as a safeguard
against any attempt to employ our courts as instruments of perse-
cution."[9] In addition, no doubt, there was also the idea that an accused should be able to have some of his friends in the courtroom
for the putative protection their presence would afford.

The Press's
Claim of a
"Right to
Know"
For years, some members of the press have claimed that the public has a "right to know" what its government is doing and, that the
press serving as the public's agent should be permitted to cover
trials virtually as they see fit to do so within the bounds of a little
decorum. The Supreme Court does not recognize the full measure
of such a claim. As the Court put it in 1965: "The free press has
been a mighty catalyst in awakening public interest in governmental affairs, exposing corruption among public officers and
employees, and generally informing the citizenry of public events
and occurrences including court proceedings. While maximum
freedom must be allowed the press in carrying on this important
function in a democratic society its exercise must necessarily be
subject to the maintenance of absolute fairness in the judicial
process."[10] Consequently, the Court has forbidden the televising of
criminal cases. After a long recital of how televising a trial inhibits
fairness, the Court went on to say: "It is said that the ever-advanc-
ing techniques of public communication and adjustment of the
public to its presence may bring about a change in the effect of
telecasting upon the fairness of criminal trials. But we are not dealing here with future developments in the field of electronics. Our
judgment cannot be rested on the hypothesis of tomorrow but
must take the facts as they are presented today."[11] Furthermore,
the Court had been quick to point out earlier in its opinion: "Nor
can the Courts be said to discriminate where they permit the news-

[8] People *v.* Blakley, 313 N.E. 2d. 763 (1974).
[9] *In re* Oliver, 333 U.S. 257, 268-270 (1948).
[10] Estes *v.* Texas, 381 U.S. 532, 539 (1965).   [11] *Ibid.*, 551-552.

paper reporter access to the courtroom. The television and radio reporter has the same privilege. They are entitled to the same rights as the general public. The press reporter is not permitted to bring his typewriter or printing press. When the advances in these arts permit reporting by printing press or by television without their present hazards to a fair trial we will have another case."[12]

While arguments about a "right to know" often begin in the context of press coverage of trials, they rarely end there; instead, they merge with a more general discussion of the basis and implications of the claimed right.[13] Consequently, it seems appropriate to discuss the issue further here. Recent decisions, in fact, would seem to make it abundantly clear that the Court distinguishes between a constitutional right to publish and the postulated "right to know." Putting to one side *statutory* guarantees of the "right to know," such as Congress's enactment of the Freedom of Information Act out of a concern for maintaining adequate publicity and openness in the rule-making process of Federal agencies[14] or the passage of "sunshine laws" by the States that open up meetings of governmental bodies to public scrutiny[15]—statutory protections that apply in limited contexts—it is clear that, *constitutionally* speaking, the Court does not recognize such a right. Just as the public generally may be excluded on certain occasions from "grand jury proceedings, . . . conferences [among Supreme Court Justices], the meetings of other official bodies in executive session, and the meetings of private organizations,"[16] so may the press. "The Constitution does not . . . accord the press special access to information not shared by members of the public generally."[17] Nor do recent decisions striking

The Public's "Right to Know"

---

[12] *Ibid.*, 540. For an interesting State court decision involving a judge closing the courtroom to press and public, *see* Oliver *v.* Poste, 331 N.Y.S. 2d. 407 (1972).

[13] *See* Wilson *v.* Chancellor, 418 F.Supp. 1358 (1976).

[14] The Freedom of Information Act was passed in 1966, 80 *Stat.* 383, and amended one year later, 81 *Stat.* 54. As originally formulated and initially amended it comprises 5 U.S.C. § 552. However, as uneasiness over governmental secrecy grew with the revelations of Watergate and the attendant cover-up, Congress again amended the Act with the Freedom of Information Act of 1974, 88 *Stat.* 1561. Those amendments not only toughened the existing law considerably, it also made it undeniably clear that those around the President came within its ambit. Particularly interesting is the question of how much leeway the Act gives for *de novo* review by the Federal courts of decisions by the CIA, for example, on the secrecy classifications given to government documents. *See* Alfred A. Knopf, Inc. *v.* Colby, 509 F. 2d. 1362 (1975) *and see* Anthony Lewis, "A Court of Appeals Decision on Prior Restraint: And a Threat to that Freedom [of Information]," *New York Times*, Feb. 16, 1975, p. 16.

[15] *See* Cathcart *v.* Andersen, 530 P. 2d. 313 (1975); *see also* Food Chemical News, Inc. *v.* Davis, 378 F.Supp. 1048 (1974).

[16] Branzburg *v.* Hayes, 408 U.S. 665, 684 (1972). *See also* Times Newspapers Ltd. *v.* McDonnell Douglas Corp., 387 F.Supp. 189 (1974).

[17] Pell *v.* Procunier, 417 U.S. 817, 834 (1974). The same point is made by the Court in Branzburg *v.* Hayes, 408 U.S. 665, 684 (1972). And, especially worth noting is the Court's statement in Zemel *v.* Rusk, 381 U.S. 1, 17 (1965), sustaining a ban on travel because "[t]he right to speak and publish does not carry with it the unrestrained right to gather information." Indeed, in other cases, where the Court has

down governmental bans on advertising the prices of prescription drugs or fees charged for routine legal services support the recognition of a "right to know."[18] Moreover, even though the Constitution guarantees the right to print, "the press is not free to publish with impunity everything and anything it desires to publish."[19]

Such a right, were it to exist, would be a right the public has. If the Court, as noted above, has time and again proclaimed that the press has no right of access independently of the public, then inescapably the press, in exercising such a right, would necessarily act in a fiduciary capacity.[20] This prospect, however, is riddled with constitutional problems of substantial magnitude. For example, it would clearly contradict the immunity the press sought to claim in *Branzburg*—that of not being forced to reveal the identity of news sources in a grand jury investigation.[21] Yet surely, if the public has a right to know, newspaper reporters as well as government officials have an obligation to tell. Further, if it is true that there is a public's right to know and the press is the instrument of the public, it is difficult to see how editorial judgment can remain in the hands of the news media,[22] especially when, as one of the Court's recent opinions observed: "The abuses of bias and manipulative reportage are . . . said to be the result of the vast accumulations of unreviewable power in the modern media empires."[23] Governmental officials, democratically chosen, could convincingly argue that they genuinely articulate what is in the public interest.

---

struck down "gag orders" or laws precluding the reporting of certain information, Cox v. Cohn, 420 U.S. 469 (1975), and Oklahoma Publ. Co. v. District Court, 430 U.S. 308 (1977), the Court has emphasized that such information was a matter of public record or that it had already been disclosed in a hearing open to the public. *See also* United States v. Mitchell, 551 F. 2d. 1252 (1976), *cert. denied* 97 S.Ct. 1578; McLaughlin v. Philadelphia Newspapers, Inc., 348 A. 2d. 376 (1975); United States v. General Motors, 352 F.Supp. 1071 (1973); *but see* State *ex rel.* Miami Herald Pub. Co. v. Rose, 271 So. 2d. 483 (1972); Sun Co. of San Bernardino v. Sup'r Ct., 105 Cal.Rptr. 873 (1973).

[18] The Court's recent decisions protecting "commercial speech," Bigelow v. Va., 421 U.S. 809 (1975), Virginia State Bd. of Pharmacy v. Virginia Citizens Consumer Council, Inc., 425 U.S. 748 (1976), Bates v. State Bar of Ariz., 97 S.Ct. 2691 (1977), are not applicable because, in these cases, the party possessing the information sought by consumers wanted to have the information disseminated.

[19] Branzburg v. Hayes, 408 U.S. 665, 683 (1972). The Court goes on to substantiate this conclusion by citing cases on libel and contempt.

[20] The Court's most recent discussion *and rejection* of the "fiduciary obligation" of the press acting as "surrogates for the public" appears in Miami Herald Pub. Co. v. Tornillo, 418 U.S. 241, 251-258 (1974).

[21] For a discussion of those claims made by the press, *see* Branzburg v. Hayes, 408 U.S. 665 (1972).

[22] As the Court said in Miami Herald Pub. Co. v. Tornillo, 418 U.S. 241, 258 (1974): "The choice of material to go into a newspaper, and the decisions made as to limitations on the size of the paper, and content, and treatment of public issues and public officials—whether fair or unfair—constitutes the exercise of editorial control and judgment. It has yet to be demonstrated how governmental regulation of this crucial process can be exercised consistent with First Amendment guarantees of a free press as they have evolved to this time."

[23] *Ibid.*, 250.

The time-honored custom of "plea-bargaining," i.e. where counsel for the defendant negotiates with the prosecutor to see if he can obtain a reduced charge at the price of pleading guilty, raises a severe question of whether or not the defendant is not in effect being enticed to bargain away his right to a trial. Justice White speaking for the Court in 1970 said: "But we cannot hold that it is unconstitutional for the State to extend a benefit to a defendant who in turn extends a substantial benefit to the State and who demonstrates by his plea that he is ready and willing to admit his crime and to enter the correctional system in a frame of mind which affords hope for success in rehabilitation over a shorter time than might otherwise be necessary." But he went on to show that he was not unmindful of the dangers involved: "This is not to say that guilty plea convictions hold no hazards for the innocent or that the methods of taking guilty pleas presently employed in this country are necessarily valid in all respects. This mode of conviction is no more foolproof than full trials to the court or to the jury. Accordingly, we take great precautions against unsound results, and we should continue to do so, whether conviction is by plea or by trial."[24]

Does Plea-Bargaining Subvert the Right to Trial?

The U.S. Court of Appeals for the Second Circuit has warned Federal judges to stay out of the plea-bargaining process, declaring that a judge's "participation . . . depreciates the image of the trial judge that is necessary to public confidence in the impartial and objective administration of criminal justice." The court's decision came on a petition of a U.S. attorney who requested the court to order the trial judge not to indicate to the defendant what sentence he would receive if he pleaded guilty. The appeals court ruling was based on its reading of Rule 11 (e) of the recently amended Federal Rules of Criminal Procedure, which provides that, while Federal judges may approve or disapprove plea bargains, they are not to participate in any discussions or agreements concerning plea bargains.[25]

In 1968, the Supreme Court held that the right to trial by jury in criminal cases was guaranteed as against the States.[26] Then, in what may fairly be characterized as a surprising decision—surprising in view of history—the Court held in 1970 "that the 12-man panel is not a necessary ingredient of 'trial by jury,' and the respondent's refusal to impanel more than six members provided for by Florida law did not violate petitioner's Sixth Amendment rights as applied to the States through the Fourteenth."[27] With respect to the widely accepted practice of requiring a unanimous verdict, the Court

An Impartial Jury

---

[24] Brady *v.* U.S., 397 U.S. 742 (1970). *See also* Peter L. Zimroth, "101,000 Defendants Were Convicted of Misdemeanors Last Year, 98,000 of Them Pleaded Guilty—To Get Reduced Sentences," *New York Times Magazine*, May 28, 1972, p. 14.
[25] *New York Times*, May 10, 1976.
[26] Duncan *v.* Louisiana, 391 U.S. 145 (1968).
[27] Williams *v.* Florida, 399 U.S. 78, 86 (1970).

wrote "We intimate no view whether or not the requirement of unanimity is an indispensable element of the Sixth Amendment jury trial."[28] But to the suggestion that "the 12-man jury gives a defendant a greater advantage since he has more 'chances' of finding a juror who will insist on acquittal and thus prevent conviction," the Court answered: ". . . The advantage might just as easily belong to the State, which also needs only one juror out of twelve insisting on guilt to prevent acquittal. What few experiments have occurred— usually in the civil area—indicate that there is no discernible difference between the results reached by the two different-sized juries."[29]

Later, in 1972, when it was squarely confronted with the issue of whether or not the Sixth Amendment required a unanimous verdict of the jury, the Court held that the requirement of unanimity "was not of constitutional stature."[30] The Court reasoned that "the purpose of trial by jury is to prevent oppression by the Government by providing a 'safeguard against the corrupt or overzealous prosecutor and against the compliant, biased, or eccentric judge.' " Consequently, it pointed out that "a requirement of unanimity does not materially contribute" to the exercise of the jury's "commonsense judgment." Further, "a jury will come to such a judgment as long as it consists of a group of laymen representative of a cross section of the community who have the duty and the opportunity to deliberate, free from outside attempts at intimidation, on the question of a defendant's guilt. In terms of this function we perceive no difference between juries required to act unanimously and those permitted to convict or acquit by votes of 10 to two or 11 to one. Requiring unanimity would obviously produce hung juries in some situations where non-unanimous juries will convict or acquit. But in either case, the interest of the defendant in having the judgment of his peers interposed between himself and the officers of the State who prosecute and judge him is equally well served."[31] In a significant concurring opinion, Justice Blackmun wrote, "I do not hesitate to say . . . that a system employing a seven-five standard, rather than a nine-three or 75% minimum, would afford me great difficulty."[32] Also, Justice Blackmun made clear that he did not think that non-unanimous verdicts were wise policy: "My vote means only that I cannot conclude that the system is constitutionally offensive. Were I a legislator, I would disfavor it as a matter of policy."

With respect to the composition of juries, the Court has long rejected the notion that a particular group in a community is entitled to representation per se,[33] and instead it has consistently interpreted

---

[28] Ibid., 100, note 46.   [29] Ibid., 101.
[30] Apodaca v. Oregon, 406 U.S. 404, 406 (1972).
[31] Ibid., 410.   [32] Ibid., 366.
[33] Or, as the Court has often preferred to phrase the issue: "Defendants are not entitled to a jury of any particular composition. . . ." See Fay v. N.Y., 332 U.S. 261, 284 (1947); Apodaca v. Oregon, 406 U.S. 404, 413 (1972).

the jury trial guarantee as mandating only that the jury will be randomly drawn from the community in a manner such that no members of any identifiable segment of the community will be precluded from the possibility of serving. Explaining the basis of the fair-cross-section requirement in a recent case, the Court said: "The purpose of a jury is to guard against the exercise of arbitrary power—to make available the commonsense judgment of the community as a hedge against the overzealous or mistaken prosecutor and in preference to the professional or perhaps over-conditioned or biased response of a judge. . . . This prophylactic vehicle is not provided if the jury pool is made up of only special segments of the populace or if large, distinctive groups are excluded from the pool. Community participation in the administration of the criminal law, moreover, is not only consistent with our democratic heritage but is also critical to public confidence in the fairness of the criminal justice system. Restricting jury service to only special groups or excluding identifiable segments playing major roles in the community cannot be squared with the constitutional concept of jury trial."[34] Court decisions have struck down State laws that excluded blacks from jury service[35] and jury selection procedures that either guaranteed the selection of no jurors at all from a given community's minority ethnic or racial groups or else held the possibility of selection to a low level clearly disproportionate to their number in the community.[36]

Reversing and remanding a conviction for aggravated kidnapping, the Supreme Court held unconstitutional Louisiana's practice of excluding women from jury duty unless they previously filed a written declaration indicating a desire to serve. The Court found that excluding an identifiable class comprising 53 percent of the population, on the grounds that women usually have pressing responsibilities at home, resulted almost always in cases being tried to all-male juries. The Court went on to conclude that such wholesale exclusion infringed a fundamental supposition of the jury trial guarantee—that the jury panels would be broadly representative of the community, at least in the sense of possibility for panel selection.[37] Justice Rehnquist dissented from the Court's decision on grounds that the defendant in the instant case had not established that *he* was "unfairly treated or prejudiced in any way by the manner in which his jury was selected." And the Court upheld an Illinois statute which provides for challenges in murder trials of jurors who admit conscientious scruples against capital punish-

[34] Taylor *v.* La., 419 U.S. 522, 530 (1975).

[35] Strauder *v.* W.Va., 100 U.S. 303 (1880).

[36] Much is summed up in the second of the Scottsboro Cases, Norris *v.* Ala., 294 U.S. 587, 589 (1935). *See also* the discussion in Taylor *v.* La., 419 U.S. 522, 526-531. The statement and application of these principles with respect to the grand jury are summarized in Castaneda *v.* Partida, 97 S.Ct. 1272 (1977). That case is particularly useful in its discussion of what constitutes a *prima facie* case of underrepresentation.

[37] Taylor *v.* La., 419 U.S. 522 (1975). The Court's holding in Taylor, however, was not made retroactive; *see* Daniel *v.* La., 420 U.S. 31 (1975).

ment.[38] In the latter case, the Court explained "We simply cannot conclude, either on the basis of the record now before us or as a matter of judicial notice, that the exclusion of jurors opposed to capital punishment results in an unrepresentative jury on the issue of guilt or substantially increases the risk of conviction. In light of the presently available information, we are not prepared to announce a *per se* constitutional rule requiring the reversal of every conviction returned by a jury selected as this one was."[39]

But in 1972 the Supreme Court decided a case involving a scheme for empaneling a grand jury in Lafayette Parish of Louisiana, which had the effect of keeping Negro representation well under its percentage of the Parish's population. The Court held that a *prima facie* case of invidious discrimination had been established that the State did not satisfactorily rebut. The Court explained: "This Court has never announced mathematical standards for the demonstration of 'systematic' exclusion of blacks but has rather emphasized that a factual inquiry is necessary in each case which takes into account all possible explanatory factors. The progressive decimation of potential Negro grand jurors is indeed striking here, but we do not rest our conclusion that petitioner has demonstrated a *prima facie* case of invidious racial discrimination on statistical improbability alone, for the selection procedures themselves were not racially neutral."[40] Noteworthy State court jury trial decisions have recently held: (1) that a one-year residency requirement for jury selection is constitutional;[41] (2) that juror selection from the roll of registered voters is not constitutionally discriminatory;[42] and (3) that, in selecting jurors, "the use of tax assessment rolls does not produce systematic exclusion of the poor."[43]

Assessing its constitutionality under the Sixth Amendment, the Supreme Court held that the Massachusetts two-tier court system did not abridge a defendant's right to trial by jury. Under that system, a person accused of certain crimes is tried initially in the lower tier without the benefit of jury trial; if convicted, he may appeal to the second tier, or, if convicted after pleading not-guilty or by "admitting sufficient findings of fact," he is entitled to jury trial *de novo* in the second tier. The Court held that while, as the appellant argued, such an arrangement "burdens the exercise of that right: (1) by imposing the financial cost of an additional trial; (2) by subjecting an accused to a potentially harsher sentence if he seeks a trial *de novo* in the second tier; and (3) by imposing the increased

---

[38] Witherspoon *v*. Illinois, 391 U.S. 510 (1968).   [39] *Ibid.*, 517-518.

[40] Alexander *v*. Louisiana, 405 U.S. 625, 630 (1972). *And see especially* Castaneda *v*. Partida, 97 S.Ct. 1272 (1977).

[41] Adams *v*. Sup'r Ct. of San Diego Cty., 524 P. 2d. 375 (1974).

[42] *See* United States *v*. Guzman, 468 F. 2d. 1245 (1972); United States *v*. Blair, 470 F. 2d. 331 (1972); State *v*. Willis, 293 N.E. 2d. 895 (1972); Brown *v*. State, 205 N.W. 2d. 566 (1973); Slaughter *v*. State, 301 So. 2d. 762 (1974).

[43] Roth *v*. State, 543 P. 2d. 939 (1975).

psychological and physical hardships of two trials," nevertheless such effects "do not impose an unconstitutional burden on the exercise of the right to a trial by jury."[44] Justice Powell concurred, finding the Court's opinion "consistent with my view that the right to a jury trial afforded by the Fourteenth Amendment is not identical to that guaranteed by the Sixth Amendment." Writing in dissent, Justice Stevens characterized as "totally irrational" the State's *requirement* that the defendant stand trial in the first tier before permitting him to have a jury trial in the second and, moreover, he concluded that the burden imposed on Sixth Amendment rights here was "significant."

(For recent developments concerning the applicability of the jury trial guarantee in contempt cases, *see* p. 206.)

A very divided Court held in 1971 that "the Due Process Clause of the Fourteenth Amendment" did not assure "the right of a trial by jury in the adjudicative phase of a state juvenile court delinquency proceeding."[45] Justice Blackmun reasoned that "accepting 'the proposition that the Due Process Clause has a role to play' . . . our taste here with respect to trial by jury, as it was in *Gault* [*see* p. 488] with respect to other claimed rights, 'is to ascertain the precise impact of the due process requirement.' "[46] In that context, Justice Blackmun concluded that "If the formalities of the criminal adjudicative process are to be superimposed upon the juvenile court system, there is little need for its separate existence. Perhaps that ultimate disillusionment will come one day, but for the moment we are disinclined to give impetus to it."[47] And as Justice Blackmun said earlier in his opinion "the applicable due process standard in juvenile proceedings . . . is fundamental fairness."[48] *(Jury Trial and Juveniles)*

One of the most vexing problems inherent in the requirement of an impartial jury is how to keep a jury free from the impact of the enormous pretrial and trial publicity the news media usually lavish on the juicier criminal cases, often aided and abetted by prosecutors and defense counsels who see advantage in taking their case to the media. To fully appreciate what this kind of publicity can do to a trial, one must read the Supreme Court's almost unbelievable account of what went on at the highly publicized trial of Dr. Sheppard some few years ago.[49] In its opinion in that case, the Court made emphatically clear that courts have an obligation to do their utmost to minimize the impact of publicity on the outcome of a trial: *(Trial by Media)*

"From the cases coming here we note that unfair and prejudicial news comment on pending trials has become increasingly prevalent. Due process requires that the accused receive a trial by an impartial jury free from outside influences. Given the pervasiveness

---

[44] Ludwig *v.* Mass., 427 U.S. 618, 626 (1976).
[45] McKeiver *v.* Pennsylvania, 403 U.S. 528, 530 (1971).
[46] *Ibid.*, 541.   [47] *Ibid.*, 551.
[48] *Ibid.*, 543.   [49] Sheppard *v.* Maxwell, 384 U.S. 333 (1966).

of modern communications and the difficulty of effacing prejudicial publicity from the minds of the jurors, the trial courts must take strong measures to ensure that the balance is never weighed against the accused. And appellate tribunals have the duty to make an independent evaluation of the circumstances. Of course, there is nothing that proscribes the press from reporting events that transpire in the courtroom. But where there is a reasonable likelihood that prejudicial news prior to trial will prevent a fair trial, the judge should continue the case until the threat abates, or transfer it to another county not so permeated with publicity. In addition, sequestration of the jury was something the judge should have raised *sua sponte* with counsel. If publicity during the proceedings threatens the fairness of the trial, a new trial should be ordered. But we must remember that reversals are but palliatives; the cure lies in those remedial measures that will prevent the prejudice at its inception. The courts must take such steps by rule and regulation that will protect their processes from prejudicial outside interferences. Neither prosecutors, counsel for defense, the accused, witnesses, court staff nor enforcement officers coming under the jurisdiction of the court should be permitted to frustrate its function. Collaboration between counsel and the press as to information affecting the fairness of a criminal trial is not only subject to regulation, but is highly censurable and worthy of disciplinary measures."[50]

Despite the Supreme Court's guidelines and the heroic work of a Committee of the American Bar Association which, wrestling with the problem, produced the highly regarded but controversial Reardon report[51] suggesting means for mitigating it, Professor John E. Stanga reports: "How does one assess the impact of the line of cases culminating in *Sheppard*? Obviously, they (and the work of groups like the American Bar Association) have had some effect: Convictions have been reversed because of the probability that prejudice might result from press comment or coverage. Protections such as change of venue have been given greater attention, and court rules to protect the accused from prejudicial publicity have been adopted in some jurisdictions. But a more comprehensive examination requires a qualified assessment of the *Rideau, Estes* and *Sheppard* line, for in the vast majority of cases the criminal justice system goes on as before, with or without press comment, and the reversal of a conviction on prejudicial press publicity grounds is the exception. Of 202 cases involving publicity issues decided over a period of about three years beginning in 1966, only 12 resulted in the setting aside or reversal of convictions."[52]

[50] *Ibid.*, 362-363.

[51] ABA Project on Minimum Standards For Criminal Justice, *Fair Trial and Free Press* (1966).

[52] John E. Stanga, Jr., "Judicial Protection of the Criminal Defendant Against Adverse Press Coverage," 13 *William and Mary Law Review*, 1 (1971).

Perhaps, it is too soon to conclude that no more will be done. The Reardon report standards were not incorporated into the new A.B.A. code of professional responsibility which became effective for its members on January 1, 1970.[53]

And, in what was clearly the Court's most significant confrontation of the fair trial–free press issue since Sheppard *v.* Maxwell a decade before, the Supreme Court reversed a ruling of the Nebraska Supreme Court that had upheld but narrowed constraints imposed by a county judge on press and media coverage of a sensational multiple murder trial. The trial judge's order, which applied only until the jury was impaneled, precluded reporting on five specific subjects: "(1) The existence or contents of a confession . . . [the defendant] had made to law enforcement officers, which had been introduced in open court at arraignment; (2) the fact or nature of statements . . . [the defendant] had made to other persons; (3) the contents of a note he had written the night of the crime; (4) certain aspects of the medical testimony at the preliminary hearing; (5) the identity of the victims of the alleged sexual assault and the nature of the assault."[54]

Recognizing the serious threat that so-called "gag orders" pose to freedom of the press, the Court indicated that "the barriers to prior restraint remain high and the presumption against its use continues intact." Yet, consistent with its view that, in resolving the conflict of First and Sixth Amendment values "[i]t is unnecessary . . . to establish a priority applicable in all circumstances," the Court looked to the circumstances and specifics of the restrictive orders at issue. Though it recognized the difficulty of any trial judge to assess realistically the impact of pretrial publicity and to devise the least restrictive measures to secure the defendant a fair trial, the Court in this case found the conclusions of the trial judge unsupported. It also faulted the judge for his apparent failure to canvass other alternatives and, at one point, raised the question of whether—given the likelihood of rumor in a small rural community—prior restraint would be largely ineffective. The Court felt especially uneasy about strictures against reporting what had taken place in open court, and pointed out that pretrial publicity was not, after all, synonymous with bias. Speaking for the Court, Chief Justice Burger concluded: "Reasonable minds can have few doubts about the gravity of the evil pretrial publicity can work but the probability that it would do so here was not demonstrated with the degree of certainty our cases on prior restraint require."

In a spirited concurring opinion in which he was joined by Jus-

---

[53] *Ibid.*, 144. *Also see* his Addendum, *ibid.*, 69ff.

[54] Nebraska Press Ass'n *v.* Stuart, 427 U.S. 539, 543-544 (1976). The prohibitions retained by the State supreme court related to: "(a) the existence and nature of any confessions or admissions made by the defendant to law enforcement officers, (b) any confessions or admissions made to any third parties, except members of the press, and (c) other facts 'strongly implicative' of the accused." *Ibid.*, 545.

tices Stewart and Marshall,[55] Justice Brennan rejected the notion that the Sixth Amendment required a balancing of First Amendment protections: "Settled case law concerning the impropriety and constitutional invalidity of prior restraints on the press compels the conclusion that there can be no prohibition on the publication by the press of any information pertaining to pending judicial proceedings or the operation of the criminal justice system, no matter how shabby the means by which the information is obtained. This does not imply, however, any subordination of Sixth Amendment rights for an accused's right to a fair trial may be adequately assured through methods that do not infringe First Amendment values." Concluded Justice Brennan: ". . . I would reject the notion that a choice is necessary, that there is inherent conflict that cannot be resolved without essentially abrogating one right or the other. . . . [J]udges possess adequate tools short of injunctions against reporting for relieving that tension."[56]

Indeed, in none of the controversies to reach the Court in recent years has it sustained the restraints on news coverage of trials imposed by trial judges.[57] And lower Federal courts appear to have understood the Court's message in these cases: that extensive pretrial publicity—even massive national pretrial publicity—does not necessarily spell bias. In both the court-martial of Lt. Calley,[58] the principal accused in the My Lai incident in Vietnam, and in the trial of the Watergate defendants,[59] Federal courts ruled that pretrial publicity had not impaired the defendants' right to a fair trial.

Judge and Jury At the common law the court was judge of the "law" and the jury was judge of the "facts"; nor could either call the other to account for its determinations within its proper sphere.[60] In actual practice, nevertheless, the judge had great freedom in advising the jury as to the merits of a case, the weight of the evidence, the reliability of

[55] Though he indicated that he wanted to hear further argument on the fair trial–free press question, Justice Stevens wrote, in a separate opinion concurring in the judgment, "I do, however, subscribe to most of what Mr. Justice Brennan says and, if ever required to face the issue squarely, may well accept his ultimate conclusion." *Ibid.*, 617.

[56] *Ibid.*, 588, 611-612. Moreover, doubt remains as to whether pretrial publicity has an impact on prospective jurors, *see Los Angeles Times*, April 14, 1976.

[57] Times-Picayune Pub. Corp. *v.* Schulingkamp, 419 U.S. 1301 (1974); Murphy *v.* Fla., 421 U.S. 794 (1975); Oklahoma Pub. Co. *v.* District Court, 97 S.Ct. 1045 (1977); Dobbert *v.* Fla., 97 S.Ct. 2290 (1977).

[58] Calley *v.* Callaway, 519 F. 2d. 184 (1975), *reversing* 382 F.Supp. 650 (1974), *stay denied* 419 U.S. 1015 (1976).

[59] United States *v.* Mitchell, 389 F.Supp. 917 (1975). *See also*, 419 U.S. 1310 (1974). In a previous ruling, the Federal district court held that media broadcasters were entitled to copies of taped conversations recorded in the White House Oval Office where such recordings were played to the jury in criminal proceedings, United States *v.* Mitchell, 386 F.Supp. 639 (1975).

[60] Coke, *Institutes of England*, Sect. 234; Bushell's Case (1670); J. B. Thayer, *Preliminary Treatise on Evidence* (Boston, 1898), 166-169. For the early history of the jury, *see ibid.*, ch. 2; A. W. Scott, *Fundamentals of Procedure* (New York, 1922), ch. 3.

witnesses, and so on.[61] And while this feature of jury trial, too, is an element of the institution as it is embodied in the Constitution, a Federal judge must always make it clear to the jury that the final determination of all matters of fact rests with them, and that his remarks on such matters are advisory only.[62] The right to trial by jury may be waived as to any offense,[63] while except by allowance of Congress it does not extend to petty offenses.[64] However, the Court has recently held: "In light of the Constitution's emphasis on jury trial, we find it difficult to understand . . . the bald proposition that to compel a defendant in a criminal case to undergo a jury trial against his will is contrary to his right to a fair trial or to due process. A defendant's only constitutional right concerning the method of trial is to an impartial trial by jury. We find no constitutional impediment to conditioning a waiver of this right on the consent of the prosecuting attorney and the trial judge when, if either refuses to consent, the result is simply that the defendant is subject to an impartial trial by jury—the very thing that the Constitution guarantees him."[65] Also, it should be recalled here that in recent years the right to trial by jury has been extended to some who were previously subject to courts-martial. (*See* pp. 115-117.)

"State and district": The jury must be drawn from the vicinage of the crime, it being assumed that this will ordinarily be the residence of the accused, who will thus be guaranteed a trial by his neighbors. But in modern conditions the vicinage of the crime may run over and beyond the boundaries of several States, and there was a time when persons charged with conspiring to violate the laws of the United States or to defraud the National Government could be dragged to the remotest parts of the Union on account of something done there by somebody else.[66] Not that Congress or the

[61] Thayer, *Preliminary Treatise*, ch. 3, passim. Thayer declares it "impossible to conceive" of jury trial existing at any stage of English history in a form that "would withhold from the jury the assistance of the court in dealing with facts. Trial by jury, in such a form as that, is not trial by jury in any historic sense of the words." *Ibid.*, 188n. "The jury works well in England because the bench is stronger than the bar." W. S. Holdsworth, *Some Lessons from Our Legal History* (New York, 1928), 85. Despite protestations of the defendants in the "Watergate Break-In" trial to the effect that Judge Sirica was biased in favor of the prosecution and that he assumed an inquisitorial role, the judge's actions at trial have been upheld by the U.S. Court of Appeals for the District of Columbia. *See* United States *v.* McCord, 509 F. 2d. 334 (1974). For Judge Sirica's response to similar charges made in the ensuing "Watergate Cover-Up" trial, *see* United States *v.* Mitchell *et al.*, 377 F.Supp. 1312 (1974).

[62] Quercia *v.* U.S., 289 U.S. 466 (1933). *See also* Glasser *v.* U.S., 315 U.S. 60 (1942); U.S. *v.* Dunmore, 446 F. 2d. 1214 (1971); U.S. *v.* Wyatt, 442 F. 2d. 858 (1971).

[63] Patton *v.* U.S., 281 U.S. 276 (1930).

[64] Schick *v.* U.S., 195 U.S. 65 (1904).

[65] Singer *v.* U.S., 380 U.S. 24 (1965); Goldstein *v.* Paulikowski, 489 P. 2d. 1159 (1971).

[66] *See* United States *v.* Johnson, 323 U.S. 273 (1944). For a succinct history *see* Justice Holmes, dissenting, in Hyde *v.* U.S., 225 U.S. 347 at 384 (1912); Jones *v.* Gasch, 404 F. 2d. 231, 234-235 (1967), *cert. denied* 390 U.S. 1414 (1968).

Government ever really had *carte blanche*. For as the Court had explained in 1944: "If an enactment of Congress equally permits the underlying spirit of the constitutional concern for trial in the vicinage to be respected rather than disrespected, construction should go in the direction of constitutional policy even though not commanded by it."[67] Starting in 1947, the Federal Rules of Criminal Procedure have set stricter guidelines for determining the venue of a Federal trial as well as the basis for granting or withholding a request for a change of venue by a defendant.[68] For example, the Rules state among other things that "the court upon motion of the defendant shall transfer the proceeding as to him to another district . . . if the court is satisfied that there exists in the district where the prosecution is pending so great a prejudice against the defendant that he cannot obtain a fair and impartial trial at any place fixed by law for holding court in that district."[69] In short, a defendant does have the right under the Rules to seek a change of venue to avoid prejudice and "for the convenience of parties and witnesses, and in the interest of justice" and Federal courts have been meticulous in considering claims to that statutory right.[70] This does not mean, however, that the defendant always gets his way, for as the Supreme Court said in 1964, in considering "the interest of justice," valid factors include: "(1) location of corporate defendant; (2) location of possible witnesses; (3) location of events likely to be in issue; (4) location of documents and records likely to be involved; (5) disruption of defendant's business unless the case is transferred; (6) expense to the parties; (7) location of counsel; (8) relative accessibility of place of trial; (9) docket condition of each district or division involved; and (10) any other special elements which might affect the transfer."[71]

For offenses against Federal laws not committed within any State, Congress has the sole power to prescribe the place of trial; such an offense is not local and may be tried at any place Congress designates.[72]

Nothing in the foregoing should becloud the fact that where all elements of an alleged crime take place in a particular State and district and the defendant insists on it, he has the constitutional right to be tried in that State and district. In the struggle to vindicate the civil rights of blacks in the South, this fact has created difficulties. Too often in the past it was virtually impossible to get juries to convict those who transgressed the rights of blacks. This led the Government at times to attempt to bypass jury trials by seeking remedies that would invoke the use of a judge's power to

Venue as a Bar to Vindicating Civil Rights

---

[67] United States *v* Johnson, 323 U.S. 273 276 (1944).

[68] 18R U.S.C. 18, 20, 21.   [69] *Ibid.*, 21.

[70] Jones *v.* Gasch, 404 F. 2d. 1231 (1967); U.S. *v.* Sweig, 316 F.Supp. 1148, 1161-1162 (1970); U.S. *v.* Price, 447 F. 2d. 23, 26 (1971).

[71] Platt *v.* Minnesota Mining & Mfg. Co., 376 U.S. 240, 243-244 (1964). *See also*, State *v.* Niccum, 190 N.W. 2d. 815 (1971).

[72] Jones *v.* U.S., 137 U.S. 202, 211 (1890); United States *v.* Johnson, 323 U.S. 273 (1944); 18 U.S.C. 3238.

punish summarily for contempt. The problems that such an approach raises were described above (pp. 206-209). Suffice it to point out here that the constitutional requirement has had at least one adverse impact on justice that the framers of the amendment had not anticipated. It was undoubtedly never intended to be a means for encouraging lawlessness.

"Nature and cause of the accusation": That is to say, the law must furnish a reasonably definite standard of guilt.[73] Applying the sense of this requirement in interpretation of the due process clause of the Fourteenth Amendment, the Court in 1939 set aside a New Jersey statute which penalized "gangsters," but later upheld a Minnesota statute which authorized proceedings against "psychopathic personalities." In the latter case the material term had been closely defined by judicial interpretation; in the former it had not.[74] Statutes prohibiting the coercion of employers to hire "unneeded" employees,[75] establishing "minimum" wages and "maximum" hours of service for persons engaged in the production of goods for interstate commerce,[76] or forbidding "undue" or "unreasonable" restraints of trade,[77] have been held to be sufficiently definite to be constitutional. Nor is a provision of the Immigration Act,[78] which makes it a felony for an alien against whom a specified order of deportation is pending to "willfully fail or refuse to make timely application in good faith for travel or other documents necessary to his departure," void, on its face, for indefiniteness.[79]

More recently in upholding obscenity legislation, the Court held that "Many decisions have recognized that these terms of obscenity statutes are not precise. This Court, however, has consistently held that lack of precision is not itself offensive to the requirements of due process. . . . 'The Constitution does not require impossible standards'; all that is required is that the language 'conveys sufficiently definite warning as to the proscribed conduct when measured by common understanding and practices. . . .' "[80] Nor did the Court find the words "under color of law" too vague to uphold indictments for a conspiracy to deprive three young civil rights workers of their Fourteenth Amendment rights by setting them up for murder.[81] In 1971, however, the Court struck down a Cincinnati ordinance which read in part: "It shall be unlawful for three or

Indefinite Charges and Illegal Presumptions

---

[73] United States v. Cohen Grocery Co., 255 U.S. 81 (1921); Coates v. City of Cincinnati, 402 U.S. 611, 616 (1971).

[74] Lanzetta v. N.J., 306 U.S. 451 (1939); Minnesota v. Probate Court, 309 U.S. 270 (1940).

[75] United States v. Petrillo, 332 U.S. 1 (1947).

[76] United States v. Darby, 312 U.S. 100, 125 (1941).

[77] Nash v. U.S., 229 U.S. 373 (1913).   [78] 8 U.S.C. 1252 (3).

[79] United States v. Spector, 343 U.S. 169 (1952).

[80] Roth v. U.S., 354 U.S. 476, 491 (1957).

[81] U.S. v. Price, 383 U.S. 787, 806 note 20 (1966). Evidently, the Federal government officials felt that a murder charge in a State court would be to no avail. Consequently, to take the case to a Federal court, they had to proceed on the basis of a Federal law; that is why the indictment was framed as it was.

more persons to assemble except at a public meeting of citizens, on any of the sidewalks . . . and there conduct themselves in a manner annoying to persons passing by, or occupants of adjacent buildings." The Court explained: "In our opinion this ordinance is unconstitutionally vague because it subjects the exercise of the right to assemble to an unascertainable standard, and unconstitutionally broad because it authorizes the punishment of constitutionally protected conduct."[82]

In a 1972 decision,[83] the Supreme Court made all so-called "vagrancy laws" constitutionally suspect when it struck down as unconstitutionally vague a particularly odious law contained in the Jacksonville, Florida, Ordinance Code which read as follows:

"Rogues and vagabonds, or dissolute persons who go about begging, common gamblers, persons who use juggling or unlawful games or plays, common drunkards, common night walkers, thieves, pilferers or pickpockets, traders in stolen property, lewd, wanton and lascivious persons, keepers of gambling places, common railers and brawlers, persons wandering or strolling around from place to place without any lawful purpose or object, habitual loafers, disorderly persons, persons neglecting all lawful business and habitually spending their time by frequenting houses of ill fame, gaming houses, or places where alcoholic beverages are sold or served, persons able to work but habitually living upon the earnings of their wives or minor children shall be deemed vagrants and upon conviciton in the Municipal Court shall be punished as provided for Class D offenses." As Justice Douglas speaking for the Court so eloquently put it: "A presumption that people who might walk or loaf or loiter or stroll or frequent houses where liquor is sold, or who are supported by their wives or who look suspicious to the police are to become future criminals is too precarious for a rule of law."

As to the indictment, the Federal Rules of Criminal Procedure require that the indictment "be a plain, concise and definite written statement of the essential facts constituting the offense charged."[84] The Supreme Court has held to the following standard for years:

"The true test of the sufficiency of an indictment is not whether it could have been made more definite and certain, but whether it contains the elements of the offense intended to be charged, 'and sufficiently apprises the defendant of what he must be prepared to meet, and, in any case any other proceedings are taken against him for a similar offence, whether the record shows with accuracy to what extent he may plead a former acquittal or conviction.' "[85]

As the Court has said: "Certain principles have remained rela-

[82] Coates *v*. City of Cincinnati, 402 U.S. 611, 614 (1971).
[83] Papachristou *et al. v*. City of Jacksonville, 405 U.S. 156 (1972).
[84] 8R U.S.C. 7 (c).
[85] U.S. *v*. Anderson, 447 F. 2d. 833 (1971); Cochrane and Sayre *v*. U.S., 157 U.S. 286 (1895); Rosen *v*. U.S., 161 U.S. 29 (1896); Hagner *v*. U.S., 285 U.S. 427 (1932); U.S. *v*. Debrow, 346 U.S. 374 (1953).

tively immutable in our jurisprudence. One of these is that where
government action seriously injures an individual, and the reasonableness of the action depends on fact findings, the evidence used
to prove the Government's case must be disclosed to the individual
so that he has an opportunity to show that it is untrue. While this is
important in the case of documentary evidence, it is even more important where the evidence consists of the testimony of individuals
whose memory might be faulty or who, in fact, might be perjurers
of persons motivated by malice, vindictiveness, intolerance, prejudice, or jealousy. We have formalized these protections in the requirements of confrontation and cross-examination. They have
ancient roots. They find expression in the Sixth Amendment which
provides that in all criminal cases the accused shall enjoy the right
'to be confronted with the witnesses against him.' This Court has
been zealous to protect these rights from erosion. It has spoken out
not only in criminal cases, . . . but also in all types of cases where
administrative and regulatory actions were under scrutiny."[86] And
in recent years there has been precious little niggling about confrontation in criminal trials.[87] Either the Government must produce the witnesses and evidence or drop the case. For example, the
Supreme Court held in 1968 that "the admission of a confession of
a co-defendant who did not take the stand deprived the defendant
of his rights under the Sixth Amendment Confrontation Clause."[88]
Nonetheless, there has "traditionally been an exception to the confrontation requirement where a witness is unavailable and has
given testimony at previous judicial proceedings against the same
defendant which was subject to cross-examination by the defendant. . . . This exception has been justified on the ground that the
right of cross-examination initially afforded provides substantial
compliance with the purposes behind the confirmation requirement."[89] In reaffirming this exception in 1972, the Court stressed
again that the witness must truly be unavailable and that the trier of
fact must be afforded "a satisfactory basis for evaluating the truth
of the prior statement."[90]

Over the defendant's arguments asserting deprivations of his
Sixth Amendment right to compulsory process and cross-

[86] Greene v. McElroy, 360 U.S. 474, 496 (1959).
[87] Cf. Illinois v. Allen, 397 U.S. 337 (1970), where it was held that privilege may be
lost by misconduct.
[88] Bruton v. U.S., 391 U.S. 123 (1968). In 1972, the Supreme Court held that a
violation of the Bruton rule could be considered harmless error where there was
overwhelming evidence of guilt and a relatively insignificant impact of the co-
defendant's statement. The Court pointed out that in Bruton it had said "a defendant is entitled to a fair trial but not a perfect one." Schneble v. Florida, 405 U.S. 427
(1972). But see dissent of Justice Marshall with whom Justices Douglas and Brennan
joined. Cf. Dutton v. Evans, 400 U.S. 74 (1970).
[89] Barber v. Page, 390 U.S. 719, 722 (1968); California v. Green, 399 U.S. 149
(1970). See also Dutton v. Evans, 400 U.S. 74 (1970) for a discussion of distinction
between the requirements of hearsay rules and the confrontation clause.
[90] Mancusi v. Stubbs, 408 U.S. 204 (1972).

examination, the Supreme Court held that where, "[i]n a criminal trial, defense counsel sought to impeach the credibility of key prosecution witnesses by testimony of a defense investigator regarding statements previously obtained from the witnesses by the investigator . . . a federal trial court may compel the defense to reveal the relevant portions of the investigator's report for the prosecution's use in cross-examining him."[91] Citing *Jencks v. United States*[92] and *United States v. Nixon*,[93] "[d]ecisions of this Court . . . recogniz[ing] the federal judiciary's inherent power to require the prosecution to produce the previously recorded statements of its witnesses so that the defense may get the full benefit of cross-examination and the truth-finding process may be enhanced,"[94] the Court, per Justice Powell, concluded in effect that "the prosecution can call upon the same power for production of witness statements that facilitate 'full disclosure of all the [relevant] facts.' " Writing further, Justice Powell explained that arguments asserting that this ruling depreciates constitutional rights "misconceives the issue," for "[t]he Sixth Amendment does not confer the right to present testimony free from the legitimate demands of the adversarial system; one cannot invoke the Sixth Amendment as a justification for presenting what might have been a half truth."

As to the defendant's absence from the courtroom, the Supreme Court has ruled that Rule 43 of the Federal Rules of Criminal Procedure is constitutional insofar as it provides that the proceedings shall continue where a defendant, accused of a non-capital offense, voluntarily absents himself from the trial.[95] And the Supreme Court of Washington has ruled that the use at trial of video-taped testimony of a robbery victim did not infringe the defendant's constitutional right under the Sixth Amendment "to be confronted with the witnesses against him."[96]

The interesting problems which have come up regarding confrontation in recent years are whether or not due process requires confrontation in administrative or legislative proceedings. The short of the matter is that the majority of the Supreme Court, over some bitter dissents, has not found that the Constitution compels the right of confrontation in these kinds of proceedings. As Chief Justice Warren put it:

"Therefore, as a generalization, it can be said that due process embodies the differing rules of fair play, which through the years, have become associated with differing types of proceedings. Whether the Constitution requires that a particular right obtain in a specific proceeding depends upon a complexity of factors. The nature of the alleged right involved, the nature of the proceeding, and the possible burden on that proceeding, are all considerations

[91] United States *v.* Nobles, 422 U.S. 225, 227 (1975).
[92] 353 U.S. 657 (1957).   [93] 418 U.S. 683 (1974).
[94] United States *v.* Nobles, 422 U.S. 225, 231 (1975).
[95] Taylor *v.* U.S., 414 U.S. 17 (1974).
[96] State *v.* Hewett, 545 P. 2d. 1201 (1976).

which must be taken into account. An analysis of these factors demonstrates why it is that the particular rights claimed by the respondents need not be conferred upon those appearing before purely investigative agencies, of which the Commission on Civil Rights is one."[97]

"Compulsory process for obtaining witnesses": The right is not as absolute as the language of the amendment suggests. Speaking of the application of Federal Rule 17b, which deals with "defendants unable to pay the fees of witnesses," an appeals court said: "Obviously, the right given the defendant is not absolute, but is to be governed by the sound discretion of the trial judge, which will not be disturbed by an appellate court unless exceptional and compelling circumstances clearly indicate an abuse of discretion."[98] Even in upholding such an important right, judges, of course, must be able to refuse patently frivolous requests in order to prevent a trial from becoming a farce.

In 1963, in the much discussed case of Gideon v. Wainwright, the Supreme Court held the right to counsel was obligatory upon the States by the Fourteenth Amendment.[99] Actually, the Supreme Court, even before *Gideon*, had held that due process alone required the right to counsel in many State cases because of particular fact situations. For example, "ignorance and illiteracy of the defendants, their youth, the circumstances of public hostility . . . and above all that they stood in deadly peril of their lives" had caused the Court to find "that the state court had a duty to assign counsel for the trial as a necessary requisite of due process of law."[100] In retrospect, the greatest impact of the *Gideon* decision was not that it made assistance of counsel mandatory on States but the kind of soul searching it inspired on the question of what is the significance of right to counsel *in the trial* if a defendant has suffered all the disadvantages of not having counsel at the earlier stages of the investigation that preceded the trial.

Protagonists for extending the right to counsel were as plentiful as they were persuasive. Yale Kamisar, Professor of Criminal Law at the University of Michigan Law School, was particularly forceful and provocative.[101] The result of the ferment has been the extension of the right to counsel to the point where "the investigation is no longer a general inquiry into an unsolved crime but has begun to focus on a particular suspect," and "the suspect has been taken into police custody." To deny the suspect the right to counsel at

Right to Counsel

[97] Hannah v. Larche, 363 U.S. 420, 442 (1960). *See also* Richardson v. Perales, 402 U.S. 389 (1971); Goldberg v. Kelly, 397 U.S. 254 (1970); Flemming v. Nestor, 363 U.S. 603 (1960).

[98] Wagner v. U.S., 416 F. 2d. 558, 564 (1969); *cert. denied*, 397 U.S. 923 (1970); People v. Nieto, 190 N.W. 2d. 579 (1971).

[99] Gideon v. Wainwright, 372 U.S. 335 (1963).

[100] Powell v. Ala., 287 U.S. 45, 71 (1932). For a discussion of other fact situations, *see* Justice Harlan's concurring opinion in *Gideon*.

[101] *See*, for example, his "Equal Justice in the Gatehouses and Mansions of American Criminal Procedure," in *Criminal Justice in our Time* (1965), 653.

that stage is to deny him his Sixth Amendment right to counsel.[102] This led inexorably to the *Miranda* decision, with the Court saying: "As for the procedural safeguards to be employed, unless other fully effective means are devised to inform accused persons of their right of silence . . . the following measures are required. Prior to any questioning, the person must be warned that he has a right to remain silent, that any statement he does make may be used as evidence against him, and that he has a right to the presence of an attorney, either retained or appointed. The defendant may waive effectuation of these rights, provided the waiver is made voluntarily, knowingly and intelligently. If, however, he indicates in any manner and at any state of the process that he wishes to consult with an attorney before speaking there can be no questioning."[103] Today there is scarcely a jurisdiction in which law enforcement officers do not carry a "Miranda card" from which they read to a suspect what his constitutional rights are, making clear, of course, that he has right to counsel.

In 1967, the Supreme Court specifically extended right to counsel to *post*-indictment police lineups.[104] In the ensuing years some lower courts extended the right to counsel to lineups in pre-arrest situations.[105] In 1972, when the Supreme Court was confronted precisely with the question of extending the exclusionary rule to "identification testimory based upon a police station showup that took place before the defendant had been indicted or otherwise formally charged with any criminal offense," it was sharply split.[106] But at least four of the majority held that "it has been firmly established that a person's right to counsel attaches only at or after the time that adversary judicial proceedings have been initiated against him."[107] But they cautioned that "What has been said is not to suggest that there may not be occasions during the course of a criminal investigation when the police do abuse identification procedures. Such abuses are not beyond the reach of the Constitution. . . . The Due Process Clause of the Fifth and Fourteenth Amendments forbids a lineup that is unnecessarily suggestive and conducive to irreparable mistaken identification."[108] While the current

[102] Escobedo *v*. Illinois, 378 U.S. 478 (1964).

[103] Miranda *v*. Arizona, 384 U.S. 436 (1966). *But see* Commonwealth *v*. Bartlett, 288 A. 2d. 796 (1972).

[104] U.S. *v*. Wade, 388 U.S. 218 (1967); Gilbert *v*. Calif., 388 U.S. 263 (1967); *see* Neil *v*. Biggers, 409 U.S. 188 (1972); *cf.* Stovall *v*. Denno, 388 U.S. 293 (1967). However, as a matter of interpreting the State constitution, the Alaska Supreme Court has held "that a suspect who is in custody is entitled to have counsel present at a pre-indictment lineup unless exigent circumstances exist so that providing counsel would unduly interfere with a prompt and purposeful investigation." Blue *v*. State, 558 P. 2d. 636, 642 (1977).

[105] State *v*. Oliver, 228 A. 2d. 81 (1971) and the cases cited therein. *But see* Zeigler *v*. Commonwealth, 186 S.E. 2d. 38 (1972).

[106] Kirby *v*. Illinois, 406 U.S. 682 (1972).

[107] *Ibid.*, 688.   [108] *Ibid.*, 690.

Court was limiting right to counsel to only the time "that adversary judicial proceedings have been initiated," it extended the right markedly where the proceedings were begun.[109] In 1972 the Court held that, "absent a knowing and intelligent waiver, no person may be imprisoned for any offense, whether classified as petty, misdemeanor or felony, unless he is represented by counsel at his trial."[110] The justices manifested a concern for the difficulties this decision would make for the administration of justice in the States. But Chief Justice Burger undoubtedly bespoke the hope of most of them in his separate opinion, where he said "The holding of the Court today may well add large new burdens on a profession already overtaxed, but the dynamics of the profession have a way of rising to the burdens placed on it."[111]

In several recent decisions concerning diverse yet significant right to counsel questions, the Supreme Court has held: (1) that the accused does not have the right to have an attorney present at a post-indictment photographic display;[112] (2) that, in a pre-*Miranda* interrogation, where police failed to observe the rule that an indigent defendant be advised he has the right to appointed counsel, in view of the fact that officers did warn him of the right to remain silent and that statements he made would be used against him, such an omission did not deprive the defendant of his privilege against self-incrimination;[113] (3) that the defendant in a State criminal proceeding has the right to defend himself without counsel if he voluntarily and intelligently elects to do so;[114] (4) that a summary court-martial was not a "criminal prosecution" and, therefore, that denial of the right to counsel to the serviceman did not effect a denial of due process;[115] and (5) that a trial judge's order preventing

[109] Argersinger v. Hamlin, 407 U.S. 25 (1972).
[110] *Ibid.*, 37.   [111] *Ibid.*, 44.
[112] United States v. Ash, 413 U.S. 300 (1973). The various opinions in the case provide a rich discussion of the meaning of right to counsel.
[113] Michigan v. Tucker, 417 U.S. 433 (1974). Speaking for the Court, Justice Rehnquist found that circumstances of the interrogation indicated no bad faith on the part of the police, and that automatic application of the exclusionary rule would serve no recognized purpose of deterring illegal police conduct. Said Justice Rehnquist: "Just as the law does not require that a defendant receive a perfect trial, only a fair one, it cannot realistically require that policemen investigating serious crimes make no errors whatsoever. The pressures of law enforcement and the vagaries of human nature would make such an expectation unrealistic." The Court found defendant's statements freely and voluntarily given.
[114] Faretta v. Calif., 422 U.S. 806 (1975). A Federal district court has ruled in a related case that a defendant in a criminal case who distrusted the organized bar and who elected to be represented by a disbarred attorney should not be prohibited from receiving such assistance. See United States v. Stockheimer, 385 F.Supp. 979 (1974). But a Federal appeals court has ruled that the defendant in a tax fraud case could not be represented at trial by his accountant; see United States v. Whitsel, 543 F. 2d. 1176 (1976). Nor does the defendant have the constitutional right to have unlicensed lay counsel assist him; see Pendell v. Amer. Bar Ass'n, 407 F.Supp. 451 (1975) *and* United States v. Kelley, 539 F. 2d. 1199 (1976).
[115] Middendorf v. Henry, 425 U.S. 25 (1976).

the defendant from consulting his own lawyer during an overnight recess, where the defendant was to continue on the stand for cross-examination, contravened the Sixth Amendment.[116]

And, amid an exchange of unusually pointed opinions, the Court decided, in probably the most controversial right-to-counsel case of recent Terms, that, where the defendant in a murder case had already been arrested and arraigned and police had promised one of defendant's attorneys not to interrogate the suspect on the drive to Des Moines (where the defendant would stand trial) but where police along the way deliberately made statements designed to elicit a response from the defendant, incriminating statements he made were not admissible under the *Miranda* rule.[117] The Court ruled that this case was controlled by Massiah *v.* U.S.,[118] where, as here, police solicited incriminating statements in the absence of defendant's counsel, depriving him of his Sixth and Fourteenth Amendment rights. The four dissenters in the case concluded the defendant had voluntarily waived the right to counsel. Chief Justice Burger among them launched another vigorous attack on the rigidity and cost of applying the exclusionary rule, intoning at one point: "Today's holding fulfills Justice Cardozo's grim prophecy that someday some court might carry the exclusionary rule to the absurd extent that its operative effect would exclude evidence relating to the body of a murder victim because of the means by which it was found. In so ruling the Court regresses to playing a grisly game of 'hide and seek,' once more exalting the sporting theory of criminal justice which has been experiencing a decline in our jurisprudence. With Justices White, Blackmun, and Rehnquist, I categorically reject the remarkable notion that the police in this case were guilty of unconstitutional misconduct, or any conduct justifying the bizarre result reached by the Court."

In noteworthy lower Federal and State court decisions, courts have held: (1) that states must grant investigative expenses or appoint investigators for indigents in criminal proceedings equal in quality to those offered by a public defender;[119] (2) that the Sixth Amendment counsel guarantee is inapplicable in civil contempt proceedings;[120] (3) that the right to counsel does not apply in pro-

[116] Geders *v.* U.S., 425 U.S. 80 (1976). The Court, per Chief Justice Burger, found plenty of less drastic alternatives available and his opinion canvasses them.

[117] Brewer *v.* Ill., 97 S.Ct. 1232 (1977). *See also* United States *v.* Valencia, 541 F. 2d. 618 (1976), where a conviction was overturned because of the intrusion on the lawyer-client relationship by a government informant who acted as the attorney's secretary. *Cf.* Hoffa *v.* U.S., 385 U.S. 293 (1966).

[118] 377 U.S. 201 (1964).

[119] Mason *v.* Ariz., 504 F. 2d. 1345 (1974). But the Supreme Court has ruled that the States can constitutionally compel the defendant to reimburse the State if he is convicted and subsequently acquires the means to bear the cost of his legal defense. Fuller *v.* Ore., 417 U.S. 40 (1974).

[120] Duval *v.* Duval, 322 A. 2d. 1 (1974). But the right to counsel does exist in proceedings that look to the loss of child custody; *see* Crist *v.* Div. of Youth and Family Serv., 320 A. 2d 203 (1974); *in re* Welfare of Luscier, 524 P. 2d. 906 (1974). One

ceedings to revoke a driver's license;[121] and (4) that neither does the right to have an attorney present extend to defendants' psychiatric examinations.[122] The courts, however, are badly split on the question of whether an individual taking a breathalyzer test has the right to counsel. Some decisions support the right,[123] provided there is no unreasonable delay in the administration of the test; others do not.[124]

No Constitutional Right to Counsel in Legislative and Administrative Proceedings

Despite the growth or right to counsel with respect to criminal law enforcement, the Court has been reluctant to find that the *Constitution* requires that legislative and administrative proceedings provide the right to counsel even where those proceedings may "lay a witness open to criminal charges."[125]

With respect to the retroactive application of right-to-counsel decisions *see* pp. 240-241.

Retro-activity

AMENDMENT VII

In suits at common law, where the value in controversy shall exceed twenty dollars, the right of trial by jury shall be preserved, and no fact tried by a jury, shall be otherwise reexamined in any court of the United States, than according to the rules of the common law.

"Suits at Common Law"

The primary purpose of this amendment was to preserve the historic line separating the province of the jury from that of the judge in civil cases, without at the same time preventing procedural improvements which did not transgress this line. Elucidating this formula, the Court has achieved the following results: It is constitutional for a Federal judge, in the course of trial, to express his opinion upon the facts, provided all questions of fact are ultimately submitted to the jury;[1] to call the jury's attention to parts of the evidence he deems of special importance,[2] being careful to distin-

---

court decision has held that the children involved in such proceedings are entitled to counsel, *see* State *ex rel.* Juvenile Dept. of Multnomah Cty. *v.* Wade, 527 P. 2d. 753 (1974). *See also in re* Rodriguez, 110 Cal.Rptr. 56 (1973).

[121] Ferguson *v.* Gathright, 485 F. 2d. 504 (1973).

[122] Stultz *v.* State, 500 S.W. 2d. 853 (1973); Armstrong *v.* State, 502 S.W. 2d. 731 (1974); Edwards *v.* Sup'r Ct. of Santa Clara Cty., 549 P. 2d. 846 (1976).

[123] Troy *v.* Curry, 303 N.E. 2d. 925 (1973), *and* Prideaux *v.* State Dept. of Public Safety, 247 N.W. 2d. 385 (1976).

[124] McNulty *v.* Curry, 328 N.E. 2d. 798 (1975), *and* State *v.* Severino, 537 P. 2d. 1187 (1975).

[125] Hannah *v.* Larche, 363 U.S. 420, 445 and Appendix (1960); *in re* Groban, 352 U.S. 330 (1957).

---

[1] Vicksburg & Railroad Co. *v.* Putnam, 118 U.S. 545, 553 (1886); United States *v.* Reading Railroad, 123 U.S. 113, 114 (1887); Ray *v.* U.S., 367 F. 2d. 258 (1966).

[2] 118 U.S. 545; where are cited Carver *v.* Jackson *ex dem.* Astor *et al.*, 4 Pet. 1, 80 (1830); Magniac *v.* Thompson, 7 Pet. 348, 390 (1833); Mitchell *v.* Harmony, 13 How. 115, 131 (1852); Transportation Line *v.* Hope, 95 U.S. 297, 302 (1877); *see also* Ray *v.* U.S., 367 F. 2d. 258 (1966).

guish between matters of law and matters of opinion in relation thereto;[3] to inform the jury when there is not sufficient evidence to justify a verdict, that such is the case;[4] to direct the jury, after plaintiff's case is all in, to return a verdict for the defendant on the ground of the insufficiency of the evidence;[5] to set aside a verdict which in his opinion is against the law or the evidence, and order a new trial;[6] to refuse defendant a new trial on the condition, accepted by plaintiff, that the latter remit a portion of the damages awarded him[7] but not, on the other hand, to deny plaintiff a new trial on the converse condition, although defendant accepted it.[8] From this point on, the line is not always easy to trace. In general, the Court has held that Federal courts of appeal must remand for retrial cases in which they reverse the verdict of a lower court, and may not substitute a judgment of their own on the merits, although more recent cases somewhat mitigate this rule, which obviously favors the law's delays.[9]

One of the liveliest disputes among Supreme Court Justices in recent decades has been whether or not the Court should review cases arising under the Federal Employers' Liability Act, cases which, when they come to the Court, generally boil down to a dispute over lower court judges' withholding cases from juries or setting aside verdicts—juries being notoriously more generous in making awards to disabled employees than are judges. An angry Justice Douglas sought to put the matter in perspective in 1959:

"It is apparent from the decisions where we refused to review cases in which lower courts withheld cases from the jury or set aside jury verdicts (or where, having granted certiorari, we sustained the lower courts in that action) that the system of judicial supervision still exists in this as in other types of cases.

"It is suggested that the Court has consumed too much of its time in reviewing these FELA cases. An examination of the 33 cases in which the Court has granted certiorari during the period of over 10 years . . . reveals that 16 of these cases were summarily reversed

[3] Games v. Dunn, 14 Pet. 322, 327 (1840); Boeing Co. v. Shipman, 411 F. 2d. 365, 380 (1969).
[4] Sparf v. U.S., 156 U.S. 51, 99-100 (1895); Pleasants v. Fant, 22 Wall. 116, 121 (1875); Randall v. Baltimore & Ohio R.R. Co., 109 U.S. 478, 482 (1883); Meehan v. Valentine, 145 U.S. 611, 625 (1892); Coughran v. Bigelow, 164 U.S. 301 (1896); Belton v. U.S., 382 F. 2d. 150 (1967).
[5] Treat Mfg. Co. v. Standard Steel & Iron Co., 157 U.S. 674 (1895); Randall v. Baltimore & Ohio R.R. Co., 109 U.S. 478, 482 (1883) and cases there cited.
[6] Capital Traction Co. v. Hof, 174 U.S. 1, 13 (1899); Southern Pacific Co. v. Guthrie, 186 F. 2d. 926 (1951).
[7] Arkansas Land & Cattle Co. v. Mann, 130 U.S. 69, 74 (1889); Gorsalitz v. Olin Corp., 429 F. 2d. 1033, 1043 (1970).
[8] Dimick v. Schiedt, 293 U.S. 474, 476-478 (1935); Gorsalitz v. Olin Corp., 429 F. 2d. 1033, 1043 (1970).
[9] Slocum v. N.Y. Life Ins. Co., 228 U.S. 364 (1913); Dimick v. Schiedt, above; Baltimore & C. Line v. Redman, 295 U.S. 654 (1935); Smith v. Illinois Central R.R. Co., 394 F. 2d. 254 (1968); Hartnett v. Brown & Bigelow, 394 F. 2d. 438 (1968).

without oral argument and without full opinions. Only 17 cases were argued during this period of more than a decade and, of these, 5 were disposed of by brief *per curiam* opinions. Only 12 cases in over 10 years were argued, briefed and disposed of with full opinions by the Court. We have granted certiorari in these cases on an average of less than 3 per year and have given plenary consideration to slightly more than 1 per year. Wastage of our time is therefore a false issue.

"The difference between the majority and minority of the Court in our treatment of FELA cases concerns the degree of vigilance we should exercise in safeguarding the jury trial—guaranteed by the Seventh Amendment and part and parcel of the remedy under this Federal Act when suit is brought in state courts. . . ."[10]

In a 1973 decision, the Court concluded "that a jury of six satisfies the Seventh Amendment's guarantee of trial by jury in *civil* cases."[11] (Emphasis added.) Three years earlier, in its disposition of a case in which it sustained the constitutionality of a Florida statute providing for six-member juries in the trial of certain criminal cases,[12] the Court wrote that it was reversing the question whether "additional references to the 'common law' that occur in the Seventh Amendment might support a different interpretation" with respect to jury trial in civil cases. In support of its subsequent decision disposing of the issue, the Court explained: "[B]y referring to the 'common law', the Framers of the Seventh Amendment were concerned with preserving the *right* of trial by jury in civil cases where it existed at common law, rather than the various incidents of trial by jury. In short, what was said in *Williams* with respect to the criminal jury is equally applicable here: constitutional history reveals no intention on the part of the Framers 'to equate the constitutional and common-law characteristics of the jury.' "[13]

The amendment governs only courts which sit under the authority of the United States,[14] including courts in the territories and the District of Columbia.[15] It does not apply to a State court even when it is enforcing a right created by Federal statute.[16] Materially it is

Limited Application of the Amendment

---

[10] Harris *v*. Penn. R.R. Co., 361 U.S. 15, 17 (1959). *See also* Rogers *v*. Missouri Pacific R.R. Co., 352 U.S. 500 (1957); Harrison *v*. Missouri Pacific R.R. Co., 372 U.S. 248 (1963); Basham *v*. Penn. R.R. Co., 372 U.S. 699 (1963); Barboza *v*. Texaco, Inc., 434 F. 2d. 121 (1970).

[11] Colegrove *v*. Battin, 413 U.S. 149, 160 (1973).

[12] Williams *v*. Fla., 399 U.S. 78 (1970).

[13] Colegrove *v*. Battin, 413 U.S. 149, 155-156.

[14] Pearson *v*. Yewdall, 95 U.S. 294, 296 (1877). *See also* Edwards *v*. Elliott, 21 Wall. 532, 557 (1874); Justices *v*. U.S. *ex rel*. Murray, 9 Wall. 274, 277 (1870); Walker *v*. Sauvinet, 92 U.S. 90 (1875); St. Louis & K.C. Land Co. *v*. Kansas City, 241 U.S. 419 (1916); *in re* Advisory Opinion to Senate, 278 A. 2d. 852, 854 (1971); Williams *v*. Williams, 186 S.E. 2d. 210 (1972).

[15] Webster *v*. Reid, 11 How. 437, 460 (1851); Kennon *v*. Gilmer, 131 U.S. 22, 28 (1889); Glidden *v*. Zdanok, 370 U.S. 530, 572 (1962).

[16] Minneapolis & St. L. R. Co. *v*. Bombolis, 241 U.S. 211 (1916), which involved the Federal Employers Liability Act of 1908. The ruling is followed in four other

"limited to rights and remedies peculiarly legal in their nature,"[17] the term "common law" being used in contradistinction to suits in which equitable rights alone were recognized at the time of the framing of the amendment.[18] Nor does it apply to cases in admiralty and maritime jurisdiction, in which the trial is by a court without a jury;[19] nor to suits to enforce claims against the United States;[20] nor to suits to cancel a naturalization certificate for fraud;[21] to orders of deportation of an alien;[22] to suits under the Longshoremen's and Harbor Workers Compensation Act.[23] In short, the Court, in its application of the amendment, until recently has followed the historic pattern of the common law. Now, substantial change may be in store as a consequence of a Supreme Court decision in 1970. The story starts back in 1934 when Congress granted the Supreme Court the power to prescribe rules for Federal courts in "civil actions at law." Congress empowered the Court to "at any time unite the general rules prescribed for cases in equity with those in actions at law so as to secure one form of civil action and procedure for both: *Provided, however*, that in such union of rules the right of trial by jury as at common law and declared by the Seventh Amendment to the Constitution shall be preserved to the parties inviolate."[24] Subsequently, the Federal Rules did provide for one form of civil action.[25] Justice White, speaking for the Court in 1970, pointed out that "Actions are no longer brought as actions at law or suits in equity. Under the Rules there is only one action—a 'civil action'—in which all claims may be joined and all remedies are available. Purely procedural impediments to the presentation of any issue by any party, based on the difference between law and equity were destroyed. . . ."[26] Consequently, the Court held that "Under the rules law and equity are procedurally combined; noth-

cases in the same volume. *See ibid.*, 241, 261, 485 and 494; Mills *v.* Louisiana, 360 U.S. 230, 237 (1959); Sharpe *v.* State, 448 P. 2d. 301 (1968), *cert. denied*, 394 U.S. 904 (1969).

[17] Shields *v.* Thomas, 18 How. 253, 262 (1856); Glidden Co. *v.* Zdanok, 370 U.S. 530, 572 (1962).

[18] Parsons *v.* Bedford, 3 Pet. 433, 447 (1830); Barton *v.* Barbour, 104 U.S. 126, 133 (1881). "It is now fundamental, though, that when legal and equitable claims are tried together, common questions of fact must be decided by the jury in order to preserve the integrity of the Seventh Amendment guarantee." Heyman *v.* Kline, 456 F. 2d. 123 (1972), and cases cited therein.

[19] Parsons *v.* Bedford, *supra*; Waring *v.* Clarke, 5 How. 441, 460 (1847). *See also* The "Sarah," 8 Wheat. 390, 391 (1823), and cases there cited.

[20] McElrath *v.* U.S., 102 U.S. 426, 440 (1880). *See also* Galloway *v.* U.S., 319 U.S. 372, 388 (1943); Glidden Co. *v.* Zdanok, 370 U.S. 530, 572 (1962).

[21] Luria *v.* U.S., 231 U.S. 9 (1913).

[22] Gee Wah Lee *v.* U.S., 25 F. 2d. 107 (1928); *cert. denied*, 277 U.S. 608 (1928). Filer & S. Co. *v.* Diamond Iron Works, 270 Fed. 489 (1921); *cert. denied*, 256 U.S. 691 (1921).

[23] Crowell *v.* Benson, 285 U.S. 22, 45, 49 (1932). The Court held that "As the Act relates solely to injuries occurring upon the navigable waters of the United States, it deals with maritime law, applicable to matters that fall within the admiralty and maritime jurisdiction. . . ." *Ibid.*, 39.

[24] 48 *Stat.* 1064 (1934).   [25] 28 R U.S.C. Rule 2.

[26] Ross *v.* Bernhard, 396 U.S. 531, 539 (1970).

ing turns now upon the form of the action or the procedural devices by which the parties happen to come before the court. . . ."[27] Three Justices sharply dissented, pointing out:

"In holding as it does that the plaintiff in a shareholder's derivative suit is constitutionally entitled to a jury trial, the Court today seems to rely upon some sort of ill-defined combination of the Seventh Amendment and the Federal Rules of Civil Procedure. Somehow the Amendment and the Rules magically interact to do what each separately was expressly intended not to do, namely, to enlarge the right to a jury trial in civil actions brought in the courts of the United States.

"The Seventh Amendment, by its terms, does not extend, but merely *preserves* the right to a jury trial '[i]n Suits at common law.' All agree that this means the reach of the Amendment is limited to those actions that were tried to the jury in 1791 when the Amendment was adopted. Suits in equity, which were historically tried to the court, were therefore unaffected by it. Similarly, Rule 38 of the Federal Rules has no bearing on the right to a jury trial in suits in equity, for it simply preserves inviolate '[t]he right of trial by jury as declared by the Seventh Amendment.' Thus this Rule, like the Amendment itself, neither restricts nor enlarges the right to jury trial. Indeed nothing in the Federal Rules can rightly be construed to enlarge the right of jury trial, for in the legislation authorizing the Rules, Congress expressly provided that they 'shall neither abridge, enlarge, nor modify the substantive rights of any litigant.' I take this plain, simple, and straightforward language to mean that after the promulgation of the Federal Rules, as before, the constitutional right to a jury trial attaches only to suits at common law. So, apparently, has every federal court that has discussed the issue. Since, as the Court concedes, a shareholder's derivative suit could be brought only in equity, it would seem to me to follow by the most elementary logic that in such suits there is no constitutional right to a trial by jury. Today the Court tosses aside history, logic, and over 100 years of firm precedent to hold that the plaintiff in a shareholder's derivative suit does indeed have a constitutional right to a trial by jury. This holding has a questionable basis in policy and no basis whatever in the Constitution."[28] Clearly, if the majority's holding continues to prevail, the right to trial by jury in civil cases will be extended considerably.

On another significant Seventh Amendment question the Court recently held that "when Congress creates new statutory 'public rights,' it may assign their adjudication to an administrative agency with which a jury trial would be incompatible, without violating the Seventh Amendment's injunction that jury trial is to be 'preserved' in 'suits at common law.' Congress is not required by the Seventh Amendment to choke the already crowded federal courts with new types of litigation nor prevented from committing some new types of litigation to administrative agencies with special competence in

[27] *Ibid.*   [28] *Ibid.*, 543-544.

the relevant field."[29] The Act created a new statutory duty on the part of employers to avoid maintaining unhealthy or unsafe working conditions and empowers the Secretary of Labor to promulgate guidelines. The statute also provides two remedies: (1) the obtaining of abatement orders to eradicate unhealthy or unsafe conditions, and (2) the awarding of civil penalties against employers maintaining such conditions. As the Court explained in support of its conclusion sustaining the constitutionality of the Act:

"The Seventh Amendment was declaratory of the existing law, for it required only that jury trial in suits at common law was to be 'preserved.' It thus did not purport to require a jury trial where none was required before. Moreover, it did not seek to change the factfinding mode in equity or admiralty nor to freeze equity jurisdiction as it existed in 1789, preventing it from developing new remedies where those available in courts of law were inadequate."[30]

AMENDMENT VIII

Excessive bail shall not be required, nor excessive fines imposed, nor cruel and unusual punishments inflicted.

The Supreme Court has had little to say with reference to excessive fines or bail. In an early case it held that it had no appellate jurisdiction to revise the sentence of an inferior court, even though the excessiveness of the fine was apparent on the face of the record.[1] Nearly one hundred and twenty years later, in 1951, however, it ruled that bail must not be excessive, that its purpose was to make reasonably sure of a defendant's appearance for trial but not so heavy that he could not give it and thereby secure his liberty for the purpose of preparing his defense.[2] According to one Federal court, the prohibition against excessive bail applies to the States.[3]

In recent years, the whole bail system has come under close scrutiny and criticism from a host of responsible persons and groups.[4] Nonetheless, interpretation of the constitutional command remains what the Supreme Court said it was in 1951.[5]

[29] Atlas Roofing Co., Inc. *v.* Occupational Safety and Health Review Com'n, 430 U.S. 442, 455 (1977).

[30] *Ibid.*, 1271. In two other recent Seventh Amendment cases, both of which were housing disputes, the Supreme Court held that the option of a jury trial applied: (1) in a civil action for recovery of damages by a black woman against white landlords for violation of the fair housing provisions of the 1968 Civil Rights Act, Curtis *v.* Loether, 415 U.S. 189 (1974); and (2) in an eviction proceeding under statutes of the District of Columbia providing summary procedures for the recovery of possession of real property, Pernell *v.* Southall Realty, 416 U.S. 363 (1974).

[1] *Ex parte* Watkins, 7 Pet. 568, 574 (1832).

[2] Stack *v.* Boyle, 342 U.S. 1 (1951); 18R U.S.C. Rule 46; Kinney *v.* Lenon, 447 F. 2d. 596 (1971); U.S. *v.* Smith, 444 F. 2d. 61 (1971).

[3] Pilkington *v.* Circuit Court, 324 F. 2d. 45, 46 (1963).

[4] *See* People *v.* Jones, 489 P. 2d. 596, 598 (1971) and works cited therein. *See also* Ronald L. Goldfarb, *Ransom: A Critique of the American Bail System* (New York, 1965); Wayne H. Thomas, *Bail Reform in America* (Berkeley, Calif., 1976).

[5] People *v.* Jones, 489 P. 2d. 596, 598 (1971); State *ex rel.* Ghiz *v.* Johnson, 183 S.E. 2d. 703 (1971); McDermott *v.* Superior Court, 97 Cal.Rptr. 171 (1971).

The ban against "cruel and unusual punishments" has received somewhat greater attention. In Wilkerson v. Utah[6] the Court observed that "difficulty would attend the effort to define with exactness the extent of the constitutional provision which provides that cruel and unusual punishments shall not be inflicted," but that it was "safe to affirm that punishment of torture, . . . and all others in the same line of unnecessary cruelty, are forbidden by that Amendment . . .";[7] but that shooting as a mode of executing the death penalty was not "cruel and unusual" within the intention of the amendment. Thirty years later a divided Court condemned a Philippine statute prescribing fine and imprisonment of from twelve to twenty years for entering a known false statement in a public record, on the ground that the gross disparity between this punishment and that imposed for other more serious offenses made it cruel and unusual, and as such, repugnant to the Bill of Rights.[8] But no constitutional infirmity was discovered in a measure punishing as a separate offense each act of placing a letter in the mails in pursuance of a single scheme to defraud.[9] Nor was it "cruel and unusual punishment," in the opinion of a divided Court, to subject one convicted of murder to electrocution after an accidental failure of equipment had rendered a previous attempt unsuccessful.[10]

"Cruel and Unusual Punishments"

Of supreme concern in recent years has been the question whether the imposition of the death penalty violates the ban on "cruel and unusual punishments." In the first phase of its answer, the Court in Furman v. Georgia[11] held that State statutes that allow the imposition of the death penalty without structuring or guiding the discretionary power of the judge or jury in the matter do violate the Eighth Amendment. The Court's majority in this ruling was a thin one, and the clarity of the Court's decision was further muddied because it was announced in a *per curiam* opinion with each of the Justices filing concurring or dissenting opinions. In his concurring opinion, Justice Douglas, articulating a variation on equal protection, argued that the racial discrimination apparent in the imposition of the death penalty made it "cruel and unusual." Justices Brennan and Marshall, also concurring, canvassed many additional arguments against the death penalty and concluded the penalty was unconstitutional *per se*. Justice Marshall, in particular, wrote that, if the public knew the facts about the imposition of the death penalty, it would not morally pass muster today. Also concurring in the judgment were Justices Stewart and White. Noting individually that they were not addressing whether the death penalty is *per se* unconstitutional they found that it was unconstitutional because, in Justice Stewart's words, it was "so wantonly and so freakishly imposed." Focusing particularly on the unguided discre-

The Death Penalty

---

[6] 99 U.S. 130 (1879).   [7] *Ibid.*, 135.
[8] Weems v. U.S., 217 U.S. 349, 371, 389 (1910).
[9] Donaldson v. Read Magazine, 333 U.S. 178, 191 (1948).
[10] Louisiana v. Resweber, 329 U.S. 459 (1947).
[11] 408 U.S. 238 (1972).

tion of the judge and jury, it was they who circumscribed the Court's holding. The dissenters primarily argued that the Court ought to have exercised self-restraint and not undertaken to make what they thought was a legislative judgment about the desirability of the death penalty.

Four years later, in the waning days of one of the longest Terms in memory, the Court handed down the second phase of its answer. Addressing at the outset the question of whether "the punishment of death for the crime of murder is, under all circumstances, 'cruel and unusual' in violation of the Eighth and Fourteenth Amendments of the Constitution," the Court held that it is not. Implicitly rejecting the proposition that constitutional evaluation of the death penalty warrants strict scrutiny, Justice Stewart, announcing the judgment of the Court in a plurality opinion, wrote: "[I]n assessing a punishment selected by a democratically elected legislature against the constitutional measure, we presume its validity. We may not require the legislature to select the least severe penalty possible so long as the penalty selected is not cruelly inhumane or disproportionate to the crime involved. And a heavy burden rests on those who would attack the judgment of the representatives of the people."[12] Rejecting arguments as to the intrinsic inhumaneness or disproportion of capital punishment for the crime of murder, the Court found support in history and precedent and pointed to the lack of convincing empirical evidence to challenge the hypothesis that it contributes to deter the commission of crime. Last but not least, Justice Stewart found, that the "standards of decency" argument, articulated four years ago in Furman v. Georgia was "undercut substantially" by eviden[ce] that a large proportion of American society continues to regard it [the death penalty] as an appropriate and necessary criminal sanction." The "most marked indication," he said, could be seen in the fact that "at least 35 States have enacted new statutes that provide for the death penalty for at least some crimes that result in the death of another person."[13]

The Court went on to sustain Georgia's capital punishment pro-

---

[12] Gregg v. Ga., 428 U.S. 153, 175 (1976). Cf., Commonwealth v. O'Neal, 339 N.E. 2d. 676 (1975), in which the Massachusetts Supreme Judicial Court struck down that state's death penalty as a matter of *state* constitutional law. Holding that "the right to life is fundamental . . . the infringement upon which triggers strict scrutiny under the compelling State interest and least restrictive means test," the Massachusetts court had specifically directed the parties to brief the question "whether the Commonwealth has a compelling interest which is served by the imposition of the death penalty in rape-murder cases, and whether such penalty is the least restrictive means for furtherance of the Commonwealth's permissible objectives." *Ibid.*, 327 N.E. 2d. 662, 668 (1975).

[13] *Ibid.*, 179-180. Justice Stewart also cited Congress's passage of the Antihijacking Act of 1974 and California's adoption of a State constitutional amendment restoring the death penalty after the State supreme court held in People v. Anderson, 493 P. 2d. 880 (1972), that it contravened the State constitution. And a recent Harris Survey shows 67 per cent of the public favors capital punishment, with 25 per cent opposed, *Minneapolis Star*, Feb. 7, 1977.

cedures, pointing out that, in addressing the infirmity previously present in *Furman*, Georgia now confined jury discretion by identifying specific guidelines to be used in the decision. Moreover, the new State procedures for automatic appeal to the State supreme court upon imposition of the death penalty, the justices held, insured that like cases would be treated alike. In an opinion that focused at length on the facts of the immediate case, Justice White, joined by Chief Justice Burger and Justice Rehnquist, joined in the Court's judgment. Justice Blackmun also concurred in the judgment on the basis of his opinion in *Furman*. Recalling the substance of their earlier opinions in *Furman*, Justices Brennan and Marshall dissented. Wrote Justice Brennan: "I emphasize only that foremost among the 'moral concepts' recognized in our cases and inherent in the Clause is the primary moral principle that the State, even as it punishes, must treat its citizens in a manner consistent with their intrinsic worth as human beings—a punishment must not be so severe as to be degrading to human dignity. A judicial determination whether the punishment of death comports with human dignity is therefore not only permitted but compelled by the Clause."[14] In two other cases, the Court sustained the constitutionality of comparable procedures in Florida[15] and Texas.[16] In these respective State schemes the Court found the discretion of the trial judge and the jury was guided by either the enumeration of aggravating factors or specified questions to be taken into account in arriving at a decision based on the particular behavior of a given defendant.

In a North Carolina case, the Court was also asked to address the question "whether a death sentence returned pursuant to a law imposing a mandatory death penalty for a broad category of homicidal offenses constitutes cruel and unusual punishment within the meaning of the Eighth and Fourteenth Amendments." To this, the Court answered "yes." Speaking once again in a plurality opinion, Justice Stewart declared: "The history of mandatory death penalty statutes in the United States . . . reveals that the practice of sentencing to death all persons convicted of a particular offense has been rejected as unduly harsh and unavoidably rigid."[17] And, responding to a defense of North Carolina's statute on grounds it provided an answer to unbridled jury discretion, Justice Stewart retorted that "mandatory statutes enacted in response to *Furman* have simply papered over the problem" since "there is general agreement that American juries have persistently refused to convict a significant portion of persons charged with first-degree murder of that offense under mandatory death penalty statutes." Finally, delimiting "a third constitutional shortcoming" of the North Carolina statute, Justice Stewart simply noted "its failure to allow the particularized consideration of relevant aspects of the character and record of each convicted defendant before the imposition upon him

---

[14] *Ibid.*, 229-230   [15] Proffitt *v*. Fla., 428 U.S. 242 (1976).
[16] Jurek *v*. Tex., 428 U.S. 262 (1976).   [17] Woodson *v*. N.C., 428 U.S. 280 (1976).

of a sentence of death." Chief Justice Burger and Justices White, Blackmun, and Rehnquist dissented. Speaking for himself, Justice Rehnquist concluded: "I do not believe that any one of these reasons singly, nor all of them together, can withstand careful analysis. Contrary to the plurality's assertions, they would import into the Cruel and Unusual Punishment Clause procedural requirements which find no support in our cases." Moreover, Justice Rehnquist continued: "Their application will result in the invalidation of a death sentence imposed upon a defendant convicted of first-degree murder under the North Carolina system, and the upholding of the same sentence imposed on an identical defendant convicted on identical evidence of first-degree murder under the Florida, Georgia, or Texas systems—a result surely as 'freakish' as that condemned in the separate opinions in *Furman*."[18] In another decision involving a comparable mandatory death penalty statute in Louisiana, the Court struck down that law.[19]

The Court tied up some of the loose ends left by its 1976 death penalty rulings with two decisions the following Term. In one case, involving the constitutionality of a State statute that imposed a mandatory death penalty for the murder of a policeman or fireman, the Court held that its prior rulings resolved this question by mandating that before any capital sentence is imposed there must be an opportunity "for consideration of whatever mitigating circumstances may be relevant to either the particular offender or the particular offense."[20] In the other, the Court held that the death sentence for the crime of rape is grossly disproportionate and, therefore, violates the ban on "cruel and unusual punishments." Two bases of support were offered for this conclusion: (1) the response of State legislatures in redesigning death penalty statutes to comply with the Court's decision in Furman *v*. Georgia was such that a far greater number of states chose to reimpose capital punishment for the crime of murder than chose to reimpose the death penalty also for the crime of rape; and (2) the evidence showed that there was a demonstrable reluctance on the part of jurors to impose the death penalty in rape cases.[21]

Students and Corporal Punishment	The Court has also recently held that the infliction of corporal punishment on students by school officials infringes neither the ban on "cruel and unusual punishments" nor the guarantee of due process. As distinguished from the context in which the Framers meant the Eighth Amendment guarantee to apply—that is, to criminals—the Court concluded that "[t]he schoolchild has little need for the protection of the Eighth Amendment" since "[t]he openness of the public school and its supervision by the community afford significant safeguards against the kinds of abuses from which the Eighth Amendment protects the prisoner." The Court

[18] *Ibid*., 309.	[19] Roberts *v*. La., 428 U.S. 325 (1976).
[20] Roberts *v*. La., 97 S.Ct. 1993, 1996 (1977).
[21] Coker *v*. Ga., 97 S.Ct. 2861 (1977).

held that the general common law precept with respect to corporal punishment, i.e., the use of reasonable but not excessive force, provides sufficient protection. In addressing the due process issue, the Court found procedural guarantees outweighed by the imposition on the school system and the interest in maintaining discipline. In the words of Justice Powell, speaking for the Court: "We conclude that the Due Process Clause does not require notice and a hearing prior to the imposition of corporal punishment in the public schools, as that practice is authorized and limited by the common law."[22]

In recent years, in keeping with a greater concern manifested for civil liberties, there have been some novel contentions as to what constitutes cruel and unusual punishments. A Georgia court of appeals held that requiring a probationer to keep his hair cut short was a violation of the First, Eighth, and Fourteenth Amendments.[23] The Supreme Court of Minnesota, however, found that a statute which did not authorize marriage between persons of the same sex did not offend the Eighth Amendment.[24] Nor did the Virginia Supreme Court find that the forfeiture of a $8,700 automobile for the owner's driving after his license was revoked an unusual punishment.[25]

But the application of the Amendment's ban on "cruel and unusual punishments" is not solely a matter of how severe the penalty is. As Justice Stewart once remarked, "Even one day in prison would be a cruel and unusual punishment for the 'crime' of having a common cold."[26] Stewart was referring to a case in which the defendant had been convicted under a California statute that made it a misdemeanor for a person to be addicted to narcotics. Holding, first, that the Eighth Amendment's ban on "cruel and unusual punishments" applied to the States as well as the Federal government, the Court ruled that criminal penalties may never be imposed for having a particular condition. In a case[27] decided six years later, the Court had to determine whether its prior ruling invalidated a Texas law making it an offense to be drunk in a public place. Speaking for a plurality in the case, Justice Marshall wrote: "On its face the present case does not fall within that holding, since appellant was convicted, not for being a chronic alcoholic, but for being in public while drunk on a particular occasion. The State of Texas thus has not sought to punish a mere status, as California did in *Robinson*." Countering an attempt by the dissenters in the case to read *Robinson* as barring punishment of an individual for having a disease, that is, something he was powerless to control, Justice Marshall continued: "*Robinson* so viewed brings this Court but a very

No Punishment of Condition or Status

---

[22] Ingraham v. Wright, 97 S.Ct. 1401, 1418 (1977).
[23] Inman v. State, 183 S.E. 2d. 413 (1971).
[24] Baker v. Nelson, 191 N.W. 2d. 185 (1971); *appeal dismissed*, 409 U.S. 810 (1972).
[25] Commonwealth v. One 1970, 2 Dr. H. T. Lincoln Auto, 186 S.E. 2d. 279 (1972).
[26] Robinson v. Calif., 370 U.S. 660, 667 (1962).
[27] Powell v. Tex., 392 U.S. 514 (1968).

small way into the substantive criminal law. And unless *Robinson* is so viewed it is difficult to see any limiting principle that would serve to prevent this Court from becoming, under the aegis of the Cruel and Unusual Punishment Clause, the ultimate arbiter of the standards of criminal responsibility, in diverse areas of the criminal law, throughout the country. . . . The entire thrust of *Robinson*'s interpretation of the Cruel and Unusual Punishment Clause is that criminal penalties may be inflicted only if the accused has committed some act, has engaged in some behavior, which society has an interest in preventing. . . . It thus does not deal with the question of whether certain conduct cannot constitutionally be punished because it is, in some sense, 'involuntary' or 'occasioned by a compulsion.' "[28] So saying, the Court rejected the attempt to frame a "constitutional doctrine of criminal responsibility" or "some sort of insanity test in constitutional terms."

Conditions of Imprisonment as "Cruel and Unusual Punishment"

Not surprisingly, in view of the saliency of the nation's prison and drug problems, our State courts have been dealing currently with a flurry of cases in which it is claimed that solitary confinement of prisoners and long prison sentences for sellers of marijuana do violence to the Eighth Amendment. The courts have upheld the use of solitary confinement, but, in doing so, one court held that a "prison inmate is entitled to relief by habeas corpus if he alleges and proves that 'excessive punishment was inflicted upon him in violation of his fundamental and basic rights' " and that, where a prisoner is segregated "under conditions of maximum security," prison authorities must offer facts to justify it.[29]

Federal courts have intensified their oversight of State penal facilities, reflecting a heightened concern with the extent to which the ills that plague so-called correctional institutions—overcrowding, understaffing, unsanitary facilities, brutality, constant fear of violence, lack of adequate medical and mental health care, poor food service, intrusive correspondence restrictions, inhumane isolation,

---

[28] *Ibid.*, 532-533. Though Justice White voted with the plurality to create the majority that refused to strike down the Texas statute in *Powell*, several observations he offered in his concurring opinion are provocative: "The fact remains that some chronic alcoholics must drink and hence must drink *somewhere*. Although many chronics have homes, many others do not. For all practical purposes the public streets may be home for these unfortunates, not because their disease compels them to be there, but because, drunk or sober, they have no place else to go and no place else to be when they are drinking. This is more a function of economic station than of disease, although the disease may lead to destitution and perpetuate that condition. For some of these alcoholics I would think a showing could be made that resisting drunkenness is impossible and that avoiding public places when intoxicated is also impossible. As applied to them this statute is in effect a law which bans a single act for which they may not be convicted under the Eighth Amendment—the act of getting drunk." *Ibid.*, 551.
[29] *In re* Hutchinson, 100 Cal.Rptr. 124, 127-128 (1972); Levier *v.* State, 497 P. 2d. 265 (1972). *Cf. In re* Henderson, 101 Cal.Rptr. 479 (1972). *See also* State *v.* Coiner, 186 S.E. 2d. 220 (1972); State *v.* Scott, 496 P. 2d. 609 (1972). For a case involving alleged mistreatment other than solitary confinement, *see* Hawthorne *v.* People, 328 N.Y.S. 2d. 488 (1971). *See also* Rosecki *v.* Gaughan, 459 F. 2d. 6 (1972).

segregation, inadequate or nonexistent rehabilitative and/or educational programs, deficient recreational opportunities—violate the Eighth Amendment ban on "cruel and unusual punishments."[30] Particularly noteworthy in this regard has been the activism of U.S. District Judge Frank Johnson, whose recent order, based upon a graphic account of the sordid, squalid conditions of Alabama prisons, details with great precision exactly what that State must do to upgrade its penal institutions to meet minimal constitutional requirements.[31]

Though many legislatures have decriminalized the personal possession of small amounts of marijuana, and the highest court in one State has held as a matter of State constitutional law that the imposition of criminal penalties for the possession of marijuana at home violates the right to privacy,[32] many of the sentences challenged as excessive follow convictions on drug offenses. Lower Federal and State courts have held that the Eighth Amendment is not violated by sentences of 100 years for possession of marijuana[33] or 1500 years for the sale of heroin.[34] The New York Court of Appeals has upheld a statute imposing a mandatory penalty of life imprison-

[30] See Costello v. Wainwright, 397 F.Supp. 20 (1975), affirmed 525 F. 2d. 1239 (1976); Detainees of Brooklyn House of Detention for Men v. Malcolm, 520 F. 2d. 392 (1975); Kimbrough v. O'Neil, 523 F. 2d. 1057 (1975); Bel v. Hall, 392 F.Supp. 274 (1975); Van Horn v. Lukhard, 392 F.Supp. 384 (1975); Dillard v. Pitchess, 399 F.Supp. 1225 (1975); Miller v. Carson, 401 F.Supp. 835 (1975); Craig v. Hocker, 405 F.Supp. 656 (1975); Alberti v. Sheriff of Harris Cty., Tex., 406 F.Supp. 649 (1975); Spain v. Procunier, 408 F.Supp. 534 (1976). See also Rhem v. Malcolm, 377 F.Supp. 995 (1974), aff'd 507 F. 2d. 333 (1974); Gates v. Collier, 501 F. 2d. 1291 (1974) and 390 F.Supp. 482 (1975); Finney v. Ark. Bd. of Correc., 505 F. 2d. 194 (1974); Battle v. Anderson, 376 F.Supp. 402 (1974); Jackson v. Allen, 376 F.Supp. 1393 (1974); Campise v. Hamilton, 382 F.Supp. 172 (1974); Clemmons v. Greggs, 509 F. 2d. 1338 (1975); Poindexter v. Woodson, 510 F. 2d. 464 (1975). The right to some constitutional minimum standards in confinement also extends to protect juvenile prisoners, see especially Morales v. Turman, 383 F.Supp. 53 (1974); see also Swansey v. Elrod, 386 F.Supp. 1138 (1975); Pena v. N.Y. State Div. for Youth, 419 F.Supp. 203 (1976). And, a Federal district court has ruled that a denial of conjugal visits does not infringe the ban on "cruel and unusual punishments." Lyons v. Gilligan, 382 F.Supp. 198 (1974). Another district court has ordered a continuation of methadone treatment during pretrial detention for addicts who had been receiving such treatment prior to their pretrail confinement, see Cudnik v. Kreiger, 392 F.Supp 305 (1974).

[31] James v. Wallace, 406 F.Supp. 318 (1976). As a parallel, see Judge Johnson's orders with respect to the deprivations visited on patients housed in the State's mental institutions, Wyatt v. Stickney, 325 F.Supp. 781 (1971), 334 F.Supp. 1341 (1971), 344 F.Supp. 373 (1972), 344 F.Supp. 387 (1972), affirmed sub nom. Wyatt v. Aderholt, 503 F. 2d. 1305 (1974). For a discussion of his judicial activism, see Steven Brill, "The Real Governor of Alabama," New York Magazine, April 26, 1976, pp. 37-41.

[32] Ravin v. State, 537 P. 2d. 494 (1975).

[33] Albro v. State, 502 S.W. 2d. 715 (1973). But a Federal appeals court found that a 20- to 40-year sentence for the sale of marijuana under an Ohio law did contravene the Eighth Amendment, Downey v. Perini, 518 F. 2d. 1288 (1975). See also People v. Lorentzen, 194 N.W. 2d. 827 (1972), but cf. State v. Chaffin, 282 N.E. 2d. 46 (1972).

[34] Rodriguez v. State, 509 S.W. 2d. 625 (1974).

ment for anyone caught trafficking in drugs,[35] but a Federal district court has ruled that deportation of a resident alien for possession of three marijuana cigarettes constituted "cruel and unusual punishment."[36] In other developments, the California Supreme Court, striking out at indeterminate sentences, has recently ruled that it is cruel and unusual punishment to imprison a person beyond a term proportionate to the offense committed.[37] Also, under new sentencing procedures approved by the Judicial Council of the U.S. Second Circuit, Federal judges will have to give reasons justifying each sentence they hand down. Said Judge Kaufman, who chairs the Council: "These rules represent a major step in the continuing effort of this circuit to bring greater openness, fairness and certainty to this important area."[38] Further, the Alaska Supreme Court rejected the Eighth Amendment challenge and sustained provisions of the State Environmental Conservation Act punishing violators with a $25,000 fine and a $1,000 fine per day for each willful violation.[39] Finally, as a result of a bizarre, governmentally sponsored experiment in which treatment was withheld from men with syphilis, the Federal government has made out-of-court settlements to the participants or their survivors.[40]

AMENDMENT IX

The enumeration in the Constitution of certain rights shall not be construed to deny or disparage others retained by the people.

Rights Anterior to the Constitution

In other words, there are certain rights of so fundamental a character that no free government may trespass upon them whether they are enumerated in the Constitution or not.[1] In point of fact, the course of our constitutional development has been to reduce fundamental rights to rights guaranteed by the sovereign from the natural rights that they once were—a development reflected especially in the history of the due process of law clause.

In an intriguing concurring opinion in the noteworthy "birth control" case, involving the constitutionality of a Connecticut stat-

---

[35] People v. Broadie, 332 N.E. 2d. 338 (1975).

[36] Lieggi v. U.S. Immig. & Nat. Serv., 389 F.Supp. 12 (1975). The court rested its holding on the premise that "an alien resident in America is protected by the Bill of Rights."

[37] In re Rodriguez, 537 P. 2d. 384 (1975).

[38] New York Times, Mar. 18, 1976.

[39] Stock v. State, 526 P. 2d. 3 (1974).

[40] San Diego Union, Dec. 17, 1974.

[1] See the language of Justice Chase, in Calder v. Bull, 3 Dall. 386, 387-389 (1798); also Justice Miller, for the Court, in Savings and Loan Asso. v. Topeka, 20 Wall. 655, 662-663 (1874); "We accept appellant's contention that the nature of political rights reserved to the people by the Ninth and Tenth Amendments are [sic] involved. The right claimed as inviolate may be stated as the right of a citizen to act as a party official or worker to further his own political views," Justice Reed, for the Court, in United Public Workers v. Mitchell, 330 U.S. 75, 94-95 (1947).

ute making it a crime for any person to use any drug or article to prevent conception, Justice Goldberg tried to breathe vitality into the Ninth Amendment:

"While this Court has had *little occasion* to interpret the Ninth Amendment '[i]t cannot be presumed that any clause in the Constitution is intended to be without effect.' . . . In interpreting the Constitution, 'real effect should be given to all the words it uses.' . . . The Ninth Amendment to the Constitution may be regarded by some as a recent discovery and may be forgotten by others, but since 1791 it has been a basic part of the Constitution which we are sworn to uphold. To hold that a right so basic and fundamental and so deep-rooted in our society as the right of privacy in marriage may be infringed because that right is not guaranteed in so many words by the first eight amendments to the Constitution is to ignore the Ninth Amendment and to give it no effect whatsoever. Moreover, a judicial construction that this fundamental right is not protected by the Constitution because it is not mentioned in explicit terms by one of the first eight amendments or elsewhere in the Constitution would violate the Ninth Amendment, which specifically states that '[t]he enumeration in the Constitution, of certain rights shall not be construed to deny or disparage others retained by the people' (emphasis added)."[2]

Justice Goldberg's argument has never commanded the assent of a majority of the Court, however. And the Ninth Amendment continues in a state of "benign neglect." Undoubtedly, the most important factor contributing to this neglect is the development of the penumbra theory of Justice Douglas, which has won the assent of a majority of the Court. Evidently, any important liberty not specifically safeguarded by the Bill of Rights can be found in the penumbra, or shadow, of a specific guarantee and thus be constitutionally protected as part of that guarantee. Let Justice Douglas explain it:

The Penumbra Theory

"The foregoing cases suggest that specific guarantees in the Bill of Rights have penumbras, formed by emanations from those guarantees that help give them life and substance. . . . Various guarantees create zones of privacy. The right of association contained in the penumbra of the First Amendment is one, as we have seen. The Third Amendment in its prohibition against the quartering of soldiers 'in any house' in time of peace without the consent of the owner is another facet of that privacy. The Fourth Amendment explicitly affirms the 'right of the people to be secure in their persons, houses, papers, and effects, against unreasonable searches and seizures.' The Fifth Amendment in its Self-Incrimination Clause enables the citizen to create a zone of privacy which government may not force him to surrender to his detriment. The Ninth Amendment provides: 'The enumeration in the Constitu-

---

[2] Griswold *v.* Connecticut, 381 U.S. 479, 490-492 (1965).

tion, of certain rights, shall not be construed to deny or disparage others retained by the people.'

"The Fourth and Fifth Amendments were described in Boyd *v.* United States, . . . as protection against all governmental invasions 'of the sanctity of a man's home and the privacies of life.' We referred in Mapp *v.* Ohio, . . . to the Fourth Amendment as creating a 'right to privacy, no less important than any other right carefully and particularly reserved to the people.' "[3]

Numerous decisions subsequent to *Griswold*, rendered by the Supreme Court and lower Federal and State courts, have implicated the Ninth Amendment in the resolution of claims alleging infringement of constitutionally protected privacy. These claims, of course, also more often invoke penumbral protection of other amendments. Precisely because Justice Stewart's criticism of the Court's handling of the privacy claim in *Griswold* continues to characterize judicial treatment of the constitutional right to privacy generally,[4] the central discussion of the right to privacy appears below under substantive due process and the Fourteenth Amendment. Because privacy claims invariably involve the due process clause of the Fourteenth Amendment,[5] but mention other amendments not at all or only occasionally, it seems both more appropriate and less repetitive to undertake the discussion there than under any or all of the amendments usually cited from the Bill of Rights.

AMENDMENT X

The powers not delegated to the United States by the Constitution, nor prohibited by it to the States, are reserved to the States respectively, or to the people.

"The Tenth Amendment was intended to confirm the understanding of the people at the time the Constitution was adopted, that powers not granted to the United States were reserved to the States or to the people. It added nothing to the instrument as originally

---

[3] *Ibid.*, 484-485. The penumbra theory has received elucidation in several U.S. courts of appeals, which in dealing with school dress codes were hard put but patently determined to find constitutional protections for boys who wanted to wear their hair long. Stull *v.* School Bd., 459 F. 2d. 339 (1972) and cases cited therein.

[4] Said Justice Stewart: "In the course of its opinion the Court refers to no less than six Amendments to the Constitution: the First, the Third, the Fourth, the Fifth, the Ninth, and the Fourteenth. But the Court does not say which of these Amendments, if any, it thinks is infringed by this Connecticut law." *Ibid.*, 527-528.

[5] Although in the very next paragraph of his dissent Stewart pointed out that the Court eschewed any reliance upon the Fourteenth, the fact is that subsequent cases clearly have, and some of them have done so exclusive of other amendments. Moreover, since the cases have been almost entirely State cases, involving the Fourteenth Amendment is inescapable. Whether the term "liberty" in the due process clause is defined to read the liberty of privacy or whether it is taken as a shorthand reference to incorporate the amendments and their penumbras and thereby make those protections applicable to the States, the fact is that the Fourteenth Amendment is inevitably involved.

ratified. . . ."[1] That this provision was not conceived to be a yardstick for measuring the powers granted to the Federal Government or reserved to the States was clearly indicated by its sponsor, James Madison, in the course of the debate which took place while the amendment was pending concerning Hamilton's proposal to establish a national bank. He declared that: "Interference with the powers of the States was no constitutional criterion of the power of Congress. If the power was not given, Congress could not exercise it; if given, they might exercise it, although it should interfere with the laws, or even the Constitution of the States."[2] Nevertheless, for approximately a century, from the death of Marshall until 1937, the Tenth Amendment was frequently invoked to curtail powers expressly granted to Congress, notably the powers to regulate interstate commerce, to enforce the Fourteenth Amendment, and to lay and collect taxes.

The first, and logically the strongest, effort to set up the Tenth Amendment as a limitation on Federal power was directed to the expansion of that power by virtue of the necessary and proper clause. In McCulloch v. Maryland,[3] the Attorney General of Maryland cited the charges made by the enemies of the Constitution that it contained ". . . a vast variety of powers, lurking under the generality of its phraseology, which would prove highly dangerous to the liberties of the people, and the rights of the states, . . ."; and he cited the adoption of the Tenth Amendment to allay these apprehensions, in support of his contention that the power to create corporations was reserved by that amendment to the States.[4] Stressing the fact that this amendment, unlike the cognate section of the Articles of Confederation, omitted the word "expressly" as a qualification of the powers granted to the National Government, Chief Justice Marshall declared that its effect was to leave the question "whether the particular power which may become the subject of contest has been delegated to the one government, or prohibited to the other, to depend upon a fair construction of the whole instrument."[5]

The States' Rights Bench which followed Marshall took a different view, and from that time forth for a full century the Court proceeded at discretion on the theory that the amendment withdrew various matters of internal police from the rightful reach of power committed to Congress. This view, which elevated the Court to the position of a quasi-arbitral body standing over and above two competing sovereignties, was initially invoked in behalf of the constitutionality of certain State acts which were alleged to have invaded the national field.[6] Not until after the Civil War was the idea that

[1] United States v. Sprague, 282 U.S. 716, 733 (1931).
[2] II Annals of Congress, col. 1897 (1791).
[3] 4 Wheat. 316 (1819).   [4] Ibid., 372
[5] Ibid., 406.
[6] See especially New York v. Miln, 11 Pet. 102 (1837); License Cases, 5 How. 504, 573-574 (1847).

the reserved powers of the States comprise an independent qualification of otherwise constitutional acts of the Federal Government actually applied to nullify, in part, an act of Congress. This result was first reached in a tax case—Collector v. Day.[7] Holding that a national income tax, in itself valid, could not be constitutionally levied upon the official salaries of State officers, Justice Nelson made the sweeping statement that ". . . The States within the limits of their powers not granted, or, in the language of the Tenth Amendment, 'reserved,' are as independent of the general government as that government within its sphere is independent of the States."[8] In 1939, Collector v. Day was expressly overruled.[9]

Outside the field of taxation, the Court proceeded more hesitantly. A year before Collector v. Day it held invalid, except as applied in the District of Columbia and other areas over which Congress has exclusive authority, a Federal statute penalizing the sale of dangerous illuminating oils.[10] It did not, however, refer to the Tenth Amendment. Instead, it asserted that the ". . . express grant of power to regulate commerce among the States has always been understood as limited by its terms; and as a virtual denial of any power to interfere with the internal trade and business of the separate States; except, indeed, as a necessary and proper means for carrying into execution some other power expressly granted or vested."[11] Similarly, in the Employers' Liability cases, [12] an act of Congress making every carrier engaged in interstate commerce liable to "any" employee, including those whose activities related solely to intrastate activities, for injuries caused by negligence, was held unconstitutional by a closely divided Court, without explicit reliance on the Tenth Amendment. At last, however, in the famous case of Hammer v. Dagenhart,[13] a narrow majority of the Court amended the amendment by inserting the word "expressly" before the word "delegated," and on this basis ruled that an act of Congress which prohibited the transportation of child-made goods in interstate commerce was not a regulation of "commerce among the States" but an invasion of the reserved powers of the States.

Judicial Amendment of the Tenth Amendment

During the twenty years following this decision, a variety of measures designed to regulate economic activities, directly or indirectly, were held void on similar grounds. Excise taxes on the profits of factories in which child labor was employed,[14] on the sale of grain futures on markets which failed to comply with Federal regulations,[15] on the sale of coal produced by non-members of a coal code established as a part of a Federal regulatory scheme,[16] and a

[7] 11 Wall. 113 (1871).   [8] Ibid., 124.
[9] Graves v. O'Keefe, 306 U.S. 466 (1939).
[10] United States v. Dewitt, 9 Wall. 41 (1870).   [11] Ibid., 44.
[12] 207 U.S. 463 (1908). See also Keller v. U.S., 213 U.S. 138 (1909).
[13] 247 U.S. 251 (1918).
[14] Bailey v. Drexel Furniture Co., 259 U.S. 20, 36, 38 (1922).
[15] Hill v. Wallace, 259 U.S. 44 (1922). See also Trusler v. Crooks, 269 U.S. 475 (1926).
[16] Carter v. Carter Coal Co., 298 U.S. 238 (1936).

tax on the processing of agricultural products, the proceeds of which were paid to farmers who complied with production limitations imposed by the Federal Government,[17] were all found to invade the reserved powers of the States. And in Schechter Poultry Corporation *v.* United States[18] the Court, holding that the commerce power did not extend to local sales of poultry brought from without the State, invoked the amendment in support of the proposition that Congress could not regulate local matters which affected interstate commerce only "indirectly." The maintenance of this rule, said Chief Justice Hughes, was essential to the maintenance of the Federal system itself.[19]

On the other hand, both before and after Hammer *v.* Dagenhart, the Court sustained Federal laws penalizing the interstate transportation of lottery tickets,[20] of women for immoral purposes,[21] of stolen automobiles,[22] of tick-infested cattle,[23] of prison-made goods.[24] Thus with some sacrifice of consistency, it still has managed to be always on the side of the angels.

At last, in 1941 the Court came full circle in its exposition of Amendment X. Having returned to the position of John Marshall four years earlier when it sustained the Social Security[25] and National Labor Relations Acts,[26] it explicitly restated Marshall's thesis in upholding the Fair Labor Standards Act in United States *v.* Darby.[27] Speaking for a unanimous Court, Chief Justice Stone wrote: "The power of Congress over interstate commerce 'is complete in itself, may be exercised to its utmost extent, and acknowledges no limitations other than are prescribed in the Constitution.' . . . That power can neither be enlarged nor diminished by the exercise or non-exercise of state power. . . . It is no objection to the assertion of the power to regulate interstate commerce that its exercise is attended by the same incidents which attend the exercise of the police power of the states. . . . Our conclusion is unaffected by the Tenth Amendment which . . . states but a truism that all is retained which has not been surrendered."[28] Hammer *v.* Dagenhart was expressly overruled.[29]

Today it is apparent that the Tenth Amendment does not shield

Triumph of the Supremacy Clause

---

[17] United States *v.* Butler, 297 U.S. 1 (1936).

[18] 295 U.S. 495 (1935).   [19] *Ibid.*, 529.

[20] Champion *v.* Ames, 188 U.S. 321 (1903).

[21] Hoke *v.* U.S., 227 U.S. 308 (1913).

[22] Brooks *v.* U.S., 267 U.S. 432 (1925).

[23] Thornton *v.* U.S. 271 U.S. 414 (1926).

[24] Kentucky Whip & Collar Co. *v.* Illinois C. R. Co., 299 U.S. 334 (1937).

[25] Steward Machine Co. *v.* Davis, 301 U.S. 548 (1937); Helvering *v.* Davis, 301 U.S. 619 (1937).

[26] National Labor Relations Board *v.* Jones & Laughlin Steel Corp., 301 U.S. 1 (1937).

[27] 312 U.S. 100 (1941). *See also* United States *v.* Carolene Products Co., 304 U.S. 144, 147 (1938); Case *v.* Bowles, 327 U.S. 92, 101 (1946).

[28] 312 U.S. 100, 114, 123, 124 (1941). *See also* Fernandez *v.* Wiener, 326 U.S. 340, 362 (1945).

[29] 312 U.S. 100, 116-117.

the States nor their political subdivisions from the impact of any authority affirmatively granted to the Federal Government. It was cited to no avail in Case v. Bowles,[30] where a State officer was forbidden to sell timber on school lands at a price in excess of the maximum prescribed by the Office of Price Administration; and when California violated the Federal Safety Appliance Act in the operation of the State Belt Railroad as a common carrier in interstate commerce, it was held liable for the statutory penalty.[31] Years earlier, indeed, the Sanitary District of Chicago was enjoined, at the suit of the Attorney General of the United States, from diverting water from Lake Michigan in excess of a specified amount. On behalf of a unanimous Court, Justice Holmes wrote: "This is not a controversy among equals. The United States is asserting its sovereign power to regulate commerce and to control the navigable waters within its jurisdiction. . . . There is no question that this power is superior to that of the States to provide for the welfare or necessities of their inhabitants."[32] Similarly, under its superior power of eminent domain, the United States may condemn land owned by a State even where the taking will interfere with the State's own project for water development and conservation.[33] Nor are rights reserved to the States invaded by a statute which requires a reduction in the amount of a Federal grant-in-aid of the construction of highways upon failure of a State to remove from office a member of the State Highway Commission found to have violated Federal law by participating in a political campaign.[34]

In a case involving the question of whether directives of the Federal Pay Board applied to limit the salary increases granted State employees by the Ohio legislature, the Court held that the Tenth Amendment was no bar to the Pay Board's action under authority of the Economic Stabilization Act of 1970. The Court, per Justice Marshall, reasoned that the act was firmly grounded in the commerce clause and that permitting a sizable segment of the economy to operate at variance from the Board's policy would imperil legitimate efforts of the Federal government to address itself to the nation's economic woes. Since the Ohio wage legislation conflicted with the Board's ruling, the supremacy clause dictated that the State was constitutionally obliged to give way.[35] Justice Rehnquist dissented. He chided the majority at one point for its seemingly contradictory remark—at least in the face of its holding—that the Tenth Amendment "is not without significance," and relying by

[30] 327 U.S. 92, 102 (1946).
[31] United States v. Calif., 297 U.S. 175 (1936).
[32] Sanitary District of Chicago v. U.S., 266 U.S. 405, 425, 426 (1925).
[33] Oklahoma v. Atkinson Co., 313 U.S. 508, 534 (1941).
[34] Oklahoma v. U.S. Civil Service Commission, 330 U.S. 127, 142-144 (1947). See also Adams v. Md., 347 U.S. 179 (1954).
[35] Fry v. U.S., 421 U.S. 542 (1975). See also United States v. Calif., 504 F. 2d. 750 (1974) for similar disposition of identical issues by the Temporary Emergency Court of Appeals in a case involving California State employees.

analogy, principally on the Court's past precedents regarding intergovernmental taxing immunities, voted to sustain the State wage legislation.

Perhaps because the result in the foregoing case seemed to be more clearly dictated by the supremacy clause, it is not, however, typical of the tone of the Court's recent decisions concerning federalism. Indeed, the drift of the Burger Court has been very much the other way.[36] More in line with the fondness expressed for "Our Federalism" in Younger *v.* Harris,[37] is the Court's decision in National League of Cities *v.* Usery.[38] Overruling the precedent of Maryland *v.* Wirtz,[39] the Supreme Court struck down the 1974 amendments to the Fair Labor Standards Act. The amendments extended to State and local public employees minimum wage and maximum hour requirements previously available only to employees engaged in interstate commerce. Speaking for the Court, Justice Rehnquist explained: "This Court has never doubted that there are limits upon the power of Congress to override state sovereignty, even when exercising its otherwise plenary powers to tax or to regulate commerce. . . . One undoubted attribute of state sovereignty is the States' power to determine the wages which shall be paid to those whom they employ in order to carry out their governmental functions, what hours those persons will work, and what compensation will be provided where these employees may be called upon to work overtime."[40] The Court concluded that the amendments impeded the States' ability to function effectively and failed to conform to the concept of a *Federal* system. Characterizing the Court's decision as "a patent usurpation of the role reserved for the political process" and "a catastrophic judicial body blow at Congress' power under the Commerce Clause," Justice Brennan dissented in an opinion that articulated doctrines of judicial self-restraint and *stare decisis* at least "in this area." Concluding that "there is an ominous portent of disruption of our constitutional structure implicit in today's mischievous decision," Justice Brennan

---

[36] *See, e.g.*, Wright *v.* Council of City of Emporia, 407 U.S. 451 (1972); San Antonio Indep. School Dist. *v.* Rodriguez, 411 U.S. 1 (1973); Miller *v.* California, 413 U.S. 15 (1973); Storer *v.* Brown, 415 U.S. 724 (1974); Hamling *v.* U.S., 418 U.S. 87 (1974); Gregg *v.* Ga., 428 U.S. 153 (1976). Very recently, in Milliken *v.* Bradley, 97 S.Ct. 2749 (1977) (*Milliken II*), the Court, affirming orders of a Federal district court aimed at remedying *de jure* segregation in Detroit's public schools by mandating joint city-state financing of programs in reading, in-service teacher training, testing, and counseling, found "no merit to petitioners' claims that the relief here ordered violates the Tenth Amendment and general principles of federalism." Said the Court: "The District Court has neither attempted to restructure local governmental entities nor to mandate a particular method or structure of state or local financing. . . . The District Court has, rather, properly enforced the guarantees of the Fourteenth Amendment consistent with our prior holdings, and in a manner that does not jeopardize the integrity of the structure or functions of state and local government." *Ibid.*, 2763.

[37] 401 U.S. 37, 44 (1971).   [38] 426 U.S. 833 (1976).
[39] 392 U.S. 183 (1968).
[40] National League of Cities *v.* Usery, 426 U.S. 833, 842, 845 (1976).

observed: "The only analysis even remotely resembling that adopted today is found in a line of opinions dealing with the Commerce Clause and Tenth Amendment that ultimately provoked a constitutional crisis for the Court in the 1930's."

"United States" means primarily the political branches of the National Government; but the term may be comprehensive enough to include any authority which was created by and which rests upon the Constitution, as for instance, the power of amending it (*see* Article V).

The States in International Law
"States" means the State governments and the people of the States, and sometimes the States territorially. In a case decided by the Supreme Court which raised the question whether the National Government or the coastal States held title to the oil lands underlying coastal submerged lands between low-water mark and the three-mile limit, numerous judicial dicta favored the State claim, but fundamental principle was on the side of the United States, and the Court held with the latter.[41] By International Law, sovereignty, which includes paramount ownership over tidewater lands, is an attribute of nationality, and so far as International Law is concerned the States do not exist.[42]

"The people" means the people of the United States as constituting one sovereign political community; that is, the same people who ordained and established the Constitution (*see* Preamble).

AMENDMENT XI

The judicial power of the United States shall not be construed to extend to any suit in law or equity, commenced or prosecuted against one of the United States by citizens of another State, or by citizens or subjects of any foreign State.

The action of the Supreme Court in accepting jurisdiction of a suit against a State by a citizen of another State in 1793, in Chisholm *v.* Georgia,[1] provoked such angry reactions in Georgia and such anxieties in other States that at the first meeting of Congress after this decision what became the Eleventh Amendment was proposed by an overwhelming vote and ratified with "vehement speed."[2] The protection afforded the States by the amendment against suits for debt extends, however, not only to those instituted "by citizens of another State," or "the citizens or subjects of a foreign State," but

---

[41] United States *v.* Calif., 332 U.S. 19 (1947). The Court held, however, that Congress could, as it did, cede to the States its right to the tidelands oil. *See* pp. 262-263. Alabama *v.* Texas, 347 U.S. 272 (1954).

[42] *See* Holmes *v.* Jennison, 14 Pet. 540, 573-576 (1840); United States *v.* Calif., 332 U.S. 19 (1947). *Cf.* Skiriotes *v.* Fla., 313 U.S. 69, 78-79 (1941).

---

[1] 2 Dall. 419 (1793).
[2] Justice Frankfurter, dissenting in Larson *v.* Domestic and Foreign Corp., 337 U.S. 682, 708 (1949).

also those brought by the State's own citizens, or by a foreign state.[3] But the bar of the Eleventh Amendment to suit in Federal court does not extend to counties and similar municipal corporations.[4]

Otherwise, the amendment has proved comparatively ineffective as a protection of States' Rights against Federal judicial power. For one thing, a suit is not "commenced or prosecuted" against a State by the appeal of a case which was instituted by the State itself against a defendant who claims rights under the Constitution or laws or treaties of the United States[5] (*see* Article III, Section II, ¶1). Nor may an officer of a State who is acting in violation of rights protected by the Constitution or laws or treaties of the United States claim the protection of the amendment, inasmuch as in so acting he loses his official and representative capacity.[6] Indeed, nowadays the amendment does not forbid the Federal courts from enjoining temporarily a State official from undertaking to enforce a State statute alleged to be unconstitutional until it has been determined finally whether the statute is constitutional or not.[7]

On the other hand, suits against the officers of a State involving what is conceded to be State property or suits asking for relief which clearly calls for the exercise of official authority cannot be maintained. Thus, in the leading case of Louisiana v. Jumel,[8] in which a holder of State bonds sought to compel the State treasurer to apply a sinking fund that had been created under an earlier constitution for the payment of the bonds to such purpose after a new constitution had abolished this provision for retiring the bonds, the proceeding was held to be a suit against the State. "The relief asked," said the Court, "will require the officers against whom the process is issued to act contrary to the positive orders of the supreme political power of the State, whose creatures they are, and to which they are ultimately responsible in law for what they do. They must use the public money in the treasury and under their official control in one way, when the supreme power has directed them to use it in another, and they must raise more money by taxation when the same power has declared that it shall be done."[9] But

State Official Immunity

---

[3] Hans v. La., 134 U.S. 1 (1890); Monaco v. Miss., 292 U.S. 313 (1934); Kirker v. Moore, 308 F.Supp. 615 (1970); Knight v. New York, 443 F. 2d. 415 (1971); Parden v. Terminal Railway, 377 U.S. 184 (1964).

[4] County of Lincoln v. Luning, 133 U.S. 529 (1890); Moor v. Cty. of Alameda, 411 U.S. 693 (1973); Mt. Healthy School Dist. v. Doyle, 97 S.Ct. 568 (1977). The State must be a real or nominal defendant. *See also* Jagnandan v. Giles, 538 F. 2d. 1166 (1976).

[5] Cohens v. Va., 6 Wheat. 264, 411-412 (1821).

[6] Osborn v. B'k of U.S., 9 Wheat. 738, 858-859, 868 (1824).

[7] *Ex parte* Young, 209 U.S. 123 (1908). *See also* Home Tel. & Tel. Co. v. Los Angeles, 227 U.S. 278 (1913); Terrace v. Thompson, 263 U.S. 197 (1923); Alabama Com. v. Southern R. Co., 341 U.S. 341 (1951); Georgia R. v. Redwine, 342 U.S. 299, 304-305 (1952); Perez v. Ledesma, 401 U.S. 82, 85, 106-108 (1971).

[8] 107 U.S. 711 (1883). *See also* Christian v. Atlantic & N.C.R. Co., 133 U.S. 233 (1890); Knight v. New York, 443 F. 2d. 415 (1971).

[9] 107 U.S. 711, 721.

mandamus proceedings to compel a State official to perform a "ministerial duty," which admits of no discretion, are held not to be suits against the State since the official is regarded as acting in his individual capacity in failing to act according to law.[10]

The immunity of a State from suit is a privilege which it may waive at pleasure by voluntary submission to suit,[11] as distinguished from appearing in a similar suit to defend its officials,[12] and by general law consenting to suit in the Federal courts. Such consent must be clear and specific and consent to suit in its own courts does not imply a waiver of immunity to suit in the Federal courts.[13] In short, in consenting to be sued, the States, like the National Government, may attach such conditions as they deem fit.[14]

In 1972, the Supreme Court reaffirmed that "an action brought by one State against another violates the Eleventh Amendment if the plaintiff State is actually suing to recover for injuries to designated individuals."[15]

Several recent decisions have explored the bounds of the amendment's general rule "that a suit by private parties seeking to impose a liability which must be paid from public funds in the state treasury is barred by the Eleventh Amendment."[16] For example, in a decision marking another turn in the stream of litigation flowing from the Kent State tragedy, the Supreme Court unanimously held, with regard to damage actions instituted under the Civil Rights Act and which named as a defendant former Ohio Governor James Rhodes, that, where a State official acts under color of State law to deprive individuals of federally protected constitutional rights, the Eleventh Amendment does not clothe him with immunity, though assessment of his *personal* liability will vary according to the scope of responsibilities and discretion attached to

[10] Board of Liquidation v. McComb, 92 U.S. 531, 541 (1876). This was a case involving an injunction, but Justice Bradley regarded mandamus and injunction as correlative to each other in cases where the official unlawfully commits or omits an act. *See also* Rolston v. Missouri Fund Commissioners, 120 U.S 390, 411 (1887), where it is held that an injunction would lie to restrain the sale of a railroad on the ground that a suit to compel a State official to do what the law requires of him is not a suit against the State.

[11] Clark v. Barnard, 108 U.S. 436, 447 (1883); Ashton v. Cameron County Water Improvement Dist., 298 U.S. 513, 531 (1936); Knight v. New York, 443 F. 2d. 415 (1971). *But see* P.T. & L. Const. Co. v. Commissioner, 288 A. 2d. 574 (1972).

[12] Farish v. State Banking Board, 235 U.S. 498 (1915); Missouri v. Fiske, 290 U.S. 18 (1933); Ford Co. v. Dept. of Treasury, 323 U.S. 459, 470 (1945).

[13] Murray v. Wilson Distilling Co., 213 U.S. 151, 172 (1909); citing Smith v. Reeves, 178 U.S. 436 (1900); Great Northern Life Ins. Co. v. Read, 322 U.S. 47 (1944); Kennecott Copper Corp. v. St. Tax Comm., 327 U.S. 573 (1946).

[14] The California Supreme Court has engendered skepticism about the concept of the doctrine of governmental immunity. *See* the brief description of the Court's and the legislature's actions in recent years in Nestle v. City of Santa Monica, 101 Cal.Rptr. 568, 575-578 (1972). *See also* Justice Traynor's brilliant and seminal opinion in Muskopf v. Corning Hospital District, 359 P. 2d. 457 (1961).

[15] Hawaii v. Standard Oil Co. of California, 405 U.S. 251, 258 note 12 (1972).

[16] Edelman v. Jordan, 415 U.S. 651, 663 (1974).

his office and the particular facts of the situation.[17] However, in a second case, the Supreme Court ruled that the Eleventh Amendment relieved Illinois from any legal obligation to honor claimants' demands for retroactive payments out of State funds where State welfare officials had withheld benefits to qualified recipients under a Federal-State program of Aid to the Aged, Blind, and Disabled in violation of both Federal statutes and the Fourteenth Amendment.[18] To be sure, it is possible that Congress may, as a condition for participation in a Federal program or in other areas legitimately the subject of its regulatory power, require the States to waive their sovereign immunity. But, said the Court: "Constructive consent is not a doctrine commonly associated with the surrender of constitutional rights, and we see no place for it here. In deciding whether a state has waived its constitutional protection under the Eleventh Amendment, we will find waiver only where stated 'by the most express language or by such overwhelming implications from the text as [will] leave no room for any other reasonable construction.' . . . The mere fact that a State participates in a program through which the Federal Government provides assistance for the operation by the State of a system of public aid is not sufficient to establish consent on the part of the State to be sued in the federal courts."[19] The Court also took care to distinguish a Federal court decree "which requires payment of state funds . . . as a necessary consequence of compliance in the future" with a substantive determination that the state has infringed federally protected rights of the plaintiffs from one that imposes a "retroactive award of monetary relief as a form of 'equitable restitution' since the latter 'is in practical effect indistinguishable in many aspects from an award of damages against the State.' "[20] Three years later, the Court found this distinction useful in sustaining a decree handed down by a district court acting to eradicate *de jure* segregation. That court ordered the city *and State* jointly to finance programs in reading, in-service teacher training, testing, and counseling. Said the Court:

[17] Scheuer v. Rhodes, 416 U.S. 232 (1974). *See also* Wood v. Strickland, 420 U.S. 308 (1975).

[18] Edelman v. Jordan, 415 U.S. 651 (1974).

[19] *Ibid.*, 673. In a case involving a suit against Missouri by State employees for overtime compensation under the Fair Labor Standards Act, the Supreme Court was unprepared to find that Congress had intended to take away the constitutional immunity of States. The Court did make clear, however, that Congress could do so in the exercise of its power under the commerce clause. *See* Employees of Dept. of Public Health & Welfare v. Mo., 411 U.S. 279 (1973).

[20] *Ibid.*, 668. In *Edelman*, the Court took particular aim at Shapiro v. Thompson, 394 U.S. 618 (1969), which along with three other cases involving summary affirmances, required State directors of public aid to make retroactive payments to several welfare recipients who had been unconstitutionally deprived of welfare eligibility by State residency requirements. Said the Court, noting that the Eleventh Amendment issue had not really been dealt with in those cases, "[W]e disapprove the Eleventh Amendment holdings of those cases to the extent that they are inconsistent with our holding today." *Ibid.*, 671.

"The educational components, which the District Court ordered into effect *prospectively*, are plainly designed to wipe out continuing conditions of inequality produced by the inherently unequal dual school system long maintained by Detroit. . . . That the programs are also 'compensatory' in nature does not change the fact that they are part of a plan that operates *prospectively* to bring about the delayed benefits of a unitary school system."[21]

Finally, addressing another exception to the immunity of the States under the Eleventh Amendment, the Court examined what limitation might be specially posed by Congressional legislation passed pursuant to Section V of the Fourteenth Amendment, which empowers Congress to "enforce, by appropriate legislation, the provisions of this article." The Supreme Court held that the Eleventh Amendment did not bar collection of back pay or attorneys' fees by certain State employees discriminated against on the basis of sex by the State of Connecticut. The plaintiffs brought suit under Title VII of the Civil Rights Act of 1964, predicated on Congress's power under §5 of the Fourteenth Amendment. Speaking for the Court, Justice Rehnquist declared: "When Congress acts pursuant to §5, not only is it exercising legislative authority that is plenary within the terms of the constitutional grant, it is exercising that authority under one section of a constitutional Amendment whose other sections by their own terms embody limitations on state authority. We think that Congress may, in determining what is 'appropriate legislation' for the purpose of enforcing the provisions of the Fourteenth Amendment, provide for private suits against States or state officials which are constitutionally impermissible in other contexts."[22]

AMENDMENT XII

The "College of Electors" So-called

¶1. The electors shall meet in their respective States and vote by ballot for President and Vice-President, one of whom, at least, shall not be an inhabitant of the same State with themselves; they shall name in their ballots the person voted for as President, and in distinct ballots the person voted for as Vice-

---

[21] Milliken *v.* Bradley, 97 S.Ct. 2749, 2762 (1977) (*Milliken II*). This case is not to be confused with the Court's decision in *Milliken I*, Milliken *v.* Bradley, 418 U.S. 717 (1974), in which the Court took up the district court's decree aimed at effecting racial balance throughout the schools of the Detroit metropolitan area. *Milliken II* was the controversy that developed on remand over the remedy to be fashioned focusing only on Detroit's public schools.

[22] Fitzpatrick *v.* Bitzer, 427 U.S. 445, 456 (1976). The Court noted that "none of these previous cases presented the question of the relationship between the Eleventh Amendment and the enforcement power granted to Congress under § 5 of the Fourteenth Amendment." *Ibid.* This point is critical in view of the fact both that the outcome here is the opposite of *Edelman* and the Court's acknowledgment that "the suit for retroactive benefits by the petitioners is in fact indistinguishable from that sought to be maintained in *Edelman*, since what is sought here is a damage award payable to a private party from the state treasury." *Ibid.*, 452.

President, and they shall make distinct lists of all persons voted for as President and of all persons voted for as Vice-President, and of the number of votes for each; which lists they shall sign and certify, and transmit sealed to the seat of the government of the United States, directed to the President of the Senate. The President of the Senate shall, in the presence of the Senate and House of Representatives, open all the certificates and the votes shall then be counted. The person having the greatest number of votes for President shall be the President, if such number be a majority of the whole number of electors appointed; and if no person have such majority, then from the persons having the highest numbers not exceeding three on the list of those voted for as President, the House of Representatives shall choose immediately, by ballot, the President. But in choosing the President the votes shall be taken by States, the representation from each State having one vote; a quorum for this purpose shall consist of a member or members from two-thirds of the States, and a majority of all the States shall be necessary to a choice. And if the House of Representatives shall not choose a President whenever the right of choice shall devolve upon them, before the fourth day of March next following, then the Vice-President shall act as President as in the case of the death or other constitutional disability of the President.

¶2. The person having the greatest number of votes as Vice-President shall be the Vice-President, if such number be a majority of the whole number of electors appointed; and if no person have a majority, then from the two highest numbers on the list the Senate shall choose the Vice-President; a quorum for the purpose shall consist of two-thirds of the whole number of Senators, and a majority of the whole number shall be necessary to a choice. But no person constitutionally ineligible to the office of President shall be eligible to that of Vice-President of the United States.

This amendment, which supersedes ¶3 of Section I of Article II of the original Constitution, was inserted on account of the tie between Jefferson and Burr in the election of 1800. The difference between the procedure which it defines and that which was laid down in the original Constitution is in the provision it makes for a separate designation by the Electors of their choices for President and Vice-President, respectively. The final sentence of ¶1, above, has been in turn superseded today by Amendments XX and XXV.

In consequence of the disputed election of 1876, Congress, by an act passed in 1887, has laid down the rule that if the vote of a State is not certified by the governor under the seal thereof, it shall not be "counted" unless both houses of Congress are favorable.[1]

[1] 3 U.S.C. 17.

It was early supposed that the House of Representatives would be often called upon to choose a President, but the political division of the country into two great parties has hitherto always prevented this, except in 1800 and 1824. Should, however, a strong third party appear, the election might be frequently thrown into Congress, with the result, since the vote would be by States, of enabling a small fraction of the population of the country to choose the President from the three candidates receiving the highest electoral vote. The situation obviously calls for a constitutional amendment.

It should be noted that no provision is made by this amendment for the situation which would result from a failure to choose either a President or Vice-President, an inadequacy which Amendment XX undertakes to cure.

Original Expecta- tions

"The mode of appointment of the Chief Magistrate of the United States," Hamilton wrote in *Federalist* No. 68, "is almost the only part of the system of any consequence, which has escaped without severe censure, or which has received the slightest mark of approbation from its opponents." Hamilton himself did not "hesitate . . . to affirm that if the manner of it be not perfect, it is at least excellent," being designed to guarantee that the choice of President should be by "a small number of persons" eminently fit to make a wise selection and to avoid "cabal, intrigue, and corruption." Actually, the so-called "College of Electors"—a college which never meets—had come by the time that Amendment XII became a part of the Constitution, to consist of party marionettes who have never exercised the least individual freedom of choice in circumstances that made their doing so a matter of the least importance in the world. Indeed, in 1872 the Democratic Electors from three States automatically cast their votes for the party candidate, Horace Greeley, on the very day he was carried to his grave.

The Actuality

In Ray *v.* Blair,[2] decided April 15, 1952, the Court had occasion to comment on the theory of the constitutional independence of the Elector, which it did in these words: "History teaches that the Electors were expected to support the party nominees. Experts in the history of government recognize the long-standing practice. Indeed, more than twenty States do not print the names of the candidates for Electors on the general election ballot." In view of such facts, the Court declined to rule that it was "unconstitutional" for one seeking nomination as an Elector in a party primary to announce his choice for President beforehand, thereby pledging himself. Justice Jackson's dissent in this case was particularly noteworthy: "No one faithful to our history can deny that the plan originally contemplated, what is implicit in its text, that electors would be free agents to exercise an independent and nonpartisan judgment as to the men best qualified for the Nation's highest offices. Certainly under that plan no state law could control the elector in perform-

[2] 343 U.S. 214, 218-219, 228-231 (1962). *See* Penton *v.* Humphrey, 264 F.Supp. 250, 252 note 1 (1967).

ance of his federal duty, any more than it could a United States Senator who also is chosen by, and represents, the State.

"This arrangment miscarried. Electors, although often personally eminent, independent, and respectable, officially became voluntary party lackeys and intellectual nonentities to whose memory we might justly paraphrase a tuneful satire:

They always voted at their Party's call
And never thought of thinking for themselves at all.

As an institution the Electoral College suffered atrophy almost indistinguishable from *rigor mortis* . . . if custom were sufficient authority for amendment of the Constitution by Court decree, the decision in this matter would be warranted. Usage may sometimes impart changed content to constitutional generalities, such as 'due process of law,' 'equal protection' or 'commerce among the states.' But I do not think powers or discretions granted to federal officials by the Federal Constitution can be forfeited by the Court for disuse. A political practice which has its origin in custom must rely upon custom for its sanctions."[3] (*See also* the discussion on p. 547.)

The impact of the "faithless elector" has been slight. There have been only eight in American history, though one has surfaced in each of the last three Presidential elections.[4]

AMENDMENT XIII

SECTION I

Neither slavery nor involuntary servitude, except as a punishment
  for crime whereof the party shall have been duly convicted, shall
  exist within the United States, or any place subject to their jurisdiction.

The historical importance of this amendment consists in the fact that it completed the abolition of African slavery in the United States, but that has not been its sole importance. The amendment is not, in the words of the Court, "a declaration in favor of a particular people. It reaches every race and every individual, and if in any respect it commits one race to the Nation, it commits every race and

---

[3] *Ibid.*, 233-234. *See also* Irish *v.* DFL Party of Minnesota, 287 F.Supp. 794 (1968). The Supreme Court's reluctance to permit the courts to interject themselves in the business of the political parties was further manifest in its decision with respect to the challenge to delegate seating at the Democratic National Convention in 1972. *See* O'Brien *v.* Brown, 409 U.S. 1 (1972), *and especially* Cousins *v.* Wigoda, 419 U.S. 477 (1975). *See* p. 338 *supra*.

[4] An independent elector cast a ballot also in the elections of 1796, 1820, 1948, 1956, and 1960. In the modern era, these have invariably been conservatives who bolted their party's choice to register a symbolic protest against the liberalism of one of the two major parties. Since 1960, all of these independent electors were elected on a Republican slate. *Congressional Quarterly Guide to U.S. Elections* (Washington, 1975), p. 207; and 1977 *Cong. Quart. Weekly Report*, 38.

every individual thereof. Slavery or involuntary servitude of the Chinese, of the Italian, of the Anglo-Saxon are as much within its compass as slavery or involuntary servitude of the African."[1]

Peonage Outlawed Moreover, "the words 'involuntary servitude' have for a long time had larger meaning than slavery."[2] Especially does this phrase ban peonage, "the essence of which is compulsory service in the payment of a debt."[3] Consequently, an Alabama statute which imposed a criminal liability and subjected to imprisonment farm laborers who abandoned their employment to enter into similar employment with other persons, was held to violate Amendment XIII, as well as national legislation forbidding peonage.[4] So it was held in 1905; and six years later the Court overturned another Alabama statute which made the refusal "without just cause" to perform the labor called for in a written contract or to refund the money advanced therefore, *prima facie* evidence of an intent to defraud and punishable as a criminal offense.[5] Subsequently other statutes of like tendency, emanating from Southern legislatures, have similarly succumbed to the Court's conception of "involuntary servitude."[6]

Interestingly enough the reserve system in baseball, which requires a player to play with a certain team or not play at all has not yet been regarded by the courts as "involuntary servitude."[7] As one Federal Court reasoned:

"A showing of compulsion is thus prerequisite to proof of involuntary servitude. Concededly, plaintiff is not compelled by law or statute to play baseball for Philadelphia. We recognize that, under the existing rules of baseball, by refusing to report to Philadelphia plaintiff is by his own act foreclosing himself from continuing a professional baseball career, a consequence to be deplored. Nevertheless, he has the right to retire and to embark upon a different enterprise outside organized baseball. The financial loss he might thus sustain may affect his choice, but does not leave him with 'no way to avoid continued service. . . .' "[8]

The Court for a time rejected what it regarded as over-extended conceptions of "involuntary servitude." Thus, the denial of admission to public places such as inns, restaurants, and theaters, or the segregation of races in public conveyances did not fall under the

---

[1] Hodges *v.* U.S., 203 U.S. 1, 16-17 (1906); Bailey *v.* Ala., 219 U.S. 219, 240-241 (1911).

[2] Slaughter House Cases, 16 Wall. 36, 69 (1873).

[3] Bailey *v.* Ala., 219 U.S. 219, 242 (1911).

[4] Clyatt *v.* U.S., 197 U.S. 207 (1905); Act of March 2, 1867, 14 *Stat.* 546.

[5] Bailey *v.* Ala., *supra.*

[6] United States *v.* Reynolds, 235 U.S. 133 (1914); Taylor *v.* Ga., 315 U.S. 25 (1942); Pollock *v.* Williams, 322 U.S. 4 (1944).

[7] Flood *v.* Kuhn, 316 F.Supp. 271, 281 (1970); *affirmed*, 443 F. 2d. 264 (1971). In its review of the case, the Supreme Court did not speak to the contention that the reserve clause resulted in involuntary servitude. Flood *v.* Kuhn, 407 U.S. 258 (1972).

[8] 316 F.Supp. 271, 281 (1970).

condemnation of Amendment XIII for many years.[9] However, in 1968 in upholding the provisions of the Civil Rights Act of 1968 to prohibit all racial discrimination, private and public, in the sale and rental of property, the Court broadened the scope of the Thirteenth Amendment by holding:

"Negro citizens, North and South, who saw in the Thirteenth Amendment a promise of freedom—freedom to 'go and come at pleasure' and to 'buy and sell when they please'—would be left with 'a mere paper guarantee' if Congress were powerless to assure that a dollar in the hands of a Negro will purchase the same thing as a dollar in the hands of a white man. At the very least, the freedom that Congress is empowered to secure under the Thirteenth Amendment includes the freedom to buy whatever a white man can buy, the right to live wherever a white man can live. If Congress cannot say that being a free man means at least this much, then the Thirteenth Amendment made a promise the Nation cannot keep."[10]

Eight years later, the Court turned its attention to the portion of the Civil Rights Act of 1866 that provides that "[a]ll persons within the jurisdiction of the United States shall have the same right in every State . . . to make and enforce contracts . . . as is enjoyed by white citizens."[11] In the spirit of its 1968 ruling, the Court held that, in prohibiting racial discrimination in the making and enforcement of private contracts, the statute therefore prohibited "private, commercially operated, nonsectarian schools from denying admission to prospective students because they are Negroes."[12]

[9] Civil Rights Cases, 109 U.S. 3 (1883); Plessy v. Ferguson, 163 U.S. 537 (1896).

[10] Jones v. Mayer Co., 392 U.S. 409, 443 (1968); Griffin v. Breckenridge, 403 U.S. 88, 104-107 (1971); cf. Palmer v. Thompson, 403 U.S. 217, 226-227 (1971). Also grounded on the Thirteenth Amendment was a Federal appeals court decision that significantly strengthened governmental efforts to ward off the phenomenon of panic selling by white home-owners which stems from the circulation of racial rumors by unscrupulous realtors who subsequently turn handsome profits when neighborhood properties are sold to incoming blacks. The U.S. Court of Appeals, Fifth Circuit, unanimously sustained the constitutionality of that provision of the Fair Housing Act of 1968, 42 U.S.C. 3604(e), which prohibited this practice of "blockbusting." See United States v. Bob Lawrence Realty, Inc., 474 F. 2d. 115 (1973). However, a recent Supreme Court decision has declared unconstitutional municipal ordinances attempting to arrest white flight from mixed neighborhoods by banning the display of "for sale" signs. Linmark Associates, Inc. v. Township of Willingboro, 97 S.Ct. 1614 (1977).

[11] 42 U.SC. § 1981.

[12] Runyon v. McCrary, 427 U.S. 160 (1976). Justice White, joined by Justice Rehnquist, in dissent argued that the legislative history of the 1866 law "confirms that the statute means what it says and no more, i.e., that it outlaws any legal rule disabling any person from making or enforcing a contract, but does not prohibit private racially motivated refusals to contract." While Justices Powell and Stevens agreed on the merits with the dissenters, they concurred with the Court's majority because that argument, said Powell, "comes too late." Though Stevens thought *Jones* and its progeny constituted "a line of authority which I firmly believe to have been incorrectly decided," he followed it, because, as he explained: "The policy of the Nation as formulated by the Congress in recent years has moved constantly in the

The Court found this reading of the statute reinforced by Congress's rejection, in enacting the Equal Employment Opportunity Act of 1972, of an amendment that would have overturned the interpretation in *Jones* "insofar as it affords private sector employees a right of action based on racial discrimination in employment." Said the Court: "There could hardly be a clearer indication of congressional agreement with the view that §1981 *does* reach private acts of discrimination." In a related case, two white employees of a transportation company brought suit under Title VII of the 1964 Civil Rights Act and under §1981 when they were fired for misappropriating cargo while a black employee, charged with the same offense was not. The Court held that the legislative history of both statutes made it clear that the ban on racial discrimination in private employment and the guarantee of contractual equality protected whites as well as non-whites.[13]

Federal courts have continued to hold that use of persons civilly committed to mental institutions for productive labor violates the constitutional prohibition on involuntary servitude where such labor programs are nontherapeutic or excessive.[14] For example, the U.S. District Court for the Eastern District of Wisconsin recently denied a motion to dismiss a complaint lodged by two mentally handicapped persons who performed productive labor in custodial treatment facilities without receiving compensation. Regarding plaintiffs' statement of a cause of action under the Thirteenth Amendment, Chief Judge John Reynolds pointed out: "Plaintiffs who wish to allege a cause of action under the thirteenth amendment must confront two substantial hurdles. First, they must allege (and ultimately prove on the merits) that their labors were performed involuntarily . . . that as a result of their mental condition they were coerced into performing designated tasks. . . . Secondly, . . . plaintiffs must allege that the work they performed was not therapeutic."[15]

Things Not Outlawed   Contracts for certain services which have from time immemorial been treated as exceptional, although involving to a certain extent the surrender of personal liberty[16] still do not fall under the condemnation of the Thirteenth Amendment; nor does "enforcement of those duties which individuals owe the State, such as service in the army, militia, on the jury, etc."[17] (But *see* pp. 111-112 for discus-

---

direction of eliminating racial segregation in all sectors of society. This Court has given a sympathetic and liberal construction to such legislation. For the Court now to overrule *Jones* would be a significant step backwards, with effects that would not have arisen from a correct decision in the first instance. Such a step would be so clearly contrary to my understanding of the *mores* of today that I think the Court is entirely correct in adhering to *Jones*."

[13] McDonald *v.* Santa Fe Trail Transp. Co., 427 U.S. 273 (1976).

[14] King *v.* Carey, 405 F.Supp. 41 (1975); Carey *v.* White, 407 F.Supp 121 (1976).

[15] Weidenfeller *v.* Kidulis, 380 F.Supp. 445, 450-451 (1974).

[16] Robertson *v.* Baldwin, 165 U.S. 275, 282 (1897).

[17] Butler *v.* Perry, 240 U.S. 328, 333 (1916); Draper *v.* Rhay, 315 F. 2d. 193, 197 (1963), *cert. denied*, 375 U.S. 915 (1963).

sion of forced military service.) Hence, "a State has inherent power to require every able-bodied man within its jurisdiction to labor for a reasonable time on public roads near his residence without compensation."[18] Nor was Mr. James C. Petrillo subjected to "involuntary servitude" when he was forbidden under the Federal Communications Act "to coerce, compel, or constrain" licensees under the act to employ unneeded persons in the conduct of their broadcasting activities.[19] And a State court recently held that a State separate maintenance statute which denied the husband "the advantages of marriage or the privileges of divorce" did not violate Amendment XIII.[20] Recently, the Supreme Court found "no substance" to the argument that paying people, held as material witnesses, $1 per day was imposing involuntary servitude on them.[21] And a Federal district court has ruled that State board of education regulations requiring that public school students be subjected to cafeteria duty neither contravened the Thirteenth Amendment nor entitled students to receive the minimum wage.[22]

SECTION II

Congress shall have power to enforce this article by appropriate
   legislation.

It should be noted that this amendment, in contrast to the opening section of the Fourteenth Amendment, just below, lays down a rule of action for private persons no less than for the States. In other words, it is legislative in character, as was the Eighteenth Amendment; and accordingly, in enforcing it, Congress may enact penalties for the violation of its provisions by private persons and corporations without paying any attention to State laws on the same subject.[1]

As the Court said in 1968: "Thus, the fact that the Congressional statute operates upon the unofficial acts of private individuals,

---

Wilson *v.* Kelley, 294 F.Supp. 1005, 1012 (1968). *See also* Arver *v.* U.S. (Selective Draft Cases), 245 U.S. 366, 390 (1918). "Work or fight" laws, such as States enacted during World War I, which required male residents to be employed during the period of that war were sustained on similar grounds, as were municipal ordinances, enforced during the Depression, which compelled indigents physically able to perform manual labor to serve the municipality without compensation as a condition of receiving financial assistance. State *v.* McClure, 7 Boyce (Del.) 265 (1919); Commonwealth *v.* Pauliot, 292 Mass. 229 (1935). For a recent case involving a conscientious objector *see* U.S. *v.* O'Brien, 391 U.S. 367, 377 (1968).

[18] Butler *v.* Perry, 240 U.S. 328 (1916).

[19] United States *v.* Petrillo, 332 U.S. 1 (1947); Act of June 19, 1934, as amended April 16, 1946; 47 U.S.C. 506; *see also* Trustees of Cal. St. Colleges *v.* Local 1352, 92 Cal. Rptr. 134 (1970); Jefferson County Teachers *v.* Bd. of Ed., 463 S.W. 2d. 627 (1971).

[20] Reese *v.* Reese, 278 N.E. 2d. 122 (1971).

[21] Hurtado *v.* U.S., 410 U.S. 578 (1973).

[22] Bobilin *v.* Bd. of Educ., 403 F.Supp. 1095 (1975).

[1] Clyatt *v.* U.S., 197 U.S. 207 (1905).

whether or not sanctioned by state law, presents no constitutional problem. If Congress has power under the Thirteenth Amendment to eradicate conditions that prevent Negroes from buying and renting property because of their race or color, then no federal statute calculated to achieve that objective can be thought to exceed the constitutional power of Congress simply because it reaches beyond state action to regulate the conduct of private individuals. The constitutional question in this case, therefore, comes to this: Does the authority of Congress to enforce the Thirteenth Amendment 'by appropriate legislation' include the power to eliminate all racial barriers to the acquisition of real and personal property? We think the answer to that question is plainly yes."[2]

AMENDMENT XIV
SECTION I

"The Great Fourteenth Amendment"

All persons born or naturalized in the United States, and subject to the jurisdiction thereof, are citizens of the United States and of the State wherein they reside. No State shall make or enforce any law which shall abridge the privileges or immunities of citizens of the United States; nor shall any State deprive any person of life, liberty or property, without due process of law; nor deny to any person within its jurisdiction the equal protection of the laws.

The opening clause of this section makes national citizenship primary and State citizenship derivative therefrom. The definition it lays down of citizenship "at birth" is not, however, exhaustive, as was pointed out in connection with Congress's power to "establish an uniform rule of naturalization."

"Subject to the jurisdiction thereof": The children born to foreign diplomats in the United States are not subject to the jurisdiction of the United States, and so are not citizens of the United States. With this narrow exception all persons born in the United States are, by the principle of the Wong Kim Ark case, entitled to claim citizenship of the United States.[1]

Judicial Repeal of the "Privileges and Immunities" Clause

"The privileges or immunities of citizens of the United States" were held in the famous Slaughter House cases, decided soon after the Fourteenth Amendment was added to the Constitution, to comprise only those privileges and immunities which the Constitution, the laws, and the treaties of the United States confer, such as the right to engage in interstate and foreign commerce, the right to appeal in proper cases to the national courts, the right to protection abroad, etc.; but not "the fundamental rights," which were said still to adhere exclusively to State citizenship.[2]

---

[2] Jones v. Mayer Co., 392 U.S. 409, 438-439 (1968); Griffin v. Breckenridge, 403 U.S. 88, 104-107 (1971); cf. Palmer v. Thompson, 403 U.S. 217, 226-227 (1971).

[1] 169 U.S. 649 (1898).

[2] 16 Wall. 36, 71, 77-79 (1873). See also Twining v. N.J., 211 U.S. 78, 97 (1908).

Following this line of reasoning, which renders the clause tautological, the Court ruled in 1920, in United States *v.* Wheeler,[3] that the right to reside quietly within the State of one's domicile is not a right which the National Government may protect against local mobs—plainly a most anomalous result. In Hague *v.* Committee for Industrial Organization,[4] however, in which a Jersey City ordinance requiring a permit for any assembly in the streets, parks, or public buildings of the city was held void, two of the Justices based their opinion on this clause. The "privilege and immunity" which they found to be infringed was the right of workingmen who are at the same time citizens of the United States to assemble for the purpose of discussing their newly acquired rights under the National Labor Relations Act; and in Edwards *v.* California four Justices agreed in 1941 that a State enactment which sought to exclude from the State indigent persons from the rest of the Union was, as to citizens of the United States, an abridgment of their privileges and immunities as such.[5] As a matter of history, there can be little question that it was the intention of the Framers of the clause to transmute all the ordinary rights of citizenship in a free government into rights of national citizenship, and thereby in effect to transfer their regulation and protection to the National Government.[6] (For further discussion of "privileges and immunities," *see* pp. 255-259.)

"Nor shall any State deprive any person of life, liberty, or property without due process of law": By "State" is meant not only all agencies of State government but those of local government as well[7] when acting under color of official authority, even though in a manner that is contrary to State law.[8] Within the meaning of the Fourteenth Amendment, the District of Columbia is not a "State," consequently "neither the District nor its officers are subject to its restrictions."[9] (While the Fourteenth Amendment has no effect *per se*, the District and its officers do, of course, come within the purview of the Fifth Amendment and the due process clause, which is a part of it. Through the Court's frequent equation of a denial of equal protection with a denial of due process, in addition to the normal, straightforward operation of that clause, most of what limits State action under the Fourteenth Amendment also limits the District under the Fifth. *See* p. 390.) More will be said about what constitutes "State action" below, pp. 518-521.

Due Process Clause

[3] 254 U.S. 281 (1920).
[4] 307 U.S. 496 (1939); *cf.* Davis *v.* Mass., 167 U.S. 43 (1897).
[5] 314 U.S. 160 (1941), where the decision overturning the State statute was based by a majority of the Court on the commerce clause. For a temporary flare-up of the "privileges and immunities" clause of Amendment XIV which was soon quenched, *cf.* Colgate *v.* Harvey, 296 U.S. 404 (1935); and Madden *v.* Ky., 309 U.S. 83 (1940).
[6] Horace Flack, *The Adoption of the Fourteenth Amendment* (Baltimore, 1908), *passim*.
[7] *Ex parte* Virginia, 100 U.S. 339 (1879); Yick Wo *v.* Hopkins, 118 U.S. 356 (1886). *See also* Trenton *v.* N.J., 262 U.S. 182 (1923).
[8] United States *v.* Classic, 313 U.S. 299 (1941); Screws *v.* U.S., 325 U.S. 91 (1945). *Cf.* Barney *v.* City of N.Y., 193 U.S. 430 (1904).
[9] District of Columbia *v.* Carter, 409 U.S. 418 (1973).

Included within the meaning of "person" are corporations[10] (see p. 516, aliens,[11] and illegitimate children.[12] However, after lengthy discussion that included a canvass of the use of the word "person" in the text of the Constitution, the Court concluded that a fetus is not a person.[13] Said the Court, "[T]he unborn have never been recognized in the law as persons in the whole sense."[14]

Effect of Amendment XIV on State Criminal Law

While, in a general way, this clause imposes on the powers of the State the same kinds of limitations that the corresponding clause of Amendment V does on the powers of the National Government, there have been conspicuous differences historically which will be spelled out below.

Application of Substantive Due Process

The earlier discussion of substantive due process under the Fifth Amendment (pp. 387-390) should be read as a backdrop to the present discussion. The concept that due process required legislatures to exercise their powers "reasonably," historically had much greater impact on State legislation than on Congressional enactments. For, as pointed out earlier, the State "police power" is not so circumscribed as the power of the National Government. The "police power" is the power of the State "to promote the public health, safety, morals, and general welfare"; or, as it has been more simply and comprehensively described, "the power to govern men and things."[15]

Judicial Supervision of the "Police Power" under Amendment XIV

Under the 1900-1937 interpretation of "liberty," "property," and "due process of law," this power was confronted at every turn by the Court's power of judicial review. Some statistics are pertinent in this connection. During the first ten years of the Fourteenth Amendment, hardly a dozen cases came before the Court under all of its clauses put together. During the next twenty years, when the *laissez-faire* conception of governmental functions was being translated by the Bar into the phraseology of Constitutional Law, and gradually embodied in the decisions of the Court, more than two hundred cases arose, most of them under the due process of law

---

[10] Santa Clara Cty. *v.* Southern Pacific R.R. Co., 118 U.S. 394 (1886).

[11] Yick Wo *v.* Hopkins, 118 U.S. 356 (1886).

[12] Levy *v.* La., 391 U.S. 68, 70 (1968).

[13] Roe *v.* Wade, 410 U.S. 113, 158 (1973).

[14] *Ibid.*, 162. Courts have been pressed increasingly for rulings as to when damage to or death of a fetus results in civil or criminal liability. Consistent with the Supreme Court's recent rulings, e.g., Planned Parenthood of Central Mo. *v.* Danforth, 428 U.S. 52, 63 (1976), they have fastened upon the point at which the fetus becomes "viable." *See* Mone *v.* Greyhound Lines, Inc., 331 N.E. 2d. 916 (1975); State *v.* Anderson, 343 A. 2d. 505 (1975); *see also Los Angeles Times*, July 1, 1976. *See also* Kilmer *v.* Hicks, 529 P. 2d. 706 (1974). *And* the Illinois Supreme Court has ruled, by a bare majority, that a child can sue for injuries suffered because of negligent acts against the mother before the child was conceived; *see San Diego Union*, Aug. 9, 1977.

[15] License Cases, 5 How. 504, 583 (1847). *See also* Charles River Bridge Co. *v.* Warren Bridge, 11 Pet. 420, 547-548 (1837); the Slaughter House cases, cited above in note 2; Barbier *v.* Connelly, 113 U.S. 27 (1885), and scores of other cases.

clause. During the ensuing twelve years this number was more than doubled—a ratio which still holds substantially.[16]

During this later period, moreover, an increasing rigor was to be discerned in the Court's standards, especially where legislation on social and economic questions was concerned. Prior to 1912 the Court had decided 98 cases involving this kind of legislation. "In only six of these did the Court hold the legislation unconstitutional. From 1913 to 1920 the Court decided 27 cases of this type and held seven laws invalid"; while between 1920 and 1930, out of 53 cases, the Court held against the legislation involved in fifteen.[17]

The same result appears from another angle when we compare an early case in this field of judicial review with a later one. In Powell v. Pennsylvania,[18] decided in 1888, the Court sustained an act prohibiting the manufacture and sale of oleomargarine, taking the ground that it could not say, "from anything of which it may take judicial cognizance," that oleomargarine was not injurious to the health, and that this being the case the legislative determination of facts was conclusive. Thirty-six years later we find the Court setting aside a Nebraska statute requiring that bread be sold in pound and half-pound loaves, on its own independent finding that the allowance made by the statute for shrinkage of the loaves was too small. Entering upon an elaborate discussion of the entire process of bread-making the Court pronounced the act "unnecessary" for the protection of buyers against fraud, and "essentially unreasonable and arbitrary."[19] In short, the case furnishes a perfect example of what was above characterized as "broad review," and that in a connection with a case which had no apparent wide-reaching implications of any sort.

Commenting upon this general development, Professor Kales once suggested that attorneys arguing "due process cases" before the Court ought to address the justices not as "Your Honors," but as "Your Lordships."[20] Similarly Senator Borah, in the Senate debate on Mr. Hughes's nomination for Chief Justice, declared that the Supreme Court had become, under the Fourteenth Amendment, "economic dictator in the United States,"[21] and in the Bread case, just mentioned, Justice Brandeis, dissenting, characterized the Court as "a superlegislature," while similar views were expressed by Justice Holmes shortly before his retirement from the Court.

The Supreme Court as "a Super-legislature"

[16] Charles W. Collins, *The Fourteenth Amendment and the States* (Boston, 1912), 188-206. *See also* Benjamin R. Twiss, *Lawyers and the Constitution: How Laissez Faire Came to the Supreme Court* (Princeton, 1942), chs. II-VII.

[17] Professor (later Justice) Felix Frankfurter, "The Supreme Court and the Public," *Forum*, 333 (June 1930).

[18] 127 U.S. 678 (1888).

[19] Burns Baking Co. v. Bryan, 264 U.S. 504 (1924). *See also* Weaver v. Palmer Bros., 270 U.S. 402 (1926).

[20] 12 *American Political Science Review*, 241 (1918).

[21] *New York Times*, February 12, 1930.

No doubt there was an element of exaggeration in some, or even all, of these expressions—no doubt, too, it would be rather difficult to indicate very precisely just wherein the exaggeration lay. The Court, of course, has no power to initiate legislation; and even before it can "veto" an act it must wait for a case to arise under it. Yet a case is sure to arise sooner or later, and as a practical matter sooner *rather* than later. One difference which lawyers are apt to stress between the point of view of a court exercising the power of judicial review and an executive exercising the veto power, is that which is supposed to result from the doctrine of *stare decisis*. A court, it is said, is apt to reflect that a present decision will be a future precedent. But then, executives are apt so to reflect too; while the fact is that in the field of Constitutional Law the doctrine of *stare decisis* is today very shaky. (*See* pp. 223-225.)

"Social Philoso- phies" of the Justices   The really distinctive thing about the Supreme Court considered as a governing body is that its make-up usually changes very gradually, so that for considerable intervals it will be found to be under the sway of a particular "social philosophy," the operation of which in important cases becomes a matter of fairly easy prediction on the part of those who follow the Court's work with some care. The Court which set aside the Income Tax Act of 1894 and which retired the Sherman Act into disuse for some years by its decision in the Sugar Trust case[22] was also the Court which ten years later in Lochner *v.* New York[23] held void as "unreasonable and arbitrary" an act regulating the hours of labor in bakeries. But another decade, and a "liberal" Court sustained without apparent effort a general ten-hour law[24] and upheld compulsory workmen's compensation.[25] Then from 1920 followed a Court of conservative outlook, a Court prone to take a decidedly astringent view of all governmental powers except its own, and to frown upon legislative projects, whether State or national, which were calculated to curtail freedom of business judgment. The outlook of the present Court, on the other hand, stems from "the Constitutional Revolution" of 1937, and is in general favorable to governmental activity at all levels. In fact, since 1940 the Court has revamped our Constitutional Law pretty thoroughly as the foregoing pages so well illustrate.

Summing up: In consequence of the doctrine of due process of law as "reasonable law," *judicial review ceased to have definite, statable limits*; and while the extent to which the Court would recanvass the factual justification of a statute under the "due process" clauses of the Constitution often varied considerably as between cases, yet this was a matter which in the last analysis depended upon the Court's own discretion, and on nothing else.

[22] United States *v.* E. C. Knight Co., 156 U.S. 1 (1895).
[23] 198 U.S. 45 (1905).
[24] Bunting *v.* Ore., 243 U.S. 426 (1917).
[25] New York Central R.R. Co. *v.* White, 243 U.S. 188 (1917).

In the famous case of Munn *v.* Illinois[26] which was decided in 1876, the Court ruled that the State's police power extended to the regulation of the prices set by "businesses affected with a public interest"; and it later held that whether a business was of this character depended on circumstances. Thus the rental of houses in the City of Washington during wartime was held to be such a business, as was the insurance business normally.[27] Later, however, the Court virtually contracted the term to public utilities,[28] holding, as we saw earlier, that their charges were subject to regulation so long as the price fixed by public authority yielded "a fair return on the value of that which is used for the benefit of the public" (*see* pp. 51-53). Then in Nebbia *v.* New York,[29] which was decided early in 1934, the Court, again altering its approach, laid down the doctrine that there is no closed category of "businesses affected with a public interest," but that the State by virtue of its police power may regulate prices whenever it is "reasonably necessary" for it to do so in the public interest; and on this basis was sustained a New York statute providing for the regulation of milk prices in that State. Commenting at the time on this decision, the Hon. James M. Beck declared, with some exaggeration, however, that the Court had "calmly discarded its decisions of fifty years," without even paying "those decisions the obsequious respect of a funeral oration."[30] Subsequent decisions further illustrate the new outlook.[31]

Ultimately, as explained earlier (pp. 389-392), the Supreme Court declined to use substantive due process as a check on economic regulation by legislatures. The truth of this statement in recent times is clearly evidenced by both the paucity of cases in which the Court has granted review and the unfailing deference the Court has shown to the legislature's judgment. In two cases involving economic regulation, the Court held: (1) that it was error for the North Dakota Supreme Court to strike down, as violative of the Fourteenth Amendment, a State statute denying a pharmacy an operating license unless the applicant was "a registered pharmacist in good standing" or "a corporation or association, the majority stock in which is owned by registered pharmacists in good standing, actively and regularly employed in and responsible for the management, supervision and operation of such pharmacy,"[32] and (2) that even if a city gross receipts tax on businesses engaged in the

[26] 94 U.S. 113.

[27] Block *v.* Hirsh, 256 U.S 135 (1921); German Alliance Co. *v.* Lewis, 233 U.S. 389 (1914).

[28] Wolff Packing Co. *v.* C't of Indust'l Relations, 262 U.S. 522 (1923).

[29] 291 U.S. 502 (1934).

[30] 78 *Cong. Rec.* 5358 (1934).

[31] Highland Farms Dairy *v.* Agnew, 300 U.S. 608 (1937); Townsend *v.* Yeomans, 301 U.S. 441 (1937); Olsen *v.* Neb., 313 U.S. 236 (1941); Federal Power Commission *v.* Hope Natural Gas Co., 320 U.S. 591 (1944).

[32] North Dakota State Bd. of Pharmacy *v.* Snyder's Drug Stores, 414 U.S. 156 (1973).

Rate and Price Regulation

parking or storage of automobiles is so excessive as to make business unprofitable, it did not contravene the guarantee of due process.[33] In a third case, the Court overruled its only use of the equal protection guarantee in the post-1937 era to strike down business regulation legislation[34] (*see* p. 516). State decisions, where there have been any, have been in accord.[35]

Substantive
Due Process
and Civil
Liberties

The Constitutional Revolution of 1937, however, did not end the Court's reliance upon substantive due process itself. Instead, after a brief lull in its activism, the Court transferred its involvement to the domain of civil liberties. As noted previously (pp. 305-308), when the circumstances of its composition permitted, the Court sallied forth wielding the "preferred freedoms" doctrine to strike down abridgments of "fundamental rights"; when its composition did not permit, the Court justified the more relaxed reception given legislative enactments by way of the balancing of interests approach. Though there is no need to recount the details of these competing modes of interpretation here, there remains the question of what rights were considered "fundamental" in the new substantive due process. Some of these rights were found explicitly in the Constitution, or, more accurately in the Bill of Rights; others were absent altogether or else seemed to be recognized only implicitly.

The Right
to Privacy

Whether the right to privacy[36] exists at the margins of several amendments or whether it is a creature of the Court's own fertile imagination remains a source of continuing controversy even among the Justices. When the right was first acknowledged by the Court in Griswold v. Connecticut[37] in 1965, Justice Douglas, speak-

---

[33] City of Pittsburgh v. Alco Parking Corp., 417 U.S. 369 (1974).

[34] City of New Orleans v. Dukes, 427 U.S. 297 (1976) *overruling* Morey v. Doud, 354 U.S. 457 (1957). The case usually cited by the Court to typify its disposition in economic regulation cases is Williamson v. Lee Optical Co., 348 U.S. 483 (1955).

[35] For example, anti-littering ordinances that require return-deposit beverage containers have been sustained, Bowie Inn, Inc. v. City of Bowie, 335 A. 2d. 679 (1975), as have countless State no-fault automobile insurance acts, *see* Manzanares v. Bell, 552 P. 2d. 1291 (1974). The Kansas Supreme Court has rejected the assertion that the no-fault insurance act abridged the right to travel as well as a host of equal protection challenges. *And see* Singer v. Sheppard, 346 A. 2d. 897 (1975); Shavers v. Atty. Gen. of Mich., 237 N.W. 2d. 325 (1975); Montgomery v. Daniels, 340 N.E. 2d. 444 (1975); Fann v. McGuffey, 534 S.W. 2d. 770 (1975). But the Illinois Supreme Court has struck down a statute placing a ceiling of $500,000 on the recovery of damages for medical malpractice. Wright v. Central Du Page Hospital Ass'n, 347 N.E. 2d. 736 (1976). The court rested its decision principally on the grounds of equal protection, however.

[36] For an extensive discussion of the right and illustrative cases, *see* P. Allan Dionisopoulos and Craig R. Ducat, *The Right to Privacy* (St. Paul, Minn, 1976).

[37] 381 U.S. 479. In a companion case, Doe v. Bolton, 410 U.S. 179 (1973), the Court considered the constitutionality of a very recently enacted Georgia statute which, while allowing abortion when the woman's life was endangered, or when the child would be born with a severe and permanent defect, or when pregnancy resulted from rape, nevertheless provided that the operation be performed in a specially state-accredited hospital, be approved by a hospital staff abortion committee, and that the attending physician's judgment be confirmed by two additional prac-

ing for the majority, observed that previous "cases suggest that specific guarantees in the Bill of Rights have penumbras, formed by emanations from those guarantees that help give them life and substance." And enumerating these guarantees which "create zones of privacy" Justice Douglas named no less than five amendments. (*See also* the discussion at pp. 441-442.) Without resting the Court's holding on any amendment in particular, but on the right to privacy in general, the Court found the marital relationship to be protected by that constitutional right.[38] Connecticut's birth control law, which trenched upon the married couple's right to make their own decision on matters of contraception, was struck down. In a subsequent case, decided on equal protection grounds, the Court declared unconstitutional a Massachusetts statute that banned the sale of contraceptive medicines or devices to all but married couples. In justifying this conclusion, the text of the Court's opinion appeared to move away from its prior position that the right to privacy inhered in a particular relationship. Speaking for the Court, Justice Brennan wrote: "It is true that in *Griswold* the right of privacy in question inhered in the marital relationship. Yet the married couple is not an independent entity with a mind and heart of its own, but an association of two individuals each with a separate intellectual and emotional make-up. If the right of privacy means anything, it is the right of the *individual*, married or single, to be free from unwarranted governmental intrusion into matters so fundamentally affecting a person as the decision whether to bear or beget a child."[39] In a subsequent ruling on the availability of contraceptives, the Court extended the right to adolescents.[40]

	Birth Control

Doubtless the most controversial of the post-*Griswold* decisions was Roe *v.* Wade,[41] in which the Court, relying on the right of privacy "founded in the Fourteenth Amendment's concept of personal liberty and restrictions upon state action" and defined since *Griswold* to be an *individual* right, concluded that such right was "broad enough to encompass a woman's decision whether or not to terminate her pregnancy." The Court emphasized that such a right was not absolute, that "a state may properly assert important inter-

Abortion

---

titioners. The Court invalidated the statutes as unjustifiably infringing on the patient's rights and unduly intruding on the right of her doctor to practice medicine.

[38] Subsequent lower court decisions emphasized this limitation. *See* Buchanan *v.* Batchelor, 308 F.Supp. 729 (1970), *reversed on other grounds sub nom.* Wade *v.* Buchanan, 401 U.S. 989 (1970). Indeed, some courts continued to rely on this interpretation despite more recent doctrinal developments. *See* Doe *v.* Commonwealth's Atty. for City of Richmond, 403 F.Supp. 1199 (1975), *aff'd* 425 U.S. 901 (1976). But see the criticism given this interpretation in Judge Merhige's dissenting opinion, *ibid.*, 1203, and see his opinion in Lovisi *v.* Slayton, 363 F.Supp. 620 (1973). The dissenting opinions on the *Lovisi* case on appeal also are critical, 539 F. 2d. 349, 352, 355 (1976).

[39] Eisenstadt *v.* Baird, 405 U.S. 438, 453 (1972).

[40] Carey *v.* Population Services International, 97 S.Ct. 2010 (1977). *See also* T‑‑‑‑‑ H‑‑‑‑‑ *v.* Jones, 425 F.Supp. 873 (1975).

[41] 410 U.S. 113 (1973).

ests in safeguarding health, in maintaining medical standards, and in protecting potential life. At some point in pregnancy, these respective interests become sufficiently compelling to sustain regulation of the factors that govern the abortion decision." Traditionally, the Court observed, this point had been marked by the viability of the fetus. Before this point is reached however, given the clear lack of consensus on the question of when life begins, the Court said, "[W]e do not agree that, by adopting one theory of life, Texas may override the rights of the pregnant woman that are at stake." Weighing the "important" interests asserted by the State against due regard for the right to privacy and in light of the traditional concept of viability which is the " 'compelling' point" in the State's interest of protecting potential life, the Court concluded: "(a) For the stage prior to approximately the end of the first trimester, the abortion decision and its effectuation must be left to the medical judgment of the pregnant woman's attending physician. (b) For the stage subsequent to approximately the end of the first trimester, the State, in promoting its interest in the health of the mother, may, if it chooses, regulate the abortion procedure in ways that are reasonably related to maternal health. (c) For the stage subsequent to viability the State, in promoting its interest in the potentiality of human life, may, if it chooses, regulate, and even proscribe, abortion except where it is necessary, in appropriate medical judgment, for the preservation of the life or health of the mother."[42]

Taking up a case it described as "a logical and anticipated corollary" to the 1973 Abortion Cases, the Supreme Court struck down several portions of Missouri's abortion law.[43] The Court held with regard to one aspect of the statute that "the State may not constitutionally require the consent of the spouse . . . as a condition for abortion during the first 12 weeks of pregnancy."[44] Reasoned the Court: "[W]e cannot hold that the State has the constitutional authority to give the spouse unilaterally the ability to prohibit the wife from terminating her pregnancy, when the State itself lacks that right." The Court ruled that the parental consent provision, where minors were concerned, also violated the Constitution. Starting from the premise that "[m]inors, as well as adults, are protected by the Constitution and possess constitutional rights," the Court explained: "It is difficult . . . to conclude that providing a parent with

[42] *Ibid.*, 164-165.

[43] Planned Parenthood of Central Missouri v. Danforth, 428 U.S. 52 (1976). In another decision, handed down the same day, the Court vacated a ruling by a Federal district court as to the unconstitutionality of a Massachusetts abortion statute, explaining that the lower court should have abstained, pending construction of the statute by the Massachusetts Supreme Judicial Court, Bellotti v. Baird, 428 U.S. 132 (1976).

[44] *Ibid.*, 69. For a State court decision upholding the woman's right to be sterilized without her husband's consent, see Ponter v. Ponter, 342 A. 2d. 574 (1975); and also Doe v. Temple, 409 F.Supp. 899 (1976); Murray v. Vandervander, 522 P. 2d 302 (1974); Meerwarth v. Meerwarth, 319 A. 2d. 779 (1974).

absolute power to overrule a determination, made by the physician and his minor patient, to terminate the patient's pregnancy will serve to strengthen the family unit. Neither is it likely that such veto power will enhance parental authority or control where the minor and the nonconsenting parent are so fundamentally in conflict and the very existence of the pregnancy already has fractured the family structure." As to other portions of the law, the Court: (1) sustained the definition of the fetus's "viability" in terms other than reference to a specific point in the gestation period; (2) upheld the requirement that the woman consent *in writing*; (3) struck down a proscription on the use of saline amniocentesis as an abortion technique; (4) approved the reporting and record-keeping requirements; and (5) declared unconstitutional provisions imposing on the physician a duty to preserve the life of the fetus whatever the stage of pregnancy on pain of civil and criminal liability.[45] Four Justices dissented in whole or in part, among them Justice White, who said at one point: "It is truly surprising that the majority finds in the United States Constitution, as it must in order to justify the result it reaches, a rule that the State must assign a greater value to a mother's decision to cut off a potential human life by abortion than to a father's decision to let it mature into a live child. Such a rule cannot be found there, nor can it be found in Roe v. Wade.... These are matters which a State should be able to decide free from the suffocating power of the federal judge, purporting to act in the name of the Constitution."

Near the conclusion of its October 1976 Term, the Court handed down several rulings directed toward answering the question of how far States and their political subdivisions had to go in facilitating elective abortions. It decided: (1) that, as a matter of statutory interpretation, Title XIX of the Social Security Act did not require that States participating in the Federal grant-in-aid Medicaid program fund the cost of non-therapeutic abortions;[46] (2) that there was no violation of the equal protection clause where States subsidize therapeutic abortions but do not agree to pay for elective abortions;[47] and (3) that a city may constitutionally refuse to permit the performance of elective abortions in city-owned hospitals while simultaneously providing hospital services to women carrying their pregnancies to childbirth.[48] Rebutting the allegation that the limi-

[45] See Commonwealth v. Edelin, 359 N.E. 2d. 4 (1976). In this much-publicized case, a Boston doctor was charged with manslaughter under a Massachusetts statute that establishes liability not for aborting a pregnant woman *per se* but for failure to sustain the life of the fetus however briefly it might have lived.

[46] Beal v. Doe, 97 S.Ct. 2366 (1977).

[47] Maher v. Roe, 97 S.Ct. 2376 (1977).

[48] Poelker v. Doe, 97 S.Ct. 2391 (1977). Actions by *private* hospitals, free of State influence and direction in their policies, are not "state actions" and therefore are *not* subject to constitutional challenge, see Greco v. Orange Memorial Hospital Corp., 374 F.Supp. 227 (1974); *and* Doe v. Bridgeton Hospital Ass'n, Inc., 327 A. 2d. 448 (1974). The same is true for an action to compel a private hospital to let a physician

tation on funding impaired the fundamental right of a woman to elect abortion, a right recognized in *Roe*, Chief Justice Burger replied in his concurring opinion: "Like the Court, I do not read any decision of this Court as requiring a State to finance a nontherapeutic abortion. The Court's holdings in *Roe* and *Doe* [*v.* Bolton] . . . simply require that a State not create an absolute barrier to a woman's decision to have an abortion. These precedents do not suggest that the State is constitutionally required to assist her in procuring it."[49] Dissenting, Justice Blackmun, the author of the Court's opinion in *Roe*, found the Court's ruling with respect to "the individual woman concerned, indigent and financially helpless," to be "punitive and tragic." He continued: "Implicit in the Court's holdings is the condescension that she may go elsewhere for her abortion. I find that disingenuous and alarming, almost reminiscent of 'let them eat cake.' "[50]

A number of noteworthy decisions by other courts have followed, drawing substantially on the interpretation given the right to privacy by *Griswold* and its progeny. A significant decision by the N.J. Supreme Court, authorizing the father of a 22-year-old comatose patient, "doomed to no more than a biologically vegetative remnant of life," to terminate life-supporting medical procedures. Said Chief Justice Hughes, speaking for the unanimous court: "Presumably this right [to privacy] is broad enough to encompass a patient's decision to decline medical treatment under certain circumstances, in much the same way as it is broad enough to encompass a woman's decision to terminate pregnancy under certain conditions. [W]e have concluded that Karen's right of privacy may be asserted on her behalf by her guardian under the peculiar circumstances here present."[51] A three-judge Federal district court ruled that Virginia's sodomy statute does not unconstitutionally trench upon any right of privacy possessed by consenting adults when they engage in sex acts with others of the same sex in private.[52] The U.S. Supreme Court summarily affirmed,[53] although that ruling took considerable criticism from Judge Merhige in dissent who pointed up considerable inconsistency with the Court-announced decisions declaring the right of privacy to be an indi-

---

sterilize a patient in the hospital, *see* Ham *v.* Holy Rosary Hospital, 529 P. 2d. 361 (1974). For a ruling where the private hospital offers religious or moral objections to permitting sterilization, *see* Chrisman *v.* Sisters of St. Joseph of Peace, 506 F. 2d. 308 (1974).

[49] Maher *v.* Roe, 97 S.Ct. 2376, 2386.

[50] Beal *v.* Doe, 97 S.Ct. 2366, 2399.

[51] Matter of Quinlan, 355 A. 2d. 647, 662-664 (1976) *reversing* 348 A. 2d. 801 (1975). The State attorney general decided not to appeal the case further, *see New York Times*, April 7, 1976. For a graphic account of the facts and issues, *see Newsweek*, Nov. 3, 1975.

[52] Doe *v.* Commonwealth's Atty. of City of Richmond, 403 F.Supp. 1199 (1975).

[53] 425 U.S. 901 (1976), *rehearing denied*, 425 U.S. 985.

vidual right.[54] In any event, whatever the disposition of the judiciary to use the right of privacy to protect sexual acts between consenting adults, the trend among the State legislatures is undeniably toward decriminalization.[55] And the Alaska Supreme Court, resting its decision on a privacy amendment added to the State constitution, has held that criminal sanctions may not be imposed for the private possession and use of marijuana within the home.[56] Contemporaneous with the legislative trend to decriminalize possession of small amounts of marijuana at the State level, President Carter has proposed that Federal criminal penalties for possession of one ounce or less should be dropped.[57] But the U.S. Supreme Court, disposing of a challenge to regulations that govern policemen's hair, beards, and moustaches, did not frame the issue in that case in terms of any privacy interest implicated and upheld the regulations as reasonable.[58]

Ruling on another claim of the right to privacy, the Court declined to hold, as a prerequisite to a suit filed under the civil rights statute, that the plaintiff's Fourteenth Amendment rights had been infringed when police distributed to local merchants a flyer on "active shoplifters" bearing the plaintiff's name and picture. The plaintiff, arguing a denial of due process, had once been arrested on shoplifting charges, but the charges had been dismissed. The Court held that the due process clause does not extend to protect a citizen from injury whenever an agent of the State commits a tort. Indeed, pointed out Justice Rehnquist, speaking for the Court: "It is hard to perceive any logical stopping place to such a line of reasoning," for, presumably, if relief were granted here, "it would be difficult to see why the survivors of an innocent bystander mistakenly shot by a policeman or negligently killed by a sheriff driving a government vehicle would not have claims equally cognizable" under the civil rights statute. Moreover, Justice Rehnquist observed: "In . . . [past] cases, as a result of the state action complained of, a right or status previously recognized by state law was distinctly altered or extinguished. It was this alteration, officially removing the interest from the recognition and protection previously afforded by the State, which we found sufficient to invoke the procedural guarantees contained in the Due Process Clause of the Fourteenth Amendment. But the interest in reputation alone which respondent seeks to vindicate in this action in federal court is

[54] See note 36, supra. These cases are enumerated in Harold W. Chase and Craig R. Ducat, 1977 Supplement to Constitutional Interpretation (St. Paul, Minn., 1977), p. 293.

[55] As of January 1, 1977, some 15 States had decriminalized private sex acts between consenting adults of the same sex; nine others made it a misdemeanor. For a listing of the States, see ibid., p. 292.

[56] Ravin v. State, 537 P. 2d. 494 (1975).

[57] 1977 Cong. Quart. Weekly Report, 1671.

[58] Kelley v. Johnson, 425 U.S. 238 (1976).

quite different from the 'liberty' or 'property' recognized in those decisions."[59] In dissent, Justice Brennan, joined by Justices Marshall and White, wrote: "The Court today holds that police officials, acting in their official capacities as law enforcers, may on their own initiative and without trial constitutionally condemn innocent individuals as criminals and thereby hound them with one of the most stigmatizing and debilitating labels in our society. If there are no constitutional restraints on such oppressive behavior the safeguards constitutionally afforded an accused in a criminal trial are rendered a sham, and no individual can feel secure that he will not be singled out for similar *ex parte* punishment by those primarily charged with fair enforcement of the law."

In other developments relative to the right of privacy, a Federal district court has held that a provision of the New York public health law, requiring physicians to report the names and addresses of patients receiving certain drugs to State authorities, is unconstitutional.[60] The new Federal Privacy Law[61] has gone into effect requiring the national government to disclose some 8,000 records systems it currently uses and affording citizens an opportunity to challenge the accuracy of data kept on them and to prevent the unwarranted dissemination of information.[62] During the same legislative session, Congress also enacted the Family Educational Rights and Privacy Act of 1974,[63] which focused upon the protection of student interests, specially preserving the confidentiality of, yet assuring student access to, their educational records.

In other cases bearing upon an asserted privacy interest, courts have ruled: (1) that prison officials who conducted a hemorrhoidectomy on an inmate without his consent and denied him necessary analgesics afterward violated "a constitutionally protected right to be secure in the privacy of one's own body against invasion by the state," absent a compelling interest;[64] (2) that a kidney might not be removed from the body of an incompetent and given to his sister who was in dire need of it;[65] (3) that an unwed mother can be compelled to identify the putative father in order to obtain welfare benefits;[66] and (4) that psychotherapists could be

[59] Paul *v*. Davis, 424 U.S. 693, 698-699, 711 (1976). Courts, however, have taken a hard look at the damage from the circulation of inaccurate arrest records. *See* Menard *v*. Saxbe, 498 F. 2d. 1017 (1974) together with Justice Rehnquist's discussion of the use of the right to privacy to vindicate personal interests in such cases in "Is an Expanded Right to Privacy Consistent with Fair and Effective Law Enforcement? Or, Privacy, You've Come a Long Way, Baby," 23 *Kansas Law Review* 1 (1974). *See also* Loder *v*. Municipal Court, 553 P. 2d. 624 (1976) especially all the articles and cases cited therein.

[60] Roe *v*. Ingraham, 403 F.Supp. 931 (1975).   [61] 88 *Stat*. 1896.

[62] *See Los Angeles Times*, Sept. 21, 1975, *and* Sept. 27, 1975.

[63] 20 U.S.C. § 1232 g.

[64] Runnels *v*. Rosendale, 499 F. 2d. 733 (1974).

[65] *In re* Guardianship of Pescinski, 226 N.W. 2d. 180 (1975).

[66] Doe *v*. Norton, 365 F.Supp. 65 (1974), *vacated and remanded sub nom.* Roe *v*. Norton, 422 U.S. 391 (1975); *see also* the Social Service Amendments of 1974 enacted by Congress, which still compel divulgence but provide no punitive sanctions, 88 *Stat*. 2337.

held liable for failure to warn an endangered victim after the patient's communications to them revealed a threat;[67] (5) that a financial disclosure statement required of certain State employees is not *per se* an unconstitutional invasion of privacy;[68] (6) that statutes proscribing prostitution[69] or requiring motorcyclists to wear safety helmets[70] do not infringe protected rights of privacy; (7) that adult adoptees have no constitutional right to satisfy their curiosity about their roots by seeing documents pertaining to their birth kept under seal;[71] (8) that no constitutional privacy interest was infringed by denial of a marriage license to two men;[72] and (9) that Navy policies mandating the discharge of any person engaging in homosexual activity is arbitrary and denies due process.[73] Finally two especially interesting cases involved claims of privacy before the Minnesota Supreme Court. In one case it remanded the controversy to a lower State court to scrutinize more thoroughly a request to order the use of the Minnesota Multiphasic Personality Inventory by a physician conducting an adverse examination of a plaintiff.[74] In the other, the court rejected a challenge to the fluoridation of public drinking water as an allegedly unjustified intrusion on an individual's bodily integrity.[75]

One of the most interesting developments in substantive due process is the formulation and enforcement of a "right to treatment" for patients languishing in State mental hospitals. Acting in response to what one State supreme court called "Dickensian squalor of unconscionable magnitudes,"[76] lower courts came increasingly to demand adequate facilities and individualized treatment for patients,[77] even to the point of threatening serious intervention in State budgeting processes to enforce this constitutional right.[78] The U.S. Supreme Court, however, has not yet confronted

The Right to Treatment

[67] Tarasoff v. Regents of the Univ. of Calif., 529 P. 2d. 553 (1974). *See also* Caesar v. Mountanos, 542 F. 2d. 1064 (1976).

[68] Illinois State Employees Ass'n v. Walker, 315 N.E. 2d. 9 (1974); *and* Montgomery County v. Walsh, 336 A. 2d. 97 (1975). *See also* Kenny v. Byrne, 365 A. 2d. 211 (1976).

[69] United States v Moses, 339 A. 2d. 46 (1975); State v. Price, 237 N.W. 2d. 813 (1976); *see also* Brown v. Brannon, 399 F.Supp. 133 (1975).

[70] State v. Beeman, 541 P. 2d. 409 (1975); People of City of Adrian v. Poucher, 247 N.W. 2d. 798 (1976); *see also* Ravin v. State, 537 P. 2d. 494, 508-509 (1975).

[71] Mills v. Atlantic City Dept. of Vital Statistics, 372 A. 2d. 646 (1977). *See also* Industrial Foundation of the South v. Texas Indus. Accident Com'n, 540 S.W. 2d. 668 (1976).

[72] Baker v. Nelson, 191 N.W. 2d. 185 (1971); *appeal dismissed*, 409 U.S. 810 (1972). *See also* Singer v. Hara, 522 P. 2d. 1187 (1974).

[73] Saal v. Middendorf, 427 F.Supp. 192 (1977); *cf.* Matlovich v. Sec'y of the Air Force, 414 F.Supp. 690 (1976).

[74] Haynes v. Anderson, 232 N.W. 2d. 196 (1975).

[75] Minnesota State Board of Health v. City of Brainerd, 241 N.W. 2d. 624 (1976).

[76] State *ex rel.* Hawks v. Lazaro, 202 S.E. 2d. 109, 120 (1974).

[77] *Ibid.*; Wyatt v. Stickney, 325 F.Supp. 781 (1971) *and* 344 F.Supp. 373 (1972); New York State Ass'n for Retarded Children v. Rockefeller, 357 F.Supp. 752 (1973); Welsch v. Likins, 373 F. Supp. 487 (1974); Donaldson v. O'Connor, 493 F. 2d. 507 (1974).

[78] Wyatt v. Stickney, 344 F.Supp. 373 (1972). Judge Johnson's ruling on the right

the issue. In one case where the Court could readily have addressed the matter, the Justices chose to narrow their consideration to focus on the criteria for commitment.[79] Reference to the case thus appears under the discussion of procedural due process. (*See* p. 490.) Chief Justice Burger, however, confronted the postulated "right to treatment" and voiced serious misgivings in his concurring opinion.[80]

Other "fundamental" rights, whose regulation has prompted "strict scrutiny" by the Court, have been the right to travel[81] and the right to vote in State elections.[82] As with the right to privacy, the constitutional sources of these rights have never been made entirely clear. Largely they have come to inhere in the broad guarantee of "liberty" in the Fifth and Fourteenth Amendments. Even at times when it has disclaimed doing so,[83] the Court's reliance ultimately on the due process clause[84] lends truth to Justice Rehnquist's contention that the Old Court's "liberty of contract" and the New Court's creations such as the right to privacy are really "sisters under the skin."[85] The Burger Court has not manifested the eagerness of the Warren Court in fashioning new "fundamental" rights, as demonstrated by sidestepping an opportunity to recognize a "right to treatment"[86] and its outright refusal to acknowledge a right to education.[87] Indeed, the Court recently has apparently come to the conclusion that "fundamental" rights have to be spelled out in the text of the Constitution or, more accurately, in the amendments.[88] These rights have been the second and surely the major source of the Court's substantive due process since the Constitutional Revolution of 1937. An activist Court's concern with broadly effectuating provisions of the Bill of Rights is twofold. First, the Court must address the scope of each civil liberty, something which we address in our discussion of the individual amendments. Second, those bent on broadly protecting civil liberties must

---

to treatment in the *Wyatt* case was subsequently affirmed by the U.S. Fifth Circuit Court of Appeals *sub nom.* Wyatt *v.* Aderholt, 503 F. 2d. 1305 (1974). (For other discussion of Judge Johnson's activism, specifically in behalf of minimal acceptable conditions in Alabama's prisons, see p. 439.)

[79] O'Connor *v.* Donaldson, 422 U.S. 563 (1975).   [80] *Ibid.*, 578.

[81] *See* Kent *v.* Dulles, 357 U.S. 116 (1964); Aptheker *v.* Secretary of State, 378 U.S. 500 (1964); U.S. *v.* Guest, 383 U.S. 745 (1965); Shapiro *v.* Thompson, 394 U.S. 618 (1969). *See especially* the discussion in Kreitzer *v.* Puerto Rico Cars, Inc., 417 F.Supp. 498 (1975).

[82] *See* Reynolds *v.* Sims, 377 U.S. 533 (1964); Harper *v.* Va. Bd. of Elections, 383 U.S. 663 (1966); Kramer *v.* Union Free School Dist. No. 15, 395 U.S. 621 (1969).

[83] Griswold *v.* Conn., 381 U.S. 479, 484-485, 528 (1965).

[84] Roe *v.* Wade, 410 U.S. 113, 153 (1973).

[85] "Is an Expanded Right to Privacy Consistent with Fair and Effective Law Enforcement? Or, Privacy, You've Come a Long Way, Baby," 23 *Kansas Law Review* 1 (1974).

[86] O'Connor *v.* Donaldson, 422 U.S. 563 (1975).

[87] Rodriguez *v.* San Antonio Indep. School Dist., 411 U.S. 1, 29-35 (1973).

[88] *Ibid.*, 33-34. *And see* Justice Marshall's rejoinder in dissent, *ibid.*, 99-117.

find a way to make those rulings applicable against State infringement. It is to the second of these matters that we now turn.

During and after the First World War many State legislatures passed acts imposing restraints upon freedom of speech, press, and teaching and learning. In deciding the question whether such measures were within the police power the Court came early to adopt the theory that the word "liberty" of the Fourteenth Amendment covers such freedoms and hence protects them against "unreasonable" State acts. A statute forbidding the teaching of subjects in any but the English language was held void as to private schools,[89] as was also an act which, by requiring that all children attend the public schools, practically forbade their attending private schools.[90] On the other hand, the Court sustained legislation penalizing advocacy of the use of violence to bring about social and political change,[91] but, in doing so, the Court said "For present purposes we may and do assume that freedom of speech and of the press—which are protected by the First Amendment from abridgment by Congress—are among the fundamental personal rights and 'liberties protected by the due process clause of the Fourteenth Amendment from impairment by the States.' "[92] Thus began the process of selective incorporation of the Bill of Rights into the Fourteenth Amendment.

Before that development reached full flower, the due process clause of the Fourteenth Amendment had an interesting history of its own with respect to law enforcement procedures. For example, it was thought that the clause did *not* subject State criminal procedure to the detailed requirements which the Fifth and Sixth Amendments lay upon the National Government. For this reason the States remained free to remodel their procedural practices, so long as they retained the essence of "due process of law," that is a fair trial in a court having jurisdiction of the case.[93] So, the mere forms of a fair trial did not suffice if the substance was lacking, as in a trial which proceeded to its foreordained conclusion under mob domination;[94] or one in which a plea of guilty or confession was obtained by misrepresentation or recourse to "third degree" methods. In judging these matters, the Court went fully into the factual record made in the trial court.[95] Likewise the Court inquired closely whether the accused was denied assistance of counsel unfairly, although whether this was because Amendment XIV

Incorporation of the Substantive Freedoms of the First Amendment

Due Process Procedures

[89] Meyer v. Neb., 262 U.S. 390 (1923).
[90] Pierce v. Society of Sisters, 268 U.S. 510 (1925).
[91] Gitlow v. N.Y., 268 U.S. 652 (1925); Whitney v. Calif., 274 U.S. 357 (1927).
[92] *Ibid.*, 666.   [93] *See* notes 94-97 below.
[94] Moore v. Dempsey, 261 U.S. 86 (1923).
[95] Brown v. Miss., 297 U.S. 278 (1936); Chambers v. Fla., 309 U.S. 227 (1940); White v. Tex., 310 U.S. 530 (1940); Smith v. O'Grady, 312 U.S. 329 (1941); Ashcraft v. Tenn., 322 U.S. 143 (1944); Malinski v. N.Y., 324 U.S. 401 (1945). Whether a confession of an accused was coerced could be left to the jury to decide. Stein v. N.Y., 346 U.S. 156 (1953).

adopted the "assistance of counsel" requirement of Amendment VI outright or only to the extent that such assistance was requisite to a "fair trial" remained somewhat uncertain.[96] The latter, more flexible test seemed to dispense with any or all of those ancient muniments of "Anglo-Saxon liberties"—indictment by grand jury, trial by jury, and immunity from self-incrimination. The Fourteenth Amendment was found not to stand in the way, provided the method of trial guaranteed, in the judgment of the Court, a fair trial.[97]

Develop-
ment of
the Doc-
trine of
Selective
Incorpora-
tion

The approach just described went by the boards once the Fifth and Sixth Amendments were incorporated into the Fourteenth. But that takes a little explaining.

A good place to begin that explanation is with the opinion of the Court, written by Justice Cardozo in the case of Palko v. Connecticut in 1937: ". . . the due process clause of the Fourteenth Amendment may make it unlawful for a state to abridge by its statutes the freedom of speech which the First Amendment safeguards against encroachment by Congress, . . . or like freedom of the press, . . . or the free exercise of religion, . . . or the right of peaceable assembly, without which speech would be unduly trammeled, . . . or the right of one accused of crime to the benefit of counsel. . . . In these and other situations immunities that are valid as against the federal government by force of the specific pledges of particular amendments have been found to be implicit in the concept of ordered liberty, and thus, through the Fourteenth Amendment, become valid as against the states."[98] It seems pretty clear that neither the Court nor Cardozo at that time was suggesting a wholesale incorporation of the Bill of Rights.[99] After all in this very case they said: "The right to trial by jury and the immunity from prosecution except as the result of an indictment may have value and importance. Even so, they are not of the very essence of a scheme of ordered liberty. To abolish them is not to violate a 'principle of justice so rooted in the traditions and conscience of our people as to be ranked as fundamental.'" The Court went on to hold with respect to double jeopardy involved in the case at hand: "Is that kind of double jeopardy to which the statute has subjected them a hardship so acute and shocking that our polity will not endure it? Does it violate those 'fundamental principles of liberty and justice which lie at the base of all our civil and political institutions'?

---

[96] Powell v. Ala., 287 U.S. 45 (1932) and Avery v. Ala., 308 U.S. 444 (1939) illustrate the care with which the Court would at times go into the facts of such cases. In Betts v. Brady, 316 U.S. 455 (1942) a divided Court found that a State was not required in every case to provide counsel for an indigent defendant. See also Gibbs v. Burke, 337 U.S. 773, 780-781 (1949).

[97] Hurtado v. Calif., 110 U.S. 516 (1884); Maxwell v. Dow, 176 U.S. 581 (1900); Twining v. N.J., 211 U.S. 78 (1908); Adamson v. Calif., 332 U.S. 46 (1947); and note particularly Justice Cardozo's words in Palko v. Conn., 302 U.S. 319 (1937).

[98] 302 U.S. 319, 324-325 (1937).

[99] Louis Henkin, " 'Selective Incorporation' in the Fourteenth Amendment," 73 Yale Law Journal, 74 (1963).

. . . The answer surely must be 'no.' " Whatever their intent, the Court and Cardozo provided a concept and a rhetoric upon which others could build, i.e. "immunities that are valid as against the federal government . . . thus through the Fourteenth Amendment, become valid as against the States."

In 1947, in an attempted *tour de force*, Justice Black argued that the Court should incorporate all of the Bill of Rights into the Fourteenth Amendment. He asserted that "history conclusively demonstrates that the language of the first section of the Fourteenth Amendment, taken as a whole, was thought by those responsible for its submission, sufficiently explicit to guarantee that thereafter no state could deprive its citizens of the privileges and protections of the Bill of Rights. Whether this Court ever will, or whether it now should, in the light of past decisions, give full effect to what the Amendment was intended to accomplish is not necessarily essential to a decision here. However that may be, our prior decisions do not prevent our carrying out that purpose, at least to the extent of making applicable to the states, not a mere part, as the Court has, but the full protection of the Fifth Amendment's provision against compelling evidence from an accused to convict him of crime."[100] However, Justice Black was unable to convince a majority of the Court to go along with him. He concluded his dissent with a telling statement of intent: "If the choice must be between the selective process of the *Palko* decision applying some of the Bill of Rights to the States, or the *Twining* rule applying none of them, I would choose the *Palko* selective process. But rather than accept either of these choices, I would follow what I believe was the original purpose of the Fourteenth Amendment—to extend to all the people of the nation the complete protection of the Bill of Rights. To hold that this Court can determine what, if any, provisions of the Bill of Rights will be enforced, and if so to what degree is to frustrate the great design of a written Constitution." He soon realized he had no choice but to use the selective process of *Palko*. And so for the next two decades he labored hard to convince a majority of the Court that the specific guarantees of the Bill of Rights each, one by one, was "implicit in the concept of ordered liberty." After all, the specifics of the concept are a subjective judgment, and, for Black, there was no reason to believe that the judgments of Cardozo and the Court of 1937 were any better than his. Black was inordinately successful in that enterprise.

Unfortunately, the rationale for incorporating the various guarantees has been difficult to divine, perhaps a predictable difficulty of the *ad hoc* approach. Did the Court read these guarantees into the word "liberty"? or "due process"? It took an erudite scholar, Professor Louis Henkin of the Columbia Law School, to find some pattern in what the Court had actually done:

"In fact, it should be clear, the Court has not read 'due process of

---

[100] Adamson *v.* California, 332 U.S. 46, 74-75 (1947).

law' as a short-hand way of referring to specifics of the Bill of Rights. (It could hardly have so read a clause which restates, identically, only one single provision of only one of the early amendments.) To find in that phrase any limitations at all it had to give meaning and content to the phrase 'due process of law.' It found protection for 'liberty,' including the liberties mentioned in the first and fourth amendments, in notions of 'substantive due process,' and, in regard to procedural due process, the Court held that the 'process' that is 'due'—say, in criminal proceedings—is what is required by the conscience of mankind. *That is the essential link* between the constitutional language and purport and all the procedural limitations which the Court applies to the states under this provision. So far as here relevant, then, all that is required of the states is that which is due because it is 'fundamental,' because its denial would shock the conscience of mankind. There is no relation—historical, linguistic or logical—between that standard and the specific provisions, or any specific provision, of the Bill of Rights. At bottom, it is difficult even to ask meaningfully whether a specific of the Bill of Rights is incorporated in ordered liberty. That a particular procedure or action is required of, or forbidden to, the federal government by a provision of the Bill of Rights is some evidence that it may be required, or forbidden, by the conscience of mankind. But this indirect relevance of the Bill of Rights to determine the content of 'due process of law' cannot support the view that any provision of the Bill of Rights, in its total federal import, is either all in, or all out of, this standard of ordered liberty. Some specifics of the Bill of Rights, in all their manifestations, may indeed be 'process' which is required by the conscience of mankind; others may not. Some elements or aspects of a specific may be required by the conscience of mankind; others may not."[101] Whatever the rationale, the results are clear: The Court has incrementally incorporated most of the provisions of the first eight amendments and supplemented these with others deemed "fundamental." Beginning with First Amendment rights, the Court later included numerous procedural guarantees and additional substantive liberties.

Breadth of an Incorporated Guarantee   From 1947 on, Justice Black took the position that when a guarantee was incorporated into the Fourteenth Amendment it was swallowed whole. Thus, once Free Speech became part of the Fourteenth, all the protections afforded that right against the National Government applied equally to the States. In Black's own words: "Now it appears that at least some of the provisions of the Bill of Rights in their very terms satisfy the Court as sound and meaningful expressions of fundamental liberty. If the Fifth Amendment's protection against self-incrimination be such an expression of fundamental liberty, I ask, and have not found a satisfactory answer, why the Court today should consider that it should

[101] Louis Henkin, " 'Selective Incorporation' . . . ," p. 78.

be 'absorbed' in part but not in full? . . . Nothing in the *Palko* opinion requires that when the Court decides that a Bill of Rights' provision is to be applied to the States, it is to be applied piecemeal. Nothing in the *Palko* opinion recommends that the Court apply part of an amendment's established meaning and discard that part which does not suit the current style of fundamentals."[102] That has been the nearly unanimous view of the members of the Court in the decade in which most of the incorporations have been accomplished.

At least three Justices have felt compelled to challenge this position. In 1952, Justice Jackson wrote: "The assumption of other dissents is that the 'liberty' which the Due Process Clause of the Fourteenth Amendment protects against denial by the States is the literal and identical 'freedom of speech or of the press' which the First Amendment forbids only Congress to abridge. The history of criminal libel in America convinces me that the Fourteenth Amendment did not 'incorporate' the First, that the powers of Congress and of the States over this subject are not of the same dimensions, and that because Congress probably could not enact this law it does not follow that the States may not."[103]

Later in 1957, Justice Harlan wrote a separate opinion in an obscenity case: "In judging the constitutionality of this conviction, we should remember that our function in reviewing state judgments under the Fourteenth is a narrow one. We do not decide whether the policy of the State is wise, or whether it is based on assumptions scientifically substantiated. We can inquire only whether the state action so subverts the fundamental liberties implicit in the Due Process Clause that it cannot be sustained as a rational exercise of power. . . . The States' power to make printed words criminal is, of course, confined by the Fourteenth Amendment, but only insofar as such power is inconsistent with our concepts of 'ordered liberty.' "[104] Generally, the other Justices have not been persuaded by the arguments of Jackson and Harlan.

However, in 1970 Justice Stewart erupted in volcanic fashion (note his language): "I substantially agree with the separate opinion Mr. Justice Harlan has filed in these cases—an opinion that fully demonstrates some of the basic errors in a mechanistic 'incorporation' approach to the Fourteenth Amendment. I cannot subscribe to his opinion in its entirety, however, if only for the reason that it relies in part upon certain dissenting and concurring opinions in previous cases in which I did not join.

"The 'incorporation' theory postulates the Bill of Rights as the substantive metes and bounds of the Fourteenth Amendment. I think this theory is incorrect as a matter of constitutional history, and that as a matter of constitutional law it is both stultifying and

[102] Adamson *v.* California, 332 U.S. 46, 86 (1947).
[103] Beauharnais *v.* Illinois, 343 U.S. 250, 288 (1952).
[104] Roth *v.* U.S., 354 U.S. 476, 501 (1957).

unsound. It is, at best, a theory that can lead the Court only to a Fourteenth Amendment dead end. And, at worst, the spell of the theory's logic compels the Court either to impose intolerable restrictions upon the constitutional sovereignty of the individual States in the administration of their own criminal law, or else intolerably to relax the explicit restrictions that the Framers actually did put upon the Federal Government in the administration of criminal justice. All this, and much more is elaborated in Mr. Justice Harlan's separate opinion. . . .

"The architect of the contemporary 'incorporation' approach to the Fourteenth Amendment is, of course, Mr. Justice Black. . . . And the separate opinion my Brother Black has filed today . . . could serve as Exhibit A to illustrate the extraordinary habits of thought into which some of us have fallen in conditioned reflex to that erroneous constitutional doctrine. 'Incorporation' has become so Pavlovian that my Brother Black barely mentions the Fourteenth Amendment in the course of an 11-page opinion dealing with the procedural rule the State of Florida has adopted for cases tried in Florida courts under Florida's criminal laws. His opinion relies instead upon the 'plain and obvious meaning' of the 'specific words' of the Fifth Amendment and other 'provisions of the Bill of Rights' which, together with 'the history surrounding the adoption of those provisions,' make clear that '[t]he Framers . . . designed' those rights 'to shield the defendant against state power.'

"Though I admire the rhetoric, I submit with all deference that those statements are, to quote their author, 'plainly and simply wrong as a matter of fact and law. . . .' If the Constitution forbids the Florida alibi-defense procedure, it is because of the Fourteenth Amendment, and not because of either the 'specific words' of the Bill of Rights or 'the history surrounding' their adoption. For as every schoolboy knows, the Framers 'designed' the Bill of Rights not against 'state power,' but against the power of the Federal Government.

"Surely Mr. Justice Harlan is right when he says it is time for the Court to face up to reality."[105]

Justice Black's rejoinder: "My Brother Harlan, . . . charges that the Court's decision . . . is evidence that the 'incorporation doctrine,' through which the specific provisions of the Bill of Rights are made fully applicable to the States under the same standards applied in federal courts will somehow result in a 'dilution' of the protections required by those provisions. He asserts that this Court's desire to relieve the States from the rigorous requirements of the Bill of Rights is bound to cause re-examination and modification of prior decisions interpreting those provisions as applied in federal courts in order simultaneously to apply the provisions equally to the State and Federal Governments and to avoid undue restrictions on the States. This assertion finds no support in today's

[105] Williams v. Florida, 399 U.S. 78, 143-145 (1970).

decision or any other decision of this Court. We have emphatically 'rejected the notion that the Fourteenth Amendment applies to the States only a "watered-down, subjective version of the individual guarantees of the Bill of Rights." . . .' Today's decision is in no way attributable to any desire to dilute the Sixth Amendment in order more easily to apply it to the States, but follows solely as a necessary consequence of our duty to re-examine prior decisions to reach the correct constitutional meaning in each case."[106] As things currently stand, the Black position prevails.

In two classes of cases "due process of law" has the meaning of *jurisdiction*, the general idea being that a State has normally no right to attempt to exercise its governmental powers upon persons and property situated beyond its boundaries.

"Due Process of Law" as Jurisdiction

The first class embraces cases in which a defendant in a personal action in a State court challenges the validity of a judgment rendered against him on the ground that, not having been within the forum State at the time, he was not served there with the proper papers. Once such a judgment was *ipso facto* void as having been rendered without jurisdiction.[107] But over a century ago, the force of this rule was broken as regards "foreign" corporations (those chartered by other States) by the doctrine that since a State may absolutely exclude such "persons," it ought to be presumed that those admitted by it had consented to be sued in its courts.[108] Then somewhat later this doctrine became impaired in turn by the doctrine that a State may not exclude "foreign" corporations from engaging in interstate commerce; while as regards natural persons who are citizens of sister States, it was never applicable anyway on account of the right of entry which is accorded them by Article IV, Section II. The result is that within the last few decades the Court has developed a much more flexible principle regarding service of process in personal actions, both those involving corporate defendants and those involving natural persons. This principle is that nowadays due process requires only that, in order to subject a defendant to a judgment *in personam*, if he be not present within the territory of the forum, he must have certain minimum contacts with it such that the maintenance of the suit does not offend "traditional notions of fair play and substantial justice." Such contacts existing, "substituted service" (i.e. other than personal service) will satisfy the requirements of the due process clause, provided "it is reasonably calculated to give him [the defendant] actual notice of the proceedings and an opportunity to be heard."[109]

Substituted service is also adequate in an action concerning land

[106] *Ibid.*, 106-107.

[107] *See* e.g. Pennoyer v. Neff, 95 U.S. 714 (1877).

[108] Lafayette Ins. Co. v. French, 18 How. 404 (1855); Arrowsmith v. United Press Int., 320 F. 2d. 219, 228-229 (1963).

[109] Milliken v. Meyer, 311 U.S. 457 (1940); International Shoe Co. v. Wash., 326 U.S. 310 (1945); Polizzi v. Cowles Mag. Inc., 345 U.S. 663 (1953); Scanapico v. RF&P R.R. Co., 439 F. 2d. 17, 19 (1970).

Substituted which is the property of a non-resident, since such actions are *in*
Service *rem* and the *res* is within the court's jurisdiction. Also, a State may by
statute make non-residents operating motor vehicles within its
borders liable to suit for any damage they do there, provided a designated State officer is served with the proper papers and a reasonable effort is made to notify the non-resident defendant of the proceedings and an opportunity thus given him to be heard.[110]

As we saw earlier, it is possible for a State court to assert jurisdiction over a suit brought by a non-resident for divorce so far as the
due process clause is concerned, but without at the same time sat-
isfying the requirements of the "full faith and credit" clause.
(*See* p. 246.)

Jurisdic-   The second class of cases referred to apply the jurisdictional
tion in principle in the field of taxation. All realty is, of course, within the
Taxation taxing jurisdiction of the State where situated. Tangible personalty,
or "movables," on the other hand, were once deemed attached to
the person of the owner (*mobilia personam sequuntur*), and hence to
be taxable at the place of his residence, but in the philosophy of the
Court this is no longer so. Today such things are taxable under the
due process clause only where they have "taxable *situs*"—a point
not always easy to determine.

As the Court held in 1962: "Nor does the Due Process Clause
confine the domiciliary State's taxing power to such proportion of
the value of the property being taxed as is equal to the fraction of
the tax year which the property spends within the State's borders.
Union Refrigerator Transit Co. *v.* Kentucky, 199 U.S. 194, held
only that the Due Process Clause prohibited ad valorem taxation by
the owner's domicile of tangible personal property permanently located in some other State. Northwest Airlines, Inc. *v.* Minnesota,
322 U.S. 292, reaffirmed the principle established by earlier cases
that tangible property for which no tax situs has been established
elsewhere may be taxed to its full value by the owner's domicile. . . .
If such property has had insufficient contact with States other than
the owner's domicile to render any one of these jurisdictions a 'tax
situs,' it is surely appropriate to presume that the domicile is the
only State affording the 'opportunities, benefits, or protection'
which due process demands as a prerequisite for taxation. . . . Accordingly, the burden is on the taxpayer who contends that some
portion of its total assets are beyond the reach of the taxing power
of its domicile to prove that the same property may be similarly
taxed in another jurisdiction. . . ."[111] (For further discussion of the
"nexus" between the thing taxed and the state doing the taxing, *see*
p. 71.)

[110] Hess *v.* Pawloski, 274 U.S. 352 (1927); Wuchter *v.* Pizzutti, 276 U.S. 13 (1928).
Chief Justice Taft's opinion in the latter case is valuable for its exposition of the law
of substituted service. *See also* Worthley *v.* Rockville Lease Car, Inc., 328 F.Supp. 185
(1971).
[111] Central R.R. Co. *v.* Penn., 370 U.S. 607, 612 (1962).

As to intangibles, the Court sought for a time, in an effort to eliminate "double taxation" of inheritances, to confine the power to tax them to the State where the decedent resided,[112] but has lately been forced by the wealth of expedients devised to avoid taxation altogether which sprang up in the wake of this rule, to abandon it.[113] And State income taxation is frequently "double," or overlapping.[114] The State in which a man is resident may tax him on his total income, while other States may tax him on such portions of it as accrued to him from property situated, or business carried on, within their respective limits; but, of course, such taxes must not be more onerous upon non-residents than upon residents.[115]

The due process clause performs yet another important function—to protect against the arbitrary action of State officials generally, where no specific constitutional guarantee affords protection. This function is best described by the Supreme Court's opinion in a case involving suspension of an automobile driver's license: "Once licenses are issued, as in petitioner's case, their continued possession may become essential in the pursuit of a livelihood. Suspension of issued licenses thus involved state action that adjudicates important interests of the licensees. In such cases the licenses are not to be taken away without that procedural due process required by the Fourteenth Amendment. . . . This is but an application of the general proposition that relevant constitutional restraints limit state power to terminate an entitlement whether the entitlement is denominated a 'right' of a 'privilege.' *Sherbert v. Verner*, 374 U.S. 398 (1963) (disqualification for unemployment compensation); *Slochower v. Board of Education*, 350 U.S. 551 (1956) (discharge from public employment); *Speiser v. Randall*, 357 U.S. 513 (1958) (denial of a tax exemption); *Goldberg v. Kelly*, 397 U.S. 254 (1970) (withdrawal of welfare benefits). . . .

Due Process as Protection Against Arbitrariness

No Right-Privilege Dichotomy

"We turn then to the nature of the procedural due process which must be afforded the licensee on the question of his fault or liability for the accident. A procedural rule that may satisfy due process in one context may not necessarily satisfy procedural due process in every case. Thus, procedures adequate to determine a welfare claim may not suffice to try a felony charge. . . . Due process re-

---

[112] *Frick v. Pa.*, 268 U.S. 473 (1925); *Blodgett v. Silberman*, 277 U.S. 1 (1928); *Farmers' Loan & T. Co. v. Minn.*, 280 U.S. 204 (1930); *Baldwin v. Mo.*, 281 U.S. 586 (1930); *First Nat'l Bk. v. Me.*, 284 U.S. 312 (1932).

[113] *Curry v. McCanless*, 307 U.S. 357 (1939); *Graves v. Elliot*, 307 U.S. 383 (1939); *Tax Com'n v. Aldrich*, 316 U.S. 174 (1942); *Greenough v. Tax Assessors*, 331 U.S. 486 (1947); *Tabacalera Severiand Jorge, S. A. v. Standard Cigar Co.*, 392 F. 2d. 706, 715 (1968); *State Loan & Finance Corp. v. D.C.*, 381 F. 2d. 895 (1967).

[114] *Guaranty Trust Co. v. Va.*, 305 U.S. 19 (1938); *Miller Bros. Co. v. Maryland*, 347 U.S. 340, 345 (1954).

[115] *Shaffer v. Carter*, 252 U.S. 37 (1920). *See also Austin v. N.H.*, 420 U.S. 656 (1975). A State may tax dividends declared outside its jurisdiction by a "foreign corporation" to the amount of the dividends which were earned within the State by the corporation. *Wisconsin v. J. C. Penney Co.*, 311 U.S. 435 (1940); *American Commuters' Association v. Levitt*, 405 F. 2d. 1148, 1152 (1969).

quires that when a State seeks to terminate an interest such as that here involved, it must afford 'notice and opportunity for hearing appropriate to the nature of the case' before the termination becomes effective."[116] But in a later case, "[t]he only question" in which was "one of timing" in according an evidentiary hearing, the Court held that, in view of the weighty public interests and the unlikelihood of error, due process did not require a hearing at the time a driver's license was initially lifted following his third conviction within a year and pending a final decision to revoke.[117]

Consistent with the flexible requirement that existence of due process guarantees afforded by the State comport with the importance of the liberty or property interest subject to deprivation, the Court upheld New York's procedures (10 days advance notice, option of requesting preremoval conference, full adversary administrative hearing subject to judicial review) for removing children placed by State agencies in foster homes.[118] And, in a case challenging a provision of New York law that establishes a rebuttable presumption that a person applying for relief within 75 days of quitting his job has done so for the purpose of qualifying for public assistance, the Court held that the State may, before granting benefits, constitutionally place the burden on the applicant to clear himself of a self-seeking motive or, alternatively, compel him to wait until such time as his motive is no longer regarded as relevant.[119] The Court has also held that a policeman, dismissed for insubordination and poor attendance at police training sessions, had no protectable Fourteenth Amendment interest in his job, beyond that conferred by State law, and that his discharge without pretermination hearing and on oral explication of the reasons, whether or not such reasons were true, did not violate due process.[120] Relying on Arnett v. Kennedy[121] identifying a "property" or "liberty" interest in such a decision when it imposes a blemish on the individual's reputation, Justice White wrote in dissent: "The ordinance plainly grants petitioner a right to his job unless there is cause to fire him. Having granted him such a right it is the Federal Con-

---

[116] Bell v. Burson, 402 U.S. 535, 538-542 (1971).

[117] Dixon v. Love, 431 U.S. 105 (1977). The decision draws heavily on some of the Court's more recent due process decisions in an administrative context with respect to the termination of welfare benefits, namely, Goldberg v. Kelly, 397 U.S. 254 (1970), and especially Mathews v. Eldridge, 424 U.S. 319 (1976), and succinctly summarizes their central principles.

[118] Smith v. Organ. of Foster Families for Equality and Reform, 97 S.Ct. 2094 (1977).

[119] Lavine v. Milne, 424 U.S. 577 (1976).

[120] Bishop v. Wood, 426 U.S. 341 (1976). This decision seems entirely consistent with the Court's renewed emphasis on respect for federalism and, hence, deference to State law.

[121] 416 U.S. 134 (1974). The thrust of this guarantee seemed appreciably limited in a subsequent decision, Codd v. Vegler, 429 U.S. 624 (1977), where the Court held no hearing was required where an untenured employee did not challenge the truth of the stigmatizing allegations.

stitution, not state law, which determines the process to be applied in connection with any state decision to deprive him of it." Nor, as discussed earlier with respect to an asserted privacy interest (p. 471), did the Court find a denial of due process where police took it upon themselves and without any procedural guarantees to circulate to local merchants a flyer identifying "active shoplifters."[122] Finally, the University of Minnesota launched a suit (marked by initial success but rebuffed on appeal) in which it argued that young athletes have a property interest in the opportunity to play college sports which they cannot be denied without due process.[123] (For some additional discussion of procedural guarantees in the administrative process, *see* p. 396; for some added cases on due process and protected liberty and property rights, *see* p. 390.)

Though the Court announced sometime ago that regard for the principles of "Our Federalism" and respect for State prerogatives in the administration of criminal justice compelled it to fashion a clear rule against intervention by Federal courts in *pending* State criminal proceedings except in truly extraordinary circumstances,[124] the Court's review of alleged denials of due process in completed State criminal proceedings have manifested a less doctrinal approach. A few examples from recent years will suffice.

Building upon its holding of five years ago in *in re* Winship, which specified that "the Due Process Clause protects the accused against conviction except upon proof beyond a reasonable doubt of every fact necessary to constitute the crime with which he is charged,"[125] the Supreme Court invalidated the constitutionality of Maine's practice governing verdicts in homicide cases. State law segregated illegal killings into two categories, murder (which carries a mandatory life sentence) and manslaughter (for which the

[122] Paul *v*. Davis, 424 U.S. 693 (1976).

[123] The suit arose from an NCAA action placing the university sports program on indefinite probation when the university refused to find three basketball players ineligible without due process hearings. A Federal district court agreed that the opportunity to participate in intercollegiate baseball at the university was a property right; *see* Regents of the University of Minnesota *v*. Nat'l Collegiate Athletic Ass'n, 422 F.Supp. 1158 (1976). The U.S. Court of Appeals for the Eighth Circuit has reversed that decision. *See Minneapolis Tribune*, Aug. 4, 1977.

[124] Younger *v*. Harris, 401 U.S. 37 (1971), and Huffman *v*. Pursue, Ltd., 420 U.S. 592 (1975). *See also* Trainor *v*. Hernandez, 97 S.Ct. 1911 (1977). The decisions in these cases reflected the Burger Court's displeasure with Dombrowski *v*. Pfister, 380 U.S. 479 (1965), a Warren Court ruling that encouraged Federal court intervention to protect "preferred freedoms" from the "chilling effects" of State prosecutions. The Court's growing deference to the States in criminal proceedings is illustrated by subsequent decisions that substantially cut back the use of Federal courts to allow prison inmates to collaterally attack their State convictions. E.g., Stone *v*. Powell, 428 U.S. 465 (1976). Said the Court even more recently: "It goes without saying that preventing and dealing with crime is much more the business of the States than it is of the Federal Government . . . and that we should not lightly construe the Constitution so as to intrude upon the administration of justice of the individual States." Patterson *v*. N.Y., 97 S.Ct. 2319, 2322 (1977).

[125] 397 U.S. 358, 364 (1970).

penalty is a fine or imprisonment not exceeding 20 years). At trial, the prosecution was required to establish that a killing was unlawful and intentional, and, only if these elements were proved, was the jury to consider the distinction between the two offenses, where-upon the burden fell to the defendant to prove by a preponder-ance of the evidence that he acted "in the heat of passion or sud-den provocation" to reduce the offense to manslaughter. Said Justice Powell speaking for a unanimous Court: "Not only are the interests underlying *Winship* implicated to a greater degree in this case, but in one respect the protection afforded those interests is less here. In *Winship* the ultimate burden of persuasion remained with the prosecution, although the standard had been reduced to proof by a fair preponderance of the evidence. In this case, by con-trast, the State has affirmatively shifted the burden of proof to the defendant. The result, in a case such as this one where the defend-ant is required to prove the critical fact in dispute, is to increase further the likelihood of an erroneous murder conviction. . . . We therefore hold that the Due Process Clause requires the prosecu-tion to prove beyond a reasonable doubt the absence of the heat of passion or sudden provocation when the issue is properly pre-sented in a homicide case."[126] (*See also* the discussion at p. 393.)

With respect to standing trial, the Supreme Court held that a de-fendant was not denied due process when, charged with a mis-demeanor carrying a possible penalty of imprisonment, he was tried before a nonlawyer, police court judge, in view of the fact that trial *de novo* was available in circuit court under Kentucky's two-tier court system. Nor did the Court find a denial of equal protection in State law that provided law-trained judges in some police courts and lay judges in others depending on the city's population.[127] The Court also rejected a due process challenge where a defendant was tried wearing identifiable prison clothes *and he failed to register an objection at trial.* While agreeing that compelling a defendant to wear prison garb in court would certainly jeopardize the prospect of a fair trial, the Court ruled that, by not objecting at the time, the accused waived his right and could not raise that question on ap-peal.[128] And the Court ruled that evidence stemming from an un-necessarily suggestive identification procedure subsequent to Stovall *v.* Denno[129] could nevertheless be admitted at trial where,

---

[126] Mullaney *v.* Wilbur, 421 U.S. 684, 700-701, 704 (1975). *Cf.* Patterson *v.* N.Y., 97 S.Ct. 2319 (1977) where the Court upheld a State statute requiring the defendant in a prosecution for second-degree murder to prove by a preponderance of the evi-dence the affirmative defense of extreme emotional disturbance to reduce the crime to manslaughter. The Court explained that such an affirmative defense "does not serve to negative any facts of the crime which the State is to prove in order to convict for murder" but constitutes a separate issue on which the defendant carries the burden of persuasion.

[127] North *v.* Russell, 427 U.S. 328 (1976).

[128] Estelle *v.* Williams, 425 U.S. 501 (1976).

[129] 388 U.S. 293 (1967).

under the totality of the circumstances, it passed the test of reliability.[130]

But among the hosts of cases in which the Supreme Court held
actions within State law enforcement systems violative of the requirements of procedural due process were the following: (1) sending a forfeiture notice to the home of a man who was in jail when
State officials should have known he could not receive it;[131] (2) trying a person for a traffic offense before a judge who was also the
mayor and thus had an interest in the collection of fines which provided a substantial portion of village funds;[132] (3) depriving a man
at trial of his only witness when the judge admonished the witness,
who was serving a jail term, that he had better tell the truth or he
would probably have to serve more time thus frightening him into
a refusal to testify;[133] and (4) revoking a probation on the grounds
that failure to report a traffic citation was tantamount to failure to
report an "arrest."[134]

Recent lower court rulings bearing on asserted denials of due
process in State criminal proceedings have held: (1) that anything
less than reciprocal alibi disclosure (i.e., in cases where the defendant offers as his defense an alibi and must disclose in advance of
trial his intention to rely on an alibi, the State must disclose to him
what witnesses it will call to refute the alibi) is unconstitutional;[135]
(2) that due process is not denied where an indigent defendant in
a criminal prosecution offers the defense of insanity but does not
have funds and is thereby precluded from hiring expert witnesses
to rebut the testimony of State-hired psychiatrists;[136] (3) that a defendant standing trial for the commission of aggravated sodomy
had no constitutional right to be tried free from the influence of a
tranquilizing drug;[137] and (4) that North Carolina's outlawry statute, which licenses the public to kill a fugitive accused of a felony if
he runs after being called on to surrender, is unconstitutional.[138]

---

[130] Manson *v.* Brathwaite, 97 S.Ct. 2243 (1977). The factors to be taken into account, enumerated in Neil *v.* Biggers, 409 U.S. 188 (1972), are, as the Court reiterated them in *Manson*: "the opportunity of the witness to view the criminal at the time
of the crime, the witness' degree of attention, the accuracy of his prior description of
the criminal, the level of certainty demonstrated at the confrontation, and the time
between the crime and the confrontation. Against these factors is to be weighed the
corrupting effect of the suggestive identification itself." *Ibid.*, 2253.

[131] Robinson *v.* Hanrahan, 409 U.S. 38 (1972).

[132] Ward *v.* Village of Monroeville, Ohio, 409 U.S. 57 (1972).

[133] Webb *v.* Texas, 409 U.S. 95 (1972).

[134] Douglas *v.* Buder, 412 U.S. 430 (1973).

[135] Cossack *v.* City of Los Angeles, 110 Cal. Rptr. 243 (1973); People *v.* Collins,
348 N.Y.S. 2d. 99 (1973); Commonwealth *v.* Contakos, 314 A. 2d. 259 (1974);
Commonwealth *v.* Jackson, 319 A. 2d. 161 (1974); People *v.* Gaines, 354 N.Y.S. 2d.
843 (1974); Allison *v.* State, 214 N.W. 2d. 437 (1974); Wright *v.* Sup'r Ct. in and for
Cty. of Maricopa, 517 P. 2d. 1261 (1974); State *v.* Grant, 519 P. 2d. 261 (1974).

[136] James *v.* State, 307 N.E. 2d. 59 (1974).

[137] State *v.* Jojola, 553 P. 2d. 1296 (1976).

[138] Autry *v.* Mitchell, 420 F.Supp. 967 (1976). The statute did not allow for judicial discretion in assessing the truth of charges set forth in the requisite affidavit, but

Juveniles   One of the clearest trends in constitutional protections within the
and Due   criminal justice system in recent years has been the extension of
Process   rights to minors who are the subject of criminal complaints. Decisions of the U.S. Supreme Court, for example, have held that
juveniles have the right to notice of charges, to counsel, to confront
and cross-examine witnesses, and to the privilege against self-
incrimination.[139] Juveniles may be convicted only on the basis of
"proof beyond a reasonable doubt"[140] and may not be put in
jeopardy twice for the same crime,[141] but they do not have a constitutional right to trial by jury.[142] Lower courts have also held: (1)
that probable cause is a constitutional standard that also protects
juveniles;[143] (2) that where a minor, taken into custody on a curfew
violation, was denied the opportunity to make a phone call, where
his parents were not notified, and where the juvenile was held for
five days in jail with adults, such actions violate constitutional
guarantees;[144] (3) that rules against the admission of hearsay evidence operate in adjudicatory proceedings of juvenile court;[145]
and (4) that a juvenile was entitled to damages from a police officer
who shot him while resisting arrest on a *misdemeanor* charge and
from the mayor who had issued a "shoot to kill" order.[146]

Prisoners'   The Supreme Court rendered a series of decisions affecting the
Rights   rights of those already in prison. Although the full panoply of
to Due   rights due the defendant in a criminal prosecution are not applica-
Process   ble in prison disciplinary proceedings where the inmate is charged
with "serious misconduct," the Court has ruled that certain procedural guarantees hold. Among these are advance written notice
of the charges, written statement justifying the decision, and the
right to produce witnesses in one's defense. The Court has not held
that the right to counsel or the right to confront witnesses inhere in
the proceedings.[147] The Court declined to reach the question of
whether such protections extended to hearings that would potentially result in an inmate's loss of privileges.[148] The Supreme Court
also held that the due process clause does not entitle a duly con-

---

compelled a judge to proclaim an accused an outlaw if, charged with a felony, he
evades arrest or conceals himself and fails to submit to process.

[139] *In re* Gault, 387 U.S. 1 (1967). The Court declined to rule on whether the Constitution also required that a juvenile defendant be provided a transcript of the proceedings or the right to appellate review.

[140] *In re* Winship, 397 U.S. 358 (1970).

[141] Breed *v.* Jones, 421 U.S. 519 (1975).

[142] McKeiver *v.* Pa., 403 U.S. 528 (1971).

[143] Cox *v.* Turley, 506 F. 2d. 1347 (1974).

[144] *Ibid.*   [145] *In re* Simon, 295 So. 2d. 473 (1974).

[146] Palmer *v.* Hall, 380 F.Supp. 120 (1974). The mayor involved was Ronnie
Thompson of Macon, Georgia. The text of the mayor's rather forthright "shoot to
kill" memorandum to the city police chief is included in the court opinion together
with an anthology of his supporting statements.

[147] *See* Wolff *v.* McDonnell, 418 U.S. 539 (1974); Baxter *v.* Palmigiano, 425 U.S.
308 (1976). *See also* the earlier decisions concerning parole and probation revocation
proceedings, Morrissey *v.* Brewer, 408 U.S. 471 (1972), and Gagnon *v.* Scarpelli,
411 U.S. 778 (1973).

[148] Baxter *v.* Palmigiano, 425 U.S. 308 (1976).

victed State prisoner to a fact-finding hearing when he is moved to a substantially less favorable penal institution in the absence of a State law conditioning such transfer on proof of misconduct or under other specified circumstances.[149] (*See also* p. 396.)

In two major decisions, the Supreme Court spoke to the question of what constitutes due process at school. The Court first heard a due process challenge to the suspension practices of some public school administrators. Drawing upon rulings establishing analogous property rights in cases involving the firing of public employees and the loss of prisoners' good time credits, the majority, speaking through Justice White, held that the State, having extended the benefits of public education, could not withdraw them from students absent procedural safeguards. Moreover, the Court reasoned, misconduct charges, if sustained, could seriously damage a student's reputation and significantly impede his later educational and employment opportunities, and therefore, student disciplinary procedures must be protected against being arbitrarily invoked. To guard against abuse, the Court held that a student who is to be suspended from school should be given notice, reasons, and a hearing prior to the administrator's action, but where the student's behavior is disruptive to the academic process, he may be suspended as long as notice, reasons, and a hearing follow as soon as is practicable.[150] Justice Powell, joined by Chief Justice Burger and Justices Blackmun and Rehnquist, dissented on the ground that, to the extent that a student's interest in education is infringed by suspension, "it is too speculative, transitory, and insubstantial to justify imposition of a *constitutional* rule." Moreover, since teachers and school administrators make many other decisions, in grading, promotion, athletics, tracking, and extracurricular activities, "claims of impairment of one's educational entitlement identical in principle to those before the Court today can be asserted with equal or greater justification." Indeed, concluded Justice Powell, "it is . . . difficult to perceive any principled limit to the new reach of procedural due process."[151]

In its second major decision, two years later, the Court, after

Due Process and Students

---

[149] Meachum v. Fano, 427 U.S. 215 (1976). *See also* Montayne v. Haymes, 427 U.S. 236 (1976).

[150] Goss v. Lopez, 419 U.S. 565 (1975). Justice White added, "We stop short of construing the Due Process Clause to require, countrywide, that hearings in connection with short suspensions must accord the student the opportunity to secure counsel, to confront and cross-examine witnesses supporting the charge and to call his own witnesses to verify his version of the incident." Such trial-type hearings, he continued, "might overwhelm administrative facilities in many places and, by diverting resources, cost more than it could save in educational effectiveness . . . [and] . . . destroy its effectiveness as part of the teaching process," *ibid.*, 583. See also *Minneapolis Tribune*, Nov. 4, 1974.

[151] *Ibid.*, 583, 586, 597, 600. Justice Powell's point appears to be borne out in at least two cases. *See* Ector Cty. Indep. School Dist. v. Hopkins, 518 S.W. 2d. 576 (1974), involving a student's expulsion for one day and her expulsion from an honor society for allegedly drinking wine during the lunch hour in violation of school rules; *see also* Wood v. Strickland, 420 U.S. 308 (1975), *and see* Warren v. Nat'l Ass'n of Secondary School Principals, 375 F.Supp. 1043 (1974).

"conclud[ing] that when public school teachers or administrators impose disciplinary corporal punishment, the Eighth Amendment is inapplicable" (*see* p. 436), turned to "[t]he pertinent constitutional question" of whether its imposition "is consistent with the requirements of due process." The Court found that due process did not require a hearing in advance of the decision to paddle students who misbehaved. Said the Court: "In view of the low incidence of abuse, the openness of our schools, and the common law safeguards that already exist, the risk of error that may result in violation of a schoolchild's substantive rights can only be regarded as minimal. Imposing additional administrative safeguards as a constitutional requirement might reduce that risk marginally, but would also entail a significant intrusion into an area of primary educational responsibility."[152]

Due Process and Confinement in Mental Institutions   At the same time judges have been exploring the constitutional dimensions of the kind of treatment given patients in mental health institutions (*see* p. 473), there has been increasing concern as to the constitutionality of the procedures by which those patients got there in the first place. Recently, the Supreme Court directed its attention to the question of "whether the State may compulsorily confine a nondangerous, mentally ill individual for the purpose of treatment." Given that "[t]he jury found that Donaldson [the plaintiff who had been confined in a Florida facility for nearly 15 years] was neither dangerous to himself nor dangerous to others, and also found that, if mentally ill, Donaldson had not received treatment," the Court held, "In short, a State cannot constitutionally confine without more a nondangerous individual who is capable of surviving safely in freedom by himself or with the help of willing and responsible family members or friends. Since the jury found, upon ample evidence, that O'Connor [the hospital superintendent], as an agent of the State, knowingly did so confine Donaldson, it properly concluded that O'Connor violated Donaldson's constitutional right to freedom."[153] The Court remanded the case to the district court to consider whether the hospital superintendent's contention that he was acting pursuant to State law in "good faith" precluded Donaldson from recovering damages on grounds of official immunity.

Recent lower Federal and State court decisions have focused on many more of the specifics of involuntary civil commitment, stressing not only the test of dangerousness, but also speedy hearing and guarantees of an adversary process.[154] In this regard, the courts

---

[152] Ingraham *v.* Wright, 97 S.Ct. 1401, 1418 (1977). The common law principle, governing the imposition of corporal punishment on students, cited by the Court with approval is that "teachers may impose reasonable but not excessive force to discipline a child."

[153] O'Connor *v.* Donaldson, 422 U.S. 563, 576 (1975).

[154] *See* Lessard *v.* Schmidt, 349 F.Supp. 1078 (1972), 379 F.Supp. 1376 (1974); *in re* Ballay, 482 F. 2d. 648 (1973); State *ex rel.* Hawks *v.* Lazaro, 202 S.E. 2d. 109 (1974); State *ex rel.* Walker *v.* Jenkins, 203 S.E. 2d. 353 (1974); Lynch *v.* Baxley, 386

have held: (1) that an individual may not be detained in a jail or hospital on an emergency basis pending examination without a timely hearing to ascertain probable cause that he is mentally ill and at which hearing he has the rights to notice, counsel, to be present unless a separate hearing finds he is incapacitated, and the assurance of a civil commitment hearing soon to follow; (2) that at a civil commitment hearing the person involved must have notice of his rights, notice of the evidence in favor of his confinement, the right to counsel, the right to be present unless he is found to be incapacitated in a separate hearing, the right to pretrial disclosure of witnesses favoring his confinement and their findings, and the right to cross-examine witnesses; (3) that the decision to commit an individual be made only upon clear and convincing evidence that the person is dangerous to others or to himself, preferably upon the decision of a jury, after the judge has canvassed the availability of a treatment program, and only if confinement is the least restrictive alternative; (4) that property of mental patients may not be taken by the State without observing procedural safeguards; and (5) that transfer to conditions of greater restraint be undertaken only after notice and hearing. In somewhat related matters, courts have also held: (1) that a former mental patient does not have the right to have access to a hospital's medical records;[155] (2) that a State may not proceed with a criminal prosecution while the defendant remains committed in a mental institution;[156] and (3) that a defendant was mentally fit to stand trial where his ability to be present and assist his counsel depended on his taking a prescribed drug.[157] Judicial review has also continued where treatments have intruded significantly on the patient's integrity as an individual.[158] These developing rights in the mental health process, moreover, have been held clearly applicable to children.[159] However, courts

---

F.Supp. 378 (1974); Kendall v. True, 391 F.Supp. 413 (1975); in re Fisher, 313 N.E. 2d. 851 (1974); in re Hodges, 325 A. 2d. 605 (1974); Doremus v. Farrell, 407 F.Supp. 509 (1975); State v. Krol, 344 A. 2d. 289 (1975); in re Andrews, 334 N.E. 2d. 15 (1975); People v. Burnick, 535 P. 2d. 352 (1975); People v. Feagley, 535 P. 2d. 373 (1975); State v. O'Neill, 545 P. 2d. 97 (1976); Stamus v. Leonhart, 414 F.Supp. 439 (1976); see also Meisel v. Kremens, 405 F.Supp. 1253 (1975) and Suzuki v. Quisenberry, 411 F.Supp. 1113 (1976). For an account of the bitterness engendered by a prisoner's transfer from a penal institution to mental hospital and his confinement there for 27 years, see United States ex rel. Schuster v. Vincent, 524 F. 2d. 153 (1975).

[155] Gotkin v. Miller, 379 F.Supp. 859 (1974) aff'd 514 F. 2d. 125 (1975); see also Wolfe v. Beale, 353 A. 2d. 481 (1976).

[156] Commonwealth v. Kohr, 323 A. 2d. 79 (1974).

[157] People v. Dalfonso, 321 N.E. 2d. 379 (1974).

[158] Price v. Sheppard, 239 N.W. 2d. 905 (1976). And see Knecht v. Gillman, 488 F. 2d. 1136 (1973); Horacek v. Exon, 357 F.Supp. 71 (1973). Also see Harper v. Cserr, 544 F. 2d. 1121 (1976), where the "wanton callousness" of those caring for the patient drove her to suicide.

[159] Bartley v. Kremens, 402 F.Supp. 1039 (1975); J. L. v. Parham, 412 F.Supp. 112 (1976). See also Kidd v. Schmidt, 399 F.Supp. 301 (1975).

have continued to uphold sterilization of the mentally ill or retarded.[160]

In other decisions, lower courts concluded that due process was denied where: (1) a municipal ordinance presumed parental responsibility for the misbehavior of their children;[161] (2) a school district refused even to consider employing a blind teacher;[162] and (3) a student was suspended because his mother struck the principal.[163] Finally, in litigation that asserted that State legislation had infringed "fundamental" personal liberty "in matters of marriage and family life," the U.S. Supreme Court found mandatory maternity leaves for teachers, enforced by school boards, "arbitrary" and "irrational" in creating an irrebuttable presumption that female teachers are incapable of fulfilling their duties beyond the fourth or fifth month of pregnancy.[164]

"Equal
Protection
of the
Laws" and
Legislative
Classifica-
tions

"Equal protection of the laws": Because statutes inevitably create distinctions as to how various people will be treated—who will receive what benefits and who will pay for them, who will assume what responsibilities and who will bear what penalties for failure to assume them—a clash seems inescapable between the reality that virtually all laws construct classifications of some sort and the Fourteenth Amendment's mandate of "equal protection of the laws." Though this protection, like those of the Fourteenth Amendment generally, was doubtless meant to protect the newly freed Negro,[165] the guarantee of equal protection of the laws has experienced far wider application as countless decisions of the Supreme Court readily illustrate. If all laws discriminate, then, which laws discriminate impermissibly? What criteria for the creation of classifications in law yield "suspect classes" that, if not sufficiently justified, result in "invidious discrimination"? Part of the answer is "none, in themselves." Even race, which is the obvious candidate for a *per se* rule,[166] has been tolerated as a basis for legitimate discrimination.[167] "Suspect classes" appear to be created in one of two ways. The term "suspect class" may characterize a "discrete and insular" group,[168] one "saddled with such disabilities, or subjected to

---

[160] *In re* Sterilization of Moore, 221 S.E. 2d. 307 (1976); North Carolina Ass'n for Retarded Children *v.* N.C., 420 F.Supp. 451 (1976). North Carolina habitually ranks first in the nation as the State with the largest annual number of forced sterilizations.

[161] Doe *v.* City of Trenton, 362 A. 2d. 1200 (1976).

[162] Gurmankin *v.* Costanzo, 411 F.Supp. 982 (1976).

[163] St. Ann *v.* Palisi, 495 F. 2d. 423 (1974).

[164] Cleveland Bd. of Educ. *v.* LaFleur, 414 U.S. 632 (1974).

[165] The Slaughterhouse Cases, 83 U.S. 36 (1873); Strauder *v.* W.Va., 100 U.S. 303 (1880).

[166] Probably the closest to a *per se* rule was the principle articulated by Justice Harlan in dissent in Plessy *v.* Ferguson, 163 U.S. 537, 552 (1896): "Our Constitution is color blind, and neither knows nor tolerates classes among citizens."

[167] Korematsu *v.* U.S., 323 U.S. 214 (1944); Hirabayashi *v.* U.S., 320 U.S. 81 (1943). *See also* discussion of "reverse discrimination" and the "benign quota" at p. 510.

[168] United States *v.* Carolene Products Co., 304 U.S. 144, 152-153, note 4 (1938).

such a history of purposeful unequal treatment, or relegated to such a position of political powerlessness as to command extraordinary protection from the majoritarian political process."[169] Usually this has meant blacks (p. 500) and aliens (*infra*), and occasionally it has included women (p. 512). Another sense in which something like a "suspect class" arises is where a statute excludes a group from the possession of a "fundamental" right. As indicated earlier (p. 466), these "fundamental" rights may be explicitly or only implicitly provided in the Bill of Rights.

In terms of the Court's bifurcated approach,[170] statutes that discriminate against "suspect classes" or invade a "fundamental" right must clear the higher hurdles in the upper tier of the Court's "two-tier model" of equal protection analysis.[171] This means the application of the "strict scrutiny" or "preferred freedoms" test. (*See* p. 306.) As Justice Marshall has observed, "If a statute is subject to strict scrutiny, the statute is always, or nearly always, . . . struck down. Quite obviously, the only critical decision is whether strict scrutiny should be invoked at all."[172] Legislation that neither yields a "suspect class" nor denies a "fundamental" right is measured by the lower hurdles of the bottom tier, what is called "the mere rationality test." This test asks whether the departure from equal treatment, provided under a given statute is reasonably justified.[173] And, as Justice Marshall observed with respect to it, "[T]hat test, too, when applied as articulated, leaves little doubt about the outcome; the challenged legislation is always upheld."[174] How consistently this schema has come to dominate the Court's equal protection analysis remains a matter of considerable dispute. In the words of Justice Marshall, "[H]appily the Court's deeds have not matched its words. Time and again, met with cases touching upon the prized rights and burdened classes of our society, the Court has acted only after a reasonably probing look at the legislative goals and means, and at the significance of the personal rights and interests invaded."[175]

Beginning with the premise that "[a]liens as a class are a prime example of a 'discrete and insular' minority," so that "classifications based on alienage . . . are inherently suspect and subject to close

Aliens

---

[169] San Antonio Indep. School Dist. *v.* Rodriguez, 411 U.S. 1, 28 (1973).

[170] *See* Gerald Gunther, "In Search of Evolving Doctrine on a Changing Court: A Model for a Newer Equal Protection," 86 *Harvard Law Review* 1 (1972).

[171] The reference to the Court's approach as "the two-tier model" is Justice Marshall's. Massachusetts Bd. of Retirement *v.* Murgia, 427 U.S. 307, 318 (1976).

[172] *Ibid.*, 319.

[173] *See* Lindsley *v.* Natural Carbonic Gas Co., 220 U.S. 61, 78 (1911); Williamson *v.* Lee Optical Co., 348 U.S. 483 (1955).

[174] Massachusetts Bd. of Retirement *v.* Murgia, 427 U.S. 307, 319 (1976).

[175] *Ibid.*, 320. In several dissenting opinions, Justice Marshall criticized at length the Court's two-tier approach and advocated a more flexible, and activist, tack for equal protection analysis. *See* Dandridge *v.* Williams, 397 U.S. 471, 508 (1970); San Antonio Indep. School Dist. *v.* Rodriguez, 411 U.S. 1, 70 (1973); Massachusetts Bd. of Retirement *v.* Murgia, 427 U.S. 307, 317 (1976).

judicial scrutiny,"[176] the Court has struck down numerous State statutes that severely restricted or entirely banned aliens from certain occupations,[177] denied or limited their receipt of educational or welfare benefits,[178] and prohibited them from holding civil service posts.[179] As indicated before, aliens were long ago held to be "persons" within the protection of the Fourteenth Amendment.[180] But the constitutional restriction on what government can do is markedly less at the Federal than the State level because of the Constitution's specific charge to Congress with respect to controlling immigration and naturalization.[181] It was not too surprising, then, when the Court, several years ago, held that the provision of the 1964 Civil Rights Act barring discrimination on the basis of "national origin" does not extend to prohibit a refusal to give equal employment opportunities on the basis of citizenship or alienage.[182]

Illegitimate Children   Though the Court has explicitly acknowledged that illegitimate children are "persons," too, within the meaning of the Fourteenth Amendment,[183] this has not converted the group into a "suspect class."[184] The bulk of the Court's decisions, however, run against

[176] Graham v. Richardson, 403 U.S. 365, 372 (1971).

[177] Yick Wo v. Hopkins, 118 U.S. 356 (1886); Truax v. Raich, 239 U.S. 33 (1915); Takahashi v. Fish and Game Com'n, 334 U.S. 410 (1948); in re Griffiths, 413 U.S. 717 (1973). See also Norwick v. Nyquist, 417 F.Supp. 913 (1976). And see Examining Bd. of Engineers, Architects, and Surveyors v. Flores de Otero, 426 U.S. 572 (1976).

[178] Graham v. Richardson, 403 U.S. 365 (1971); Nyquist v. Mauclet, 97 S.Ct. 2120 (1977); cf. Mathews v. Diaz, 426 U.S 67 (1976).

[179] Sugarman v. Dougall, 413 U.S. 634 (1973). See also Hampton v. Mow Sung Wong, 426 U.S. 88 (1976).

[180] Yick Wo. v. Hopkins, 118 U.S. 356 (1886). Before the Court's regular adherence to the strict scrutiny approach, States were not obliged to include aliens in the distribution of public welfare or benefits, see Truax v. Raich, 239 U.S. 33, 39-40 (1915), but this exception was overtaken with the general demise of the right-privilege distinction in Constitutional Law. See Graham v. Richardson, 403 U.S. 365, 372-376 (1971).

[181] The Court sums it up in Takahashi v. Fish and Game Com'n, 334 U.S., at 419. See Chinese Exclusion Case, 130 U.S. 581 (1889); Fong Yue Ting v. U.S., 149 U.S. 698 (1893); Harisiades v. Shaughnessy, 342 U.S. 580 (1952); Shaughnessy v. U.S. ex rel. Mezei, 345 U.S. 206 (1953); Galvan v. Press, 347 U.S. 522 (1954). In equal protection terms, the difference between the Federal and State jurisdictions becomes readily apparent where residency requirements are imposed as a condition for Medicare or education benefits; the restriction on aliens (i.e., the imposition of a residency requirement) was sustained in the Federal case, Mathews v. Diaz, 426 U.S 67 (1976), but not the State case, Nyquist v. Mauclet, 97 S.Ct. 2120 (1977).

[182] Espinoza v. Farah Mfg. Co., 414 U.S. 86 (1973).

[183] Levy v. La., 391 U.S. 68, 70 (1968).

[184] Indeed, the Court has held explicitly to the contrary; see Mathews v. Lucas, 427 U.S. 495, 504-506 (1976). Consequently, though sentiments of the Warren Court might have been in the other direction, see Levy v. La., 391 U.S. 68 (1968), the focus of the Court's analysis currently is on the arbitrariness of the distinction. This necessarily leads the Court to adopt an interest-balancing approach. That the sentiments of the Warren Court were in favor of holding that illegitimates constituted a "suspect class" is reinforced by the dissenting opinion of Justice Brennan in Labine v. Vincent, 401 U.S. 532, 541 (1971).

distinctions created in State law that cut against illegitimates, such as those in (1) a wrongful death statute allowing only legitimate children to recover damages for the death of a parent;[185] (2) a workmen's compensation law allowing legitimates to first claim, prioritizing illegitimates with "other dependents," and awarding payment only if first-priority claimants do not exhaust the collectable limit;[186] and (3) a statute creating a judicially enforceable right to support for legitimate children from their natural fathers but denying such a claim by illegitimates.[187] But the Court has upheld distinctions in State or Federal law that: (1) gave priority to others (including illegitimates who had been legitimated) over illegitimates who had merely been acknowledged in intestate succession;[188] and (2) required children other than those who were legitimate, adopted, or eligible to inherit property from the insured under State law (these were automatically qualified) to show dependency (as defined in the statute) on the deceased before being declared eligible to collect surviving children's benefits under the Social Security Act.[189] The Court, in large measure, has justified reaching different conclusions in these various cases by pointing out that some State interests are weightier than others in overriding the equal protection claim of the illegitimates[190] (especially the State interest in preventing spurious claims to estates) and that some statutes create "insurmountable barriers" to illegitimates while others allow the parents to legitimate those children born out of wedlock such that they can share alike under the law with legitimates.

In the text of a 1977 decision in which the Court ruled that States are not constitutionally obliged by the equal protection clause to fund elective as well as therapeutic abortions for indigent women, it observed: "In a sense, every denial of welfare to an indigent creates a wealth classification as compared to nonindigents who are able to pay for the desired goods or services. But this Court has never held that financial need alone identifies a suspect class for purposes of equal protection analysis. . . . Accordingly, the central question . . . is whether the regulation 'impinges upon a fundamental right explicitly or implicitly protected by the Constitution.' "[191]

Indigency

[185] Levy v. La., 391 U.S. 68 (1968).

[186] Weber v. Aetna Casualty and Surety Co., 406 U.S. 164 (1972). Or a State statute designed to deny illegitimates welfare benefits legitimate children could obtain, see New Jersey Welfare Rights Organ. v. Cahill, 411 U.S. 619 (1973).

[187] Gomez v. Perez, 409 U.S. 535 (1973).

[188] Labine v. Vincent, 401 U.S. 532 (1971). But the Court has struck down an Illinois statute which allows legitimate children to inherit by intestate succession from both parents but allows illegitimates to inherit in the absence of a will only from the mothers. Trimble v. Gordon, 97 S.Ct. 1459 (1977).

[189] Mathews v. Lucas, 427 U.S. 495 (1976).

[190] See Jimenez v. Weinburger, 417 U.S. 628 (1974); though the Court in this case struck down a provision of the Social Security Act and not a State statute, the balancing approach is apparent.

[191] Maher v. Roe, 97 S.Ct. 2376, 2381 (1977).

The statement seems entirely correct and substantially distinguishes statutes the Court struck down from those it upheld. For example, in cases where the poll tax was declared unconstitutional,[192] or where a State residency requirement was invalidated as a condition that could be imposed for the receipt of welfare benefits,[193] the "fundamental" rights of voting and travel were respectively at stake. Further, the group of cases where the highest proportion of equal protection claims was sustained by the Court directly implicated due process[194] in the operation of the criminal or civil justice system. Thus the Court held that equal protection was denied where indigent would-be appellants' access to the courts was cut off,[195] where poor defendants, convicted of offenses that carried a fine for those who could pay, were sentenced to "work off" their sentences in jail,[196] and where indigent defendants were denied certain protective exemptions that other civil judgment debtors were accorded.[197] The Court has long held that equal protection was infringed where punishment under a statute could be implicitly class-based.[198] But the Court did not find a denial of equal protection where a State statute conditioned parole in part on an indigent's willingness to reimburse the county for expenses it incurred in furnishing him with counsel and an investigator at trial.[199] Clearly, the Court has been much less receptive to claims that welfare benefits have been denied.[200] Nor has the Court found any infringement of equal protection where the State constitution conditioned the construction of low-cost public housing upon majority approval in a referendum.[201] But the New Jersey Su-

[192] Harper v. Va. State Bd. of Elections, 383 U.S. 663 (1966).

[193] Shapiro v. Thompson, 394 U.S. 618 (1969). *See also* Memorial Hosp. v. Maricopa Cty., 415 U.S. 250 (1974).

[194] To Justice Harlan, who dissented in both *Harper* and *Shapiro*, the due process focus was critical. Indeed, in several of the cases bearing upon the operation of the criminal justice system, Justice Harlan concurred in the result reached by the Court not because, as the majority argued, the indigent defendant or would-be appellant was treated differently from those who could pay, but because it jeopardized the possibility of the system doing legal justice; hence, it impaired due process not equal protection. *See Griffin* v. Ill., 351 U.S. 12, 29 (1956) (dissenting opinion); Douglas v. Calif., 372 U.S. 353, 360 (1963) (dissenting opinion); Williams v. Ill., 399 U.S. 235, 259 (1970) (concurring opinion); Tate v. Short, 401 U.S. 395, 401 (1971) (statement concurring in the judgment).

[195] Griffin v. Ill., 351 U.S. 12 (1956); Douglas v. Calif., 372 U.S. 353 (1963); Bounds v. Smith, 97 S.Ct. 1491 (1977). *See also* Lane v. Att'y Gen. of the U.S., 477 F. 2d 847 (1973).

[196] Williams v. Ill., 399 U.S. 235 (1970); Tate v. Short, 401 U.S. 395 (1971).

[197] James v. Strange, 407 U.S. 128 (1972).

[198] Skinner v. Okla. *ex rel.* Williamson, 316 U.S. 535 (1942).

[199] Fuller v. Ore., 417 U.S. 40 (1974).

[200] Dandridge v. Williams, 397 U.S. 471 (1970); Rosado v. Wyman, 397 U.S. 397 (1970); Jefferson v. Hackney, 406 U.S. 535 (1972); Ortwein v. Schwab, 410 U.S. 656 (1973); Ohio Bureau of Employment Services v. Hodory, 97 S.Ct. 1898 (1977); Batterton v. Francis, 97 S.Ct. 2399 (1977).

[201] James v. Valtierra, 402 U.S. 137 (1971). Lower courts have evinced mixed sympathies toward the claims of lower income groups endeavoring to compel local government to follow through in the construction of public housing. Most of the

preme Court has been especially receptive to constitutional challenges attacking zoning ordinances that seek to keep out those of lesser means by requiring certain minimum lot sizes.[202] (*See also* discussion of the constitutionality of property-tax funding of public schools, p. 509.)

While agreeing that "the treatment of the aged in this Nation has Age
not been wholly free of discrimination," the Court, refusing to find that such people constituted a "suspect class," concluded that "unlike, say, those who have been discriminated against on the basis of race or national origin, [the aged] have not experienced a 'history of purposeful unequal treatment' or been subject to unique disabilities on the basis of stereotyped characteristics not truly indicative of their abilities."[203] Rather, the Court pointed out, "it marks a stage that each of us will reach if we live out our normal span." Applying the test of "reasonableness," the Court went on to hold that a State statute compelling uniformed officers in the state police to retire at age 50 did not contravene the equal protection clause. "Since physical ability generally declines with age, mandatory retirement at 50 serves to remove from police service those whose fitness for uniformed work presumptively has diminished with age." Congress, however, in passing the Age Discrimination in Employment Act has prohibited private employers from discharging any individual between the ages of 45 and 60 because of age or from discriminating on that basis in hiring.[204] The courts have universally upheld mandatory retirement plans. And, reversing a superior court decision, the New Jersey Supreme Court has upheld "spot zoning" of "trailer parks" that limit occupancy to persons 52 years of age or older.[205] In other decisions, lower courts have held unconstitutional both a law excluding persons over 65 and under 18

decisions run against the claims of the low income groups, *see* Acevedo *v.* Nassau Cty., N.Y., 500 F. 2d. 1078 (1974); Citizens Comm. for Faraday Wood *v.* Lindsay, 507 F. 2d. 1065 (1974); Yarborough *v.* City of Warren, 383 F.Supp. 676 (1974). *But see* Garrett *v.* City of Hamtramck, 503 F. 2d. 1236 (1974).

[202] That court held that zoning ordinances that permit only "relatively high-priced, single-family detached dwellings on sizable lots and . . . expensive apartments" violate the State constitution. So. Burlington Cty. NAACP *v.* Township of Mount Laurel, 336 A. 2d. 713, 717 (1975); *see also* Oakwood at Madison, Inc. *v.* Township of Madison, 371 A. 2d. 1192 (1977); *but cf.* Ybarra *v.* Town of Los Altos Hills, 503 F. 2d. 250 (1974). The U.S. Supreme Court, however, declined to reach the merits in such a case, *see* Warth *v.* Seldin, 422 U.S. 490 (1975). *See also*, Construction Industry Ass'n of Sonoma Cty. *v.* City of Petaluma, 522 F. 2d. 897 (1975). Though this is, strictly speaking, a due process case, there are distinct implications in it for zoning cases which have raised clear equal protection issues. And the New Hampshire Supreme Court has ruled that a State tax exemption law that, in effect, shifts more of the property tax burden from moderate income homeowners to those at both ends of the economic scale, violates that State's constitution. Felder *v.* City of Portsmouth, 324 A. 2d. 708 (1974).

[203] Massachusetts Bd. of Retirement *v.* Murgia, 427 U.S. 307, 313 (1976).

[204] 29 U.S.C. §§ 621, *et seq. See also* McMann *v.* United Air Lines, 542 F. 2d. 217 (1976).

[205] Taxpayers Ass'n of Weymouth Twshp. *v.* Weymouth Twshp., 364 A. 2d. 1016 (1976).

from general relief benefits[206] and a local ordinance prohibiting loitering by boys and girls under 18 years of age after 10 p.m.[207]

Residency   A clash with "fundamental" rights would appear both natural and likely where the State creates classifications in law based on residency. Indeed, in cases challenging restrictions on electoral participation[208] and eligibility for welfare benefits,[209] the Court struck down such residency requirements as they trenched upon the right to vote and the right to travel. The Court's approach to adjudication, as might be expected, has been marked by a weighing of the interests put forth by the State. Thus the Court held in 1973 that "since Connecticut purports to be concerned with residency in allocating the rates for tuition and fees at its university system, it is forbidden by the Due Process Clause to deny an individual the resident rates on the basis of a permanent and irrebuttable presumption of nonresidence, when that presumption is not necessarily or universally true in fact, and when the state has reasonable alternative means of making the crucial determination."[210] Deciding two years later to uphold Iowa's one-year residency requirement as a prerequisite to initiating divorce proceedings, the Court distinguished the cases referred to above: "What those cases had in common was that the durational residency requirements they struck down were justified on the basis of budgetary or record-keeping considerations which were held insufficient to outweigh the constitutional claims of the individuals. But Iowa's divorce residency requirement is of a different stripe." Continued the Court, "Iowa's residency requirement may reasonably be justified on grounds other than purely budgetary considerations or administrative convenience."[211] Among those other grounds elaborated by the Court was the State's interest in preventing collateral attack on its divorce decrees. And, in a residency issue which has come to the fore in urban areas, lower courts have upheld as constitutional a simultaneous residency requirement imposed on those who are employed in city government.[212]

Equal Protection and the Electoral Process   Prefacing that portion of its opinion in the campaign finance reform case that addressed the equal protection challenge to public funding of presidential campaigns, the Court observed: "In several situations concerning the electoral process, the principle has been developed that restrictions on access to the electoral process must survive exacting scrutiny. The restriction can be sustained only if it

[206] Morales v. Minter, 393 F.Supp. 88 (1975).

[207] *In re* Doe, 513 P. 2d. 1385 (1973). But a Federal district court has upheld a minimum age for admission to public school as reasonable; Hammond v. Marx, 406 F.Supp. 853 (1975).

[208] Dunn v. Blumstein, 405 U.S. 330 (1972).

[209] Shapiro v. Thompson, 394 U.S. 618 (1969); Memorial Hosp. v. Maricopa Cty., 415 U.S. 250 (1974).

[210] Vlandis v. Kline, 412 U.S. 441, 452 (1973).

[211] Sosna v. Iowa, 419 U.S. 393, 406 (1975).

[212] Wright v. City of Jackson, Miss., 506 F. 2d. 900 (1975); *see also* Town of Milton v. Civil Service Com'n, 312 N.E. 2d. 188 (1974).

furthers a 'vital' governmental interest . . . that is 'achieved by a means that does not unfairly or unnecessarily burden either a minority party's or an individual candidate's equally important interest in the continued availability of political opportunity."[213] Applying this precept in previous cases, the Court had struck down State statutes that: (1) gave built-in advantages to the two major political parties while making it virtually impossible for minor parties to get on the ballot;[214] and (2) required the payment of a filing fee as an absolute prerequisite to a candidate's appearance on the ballot.[215] But, as in other cases where the Court found that statutory provisions may have favored a two-party system but did not erect impenetrable barriers to other parties or candidates,[216] the Court sustained the constitutionality of the public funding provisions. Said the Court: "Any risk of harm to minority interests is speculative due to our present lack of knowledge of the practical effects of public financing and cannot overcome the force of the governmental interests against the use of public money to foster frivolous candidacies, create a system of splintered parties, and encourage unrestrained factionalism."[217] Moreover, applying "strict scrutiny" to restrictions on voter participation, the Court held unconstitutional State statutes that disenfranchised entire classes of people such as servicemen,[218] non-property-owners,[219] newly arrived residents,[220] some Federal employees,[221] and those who were unable or failed to pay a poll tax.[222] On the other hand, the Court found constitutional violation in California's denial of the franchise to ex-felons.[223] Further, the California Supreme Court invalidated a statute that required that the names of incumbents appear first

---

[213] Buckley v. Valeo, 424 U.S. 1, 93-94 (1976), quoting Lubin v. Panish, 415 U.S. 709, 716 (1974).

[214] Williams v. Rhodes, 393 U.S. 23 (1968); American Party of Texas v. White, 415 U.S. 767 (1974) (striking down the State's practice of putting on absentee ballots the names of candidates nominated by the two major parties).

[215] Jenness v. Fortson, 403 U.S. 431 (1971); Storer v. Brown, 415 U.S. 724 (1974); American Party of Texas v. White, 415 U.S. 767 (1964). Storer rejected an equal protection challenge to a California law, aimed at preventing excessive factionalism in the political process, which required that, as a prerequisite of independent candidacy for office, a person seeking a position on the ballot be unaffiliated with any party during the previous year and that he file nomination papers bearing a number of signatures equal to 5 to 6% of the entire vote cast in the preceding general election in the constituency from which the petitioner seeks election. White upheld State regulations that, among other things, limited the number of candidates who could appear on the ballot, compelled minority party office-seekers to disclose candidacy early and financed primaries for only parties that drew 200,000 votes or more in the preceding gubernatorial election.

[216] Bullock v. Carter, 405 U.S. 134 (1972); Lubin v. Panish, 415 U.S. 709 (1974).

[217] Buckley v. Valeo, 424 U.S. 1, 101 (1976).

[218] Carrington v. Rash, 380 U.S. 89 (1965).

[219] Kramer v. Union Free School Dist. No. 15, 395 U.S. 621 (1969); Cipriano v. City of Houma, 395 U.S. 701 (1969); Phoenix v. Kolodziejski, 399 U.S. 204 (1970).

[220] Dunn v. Blumstein, 405 U.S. 330 (1972).

[221] Evans v. Cornman, 398 U.S. 419 (1970).

[222] Harper v. Va. State Bd. of Elections, 383 U.S. 663 (1966).

[223] Richardson v. Ramirez, 418 U.S. 24 (1974).

on the ballot.[224] And a Federal appeals court has ruled that the Republican-controlled Arizona House of Representatives did not infringe the equal protection clause when Democratic members were not given seats on legislative committees and subcommittees proportionate to their voting strength in the House.[225] (For a discussion of equal protection in reapportionment, *see* p. 521. For a discussion of race and electoral discrimination, *see* the discussion of voting rights under the Fifteenth Amendment, at p. 522ff.)

A number of other equal protection issues are worth noting. First, courts have had no difficulty upholding the preference given to veterans in public employment.[226] Nor has the Supreme Court seen any equal protection trouble with zoning ordinances that distinguish between unrelated individuals and family members in the occupation of single dwelling units.[227] Lower courts have been quick to strike down discrimination against married persons.[228] Finally, legal appreciation of the rights of the mobility handicapped especially in access to public transportation may well be emerging.[229]

School Desegregation

In 1896 it was held in Plessy *v.* Ferguson[230] that it was reasonable for a State to require, in the interest of minimizing occasions for race friction, that white and colored persons travelling by rail be assigned separate coaches, the quality of the accommodations afforded the two races being substantially equal; and in due course

---

[224] Gould *v.* Grubb, 536 P. 2d. 1337 (1975). See also Williamson *v.* Fortson, 376 F.Supp. 1300 (1974). But cf. Clough *v.* Guzzi, 416 F.Supp. 1057 (1976).

[225] Davids *v.* Akers, 549 F. 2d. 120 (1977).

[226] See Koelfgen *v.* Jackson, 355 F.Supp. 243 (1972); Feinerman *v.* Jones, 356 F.Supp. 252 (1973); Williams *v.* State Civil Service Com'n, 300 A. 2d. 799 (1973); Rios *v.* Dillman, 499 F. 2d. 329 (1974). But cf. Anthony *v.* Mass., 415 F.Supp. 485 (1976). Further, the Supreme Court sustained a Federal statue not extending veterans' educational benefits to conscientious objectors who fulfilled their alternative service commitments. Speaking for the Court, Justice Brennan held that the denial of such benefits to draftees who performed social service work while allowing draftees who completed active military service to take full advantage of the benefits did not constitute invidious discrimination. On the contrary, the Court held that such a policy was within Congress's power to make military service more attractive, and bore a rational relationship to the greater risk and inconvenience placed on those who served in the Armed Forces. Johnson *v.* Robison, 415 U.S. 361 (1974).

[227] See Village of Belle Terre *v.* Boraas, 416 U.S. 1 (1974) *and* Moore *v.* City of East Cleveland, 97 S.Ct. 1932 (1977). Though the zoning restriction challenged in *Moore* was held unconstitutional it was because it arbitrarily defined "family" in too narrow terms, not because of an impermissible discrimination between the nuclear family and unrelated persons. For a critique of "family" relationships as the basis of zoning ordinances, see the dissenting opinion of Justice Brennan in *Moore*.

[228] See O'Neill *v.* Dent, 364 F.Supp. 565 (1973), where the Merchant Marine Academy's regulation prohibiting attendance by married cadets was struck down; Bell *v.* Lone Oak Indep. School Dist., 507 S.W. 2d. 636 (1974), where a high school regulation precluding married students from participation in extracurricular activities was declared unconstitutional. See also the Supreme Court's decision in U.S. Dept. of Agriculture *v.* Moreno, 413 U.S. 528 (1973), where a denial of food stamps to any household containing an individual unrelated to any other member of the household did not survive constitutional scrutiny.

[229] Bartels *v.* Biernat, 405 F.Supp. 1012 (1975); *but see* Snowden *v.* Birmingham-Jefferson Cty. Transit Auth., 407 F.Supp. 394 (1975).

[230] 163 U.S. 537.

the same ruling was extended to public-supported institutions of learning.[231] This enlarged application of the "separate but equal" formula is, of course, no longer law of the land. It was first repudiated by the Court as to professional schools and schools of higher learning on the ground that for financial and other reasons, such as scarcity of available teaching talent, it was impossible for certain States to provide equal facilities for the two races in these fields of instruction.[232] Moreover, said the Court, in 1950, speaking with reference to a segregated Negro law school, such an institution could not offer its students "those qualities which are incapable of objective measurement but which make for greatness in a law school."[233] In the celebrated *"Brown"* case, decided in 1954, it was held that like considerations "apply with added force to children in grade and high schools. To separate them," said Chief Justice Warren, speaking for a unanimous Court, "from others of similar age and qualifications solely because of their race generates a feeling of inferiority as to their status in the community that may affect their hearts and minds in a way unlikely ever to be undone. . . . We conclude that in the field of education the doctrine of 'separate but equal' has no place. Separate educational facilities are inherently unequal."[234]

That the Court was headed for some such result without the

[231] Cumming *v*. C'ty B'd of Educ., 175 U.S. 528 (1899); Gong Lum *v*. Rice, 275 U.S. 78 (1927).

[232] Missouri *ex rel*. Gaines *v*. Canada, 305 U.S. 337 (1938); Sipuel *v*. Okla., 332 U.S. 631 (1948); Sweatt *v*. Painter, 339 U.S. 629 (1950); McLaurin *v*. Okla. St. Regents, 339 U.S. 637 (1950).

[233] 339 U.S. 637, 634.

[234] Brown *v*. Topeka, 347 U.S. 483, 495. The cases originated in Kansas, South Carolina, Virginia, and Delaware. They first reached the Court in 1952 and were put over for reargument in the 1953 Term. Of this reargument the Chief Justice remarked: "It was largely devoted to the circumstances surrounding the adoption of the Fourteenth Amendment in 1868. It covered, exhaustively, consideration of the Amendment in Congress, ratification by the states, then existing practices in racial segregation, and the views of proponents and opponents of the Amendment.

"This discussion and our own investigation convince us that, although these sources cast some light, it is not enough to resolve the problem with which we are faced.

"At best, they are inconclusive. The most avid proponents of the post-war Amendments undoubtedly intended them to remove all legal distinctions among 'all persons born or naturalized in the United States.'

"Their opponents, just as certainly, were antagonistic to both the letter and the spirit of the Amendments and wished them to have the most limited effect. . . .

"An additional reason for the inclusive nature of the Amendment's history with respect to segregated schools, is the status of public education at that time. In the South, the movement toward free common schools, supported by general taxation, had not yet taken hold. Education of white children was largely in the hands of private groups. Education of Negroes was almost nonexistent, and practically all of the race was illiterate. In fact, any education of Negroes was forbidden by law in some states.

"Today, in contrast, many Negroes have achieved outstanding success in the arts and sciences as well as in the business and professional world. It is true that public education had already advanced further in the North, but the effect of the Amendment on Northern States was generally ignored in the Congressional debates.

"Even in the North, the conditions of public education did not approximate those

necessity of invoking "sociological data" is indicated by certain earlier holdings, including those reached by it in implementing the
"separate but equal" rule (*see* note 232 *supra*). Thus, even under the
law as it stood when the Desegregation cases were decided, the two
races could not be segregated by public authority as to their places
of abode; and while private covenants forbidding the transfer of
real property to persons of a designated race or color had been
held to be "lawful,"[235] the enforcement thereof by a State through
its courts, being a State act, was held to violate the "equal protection" clause.[236] And, of course, even at that time neither race could
be denied the generally recognized "civil rights," the right to own
and possess property, to make contracts, to serve on juries,[237] etc.

The story of the attempt to make good the promise of the
Court's decision in the *Brown* case is not a pretty nor encouraging
one. That story was concisely told by Justice Burger in 1971:

"Nearly 17 years ago this Court held, in explicit terms, that state-
imposed segregation by race in public schools denies equal protection of the laws. At no time has the Court deviated in the slightest
degree from that holding or its constitutional underpinnings.
None of the parties before us questions the Court's 1955 holding in
Brown II, that 'School authorities have the primary responsibility
for elucidating, assessing, and solving these problems; courts will
have to consider whether the action of school authorities consti-

---

existing today. The curriculum was usually rudimentary; ungraded schools were
common in rural areas; the school term was but three months a year in many states;
and compulsory school attendance was virtually unknown.

"As a consequence, it is not surprising that there should be so little in the history
of the Fourteenth Amendment relating to its intended effect on public education."

Later he adds: "Today, education is perhaps the most important function of state
and local governments. Compulsory school attendance laws and the great expenditures for education both demonstrate our recognition of the importance of education to our democratic society. It is required in the performance of our most basic
public responsibilities, even service in the armed forces. It is the very foundation of
good citizenship. . . .

"Today, it is a principal instrument in awakening the child to cultural values, in
preparing him for later professional training, and in helping him to adjust normally
to his environment," citing the following works: K. B. Clark, *Effect of Prejudice and
Discrimination on Personality Development* (Midcentury White House Conference on
Children and Youth, 1950); Witmer and Kotinsky, *Personality in the Making* (1952),
ch. 6; Deutscher and Chein, "The Psychological Effects of Enforced Segregation: A
Survey of Social Science Opinion," 26 *J. Psychol.*, 259 (1948); Chein, "What Are the
Psychological Effects of Segregation Under Conditions of Equal Facilities?" 3 *Int. J.
Opinion and Attitude Res.* 229 (1949); Brameld, *Educational Costs in Discrimination and
National Welfare* (McIver, ed., 1949), 44-48; Frazier, *The Negro in the United States*
(1949), 674-681; and Myrdal, *An American Dilemma* (1944); 347 U.S. 483, 489-496.

A fifth case from the District of Columbia was disposed of in line with the holdings in the State cases under the "due process" clause of Amendment V. *See* Bolling
v. Sharpe, 347 U.S. 497 (1954).

[235] Buchanan *v.* Warley, 245 U.S. 60 (1917); Corrigan *v.* Buckley, 271 U.S. 323
(1926).

[236] Shelley *v.* Kramer, 334 U.S. 1 (1948); aff'd in Barrows *v.* Jackson, 346 U.S. 249
(1953).

[237] Strauder *v.* W.Va., 100 U.S. 303 (1880).

tutes good faith implementation of the governing constitutional principles. Because of their proximity to local conditions and the possible need for further hearings, the courts which originally heard these cases can best perform this judicial appraisal. Accordingly, we believe it appropriate to remand the cases to those courts.

" 'In fashioning and effectuating the decrees, the courts will be guided by equitable principles. Traditionally, equity has been characterized by a practical flexibility in shaping its remedies and by a facility for adjusting and reconciling public and private needs. These cases call for the exercise of these traditional attributes of equity power. At stake is the personal interest of the plaintiffs in admission to public schools as soon as practicable on a nondiscriminatory basis. To effectuate this interest may call for elimination of a variety of obstacles in making the transition to school systems operated in accordance with the constitutional principles set forth in our May 17, 1954, decision. Courts of equity may properly take into account the public interest in the elimination of such obstacles in a systematic and effective manner. But it should go without saying that the vitality of these constitutional principles cannot be allowed to yield simply because of disagreement with them.' Brown v. Board of Education, 349 U.S. 294, 299-300 (1955)." It should be noted that it was in *Brown II* that the Court also said "The . . . cases are remanded . . . to take such proceedings and enter such orders and decrees consistent with this opinion as are necessary and proper to admit to public schools on a racially nondiscriminatory basis *with all deliberate speed* the parties to these cases (emphasis supplied)."

"Over the 16 years since *Brown II*, many difficulties were encountered in implementation of the basic constitutional requirement that the State not discriminate between public school children on the basis of their race. Nothing in our national experience prior to 1955 prepared anyone for dealing with changes and adjustments of the magnitude and complexity encountered since then. Deliberate resistance of some to the Court's mandates has impeded the good-faith efforts of others to bring school systems into compliance. The detail and nature of these dilatory tactics have been noted frequently by this Court and other courts.

"By the time the Court considered Green v. County School Board, 391 U.S. 430, in 1968, very little progress had been made in many areas where dual school systems had historically been maintained by operation of state laws. In *Green*, the Court was confronted with a record of a freedom-of-choice program that the District Court had found to operate in fact to preserve a dual system more than a decade after *Brown II*. While acknowledging that a freedom-of-choice concept could be valid remedial measure in some circumstances, its failure to be effective in *Green* required that:

" 'The burden on a school board today is to come forward with a plan that promises realistically to work . . . *now* . . . until it is clear

that state-imposed segregation has been completely removed.'
Green, supra, at 439.

"This was plain language, yet the 1969 Term of Court brought
fresh evidence of the dilatory tactics of many school authorities.
Alexander *v.* Holmes County Board of Education, 396 U.S. 19, restated the basic obligation asserted in Griffin *v.* School Board, 377
U.S. 218, 234 (1964), and *Green, supra*, that the remedy must be
implemented *forthwith*."[238]

It was this dismal record which led Justice Black in an unprecedented television interview[239] to observe that in retrospect he felt
that the Court should have decided *Brown I* like any other law case,
make its decision, and let the other branches of government figure
out how to vindicate the rights established by the decision rather
than to endeavor to do it through the judicial process. Surely, the
record shows how inadequate the judicial process is to the task.
The judicial effort with all of the attendant difficulties led inexorably to the Supreme Court's effort to formulate guidelines for the
lower courts in 1971. As Chief Justice Burger put it: "The problems encountered by the district courts and courts of appeals make
plain that we should now try to amplify guidelines, however in-
complete and imperfect, for the assistance of school authorities and
courts."[240] In doing so, Chief Justice Burger continued: "This
Court, in *Brown I*, appropriately dealt with the large constitutional
principles; other federal courts had to grapple with the flinty in-
tractable realities of day-to-day implementation of those constitutional commands. Their efforts of necessity, embraced a process of
'trial and error,' and our effort to formulate guidelines must take
into account their experience."[241]

The guidelines which the Court set forth were these:

(1) "Racial Balances or Racial Quotas. . . . In sum, the very lim-
    ited use made of mathematical ratios was within the equita-
    ble remedial discretion of the District Court."
(2) "One-race Schools. . . . The district judge or school au-
    thorities should make every effort to achieve the greatest
    possible degree of actual desegregation and will thus neces-
    sarily be concerned with the elimination of one-race schools.
    . . . An optimal majority-to-minority transfer provision has
    long been recognized as a useful part of every desegregation
    plan."
(3) "Remedial Altering of Attendance Zones. . . . We hold that
    the pairing and grouping of non-contiguous school zones is
    a permissible tool and such action is to be considered in light
    of the objectives sought."

[238] Swann *v.* Board of Education, 402 U.S. 1, 11-13 (1971).
[239] For the text of the interview, *see* 1969 *Cong. Quart. Weekly Report*, 6-11.
[240] Swann *v.* Board of Education, 402 U.S. 1, 11-13 (1971).
[241] *Ibid.*, 6.

(4) "Transportation of Students. . . . In these circumstances [situations in Charlotte, N.C., and Mobile, Ala.], we find no basis for holding that the local school authorities may not be required to employ bus transportation as one tool of school desegregation. Desegregation plans cannot be limited to the walk-in school."[242]

Though the Court in *Swann* canvassed the options open to the lower courts in the quest to "eliminate dual systems and establish unitary systems," that is to "eliminate from the public schools all vestiges of state-imposed segregation,"[243] subsequent Supreme Court decisions spelled out more emphatically what occasions warranted intervention by Federal courts. What, exactly, identified a "dual system"? Would a finding of impermissible discrimination with respect to one or two schools in a public school system carry implications for the system as a whole? Then, in June 1973, the Court decided the Denver case which, as Justice Powell pointed out in his separate opinion, was "the first school desegregation case to reach this Court which involves a major city outside the South."[244] The Supreme Court, speaking through Justice Brennan, held "that a finding of intentionally segregative school board actions in a meaningful portion of a school system, as in this case, creates a presumption that other segregated schooling within the system is not adventitious. It establishes, in other words, a *prima facie* case of unlawful segregative design on the part of school authorities, and shifts to those authorities the burden of proving that other segregated schools within the system are not also the result of intentionally segregative actions. . . . We emphasize that the differentiating factor between *de jure* segregation and so-called *de facto* segregation to which we referred in Swann is *purpose* or *intent* to segregate."[245] The case was remanded to the district court to afford the school board an opportunity to prove it was not deliberately segregating students. But, the Court said, if it is determined, that the Denver school system is a dual school system then the "School Board has the affirmative duty to desegregate the entire system 'root and branch.'" The Court also held that the district court had been wrong in "separating Negroes and Hispanos for purposes of defining a 'segregated' school," suggesting that a school with "a combined predominance of Negroes and Hispanos" might very well be considered a segregated school.

Underscoring the point that only *de jure* segregation could prompt the exercise of equity powers by Federal courts, the Supreme Court overturned lower Federal court decisions that had directed the consolidation of the Detroit public school system with the systems of 53 surrounding suburbs and had ordered the busing of

[242] Ibid., 22-31.   [243] 402 U.S. 1, 6, 15 (1971).
[244] Keyes *v.* School Dist. No. 1, Denver, Colo., 413 U.S. 189, 217 (1973).
[245] *Ibid.*, 208.

students on a massive scale among them for the purpose of achieving racial balance.[246] Despite the fact that only the city system was found to contain vestiges of *de jure* segregation, the lower courts found that a solution confined to a Detroit-only plan would result in maintaining a central city area comprised of virtually all-black schools ringed by suburban systems of all-white schools. By a 5-4 vote, the Court, speaking through Chief Justice Burger, rejected the judicial creation of a unitary metropolitan system. The majority held that, absent any showing of *de jure* segregation on the part of the suburban schools, there was no constitutional authority for erasing local school district lines, and the previous decision in *Swann* was not to be read as standing for the proposition that district lines were merely a political convenience susceptible to judicial alteration in the interest of promoting racial integration. Without any evidence that the state had drawn school district lines with a segregative intent, the Court held that deference should be shown to the traditional value of local control over education. In sum, the Court concluded that the relief should have been confined within the boundaries of the city school district: "The constitutional right of the Negro respondents residing in Detroit is to attend a unitary school system in that district. Unless petitioners drew the district lines in a discriminatory fashion, or arranged for White students residing in the Detroit district to attend schools in Oakland and Macomb Counties, they were under no constitutional duty to make provisions for Negro students to do so. The view of the dissenters, that the existence of a dual system *in Detroit* can be made the basis for a decree requiring cross-district transportation of pupils cannot be supported on the grounds that it represents merely the devising of a suitably flexible remedy for the violation of rights already established by our prior decisions. It can be supported only by drastic expansion of the constitutional right itself, an expansion without any support in either constitutional principle or precedent."

Calling the decision "a giant step backwards," the dissenters, Justices Douglas, Brennan, White, and Marshall, argued that there was ample evidence in the record to demonstrate that Michigan's educational system was not one primarily of local control but rather one that reflected a highly centralized approach and that state officials had taken numerous "thinly disguised" actions, principally with regard to financing and the provision of facilities, which resulted not only in contributing to discrimination within the Detroit system but also in promoting inter-district segregation. The dissent-

---

[246] Milliken *v.* Bradley, 418 U.S. 717 (1974). *See also* Wright *v.* Council of the City of Emporia, 407 U.S. 451 (1972). The Court, or a sizable minority of Justices on it in the *Emporia* case, has endeavored to minimize Federal court action which dismantles local government boundaries. As the Court said, with obvious satisfaction, in the *Milliken* case on appeal of the district court's subsequent decree on remand, "The District Court has neither attempted to restructure local government entities nor to mandate a particular method or structure of state or local financing." 433 U.S. 267, 291 (1977). *See also* San Antonio Indep. School Dist. *v.* Rodriguez, 411 U.S. 1 (1973).

ers concluded that a metropolitan area-wide remedy was not only justified by the *de jure* segregative practices of *both* city *and* state authorities but embodied a far sounder solution in effectively dismantling and preventing the regeneration of a dual system. On appeal from an order by the district court on remand, the Supreme Court subsequently affirmed that, in formulating a comprehensive decree to abolish a dual system and to remedy its effects, a Federal court could constitutionally order the city and State to finance jointly a range of compensatory educational programs, including reading, in-service teacher training, testing, and counseling and career guidance.[247]

Following close on the heels of the Court's initial ruling in *Milliken*, Congress enacted, as Title II of the Education Amendments of 1974,[248] a series of strict limitations on the use of busing and other remedial techniques by Federal courts. Included in the act were some provisions that: (1) precluded the use of desegregative techniques solely to achieve "racial balance" (i.e., to remedy *de facto* segregation); (2) directed the courts to select from a priority of remedial techniques that would keep children in schools closest to their own neighborhoods; (3) prohibited the start of forced busing during the school year; (4) mandated that no transfer or transportation of students begin until all appeals or the time for appeals has been exhausted; and (5) denied any funding for the purpose of achieving "racial balance."

In another suit, where on appeal a U.S. circuit court had ordered a district court to formulate a decree for the Chicago metropolitan area that would reach beyond the city limits in disestablishing segregation in public housing, the Court held that a Federal district court could order the construction of low income public housing in white suburban neighborhoods where it was found that the Chicago Housing Authority and the U.S. Department of Housing and Urban Development combined to "avoid the placement of Negro families in white neighborhoods." Distinguishing the facts of this case from Milliken v. Bradley, where "the District Court's proposed remedy . . . was impermissible because of the limits on the federal judicial power to interfere with the operation of state political entities that were not implicated in unconstitutional conduct," the Supreme Court held: "Here . . . a judicial order directing relief beyond the boundary lines of Chicago will not necessarily entail coercion of uninvolved governmental units, because both CHA and HUD have the authority to operate outside the Chicago city limits."[249]

If these cases tell us when judicial intervention in the name of equal protection begins, a natural sequel is to inquire when control by the Federal courts ends. The answer, in short, is when a scheme of *de jure* segregation has been dismantled. Once this has been ac-

---

[247] 97 S.Ct. 2749 (1977).   [248] 88 *Stat.* 484.
[249] Hills *v.* Gautreaux, 425 U.S. 284, 298 (1976).

complished, oversight by the Federal courts concludes. In the case of public school desegregation, for example, if, just as the last vestiges of a dual system have been dismantled, the composition of the city's population changes significantly, yielding lopsided racial distributions in the students attending various schools, the result is the product of *de facto* segregation and Federal courts do not retain jurisdiction with the continued option of redrawing attendance zone lines or busing students to achieve "racial balance."[250]

Implementing the equal protection guarantee in the face of *de jure* discrimination, lower courts have: (1) been vigorously backed by the Supreme Court when busing decrees brought violence and rioting in northern cities, particularly Boston;[251] (2) enjoined Federal revenue-sharing funds to Chicago in the face of racial bias in its procedures for hiring police officers;[252] and (3) turned thumbs down on efforts in the Dallas public schools to convert from a dual to a unitary school system by interracial contact via television between separate classrooms with weekly personal visits.[253] In the same vein of enforcing desegregation, the Supreme Court ruled that Mississippi could not provide free textbooks to students in private as well as public schools when the private schools practice racial discrimination.[254]

It is worth reflecting on the importance of the requirement, elaborated in *Keyes* and reiterated in subsequent decisions, that to be prohibited, discrimination must evidence intention or willfulness. In fact, intent may be very difficult to demonstrate. Palmer *v.* Thompson[255] was a case in point. There, under a court order to desegregate public facilities, the city council, ostensibly for budgetary reasons, closed the city's swimming pools. Reasoning that "[i]t is not a case where a city is maintaining different sets of facilities for blacks and whites and forcing the races to remain separate in recreational or educational activities," the Court concluded, "Nothing in the history or the language of the Fourteenth Amendment nor in any of our prior cases persuades us that the closing of the

[250] Pasadena City Bd. of Educ. *v.* Spangler, 427 U.S. 424 (1976). *See also* § 215(c) of the Education Amendments of 1974.

[251] Morgan *v.* Hennigan, 379 F.Supp. 410 (1974), *affirmed sub nom.* Morgan *v.* Kerrigan, 509 F. 2d. 580 (1974), *cert. denied*, 421 U.S. 963 (1975). *See also* Morgan *v.* Kerrigan, 401 F.Supp. 216 (1975), *affirmed* 530 F. 2d. 401, *cert. denied* 426 U.S. 935 (1976). Commentary on events in the Boston cases and actions of the State legislature also appears in School Comm. of Springfield *v.* Bd. of Educ., 319 N.E. 2d. 427 (1974). Of interest, too, is a California case involving an attempt to unseat a school board and force compliance with an initiative measure barring the assignment of pupils on the basis of race, *see* Santa Barbara School Dist. *v.* Superior Ct., 530 P. 2d. 605 (1975). *But see* the Court's handling of the controversial Indianapolis case, Bd. of School Com'rs of Indianapolis *v.* Buckley, 97 S.Ct. 802 (1977) and Housing Auth. of Indianapolis *v.* Buckley, 97 S.Ct. 802 (1977). *See also Minneapolis Tribune*, Jan 26, 1977.

[252] United States *v.* Chicago, 411 F.Supp. 218 (1976), *aff'd in part and reversed in part and remanded* 549 F. 2d. 415 (1977).

[253] Tasby *v.* Estes, 517 F. 2d. 92 (1975).

[254] Norwood *v.* Harrison, 413 U.S. 455 (1973).   [255] 403 U.S. 217 (1971).

Jackson swimming pools to all its citizens constitutes a denial of "the equal protection of the laws." Sometimes, of course, the effects of discriminatory action are so clear that they reveal an unmistakable intent, as when the boundaries of a city, once in the shape of a square, are contorted to a 28-sided figure coincidentally excluding all of the black neighborhoods.[256] As the Court has made clear, however, disproportionate racial impact alone does not by itself prove *de jure* discrimination. It is crucial because it furnishes the part of the circumstantial evidence from which a pattern and, hence, motive can be discerned.[257] Nor does the racial motive need to have been the sole, or dominant, or even primary motive; it is enough that it was a consideration, for, as the Court observed, while "legislators and administrators are properly concerned with balancing numerous competing considerations" in reaching policy decisions, "racial discrimination is not just another competing consideration."[258] Likewise, the Court has demonstrated continuing concern that employment testing be job-related and not stray widely from the mark so as to wantonly exclude minorities.[259]

Another momentous problem involving schools and equal protection surfaced in the early 'seventies. In 1971, both a Federal district court in Texas and the California Supreme Court held that a State school financing system which relied heavily on local property taxes was unconstitutional in that it results in invidious discrimination against the poor as to the quality of the schools which their children attend.[260] On appeal, the Supreme Court in *Rodriguez*, the Texas case, held that the interdistrict disparity in property tax revenues used to finance public education did not constitute a violation of equal protection. Recalling that its opinion in *Brown I* had underscored the importance of education as a function of State and local government, the Court nevertheless asserted, "But the importance of a service performed by the State does not determine whether it must be regarded as fundamental for purposes of examination under the Equal Protection Clause."[261] Moreover, the

Public
School
Financing
and Equal
Protection

[256] Gomillion *v*. Lightfoot, 364 U.S. 339 (1960).

[257] Washington *v*. Davis, 426 U.S. 229 (1976); Village of Arlington Heights *v*. Metro. Housing Dev. Corp., 429 U.S. 252 (1977). *Also see* the jury selection cases, in which racial bias was alleged, where the standard was whether jury procedures allowed "a fair possibility for obtaining a representative cross-section of the community": Peters *v*. Kiff, 407 U.S. 493 (1972); Alexander *v*. La., 405 U.S. 625 (1972). *And see* the discussion at p. 410ff.

[258] Village of Arlington Heights *v*. Metro. Housing Dev. Corp., 429 U.S. 252, 265 (1977).

[259] *See, e.g.*, Griggs *v*. Duke Power Co., 401 U.S. 424 (1971); Albermarle Paper Co. *v*. Moody, 422 U.S. 405 (1975); Washington *v*. Davis, 426 U.S. 229 (1976). *See also* Walston *v*. County School Bd. of Nansemond Cty., Va., 492 F. 2d. 919 (1974); Vulcan Society of the New York City Fire Dept. *v*. Civil Service Com'n, 360 F.Supp. 1265 (1973); Shield Club *v*. City of Cleveland, 370 F.Supp. 251 (1972); Commonwealth of Pennsylvania *v*. Glickman, 370 F.Supp. 724 (1974); Officers for Justice *v*. Civil Service Com'n, 371 F.Supp. 1328 (1973).

[260] Serrano *v*. Priest, 487 P. 2d. 1241 (1972) *and* Rodriguez *v*. San Antonio School Dist., 337 F.Supp. 280 (1971).

[261] San Antonio Indep. School Dist. *v*. Rodriguez, 411 U.S. 1, 30 (1973).

majority asked, were the right to education declared a fundamental right, would such a fundamental claim not also exist on food and shelter? And, how much provision of these important functions by the State would constitute the constitutional minimum? Neither, reasoned the Court, did the postulated connection between education and voting, by way of assuring an informed electorate, create the necessity to strictly scrutinize property tax funding of public schools. Rather, the Court found the property tax, supplemented by State and Federal subsidy, a reasonable approach, reflecting a commitment to local involvement and warranting deference under the Federal principle.

Serrano, the California case, ultimately reached the opposite conclusion. Though the U.S. Supreme Court declined to hear the case on the basis of its ruling in *Rodriguez*, the California Supreme Court subsequently held that "the California public school financing system for public elementary and secondary schools . . . while not in violation of the equal protection clause of the Fourteenth Amendment to the United States Constitution, is invalid *as being in violation of . . . the equal protection of the laws provisions of our state Constitution*" (emphasis supplied).[262] Reasoning from premises exactly opposite of those adopted by the Court in *Rodriguez*, namely "(1) discrimination in educational opportunity on the basis of district wealth involves a suspect classification, and (2) education is a fundamental interest," the California court concluded the public school financing system at issue was "not . . . shown by the state to be necessary to achieve a compelling state interest." State supreme court decisions are split, however, on whether to follow the reasoning in *Rodriguez* or *Serrano* in the interpretation of their own State constitutional provisions.[263]

The
Benign
Quota

In the struggle to eliminate *invidious* discrimination, officials have sometimes seen fit to establish quotas in various enterprises such as housing, education, and employment to ensure a better representation of groups which are commonly discriminated against. To those, not members of minority groups, who find themselves excluded by these efforts at affirmative action, this appears to be discrimination in reverse, indistinguishable in principle from the invidious treatment on the basis of race, sex, or ethnicity that heretofore disadvantaged the minorities. Though Federal courts for years have acted to implement statutorily imposed minority group employment by quota,[264] the day is fast approaching for a

---

[262] Serrano v. Priest, 557 P. 2d. 929, 957-958 (1976).

[263] The Washington Supreme Court adopted a *Rodriguez* view of its State's equal protection clause in Northshore School Dist. No. 417 v. Kinnear, 530 P. 2d. 178 (1974); the New Jersey Supreme Court, on the other hand, adopted an outlook like that of *Serrano* in its decision of Robinson v. Cahill, 303 A. 2d. 273 (1973). In *in re* G. H., 218 N.W. 2d. 441 (1974), the North Dakota Supreme Court held that a provision of the State constitution providing every child a right to a public school education guaranteed equal educational opportunity for handicapped children.

[264] *See* Contractors Ass'n v. Sec'y of Labor, 442 F. 2d. 159 (1971); Southern Illinois Builders Ass'n v. Ogilvie, 471 F. 2d. 680 (1972); United States v. Local Union No.

judgment on the constitutionality of the enterprise; the Court has set the question for argument at its October 1977 Term.[265]

The Court will have a wide variety of constitutional responses from which to select.[266] Among the options apparent from lower court decisions are: (1) finding that this is discrimination on the basis of race, which creates a "suspect class" but which is justified by compelling State interests;[267] (2) holding that application of the "strict scrutiny" test would be contrary to the salutary purposes for which the Fourteenth Amendment was intended" and concluding that use of the quota was *reasonably* justified;[268] (3) reasoning that quotas create "suspect classes" which are not supported by any compelling State interest;[269] and (4) concluding that race as a basis for creating classifications in law is *per se* unconstitutional thus adopting Justice Harlan's dissenting view in *Plessy* that "the Constitution is color blind."[270]

A closely related problem was presented in a wave of lawsuits spawned by the recession of the mid-1970s. The suits challenged the labor-management "last man hired is the first man fired" policy because it resulted in the layoff of a disproportionate number of

---

212, Etc., 472 F. 2d. 634 (1973); United States *v* Wood, Wire & Metal Lathers Int'l Union, Local No. 46, 471 F. 2d. 408 (1973); Sims *v*. Sheet Metal Workers Int'l Ass'n Local Union No. 65, 353 F.Supp. 22 (1972); Assoc. General Contractors of Mass., Inc. *v*. Altschuler, 490 F. 2d. 9 (1973); Anderson *v*. San Francisco Unified School Dist., 357 F.Supp. 248 (1972); Erie Human Relations Com'n *v*. Tullio, 357 F.Supp. 422 (1973); Oburn *v*. Shapp, 521 F. 2d. 142 (1975); Equal Employment Opportunity Com'n *v*. Local 638 . . . Local 28 of Sheet Metal Workers' Int'l Ass'n, 532 F. 2d. 821 (1976); United States *v*. City of Chicago, 411 F.Supp. 218 (1976), *aff'd in part and reversed in part and remanded* 549 F. 2d. 415 (1977). *But cf.* Kirkland *v*. N.Y. State Dept. of Correctional Services, 520 F. 2d. 420 (1975).

[265] Bakke *v*. Regents of the University of California, 553 P. 2d. 1152 (1976), *cert. granted* 97 S.Ct. 1098 (1977).

[266] *See* Boris I. Bittker, "The Case of the Checker-Board Ordinance: An Experiment in Race Relations," 71 *Yale Law Journal*, 1387 (1962).

[267] DeFunis *v*. Odegaard, 507 P. 2d. 1169 (1973), *vacated and remanded*, 416 U.S. 312 (1974), *judgment reinstated*, 529 P. 2d. 438 (1974). This is not to say that the court in *DeFunis* overlooked the distinction in purpose between benign quotas and *invidious* discrimination; it was a matter addressed at length by the Washington Supreme Court in *DeFunis I*. Said the court: "*Brown* did not hold that all racial classifications are *per se* unconstitutional; rather, it held that invidious racial classifications—i.e., those that stigmatize a racial group with the stamp of inferiority—are unconstitutional. Even viewed in a light most favorable to the plaintiff, the 'preferential' minority admissions policy administered by the law school is clearly not a form of invidious discrimination. The goal of this policy is not to separate the races, but to bring them together." The court went on to observe that the decision of the U.S. Supreme Court in *Swann* confirmed this conclusion.

[268] Alevy *v*. Downstate Medical Center, 348 N.E. 2d. 537 (1976).

[269] Bakke *v*. Regents of the University of California, 553 P. 2d. 1152 (1976). A number of other decisions have also run against upholding affirmative action; *see* Lige *v*. Town of Montclair, 367 A. 2d. 833 (1976); Flanagan *v*. President and Directors of Georgetown College, 417 F.Supp. 377 (1976); Cramer *v*. Virginia Commonwealth Univ., 415 F.Supp. 673 (1976); Hupart *v*. Bd. of Higher Educ. of City of New York, 420 F.Supp. 1087 (1976).

[270] *See* DeFunis *v*. Odegaard, 507 P. 2d. 1169, 1189 (1973) (dissenting opinion of Chief Justice Hale in which Justice Hunter joined).

black workers. Lower Federal court decisions had held that the courts were without jurisdiction to alter labor-management agreements that employees be dismissed on the basis of seniority, regardless of the fact that, given the racially discriminatory hiring practices that prevailed for years, such a procedure overwhelmingly favored whites.[271] In 1976, the Supreme Court held, as a matter of statutory construction, that Title VII of the 1964 Civil Rights Act empowers Federal courts to award retroactive seniority to black victims of job discrimination.[272] The award applies to workers who sought employment, were rejected because of race, and who subsequently were hired by the same employer. Speaking for the Court, Justice Brennan wrote: "Without an award of seniority dating from the time at which he was discriminatorily refused employment, an individual . . . will never obtain his rightful place in the hierarchy of seniority." Acknowledging that such an award need not be made "in all circumstances," Justice Brennan went on to point out that, given Congress's purpose in Title VII to vest Federal courts with a sufficient store of remedies with which to make victims of discrimination whole again, "we find untenable the conclusion that this form of relief may be denied merely because the interests of other employees may thereby be affected." Justice Powell, dissenting, criticized the Court's decision as ignoring the equities of innocent employees who were being penalized by the effect of such awards for discrimination for which they were not responsible. Chief Justice Burger, also dissenting, would have been more receptive to monetary awards.

Discrimina-
tion Based
on Sex
Since the Court's maiden voyage into the world of gender-based distinctions in law in 1971, an increasing share of the Court's equal protection cases have involved challenges to statutes that contained classifications based on sex. While the Court has several times struck down such statutes, those occasions have been proportionately far fewer than in suits challenging classifications based on race. Attendant to this growth in the law has been a disconcerting unpredictability. In large part, the unpredictability of the Court's response to gender-based legislation stems from the contradiction between the Court's two principal precedents. The first of those precedents was Reed v. Reed,[273] the Court's initial effort in the

---

[271] Franks v. Bowman Transp. Co., 495 F. 2d. 398 (1974); Waters v. Wisc. Steel Wkrs. of Int'l Harvester Co., 502 F. 2d. 1309 (1974); Jersey Central Power and Light Co. v. Local Unions of IBEW, 508 F. 2d. 687 (1975).

[272] Franks v. Bowman Transp. Co., 424 U.S. 747. The following year, in a suit alleging that blacks and Spanish-surnamed persons had been discriminated against in employment by a trucking company, the Court held that the government had sustained the burden of showing such a pattern or practice of discrimination, that retroactive seniority would be awarded as relief even if the labor-management agreement in effect made no such provision, and that the seniority systems, which tended to lock employees into less desirable non-line driver positions, did not run afoul of the law because "[i]t applies equally to all races and ethnic groups." Int'l Bro. of Teamsters v. U.S., 431 U.S. 324 (1977).

[273] 404 U.S. 71 (1971).

field. Invalidating an Idaho statute that gave men preference over women in the appointment of administrators of estates of persons who die intestate, the Court unanimously ruled that the gender-based distinction in that law was arbitrary, and therefore unconstitutional, because it bore no fair or substantial relation to the object of the legislation.

To some, *Reed* stood, then, for the proposition that the test of a gender-based classification was reasonableness; the Idaho statute having flunked the test because it was unreasonable. But two years later, in Frontiero *v.* Richardson,[274] a plurality, speaking through Justice Brennan, read *Reed* to announce a "departure from 'traditional' rational-basis analysis with respect to sex-based classifications." Said Justice Brennan, "[S]ince sex, like race and national origin, is an immutable characteristic determined solely by the accident of birth, the imposition of special disabilities upon the members of a particular sex because of their sex would seem to violate 'the basic concept of our system that legal burdens should bear some relationship to individual responsibility.' " Hence, "classifications based upon sex . . . are inherently suspect, and must therefore be subjected to strict judicial scrutiny." By this test, the Court declared unconstitutional a Federal statute that automatically qualified married servicemen to receive increased quarters allowances and medical and dental benefits for their wives, but accorded these fringe benefits to the husbands of female military personnel only if they were dependent on their servicewomen spouses for over one-half their support.

Of the Court's subsequent decisions, two cited *Frontiero*, five relied on *Reed* or its progeny, and four refrained from discussing either. Applying the "strict scrutiny" analysis, announced in *Frontiero*, the Court struck down two provisions of the Social Security Act: one granted survivor's benefits to widows and minor children but only to minor children in the case where a husband survives his working spouse;[275] the other paid survivor's benefits to a widow based on the earnings of her deceased husband, but such benefits on the earnings of a deceased wife were not paid to a widower unless he was receiving half his support from her.[276] The bulk of the cases citing *Reed* ran the other way. The Court upheld a Florida law giving widows but not widowers a $500 property tax exemption,[277] a Federal statute providing for mandatory discharge of naval officers that deals with men and women differently (women are guaranteed 13 years of service; men have no such guarantee),[278] and a formula for the computation of old-age benefits allowing women to exclude from computation of their "average monthly wage" three

---

[274] 411 U.S. 677 (1973).
[275] Weinberger *v.* Wiesenfeld, 420 U.S. 636 (1975).
[276] Califano *v.* Goldfarb, 430 U.S. 199 (1977).
[277] Kahn *v.* Shevin, 416 U.S. 351 (1974).
[278] Schlesinger *v.* Ballard, 419 U.S. 498 (1975).

more lower earning years than similarly situated men.[279] But, citing *Reed*, the Court struck down as irrational a Utah law that specified a lower age of majority for girls than boys in the context of a parent's obligation to pay child support[280] and an Oklahoma statute prohibiting the sale of 3.2-per cent beer to females under 18 and males under 21.[281] Relying on neither *Reed* nor *Frontiero*, the Court upheld: (1) a State disability insurance benefit plan that pays benefits to disabled private employees but excludes pregnancy from coverage;[282] (2) a private disability plan with the same exclusion;[283] and (3) a Social Security Act provision that grants benefits to a married woman whose husband retires or is disabled if she has a minor or dependent child in her care but not to a divorced woman in similar circumstances.[284] In the fourth case, the Court upheld part of an Alabama law establishing explicit gender-criterion for the assignment of prison guards to maximum security prisons where they would be in "contact positions" but striking down the law's minimum height and weight requirements.[285] The Court's two-tiered treatment of gender-based distinctions, however has implications that go beyond the Fourteenth Amendment. Supporters of the Equal Rights Amendment have made much of the argument that the limitations of equal protection analysis are manifest and adoption of the proposed constitutional amendment would significantly clarify matters by making sex a "suspect class."

In a somewhat related case, decided on Sixth Amendment grounds, the Court held unconstitutional Louisiana's practice of categorically excluding women from jury service unless they filed a written declaration of a desire to serve.[286] The Court concluded that excluding an identifiable class that constituted 53 per cent of the population infringed the requirement that jury panels be drawn from a cross-section of the community. In a related First Amendment case, the Court upheld a human relations commission's order forbidding newspapers to carry sex-designated want ads.[287]

Furthermore, numerous lower court decisions have held that girls may not be barred from competing with boys in high school non-contact sports.[288] And, implementing the Education Amend-

---

[279] Califano v. Webster, 430 U.S. 313 (1977).
[280] Stanton v. Stanton, 421 U.S. 7 (1975).
[281] Craig v. Boren, 429 U.S. 191 (1976).
[282] Geduldig v. Aiello, 417 U.S. 484 (1974).
[283] General Electric Co. v. Gilbert, 429 U.S. 125 (1976).
[284] Mathews v. deCastro, 429 U.S. 181 (1976).
[285] Dothard v. Rawlinson, 433 U.S. 321 (1977).
[286] Taylor v. La., 419 U.S. 522 (1975).
[287] Pittsburgh Press Co. v. Pittsburgh Com'n on Human Relations, 413 U.S. 376 (1973).
[288] *See* Morris v. Michigan State Bd. of Educ., 472 F. 2d. 1207 (1973); *and* Haas v. South Bend Community School Corp., 289 N.E. 2d. 495 (1972); Fortin v. Darlington Little League, 514 F. 2d. 344 (1975); *and* Darrin v. Gould, 540 P. 2d. 882 (1975); *but cf.* Bucha v. Illinois High School Ass'n, 351 F.Supp. 69 (1972). Such cases

ments of 1972 Title IX of which bars discrimination on the basis of sex in any education program receiving Federal financial assistance,[289] the Department of Health, Education, and Welfare issued a welter of non-discrimination regulations.[290] Controversy quickly centered on the guidelines dealing with athletics. Those regulations, permitting separate men's and women's teams in contact sports but simultaneously mandating equal athletic opportunities,[291] have raised the ire of college football coaches who see the resources of the revenue-raising men's teams being cut to fund non-revenue-producing women's teams.[292]

In other decisions, lower courts have found impermissible gender-based discrimination in practices that: (1) exclude women from bars open to the public that serve "men only";[293] (2) saddle women employees in bars with restrictions additional to those imposed on male employees;[294] (3) make the residency of a married woman that of her husband for purpose of determining eligibility to attend college at in-state tuition rates;[295] (4) differentiate between women and men in the structure of insurance or retirement benefits based on the greater longevity of women;[296] (5) fix the presumption of fitness with the mother in child custody cases;[297] and (6) award veterans a preference in civil service employment.[298] Courts have upheld: (1) a hospital's policy of not allowing fathers in the delivery room;[299] (2) a statute requiring a natural mother's but not father's consent to adoption;[300] (3) a woman's right after marriage to continue to use her maiden name;[301] and (4) the obligation

---

involve determination of critical questions of "state action," *see* Magill v. Avonworth Baseball Conference, 516 F. 2d. 1328 (1975). *See also* Cape v. Tenn. Secondary School Athletic Ass'n, 424 F.Supp. 732 (1976).

[289] 20 U.S.C. §§ 1681 *et seq.*   [290] 40 F. R. 24127 (1975).

[291] § 86.41(b) and (c).

[292] It is interesting to note how the guidelines, at least with regard to athletics, appear to revive the heretofore discredited "separate but equal" doctrine, enunciated by the Court in Plessy v. Ferguson and repudiated by it over twenty years ago.

[293] Bennett v. Dyer's Chop House, Inc., 350 F.Supp. 153 (1972); Johnston v. Heinemann Candy Co., Inc., 402 F.Supp. 714 (1975); Cross v. Midtown Club, Inc., 365 A. 2d. 1227 (1976). *See also* Women's Liberation Union of R.I. v. Israel, 379 F. Supp. 44 (1974), *aff'd* 512 F. 2d 106 (1975).

[294] White v. Flemming, 374 F.Supp. 267 (1974), *aff'd* 522 F. 2d. 730 (1975). One court dismissed the complaint of a waitress who had been fired for refusing to shave the long hair on her legs to which customers objected despite her contention that male employees were not required to shave their legs. *San Diego Evening Tribune*, June 5, 1975.

[295] Samuel v. Univ. of Pittsburgh, 538 F. 2d 991 (1976).

[296] Rosen v. Public Service Electric and Gas Co., 477 F. 2d. 90 (1973); Manhart v. City of Los Angeles, Dept. of Water and Power, 553 F. 2d. 581 (1976); Reilly v. Robertson, 360 N.E. 2d. 171 (1977).

[297] State *ex rel.* Watts v. Watts, 350 N.Y.S. 2d. 285 (1973).

[298] Anthony v. Massachusetts, 415 F.Supp. 485 (1976).

[299] Fitzgerald v. Porter Mem. Hosp., 523 F. 2d. 716 (1975).

[300] *In re* Adoption of Malpica-Orsini, 331 N.E. 2d. 486 (1975).

[301] Kruzel v. Podell, 226 N.W. 2d. 458 (1975); Dunn v. Palermo, 522 S.W. 2d. 679 (1975); *see also in re* Natale, 527 S.W. 2d. 402 (1975); Laks v. Laks, 540 P. 2d. 1277 (1975). *But cf.* Application of Halligan, 350 N.Y.S. 2d. 63 (1973).

of a man who had sex reassignment surgery to support his former wife.[302] Moreover, the U.S. Supreme Court has affirmed by an equally divided vote an appeals court decision upholding a school district's maintenance of some all-girls and all-boys schools so long as attendance is voluntary and the educational opportunities are equal[303] and a Federal appeals court has held that a Congressman infringed equal protection when he fired a female staff member because of her sex.[304] Finally, reversing a district court decision, another appeals court held that the selective service statute did not unconstitutionally discriminate on the basis of sex.[305]

Corpora-
tions as
"Persons"

As was remarked earlier, corporations are "persons" within the meaning of the Fourteenth Amendment, and so are entitled to the "equal protection of the laws." But for a "foreign" corporation to be entitled to equal treatment with the corporations chartered by a State it must be "subject to the jurisdiction thereof."[306] The importance, moreover, of this reading of the term, the historical validity of which has been disputed,[307] is much less than is sometimes supposed. It does not mean that the law may not exact special duties of corporations, but it does mean that such duties must bear some reasonable relation to the fact that they are corporations and to the nature of the business in which they are engaged. Thus, in view of the special dangers to which the railroad business exposes the public, railroad companies may be required to stand the heavy expense of elevating their grade crossings.[308] On the other hand, a railroad may not be required to carry selected commodities at a loss.[309]

Equal
Protection
as to
Persons in
the Same
Business

The Supreme Court in a single Term recently turned back four equal protection challenges in business regulation cases, underscoring the long-established theme of judicial self-restraint by overruling Morey v. Doud,[310] "the only case in the last half century to invalidate a wholly economic regulation solely on equal protection grounds."[311] The Court upheld: (1) a Texas statute allowing wider venue in suits against foreign than domestic corporations;[312] (2) a Maryland law treating foreign and domestic scrap processors differently in a complex carrot-and-stick effort to rid the State of

---

[302] M. T. v. J. T., 355 A. 2d. 204 (1976). On a related matter, the courts have held that the ban on sex discrimination in the Civil Rights Act does not extend to cover transsexuals, see Voyles v. Ralph K. Davies Medical Center, 403 F.Supp. 456 (1975).

[303] Vorchheimer v. School Dist. of Philadelphia, 532 F. 2d. 880 (1976), aff'd 97 S.Ct. 1671 (1977).

[304] Davis v. Passman, 544 F. 2d. 865 (1977).

[305] United States v. Reiser, 532 F. 2d. 673 (1976), reversing 394 F.Supp. 1060.

[306] Santa Clara County v. So. Pac. R.R. Co., 118 U.S. 394 (1886); Hanover Fire Ins. Co. v. Carr, 272 U.S. 494 (1926); cf. WHYY v. Glassboro, 393 U.S. 117 (1968).

[307] See the interesting dissenting opinion of Justice Black in Connecticut Gen. L. Ins. Co. v. Johnson, 303 U.S. 77 at 82 (1938), and references.

[308] Chicago & Alton R.R. Co. v. Tranbarger, 238 U.S. 67 (1915), and cases there cited. Cf. Robertson v. California, 328 U.S. 440, 456-457 (1946).

[309] Northern Pacific Ry. v. No Dak., 236 U.S. 585 (1915).

[310] 354 U.S. 457 (1957).

[311] City of New Orleans v. Dukes, 427 U.S. 297, 306 (1976).

[312] American Motorists Insurance Co. v. Starnes, 425 U.S. 637 (1976).

abandoned automobiles;[313] (3) a Detroit zoning ordinance designed to prevent a skid-row atmosphere from developing by spreading out certain "regulated uses" of property (e.g., adult theaters, adult bookstores, bars, hotels, cabarets);[314] and (4) a New Orleans ordinance, with a grandfather clause provision, regulating pushcart vendors engaged in the sale of foodstuffs in the city's French Quarter.[315]

The clause is also ineffective as a restraint on the taxing power of the States. Almost any classification made in a tax measure will be sustained by the Court, whether it is relevant to the business of raising revenue or proceeds from some ulterior motive.[316] As the Court said in 1959: "Of course, the States, in the exercise of their taxing power, are subject to the requirements of the Equal Protection Clause of the Fourteenth Amendment. But that clause imposes no iron rule of equality, prohibiting the flexibility and variety that are appropriate to reasonable schemes of state taxation. The State may impose different specific taxes upon different trades and professions and may vary the rate of excise upon various products. It is not required to resort to close distinctions or to maintain a precise, scientific uniformity with reference to composition, use or value. . . . But there is a point beyond which the State cannot go without violating the Equal Protection Clause. The State must proceed upon a rational basis and may not resort to a classification that is palpably arbitrary."[317] If there is such "a point," however, it must be more theoretical than real. Indeed, in the course of its opinion addressing an equal protection challenge to an Illinois constitutional provision that subjected corporations but not individuals to an *ad valorem* personal property tax, the Court, quoting the foregoing passage from *Bowers*, failed to mention the sentence beginning "But there is a point . . .".[318] Said the Court: "Where taxation is concerned and no specific federal right, apart from equal protection, is imperiled, the States have large leeway in making classifications and drawing lines which in their judgment produce reasonable systems of taxation."[319]

Taxation

[313] Hughes v. Alexandria Scrap Corp., 426 U.S. 794 (1976).

[314] Young v. American Mini Theatres, Inc., 427 U.S. 50 (1976). Other cities have also followed suit, see *New York Times*, Nov. 28, 1976.

[315] City of New Orleans v. Dukes, 427 U.S. 297 (1976).

[316] See State Tax Com'rs v. Jackson, 283 U.S. 527 (1931); and Great Atlantic and Pacific Tea Co. v. Grosjean, 301 U.S. 412 (1937); and cases cited there.

[317] Allied Stores of Ohio v. Bowers, 358 U.S 522, 526-527 (1959); Flores v. Government of Guam, 444 F. 2d. 284, 288 (1971); State v. Kelly, 285 A. 2d. 571 (1972).

[318] Lenhausen v. Lake Shore Auto Parts, Inc., 410 U.S. 356, 360 (1973).

[319] *Ibid.*, 359. *See also* City of Pittsburgh v. Alco Parking Corp., 417 U.S. 369 (1974). A recent illustration of one such claim, which the Court called "patently frivolous," appeared in a portion of an opinion disposing of an action brought by a gasoline distributor who was forced to pay a State sales tax on the gross proceeds of retail sales without first deducting Federal and State gasoline excise taxes, the Supreme Court rejected the distributor's argument that the imposition of the sales tax constituted a denial of equal protection since other States permitted such excise taxes to be deducted. The Court pointed out: "The prohibition of the Equal Protec-

Expansion of the Concept of State Action

As we saw above, the term "State" in this clause meant for years any agency whereby the State exercised its powers. It thus included any State or local official when acting under color of his office,[320] and in deciding whether a State has violated the above provisions, the Court has always been free to go behind the face of the law and inquire into the fairness of its actual enforcement.[321] This rule, originally laid down in Yick Wo v. Hopkins, was illustrated some years ago in one of the *Scottsboro* cases, where an indictment returned by a grand jury of whites in a county of Alabama in which no member of a considerable Negro population had ever been called for jury service, was held void, although the Alabama statute governing the matter contained no discrimination between the two races.[322]

In recent years, the concept of what constitutes State action has been broadened dramatically, though not suddenly.[323] Case by case, the Court moved from its position in Shelley v. Kraemer (1948) that "action inhibited by the first section of the Fourteenth Amendment is only action which may fairly be said to be that of the States"[324] to its present position which is worth quoting at length: "Is there sufficient state action to prove a violation of petitioner's Fourteenth Amendment rights if she knows that Kress [S. H. Kress and Co.] refused her service because of a state-enforced custom compelling segregation of the races in Hattiesburg restaurants?

"In analyzing this problem, it is useful to state two polar propositions, each of which is easily identified and resolved. On the one hand, the Fourteenth Amendment plainly prohibits a State itself from discriminating because of race. On the other hand, §1 of the

---

tion Clause is against its denial by the State, here Mississippi, as between taxpayers subject to its laws. Petitioner makes no claim of unconstitutional discrimination by Mississippi of its sales tax among taxpayers subject to that tax." Gurley v. Rhoden, 421 U.S. 200, 212 (1975). The Supreme Court also rejected the notion that the sales tax was a tax on the excise taxes, observing that both excise taxes attached to the producer, not the consumer, and prior to the point of retail sale.

[320] *Ex parte* Virginia, 100 U.S. 339 (1879); Screws v. U.S., 325 U.S. 91 (1945); Shelley v. Kraemer, 334 U.S. 1 (1948).

[321] Yick Wo v. Hopkins, 118 U.S. 356 (1886); Reagan v. Farmers' Loan & T. Co., 154 U.S. 362 (1894); Tarrance v. Fla., 188 U.S. 519 (1903).

[322] Norris v. Ala., 294 U.S. 587 (1935). To the same effect were Hale v. Ky., 303 U.S. 613 (1938); Pierre v. La., 306 U.S. 354 (1939); *and* Smith v. Tex., 311 U.S. 128 (1940); Avery v. Ga., 345 U.S. 559 (1953). *Cf.* Brown v. Allen, 344 U.S. 443 (1953).

[323] "State action" was found to inhere in all of the following: (1) court enforcement of a restrictive covenant, Shelley v. Kraemer, 334 U.S. 1 (1948); (2) exclusion of blacks from membership in a private "club" which endorsed candidates for the primary election, Terry v. Adams, 345 U.S. 461 (1953); (3) receipt of rent by a municipal corporation from "whites only" restaurant located in a public parking garage, Burton v. Wilmington Parking Auth., 365 U.S. 715 (1961); (4) city ordinance requiring separate facilities for the races, Peterson v. City of Greenville, 373 U.S. 244 (1963); (5) oral statements by city officials proclaiming a policy of segregation, Lombard v. La., 373 U.S. 267 (1963); (6) upkeep of an all-white park by a city, Evans v. Newton, 382 U.S. 296 (1966); and (7) amendment of a State constitution so as to preserve the absolute independence of a lessor to rent property to whomever he chooses, Reitman v. Mulkey, 387 U.S. 369 (1967).

[324] Shelley v. Kraemer, 334 U.S. 1, 13 (1948).

Fourteenth Amendment does not forbid a private party, not acting against a backdrop of state compulsion or involvement, to discriminate on the basis of race in his personal affairs as an expression of his own personal predilections. As was said in Shelley *v.* Kraemer . . . §1 of '[t]hat Amendment erects no shield against merely private conduct however discriminatory or wrongful.'

"At what point between these two extremes a State's involvement in the refusal becomes sufficient to make the private refusal to serve a violation of the Fourteenth Amendment, is far from clear under our case law. If a State had a law requiring a private person to refuse service because of race, it is clear beyond dispute that the law would violate the Fourteenth Amendment and could be declared invalid and enjoined from enforcement. Nor can a State enforce such a law requiring discrimination through either convictions of proprietors who refuse to discriminate, or trespass prosecutions of patrons who, after being denied service pursuant to such a law, refuse to honor a request to leave the premises. . . .

"For state action purposes it makes no difference of course whether the racially discriminatory act by the private party is compelled by a statutory provision or *by a custom having the force of law*—in either case it is the State that has commanded the result by its law. Without deciding whether less substantial involvement of a State might satisfy the state action requirement of the Fourteenth Amendment, we conclude that petitioner would show an abridgment of her equal protection right, if she proves that Kress refused her service because of a state-enforced custom of segregating the races in public restaurants"[325] (emphasis supplied).

But the Court in 1972 narrowed somewhat the concept of what constitutes State action. In the attention-getting case involving the Negro guest who was denied service in a Moose Lodge, Justice Rehnquist speaking for the Court stated the view that "Our holdings indicate that where the impetus for discrimination is private, the State must have 'significantly involved itself with invidious discriminations,' in order for the discriminating action to fall within the ambit of the constitutional prohibition."[326] The Court did not find the act of liquor licensing (on which the contention of State action was based) such a significant involvement. As the Court saw it, with a minor exception the State Liquor Control Board "plays absolutely no part in establishing or enforcing the membership or guest policies of the club which it licenses to serve liquor."[327]

[325] Adickes *v.* Kress and Co., 398 U.S. 144, 169-171 (1970).
[326] Moose Lodge No. 107 *v.* Irvis, 407 U.S. 163, 173 (1972).
[327] *Ibid.*,175. The Court was troubled by the fact that the Board did have regulations which required that "every club licensee shall adhere to all the provisions of its constitution and by-laws." Of course, this could have the effect of enforcing discriminations spelled out in the constitution and by-laws. But parties to the suit conceded that the purpose of these regulations was to keep public accommodations from masquerading as private clubs. Nonetheless, the Court held that the discriminated-against guest was entitled to a decree enjoining the enforcement of those regulations, "He was entitled to no more." *Ibid.*, 179. Subsequently, the Pennsylvania Supreme Court upheld an order that the Harrisburg Moose Lodge drop a

Where a customer sued under the Civil Rights Act for damages alleging a violation of her constitutional rights to notice, a hearing, and an opportunity to pay all amounts in arrear before termination of electric service by the power company, the Supreme Court also found no "state action."[328] Speaking for the six-man majority, Justice Rehnquist concluded: "All of petitioner's arguments taken together show no more than that Metropolitan was a heavily regulated private utility, enjoying at least a partial monopoly in the providing of electrical service within its territory, and that it elected to terminate service to petitioner in a manner which the Pennsylvania Public Utilities Commission found permissible under state law. Under our decision this is not sufficient to connect the State of Pennsylvania with respondent's action so as to make the latter's conduct attributable to the State for purposes of the Fourteenth Amendment." Though Justices Douglas, Brennan, and Marshall each dissented separately, their common objections to the majority position are perhaps best covered by the opinion of Justice Marshall. He lamented that "this case is a very poor vehicle for resolving the difficult and important questions presented," and voted to dismiss the writ of certiorari as improvidently granted since "it [is] unclear whether petitioner has a property right under state law to the service she was receiving from the . . . company." Forced to reach the "state action" issue, however, he discerned factors which, in the aggregate, mandated the opposite conclusion. Wrote Marshall: "Our state action cases have repeatedly relied on several factors clearly presented by this case: a state-sanctioned monopoly; an extensive pattern of cooperation between the 'private' entity and the state; and a service uniquely public in nature." What would the Court's conclusion be, wondered Justice Marshall, with regard to "state action," where "a company . . . refused to extend service to Negroes, welfare recipients, or any other group that the company preferred, for its own reasons, not to serve"?

Where medical boards deny hospital privileges to doctors who then assert due process challenges to the method of such termination, courts have focused on the degree to which the actions of such boards are "state action" as a prerequisite to examining the validity of the due process claims.[329] Also addressing contentions of dis-

---

ban against serving Negro guests. 294 A. 2d. 594 (1972); *appeal dismissed*, 409 U.S. 1052 (1972).

[328] Jackson *v.* Metro. Edison Co., 419 U.S. 345 (1974). *See also* Dawes *v.* Philadelphia Gas Com'n, 421 F.Supp. 806 (1976); *but see* Uhl *v.* Ness City, Kan., 406 F.Supp. 1012 (1975).

[329] Much of the judicial analysis in dealing with the "state action" question concentrates on the amount of public funding (Federal and State), though courts have disagreed as to how much is enough and to what degree this single factor is determinative. *See* Christhilf *v.* Annapolis Emergency Hosp. Ass'n, Inc., 496 F. 2d. 174 (1974); Poe *v.* Charlotte Memorial Hospital, 374 F.Supp. 1302 (1974), which found "state action"; *and contra see* Slavcoff *v.* Harrisburg Polyclinic Hospital, 375 F.Supp. 999 (1974); Barrett *v.* United Hospital, 376 F.Supp. 791 (1974); Barrio *v.* McDonough Dist. Hospital, 377 F.Supp. 317 (1974); Hoberman *v.* Lock Haven Hospital, 377 F.Supp. 1178 (1974).

criminatory treatment by ostensibly private organizations, Federal courts have found "state action" to adhere in the behavior of a charitable foundation that was substantially dependent on its tax exempt status,[330] and a private university that was characterized as having a "symbiotic relationship" with the State,[331] but not in that of a national non-profit business organization even though 31.4 per cent of its budget came from Federal funds and it enjoyed tax exempt status.[332] And, reversing a lower court decision which it characterized as "the first time in the history of Fourteenth Amendment jurisprudence that a Federal district court has undertaken the supervision of membership policies in a genuinely private club," the U.S. Court of Appeals, Fifth Circuit, failed to find the requisite "state action." The yacht club, which excluded blacks and Jews from membership, leased from the City of Miami "the bay bottom land underlying club-constructed and club-maintained dock facilities connected to the club lands on shore." The appeals court, sitting *en banc*, concluded by a 9-5 vote, that there was insufficient State involvement because: (1) the club had been in existence longer than the city, and had constructed and maintained its docks for 30 years before the city asserted title to the bay bottom land; and (2) the city's involvement was limited to receipt of a payment from the club of $1 per year for lease of the bay bottomlands.[333]

The equal protection clause served as the basis for the breakthrough in 1962 on the reapportionment issue. As pointed out earlier, p. 219, until then the matter of legislative districting was considered by the Court to be a "political question." As a practical matter this left it to the State legislatures and Congress to change a situation which would upset a political power balance in which many of the legislators were themselves beneficiaries.[334] And it was clear by the 1960's that it just would not be done.[335] Consequently, gross inequities in the worth of citizens' votes abounded throughout the political system.[336]

At length, in Baker *v.* Carr (1962), the Court held that: "the complaint's allegations of a denial of equal protection present a justiciable constitutional cause of action upon which appellants are entitled to a trial and a decision. The right asserted is within the reach

The Right to Have Votes Count Equally

[330] Jackson *v.* Statler Foundation, 496 F. 2d. 623 (1974).
[331] Rackin *v.* Univ. of Penn., 386 F.Supp. 992 (1974).
[332] New York City Jaycees, Inc. *v.* U.S. Jaycees, Inc., 377 F.Supp. 481 (1974), *reversed*, 512 F. 2d. 856 (1975); Junior Chamber of Commerce of Kansas City, Mo. *v.* Missouri State Chamber of Commerce, 508 F. 2d. 1031 (1975); Junior Chamber of Commerce of Rochester, N.Y. *v* U.S. Jaycees, 495 F. 2d. 883 (1974). *See also* Stearns *v.* Veterans of Foreign Wars, 353 F.Supp. 473 (1972).
[333] Golden *v.* Biscayne Bay Yacht Club, 530 F. 2d. 16 (1976), *reversing* 370 F.Supp. 1038; the *en banc* decision also overturned a previous decision by a three-judge circuit court panel, 521 F. 2d. 344 (1975), which had affirmed the distrist court's judgment.
[334] Carl A. Auerbach, "The Reapportionment Cases: One person, One Vote-One Vote, One Value," 1964 *Supreme Court Review*, 1, 68-70.
[335] *Ibid.*   [336] Baker *v.* Carr, 369 U.S. 186, 253-255 (1962).

of judicial protection under the Fourteenth Amendment."[337] Once the Court found that such complaints were justiciable, much of what followed with respect to having votes count equally was predictable. After all, it was the meaning of the *equal* protection clause which was being decided in most of the cases that followed. However, in the first case after Baker *v.* Carr, Wesberry *v.* Sanders (1964), the Court held with respect to Congressional districts "the command of Art. I §2 that the Representatives be chosen 'by the People of the several States' means that as nearly as practicable one man's vote in a congressional election is to be worth as much as another's," and explicitly said it was not deciding the issue on the basis of the Fourteenth Amendment.[338] This decision was followed quickly by Reynolds *v.* Sims (1964), in which the Court held that "the Equal Protection Clause guarantees the opportunity for equal participation by all voters in the election of state legislators. Diluting the weight of votes because of place of residence impairs basic constitutional rights just as much as invidious discriminations based upon factors such as race . . . or economic status. . . . We hold that, as a basic constitutional standard, the Equal Protection Clause requires that the seats in both houses of a bicameral state legislature must be apportioned on a population basis. Simply stated, an individual's right to vote for state legislators is unconstitutionally impaired when its weight is in a substantial fashion diluted when compared with votes of citizens living in other parts of the State."[339]

One can only wonder if the Court fully appreciated the difficulties in store for the courts of the United States in attempting to resolve the myriad of complex practical questions which would arise upon the interpretation that the equal protection clause required that one man's vote be worth the same as every other man's. They certainly would never be able to say that they were not warned. In a long, artful, and powerful dissent in Baker *v.* Carr, Justice Frankfurter had alerted them to the pitfalls:

"A hypothetical claim resting on abstract assumptions is now for the first time made the basis for affording illusory relief for a particular evil even though it foreshadows deeper and more pervasive difficulties in consequence. The claim is hypothetical and the assumptions are abstract because the Court does not vouchsafe the lower courts—state and federal—guidelines for formulating specific, definite, wholly unprecedented remedies for the inevitable litigations that today's umbrageous disposition is bound to stimulate in connection with politically motivated reapportionments in so many States. In such a setting to promulgate jurisdiction in the abstract is meaningless. It is as devoid of reality as 'a brooding omnipresence in the sky,' for it conveys no intimation what relief, if

---

[337] *Ibid.*, 237.
[338] Wesberry *v.* Sanders, 376 U.S. 1, 8 and note 10 (1964).
[339] Reynolds *v.* Sims, 377 U.S. 533, 566-568 (1964).

any, a District Court is capable of affording that would not invite legislatures to play ducks and drakes with the judiciary. For this Court to direct the District Court to enforce a claim to which the Court has over the years consistently found itself required to deny legal enforcement and at the same time to find it necessary to withhold any guidance to the lower court how to enforce this turnabout, new legal claim, manifests an odd—indeed an esoteric—conception of judicial propriety. One of the Court's supporting opinions, as elucidated by commentary, unwittingly affords a disheartening preview of the mathematical quagmire (apart from divers judicially inappropriate and elusive determinants) into which this Court today catapults the lower courts of the country without so much as adumbrating the basis for a legal calculus as a means of extrication. Even assuming the indispensable intellectual disinterestedness on the part of judges in such matters, they do not have accepted legal standards or criteria or even reliable analogies to draw upon for making judicial judgments. To charge courts with the task of accommodating the incommensurable factors of policy that underlie these mathematical puzzles is to attribute, however flatteringly, omnicompetence to judges."[340]

Three basic problems have plagued the courts with respect to reapportionment: (1) how much deviation from absolute equality will be permitted because of practical considerations? (2) what kinds of elections are required to pass the muster of equal protection? (3) what remedies should be applied by courts to force recalcitrant legislatures to reapportion?

As to the first problem, the Court's most recent pronouncement is that " 'Mathematical exactness or precision is hardly a workable constitutional requirement,' . . . but deviations from population equality must be justified by legitimate state considerations. . . ."[341] That, of course, still leaves it up to the courts to determine what is a legitimate State consideration and how much deviation to allow for it. The Court has never announced a constitutionally excusable range of deviation from absolute equality. Rather, it has weighed the magnitude of any given deviation against the justification proffered by the State on a case by case basis. In a 1977 ruling in which the Court made the point that court-drawn apportionments were subject to stiffer expectations than plans devised by legislative bodies, it observed: "The maximum population deviations of 16.5% in the Senate districts and 19.3% in the House districts can hardly be characterized as *de minimis*; they substantially exceed the 'under-10%' deviations the Court has previously considered to be of prima facie constitutional validity only in the context of legislatively enacted apportionments. . . . [E]ven a legislatively crafted apportionment with deviations of this magnitude could be justified

[340] Baker v. Carr, 369 U.S. 186, 267-268 (1962).
[341] Abate v. Mundt, 403 U.S. 182, 185 (1971). *See also* Witcomb v. Chavis, 403 U.S. 124 (1971).

only if it were 'based on legitimate considerations incident to the effectuation of a rational state policy.' "[342] In addition to the compactness and contiguousness of districts and some respect for lines dividing subordinate units of government, other "legitimate considerations," acknowledged by the Court, have included both the protection of incumbents[343] and the approximation of State-wide party strength[344] (to provide balance and an assured base of party representation) in the design of legislative districts. Representation of racial minorities, too, is a valid consideration (*see* the discussion under Amendment XV at p. 537). Because of the added impact of Article I, Section II, which mandates that Representatives be chosen on a population basis, apportionment plans for Congressional districts are subject to greater scrutiny.[345]

Addressing the second question, the Court has held that the "one man, one vote" principle is applicable to local governmental units, too, since they are creations of the State.[346] But for what *types* of institutions is it mandatory? In 1970, the Supreme Court attempted to dispose of the problem: "It has also been urged that we distinguish for apportionment purposes between elections for 'legislative' officials and those for 'administrative' officers. Such a suggestion would leave courts with an equally unmanageable principle since governmental activities 'cannot easily be classified in the neat categories favored by civics texts,' . . . and it must also be re-

---

[342] Connor v. Finch, 97 S.Ct. 1828, 1835 (1977). In the dissenting opinion to Gaffney v. Cummings, 412 U.S. 772 (1973), a majority on the Court was accused by Justices Douglas, Brennan, and Marshall of retreating from the precept enunciated in Kirkpatrick v. Preisler, 394 U.S. 526 (1969) and Wells v. Rockefeller, 394 U.S. 542 (1969) in which Justice Brennan, speaking for the Court rejected the notion "that there is a fixed numerical or percentage population variance small enough to be considered *de minimis* and to satisfy without question the 'as nearly as practicable' standard" in district equality. Instead, "the 'as nearly as practicable' standard requires that the state make a good-faith effort to achieve precise mathematical equality." Continued Justice Brennan, "Unless population variances among congressional districts are shown to have resulted despite such effort, the State must justify each variance, no matter how small." Concurring in White v. Weiser, 412 U.S. 783 (1973), where the maximum deviation in congressional districts was two and one-half per cent, Justice Powell observed, "[M]ore recent cases have allowed modest variations from theoretical 'exactitude' in recognition of the impracticality of applying the *Kirkpatrick* rule as well as deference to legitimate state interests." Though the Court has rejected variances that go as high as 30 or 40 per cent among districts, *see* Swann v. Adams, 385 U.S. 440 (1967), the Court recently sustained a variance of over 16 per cent in Mahan v. Howell, 410 U.S. 315 (1973). Said the Court in *Mahan*, where the apportionment plan was devised by the legislature, "While this percentage may well approach tolerable limits, we do not believe it exceeds them." But in Chapman v. Meier, 420 U.S. 1 (1975), where a Federal district court was imposing its plan on the North Dakota legislature, the Court found that a total variance of 20 per cent was not *de minimis* and could not stand absent persuasive justification.

[343] White v. Weiser, 412 U.S. 783 (1973).

[344] Gaffney v. Cummings, 412 U.S. 735 (1973).

[345] Wesberry v. Sanders, 376 U.S. 1 (1964); Mahan v. Howell, 410 U.S. 315 (1973); White v. Regester, 412 U.S. 755 (1973).

[346] Avery v. Midland Cty., Tex., 390 U.S. 474 (1968).

jected. We therefore hold today that as a general rule, whenever a state or local government decides to select persons by popular election to perform governmental functions, the Equal Protection Clause of the Fourteenth Amendment requires that each qualified voter must be given an equal opportunity to participate in that election, and when members of an elected body are chosen from separate districts, each district must be established on a basis that will insure, as far as is practicable, that equal numbers of voters can vote for proportionally equal numbers of officials. It is of course possible that there might be some case in which a State elects certain functionaries whose duties are so far removed from normal governmental activities and so disproportionately affect different groups that a popular election . . . might not be required. . . ."[347]

But, with respect to delegate apportionment and selection for the national nominating conventions, Federal courts have upheld both the awarding of bonus delegates[348] (affording extra delegates to States which cast their electoral votes for the party's last Presidential candidate and which have recently elected a governor or a senator with the party's affiliation) and winner-take-all primaries.[349] And in two interesting cases decided by the U.S. Court of Appeals for the Eighth Circuit, the "one man, one vote" rule was held applicable to malapportioned Indian tribal councils.[350]

As was predictable, the courts have had great difficulty with legislatures which in Frankfurter's words have played "ducks and drakes with the judiciary." After canvassing what courts have used for remedies, Professor David R. Berman wrote in a splendid article: "By the end of March 1966, all indications were that the favorite form of positive judicial relief was the foundation of a court plan, with all the bi-partisan and non-partisan assistance possible."[351] One such plan devised by the U.S. District Court of Minnesota came a cropper in the Supreme Court. The District Court sharply reduced the size of the legislature in devising its apportionment order. The Supreme Court held *per curiam*: "We know of no federal constitutional principle or requirement that authorizes a federal reapportioning court to go as far as the District Court did and, thus, to by-pass the State's formal judgment as to the proper size of its legislative bodies. No case decided by this Court has gone that far and we have found no district court decision that has employed such radical surgery in reapportionment. There are cases where judicial reapportionment has effectuated minor changes in a

---

[347] Hadley v. Junior College District, 397 U.S. 50, 55-56 (1970). The Supreme Court recently affirmed a lower court decision that the "one man, one vote" rule was inapplicable to judicial elections. Holshouser v. Scott, 409 U.S. 807 (1972).

[348] Ripon Society v. Nat'l Republican Party, 525 F. 2d. 567 (1975), *vacating* 525 F. 2d. 548, *reversing and remanding* 369 F.Supp. 368; *cert. denied* 424 U.S. 933.

[349] Graham v. Fong Eu, 403 F.Supp. 37 (1975), *affirmed* 423 U.S. 1067 (1976).

[350] White Eagle v. One Feather, 478 F. 2d. 1311 (1973); *and* Daly v. U.S., 483 F. 2d. 700 (1973).

[351] 1970 *Law and the Social Order*, 519, 536.

legislature's size. . . . We do not disapprove a court-imposed minor variation from a State's prescribed figure when that change is shown to be necessary to meet constitutional requirements."[352] The Court has also emphasized that, in formulating reapportionment plans, Federal courts should eschew multimember districts and at-large elections in favor of single-member districts,[353] for the effect of other formats of representation on the political power of minorities has been a constant source of concern[354] (*see* the discussion at p. 537).

A decade after he penned the Court's opinion in *Baker*, Justice Brennan concluded that, while compliance in reapportionment had been slow and uncertain at the start, "[t]he improvement in the post-1969 years could not have been more dramatic." With respect to State legislative districts Justice Brennan observed: "[I]n almost one-half of the States the total variance in population of senatorial districts was within 5% to zero. Of the 45 States as to which information was available, 32 had reduced the total variance below 10% and only eight had failed to bring the total variance below 15%. With regard to House districts the improvement is similar. On the basis of information concerning 42 States, it appears that 20 have achieved a total variance of less than 5% and only 14 retained districts with a total variance of more than 15% from the constitutional ideal."[355] This "encouraging development," he asserted was jeopardized by the Court's *de minimis* approach. Whether that is so remains to be seen. The slow progress, however, in reapportionment again raises the question of the efficacy of the judicial process for resolving certain kinds of problems as it did in the school desegregation issue. But here, there literally was no other way. As Justice Clark pointed out in Baker *v*. Carr:

"Although I find the Tennessee apportionment statute offends the Equal Protection Clause, I would not consider intervention by this Court into so delicate a field if there were any other relief available to the people of Tennessee. But the majority of the people of Tennessee have no 'practical opportunities for exerting their political weight at the polls' to correct the existing 'invidious discrimination.' Tennessee has no initiative and referendum. I have searched diligently for other 'practical opportunities' present under the law. I find none other than through the federal courts. The majority of the voters have been caught up in a legislative strait jacket. Tennessee has an 'informed, civically militant electorate' and 'an aroused popular conscience,' but it does not sear 'the conscience of the people's representatives.' This is because the legislative policy has riveted the present seats in the Assembly to

[352] Sixty-Seventh Minn. State Senate *v*. Beens, 406 U.S. 187, 198 (1972).
[353] Chapman *v*. Meier, 420 U.S. 1 (1975).
[354] *See* Mahan *v*. Howell, 410 U.S. 315 (1973); White *v*. Regester, 412 U.S. 755 (1973).
[355] Gaffney *v*. Cummings, 412 U.S 772, 780 (1973).

their respective constituencies, and by the votes of their incumbents a reapportionment of any kind is prevented. The people have been rebuffed at the hands of the Assembly; they have tried the constitutional convention route, but since the call must originate in the Assembly, it, too, has been fruitless. They have tried Tennessee courts with the same result, and Governors have fought the tide only to flounder. It is said that there is recourse in Congress and perhaps that may be, but from a practical standpoint this is without substance. To date Congress has never undertaken such a task in any State. We therefore must conclude that the people of Tennessee are stymied and without judicial intervention will be saddled with the present discrimination in the affairs of their state government. . . ."[356]

Often in special elections, particularly referenda on bond issues, the law has restricted who may vote or has required approval of the question put before the voters by a super-majority. With respect to voting restrictions, the Court struck down statutes that allowed only real property taxpayers to participate in bond elections[357] and limited the franchise in school board elections to parents or individuals who owned taxable real property in the district.[358] These, the Court held were elections of "general interest" and the State had failed to establish any compelling interest for excluding a whole class from the electorate. But the Court sustained restrictions on participation in elections of "special interest." It held that the California voter qualification laws for water storage district elections, limiting voting to landholders in proportion to the value of their lands, were rationally based and therefore not in violation of the equal protection clause.[359] Similarly, the Court upheld a Wyoming statute limiting voting in a watershed improvement district to landowners in proportion to the acreage they held.[360]

"Special Interest" Elections

As for rules governing bond referenda that require voter ratification by a super-majority, the Court held constitutional a State requirement that approval of 60% of the voters was needed on bond issues and increases in tax rates in its political subdivisions. The Court reasoned: "that so long as such provisions do not discriminate against or authorize discrimination against any identifiable class they do not violate the Equal Protection Clause. We see no meaningful distinction between such absolute provisions on debt, changeable only by constitutional amendment, and provisions that legislative decisions on the same issues require more than a majority vote in the legislature. On the contrary, these latter provisions

[356] Baker v. Carr, 369 U.S. 186, 259 (1962).
[357] Cipriano v. City of Houma, 395 U.S. 701 (1969); Phoenix v. Kolodziejski, 399 U.S. 204 (1970).
[358] Kramer v. Union Free School Dist. No. 15, 395 U.S. 621 (1969).
[359] Salyer Land Co. v. Tulare Lake Basin Water Storage Dist., 410 U.S. 719 (1973).
[360] Associated Enterprises, Inc. v. Toltec Watershed Improvement Dist., 410 U.S. 743 (1973).

may, in practice, be less burdensome than the amendment process. Moreover, the same considerations apply when the ultimate power, rather than being delegated to the legislature remains with the people, by way of a referendum."[361] A related question presented to the Court has been the constitutionality of statutes requiring approval of issues on the ballot by a concurrent majority. A Texas "dual box" election procedure for local bond elections required that property taxpayers deposit their votes in one box and all other registered voters deposit their ballots in a separate box, with a majority affirmative vote in both boxes required to pass a bond issue. The Court concluded that this arrangement "erects a classification that impermissibly disenfranchises persons otherwise qualified to vote, solely because they have not rendered some property for taxation."[362] However, the Court upheld a State law that required a majority of voters within city limits and a majority of those living outside the city to approve a new county charter. The Court explained, "The provisions of New York law here in question no more than recognize the realities of these substantially different electoral interests."[363]

SECTION II

Representatives shall be apportioned among the several States according to their respective numbers, counting the whole number of persons in each State, excluding Indians not taxed. But when the right to vote at any election for the choice of electors for President and Vice-President of the United States, Representatives in Congress, the executive and judicial officers of a State, or the members of the legislature thereof, is denied to any of the male inhabitants of such State, being twenty-one years of age, and citizens of the United States, or in any way abridged, except for participation in rebellion, or other crime, the basis of representation therein shall be reduced in the proportion which the number of such male citizens shall bear to the whole number of male citizens twenty-one years of age in such State.

In the struggle to vindicate the legal rights of black Americans, it was a natural reaction to attempt to breathe life into this provision of the Constitution, despite the fact that it had never been successfully implemented.[1] Senator Pat McNamara of Michigan led an abortive effort in the late 1950's to enact legislation designed to reduce the number of Representatives from States which restricted voting rights.[2] And in the 1960's there was an effort to include such

---

[361] Gordon v. Lance, 403 U.S. 1, 7 (1971).
[362] Hill v. Stone, 421 U.S. 289, 300 (1975).
[363] Town of Lockport v. Citizens for Community Action, 97 S.Ct. 1047, 1055 (1977).

---

[1] George D. Zuckerman, "A Consideration of the History and Present Status of Section 2 of the Fourteenth Amendment," 30 *Fordham Law Review*, 93, 124 (1961).
[2] *Ibid.*, 120-124.

a provision in the Civil Rights Act of 1964, an effort which failed.[3] As recently as 1965, a group of citizens went to a Federal district court seeking a declaratory judgment against the Secretary of Commerce and the Director of the Census Bureau to compile at the next census figures as to the denial of the right to vote and to figure the apportionment for the House of Representatives on the basis of those figures. Although the District Court held that the citizens who brought the case lacked standing it did go to the merits of the Fourteenth Amendment argument and cited with approval the language of a Circuit Court in an earlier case: "Irrespective of the Fourteenth Amendment's mandate the Congress, in the present state of the law, is not required to prescribe that census-takers ascertain information relative to disenfranchisement. . . . There was nothing unconstitutional in the omission from the census form of a question relating to disenfranchisement."[4]

Presumably, the efficacy of the other efforts to vindicate the right to vote, precludes any further effort to invoke this provision of the Constitution.[5] (*See* pp. 535-539.)

SECTION III

No person shall be a Senator or Representative in Congress, or elector of President and Vice-President, or hold any office, civil or military, under the United States or under any State, who, having previously taken an oath as a member of Congress, or as an officer of the United States, or as a member of any State legislature, or as an executive or judicial officer of any State, to support the Constitution of the United States, shall have engaged in insurrection or rebellion against the same, or given aid or comfort to the enemies thereof. But Congress may, by a vote of two-thirds of each house, remove such disability.

SECTION IV

The validity of the public debt of the United States, authorized by law, including debts incurred for payment of pensions and bounties for services in suppressing insurrection or rebellion, shall not be questioned. But neither the United States nor any State shall assume or pay any debt or obligation incurred in aid of insurrection or rebellion against the United States, or any claim for the loss or emancipation of any slave; but all such debts, obligations and claims shall be held illegal and void.

These sections are today, for the most part, of historical interest only.

[3] 1964 U.S. *Cong. & Adm. News*, 2422ff.
[4] Lampkin *v.* Connor, 239 F.Supp. 757, 766 (1965), *affirmed*, 360 F. 2d. 505 (1966); U.S. *v.* Sharrow, 409 F. 2d. 77 (1962), *cert. denied*, 372 U.S. 949 (1963).
[5] *But see* Zuckerman, "A Consideration of the History and Present Status of Section 2 of the Fourteenth Amendment," pp. 128-135.

SECTION V

The Congress shall have power to enforce, by appropriate legislation, the provisions of this article.

Congres-
sional En-
forcement
of the
Amend-
ment

The full extent of the powers of Congress under this section, in the regulation and protection of civil rights, has never been conclusively determined.[1] In the famous Civil Rights cases,[2] decided nearly three quarters of a century ago, the Court held void an act of Congress forbidding inns, railroads, and theaters to discriminate between persons on the ground of race, the basis of the decision being the proposition that the prohibitions of the opening section of the Fourteenth Amendment were intended to reach only positive acts of State authorities derogatory of the rights protected by the amendment—not acts of private individuals or acts of omission by the State itself. In the case of Truax *v.* Corrigan,[3] on the other hand, which was decided in 1921, the Court declared that the same clauses require a certain minimum of protection from the State for all classes and persons. In 1966, to the argument that "an exercise of congressional power under §5 of the Fourteenth Amendment that prohibits the enforcement of a state law can only be sustained if the judicial branch determines that the state law is prohibited by the provisions of the Amendment that Congress sought to enforce," the Court said "We disagree. Neither the language nor history of §5 supports such a construction. . . . 'Congress is authorized to *enforce* the prohibitions by appropriate legislation. Such legislation is contemplated to make the amendment fully effective.' A construction of §5 that would require a judicial determination that the enforcement of the state law precluded by Congress violated the Amendment, as a condition of sustaining the congressional enactment, would depreciate both congressional resourcefulness and congressional responsibility for implementing the legislative power in this context to the insignificant role of abrogating only those state laws that the judicial branch was prepared to adjudge unconstitutional, or of merely informing the judgment of the judiciary by particularizing the 'majestic generalities' of §1 of the Amendment."[4]

Nor is it only the equal protection clause which Congress is empowered to implement by "appropriate legislation," but all the "provisions of this article." The outstanding legislation having this purpose was first enacted in 1866 and, as since amended, appears today in Title 18 of the United States Code.[5] It reads thus: "Whoever, under color of any law, statute, ordinance, regulation, or custom, willfully subjects . . . any inhabitant of any State, Territory, or District to the deprivation of any rights, privileges, or immunities

[1] Griffin *v.* Breckenridge, 403 U.S. 88, 107 (1971).
[2] 109 U.S. 3 (1883).   [3] 257 U.S. 312 (1921).
[4] Katzenbach *v.* Morgan, 384 U.S. 641, 648-649 (1966).
[5] 18 U.S.C. 242. *See also* 18 U.S.C. 371.

secured or protected by the Constitution and the laws of the United States, or to different punishments, pains, or penalties, on account of such inhabitant being an alien, or by reason of his color, or race, than are prescribed for the punishment of citizens shall be fined not more than $1,000, or imprisoned not more than one year, or both."

After lying dormant for many years, this provision was resusci- Re-
tated and reanimated in 1941 by the decision in the *Classic* case (*see* suscitation
p. 534). It was given added vitality by the Court's decision in the of this
attention-getting case, Screws *v*. United States.[6] Speaking for the Power
Court, Justice Douglas recited the circumstances of a case of extreme and wanton brutality by a Georgia sheriff and two assistants
in effecting the arrest of a young Negro, who died in consequence
of this treatment.

Screws and his co-defendants were indicted for having, under color of the laws of Georgia, "willfully" caused Hall to be deprived of "rights, privileges, or immunities secured or protected" to him by the Fourteenth Amendment—the right not to be deprived of life without due process of law; the right to be tried upon the charge on which he was arrested by due process of law, and if found guilty to be punished in accordance with the laws of Georgia.

While the indictment was held to fall within the terms of the Federal law quoted above, the conviction of Screws and his com- panions was reversed on the ground that the trial judge should have charged the jury that to convict they must find the accused to have had the "*specific* intention" of depriving Hall of his constitu- tional rights. This charge being given in a second trial, the jury ac- quitted. Later decisions, however, qualified the requirement of "specific intention" with the doctrine of the common law, that "the intent is presumed and inferred from the result of the action."[7]

Significantly (and curiously in view of the Court's position with respect to Congress's power under the Thirteenth Amendment; *see* pp. 459-460), the Court in 1971 seemed to go out of its way to avoid deciding that Congress could impose liabilities on private persons under the Fourteenth Amendment. Because the case involved an assault on travelers on the highway, the Court was able to hold that "Our cases have firmly established that the right of interstate travel is constitutionally protected, does not necessarily rest on the Four- teenth Amendment, and is assertable against private as well as gov- ernmental interference. . . ."[8] (*See* pp. 257-259.)

To emphasize its point, the Court concluded with this statement: "More specifically, the allegations of the complaint in this case have not required consideration of the scope of the power of Congress

---

[6] 325 U.S. 91 (1945).
[7] *See* Williams *v*. U.S., 341 U.S. 97 (1951); Koehler *v*. U.S., 342 U.S. 852 (1951); *also* Robert L. Hale, "Unconstitutional Acts as Federal Crimes," 60 *Harvard Law Re- view*, 65 (1946). *But see* Griffin *v*. Breckenridge, 403 U.S. 88, 102 note 10 (1971).
[8] Griffin *v*. Breckenridge, 403 U.S. 88, 105 (1971).

under §5 of the Fourteenth Amendment."[9] A clue as to what bothered the Court about deciding once and for all and in the broadest terms, that the Fourteenth Amendment permitted Congress to reach private action can be found in the fears it expressed about having the particular law involved in the case become a general Federal tort law: "The constitutional shoals that would lie in the path of interpreting [the law] as a general federal tort law can be avoided. . . ."[10] The implication seems to be that unless the Court is careful in finding power for Congress under the Fourteenth Amendment, Congress could become involved in regulation of activities which have normally been regarded as State matters. The Court referred, for example, to punishing an assault committed by two or more persons within a State.[11] But the Court's own language in the case suggests that such fears are exaggerated. After all, the only warrant for Congressional action even under a broadened scope for §5 would be that it comported with the purpose of the Fourteenth Amendment—to end invidious discrimination. It is one thing for Congress to pass a law making it a Federal crime to assault someone in an effort to keep him from exercising a constitutional right; it is quite another for Congress to attempt to pass a law making a simple assault occurring within a State a Federal crime.[12]

AMENDMENT XV

SECTION I

The right of citizens of the United States to vote shall not be denied or abridged by the United States or by any State on account of race, color or previous condition of servitude.

An Affirma-   At the outset the Court emphasized only the negative aspects of
tive Grant   this amendment. "The Fifteenth Amendment," it asserted, did
of Rights   "not confer the right . . . [to vote] upon any one," but merely "invested the citizens of the United States with a new constitutional right which is . . . exemption from discrimination in the exercise of the elective franchise on account of race, color, or previous condition of servitude."[1] Within less than ten years, however, in *ex parte* Yarbrough,[2] the Court ventured to read into the amendment an affirmative as well as a negative purpose. Conceding "that this article" had originally been construed as giving "no affirmative right to

---

[9] *Ibid.*, 107.   [10] *Ibid.*, 101.
[11] *Ibid.*
[12] *See* Justice Black's words in Oregon *v.* Mitchell, 400 U.S. 112, 128 (1970).

---

[1] United States *v.* Reese, 92 U.S. 214, 217-218 (1876); United States *v.* Cruikshank, 92 U.S. 542, 556 (1876).
[2] 110 U.S. 651, 665 (1884); citing Neal *v.* Delaware, 103 U.S. 370, 389 (1881). This affirmative view was later reiterated in Guinn & Beal *v.* U.S., 238 U.S. 347, 363 (1915).

the colored man to vote," and as having been "designed primarily to prevent discrimination against him," Justice Miller, in behalf of his colleagues, conceded "that under some circumstances it may operate as the immediate source of a right to vote. In all cases where the former slave-holding States had not removed from their Constitutions the words 'white man' as a qualification for voting, this provision did, in effect, confer on him the right to vote, because . . . it annulled the discriminating word *white*, and thus left him in the enjoyment of the same right as white persons. And such would be the effect of any future constitutional provision of a State which should give the right of voting exclusively to white people. . . ."

The early history (i.e. before 1957) of the Fifteenth Amendment was largely a record of belated judicial condemnation of various attempts by States to disfranchise the Negro either overtly through statutory enactment, or covertly through inequitable administration of their electoral laws or by toleration of discriminatory membership practices of political parties. Of several such devices, one of the first to be held unconstitutional was the "grandfather clause." Without expressly disfranchising the Negro, but with a view to facilitating the permanent placement of white residents on the voting lists while continuing to interpose severe obstacles upon Negroes seeking qualification as voters, several States, beginning in 1895, enacted temporary laws whereby persons who were voters, or descendants of voters on January 1, 1867, could be registered notwithstanding their inability to meet any literacy requirements. Unable because of the date to avail themselves of the same exemption, Negroes were thus left exposed to disfranchisement on grounds of illiteracy while whites no less illiterate were enabled to become permanent voters. With the achievement of this intended result, most States permitted their laws to lapse; but Oklahoma's grandfather clause was enacted as a permanent amendment to the State constitution; and when presented with an opportunity to pass on its validity, a unanimous Court condemned the standard of voting thus established as recreating and perpetuating "the very conditions which the [Fifteenth] Amendment was intended to destroy."[3] Nor, when Oklahoma in 1916 followed up this defeat with a statute which provided that all persons, except those who voted in 1914, who were qualified to vote in 1916 but who failed to register between April 30 and May 11, 1916, should be perpetually disfranchised, did the Court experience any difficulty in holding the same to be repugnant to the amendment.[4] That amendment, Justice Frankfurter declared, "nullifies sophisticated as well as simple-minded modes of discrimination. It hits onerous procedural requirements which effectively handicap exercise of the franchise by the colored race although the abstract right to vote may remain unrestricted as to race."[5]

Disallowance of Nullifying Expedients

---

[3] Guinn & Beal *v.* U.S., 238 U.S. 347, 360, 363-364 (1915).
[4] Lane *v.* Wilson, 307 U.S. 268 (1939).   [5] *Ibid.*, 275.

Primaries   When, however, it was first called upon to deal with the exclusion
as Elections   of Negroes from participation in primary elections, the Court displayed indecision. Prior to its becoming convinced that primary
contests were in fact elections,[6] the Court had relied upon the
equal protection clause to strike down a Texas White Primary
Law[7] and a subsequent Texas statute which contributed to a like
exclusion by limiting voting in primaries to members of State political parties as determined by the central committees thereof.[8]
When exclusion of Negroes was thereafter maintained by political
parties acting not in obedience to any statutory command, this discrimination was for a time viewed as not constituting State action
and so as not prohibited by either the Fourteenth or the Fifteenth
Amendments.[9] Nine years later this holding was reversed when the
Court, in Smith v. Allwright,[10] declared that where the selection of
candidates for public office is entrusted by statute to political parties, a political party in making its selection at a primary election is a
State agency, and hence may not under this amendment exclude
Negroes from such elections.

Initially the Court held that literacy tests drafted so as to apply
alike to all applicants for the voting franchise would be deemed to
be fair on their face, and in the absence of proof of discriminatory
enforcement could not be viewed as denying the equal protection
of the laws guaranteed by the Fourteenth Amendment.[11] Later
however, the Boswell amendment to the constitution of Alabama,
which provided that only persons who understood and could explain the Constitution of the United States to the reasonable satisfaction of boards of registrars, was found, both in its object as well
as in the manner of its administration, to be contrary to the Fifteenth Amendment. The legislative history of the Alabama provision disclosed, said the Court, that "the ambiguity inherent in the
phrase 'understand and explain' . . . was purposeful . . . and . . .
intended as a grant of arbitrary power in an attempt to obviate the
consequences of" Smith v. Allwright.[12]

---

[6] United States v. Classic, 313 U.S. 299 (1941); Smith v. Allwright, 321 U.S. 649
(1944).

[7] Nixon v. Herndon, 273 U.S. 536 (1927).

[8] Nixon v. Condon, 286 U.S. 73, 89 (1932).

[9] Grovey v. Townsend, 295 U.S. 45, 55 (1935).

[10] 321 U.S. 649 (1944). Notwithstanding that the South Carolina legislature,
after the decision in Smith v. Allwright, repealed all statutory provisions regulating
primary elections and political organizations conducting them, a political party thus
freed of control is not to be regarded as a private club and for that reason exempt
from the constitutional prohibitions against racial discrimination contained in
Amendment XV. Rice v. Elmore, 165 F. 2d. 387 (1947); cert. denied, 333 U.S. 875
(1948). A South Carolina political party, which excluded Negroes from membership, required that white as well as Negro qualified voters, as a prerequisite for voting in its primary, take an oath that they would support separation of the races. Not
surprisingly, this ingenious (?) maneuver was held void. Terry v. Adams, 345 U.S.
461 (1953).

[11] Williams v. Miss., 170 U.S. 213, 220 (1898).

[12] Davis v. Schnell, 81 F.Supp. 872, 878, 880 (1949); affirmed, 336 U.S. 933
(1949).

Starting in 1957, Congress has taken a strong, positive, and leading role in the effort to vindicate voting rights, as will be shown below.

SECTION II

The Congress shall have power to enforce this article by appropriate legislation.

In the protection of the right conferred by this amendment Congress passed the Enforcement Act of 1870, which, however, was largely nullified by a Supreme Court decision in 1876.[1] Congress finally endeavored to remedy the situation by enacting the Civil Rights Act of 1957. The measure created a Commission on Civil Rights, whose duty it is to investigate allegations that certain citizens of the United States are being deprived of the right to vote and have their votes counted on account of race, color, religion or national origin; and, when such allegations are found to be substantiated, the Attorney General may institute "a civil action or other proper proceeding for preventive relief," including under some circumstances prosecutions for criminal contempt by a judge acting without a jury.[2] (*See* p. 206.)

Continued State resistance forced Congress to seek constantly new and ingenious ways to vindicate the right to vote.[3] For example, in 1964 Congress made it a presumption (albeit a rebuttable presumption) "that any person who has not been adjudged an incompetent and who has completed the sixth grade in a public school . . . possesses sufficient intelligence to vote in any Federal election."[4] The purpose, of course, was to make it easier to register large numbers of voters quickly and put the burden on the States to show that particular individuals were not qualified after they were registered. More powerful medicine was administered by Congress in the Voting Rights Act of 1965.[5] The remedial provisions of the act applied to any State or its political subdivision found by the U.S. Attorney General to have maintained a "test or device" (e.g., literacy test, constitution interpretation test, requirement that the voter possess "good moral character," etc.) as a prerequisite to voting on November 1, 1964, and which was determined by the director of the census to have less than 50 per cent of its voting-age residents registered or voting in the November 1964 election.[6] The

---

[1] In the early case of United States *v.* Reese, 92 U.S. 214, 218 (1876), the Enforcement Act of 1870 (16 *Stat.* 140), which penalized State officers for refusing to receive the vote of any qualified citizen, was held to be constitutionally inapplicable to support a prosecution of such officers for having prevented a qualified Negro from voting.

[2] 71 *Stat.* 634 (1957).

[3] 74 *Stat.* 88 (1969); 78 *Stat.* 241 (1964); 79 *Stat.* 437 (1965). For a good, concise description of this effort, *see* 2 U.S. *Cong. & Admin. News*, 2437-2582 (1965).

[4] 78 *Stat.* 241 (1964).   [5] 79 *Stat.* 437 (1965).

[6] So as to further cut the prospect of delay, the act provided that the actions of the Attorney General and the Director of the Census would be unreviewable. The

act provided, among other remedies, for prompt suspension of such tests and devices, the assignment of Federal registrars and poll-watchers, and that States identified through the procedures described above obtain the approval of either the U.S. Attorney General or a declaratory judgment from the U.S. District Court for the District of Columbia approving any "proposed change" adding a "test or device" before it would become effective. These Congressional efforts were, of course, challenged on constitutional grounds, but such challenges were unsuccessful.[7] But even so stout a protagonist of civil rights as Justice Black expressed concern about a "federal law which assumes the power to compel the States to submit in advance any proposed legislation they have for approval by federal agents." He said it "approaches dangerously near to wiping the States out as useful and effective units in the government of our country. I cannot agree to any constitutional interpretation that leads inevitably to such a result."[8] The majority held otherwise, however, concluding that "In the oft-repeated words of Chief Justice Marshall, referring to another specific legislative authorization in the Constitution, 'This power, like all others vested in Congress, is complete in itself, may be exercised to its utmost extent and acknowledges no limitations other than are prescribed in the constitution.' "[9]

Nor was the majority being cavalier in its holding. They recited the problems Congress had faced in attempting to vindicate voting rights and indicated the need for inventiveness: "Congress exercised its authority under the Fifteenth Amendment in an inventive manner when it enacted the Voting Rights Act of 1965. First: The measure prescribes remedies for voting discrimination which go into effect without any need for prior adjudication. This was clearly a legitimate response to the problem, for which there is ample precedent under other constitutional provisions. . . . Congress had found that case-by-case litigation was inadequate to combat widespread and persistent discrimination in voting, because of the inordinate amount of time and energy required to overcome the obstructionist tactics invariably encountered in these lawsuits. After enduring nearly a century of systematic resistance to the Fifteenth Amendment, Congress might well decide to shift the advantage of time and inertia from the perpetrators of the evil to its victims. The question remains, of course, whether the specific remedies prescribed in the Act were an appropriate means of combatting the evil, and to this question we shall presently address ourselves."[10]

Court subsequently affirmed this as a constitutional power of Congress to enforce the guarantee of the Fifteenth Amendment. *See* Morris *v.* Gressette, 97 S.Ct. 2411 (1977); Briscoe *v.* Bell, 97 S.Ct. 2428 (1977).

[7] South Carolina *v.* Katzenbach, 383 U.S. 301 (1966) and cases cited at 326; Katzenbach *v.* Morgan, 384 U.S. 641 (1966).

[8] South Carolina *v.* Katzenbach, 383 U.S. 301, 360 (1966).

[9] *Ibid.*, 327.   [10] *Ibid.*

In 1970 Congress amended the Voting Rights Act by banning until August 6, 1975, a literacy test in any national, State, or local election in any area of the United States where such a test is not already prescribed by the basic acts.[11] The Court unanimously upheld the constitutionality of that provision.[12] Five years later, Congress again renewed the act, this time for a ten-year period, and broadened its provisions still further to cover language minorities.[13]

Over the course of its last three Terms, the Supreme Court has encountered several cases alleging attempts to water down the voting power of minorities through the annexation of new territory by cities and the use of at-large elections. The prophylactic effects of the Voting Rights Act of 1965 were held by the Supreme Court in 1971 to extend to annexation where that had become a racially discriminatory electoral device.[14] Four years later, the Supreme Court was confronted with a suit challenging Richmond, Virginia's annexation of adjacent county land, which reduced the proportion of blacks in the city from 52 to 42 per cent. Speaking for the Court, Justice White, however, held that the fact that Richmond's plan to elect city councilmen from single-member districts distinguished this situation from the earlier case where annexation had been followed by at-large elections. Justice White continued: "As long as the ward system fairly reflects the strength of the Negro community as it exists after the annexation, we cannot hold, without more specific legislative directions, that such an annexation is nevertheless barred. . . . It is true that the black community, if there is bloc racial voting, will command fewer seats on the city council; and the annexation will have effected a decline in the Negroes' relative influence in the city. But a different city council and an enlarged city are involved after the annexation. . . . To hold otherwise would be either to forbid all such annexations or to require, as the price for approval of the annexation, that the black community be assigned the same proportion of council seats as before, hence perhaps permanently overrepresenting them and underrepresenting other elements in the community, including the nonblack citizens in the annexed area."[15] Justice Brennan in dissent argued that the city's past history of racial discrimination and its clear intent to dilute black voting power made talk of the "objective justifications" for annexation a "sort of post hoc rationalization." Joined by Justices Douglas and Marshall, Justice Brennan maintained that "the dilutive effect of Richmond's annexation is clear." Pointing out that blacks, who previously had constituted 44.8 per cent of the city's voting age population, would now make up 37.3 per cent, he concluded: "I cannot agree that such a significant dilution of black voting strength can be remedial . . . simply by allocating to blacks a

[11] 84 *Stat.* 314 (1970).   [12] Oregon *v.* Mitchell, 400 U.S. 112, 118 (1970).
[13] 89 *Stat.* 400.   [14] Perkins *v.* Matthews, 400 U.S. 379 (1971).
[15] City of Richmond *v.* U.S., 422 U.S. 358, 371 (1975).

reasonably proportionate share of voting power within the postan-
nexation community."

In 1976, despite a prior adverse determination by both the Attorney General and the U.S. District Court, District of Columbia, as
to the dilutive effect on the black vote, the Supreme Court sustained the validity of a plan governing the election of members of
the New Orleans city council. The Court approved the continuation of electing two of the seven councilmen at large, since that feature was not a "proposed change" in voting arrangements covered
by the 1965 Voting Rights Act. The Court also held the decennial
reapportionment of the remaining five single-member districts to
be constitutional. Reasoning from the premise "that a legislative
reapportionment that enhances the position of racial minorities
with respect to their effective exercise of the electoral franchise can
hardly have the 'effect' of diluting or abridging the right to vote on
account of race," the Court found in the case at hand: "Under the
apportionment of 1961 none of the five councilmanic districts had
a clear Negro majority of registered voters, and no Negro has been
elected to the New Orleans City Council while that apportionment
system has been in effect. Under Plan II, by contrast, Negroes will
constitute a majority of the population in two of the five districts
and a clear majority of the registered voters in one of them. Thus,
there is every reason to predict . . . that at least one and perhaps
two Negroes may well be elected to the Council."[16] In dissent, Justice Marshall concluded that, by focusing on whether the proposed
plan was better or worse than the preexisting state of affairs, "the
Court dilutes the meaning of unconstitutionality . . . to the point
that the congressional purposes . . . are no longer served and the
sacred guarantees of the Fourteenth and Fifteenth Amendments
emerge badly battered." For Justice Marshall, the question to be
answered was: "when does a redistricting plan have the effect of
'abridging' the right to vote on account of race or color?" Looking
to "the effect of the plan itself, rather than the effect of the change
in plans" and focusing on "representation on the entire council" instead of in terms of the five single-member districts, Justice Marshall concluded that the plan violated the Voting Rights Act because the gap between blacks' proportion of the population and
their possible portion of the council seats was not justified by any
compelling governmental interest in maintaining voting arrangements under the plan.

In a second case, decided the same year, the Supreme Court held
that a Federal district court erred in ordering at-large elections for
school board and police jury positions. Given the effect of at-large
elections in minimizing the electoral influence of blacks and other
minorities, the Court held that the district court had an obligation
at the outset, unless it infringed protected rights, to pursue the use

[16] Beer *v.* U.S., 425 U.S. 130, 141-142 (1976).

of single-member districts.[17] In a covey of decisions, Federal courts have reacted very negatively to at-large elections because they disadvantaged black voters, who were invariably in the minority.[18]

And, in a significant ruling one year later, the Court upheld New York's use of a racial quota in the design of certain legislative districts. The result of altering white majorities in some of the state senate districts to create substantial black majorities had been to partition and thus dilute the political impact of New York City's Hasidic Jewish community, previously contained within one district. Said the Court: "Implicit in *Beer* and *City of Richmond* . . . is the proposition that the Constitution does not prevent a State subject to the Voting Rights Act from deliberately creating or preserving black majorities in particular districts in order to ensure that its reapportionment plan complies with §5 [of the Act]. . . . [N]either the Fourteenth nor the Fifteenth Amendment mandates any *per se* rule against using racial factors in districting and apportionment. Nor is . . . [t]he permissible use of racial criteria . . . confined to eliminating the effects of past discriminatory districting or apportionment."[19]

AMENDMENT XVI

The Congress shall have power to lay and collect taxes on incomes, from whatever source derived, without apportionment among the several States, and without regard to any census or enumeration.

A Judicial Decision "Recalled"

The ratification of this amendment was the direct consequence of the decision in 1895[1] whereby the attempt of Congress the previous year to tax incomes uniformly throughout the United States[2] was held by a divided Court to be unconstitutional. A tax on incomes derived from property,[3] the Court declared, was a "direct tax" which Congress under the terms of Article I, Section II, clause 3, and Section XI, clause 4, could impose only by the rule of apportionment according to population; although scarcely fifteen years

---

[17] East Carroll Parish School Board *v*. Marshall, 424 U.S. 636 (1976).

[18] Wallace *v*. House, 515 F. 2d 619 (1975); Kendrick *v*. Walder, 527 F. 2d 44 (1975); Stewart *v*. Waller, 404 F.Supp. 206 (1975); Paige *v*. Gray, 399 F.Supp. 459 (1975); *but cf.* Wilson *v*. Vahue, 403 F.Supp. 58 (1975).

[19] United Jewish Organizations of Williamsburgh, Inc. *v*. Carey, 430 U.S. 144 (1977).

---

[1] Pollock *v*. Farmers' Loan & Trust Co., 157 U.S. 429 (1895); 158 U.S. 601 (1895).

[2] 28 *Stat.* 509.

[3] The Court conceded that taxes on incomes from "professions, trades, employments, or vocations" levied by this act were excise taxes and therefore valid. The entire statute, however, was voided on the ground that Congress never intended to permit the entire "burden of the tax to be borne by professions, trades, employments, or vocations" after real estate and personal property had been exempted. 158 U.S. 601, 635 (1895).

prior the Justices had unanimously sustained[4] the collection of a similar tax during the Civil War.[5]

Decisions Undermining the Pollock Case
During the interim between the *Pollock* decision in 1895, and the ratification of the Sixteenth Amendment in 1913, the Court gave evidence of a growing awareness of the dangerous consequences to national solvency which that holding threatened, and partially circumvented it, either by taking refuge in redefinitions of "direct tax" or, and more especially, by emphasizing, virtually to the exclusion of the former, the history of excise taxation. In a series of cases, including Nicol *v.* Ames,[6] Knowlton *v.* Moore,[7] and Patton *v.* Brady,[8] the Court held the following taxes to have been levied merely upon one of the "incidents of ownership" and hence to be excises: a tax which involved affixing revenue stamps to memoranda evidencing the sale of merchandise on commodity exchanges, an inheritance tax, and a war revenue tax upon tobacco on which the hitherto imposed excise tax had already been paid and which was held by the manufacturer for resale.

Thanks to these endeavors, the Court found it possible in 1911 to sustain a corporate income tax as an excise "measured by income" on the privilege of doing business in corporate form.[9] But while the adoption of the Sixteenth Amendment put a stop to speculation whether the Court would eventually overrule *Pollock*, it is interesting to note that in its initial appraisal of the amendment it characterized income taxes as "inherently indirect" and hence subject to the rule of uniformity, the same as excises, duties and imports until they were "removed" therefrom and "placed under the direct class"—removed, that is, by the Court itself.[10]

The Court's Interpretation of Amendment XVI
Building upon definitions formulated in cases construing the Corporation Tax Act of 1909, the Court initially described income as the "gain derived from capital, from labor, or from both combined," inclusive of the "profit gained through a sale or conversion of capital assets."[11] Moreover, any gain not accruing prior to 1913 was held to be taxable income for the year in which it was realized by sale or conversion of the property to which it had accrued;[12] while corporate dividends in the shape of money or of the stock of another corporation were held to be taxable income of the stockholder for the year in which he received them, regardless of when the profits against which they were voted had accrued to the corpo-

---

[4] Springer *v.* U.S., 102 U.S. 586 (1881).
[5] 13 *Stat.* 223 (1864).   [6] 173 U.S. 509 (1899).
[7] 178 U.S. 41 (1900).   [8] 184 U.S. 608 (1902).
[9] Flint *v.* Stone Tracey Co., 220 U.S. 107 (1911).
[10] Brushaber *v.* Union Pac. R. Co., 240 U.S. 1, 18-19 (1916). *See also* Stanton *v.* Baltic Min. Co., 240 U.S. 103, 112 (1916).
[11] Stratton's Independence *v.* Howbert, 231 U.S. 399, 415 (1914); Doyle *v.* Mitchell Bros. Co., 247 U.S. 179 (1918).
[12] Eisner *v.* Macomber, 252 U.S. 189 (1920); Bowers *v.* Kerbaugh-Empire Co., 271 U.S. 170 (1926).

ration.[13] A stock dividend issued against a corporate surplus, however, was held not to be "income" in the hands of the stockholder,
since it left the stockholder's share of the surplus still under the
control of the corporate management.[14] That decision, of course,
narrowed the definition of "income" and has proved troublesome.[15] Nor has Congress in its efforts to mitigate the troubles been
free to ignore the Court's holding for as the Court said in that decision: "Congress cannot by any definition it may adopt conclude the
matter, since it cannot by legislation alter the Constitution, from
which alone it derives its power to legislate, and within whose limitations alone that power can be lawfully exercised." That decision
laid down in 1920 is still good law,[16] and Congress has endeavored
to get around it by shifting liability from stockholders to the corporations.[17]

Although empowered to tax incomes "from whatever source derived," Congress is not precluded from leaving some incomes un-
taxed.[18] Conversely, it may "condition, limit or deny deductions
from gross income to arrive at the net that it chooses to tax";[19] and
in 1927 the Court ruled that gains derived from illicit traffic in liquor were taxable income under the Act of 1921.[20] Said Justice
Holmes for the unanimous Court: "We see no reason . . . why the
fact that a business is unlawful should exempt it from paying the
taxes that if lawful it would have to pay."[21] However, in Commissioner v. Wilcox,[22] decided in 1946, Justice Murphy, speaking for a
majority of the Court, held that embezzled money was not taxable
income to the embezzler, although any gain he derived from the
use of it would be. Justice Burton dissented on the basis of the
Sullivan case; and in 1952, a sharply divided Court, cutting loose
from the metaphysics of the Wilcox case, held that Congress had
the power under Amendment XVI to tax as income monies received by an extortioner.[23] In 1961, the Court expressly overruled
Wilcox.[24]

[13] Lynch v. Hornby, 247 U.S. 339 (1918).

[14] Eisner v. Macomber, cited above. Helvering v. Griffiths, 318 U.S. 371 (1943),
which maintained the rule laid down in Eisner v. Macomber, was based immediately
on 53 Stat. 1, Sect. 115a (1); see also Moline Properties, Inc. v. Com'r of Int. Rev., 319
U.S. 436 (1943), where the corporate entity conception, which is basic to the decision in the Eisner holding, is endorsed. For recent citations to Eisner see Connor v.
U.S, 439 F. 2d. 974, 980 (1971) and cases cited therein; Kem v. C.I.R., 432 F. 2d.
961, 962 (1970).

[15] Ibid. Also U.S. v. Davis, 397 U.S. 301, 308-311 (1970).

[16] See notes 14 and 15 supra.

[17] Motor Fuel Carriers Inc. v. U.S., 420 F. 2d. 702, 704 (1970).

[18] Brushaber v. Union Pac. R. Co., 240 U.S. 1 (1916); Moritz v. C.I.R., 55 T.C.
113, 115 (1970); Shinder v. C.I.R., 395 F. 2d. 222 (1968).

[19] Helvering v. Independent L. Ins. Co., 292 U.S. 371, 381 (1934); Helvering v.
Winmill, 305 U.S. 79, 84 (1938); Moritz v. C.I.R., 55 T.C. 113, 115 (1970); Shinder
v. C.I.R., 395 F. 2d. 223 (1968).

[20] United States v. Sullivan, 274 U.S. 259 (1927).   [21] Ibid., 263.

[22] 327 U.S. 404 (1946).   [23] Rutkin v. U.S., 343 U.S. 130 (1952).

[24] James v. U.S., 366 U.S. 213 (1961). See also Urban v. U.S., 445 F. 2d. 641 (1971).

While Congress's power to tax incomes is relieved by this amendment from the rule of apportionment, it still remains subject to the due process clause of Amendment V, which would forbid any obviously arbitrary classification for this purpose. Thus an act of Congress which taxed incomes of Republicans at a higher rate than those of Democrats would, presumably, be invalid. But incomes of corporate persons may be taxed on a different basis than those of natural persons, and large incomes may be, and are, taxed at progressively higher rates than smaller incomes. Also, Congress may, in order to compel corporations to distribute their profits and thereby render them taxable in the hands of stockholders, levy a special tax on such accumulated profits in the hands of the corporation, without transcending its powers under the Sixteenth Amendment,[25] or violating the Fifth Amendment. And Congress without violating the Fifth Amendment "may provide for retroactive operation of income tax legislation."[26]

The question has been occasionally mooted whether the separate incomes of a husband and wife may be taxed as one joint income and so, in effect, at *a higher rate* than incomes of the same size of unmarried persons, the tax being "progressive." Some years ago the Court overturned a Wisconsin tax of this description on the ground that the due process clause of Amendment XIV forbade the taxation of one person's income of property by reference to those of another person. Three Justices, however, dissented in an opinion by Justice Holmes, which argued that such a tax was constitutional, first, in the light of "a thousand years of history," the reference being to the common law doctrine that the income and property of the wife were at the disposal of the husband; secondly, because husbands and wives do actually get the benefit of one another's income; thirdly, as a means of avoiding tax evasions.[27] The second and third reasons, at least, are persuasive that such a classification for purposes of income taxation would not be so utterly unreasonable as to fall under the ban of the Fifth Amendment, which, it should be remembered, does not contain an equal protection clause, and a later decision which held that the entire value of "community property" (property held in common by husband and wife) may be subjected to the Federal estate tax upon the death of either spouse, confirms this conclusion.[28]

It should be understood that as a general proposition most income tax litigation does not involve constitutional questions and, when it is contended that it does, the "long established policy of the Court" is to defer, "where possible, to Congressional procedures in the tax field."[29]

[25] Helvering *v*. National Grocery Co., 304 U.S. 282 (1938); Helvering *v*. National Steel Rolling Mills, Inc., 311 U.S. 46 (1940); Motor Fuel Carriers Inc. *v*. U.S., 420 F. 2d. 702, 704 (1970) and cases cited therein.
[26] Shanahan *v*. U.S., 447 F. 2d. 1082 (1971) and cases cited therein.
[27] Hoeper *v*. Tax Com. of Wis., 284 U.S. 206 (1931).
[28] Fernandez *v*. Wiener, 326 U.S. 340 (1945).
[29] Schlude *v*. C.I.R., 372 U.S. 129, 135 (1963).

As indicated earlier the requirement to keep tax records does not offend the Fifth Amendment's privilege against self-incrimination (p. 382). Recently, a Federal court held that an embezzler was required to report embezzlement income despite his Fifth Amendment right not to be compelled to be a witness against himself.[30]

AMENDMENT XVII

¶1. The Senate of the United States shall be composed of two Senators from each State, elected by the people thereof, for six years; and each Senator shall have one vote. The electors in each State shall have the qualifications requisite for electors of the most numerous branch of the State legislatures.

¶2. When vacancies happen in the representation of any State in the Senate, the executive authority of such State shall issue writs of election to fill such vacancies: Provided, That the legislature of any State may empower the executive thereof to make temporary appointments until the people fill the vacancies by election as the legislature may direct.

¶3. This amendment shall not be so construed as to affect the election or term of any Senator chosen before it becomes valid as part of the Constitution.

This amendment, as was noted before, supersedes Article I, Section III, ¶1. Very shortly after its ratification the point was established that if a person possessed the qualifications requisite for voting for a Senator, his right to vote for such an officer was not derived merely from the constitution and laws of the State in which they are chosen but has its foundation in the Constitution of the United States.[1] Consistently with this view, Federal courts years ago declared that when local party authorities, acting pursuant to regulations prescribed by a party's State executive committee, refused to permit a Negro, on account of his race, to vote in a primary to select candidates for the office of United States Senator, they deprived him of a right secured to him by the Constitution and laws, in violation of this amendment.[2]

The politics of New York State gave rise to two recent cases involving interpretation of the Seventeenth Amendment. When Senator James Buckley won only a plurality in the three-cornered 1970 Senate race, the Committee for Fair Play for Voters went to Federal court contending that their right under the Seventeenth Amendment "to be represented by a senator who is elected by a majority vote" had been abridged, seeking a run-off between the top two candidates. The court held that the Seventeenth

---

[30] U.S. v. Milder, 329 F.Supp. 759 (1971).

[1] United States v. Aczel, 219 F. 917 (1915), citing ex parte Yarbrough, 110 U.S. 651 (1884).

[2] Chapman v. King, 154 F. 2d. 460 (1946); cert. denied, 327 U.S. 800 (1946).

Amendment contained no provision that a Senator must win a majority of the vote.[3]

When Senator Robert F. Kennedy was assassinated on June 6, 1968, groups of New York voters brought three suits seeking to have the vacancy filled in the November 1968 election. Under New York law, if there was less than 60 days left prior to New York's regular spring primary in an even-numbered year, the vacancy was to be filled by election in the next even-numbered year, which in this situation was November 1970. In the meantime, the Governor was empowered to make a temporary appointment. The court held that "the Seventeenth Amendment's vacancy provision explicitly confers upon state legislatures discretion concerning the timing of vacancy elections" and dismissed the complaints.[4]

AMENDMENT XVIII

SECTION I

After one year from the ratification of this article the manufacture, sale or transportation of intoxicating liquors within, the importation thereof into, or the exportation thereof from the United States and all territory subject to the jurisdiction thereof for beverage purposes is hereby prohibited.

SECTION II

The Congress and the several States shall have concurrent power to enforce this article by appropriate legislation.

SECTION III

This article shall be inoperative unless it shall have been ratified as an amendment to the Constitution by the Legislatures of the several States, as provided in the Constitution, within seven years from the date of the submission hereof to the States by the Congress.

This final section was no proper part of the amendment but was really a part of the Congressional resolution of submission, and was rightly so treated by the Supreme Court.[1] How, indeed, could an inoperative amendment operate to render itself inoperative?

The entire amendment was repealed in 1933 by the Twenty-First Amendment (*see* below, pp. 548-550). Some of the questions, however, which were raised under Article V and the Fourth and Fifth Amendments by the efforts, first to enforce, and then to get rid of,

---

[3] Phillips *v.* Rockefeller, 321 F.Supp. 516 (1970), *affirmed*, 435 F. 2d. 976 (1970).
[4] Valenti *v.* Rockefeller, 292 F.Supp. 851 (1968). *affirmed*, 393 U.S. 405 (1969), *rehearing denied*, 393 U.S. 1124 (1969).

[1] Dillon *v.* Gloss, 256 U.S. 368 (1921).

National Prohibition, contributed significantly to the development of the meaning of those two amendments.[2]

In 1934, the Supreme Court held that "Upon ratification of the Twenty-first Amendment, the Eighteeenth Amendment became inoperative. Neither the Congress nor the courts could give it continued vitality. The National Prohibition Act, to the extent that its provisions rested upon grant of authority to the Congress by the Eighteenth Amendment, immediately fell with the withdrawal by the people of the essential constitutional support."[3] Consequently, even prosecution for acts committed while the law was in force could not be prosecuted after the date of adoption of the new amendment. "In case a statute is repealed or rendered inoperative, no further proceedings can be had to enforce it in pending prosecutions unless competent authority has kept the statute alive for that purpose."

AMENDMENT XIX

The right of citizens of the United States to vote shall not be denied or abridged by the United States or by any State on account of sex.

Congress shall have power to enforce this article by appropriate legislation.

This amendment, which consummated a reform that had been long under way in the States, was passed by the House on May 21, 1919, and by the Senate on June 4, 1919. It was ratified by the required number of States in time for the Presidential election, November 1920. An objection that the amendment, by enlarging the electorate without a State's consent, destroyed its autonomy and hence exceeded the amending power, was overruled by the Court by pointing to the precedent created by the adoption of the Fifteenth Amendment.[1]

The Nineteenth Amendment has given rise to some novel contentions in Federal and State courts in recent years. One woman, protesting that there were only males on the ballot, contended that she had the right "to vote only for women candidates, and to withhold her vote from male candidates";[2] a seventeen-year-old male contended that a State delinquency law which defined a delinquent child as a male under 16 and a female under 18 years of age violated the Nineteenth Amendment.[3] The courts have made short

---

[2] Amos v. U.S., 255 U.S. 313 (1921); Carroll v. U.S., 267 U.S. 132 (1925); Taylor v. U.S., 286 U.S. 1 (1932); Hester v. U.S., 265 U.S. 57 (1924); Olmstead v. U.S., 277 U.S. 438 (1928).

[3] U.S. v. Chambers, 291 U.S. 217, 222-223 (1934).

[1] Leser v. Garnett, 258 U.S. 130 (1922).

[2] Boineau v. Thornton, 235 F.Supp. 175 (1964); *affirmed*, 379 U.S. 15 (1964).

[3] Coyle v. Oklahoma, 489 P. 2d. 223 (1971); Benson v. Oklahoma, 488 P. 2d. 383 (1971).

shrift of such arguments. But a Federal court did give broader meaning to the Amendment than appears called for by its words in saying "Whatever the ancient doctrine [of domicile], a wife is capable of acquiring a domicile separate from that of her husband; at least to this extent legal equality of the sexes is embodied in the Fourteenth and Nineteenth Amendments."[4]

Patently, as a weapon against State discriminations other than on the basic right to vote, the Fourteenth Amendment is more effective than the Nineteenth Amendment.

AMENDMENT XX

SECTION I

The terms of the President and Vice-President shall end at noon on the 20th day of January, and the terms of Senators and Representatives at noon on the 3d day of January, of the years in which such terms would have ended if this article had not been ratified; and the terms of their successors shall then begin.

SECTION II

The Congress shall assemble at least once in every year, and such meeting shall begin at noon on the 3d day of January, unless they shall by law appoint a different day.

SECTION III

If, at the time fixed for the beginning of the term of the President, the President-elect shall have died, the Vice-President-elect shall become President. If a President shall not have been chosen before the time fixed for the beginning of his term or if the President-elect shall have failed to qualify, then the Vice-President-elect shall act as President until a President shall have qualified; and the Congress may by law provide for the case wherein neither a President-elect nor a Vice-President-elect shall have qualified, declaring who shall then act as President, or the manner in which one who is to act shall be selected, and such person shall act accordingly until a President or Vice-President shall have qualified.

SECTION IV

The Congress may by law provide for the case of the death of any

[4] Spindel *v.* Spindel, 283 F.Supp. 797 (1968). A three-judge Federal district court has held that a Georgia statute creating an irrebuttable presumption that the domicile of a married woman was that of her husband, thus automatically precluding from voter registration a married woman whose husband claimed residence and voted in New Jersey, violated the guarantee of female suffrage under the Nineteenth Amendment, Kane *v.* Fortson, 369 F.Supp. 1342 (1973).

of the persons from whom the House of Representatives may choose a President whenever the right of choice shall have devolved upon them and for the case of death of any of the persons from whom the Senate may choose a Vice-President whenever the right of choice shall have devolved upon them.

SECTION V

Sections 1 and 2 shall take effect on the 15th day of October following the ratification of this article.

SECTION VI

This article shall be inoperative unless it shall have been ratified as an amendment to the Constitution by the legislatures of three-fourths of the several States within seven years from the date of its submission.

This, the so-called Norris "Lame Duck" Amendment, was proposed by Congress March 2, 1932, to the legislatures of the States, and was proclaimed by the Secretary of State February 6, 1933, having then been ratified by 39 States. By October 15, 1933, it had been ratified by all the States. Its primary purpose was to eliminate the so-called short session of Congress which used to follow after an election and in which defeated Congressmen ("Lame Ducks") participated. A constitutional amendment was required because adoption of the Amendment did in fact shorten the full constitutional terms of the President, Vice-President, and Congressmen then in office.[1] The original date selected and used before this amendment, of course, reflected the rudimentary state of communications and transportation of a much earlier day.[2] (*See* p. 149.)

Congress has fulfilled its obligations under Section III by enacting from time to time legislation dealing with Presidential succession.[3] The latest version provides among other things that where a President-elect is not qualified the Speaker of the House will act as President until a President or Vice-President qualifies.[4] One can only shudder at a prospect possible under the amendment and the law. Suppose an election goes to the House for resolution under the Twelfth Amendment and a wrangle ensues and for weeks none of the three candidates from which the House must select can command the necessary vote to be qualified (nor can a Vice-President be chosen). Suppose a large number of the members of the House prefer the Speaker to the regular candidates! What would be their incentive to settle the election and qualify a President?[5]

[1] U.S., 72d Cong., 1st Sess., Senate, Report No. 26 (1932).
[2] *Ibid.*   [3] 3 U.S.C. 19.
[4] *Ibid.*
[5] 1947 *U.S. Cong. Serv.* 1310; Edward S. Corwin, *The President, Office and Powers,* pp. 56-58.

AMENDMENT XXI
SECTION I

The eighteenth article of amendment to the Constitution of the United States is hereby repealed.

SECTION II

The transportation of importation into any State, Territory, or possession of the United States for delivery or use therein of intoxicating liquors, in violation of the laws thereof, is hereby prohibited.

SECTION III

This article shall be inoperative unless it shall have been ratified as an amendment to the Constitution by conventions in the several States, as provided in the Constitution, within seven years from the date of the submission hereof to the States by the Congress.

This amendment was proposed by Congress February 20, 1933, to conventions to be called in the several States, and was proclaimed to be in effect December 5 of the same year, having been ratified by 36 States, a record for celerity.

Decisions Interpreting the Amendment

Decisions interpreting the amendment to date fall into two general categories: decisions which assert the unlimited character of State power within the precincts marked out by Section II; decisions which define those precincts with greater particularity. On the one hand, the Court has said, the amendment authorizes a State to impose a license fee upon the importation into it of liquor from without;[1] to discriminate as to what liquors it shall permit to be imported;[2] to retaliate against such discriminations;[3] and in general to legislate, unfettered by "traditional Commerce Clause limitations" or any other clause of the Constitution, respecting liquor introduced into it from without.[4] On the other hand, the amendment does not, the Court holds, enable a State to regulate the sale of liquor in a national park over which it had ceded jurisdiction to the United States;[5] nor does it disable Congress from regulating the importation of liquors from abroad;[6] nor does it permit a State to tax imported Scotch whiskey still in the original package

[1] State Bd. of Equalization *v.* Young's Market Co., 299 U.S. 59 (1936).

[2] Mahoney *v.* Joseph Triner Corp., 304 U.S. 401 (1938).

[3] Indianapolis Brewing Co. *v.* Liquor Control Com'n of Mich., 305 U.S. 391 (1938).

[4] Hostetter *v.* Idlewild Bon Voyage Liquor Corp., 377 U.S. 324, 330 (1964); *but see* Justice Black's dissent, *ibid.*, 334; Ziffrin *v.* Reeves, 308 U.S. 132 (1939); Joseph E. Seagram & Sons, Inc. *v.* Hostetter, 384 U.S. 35, 42 (1966).

[5] Collins *v.* Yosemite Park and Curry Co., 304 U.S. 518 (1938).

[6] Jameson & Co. *v.* Morgenthau, 307 U.S. 171 (1939); Hostetter *v.* Idlewild Bon Voyage Liquor Corp., 377 U.S. 324 (1964).

in the hands of the original importer;[7] nor does it prevent the enforcement of the Sherman Anti-Trust Act against a conspiracy to raise prices;[8] and when a State seeks to control the passage *through* it of liquor coming from another State and destined for a third State, it is no longer exercising any power granted it by the amendment, but its customary police power. Its regulations, therefore, must be "reasonable" in the judgment of the Court, and may be set aside by Congress under the commerce clause.[9]

In 1972, the Supreme Court rendered its controversial "bottomless" dancers decision. Justice Rehnquist, speaking for the Court said: ". . . we conceive the State's authority in the area to be somewhat broader than did the District Court. This is not to say that all such conduct and performance is without the protection of the First and Fourteenth Amendments. But we would poorly serve both the interests for which the State may validly seek vindication and the interests protected by the First and Fourteenth Amendments were we to insist that the sort of Bacchanalian revelries which the Department sought to prevent by these liquor regulations were the constitutional equivalent of a performance by a scantily clad ballet troupe in a theater.

"The Department's conclusion, embodied in these regulations, that certain sexual performances and the dispensation of liquor by the drink ought not to occur simultaneously at premises which have licenses was not an irrational one. Given the added presumption in favor of the validity of the state regulation in this area which the Twenty-first Amendment requires, we cannot hold that the regulations on their face violate the Federal Constitution."[10]

In addition to the *LaRue* case, the Supreme Court the same Term decided three other Twenty-First Amendment cases. One, it held that *incident to a valid scheme of regulating the sale of liquor*, a State could require that a liquor manufacturer, as a condition of doing business in the State, do more than merely solicit sales.[11] Two, it held that a district court had erred "in ruling that the Twenty-first Amendment empowered the State Tax Commission . . . [to take a] markup . . . [on] transactions between out-of-state distillers and nonappropriated fund activities [military officers' clubs] located on the two exclusively federal enclaves."[12] Three, the Court let stand a Maine law barring State liquor and food licenses to "whites only" private clubs.[13] Striking down an Oklahoma statute, three years later, which prohibited the sale of 3.2-per cent beer to females

---

[7] Department of Revenue *v.* James Beam Co., 377 U.S. 341 (1964); "The tax here in question is clearly the kind prohibited by the Export-Import Clause [Art. I § 10, ch. 2]," *ibid.*, 343.

[8] Joseph E. Seagram & Sons, Inc. *v.* Hostetter, 384 U.S. 34, 45 (1966).

[9] Duckworth *v.* Ark., 314 U.S. 390 (1941); Carter *v.* Va., 321 U.S. 131 (1944).

[10] California *v.* LaRue, 409 U.S. 109, 118-119 (1972).

[11] Heublein, Inc. *v.* South Carolina Tax Com'n, 409 U.S. 275 (1972).

[12] United States *v.* State Tax Com'n of Mississippi, 412 U.S. 363, 381 (1973).

[13] B.P.O.E. Lodge No. 2043 *v.* Ingraham, 411 U.S. 924 (1973).

under 18 and to males under 21, the Court said of this gender-based distinction: "As one commentator has remarked, '[n]either the text nor the history of the Twenty-first Amendment suggests that it qualifies individual rights protected by the Bill of Rights and the Fourteenth Amendment where the sale or use of liquor is concerned.' . . . In sum, the principles in the Equal Protection Clause are not to be rendered inapplicable by statistically-measured but loose-fitting generalities concerning the drinking tendencies of aggregate groups. We thus hold that the operation of the Twenty-first Amendment does not alter the application of equal protection standards that otherwise govern this case."[14] The courts have also continued to hold that AMTRAK is bound to honor State prohibition statutes where its trains discharge or board passengers in States which prohibit the sale of alcoholic beverages.[15]

AMENDMENT XXII

No person shall be elected to the office of President more than twice, and no person who has held the office of President, or acted as President, for more than two years of a term to which some other person was elected President shall be elected to the office of President more than once. But this article shall not apply to any person holding the office of President when this article was proposed by the Congress, and shall not prevent any person who may be holding the office of President, or acting as President, during the term within which this article becomes operative from holding the office of President or acting as President during the remainder of such term.

This amendment was proposed by Congress on March 24, 1947; and ratification of it by the required three-fourths of the States was completed on February 27, 1951. On March 1st, Jess Larson, Administrator of General Services, certified its adoption.[1] Formerly this service was performed by the Secretary of State.

The Twenty-Second Amendment was a response to President Franklin D. Roosevelt's successful defiance of the no third-term tradition. It is difficult to resist the temptation to observe that much of the impetus for the amendment came from Republicans who wanted to punish Roosevelt posthumously.[2] But the debate in Congress which was a prelude to the proposal seems to have been on the merits.[3] There were fears that the amendment would make the President a lame-duck President in the last two years of his sec-

---

[14] Craig v. Boren, 97 S.Ct. 451, 461, 463 (1976).
[15] Nat'l Railroad Passenger Corp. v. Miller, 358 F.Supp. 1321 (1973); Nat'l Railroad Passenger Corp. v. Harris, 490 F. 2d. 572 (1974).

---

[1] 16 *Fed. Reg.* 2019.
[2] Edward S. Corwin, *The President*, 38; Henry S. Commager, "Only Two Terms for a President?" *New York Times Magazine*, April 27, 1947, p. 73.
[3] Everett S. Brown, "Terms of Office of the President," 41 *American Political Science Review*, 447 (1947).

ond term and less effective. Such does not seem to have happened. As Malcolm Moos, an aide to President Eisenhower, observed, ". . . it may be that the President is using the Twenty-second amendment as a political weapon aimed at Congress. In other words, the President can gain support for his policies because he can convince the people he has nothing to gain personally. The amendment eliminates self-interest."[4] President Lyndon B. Johnson's announcement that he would not run again speaks to the same point.

During the Eisenhower years, there was some effort to repeal the amendment.[5] Such efforts now have abated.

AMENDMENT XXIII

SECTION I

The District constituting the seat of Government of the United States shall appoint in such manner as the Congress may direct:
A number of electors of President and Vice-President equal to the whole number of Senators and Representatives in Congress to which the District would be entitled if it were a State, but in no event more than the least populous State; they shall be in addition to those appointed by the States, but they shall be considered, for the purposes of the election of President and Vice-President, to be electors appointed by a State; and they shall meet in the District and perform such duties as provided by the twelfth article of amendment.

SECTION II

The Congress shall have power to enforce this article by appropriate legislation.

This amendment was proposed by Congress in 1960 and was declared by the Administrator of General Services on April 3, 1961, to have been ratified.[1] The clear purpose of the amendment was "to provide the citizens of the District of Columbia with appropriate rights of voting in national elections for President and Vice President of the United States"[2] and was in keeping with the developing ideas of "one man–one vote" of the period. (*See* p. 522.)

AMENDMENT XXIV

SECTION I

The right of citizens of the United States to vote in any primary or other election for President or Vice-President, for electors for

---

[4] Malcolm Moos, "The President and the Constitution," 48 *Kentucky Law Journal*, 103, 120 (1959).
[5] Edward S. Corwin, *The President*, pp. 37-38 and 338.

---

[1] U.S.C. Amend. 23.   [2] 1 *U.S. Cong. & Adm. News*, 1459, 1460 (1960).

President or Vice-President, or for Senator or Representative in Congress, shall not be denied or abridged by the United States or any State by reason of failure to pay any poll tax or other tax.

SECTION II

The Congress shall have power to enforce this article by appropriate legislation.

This amendment was proposed by Congress in 1962 and declared ratified on February 4, 1964.[1]

As the House Report accompanying the proposal indicated: "Federal legislation to eliminate poll taxes, either by constitutional amendment or statute, has been introduced in every Congress since 1939."[2] Yet five States still required the payment of a poll tax by voters. In a test case in 1965, the Supreme Court held that "For federal elections, the poll tax is abolished absolutely as a prerequisite to voting, and no milder substitute may be imposed."[3] When Virginia sought to retain the poll tax for those who vote in State elections, a sharply-divided Court struck it down in 1966 as a violation of the equal protection clause: "In a recent searching reexamination of the Equal Protection Clause, we held, . . . that 'the opportunity for equal participation by all voters in the election of state legislators' is required. . . . We decline to qualify that principle by sustaining this poll tax."[4]

AMENDMENT XXV

SECTION I

In case of the removal of the President from office or of his death or resignation, the Vice-President shall become President.

SECTION II

Whenever there is a vacancy in the office of the Vice-President, the President shall nominate a Vice-President who shall take office upon confirmation by a majority vote of both Houses of Congress.

SECTION III

Whenever the President transmits to the President pro tempore of the Senate and the Speaker of the House of Representatives his

[1] U.S.C. Amend. 24.
[2] 1962 *U.S. Cong. & Adm. News*, 4033, 4034. *See also* Congressional Quarterly Service, *Congress and the Nation* (Washington, 1969), II, 360 and 353.
[3] Harman *v.* Forssensius, 380 U.S. 528, 542 (1965).
[4] Harper *v.* Virginia Bd. of Elections, 383 U.S. 663 (1966).

written declaration that he is unable to discharge the powers and duties of his office, and until he transmits to them a written declaration to the contrary, such powers and duties shall be discharged by the Vice-President as Acting President.

SECTION IV

Whenever the Vice-President and a majority of either the principal officers of the executive departments or of such other body as Congress may by law provide, transmit to the President pro tempore of the Senate and the Speaker of the House of Representatives their written declaration that the President is unable to discharge the powers and duties of his office, the Vice-President shall immediately assume the powers and duties of the office as Acting President.

Thereafter, when the President transmits to the President pro tempore of the Senate and the Speaker of the House of Representatives his written declaration that no inability exists, he shall resume the powers and duties of his office unless the Vice-President and a majority of either the principal officers of the executive department or of such other body as Congress may by law provide, transmit within four days to the President pro tempore of the Senate and the Speaker of the House of Representatives their written declaration that the President is unable to discharge the powers and duties of his office. Thereupon Congress shall decide the issue, assembling within forty-eight hours for that purpose it not in session. If the Congress, within twenty-one days after receipt of the latter written declaration, or, if Congress is not in session, within twenty-one days after Congress is required to assemble, determines by two-thirds vote of both Houses that the President is unable to discharge the powers and duties of his office, the Vice-President shall continue to discharge the same as Acting President; otherwise, the President shall resume the powers and duties of his office.

This amendment was proposed in 1965 and ratified in 1967.[1] It was an attempt to resolve one of the thorniest problems of the American political system—what to do when a President is disabled.[2] How important that problem is can be measured by the fact that in the twentieth century, two Presidents, Wilson and Eisenhower, lay gravely ill while in office. Another, Franklin D. Roosevelt, was apparently very ill in his last days, and John F. Kennedy lay mortally wounded for a short time.

For several Presidencies prior to enactment of the amendment,

[1] U.S.C. Amend. 25.
[2] Edward S. Corwin, *The President*, 53-59, 345-346; Ruth C. Silva, "Presidential Succession and Disability," 21 *Law and Contemporary Problems*, 646 (1956); U.S., 88th Congress, 2nd Sess., Senate, Report No. 1382 (1964).

Presidents and Vice-Presidents exchanged letters specifying how and under what terms the President would relinquish the reins of office if disabled.[3] This arrangement begged some of the basic issues in the disability problem. For one thing, it made it appear that only the President and Vice-President had an interest in what was done. Certainly, the people of the United States have a big concern in a President's fitness to hold office. Also, those agreements were vague as to what was to be done if a President were not in a condition to determine his own fitness. Suppose a President became mentally ill? The amendment supposedly takes care of those issues by not relying on the President's judgment alone. But this does not resolve the practical political dynamics which will be involved every time a President is gravely ill. Typically, the Vice-President is from another wing of the party chosen to give the ticket "balance." The President's advisors are more generally picked on the basis of political views similar to the President's. It would be in their interest at least on some occasions to shield the office from a Vice-President of differing political views. It may not be impossible to "protect" a disabled President and profess to be doing his bidding. We are told that Mrs. Wilson did so rather successfully.[4] In brief, whenever a President is stricken, we can still anticipate the kind of power struggle which took place at the bedside of President Eisenhower between Presidential aide Sherman Adams and Vice-President Richard Nixon.[5] Nor is this to suggest ill will on the part of those participating in the struggle. The stakes are high in terms of ability to do well by the nation, and it is natural for political rivals to view themselves as the salvation of the nation and their rivals as menaces.

With the resignation of President Nixon in August 1974 and the precipitous drop in President Ford's popularity one month later, when he granted Nixon a "full, free and absolute pardon . . . for all offenses against the United States which he . . . has committed or may have committed" while in office, the Twenty-Fifth Amendment became the subject of heightened concern. Following Theodore Roosevelt's enunciation of the stewardship view of the Presiden-

---

[3] Congressional Quarterly Service, *Congress and the Nation* (Washington, 1965), 1436, II, p. 647. The following was the agreement made by Eisenhower-Nixon, Kennedy-Johnson, and Johnson-Humphrey: "(1) In the event of inability the President would—if possible—so inform the Vice President, and the Vice President would serve as Acting President, exercising the powers and duties of the office until the inability had ended. (2) In the event of an inability which would prevent the President from so communicating with the Vice President, the Vice President, after such consultation as seems to him appropriate under the circumstances, would decide upon the devolution of the powers and duties of the office and would serve as Acting President until the inability had ended. (3) The President, in either event, would determine when the inability had ended and at that time would resume the full exercise of the powers and duties of the office."

[4] Ruth C. Silva, "Presidential Succession, " p. 652.

[5] Jack Bell, *The Splendid Misery* (New York, 1960), 384ff.

tial office, Woodrow Wilson justified the respect due the Chief Executive's actions in the public interest on the grounds that the President was the only Federal official elected by all the people.[6] That the Twenty-Fifth Amendment was used twice in two years with the effect of filling both the Presidency and Vice-Presidency with individuals who were not so elected, in the view of some critics, compromised the legitimacy of those offices. Moreover, in light of the lengthy hearings preceding Nelson Rockefeller's nomination to the Vice-Presidency, other critics have faulted the amendment for its failure to call for an up or down vote on the nominee within a certain time period.[7] Whether the advantages of the amendment, particularly that of assuring that the Vice-President would be of the President's own party,[8] outweigh these inadequacies is a matter of on-going debate. Recently, Senator Kennedy proposed that we "have a special election for the Presidency either after the death or disability of a President or after a vote of no-confidence in him by two-thirds of both houses. The election would be to fill out the remainder of the term and the Secretary of State would serve as an 'acting President' in the interim."[9] Said Senator Birch Bayh, who proposed the amendment: "Neither I, nor, I think, any other member of Congress foresaw that the provisions we drafted for the filling of a vacancy in the Vice Presidency would be used in a situation in which a person chosen under its terms would succeed to the White House after the resignation of both the President and the Vice President under the circumstances in which Mr. Nixon and Mr. Agnew left office. If one looks back at the amendment's legislative history, the principal focus of controversy was on Presidential disability rather than on a Vice Presidential vacancy. It is easy to find fault with the 25th Amendment; it is much more difficult to envision an alternative solution that does not present further faults."[10]

AMENDMENT XXVI

SECTION I

The right of citizens of the United States, who are eighteen years of age or older, to vote shall not be denied or abridged by the United States or by any State on account of age.

[6] *See* Edward S. Corwin, *The President: Office and Powers* (New York: New York University Press, 1957), pp. 152-153; *and* Woodrow Wilson, *Constitutional Government* (New York, 1908), pp. 67-68.

[7] *New York Times*, Nov. 17, 1974.

[8] Columnist William F.Buckley, Jr. has argued that the amendment's "principal failure . . . is in inviting members of the political party other than the President's to participate in the confirmation." *San Diego Union*, Nov. 26, 1974.

[9] *New York Times*, Nov. 17, 1974.

[10] *New York Times*, Aug. 25, 1974. For a comprehensive treatment of the history and early applications of the amendment, *see* John D. Feerick, *The Twenty-Fifth Amendment* (Bronx, N.Y., 1977).

SECTION II

The Congress shall have power to enforce this article by appropriate legislation.

This amendment was proposed and ratified in 1971.[1] The impetus for the amendment was explained in the Senate report accompanying the proposal this way: "Thus the Committee is convinced that the time has come to extend the vote to 18-year-olds in all elections: because they are mature enough in every way to exercise the franchise; they have earned the right to vote by bearing responsibilities of citizenship; and because our society has so much to gain by bringing the force of their idealism and concern and energy into the constructive mechanism of elective government."[2]

It is significant that prior to enactment of the Twenty-Sixth Amendment, Congress in the Voting Rights Act of 1970[3] had already lowered the minimum age of voters from 21 to 18 in both State and Federal elections. But the Supreme Court decided in 1970 that "the 18-year-old vote provisions of the Act are constitutional and enforceable insofar as they pertain to federal elections and unconstitutional and unenforceable insofar as they pertain to state and local elections."[4] For a short time, this created administrative confusion in the States and undoubtedly explains why the Twenty-Sixth Amendment was ratified so swiftly.

The passage of the amendment set in force strong efforts to register young voters.[5] One of the sticky problems in registering young voters, at the outset, was to determine whether students should be required to vote where they went to school or where their parents lived. In 1972, the Supreme Court upheld a lower Federal court ruling that students unable to register in their school communities would have to take their cases to court as individuals and not seek redress in a class action.[6] The lower court had held that "This is not a class action [within the Federal Rules]. The facts and circumstances controlling the right of applicants to register may vary in respect to each of them, especially in such matters as residence and domicile, as well as in regard to the nature and content of the questions propounded to them by their respective registrars at the time they first sought registration. Therefore, the plaintiffs here cannot be said to be representative of other students desiring registration."[7] Prior to the election of 1972, we were assured by the *New York Times* that most States do in fact aid student voters.[8]

[1] U.S.C. Amend. 26.

[2] 3 *U.S. Cong. News*, 367 (1971). The whole report is worthy of attention. *See also* 1971 *Cong. Quart. Weekly Report*, 1436-1439 and 2296-2300.

[3] 84 *Stat.* 314.   [4] *Oregon v.* Mitchell, 400 U.S. 112, 118 (1970).

[5] Jules Witcover, "The Youth Vote: A Question Mark—25 Million Potential," *Washington Post*, Sept. 8, 1971.

[6] Manard *v.* Miller, 405 U.S. 982 (1972).

[7] Manard *v.* Miller, 53 F.R.D. 610 (1971).

[8] "Most States Aid Student Voters," *New York Times*, June 4, 1972.

Several important State court decisions have held that requiring a minimum age over 18 for holding office or for serving on juries did not violate the Twenty-Sixth Amendment.[9] However, the Colorado Supreme Court held that qualified electors between the ages of eighteen and twenty could not be precluded by law from signing and circulating initiative petitions.[10]

Federal courts have ruled: (1) that an Illinois statute setting 21 as the minimum age for election to school boards is not violative of constitutional rights;[11] (2) that this amendment is not applicable to tribal elections;[12] (3) that voting age students cannot be made to meet a more rigorous residency test than other persons;[13] (4) that the action of a town council scheduling a municipal election for a date on which the local college would be in recess did not violate students' Twenty-Sixth Amendment rights.[14]

PROPOSED CONSTITUTIONAL AMENDMENT

The following resolution was passed by Congress on March 22, 1972, submitting the proposed Equal Rights Amendment to the States for ratification:

Resolved by the Senate and House of Representatives of the United States of America in Congress assembled (two-thirds of each House concurring therein), That

The following article is proposed as an amendment to the Constitution of the United States, which shall be valid to all intents and purposes as part of the Constitution when ratified by the legislature of three-fourths of the several States within seven years from the date of its submission by the Congress:

"Article—

"Section 1. Equality of rights under the law shall not be denied or abridged by the United States or by any State on account of sex.

[9] Opatz v. St. Cloud, 196 N.W. 2d. 298 (1972); State v. Silva, 259 So. 2d. 153 (1972); Johnson v. State, 260 So. 2d. 436 (1972); Shelby v. State, 479 S.W. 2d. 31 (1972); Hopkins v. State, 311 A. 2d. 483 (1973); People v. Scott, 309 N.E. 2d. 257 (1974); Reed v. State, 292 So. 2d. 7 (1974); Vasquez v. State, 500 S.W. 2d. 518 (1973); Nichols v. State, 501 S.W. 2d. 333 (1973).
[10] Colorado Project-Common Cause v. Anderson, 495 P. 2d. 220 (1972).
[11] Blassman v. Markworth, 359 F.Supp. 1 (1973). *See also* Human Rights Party v. Sec'y of State for Mich., 370 F.Supp. 921 (1973).
[12] Wounded Head v. Tribal Council of the Oglala Sioux Tribe of Pine Ridge Reservation, 507 F. 2d. 1079 (1975); Cheyenne River Sioux Tribe v. Kleppe, 424 F.Supp. 448 (1977).
[13] Sloane v. Smith, 351 F.Supp. 1299 (1972). As to the liberality of construing the amendment, see Hershkoff v. Bd. of Registrars of Voters of Worcester, 321 N.E. 2d. 656 (1974); *but cf.* the more strict assessment of domicile in Dyer v. Huff, 382 F.Supp. 1313 (1973).
[14] Walgren v. Bd. of Selectmen of Town of Amherst, 519 F. 2d. 1364 (1975).

"Section 2. The Congress shall have the power to enforce, by appropriate legislation, the provisions of this article.

"Section 3. This amendment shall take effect two years after the date of ratification."

The House Report which accompanied the resolution explained the purpose of the proposed amendment in these words:

"In recommending the proposed amendment to the Constitution, your Committee recognizes that our legal system currently contains the vestiges of a variety of ancient common law principles which discriminate unfairly against women. Some of these discriminatory principles are based on the old common law doctrine of 'coverture' which treated the husband and wife as a single legal entity, but which regarded the husband alone as 'the one.' Other discriminatory principles still discernible in our legal system are based on an invidious and outmoded double-standard which affords men a greater freedom than women to depart from conventional moral standards. Still other forms of discriminatory laws have their origins in obsolete and often irrational notions of chivalry which in a modern context regard women in a patronizing or condescending light. Regardless of the historical antecedents of these varieties of sex discrimination, they are in many cases without rational justification and are no longer relevant to our modern democratic institutions. Their persistence even in vestigial form creates disharmony between the sexes. Therefore, we strongly recommend that all irrational discrimination on the basis of sex be eliminated."[1]

Significantly, the report conceded that "These discriminatory features of our legal system could be eliminated without amending the Constitution if the Supreme Court were eventually to accord women the full benefit of the equal protection clause." But the report went on to include the observation that "to date the case law in this area has not been thoroughly developed. As a result, it is your Committee's view that the proposed Constitutional amendment would be a means of articulating a National policy against sex discrimination which is needed and has not yet been fully articulated by the judicial system."[2] In the report and, indeed, in the long and interesting debate in the Senate, fears were expressed that the amendment would require *identical* legal treatment for men and women. If such would be the case, it was suggested that "Such a per se rule would be undesirably rigid because it would leave no room to retain statutes which may reasonably reflect differences between the sexes. . . . For example, not only would women, including mothers be subject to the draft but the military would be compelled to place them in combat units alongside of men. The same rigid interpretation could also require that work protective laws reason-

---

[1] U.S., 92d Congress, *House Report* 92-359 (1971).   [2] *Ibid.*

ably designed to protect the health and safety of women be invalidated. . . ."[3]

Indiana's approval in January 1977 brings the total number of states that have ratified the ERA to 35—three short of the three-fourths majority needed before the March 1979 deadline.[4] But two states, Nebraska and Tennessee, have voted to rescind their earlier approval.[5] Although, one Gallup Poll shows 58 per cent of the public favors the amendment,[6] the ERA has "bogged down in the trenches of Southern and rural state legislatures."[7] Though it would not be prudent to forecast whether the ERA will pass, it is safe to predict that, if ratified, the Court will be busy for years spelling out its meaning. A clue to what may be in store is presented by State court decisions interpreting ERA amendments to their State constitutions. The Pennsylvania Supreme Court has continued to hold that that State's equal rights amendment mandates that the support of children is the *equal* responsibility of the mother and father in accordance with the capacity of each to contribute and not an obligation that is necessarily presumed to lie with the father.[8] A State appellate court has ruled, however, that the effect of Washington's ERA does not extend to allowing persons of the same sex to marry.[9] And, while some have argued that one of the effects of the proposed amendment would be to make women liable for compulsory military service if the draft were to be restored in the

---

[3] *Ibid. See also* the fascinating debate in the Senate in 188 *Cong. Rec.* No. 42, pp. S4247-S4273 and No. 44, S4531-S4537. *See* particularly statement of Paul Freund, Dean Pound and other lawyers and legal scholars. *Ibid.*, S4263-S4264. *Also see* 1971 *Cong. Quart. Weekly Report*, 692ff.

[4] 1977 *Cong. Quart. Weekly Report*, 179.

[5] As recent law review comments suggest, a lively debate still continues as to the legal effect of a vote by a State legislature to rescind its earlier ratification of a proposed constitutional amendment, *see* "Constitutional Amendments—The Justiciability of Ratification and Retraction," 41 *Tennessee Law Review*, 93 (1973), *and* "The Equal Rights Amendment: Will States Be Allowed to Change Their Minds?" 49 *Notre Dame Lawyer*, 657 (1974).

[6] Interestingly enough, poll results show that men favor the amendment's passage more than women (63 per cent as against 54 per cent). The amendment receives least support in the South. *New York Times*, March 27, 1975.

[7] Nick Thimmesch, "The Sexual Equality Amendment," *New York Times Magazine*, June 24, 1973, p. 8. Some formidable arguments pro and con are contained in the article and other articles mentioned therein. *See also* Hazel Greenberg, ed., *The Equal Rights Amendment: A Bibliographic Study* (Westport, Conn., 1976). Of the 15 states that have not yet ratified the ERA, nine are in the South (only Tennessee and Texas have approved the amendment), two are in the Midwest (Illinois and Missouri), and four are in the Far West (Arizona, Oklahoma, Utah, and Washington).

[8] Conway *v.* Dana, 318 A. 2d. 324 (1974); but the effects of such an amendment are not retroactive, *see* People *v.* Elliott, 525 P. 2d. 457 (1974). *See also* Wiegand *v.* Wiegand, 310 A. 2d. 426 (1973), where a Pennsylvania Superior Court held, in applying the equality of rights amendment to the State constitution, that provisions of the State's divorce law, which give wives but not husbands the right to obtain divorces from bed and board, to alimony, and to costs in a divorce action, are no longer constitutional.

[9] Singer *v.* Hara, 522 P. 2d. 1187 (1974).

future, one Federal appeals court has rejected the conclusion, though on the basis of the Fifth Amendment's due process clause, in holding that the Selective Service Act as applied only to men is constitutional.[10]

EPILOGUE

One cannot parse the meaning of the Constitution without coming away from it with great admiration and respect for the document and its authors. Yet, as one canvasses the problems of the 1970's, one cannot help but wonder if a restructuring of our governmental system is not in order. This is said as no disrespect to the Framers. For, as Professor James M. Burns pointed out (*see* quote, p. 200), the Constitution has, indeed, served us well for nearly two hundred years. But that fact in itself does not mean that it will continue to serve us well as our problems change. For example, are the separation of powers principle and the inordinate series of checks and balances as viable for our maturity as a nation with all the responsibility maturity brings, as they were in our birth and youth? We do not pass judgment on that question; we respectfully suggest that we should be thinking about it. We make no claim to novelty in offering our suggestion. Professor Corwin as early as 1948 and James M. Burns as late as 1972 were suggesting the same thing.[1] Nor do we make the suggestion light-heartedly. We find ourselves much in accord with the ambivalent feelings expressed by McGeorge Bundy a few years ago: ". . . it is not unthinkable (I want to be careful how I say this)—it is something to be thought about— that this country may need a new or radically amended Constitution. If I had to vote on this question today, I would vote No, because I believe that we very likely could not do better, even now, than our forefathers. One can easily conceive of constitutions very much worse than the one we have, and it is at least possible that some of the parts of the Constitution, that all of us here prize most, might fail in a truly democratic test today. Would we pass the Bill of Rights? But as I express doubt and register this tentative negative, I worry about my own worries. If mistrust of our government is part of our problem, it is at least possible that mistrust of our capacity to change our government is a deeper error still. Our universities and colleges are surely in a time of constitutional reform. Is there no parallel need for the nation? This question is already being asked, and I think rightly, on the issue of the direct election of Presidents. But what about the powers of states and the needs of the growing

---

[10] United States *v.* Reiser, 532 F. 2d. 673 (1976), *reversing* 394 F.Supp. 1060 (1975). *See also* United States *v.* Fallon, 407 F. 2d. 621 (1969), *cert denied* 395 U.S. 908 (1969); United States *v.* Baechler, 509 F. 2d. 13 (1974).

---

[1] Edward S. Corwin, "Our Constitutional Revolution and How to Round It Out," 19 *Penn. Bar Assoc. Quarterly*, 261 (1948), and James M. Burns, *Uncommon Sense* (New York, 1972).

number of great cities that cross state boundaries in all of our real economic and social life? And at another level, what about the need to prepare for a time when certain basic powers of government should be exercises above the level of the nation-state?

"I say these things are not unthinkable. I do not say that a new constitution is right. It may well turn out, even on issues as large as these, that precisely because it is a *constitution* with which we are living, a *constitution* which the Justices are expounding, precisely because a *constitution* can fit itself to new times, new duties, that even these issues can be met within the four corners of the document of 1787. But it is not certain, and it does need thought."[2]

[2] Mt. Holyoke College, *The Inauguration Issue* (South Hadley, Mass., 1969), pp. 54-55.

THE CONSTITUTION

PREAMBLE

W E, the people of the United States, in order to form a more perfect union, establish justice, insure domestic tranquillity, provide for the common defense, promote the general welfare, and secure the blessings of liberty to ourselves and our posterity, do ordain and establish this Constitution for the United States of America.

ARTICLE I

SECTION I

All legislative powers herein granted shall be vested in a Congress of the United States, which shall consist of a Senate and House of Representatives.

SECTION II

[1] The House of Representatives shall be composed of members chosen every second year by the people of the several States, and the electors in each State shall have the qualifications requisite for electors of the most numerous branch of the State legislature.

[2] No person shall be a Representative who shall not have attained to the age of twenty-five years, and been seven years a citizen of the United States, and who shall not, when elected, be an inhabitant of that State in which he shall be chosen.

[3] Representatives and direct taxes shall be apportioned among the several States which may be included within this Union, according to their respective numbers, which shall be determined by adding to the whole number of free persons, including those bound to service for a term of years, and excluding Indians not taxed, three-fifths of all other persons. The actual enumeration shall be made within three years after the first meeting of the Congress of the United States, and within every subsequent term of ten years, in such manner as they shall by law direct. The number of Representatives shall not exceed one for every thirty thousand, but each State shall have at least one Representative; and until such enumeration shall be made, the State of New Hampshire shall be entitled to choose three; Massachusetts, eight; Rhode Island and Providence Plantations, one; Connecticut, five; New York, six; New Jersey, four; Pennsylvania, eight; Delaware, one; Maryland, six; Virginia, ten; North Carolina, five; South Carolina, five; and Georgia, three.

[4] When vacancies happen in the representation from any State, the executive authority thereof shall issue writs of election to fill such vacancies.

[5] The House of Representatives shall choose their Speaker and other officers, and shall have the sole power of impeachment.

SECTION III

[1] The Senate of the United States shall be composed of two Senators from each State, chosen by the legislature thereof for six years; and each Senator shall have one vote.

[2] Immediately after they shall be assembled in consequence of the first election, they shall be divided as equally as may be into three classes. The seats of the Senators of the first class shall be vacated at the expiration of the second year, of the second class at the expiration of the fourth year, and of the third class at the expiration of the sixth year, so that one-third may be chosen every second year; and if vacancies happen by resignation or otherwise during the recess of the legislature of any State, the executive thereof may make temporary appointments until the next meeting of the legislature, which shall then fill such vacancies.

[3] No person shall be a Senator who shall not have attained to the age of thirty years, and been nine years a citizen of the United States, and who shall not, when elected, be an inhabitant of that State for which he shall be chosen.

[4] The Vice-President of the United States shall be President of the Senate, but shall have no vote, unless they be equally divided.

[5] The Senate shall choose their other officers and also a President *pro tempore* in the absence of the Vice-President, or when he shall exercise the office of President of the United States.

[6] The Senate shall have the sole power to try all impeachments. When sitting for that purpose, they shall be on oath or affirmation. When the President of the United States is tried, the Chief Justice shall preside; and no person shall be convicted without the concurrence of two-thirds of the members present.

[7] Judgment in cases of impeachment shall not extend further than to removal from office, and disqualification to hold and enjoy any office of honor, trust, or profit under the United States; but the party convicted shall, nevertheless, be liable and subject to indictment, trial, judgment, and punishment, according to law.

SECTION IV

[1] The times, places, and manner of holding elections for Senators and Representatives shall be prescribed in each State by the legislature thereof; but the Congress may at any time by law make or alter such regulations, except as to the places of choosing Senators.

[2] The Congress shall assemble at least once in every year, and such meeting shall be on the first Monday in December, unless they shall by law appoint a different day.

SECTION V

[1] Each House shall be the judge of the elections, returns, and qualifications of its own members, and a majority of each shall constitute a quorum to do business; but a smaller number may adjourn from day to day, and may be authorized to compel the attendance of absent members, in such manner, and under such penalties, as each House may provide.

[2] Each House may determine the rules of its proceedings, punish its members for disorderly behavior, and with the concurrence of two-thirds, expel a member.

[3] Each House shall keep a journal of its proceedings, and from time to time publish the same, excepting such parts as may in their judgment require secrecy, and the yeas and nays of the members of either House on any question shall, at the desire of one-fifth of those present, be entered on the journal.

[4] Neither House, during the session of Congress, shall, without the consent of the other, adjourn for more than three days, nor to any other place than that in which the two Houses shall be sitting.

SECTION VI

[1] The Senators and Representatives shall receive a compensation for their services, to be ascertained by law and paid out of the Treasury of the United States. They shall, in all cases except treason, felony, and breach of the peace, be privileged from arrest during their attendance at the session of their respective Houses, and in going to and returning from the same; and for any speech or debate in either House they shall not be questioned in any other place.

[2] No Senator or Representative shall, during the time for which he was elected, be appointed to any civil office under the authority of the United States, which shall have been created, or the emoluments whereof shall have been increased during such time; and no person holding any office under the United States shall be a member of either House during his continuance in office.

SECTION VII

[1] All bills for raising revenue shall originate in the House of Representatives; but the Senate may propose or concur with amendments as on other bills.

[2] Every bill which shall have passed the House of Representatives and the Senate shall, before it become a law, be presented to the President of the United States; if he approve he shall sign it, but if not he shall return it, with his objections, to that House in which it shall have originated, who shall enter the objections at large on their journal and proceed to reconsider it. If after such reconsideration two-thirds of that House shall agree to pass the bill, it shall be sent, together with the objections, to the other House, by which it

shall likewise be reconsidered, and if approved by two-thirds of that House it shall become a law. But in all such cases the vote of both Houses shall be determined by yeas and nays, and the names of the persons voting for and against the bill shall be entered on the journal of each House respectively. If any bill shall not be returned by the President within ten days (Sundays excepted) after it shall have been presented to him, the same shall be a law, in like manner as if he had signed it, unless the Congress by their adjournment prevent its return, in which case it shall not be a law.

[3] Every order, resolution or vote to which the concurrence of the Senate and House of Representatives may be necessary (except on a question of adjournment) shall be presented to the President of the United States; and before the same shall take effect shall be approved by him, or being disapproved by him, shall be repassed by two-thirds of the Senate and House of Representatives, according to the rules and limitations prescribed in the case of a bill.

SECTION VIII

[1] The Congress shall have power to lay and collect taxes, duties, imposts and excises, to pay the debts and provide for the common defense and general welfare of the United States; but all duties, imposts and excises shall be uniform throughout the United States;

[2] To borrow money on the credit of the United States;

[3] To regulate commerce with foreign nations, and among the several States, and with the Indian tribes;

[4] To establish an uniform rule of naturalization, and uniform laws on the subject of bankruptcies throughout the United States;

[5] To coin money, regulate the value thereof, and of foreign coin, and fix the standard of weights and measures;

[6] To provide for the punishment of counterfeiting the securities and current coin of the United States;

[7] To establish post offices and post roads;

[8] To promote the progress of science and useful arts by securing for limited times to authors and inventors the exclusive right to their respective writings and discoveries;

[9] To constitute tribunals inferior to the Supreme Court;

[10] To define and punish piracies and felonies committed on the high seas and offenses against the law of nations;

[11] To declare war, grant letters of marque and reprisal, and make rules concerning captures on land and water;

[12] To raise and support armies, but no appropriation of money to that use shall be for a longer term than two years;

[13] To provide and maintain a navy;

[14] To make rules for the government and regulation of the land and naval forces;

[15] To provide for calling forth the militia to execute the laws of the Union, suppress insurrections, and repel invasions;

[16] To provide for organizing, arming and disciplining the

militia, and for governing such part of them as may be employed in the service of the United States, reserving to the States respectively the appointment of the officers, and the authority of training the militia according to the discipline prescribed by Congress;

[17] To exercise exclusive legislation in all cases whatsoever over such district (not exceeding ten miles square) as may, by cession of particular States and the acceptance of Congress, become the seat of the Government of the United States, and to exercise like authority over all places purchased by the consent of the legislature of the State in which the same shall be, for the erection of forts, magazines, arsenals, dockyards, and other needful buildings;

[18] To make all laws which shall be necessary and proper for carrying into execution the foregoing powers, and all other powers vested by this Constitution in the Government of the United States, or in any department or officer thereof.

SECTION IX

[1] The migration or importation of such persons as any of the States now existing shall think proper to admit shall not be prohibited by the Congress prior to the year one thousand eight hundred and eight, but a tax or duty may be imposed on such importation, not exceeding ten dollars for each person.

[2] The privilege of the writ of habeas corpus shall not be suspended, unless when in cases of rebellion or invasion the public safety may require it.

[3] No bill of attainder or ex post facto law shall be passed.

[4] No capitation or other direct tax shall be laid, unless in proportion to the census or enumeration hereinbefore directed to be taken.

[5] No tax or duty shall be laid on articles exported from any State.

[6] No preference shall be given by any regulation of commerce or revenue to the ports of one State over those of another; nor shall vessels bound to or from one State be obliged to enter, clear or pay duties in another.

[7] No money shall be drawn from the Treasury but in consequence of appropriations made by law; and a regular statement and account of the receipts and expenditures of all public money shall be published from time to time.

[8] No title of nobility shall be granted by the United States; and no person holding any office of profit or trust under them shall, without the consent of the Congress, accept of any present, emolument, office, or title of any kind whatever from any king, prince, or foreign state.

SECTION X

[1] No State shall enter into any treaty, alliance, or confederation; grant letters of marque and reprisal; coin money, emit bills of

credit; make anything but gold and silver coin a tender in payment of debts; pass any bill of attainder, ex post facto law or law impairing the obligation of contracts, or grant any title of nobility.

[2] No State shall, without the consent of the Congress, lay any imposts or duties on imports or exports, except what may be absolutely necessary for executing its inspection laws; and the net produce of all duties and imposts, laid by any State on imports or exports, shall be for the use of the Treasury of the United States; and all such laws shall be subject to the revision and control of the Congress.

[3] No State shall, without the consent of Congress, lay any duty of tonnage, keep troops and ships of war in time of peace, enter into any agreement or compact with another State or with a foreign power, or engage in war, unless actually invaded or in such imminent danger as will not admit of delay.

ARTICLE II

SECTION I

[1] The executive power shall be vested in a President of the United States of America. He shall hold his office during the term of four years, and together with the Vice-President, chosen for the same term, be elected as follows:

[2] Each State shall appoint, in such manner as the legislature thereof may direct, a number of Electors, equal to the whole number of Senators and Representatives to which the State may be entitled in the Congress; but no Senator or Representative, or person holding an office of trust or profit under the United States, shall be appointed an Elector.

[3] The Electors shall meet in their respective States and vote by ballot for two persons, of whom one at least shall not be an inhabitant of the same State with themselves. And they shall make a list of all the persons voted for, and of the number of votes for each; which list they shall sign and certify, and transmit sealed to the seat of government of the United States, directed to the President of the Senate. The President of the Senate shall, in the presence of the Senate and House of Representatives, open all the certificates, and the votes shall then be counted. The person having the greatest number of votes shall be the President, if such number be a majority of the whole number of Electors appointed; and if there be more than one who have such majority, and have an equal number of votes, then the House of Representatives shall immediately choose by ballot one of them for President; and if no person have a majority, then from the five highest on the list the said House shall in like manner choose the President. But in choosing the President the votes shall be taken by States, the representation from each State having one vote; a quorum for this purpose shall consist of a member or members from two-thirds of the States, and a majority

of all the States shall be necessary to a choice. In every case, after the choice of the President, the person having the greatest number of votes of the Electors shall be the Vice-President. But if there should remain two or more who have equal votes, the Senate shall choose from them by ballot the Vice-President.

[4] The Congress may determine the time of choosing the Electors and the day on which they shall give their votes, which day shall be the same throughout the United States.

[5] No person except a natural-born citizen, or citizen of the United States at the time of the adoption of this Constitution, shall be eligible to the office of President; neither shall any person be eligible to that office who shall not have attained to the age of thirty-five years, and been fourteen years a resident within the United States.

[6] In case of the removal of the President from office, or of his death, resignation, or inability to discharge the powers and duties of the said office, the same shall devolve on the Vice-President, and the Congress may by law provide for the case of removal, death, resignation, or inability, both of the President and Vice-President, declaring what officer shall then act as President, and such officer shall act accordingly until the disability be removed or a President shall be elected.

[7] The President shall, at stated times, receive for his services a compensation, which shall neither be increased nor diminished during the period for which he shall have been elected, and he shall not receive within that period any other emolument from the United States or any of them.

[8] Before he enter on the execution of his office he shall take the following oath or affirmation:

"I do solemnly swear (or affirm) that I will faithfully execute the office of President of the United States, and will to the best of my ability preserve, protect, and defend the Constitution of the United States."

SECTION II

[1] The President shall be Commander-in-Chief of the Army and Navy of the United States, and of the militia of the several States when called into the actual service of the United States; he may require the opinion, in writing, of the principal officer in each of the executive departments, upon any subject relating to the duties of their respective offices, and he shall have power to grant reprieves and pardons for offenses against the United States, except in cases of impeachment.

[2] He shall have power, by and with the advice and consent of the Senate, to make treaties, provided two-thirds of the Senators present concur; and he shall nominate, and, by and with the advice and consent of the Senate, shall appoint ambassadors, other public

ministers and consuls, judges of the Supreme Court, and all other officers of the United States whose appointments are not herein otherwise provided for, and which shall be established by law; but the Congress may by law vest the appointment of such inferior officers, as they think proper, in the President alone, in the courts of law, or in the heads of departments.

[3] The President shall have power to fill up all vacancies that may happen during the recess of the Senate, by granting commissions which shall expire at the end of their next session.

SECTION III

He shall from time to time give to the Congress information of the state of the Union, and recommend to their consideration such measures as he shall judge necessary and expedient; he may, on extraordinary occasions, convene both Houses, or either of them, and in case of disagreement between them with respect to the time of adjournment, he may adjourn them to such time as he shall think proper; he shall receive ambassadors and other public ministers; he shall take care that the laws be faithfully executed, and shall commission all the officers of the United States.

SECTION IV

The President, Vice-President and all civil officers of the United States shall be removed from office on impeachment for and conviction of treason, bribery, or other high crimes and misdemeanors.

ARTICLE III

SECTION I

The judicial power of the United States shall be vested in one Supreme Court, and in such inferior courts as the Congress may from time to time ordain and establish. The judges, both of the Supreme and inferior courts, shall hold their offices during good behavior, and shall, at stated times, receive for their services a compensation which shall not be diminished during their continuance in office.

SECTION II

[1] The judicial power shall extend to all cases, in law and equity, arising under this Constitution, the laws of the United States, and treaties made, or which shall be made, under their authority; to all cases affecting ambassadors, other public ministers, and consuls; to all cases of admiralty and maritime jurisdiction; to controversies to

which the United States shall be a party; to controversies between
two or more States; between a State and citizens of another State;
between citizens of different States; between citizens of the same
State claiming lands under grants of different States, and between a
State, or the citizens thereof, and foreign states, citizens, or subjects.

[2] In all cases affecting ambassadors, other public ministers and
consuls, and those in which a State shall be party, the Supreme
Court shall have original jurisdiction. In all the other cases before
mentioned the Supreme Court shall have appellate jurisdiction,
both as to law and fact, with such exceptions and under such regulations as the Congress shall make.

[3] The trial of all crimes, except in cases of impeachment, shall
be by jury; and such trial shall be held in the State where the said
crimes shall have been committed; but when not committed within
any State, the trial shall be at such place or places as the Congress
may by law have directed.

SECTION III

[1] Treason against the United States shall consist only in levying
war against them, or in adhering to their enemies, giving them aid
and comfort. No person shall be convicted of treason unless on the
testimony of two witnesses to the same overt act, or on confession in
open court.

[2] The Congress shall have power to declare the punishment of
treason, but no attainder of treason shall work corruption of blood
or forfeiture except during the life of the person attainted.

ARTICLE IV

SECTION I

Full faith and credit shall be given in each State to the public acts,
records, and judicial proceedings of every other State. And the
Congress may by general laws prescribe the manner in which such
acts, records, and proceedings shall be proved, and the effect
thereof.

SECTION II

[1] The citizens of each State shall be entitled to all privileges and
immunities of citizens in the several States.

[2] A person charged in any State with treason, felony, or other
crime, who shall flee from justice, and be found in another State,
shall, on demand of the executive authority of the State from which
he fled, be delivered up, to be removed to the State having jurisdiction of the crime.

[3] No person held to service or labor in one State, under the
laws thereof, escaping into another, shall, in consequence of any

law or regulation therein, be discharged from such service or labor, but shall be delivered up on claim to the party to whom such service or labor may be due.

SECTION III

[1] New States may be admitted by the Congress into this Union; but no new State shall be formed or erected within the jurisdiction of any other State; nor any State be formed by the junction of two or more States or parts of States, without the consent of the legislatures of the States concerned as well as of the Congress.

[2] The Congress shall have power to dispose of and make all needful rules and regulations respecting the territory or other property belonging to the United States; and nothing in this Constitution shall be so construed as to prejudice any claims of the United States or of any particular State.

SECTION IV

The United States shall guarantee to every State in this Union a republican form of government, and shall protect each of them against invasion, and on application of the legislature, or of the executive (when the legislature cannot be convened), against domestic violence.

ARTICLE V

The Congress, whenever two-thirds of both Houses shall deem it necessary, shall propose amendments to this Constitution, or, on the application of the legislatures of two-thirds of the several States, shall call a convention for proposing amendments, which in either case shall be valid to all intents and purposes as part of this Constitution, when ratified by the legislatures of three-fourths of the several States, or by conventions in three-fourths thereof, as the one or the other mode of ratification may be proposed by the Congress; provided that no amendment which may be made prior to the year one thousand eight hundred and eight shall in any manner affect the first and fourth clauses in the Ninth Section of the First Article; and that no State, without its consent shall be deprived of its equal suffrage in the Senate.

ARTICLE VI

[1] All debts contracted and engagements entered into, before the adoption of this Constitution, shall be as valid against the United States under this Constitution as under the Confederation.

[2] This Constitution, and the laws of the United States which shall be made in pursuance thereof, and all treaties made, or which shall be made, under the authority of the United States, shall be the

supreme law of the land; and the judges in every State shall be bound thereby, anything in the Constitution or laws of any State to the contrary notwithstanding.

[3] The Senators and Representatives before mentioned and the members of the several State legislatures, and all executive and judicial officers both of the United States and of the several States, shall be bound by oath or affirmation to support this Constitution; but no religious test shall ever be required as a qualification to any office or public trust under the United States.

ARTICLE VII

The ratification of the conventions of nine States shall be sufficient for the establishment of this Constitution between the States so ratifying the same.

AMENDMENT I

Congress shall make no law respecting an establishment of religion, or prohibiting the free exercise thereof; or abridging the freedom of speech or of the press; or the right of the people peaceably to assemble, and to petition the government for a redress of grievances.

AMENDMENT II

A well-regulated militia being necessary to the security of a free State, the right of the people to keep and bear arms shall not be infringed.

AMENDMENT III

No soldier shall, in time of peace, be quartered in any house without the consent of the owner, nor in time of war, but in a manner to be prescribed by law.

AMENDMENT IV

The right of the people to be secure in their persons, houses, papers, and effects, against unreasonable searches and seizures, shall not be violated, and no warrants shall issue but upon probable cause, supported by oath or affirmation, and particularly describing the place to be searched, and the persons or things to be seized.

AMENDMENT V

No person shall be held to answer for a capital, or otherwise infamous crime, unless on a presentment or indictment of a grand jury, except in cases arising in the land or naval forces, or in the militia, when in actual service in time of war or public danger; nor shall any person be subject for the same offense to be twice put in jeopardy of life or limb; nor shall be compelled in any criminal case to be a witness against himself, nor be deprived of life, liberty or property, without due process of law; nor shall private property be taken for public use without just compensation.

AMENDMENT VI

In all criminal prosecutions, the accused shall enjoy the right to a speedy and public trial, by an impartial jury of the State and district wherein the crime shall have been committed, which district shall have been previously ascertained by law, and to be informed of the nature and cause of the accusation; to be confronted with the witnesses against him; to have compulsory process for obtaining witnesses in his favor, and to have the assistance of counsel for his defense.

AMENDMENT VII

In suits at common law, where the value in controversy shall exceed twenty dollars, the right of trial by jury shall be preserved, and no fact tried by a jury shall be otherwise re-examined in any court of the United States, than according to the rules of the common law.

AMENDMENT VIII

Excessive bail shall not be required, nor excessive fines imposed, nor cruel and unusual punishments inflicted.

AMENDMENT IX

The enumeration in the Constitution of certain rights shall not be construed to deny or disparage others retained by the people.

AMENDMENT X

The powers not delegated to the United States by the Constitution, nor prohibited by it to the States, are reserved to the States respectively, or to the people.

AMENDMENT XI

The judicial power of the United States shall not be construed to extend to any suit in law or equity, commenced or prosecuted against one of the United States by citizens of another State, or by citizens or subjects of any foreign state.

AMENDMENT XII

[1] The Electors shall meet in their respective States and vote by ballot for President and Vice-President, one of whom, at least, shall not be an inhabitant of the same State with themselves; they shall name in their ballots the person voted for as President, and in distinct ballots the person voted for as Vice-President, and they shall make distinct lists of all persons voted for as President and of all persons voted for as Vice-President, and of the number of votes for each; which lists they shall sign and certify, and transmit sealed to the seat of the government of the United States, directed to the President of the Senate. The President of the Senate shall, in the presence of the Senate and House of Representatives, open all the certificates and the votes shall then be counted. The person having the greatest number of votes for President shall be the President, if such number be a majority of the whole number of Electors appointed; and if no person have such majority, then from the persons having the highest numbers not exceeding three on the list of those voted for as President, the House of Representatives shall choose immediately, by ballot, the President. But in choosing the President the votes shall be taken by States, the representation from each State having one vote; a quorum for this purpose shall consist of a member or members from two-thirds of the States, and a majority of all the States shall be necessary to a choice. And if the House of Representatives shall not choose a President whenever the right of choice shall devolve upon them, before the fourth day of March next following, then the Vice-President shall act as President, as in the case of the death or other constitutional disability of the President.

[2] The person having the greatest number of votes as Vice-President shall be the Vice-President, if such number be a majority of the whole number of Electors appointed; and if no person have a majority, then from the two highest numbers on the list the Senate shall choose the Vice-President; a quorum for the purpose shall consist of two-thirds of the whole number of Senators, and a majority of the whole number shall be necessary to a choice. But no person constitutionally ineligible to the office of President shall be eligible to that of Vice-President of the United States.

AMENDMENT XIII

SECTION I

Neither slavery nor involuntary servitude, except as a punishment for crime whereof the party shall have been duly convicted, shall exist within the United States, or any place subject to their jurisdiction.

SECTION II

Congress shall have power to enforce this article by appropriate legislation.

AMENDMENT XIV

SECTION I

All persons born or naturalized in the United States, and subject to the jurisdiction thereof, are citizens of the United States and of the State wherein they reside. No State shall make or enforce any law which shall abridge the privileges or immunities of citizens of the United States; nor shall any State deprive any person of life, liberty or property, without due process of law; nor deny to any person within its jurisdiction the equal protection of the laws.

SECTION II

Representatives shall be apportioned among the several States according to their respective numbers, counting the whole number of persons in each State, excluding Indians not taxed. But when the right to vote at any election for the choice of Electors for President and Vice-President of the United States, Representatives in Congress, the executive and judicial officers of a State, or the members of the legislature thereof, is denied to any of the male inhabitants of such State, being twenty-one years of age, and citizens of the United States, or in any way abridged except for participation in rebellion or other crime, the basis of representation therein shall be reduced in the proportion which the number of such male citizens shall bear to the whole number of male citizens twenty-one years of age in such State.

SECTION III

No person shall be a Senator or Representative in Congress, or elector of President and Vice-President, or hold any office, civil or military, under the United States or under any State, who, having previously taken an oath as a member of Congress, or as an officer of the United States, or as a member of any State legislature, or as an executive or judicial officer of any State, to support the Constitution of the United States, shall have engaged in insurrection or rebellion against the same, or given aid or comfort to the enemies thereof. But Congress may, by a vote of two-thirds of each House, remove such disability.

SECTION IV

The validity of the public debt of the United States, authorized by law, including debts incurred for payment of pensions and bounties for services in suppressing insurrection or rebellion, shall not be questioned. But neither the United States nor any State shall assume or pay any debt or obligation incurred in aid of insurrection or rebellion against the United States, or any claim for the loss or emancipation of any slave; but all such debts, obligations, and claims shall be held illegal and void.

SECTION V

The Congress shall have power to enforce, by appropriate legislation, the provisions of this article.

AMENDMENT XV

SECTION I

The right of citizens of the United States to vote shall not be denied or abridged by the United States or by any State on account of race, color, or previous condition of servitude.

SECTION II

The Congress shall have power to enforce this article by appropriate legislation.

AMENDMENT XVI

The Congress shall have power to lay and collect taxes on incomes, from whatever source derived, without apportionment among the several States, and without regard to any census or enumeration.

AMENDMENT XVII

SECTION I

The Senate of the United States shall be composed of two Senators from each State, elected by the people thereof, for six years; and each Senator shall have one vote. The electors in each State shall have the qualifications requisite for electors of the most numerous branch of the State legislatures.

SECTION II

When vacancies happen in the representation of any State in the Senate, the executive authority of such State shall issue writs of election to fill such vacancies: Provided, that the legislature of any State may empower the executive thereof to make temporary appointments until the people fill the vacancies by election as the legislature may direct.

SECTION III

This amendment shall not be so construed as to affect the election or term of any Senator chosen before it becomes valid as part of the Constitution.

AMENDMENT XVIII

SECTION I

After one year from the ratification of this article the manufacture, sale or transportation of intoxicating liquors within, the importation thereof into, or the exportation thereof from the United States and all terrritory subject to the jurisdiction thereof, for beverage purposes, is hereby prohibited.

SECTION II

The Congress and the several States shall have concurrent power to enforce this article by appropriate legislation.

SECTION III

This article shall be inoperative unless it shall have been ratified as an amendment to the Constitution by the legislatures of the several States, as provided in the Constitution, within seven years from the date of the submission hereof to the States by the Congress.

AMENDMENT XIX

SECTION I

The right of citizens of the United States to vote shall not be denied or abridged by the United States or by any State on account of sex.

SECTION II

Congress shall have power to enforce this article by appropriate legislation.

AMENDMENT XX

SECTION I

The terms of the President and Vice-President shall end at noon on the 20th day of January, and the terms of Senators and Representatives at noon on the 3d day of January, of the years in which such terms would have ended if this article had not been ratified; and the terms of their successors shall then begin.

SECTION II

The Congress shall assemble at least once in every year, and such meeting shall begin at noon on the 3d day of January, unless they shall by law appoint a different day.

If, at the time fixed for the beginning of the term of the President, the President-elect shall have died, the Vice-President-elect shall become President. If a President shall not have been chosen before the time fixed for the beginning of his term or if the President-elect shall have failed to qualify, then the Vice-President-elect shall act as President until a President shall have qualified; and the Congress may by law provide for the case wherein neither a President-elect nor a Vice-President-elect shall have qualified, declaring who shall then act as President, or the manner in which one who is to act shall be selected, and such person shall act accordingly until a President or Vice-President shall have qualified.

The Congress may by law provide for the case of the death of any of the persons from whom the House of Representatives may choose a President whenever the right of choice shall have devolved upon them, and for the case of death of any of the persons from whom the Senate may choose a Vice-President whenever the right of choice shall have devolved upon them.

Sections I and II shall take effect on the 15th day of October following the ratification of this article.

This article shall be inoperative unless it shall have been ratified as an amendment to the Constitution by the legislatures of three-fourths of the several States within seven years from the date of its submission.

AMENDMENT XXI

The eighteenth article of amendment to the Constitution of the United States is hereby repealed.

The transportation or importation into any State, territory, or possession of the United States for delivery or use therein of intoxicating liquors, in violation of the laws thereof, is hereby prohibited.

This article shall be inoperative unless it shall have been ratified as an amendment to the Constitution by conventions in the several States, as provided in the Constitution, within seven years from the date of the submission hereof to the States by the Congress.

AMENDMENT XXII

No person shall be elected to the office of President more than twice, and no person who has held the office of President, or acted as President, for more than two years of a term to which some other person was elected President shall be elected to the office of President more than once. But this Article shall not apply to any person holding the office of President when this Article was proposed by the Congress, and shall not prevent any person who may be holding the office of President, or acting as President, during the term within which this Article becomes operative from holding the office of President or acting as President during the remainder of such term.

AMENDMENT XXIII

SECTION I

The District constituting the seat of Government of the United States shall appoint in such manner as the Congress may direct:

A number of electors of President and Vice-President equal to the whole number of Senators and Representatives in Congress to which the District would be entitled if it were a State, but in no event more than the least populous State; they shall be in addition to those appointed by the States, but they shall be considered, for the purposes of the election of President and Vice-President, to be electors appointed by a State; and they shall meet in the District and perform such duties as provided by the twelfth article of amendment.

SECTION II

The Congress shall have power to enforce this article by appropriate legislation.

AMENDMENT XXIV

SECTION I

The right of citizens of the United States to vote in any primary or other election for President or Vice-President, for electors for

President or Vice-President, or for Senator or Representative in Congress, shall not be denied or abridged by the United States or any State by reason of failure to pay any poll tax or other tax.

SECTION II

The Congress shall have power to enforce this article by appropriate legislation.

AMENDMENT XXV

SECTION I

In case of the removal of the President from office or of his death or resignation, the Vice-President shall become President.

SECTION II

Whenever there is a vacancy in the office of the Vice-President, the President shall nominate a Vice-President who shall take office upon confirmation by a majority vote of both Houses of Congress.

SECTION III

Whenever the President transmits to the President pro tempore of the Senate and the Speaker of the House of Representatives his written declaration that he is unable to discharge the powers and duties of his office, and until he transmits to them a written declaration to the contrary, such powers and duties shall be discharged by the Vice-President as Acting President.

SECTION IV

Whenever the Vice-President and a majority of either the principal officers of the executive departments or of such other body as Congress may by law provide, transmit to the President pro tempore of the Senate and the Speaker of the House of Representatives their written declaration that the President is unable to discharge the powers and duties of his office, the Vice-President shall immediately assume the powers and duties of the office as Acting President.

Thereafter, when the President transmits to the President pro tempore of the Senate and the Speaker of the House of Representatives his written declaration that no inability exists, he shall resume the powers and duties of his office unless the Vice-President and a majority of either the principal officers of the executive department or of such other body as Congress may by law provide, transmit within four days to the President pro tempore of the Senate and the Speaker of the House of Representatives their written declaration that the President is unable to discharge the powers and duties of his office. Thereupon Congress shall decide the issue, assembling within forty-eight hours for that purpose if not in session. If the Congress, within twenty-one days after receipt of the latter written declaration, or, if Congress is not in session, within twenty-one days after Congress is required to assemble, determines by two-thirds vote of both Houses that the President is unable to discharge the powers and duties of his office, the Vice-President shall continue to discharge the same as Acting President; otherwise, the President shall resume the powers and duties of his office.

AMENDMENT XXVI

SECTION I

The right of citizens of the United States, who are eighteen years of age or older, to vote shall not be denied or abridged by the United States or by any State on account of age.

SECTION II

The Congress shall have power to enforce this article by appropriate legislation.

TABLE OF CASES

INDEX

Goldberg, Arthur J. (*cont.*)
Amendment, 441; on right to assemble and to petition, 333
Gorham, Nathaniel, 284
Graham, Fred P., 184n, 365n
"grandfather clause," 517, 533
grand jury, 31, 184, 368, 373, 376, 381, 386, 408, 476; courts-martial excepted from, 368-369; exclusionary rule, use of, 363, 379; provisions for, 368; selection of, 412
grants-in-aid, 44n, 145
Gravel, Mike, 27-28
Graves, Thomas J., 160n
Gray, Horace, 41
Great Britain, 89, 149; agreements with, 264; impressment of seamen, 88
Great Lakes, 174, 227
Great Writ, 126
Greeley, Horace, 454
Greenberg, Hazel, 559n
Greytown, Nicaragua, 196
Griswold, A. W., 314n
Grodzins, Morton, 283n
Groppi, James E., 24n
Gross, Leo, 131n
Gross National Debt, 45
Guam, 210n, 211, 88; Bill of Rights of, 285n; courts of, 265; unincorporated territory, 266
Guffey Coal Conservation Act of 1935, 62
Gun Control Act of 1968, 359
Gunther, Gerald, 493n

habeas corpus, 124, 126n, 114, 161n; availability of writ of, 105-106, 239; background on, 126; curtailed relief to State prisoners, 363, 438; *in forma pauperis* and, 126; suspension of, 124-127; use of, 279, 387
Hague Conventions, 169
Haig, Alexander M., 34
"Hair," 318n
hair length, and First, Eighth, and Fourteenth Amendments, 442; and penumbra theory, 442n; and reservists, 117
Hale, Robert L., 531n
Hall, Robert, 531
Hamilton, Alexander, 43, 103, 167, 196, 284, 443; on executive power, 148; on freedom of press, 303; on judicial

review, 221; on President, as Commander-in-Chief, 157; on Presidential election, 454; on State aid in National Law enforcement, 280
Hand, Learned, 307
handicapped, rights of, 500
Hanoi, 175
Harlan, John M. (1833-1911), 57
Harlan, John Marshall (1899—), 27, 308, 511; on conscientious objectors' cases, 295; on incorporation of Bill of Rights, 479-480
Harris, Joseph, 188n
Harrison, William H., 155
Harris Poll, 317n
Hart, James, 283n
Hartke, Vance, 19
Hatalkts, Alfred C., 260
Hatch Act, 180, 336
Hayburn's case, 205n
Headquarters Agreement, 236
Health, Education, and Welfare, Department of, 49, 137
Hearst, Patricia, 332
Henkin, Lewis, 476n, 477
Heublein, Inc., 75
"high crimes and misdemeanors," 14, 201
Higher Education Facilities Act of 1963, 289
Highway Beautification Act of 1956, 401n
Hinds, Asher C., 10n, 20n
Hiroshima, 160
Hiss, Alger, 131n
Hiss Act, 131n
"hit and run" statute, 382-383
Hoffman, Judge, 207
Holdsworth, W. S., 417n
Holland, T. E., 387n
Hollins, George N., 196
Holmes, Oliver W., 170, 232, 262; on commerce, 64, 446, 463; on freedom of speech and press, 303-305; on judicial review, 223; on self-incrimination, 382, 385; income tax returns, 541; on taxation, 542; on Tenth Amendment, 446
homosexuals, cases involving, 317, 473; marriage, 437
Hoover, Herbert, 155
Hoover Dam, 273
Horn, Stephen, 164n

Library of Congress Cataloging in Publication Data

Corwin, Edward Samuel, 1878-1963.
    Edward S. Corwin's The Constitution and what it means
today.

    Includes bibliographical references and indexes.
    1.   United States—Constitutional law.   I.   Chase,
Harold William, 1922-   II.   Ducat, Craig R.
III.   Title.   IV.   Title: The Constitution and what it
means today.
KF4550.C64 1978   342'.73'023   78-53809
ISBN 0-691-09240-0
ISBN 0-691-02758-7 pbk.